THE PRIDE OF HAVANA

The Pride of Havana
A History of Cuban Baseball

Roberto González Echevarría

OXFORD
UNIVERSITY PRESS

For my late son, Carlos,
courageous and graceful to the end,
and to Dr. Dennis Cooper, anargyros,
for his compassion and wisdom

OXFORD
UNIVERSITY PRESS

Athens   Auckland   Bangkok   Bogotá   Buenos Aires   Calcutta
Cape Town   Chennai   Dar es Salaam   Delhi   Florence   Hong Kong   Istanbul
Karachi   Kuala Lumpur   Madrid   Melbourne   Mexico City   Mumbai   Nairobi   Paris
São Paulo   Shanghai   Singapore   Taipei   Tokyo   Toronto   Warsaw

and associated companies in
Berlin   Ibadan

Copyright © 1999 by Roberto González Echevarría

First published by Oxford University Press, Inc., 1999
198 Madison Avenue, New York, New York 10016

First issued as an Oxford University Press paperback, 2001

Oxford is a registered trademark of Oxford University Press

Library of Congress Cataloging-in-Publication Data
González Echevarría, Roberto.
The pride of Havana : a history of Cuban baseball / by Roberto
González Echevarría.
p.   cm.
Includes bibliographical references (p.   ) and index.
ISBN 0-19-506991-9 (Cloth)
ISBN 0-19-514605-0 (Pbk.)
1. Baseball—Cuba—History.   2. Baseball—Social aspects—Cuba.
I. Title.
GV863.25.A1G65   1999
796.357'097291—dc21   98-20779

1 3 5 7 9 10 8 6 4 2

Printed in the United States of America
on acid-free paper

Contents

Illustrations follow pages 144 and 304.

A Note to the Paperback Edition

The publication of *The Pride of Havana* in the spring of 1999 coincided with the home and away series that the Baltimore Orioles played against the Cuban National Team. The Orioles beat the Cubans narrowly in Havana before a handpicked crowd of the regime's faithful. A month later, in Baltimore, a pumped-up Cuban team routed the listless Orioles, who were last in the American League and reluctant to play on an off-day. The media saw it as a historic event; those who took the time to read *The Pride of Havana* knew that major league teams had lost regularly over the years to both professional and amateur Cuban squads. In 1939, Juanito Decall defeated the Red Sox in Havana pitching for a selection drawn from the Amateur League. And in 1908, José de la Caridad Méndez, "The Black Diamond," had pitched twenty-five scoreless innings against the Reds in two shutouts and a long relief stint.

Still, the excellent performance of the Cuban team seemed to show that baseball on the island was recovering from the slump suffered in the nineties, during the "special period," meaning the further deterioration of the dependent Cuban economy after the collapse of the Soviet Union. For a while, preventive penalties levied against potential defectors stemmed the tide of players leaving for the United States by whatever means. Interest in Cuban baseball sparked by the Orioles games also restored some of the prestige the Cuban game had enjoyed. But players continued to find their way to freedom. Andy Morales, who hit a memorable homer against the Orioles in Camden Yards, had to escape twice to be able to remain in the Unites States. Adrián "Duquesito" Hernández, a clone of Orlando "El Duque" Hernández (to whom he is not related), was first reported to have sneaked out of Havana in drag. Like his model, he signed with the Yankees, as Morales appears about to do. Danny Báez, a young fireballer with the Cuban team at the Pan American Games in Winnipeg, left to sign a six-million-dollar contract with the Indians. He is on the verge of breaking into the majors, as are several other Cubans with various organizations. In Cuba, successful defectors, particularly "El Duque," are revered by the fans, who follow their exploits with devotion. It is safe to assume that as the Castro era finally comes to an end, the flow of Cuban talent into Organized Baseball will increase dramatically.

Cuban baseball suffered a serious setback in the 2000 Olympics. They were defeated by a Team USA made up of very young or very old professionals (players not in major league forty-man rosters), led by the voluble Tom Lasorda, the old Almendares Blues' stalwart. It was like the revenge of the old Cuban Winter Professional League. Cuba also lost a game to the Netherlands! As in Atlanta in 1996, Cuba's team was made up of veterans, perhaps because the regime thought that they would not be tempting to professional scouts. But the four years elapsed may have made them too old. Linares, Mesa, and Kindelán, players well past their prime, could not do to the American Olympians what they had done to the Orioles. Some of the younger players that the team did carry, like fastball artist Maels Rodríguez, who can throw a ball one hundred miles an hour, do seem ready for advanced professional competition.

At the end of *The Pride of Havana* I noted that there was a shift in Cuban baseball in the direction of major league–style play, meaning fast pitching and long ball hitting, as opposed to the more tactical traditional Cuban game. This has continued. It is sport as spectacle for profit, precisely the kind decried in the regime's earlier propaganda. Reportedly, training methods have been revised to accommodate this change, in which ninth-place hitters go for the fences with increasing success. The usual complaints about a juiced-up ball have been heard. A clear sign of the shift is the return to wooden bats in Cuban competition, an indication that the players are being prepared for professional baseball in the United States and elsewhere. I still believe that the plan is to accomplish this while the Castro regime is still in power, a doubtful proposition.

Since *The Pride of Havana* appeared there have been some important accomplishments by Cuban players in the United States. Tony Pérez was finally inducted into the Hall of Fame, joining Martín Dihigo as one of only two Cubans there. "El Duque" Hernández has settled in as a star with the Yankees, Rey Ordóñez has won three Gold Gloves, and Liván Hernández had a superb 2000 season with the Giants. Rafael Palmeiro continues to pile up numbers that will certainly take him to the Hall of Fame. José Canseco, although he has lost the speed and arm that made him a great base stealer and better than average outfielder, retains his shocking power at the plate and is closing in on 500 home runs, giving him a sure ticket to Cooperstown also. Adolfo Luque, "The Pride of Havana," should be recognized as well, not just for his accomplishments as a player in the majors, but also in Cuba and Mexico, where he was a successful manager too. Luque was one of the greats of Latin American baseball, and Latin American baseball is now an integral part of Organized Baseball.

Acknowledgments

Accustomed to dealing mostly with written texts in my work as a literary critic and historian, researching *The Pride of Havana* often took me instead to people, not a few of whom eagerly volunteered to assist as soon as they found out my topic, which was so close to their hearts. I suspect that most would have liked to have been the ones writing the book; ironically they were, without knowing it. Though every single one of those I interviewed (complete list in Bibliography) lent precious assistance, a few deserve special mention. I recorded two long conversations with Agapito Mayor, but we talked many other times over lunch or on the telephone. He also put at my disposal two large boxes of clippings and memorabilia that he allowed me to take home to rummage through at my leisure. He was my chief informant. Rodolfo Fernández I interviewed on tape in the early stages of research and several other times informally and via the telephone as I learned more about the subject. He was like a patient, wise teacher making suggestions, pointing out promising leads, and tactfully correcting mistakes. Rodolfo also sent me magazines, pictures, and clippings, and maintained with me a lively correspondence in his impeccable Spanish and enviable handwriting. Rocky and Alberta Nelson received me enthusiastically in Portsmouth, Ohio, and allowed me to cart away yet another box of clippings and memorabilia that I was able to sift through and copy at home. I recorded an interview with Rocky and spent several hours with him and Alberta reminiscing about Havana and trying to learn his awkward but effective batting stance. Max Lanier coaxed a friendly motel owner in Dunellon, Florida, into making a room available to record our interview in a quiet environment, gave me clippings and memorabilia to keep, and spent a long lunch with me recalling the final game. José Valdivielso, an educated man of exquisite manners, took me into his home, recorded an interview with me, and let me copy pictures and other materials. I continue to rely on his generosity, knowledge, and intelligence to this day. Emilio de Armas, entrepreneur extraordinaire, from the vantage point of his ninety-plus years of age, surveyed for me the history of professional baseball. He sat with me for several interviews and allowed me to copy books, clippings, and magazines. He was also gracious enough to answer my telephone calls when I needed to verify a detail or two. With him I was able not only to learn about but also to capture the atmosphere of Cuban baseball in the twenties and thirties. Fausto Miranda was another mine of information and a gracious host, who not only allowed himself to be interviewed twice but also answered my calls, helped me with elusive facts, and allowed me to reproduce several pictures and to consult a Havana telephone book from the fifties that he owns. Charles Monfort, collector and archivist, selflessly put in my hands his entire collection and no less valuable recollections, and shared as well his scrupulous devotion to accuracy.

I spent two afternoons in Havana with Eddy Martin, the island's leading sportscaster, a patient and solicitous gentleman who took time from his crowded schedule to roam with me through the Gran Stadium, sat for a long interview, and answered all my questions. I saw Jorge Fuentes, then manager of the Cuban National Team, several times, and recorded a two-hour interview that yielded much information about the game in the post-revolutionary period. At the stadium, Raúl Esteban Pérez, a physical education instructor at the University of Havana, and former professional players Ernesto Morilla and Asdrúbal Baró helped me acquaint myself with the new rituals of that temple.

It pains me to have to report that several of my informants have died since I talked to them: Napoleón Reyes, Fermín Guerra, Quilla Valdés, Dick Sisler, and Claro Duany, as far as I know. I treasure now even more their memory and the knowledge and wisdom they passed on to me.

I cannot give enough thanks to three friends in Havana who made all my work there possible. The first is Miguel Barnet, who used his charm and influence to give me access to anything I needed or wanted related to this project. I must also record here my admiration and gratitude for all I learned from Barnet the writer in my effort to record oral history by making my informants "speak" in the first person. I even had the luxury of having Barnet himself go over the script of the first-person testimonies included in this book. Araceli García Carranza, the most distinguished librarian and bibliographer in Cuban history and one of the leading ones in all of Latin America today, put the holdings of the José Martí National Library within my reach. The discovery of all those nineteenth-century journals devoted to literature and baseball I owe to her. Abel Prieto, now minister of culture but president of the Writers' Union at the time I was working on *The Pride of Havana,* went to great lengths to ensure that I had access to anything I needed without hindrance, restriction, or supervision of any kind. Lázaro Rolo and Antonieta Fernández Hernández, of the National Library, and Ana Cairo, professor at the University of Havana, also lent assistance and support.

In New Haven, my son Roberto E. González, who is a sportswriter for the *Hartford Courant,* gave me information on current developments in the Eastern League involving Cuban players, and told me about breaking news of any kind. Carlos A. González, my late son, to whose cherished memory *The Pride of Havana* is dedicated, helped me organize Cuban ballplayers by age. His friend Tony Carbone gave me valuable information on mobsters with connection to Cuba. Isabel, my wife, transcribed several interviews, struggling heroically with the idiosyncratic pronunciation of some of the old Cuban and American players. She was also the first reader of the entire manuscript and made keen suggestions about content, style, and usage. At Yale, César Rodríguez, Latin American librarian and valued friend, and the staffs of Sterling Memorial Library, Beinecke Rare Book and Manuscript Library, and Seely Mudd Library helped me with the bulk of my research. Judge José A. Cabranes, longtime friend and baseball fan, encouraged me with the project, passed on clippings with current information, and lectured me on the advisability of writing for an audience beyond the limited academic one (which he characterized with a pungent Puerto Rican term). John M. Merriman was among the first to urge me to write this book, got me in touch with publishers, and infused me with his boundless enthusiasm. Richard H. Brodhead, now dean of Yale College but first and foremost a good friend and a scholar of American literature and culture, kept asking for updates and summaries that helped me plot my course. Richard C. Levin, Yale president and San Francisco Giant fan, showed sincere interest in my project and was one of the several supportive colleagues with whom I could converse about it. I cannot fail to recall here that his predecessor, my long lamented friend and partner in vice Bart Giammati, was among the first to inspire me to write about baseball. Harold Bloom, the most devoted Yankee fan I know and a dear and longtime friend, has shared with me for years the pleasures and pains of the baseball calendar. María Rosa Menocal, not just a colleague but also a sisterly presence, exhorted me, often shrilly, to write about popular culture without shame. Giuseppe Mazzotta, in our by now institutional more than constitutional walks, followed my progress and kept up my spirits with his wit and humor. My teammates on the Madison Ravens, of the Connecticut

Senior Baseball League, particularly Marc Wortman, Will Armster, Walter Smith, Edward Vescovi, Dennis Cooper, and Luis Muriel, gave me again the feel for the real game.

At the New York Public Library, Denise A. Hibay, a consummate professional, helped me make the best possible use of that institution's outstanding Cuban and baseball collections. Carlos R. Hortas, former classmate at Yale and virtually lifelong friend, made possible many of my adventures in New York, serving as guide in that sometimes baffling but always exciting city. He also contributed valuable recollections of Puerto Rican baseball.

In Tampa Carlos J. Cano led me though some of our old haunts, found Agapito Mayor for me, and offered his hospitality. In Miami Pedro Yanes and Manuel García were my advisers, guides, and hosts. I owe to them almost everything I accomplished in that second largest of Cuban cities. Also in Miami, Bernardo Iglesias, photographer extraordinaire, shared with me his vivid memories of the Gran Stadium. At Johns Hopkins University, in Baltimore, Eduardo G. González, brother more than uncle, and his daughter, my cousin Eva, provided no small measure of assistance in things Cuban, and Eduardo helped me recall some of our shared baseball past.

Georgina Dopico-Black, then my research assistant and now my admired colleague, helped me tremendously in rummaging through Yale's Cuban collection, and gave me encouragement in difficult times. Another graduate assistant, Christine Dolan, helped both with research and in taking some of the pictures included here.

Amauri Pi González, Spanish voice of the San Francisco Giants, allowed me to see the game from the perspective of the broadcast booth and gave me access to the locker room, where I met several times with their generous manager, Dusty Baker. Amauri's kindness made it possible for me to talk to recent Cuban defectors Osvaldo Fernández and Rey Ordóñez, and to veteran Octavio (Cookie) Rojas, now a coach with the New York Mets.

Generous and sometimes copious help often came through the mail from Isabel Alvarez-Borland, Tom Miller, Antonio Madrigal, Enrique Sacerio Garí, Gustavo Pérez Firmat, Rob Ruck, Jorge Pérez López, Mel R. Martínez, Miguel A. Sánchez, Roberto Ruiz, Alberta Nelson, Everardo Santamarina, Enrique V. Menocal, Narciso Camejo, Peter Bjarkman, Raúl Esteban Pérez, and Ana Cairo. Among the former players, in addition to those already mentioned, I received correspondence from Bobby Bragan, Rafael Noble, and Manuel "Cocaína" García. I have never met in person some of these benefactors, and I regret to say that some, as with the interviewed players, have passed away ("Cocaína," Santamarina). May their mention here help preserve the memory of their accomplishments as well as of their generosity of spirit.

I had two strictly telephone informants: Preston Gómez and Narciso Camejo. Gómez, from his home in California, recalled in exquisite detail his years playing sugarmill and amateur baseball in Cuba. Camejo, the last president of the professional Cuban League, evoked from Puerto Rico the process by which the revolutionary takeover brought about the demise of that proud circuit. I hope to meet these gentlemen in person someday soon.

A writer should record his gratitude to those who inspired him and served as his models. I happily do so here to Roger Kahn for *The Boys of Summer,* Jim Brosnan for *The Long Season,* Jim Bouton for *Ball Four,* Robert Peterson for *Only the Ball Was White,* Arnold Hano for *A Day in the Bleachers,* John Holway for *Voices from the Great Black Leagues,* Tomás Morales Fernández for *Los grandes juegos,* and Rob Ruck for *Sandlot Seasons.*

This book was begun under the stewardship of Sheldon Meyer, but by the time I finished it he had retired and his place was taken by Peter Ginna. I owe Peter not a small debt of gratitude for his editorial suggestions concerning the first two chapters. He and his able assistant, Isabella Robertson, did much to improve the manuscript. To Joellyn Ausanka, a doctor of details, I owe a great debt of gratitude for seeing the book through its final stages.

I am grateful for the assists, and take the credit for any hits and the blame for errors and men left on base.

HAVANA

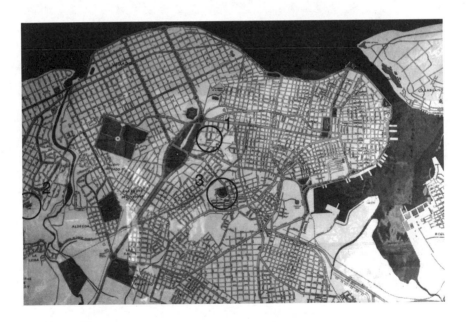

1. Area where Almandares Park stood
2. La Tropical
3. El Gran Stadium (now Latinoamericano)

THE PRIDE OF HAVANA

1	2	3	4	5	6	7	8	9	R	H	E

First Pitch

Alonso de Ojeda, one of the first conquistadors to rush to the Caribbean in the wake of Columbus, was a man of great physical strength and skill. Lore has it that one of his favorite feats was to stand at the base of the Giralda Tower in Seville, which is a full 250 feet high, and hurl an orange clear over the statue on top of it. Almost 500 years later, in 1965, Pedro Ramos, a Cuban pitcher with the Yankees at the time, tried to reach the ceiling of the Houston Astrodome (208 feet) with a baseball before the first game ever played there. Ojeda's stunt uncannily anticipated that throwing a round object would become a passion of the variegated progeny he and others were to leave in the Caribbean. It is among the first things a boy learns in the region.

In the provinces of Cuba I grew up throwing stones at cans, bottles, trees, fruits, and animals. Some of my friends routinely killed birds by picking them off trees with stones. Their accuracy or *puntería* was, as I recall it now, truly remarkable. A good deal of worth was attached to how well one could throw, and how far. We often engaged in battles using the entire cornucopia of tropical fruits or mudballs, which when laced with a stone caused real damage. We could throw even before a baseball entered our lives. And it did early. Middle- and upper-class boys could expect baseball equipment as Christmas gifts, particularly because the professional baseball season coincided with the holidays. Baseball was literally in the air, broadcast by several radio stations throughout the island, and later by television. Poorer boys made their own balls and bats using various materials, or got their hands on equipment in a variety of ways (including, of course, stealing it). We played baseball, which in Cuba is familiarly known as *pelota* or ball, all year. But we were in a baseball frenzy during the winter because of the professional season, which polarized us mostly into Habanistas (followers of the Habana Leones or Lions), whose color was red, and Almendaristas (followers of the Almendares Alacranes or Scorpions), whose color was blue. There was a smattering of followers of Marianao (the Tigers), who wore orange and black, and of Cienfuegos (the Elephants), who wore green. I should confess from the start that I was, that I still am, an Habanista.

As young boys we played anywhere: in open fields, in roads and city streets, in schoolyards. We also played in a variety of ways to adjust to the number of players available, the size of the field, and the time available. We sometimes played to a given number of runs, or more conventionally to a set number of innings. I have played hundreds of games with only two bases and home plate, and quite a few with only one base and home. It was slow-pitch, *a la floja*, for the most part, and the number of bases off a hit depended on the kind of field. Equipment was apportioned according to ownership, ability, and position. The first baseman, not to mention the catcher, had to have a glove to catch the throws if we were playing *a la dura*, or hardball. Outfielders often had no glove. We used many kinds of balls; some we made ourselves wrapping twine around a small rubber ball and covering the finished product with adhesive tape. But we often had a real baseball, which we called *pelotas poli*, "poli" being a deformation of Spalding, which was the most popular brand early in Cuban baseball. By my time the ball we coveted was the Wilson, used by the professional league, which I will always call here the Cuban League. Although we played mostly pickup games, we took them seriously, particularly if they attracted a crowd of idlers and passersby. I remember games in which the spectators (a taxi driver taking a break and a few loafers) placed bets, adding to the pressure. At school we divided into several squads and later joined neighborhood teams.

Adult supervision at this stage was minimal or nonexistent. We organized the games, later the teams, with undisguised ruthlessness. If one was afraid of the ball, could not field, or struck out often, these weaknesses were brought up loudly and without mercy whenever it came time to choose up sides or to make up a team. It was survival of the fittest all the way. We did not learn baseball the way kids do in Little League. We were like artisans learning a craft: We watched and imitated others with more skill. We had no special drills and no formal instruction. One just had to learn to do things the right way. An older boy might tell you if you did something wrong, but most likely he would make fun of you.

Nobody gave a thought to baseball being American or Cuban. We revered the great players we heard about and whose pictures we saw in newspapers and magazines, no matter what their nationality or race. The pickup games we played and the neighborhood teams we organized may have been poor in supervision and equipment, but they were rich in experience: On a good week I might get fifty at-bats, whereas many a kid in the U.S. Little League comes to the plate two or three times in the same period. Later we moved up in baseball through different channels. Some might make the school teams and then move up to the Juveniles (under-twenty league), and later the amateurs, the teams in what I will always call here the Amateur League. Others might play for a sugarmill team, or one sponsored by a store or factory in a semipro league. Race would then enter into the picture. But childhood baseball in the Cuba of the fifties and earlier was truly a child's world, stratified by skill, strength, and bravado, not by color or class. This was the world I left behind with the advent of the revolution in 1959, when we came as exiles to Tampa, Florida. It remains pristine and self-enclosed in my memory, along with recollections of the Cuban League and my beloved Habana Lions (I will write Habana when referring to the baseball club).

This book is an attempt to recover those feelings and memories, inevitably filtered through the mind of the literature professor I have become in the interim. I have tried not to disguise the clash between personal memories and the academic discourse that has allowed me to fully evoke them. I have often hesitated to continue my research for fear that learning too much about Cuban baseball would destroy the pleasure of my intimate reminiscences. Yet I cannot still the voice that learned to write history in libraries, graduate seminars, professional conventions, and teaching undergraduate classes. Hence I have tried as best as I can to get it right, by going to the newspapers, talking to participants, and reconstructing a cultural and socioeconomic context. I have attempted to write a history of Cuban baseball from its inception in the 1860s to the present, trying to figure out, using the full array of my intellectual equipment, the significance of the game in the nation's culture. This is the part of baseball about which I had no interest or clue as a child but that beckoned now as a mystery, a huge historical irony to be analyzed: that my country's political evolution, fueled by intense anti-Americanism, had continued to embrace the most American of games as its own. But I have not left myself, or the child I was, out of this research project, as one often pretends to do in academic writing. On the contrary, I have tried to weave my personal memories as a witness and participant (both as player and as fan) into the narrative.

The dialogue between the professor and the child is not the only one at the center of this book; a more intense debate within myself has been about whether to write it in English or Spanish. In English there is a certain style of writing about Latin American baseball that involves much condescension and humor of questionable taste. The differences of attitude, rituals, and customs are portrayed by sportswriters who think themselves quite free of prejudice, as being funny, or as instances of the zany spirit of Latin people. All this is written from an implicitly supercilious position that assumes that in the United States there is an order in what is, after all, Organized Baseball, that would not allow for any shenanigans. I believe that in most cases the writers or broadcasters who are most guilty of this are simply covering up their own ignorance and sense of uncanniness at seeing a game they consider theirs played by strangers. Writing in English, I sometimes feared, would inevitably contaminate my discourse with this built-in racism. Another apprehension was to write too much in an effort to correct the distortions of Cuban, and by extension Latin American, baseball in the United States. In a polemic, one's emphases can be dictated by the opponent's biases, and this in itself can lead to distortions. Spanish beckoned because I could write for my own audience, without need for explanations. The solution was to write in both. There are pages of this book that I first wrote in Spanish and later translated into English to avoid a certain point of view imposed by the language in which one first thinks of something. I realized that I was also an American baseball fan and that I had to let both the Cuban and the American sides of me speak.

I have written a book that I hope will correct some of the views Americans and others have of Cuban baseball. To me, the most vexing example of how lightly and condescendingly the history of Latin baseball is dealt with in the United States involves a story about Fidel Castro that I would like to set straight here once and for all. Every time I mentioned that I was writing a book about Cuban baseball, the first thing Americans said had to do with Fidel's (which is how we Cubans call him, never "Castro") alleged prowess in the sport, and the irony that, had he been signed by the Senators or the Giants, there would have been no Cuban Revolution. This story even worked itself into a book by eminent historian John M. Merriman, one of my closest friends and batterymate in the Yale Intramural Baseball League.[1] The whole thing is a fabrication by an American journalist whose name is now lost, and it is never told in Cuba because everyone would know it to be false. Let it be known here that Fidel Castro was never scouted by any major-league team, and is not known to have enjoyed the kind of success in baseball that could have brought a scout's attention to him. In a country where sports coverage was broad and thorough, in a city such as Havana with a half-dozen major newspapers (plus dozens of minor ones) and with organized leagues at all levels, there is no record that Fidel Castro ever played, much less starred, on any team. No one has produced even one team picture with Fidel Castro in it. I have found the box score of an intramural game played between the Law and the Business Schools at the University of Havana where a certain F. Castro pitched and lost, 5–4, in late November 1946; this is likely to be the only published box score in which the future dictator appears (*El Mundo,* November 28, 1946).[2] Cubans know that Fidel Castro was no ballplayer, though he dressed himself in the uniform of a spurious, tongue-in-cheek team called Barbudos (Bearded Ones) after he came to power in 1959 and played a few exhibition games. There was no doubt then about his making any team in Cuba. Given a whole country to toy with, Fidel Castro realized the dream of most middle-aged Cuban men by pulling on a uniform and "playing" a few innings.[3]

Even well-meaning writers distort Cuban and Latin American baseball when they plea for the acceptance of its exuberant, flashy, and carefree style of play, which they often liken to their (also faulty) understanding of Latin music and dance. In other words, they argue in favor of allowing the Latin players to live up to American stereotypes about them. The fact is that Cuban (and most Latin) baseball has always been conservative, highly strategic, and has frowned on flamboyant players, who are derisively called *postalitas.* The word means "little post card," I presume because it is thought that the player is posturing, as if posing for a picture. As the reader will discover here, Cuba's style of "inside" baseball, consisting of bunting, slapping a grounder past a charging infielder, almost no base-stealing, and patience at the plate was derived from the pioneers of Negro Leagues baseball, who had much influence in Cuba during the early part of the twentieth century. With exceptions, Cuban players have been small, not the slugger type; hence the game adopted a patient strategy, and there was even a snobbish disdain for the home-run mentality. Pitching, because of the general lack of overpowering speed, depends on guile, junk, and much control. Given the pervasiveness of betting at all levels of Cuban baseball throughout history (to the present), it has never been prudent to jeopardize somebody else's money by being reckless. Like baseball everywhere, Cuban baseball is not lacking in amusing anecdotes, so there is no need for fabrication. I have told or retold some of these, but my aim has been to stick to the truth, or as close to it as I can get by going to the written record and oral sources.

Another reason for writing the book, a powerful incentive for someone like me trained in philology and literary criticism, was to undo some of the abuse visited on the names of Cuban ballplayers over the years by American sportswriters, broadcasters, and even sports historians. Three kinds of errors mar the historical record. First, the American press has simply misspelled the names of countless Cuban (and other Latin) ballplayers. I have seen Cristóbal Torriente's rather elegant name appear as Cristebal Torrienti, to take just one example. Second, the names of Cuban players have often been truncated by American teammates, or even the front offices of the teams they played for, perhaps because Americans find long names pretentious. In Spanish it is common practice (even a legal requirement) to have two surnames, as I do; the first is my father's, González; the second, my mother's maiden name, Echevarría. In informal situations it is the second surname that would be dropped. Thus the late Cuban infielder Hiraldo Sablón Ruiz was known as "Hiraldo Sablón" by his countrymen. Americans, however, bewildered Cuban fans by referring to him as "Chico Ruiz," adding insult to injury by giving him a generic nickname.

The nicknames given to Latin players are the third kind of offense, in this case both to historical accuracy and to their dignity. They have typically combined ignorance and condescension. "Chico" or "chica" is one way Cubans (and other Spanish speakers) might familiarly call for each other's attention, somewhat like "buddy" or "mac" in American idiom. Naming a player "Chico" because one of his teammates used the word would be like calling the Yankee star "Buddy" Mantle because someone said, "Way to go, buddy!" when he hit a homer. Yet this nickname has stuck to many Latin American athletes, from Chico Fernández, known in Cuba by his rather serious name Humberto Fernández, to the Panamanian Chico Salmón, and to countless others. There was even a "Chica."[4] Other nicknames infantilize athletes: Orestes Miñoso, with his proud classical name, became "Minnie" Minoso in the United States; Edmundo Amorós, "Sandy" Amoros; while that patriarch of Cuban baseball Miguel Angel González was reduced to "Mike" Gonzalez (or worse, Gonzales). The list of indignities, the worst of which was perhaps calling Luis Tiant "El Tiante," could go on and on. In this book I have preserved the names of all players in the original Spanish form (as they were known in Cuba, or other Latin country of origin), but included in parentheses, the first time he is mentioned or when relevant, the nickname in the United States. I could not have written a whole book referring to Orestes Miñoso as "Minnie."

But the most powerful reason to write the book was to preserve and exalt the memory of Cuban, Latin American, and American players who played in Cuba and performed feats worthy of remembrance. This is the epic side of my work, and the reason for the Homeric lists that sometimes appear in it. Given the recent history of Cuba, including the diaspora and the separation of Cubans inside and outside the island, preservation of a common memory such as baseball is an important, even urgent endeavor. In Cuba itself, the effort to bolster the achievements of the revolution have led to an erasure of our baseball memory, a sort of cultural lobotomy. Foreign historians of Cuban sports have often bought into the idea that Cuba's sports history begins in 1959 and mouth the propaganda churned out by bureaucrats and ideologues. But the fact is that Cuba has a rich sports history and that the country's emphasis on sports is something derived from its proximity to the United States. While touting its achievements and triumphs, the current Cuban regime has really profited from the strength of Cuban sports before 1959, and the importance Cubans attach to sports, particularly to baseball. The regime, as in the arts (ballet, literature, painting, music), has really been invested in Cuba's strengths as far back as the nineteenth century. Rather than a break, as they claim, Cuba's achievements in these areas after 1959 are really continuities and retentions. My aim is to preserve the common memory.

Naive social scientists who study Cuban sports in an intellectual and cultural vacuum only see the games for their educational or health benefits, and are wont to focus excessively on issues of social justice. It is easy to criticize pre-1959 sports in Cuba not only because of the country's indisputable failings, which were not exceptional, but also because the past appears as inert and absolute, disconnected from the present. In other words, Cuba's flaws up to 1959 would have continued unimproved until today had the revolution not taken place. This is a very facile sort of speculation not supported by the facts or by common sense. Besides, as stated, the revolution profited from much of that past's projection into the future. More importantly, one need not accept the doctrine that turns sports into healthy, pedagogical activities aimed at producing more perfect citizens according to the models provided by the state. This idea, which fueled the Nazi, Soviet, and Cuban sports apparatuses, ignores deeper aspects of sports. Games involve eros as well as heroes, ignite the group-bonding impulses in all of us, and release them in mock wars, generating the kind of adoration of exceptional individuals commonly expressed in epic poems as well as in sacred texts. People do not play games to get healthy but to feel good in the performance of physical acts. And feeling good involves defeating an opponent in a physical contest fraught with real as well as fake violence, sparked by sublimated hatred and lust at various levels of symbolization. Feeling good also involves being idolized by others. The memory of athletic feats, like that of wars and other heroic activities, is an essential component of the nation.

This book encompasses both the history and the lore of Cuban baseball. The history is, as accurately as I can get it, what happened, when, and in what political, social, and economic context. The lore is made up of two kinds of stories: a sort of "official" history, which is often tied up to national myth-making; and then the stories about deeds and dudes—great feats, wacky anecdotes, hyperbole, and gossip.

The Cuban League's last game was in February 1961. The league has been dead for thirty-seven years. Because its heroes have not been extolled in newspapers, magazines, radio, or television on the island, the history of the Cuban League dies a little every day as those of us who lived by it pass. In Miami, journalists such as Fausto Miranda, collectors such as Charles Monfort, and others have kept the lore of the Cuban League alive, and through word of mouth many ordinary Cubans have done the same. But memories fade, and the will to go through crumbling newspapers or grainy reels of microfilm is rare. With the fading memory, a valuable component of Cuban—of human—culture is lost. I have done my best here to salvage as much as my abilities, time, energy, and resources have allowed me. There will be some in the future, I hope, better equipped than I to complete the task.

Playing hardball again for the past five summers in an over-thirty league (I qualified amply) brought me back in touch with a process that can serve as metaphor for my method in writing this book: breaking in a new glove. A new glove is stiff. It is made for an abstract hand, and the leather is slick and hard. A new glove is broken in by the blows of baseballs caught with it and by pounding your own fist against it; by punching, as it were, your own hand while it is in the glove. Some oil and water help, but it is mostly your own body warmth, your sweat and spit that begin to mold the leather to the contours of your hand, and to the spot where you prefer to catch the ball. The glove becomes almost a part of you, but not quite; it is shaped by your hand, but it mediates between you and the ball. I have done something similar in writing this book. I have bypassed learning the proper ethnographic techniques to interview informants. I have devised my own questionnaires to suit my interests and let the conversations take their course. I have written to some informants who have been kind enough to reply, often at length. I have dealt with their responses as documents and evidence, according to my own understanding of both. I have consulted friends and family members and have become the friend of some of my informants. My interests have shaped all of these investigations, but the very process has also shaped my interests. Like the ball hitting the glove and leaving an imprint, which is in turn molded by the shape of my hand and my own secretions, the history, my history, and the story of my work itself have converged as an interplay of forms to yield the book. There has been joy and pain in the process, as there is exhilaration and sometimes hurt in catching a ball. Some of my informants have died, others have told me very moving stories about their lives, yet others are so physically diminished by time and the relentless decay of the body that I have felt their pain as my own.

A glove is not a hand, no matter how much you try to break it in. It is still a form between your hand and the ball. Writing history, particularly cultural history, has its patterns and procedures as well as a narrative shape. My forays through libraries, particularly Yale's, the Cuban National Library in Havana, and the New York Public Library's extraordinary Cuban collections have been guided by years of academic training. I have pursued facts with as much care as I have in other books of mine, but here the discrete boundaries of my field of study have been widened. I have been as interested in the advertisements in journals as in the articles, and followed leads not only about politics but also about radio broadcasting. In a sense cultural history has no discrete limits; presumably anything can be relevant in a nonhierarchical way. I have let my narrative focus dictate the boundaries, more as if I were writing a novel about Cuban baseball than a treatise about it. If the reader and I are interested in the history of Cuban baseball, then there is only so much that we really want to know about its relationship to

Cuban popular music or Afro-Cuban religion. I have delved into politics, labor and racial problems, or financial scandals only insofar as they impinged unambiguously on baseball.

My method, then, ultimately is literary: the narrative flow of the book, which contains both epic elements, with heroes, fables, and lore, and more analytic components that weave in and out, trying to tease out the hidden, prime mover of history. The epic part is as crucial to my story as it is to baseball everywhere. Baseball is very much a male ritual involving fathers and sons. It is a modern way in which men reenact military exercises, a form of civilized, mock warfare with its ceremonies, physical training, and lore. It has to do with physical and moral prowess and its collective recall, and with the actual or vicarious enjoyment of ritualized violence. These are the reasons why sports, particularly team sports, can be absorbed into a national mythology and its champions confused with military heroes, or its coaches with statesmen. But my book has more of the novel than the epic because it has a critical component that refuses to slide into hero-worship, or become moralistic about evil and evildoers. My story is full of the ambiguity and complexity of life itself. Even when accounts of deceit, political corruption, or any other manifestation of the human condition appear, they are not intended to pass judgment.

I have avoided theorizing or tying down my story to a master narrative, such as economic history or the history of American imperialism. These factors are present as a backdrop. But I have not wished to belabor the obvious or to make Cuban baseball appear entirely dependent on them. The problem with much cultural history today is that it is still informed by the Marxist dogma that every single phenomenon of social life can be traced back to economic factors. Hence much history has been written in a spirit of sleuthing for the guilty parties of what inevitably turns out to be a major conspiracy promoted by one principal evil force, be it capitalism or the United States or both. This kind of pious approach does not appeal to me because I am bored by the predictable, but above all because I am too agnostic to believe even in the devil.

Having said this, I must add that in some important ways this book includes the history of the United States, too. Though an island, Cuba is really a frontier. In colonial times it was the first border between the Old and the New Worlds, later the embattled line between the Spanish Empire and the other European powers. Since the nineteenth century, and most poignantly in the past forty years, it has been either a bridge or a wall between itself and the United States. Crossings in either direction have always entailed a more or less radical transformation, at times to sharpen the differences, at others to erase them, or, more often than not, to mask them. Though this play of transformations, fueled by powerful feelings of attraction and rejection, finds a stage in politics, literature, and the arts, its most visible and telling exhibition is found in popular culture and sports, particularly baseball and music. This book, therefore, is the partial history of a border, an account of the transformations that occur in that border.

The overall thesis of this book is that American culture is one of the fundamental components of Cuban culture, even when historically there have been concerted and painful attempts to fight it off or deny it. I mean that even in periods, such as after the revolution, when Cuban culture tried to separate itself from American culture, it was being defined by it. Baseball is the clearest indication of this, but not the only one. It is a process in which the antagonist is absorbed instead of repelled, which shows that in any relationship of cultures, even rejection is mutually influencing, because cultures are dynamic ensembles.

Cuba's culture is one in which the clash of the modern and the pre-modern took place most recently and fruitfully. Slavery in Cuba was legal until 1886 (when baseball was already present on the island), with large numbers of Africans from various regions of that continent having been brought to toil in the production of sugar. Neo-African cultures in Cuba learned to adapt and adopt what they found around them, including the beliefs and practices of other neo-African cultures, but mostly the ways of the mainstream Spanish, or Spanish-origin hegemonic class. This process made them permeable to the alien in ways most traditional cultures, in situ, are not. The most profound and enduring contribution of neo-African cultures to Cuban culture as a whole is that capacity for absorption of the foreign, even the hostile. Traditional cultures are conservative, retentive, creating meaning through repetition. The repeated becomes familiar, the familiar becomes tradition. Cuba faced the most aggressive of modern capitalist cultures: the expanding United States of the nineteenth and the first half of the twentieth century. The absorptive quality of Cuban culture assimilated this element, which clashed with the conservative element of traditional cultures that is also part of its makeup. But these had already been dominated and molded by the process of adaptation and adoption mentioned.

The most combustive meeting of the traditional and the modern is at the level of popular culture, where economic forces, technology, and social mixing promote mutual contamination. By virtue of being a collective activity baseball is also, like all sports, a ritual that retains an aura of sacredness. Players perform prescribed motions in which the timeless enigmas and the perplexing human predicaments interpreted by religion are literally in play: chance, fate, providence, the struggle against evil, victory, shameful defeat, human weakness, bodily prowess, and physical limitation. Repetition of expected gestures lends the spectacle of the baseball game a greater religious inflection. Some of the plays, such as the "sacrifice," even have religious names. But since we live in modern, secular societies, this sacredness is sublimated or deflected into nationalism; contests often involve flags, parades, national anthems, and the presence of political leaders at the stadiums. Sacredness wanes, however, as the game is incorporated into popular culture and becomes spectacle, entertainment, fun. In this, Cuban baseball loosely follows the model of Afro-Cuban music, though much of this music does have a true liturgical function and hence is even more sacred to begin with. Afro-Cuban priests, musicians, and other keepers of the tradition released secrets and adulterated practices to conform to the needs of mainstream society, particularly as this became dominated by foreign influences brought in by tourism. But before anyone laments the loss of purity, one should not forget that it was this desacralized, contaminated music that became what is known as Cuban music. The process was aided by the mass media: the gramophone, the radio, the movies, and more recently television. Cuban culture, perhaps all modern cultures, are the unholy sites of sacrilege, defilement, and profanation. Ojeda's tossing an orange over a church spire in the sixteenth century also uncannily anticipated the pleasures of impiety. There is no turning back.

1	2	3	4	5	6	7	8	9	R	H	E

The Last Game

"Who is the greatest manager, really, Luque or
Mike González?"
"I think they are equal."
　　—Ernest Hemingway, *The Old Man and the Sea*

Dawn was cool and bright in Havana on Tuesday, February 25, 1947. A brisk wind whipped away the high clouds remaining from yesterday's rains as a golden glow began to unveil the skyline of the city. Newspaper vendors broke the silence with their cries, and bottles clinked on sidewalks and in doorways as milkmen completed their rounds. The rumble of buses and the clanging of streetcars were just beginning. Soon, as if driven by a sudden migratory urge, thousands would board them, joining others on foot and in cars. The thousands would head to the Gran Stadium de la Habana, the new baseball park built not far from downtown, to the south. The most dramatic ending in the nearly seventy-year history of the Cuban League was about to take place that afternoon, in a contest that—no one knew it then—would be the most important baseball game yet played on the island, perhaps the last of such portent.

In Santos Suárez, a middle-class suburb of Havana developed mostly in the twenties in a style reminiscent of California, a man of thirty got up to have breakfast. He wanted to make it early to the stadium to find a seat, or merely to be able to get in. The man's three-year-old son began his plea to be taken along to the game. It was not heeded; hence I have been left to reconstruct what happened that afternoon. My father (and namesake) was to tell me years later, while I was still disconsolate and reproachful for not having been at the game with him, that he found the stands half full by midmorning (for the 3:00 P.M. game), and a carnival atmosphere that was pierced by the cries of bettors hawking their early odds. (Gambling at the park was allowed until the end of professional baseball in Cuba and has reappeared openly in recent years.) By the time the game began, he said, intimating how dangerous the whole thing would have been for me at my tender age, spectators were on the field, separated from the players by ropes, while others, more intrepid, climbed the light towers by the dozen.

February is a glorious month in the Caribbean, a sudden spring, particularly for those who have endured the bitter cold of the North and its depressing darkness. There is a soothing, cool air and a soft brightness, particularly enjoyable to natives who suffer every year the blistering, humid days of summer. A February afternoon in Havana is perfect for a ball game, and today's would be a memorable one. Known to those hurrying to the ballpark was that the match would decide the 1946–47 championship in favor of one of the two bitter rivals, the Habana Reds and the Almendares Blues; that the two most revered managers in the history of Cuban baseball would face each other for the first time in a game with everything at stake; and that the exciting pennant race about to close marked the end of the most successful season of the Cuban League, one in which a brand-new stadium of major-league quality had been repeatedly filled. Once they got to the stadium, the fans would discover that the pitcher for Almendares, Max Lanier, who had defeated Habana only forty-eight hours before, was going to take the mound again to attempt a rare feat of endurance and will.

What not even the most knowledgeable fans could know was that that afternoon's game was fraught with portents for Cuban baseball and was a crucial battle in a larger war involving organized baseball, the Mexican League, and Caribbean baseball in general. The Mexican League had challenged American baseball's monopoly of talent, and impending racial integration of the major leagues was to change for good the traditional ties between the Cuban League and the Negro Leagues. Labor unrest among players and the emergence of a rival league in Cuba to challenge the established professional circuit had created some instability, and the Cuban League's relative independence from organized baseball was about to come to an end. Never would established American major leaguers play in the Cuban League, and native stars would be sporadically banned from it in the future. Some of the Cuban stars, in fact, would be declared ineligible in Cuba as punishment for having played in Mexico. Other unknowns, these the products of chance, were that never would Habana and Almendares engage in a pennant race such as this, and never would the patriarchs of Cuban baseball, Miguel Angel González and Adolfo Luque, square off in such a momentous confrontation as the one about to take place at the Gran Stadium.

As fate would have it, the game on the afternoon of February 25 would be witnessed by some of the protagonists of the historic struggles taking place at the time in Organized Baseball. The Brooklyn Dodgers, led by the irascible Leo Durocher and the pompous Branch Rickey, had landed in Havana on the twentieth to begin spring training at the new Gran Stadium. With them came glamorous Laraine Day, the movie actress whom Durocher had married after a well-publicized scandal, and Jackie Robinson, fresh from a terrific first season in organized baseball as a member of the Montreal Royals, the Dodger farm team in the International League. Rickey, who had carefully arranged Robinson's entry into Organized Baseball, had chosen Havana as the site for this particularly crucial spring training because of its less restrictive racial relations. Besides, this was not the first time the Dodgers had come to train in Havana and enjoyed its spring weather. Since the early forties Havana had been a favorite training site, abandoned only due to wartime travel restrictions. The Dodger bunch would make news soon as Durocher, spotted with some gamblers at Gran Stadium during an exhibition against the New York Yankees, was suspended by Commissioner A. B. (Happy) Chandler.[1]

It was anticipated that soon Robinson would be moved up from the Royals to the Dodger roster, thus officially breaking the color barrier in modern major-league baseball. Robinson's presence in Havana could not be more significant for Cuban professional baseball. His signing the year before was one of several major changes in the sport that would make the 1946–47 season of the Cuban League the end of an era and the beginning of another. With Robinson, and the small number of blacks entering organized baseball in the next decade, the Negro Leagues (one of the major sources of talent for the Cuban League) entered a period of slow but irreversible decline, jeopardizing the careers of many mature black players who were not signed by teams in the majors or minors. On a strictly business level, the racial integration of organized baseball was one of a series of monopolistic moves by the major leagues that would deeply affect professional baseball in Cuba and elsewhere in the Caribbean, Mexico, and Central and South America. Another related factor was the rise of the Mexican League under the leadership of Jorge Pasquel, which threatened the absolute control team owners in the United States had over their players. Cuba and Mexico were reaping the rewards of a postwar economic boom, as well as a surfeit of quality players, while in the United States, returning veterans swelled the rosters of major- and minor-league teams. The availability of so much talent, capable of spilling over into leagues not governed by Organized Baseball, led to a far-reaching conflict in which the stronger American interests eventually prevailed. The Cuban League's 1946–47 season reflected this struggle, which culminated with a formal agreement between Cuban and U.S. baseball in early summer. This pact changed the nature of the Cuban League until its demise in 1961, brought about by the revolution led by Fidel Castro. But in Havana, in all of Cuba, and indeed in a good part of the Caribbean and Central America reached by the radio broadcasts, the focus of attention on this Tuesday, February 25 was the game that afternoon between Habana and Almendares at Gran Stadium, not the Dodgers and the problems of American baseball.

The new stadium in El Cerro, once an aristocratic neighborhood of Havana but now a popular barrio, was the most tangible symbol of the recent changes in Cuban professional baseball. The new facility seated more than thirty thousand, whereas La Tropical (Gran Stadium Cervecería Tropical), where the league had played since the early thirties, only seated about fifteen thousand. More importantly, La Tropical, as the park was then known in Cuba, was part of a beer garden that included dance halls and other amenities and belonged to old Cuban money. The brewery was owned by Don Julio Blanco Herrera, a patriarch sportsman who had built the stadium to allow Cuba to host the 1930 Second Central American games. The bucolic setting and enormous expanses needed to accommodate track and field and other sports made La Tropical a beautiful sports arena. But it was not suited for expansion without changing its character completely. The new stadium, on the other hand, was built by Roberto (Bobby) Maduro and Miguel (Miguelito) Suárez, scions of new Cuban millionaire families whose wealth was in insurance, with strong ties to American interests. The league's leaving La Tropical for the Gran Stadium in El Cerro was a major business challenge that did not go unanswered: An alternative Cuban League, called Liga de la Federación, mostly financed by Don Julio and which competed for talent (both foreign and domestic) with the established league, operated in the older park during the 1946–47 season.

The transfer from La Tropical to the Gran Stadium reflected the prosperity and stability that Cuba enjoyed under Fulgencio Batista's constitutional presidency (1940–44) during World War II, as well as the increased closeness with the United States brought about by the conflict. The war raised prices and demand for sugar, and the U.S. military set up air bases on the island, built or rebuilt airports at Camagüey, Cienfuegos, and San Antonio de los Baños, near Havana, and maintained troops in strategic installations such as the nickel mines in Nicaro. Batista had been elected and supported by a broad coalition that included the Communists. He enjoyed enormous popularity, particularly among lower-class, nonwhite Cubans, for he was a light mulatto. Batista covered himself with a mantle of democratic glory by peacefully turning power over to his successor and rival, Dr. Ramón Grau San Martín, in 1944. The precarious truce enforced by Batista's personality and power within the army began to unravel soon under the inept and diffident former professor of physiology from the University of Havana. There was still relative plenty, but political chaos threatened to erupt under Grau's vacillating regime, which was nominally trying to bring about some of the policies propounded by the failed revolution of 1933. Don Julio Blanco Herrera, who had enjoyed Batista's favor, now found himself looking for Grau's when the Cuban League abandoned his park and patronage.

All of this was simmering below the surface as the entire country paused for the epic struggle between Habana and Almendares. In the early morning the Dodgers would go through light drills at the Gran Stadium, most of them probably oblivious to the partisan frenzy surrounding them and the import of the game that would take place on that very turf that afternoon. As dawn broke, on February 25, Max Lanier, who would be the protagonist of that afternoon's drama and who was once the torment of Durocher's Dodgers when he pitched for the Cardinals, stirred in his apartment. He was to tell me many years later that he was not awed by the importance of the game, nor really invested in the Habana-Almendares rivalry, which was a Cuban thing. Half-packed bags lay all around; Lanier had reservations for a night flight back to Florida and to his family in St. Petersburg, no matter what the outcome that afternoon. He would leave mourning or celebrating to others. Lanier's baseball season had been crucial for more important reasons than a mere game in a foreign land. It had taken him not merely outside Organized Baseball but also away from the United States. As one of the most notorious "jumpers" from the major leagues to the Mexican League, back home Lanier was something of a traitor. A truly outstanding major leaguer, he had pitched in two World Series, and had won six in a row in 1946 before deciding to leave the Cardinals and accept Pasquel's offer. Lanier had won a do-or-die game on Sunday against Habana to put his Almendares team within reach of a tie with the Reds. Almendares would actually go a half a game ahead on Monday in a game fraught with difficult strategic decisions that fans were to argue over for decades to come. Tuesday's game would decide the championship.

The anticipated battle pitted what the frenzied national press called, with characteristic hyperbolic license, the "eternal rivals": the Rojos or Leones of Habana, and the Azules or Alacranes of Almendares. The Reds or Lions and the Blues or Scorpions. The exaggeration by the excited writers and radio broadcasters was, in the relative terms of baseball's short history, not really that far off the mark. The teams facing each other that afternoon were older than most major-league teams: The Habana Reds and the Almendares Blues had existed since the 1860s, and had begun to play each other regularly in 1878, when the Cuban League was founded, and twenty years before Cuba became independent from Spain. The 1946–47 season had seen them battle through ups and downs that saw the Reds prevail from midseason on and the Blues rush to catch them at the end, while Cienfuegos and Marianao, the also-rans, provided keen competition for both and were also involved in crucial games. All four squads were not only of high quality, but also their rosters were studded with legendary Cuban players whose careers reached back to the twenties. There were also many great American, Mexican, and even a Venezuelan player. The Cuban season had seen the best of Caribbean baseball in action that winter.

As in all epic battles, Habana and Almendares, with a following to which the word "fanatic" cannot do justice, were led by larger-than-life heroes, two of the patriarchs of modern Cuban baseball. Habana was managed by none other than Miguel Angel (Mike) González, an alumnus of the Cardinals' Gas House Gang and their manager for part of the 1938 season. Almendares, named after a suburb of the capital, had the largest following in the country and the whole Caribbean basin because of radio broadcasts. It was managed by Adolfo (Dolf) Luque, the "Havana Perfecto" or "The Pride of Havana" (after a Cuban cigar, of course) to Americans, "Papá Montero" (a folkloric Afro-Cuban dancer and pimp) to Cubans. In 1923 Luque had won 27 games for the Cincinnati Reds and had gone on to compile 194 wins for them, the New York Giants, and the Brooklyn Dodgers from 1918 to 1935.

González's and Luque's careers stretched back to the early years of the century and were intertwined with the Cuban League's modern history. Luque was known for his explosive temper and caustic tongue as well as his head-hunting style of pitching. He was reputed to carry a gun, even while in uniform, and was something of a drinker and a carouser. Luque lived for the day. A light-hitting but outstanding defensive catcher, Miguel Angel was a quiet, studious type with a good business sense; he wound up owning the Habana team and amassing quite a fortune. A lanky man with protruding ears, he looked, in his youth, like an oversized Laurel, of the Laurel and Hardy team. He was then called "Pan de Flauta" because he was thin and long like a baguette, or "Canillitas" because of his skinny calves, and probably because he walked like Charlie Chaplin, who was known by that name.

On the morning of February 25, Luque and Miguel Angel had not yet made up their lineups. Both had to make crucial choices on their pitching. Loud arguments about decisions made in the previous two days could still be heard in the stands. The Reds' slide and the loss on Monday had made Miguel Angel the goat. But one victory could redeem him, and Habana had won so often during the season that one more win could not be denied. Almendares, on the other hand, had spent itself getting to this day: Its two left-handed aces, Agapito Mayor and Lanier, were exhausted. The "Triple Feo" (The Thrice Ugly, as Mayor was known) had beaten Habana the day before. Who would start for them? A review of the season will show what options faced the two patriarchs of Cuban baseball as they squared off on the afternoon of February 25, 1947, and the larger forces that helped to shape the season's outcome.

⊖

The news during the spring and summer of 1946 had been Jorge Pasquel's efforts to upgrade the Mexican League by signing American stars from the major leagues. The Mexican League had existed since the thirties, and baseball had been played in Mexico since the nineteenth century. But in the later thirties and early forties the Mexican League had begun attracting increasing numbers of American black players, as well as Cubans of all colors and Latin Americans from other countries. With these recruits and the local players, the Mexican League was a fairly strong circuit, and an alternative to players who did not feel comfortable in the United States. These were mostly black Cubans, Puerto Ricans, Venezuelans, and Dominicans, but also a few whites from those countries. By far the greatest number were American and Cuban blacks.

What Pasquel attempted to do was to improve the quality of play by signing American major leaguers, and to boost the image of Mexican baseball by stealing as many glittering names as possible. He had first bought the Veracruz team, which wore blue, and resettled it (without changing its name) in Mexico City, which had a huge population and was home to his team's traditional rivals, the Mexico City Reds. He soon discovered that he needed to shore up the other teams in the league to have a more balanced and attractive competition as well as to reach a wider market. As president and virtual czar of the league he stocked teams with talent, got others to invest in local teams, and even imported umpires Raúl (Chino) Atán and Amado Maestri from Cuba.[2] Pasquel went around literally flashing wads of dollars at American stars, and even sending a signed blank check to Bob Feller. His stunts did not fail to attract attention to himself and the Mexican League, particularly when a few of the American players decided to take the money, hence breaking their contracts with their teams and Organized Baseball.

Jorge Pasquel, who had played and briefly managed in the Mexican League, was a multimillionaire with expensive tastes, a zest for life, and deep nationalistic pride. One of five brothers, he was a rich man in the mold of George Steinbrenner and Ted Turner, except for his exquisite politeness and cosmopolitan air. He traveled in a private plane, had a fabulous wardrobe purchased in New York, London, and Paris, and had a strong interest in the substantial Mexican movie industry. The latter provided the usual perks, including the availability of starlets for him and his cronies. His homes, his celebrity friends, and his travels were the stuff of legend. Pasquel was also well connected in the government. He was a close friend of President Manuel Avila Camacho and other high-ranking members of the ruling Partido Revolucionario Institucional. He considered himself to be, at the very least, on an equal footing with American baseball magnates, some of whom were certainly not as rich, refined, and powerful as he was.

Mexico's postwar prosperity and stability (the revolution was forty years old) as well as its booming oil industry allowed Pasquel to dream of parity with U.S. baseball. Mexico was, after all, one of the prime bullfighting sites in the world, second only to Spain, and a considerable soccer power. Why not achieve the same standards in baseball? In a capitalist market it was a question of having the money, and he and his brothers had plenty. As far as I have been able to ascertain, the Pasquels controlled Mexico's customs and got a cut on all imports. But Pasquel failed to consider that his nationalism had a strong counterpart in the United States, where many team owners thought that the game belonged to them. Baseball was, after all, the national game and part of the American heritage. Pasquel also failed to take into account racism, and the widespread contempt for things Mexican in the United States.

It is not surprising that Pasquel should have had the greatest success in luring away quality players from the St. Louis Cardinals—in addition to Lanier, pitcher Fred Martin and promising infielder Lou Klein had also gone South. Under Branch Rickey during the thirties, the Cardinals had been the first team to create a "farm system," consisting of many minor-league teams in which hundreds of players toiled for very low salaries and with little hope of reaching the majors. Cardinal salaries were notoriously skimpy, and there always seemed to be several players ready and eager to take one's place. Lanier, Martin, and Klein could hardly resist the Mexican offer. Pasquel gave Lanier $20,000 a year for five years and a cash bonus to sign! This was a fabulous sum in 1947. It was also from the Cardinals that Pasquel enjoyed the kind of response he was looking for. In defiance of other baseball magnates, Sam Breadon, owner of the Cardinals, took a plane to Mexico to pay Pasquel a courtesy visit. They went together to a game and were photographed at the ballpark. The Mexican was getting the kind of respect he felt he deserved. In an interview in the fall of 1946 Pasquel proclaimed that Mr. Breadon was a gentleman and that he would henceforth leave the Cardinals alone, but that he was still going for players on all other teams.[3] In that same interview, Pasquel also boasted to Luis Orlando Rodríguez, head of the Cuban Federación Nacional de Deportes y Educación Física, that he had been given several opportunities to buy major-league teams. But Pasquel said he had no interest in buying a major-league team because the other owners would try to squeeze him out, and besides, his aim was to bring the Mexican League to parity with major-league baseball. (In the face of the recent uproar caused by the sale of the Seattle Mariners to Japanese interests, one wonders what would have happened if Pasquel had attempted to buy a team in the majors.)

Organized Baseball reacted with a fit of protectionist xenophobia to the Mexican challenge, banning for five years all players who signed with Pasquel and issuing threats to anyone doing business with him. Pasquel persisted by waving rolls of American dollars to American players, who grabbed them and headed down to Mexico. Other than the three Cardinals, the Dodgers lost Mickey Owen, Puerto Rican star Luis Rodríguez Olmo, and Canadian outfielder Roland Gladu. The Giants were hit hard, losing Cubans Napoleón Reyes and Adrián Zabala as well as Sal Maglie, Roy Zimmerman, George Hausmann, Danny Gardella, Ace Adams, and Harry Feldman. The Phillies lost Cuban René Monteagudo, and the Reds Cuban pitcher Tomás de la Cruz. Cleveland lost catcher Jim Steiner, the Athletics Cuban outfielder Roberto Estalella, Detroit infielder Murray Franklin, and the White Sox gave up Alejandro Carrasquel. The Senators lost Cuban slugger Roberto Ortiz and the Browns Vern Stephens. But these were only the players on major-league rosters. Many others, such as Hayworth and Mayor, who were in the minors, also went to Mexico, not to mention many players from the Negro Leagues.

For American blacks the lure of the Mexican League was clear. In Mexico they were celebrities on a national scale, treated as equals and with access to everything. Adjusting to the language, the food, and the culture in general may have been difficult, but the sense of freedom and the recognition must have been exhilarating. For Cuban players, both black and white, the attraction was even greater. In Mexico they did not have to suffer any discrimination and were not hampered by a language barrier. In the case of the black Cuban players it was actually better than being at home because, except for perhaps the very highest levels of society, blacks enjoyed an equality in Mexico that was unknown in Cuba; they could not be turned away from certain hotels, clubs, restaurants, or bars, as they could in Cuba. Several prominent black Cuban players not only played in Mexico but also settled there and married Mexican women: Santos Amaro, Pedro Orta, Avelino Cañizares, and Héctor Rodríguez, among others.[4]

Cuban whites also enjoyed Mexico, and many listened to Pasquel's call, "jumping" their contracts with organized baseball. Andrés Fleitas recalled when I talked to him: "So then I got the contract from the Giants, to be their second catcher, because they had traded their regular catcher, Mancuso, and had Westrum as first catcher. They offered me, I think, $500 or $600 a month, and Pasquel offered me $5,000 for the season. And seeing that Tomás de la Cruz had gone, and Roberto Ortiz had gone, I signed a three-year contract for $15,000, which they later raised to $18,000. I played there in '45, '46, and '47 for Monterrey." Napoleón Reyes, who was with the Giants, also went, after Pasquel offered him a fabulous sum that allowed him to buy an apartment building in Havana. Reyes also remembers having a great time in Mexico, particularly in Acapulco, where he took full advantage of Pasquel's connections with the movie industry and its supply of starlets.

Mexico's allure to *non*-American players is a factor not generally considered when assessing the reaction of organized baseball to Pasquel's "raids." The Mexican League attracted many Latin American players who were under contract in the United States. The majority of these, like Agapito Mayor, Sandalio Consuegra, and Andrés Fleitas, were Cuban. But there were also Puerto Ricans and Venezuelans. Not to mention, of course, that any Mexican talent being developed would most likely remain at home. At the beginning of the 1946–47 Cuban League season the best Latin American players were affiliated with Mexican teams and went to Havana for the winter. Most were making more money that way than many players in the majors and far more than they could hope to earn in the minors. Organized baseball was not only in danger of losing its own stars, but also the increasingly abundant Latin pool, particularly rich now that Latin blacks (such as Orestes Miñoso) would be allowed to sign with major-league teams.

Pasquel also caused political problems in Cuban baseball that were exacerbated by the move from La Tropical to the Gran Stadium de La Habana in El Cerro. Don Julio Blanco Herrera was left without professional baseball in his well-known park, and he was not happy about it. The story goes that the owners and leasers of teams in the Cuban League asked the old man, given the excellent attendance during the war years, to upgrade La Tropical, or else they would build a new stadium. Don Julio is reported to have answered that nobody "built a stadium on him," or words to that effect, and furthermore that he would not remodel his park. Whereupon Suárez and Maduro, aided by wizard promoter Emilio de Armas, formed a corporation and built the new stadium in a year. Still, as a gesture of reconciliation, they offered La Tropical brewery exclusive rights to sell its beer at the Gran Stadium. Quixotically, Don Julio refused. The new stadium's scoreboard was built with huge adds for rival Hatuey Beer and the Bacardí Company that made it. Given this state of affairs and the fears of the players who did not want to be associated with those who had played in Pasquel's league, Don Julio agreed to help organize and finance the alternative league, the Liga de la Federación, which would play at La Tropical.

The Dirección (or Federación) Nacional General de Deportes y Educación Física had been founded at Batista's urging, and his associate Colonel Jaime Mariné was chosen as its head. He was to promote physical education programs throughout the country and oversee sports. Mariné was instrumental in bringing the Cuban League out of the depressed thirties. When Batista's presidential term ended in 1944 and Grau San Martín assumed the presidency, he named Luis Orlando Rodríguez to Mariné's position. Luis Orlando was the colonel's opposite—indeed, an opponent who had been hunted by Batista's police.[5] A handsome, charismatic, and eloquent young man, Luis Orlando found himself in the middle of the baseball war.

Though Grau, an aging revolutionary himself, did give the position to Luis Orlando, he assigned nearly no budget to the Federación. But Rodríguez was a born politician and public-relations man. Don Julio Blanco Herrera made available to him funds from concessions and other ventures earned in the last and very lucrative baseball season at La Tropical, which he used to launch the new league. The Liga de la Federación Nacional de

Educación Física y Deportes, or simply Liga de la Federación, would operate as a cooperative, with earnings shared fairly among the players. This plan soon went awry, when, to compete with the Cuban League, what reporters at the time called "fabulous salaries" were offered to American players Ray (Talúa) Dandridge and Booker McDaniels, both of whom left Marianao at the Gran Stadium to play in La Tropical. This caused a scandal, and the rivalry between the two leagues turned ugly.

The political struggle intensified when two opposing laws were brought before the Cuban congress to deal with the situation. One, obviously drawn up by those favorable to the Federación, would allocate that organization a budget of $700,000 and the power to regulate professional baseball. The opposing law would create the position of commissioner of baseball, but with no connections to the Federación. In the end, the only money assigned to Luis Orlando Rodríguez by the government was a small stipend drawn from proceeds of the national lottery. In spite of the cash given him by Don Julio his powers were limited, as was soon evident when he tried to suspend pitcher Pedro "Natilla" (Custard) Jiménez for not fulfilling his contract with the Liga de la Federación. The Cuban League (in which he played for Habana) replied that it did not recognize the Federación's jurisdiction, and Jiménez was kept on the active roster undisturbed.

Ironically, the Federación and the Liga de la Federación that it promoted were fighting the monopoly of the Cuban League by defending the much larger monopoly of American Organized Baseball. Teams at La Tropical fielded players free of connections with Mexico, while most of those at the Gran Stadium had played or managed there. Maduro, Suárez, and Miguel Angel González, all of whom had strong ties with organized baseball, were doing Pasquel's bidding by attempting to preserve the independence of the Cuban League. Confusion reigned supreme. Perhaps to keep their players in line, the Cuban League announced that it was about to raise the number of Americans each team could carry on its roster, creating panic among Cuban ballplayers, who feared for their jobs. This move brought home the feeling that unionization was needed. Tomás de la Cruz and Napoleón Reyes took the initiative, formally and legally creating the Asociación Nacional de Peloteros Profesionales de Cuba. At first they claimed that this would be mostly a social organization, but the owners were not fooled and agreed immediately to a series of demands on salaries and working conditions. Another gesture of appeasement was to set the date for a game, in late January 1947, at the Gran Stadium, between "The Best Habana" and "The Best Almendares" (both selected by the fans), with earnings going to the Asociación. This turned out to be a tremendous success, particularly when Luque and Miguel Angel played as a battery in the last inning, a "historic" event, as the press called it. Although they did get one hit off "Papá Montero," he still pitched a scoreless inning against active players half his age!

By late January Luque and Miguel Angel were engaged in a bitter struggle for the championship of the Cuban League, with Habana beginning to slide back from its leading position.

☺

The Liga de la Federación championship, for all its difficulties, was fairly successful and attacked the Cuban League on its weakest flank, which was that all its teams played exclusively in Havana. Even Cienfuegos, though a city in central Cuba, played its home games at the Gran Stadium. The Federación season began with three teams: Havana Reds (the name in English to avoid legal problems); Oriente (with blue uniforms, thus playing on the Habana-Almendares rivalry), which based in Santiago, on the eastern end of Cuba; and Matanzas. But the Liga de la Federación added Camagüey in December for a "second round," and announced plans to have the winning team go to a playoff against its counterpart in yet another professional championship, being played in Oriente Province. This championship consisted of four teams: Contramaestre, Santiago, Holguín, and Camagüey. These plans did not come to fruition, but the eastern championship continued through January. And while the inclusion of a Camagüey team in the Liga de la Federación attracted many fans to the games played at the provincial capital of that name, the experiment was short-lived and ended in acrimony, with players refusing to take the field for a doubleheader unless they were paid in advance. But what really turned out to be a hit was the Matanzas team, which played its games at the "historic" Palmar del Junco, the park where supposedly the first baseball game ever in Cuba was staged. Led by Silvio García, who managed, pitched, and played shortstop, the team gave a good account of itself and drew enthusiastic crowds.

The new league was stocked mainly with Cuban players who belonged to teams in U.S. organized baseball and feared (with reason) that playing with and against Americans who had already been banned for five years by Commissioner Chandler would jeopardize their own careers. This was the case with catcher Fermín (Mike) Guerra, who belonged to the Senators and was traded during the winter to the Philadelphia Athletics; Gilberto (Gil) Torres, an infielder and pitcher who played for the Senators; and first baseman Regino Otero, who was playing with Los Angeles, of the Pacific Coast League. Others who were under contract, but in the minor leagues, were Angel Fleitas (Andrés's brother, who belonged to the Senators), José Antonio (Tony) Zardón, Luis (Witto) Alomá, and Manuel (Chino) Hidalgo, all Senators, too. The two greatest attractions of this championship were Julio (Jiquí) Moreno (nicknamed after a Cuban hardwood), who was among the greatest amateur pitchers in Cuban history while playing for Círculo de Artesanos of San Antonio de los Baños (near Havana), and Conrado Marrero, who was the most popular amateur pitcher ever. Marrero made his debut in Cuban professional baseball with Oriente and had a great season. In the forties, with the possible exception of Roberto Ortiz, there was no more popular player in Cuba than Marrero, whose intelligence, control, and vast repertory of pitches had made him the most successful hurler in the history of Cuban amateur baseball. A bit plump, of less than average height, with short arms and small hands, Marrero looked, in uniform, like someone in a baseball costume, not a player. He looked more like a Spanish grocer or peasant than an athlete. Marrero was already thirty-five by 1946, yet he went on to have a long and distinguished career in the Cuban League with Almendares and in the American League with the Senators. He and others "jumped" to the Cuban League when the Liga de la Federación finished in January 1947.

But the championship that captivated everyone's attention was the Cuban League's at El Cerro. In addition to Habana and Almendares, the other two teams were the Elefantes of Cienfuegos, representing that most beautiful city on the Cuban southern coast, known in Cuba as "The Pearl of the South," and the Frailes of Marianao, representing the municipality adjoining Havana where La Tropical Stadium stands. Cienfuegos, which had won the 1945–46 season under Luque, was led in 1946–47 by the best Cuban baseball player of all time, Martín "El Maestro" (or "El Inmortal") Dihigo, who was to be enshrined in three halls of fame: the American, the Mexican, and the Cuban. An overpowering pitcher who starred in the American Negro Leagues, Dihigo was also an accomplished hitter and was capable of playing every position. He once led the Mexican League in pitching and hitting in the same season. Dihigo was a tall black man with the physique of today's Dave Winfield, but with the grace of movement and agility of a Roberto Clemente, and just as proud. A standout everywhere he played, Dihigo, a man of truly superlative talents, and not just in baseball terms, was (and is) a revered figure in Cuba. Along with González and Luque, Dihigo's story spans the golden era of Cuban baseball, the age of heroes and titans. He was still on the active roster and pitched some in 1946–47.

Marianao was led by another patriarch for most of the season, Armando Marsans, once a superb outfielder, and one of the first Cubans to play in the major leagues (with the Cincinnati Reds). In the summer of 1946 Marsans, a quiet and effective leader, had managed the powerful Alijadores de Tampico in the Mexican League. Many of his players there followed him to Marianao. The four Cuban teams were a composite of the cream of Cuban baseball as well as some of the best talent from the American Negro Leagues, the Mexican League, and the most prominent players from American organized baseball who had signed with Pasquel.

Habana boasted Leonard (Lennox) Pearson at first base, a large, powerful, right-handed slugger from the Newark Eagles. Hank (Machine Gun) Thompson, from the Kansas City Monarchs and eventually the New York Giants, was at short; he hit from the left. Lou Klein, who had gone from the St. Louis Cardinals to Mexico, was at third. He was a solid right-handed hitter and a favorite in Cuba. Heberto Blanco, a Cuban black from the

New York Cubans (in the Negro Leagues) and the Mexican League, played second. Some considered him the best Cuban ever at the position. His brother Carlos was a backup infielder. In the outfield Habana had the popular Pedro "Perico" (or Perucho) Formental in center, a left-handed Cuban slugger with the Memphis Red Sox, of the Negro Leagues, and also a standout in the Mexican League. Henry Kimbro, another left-handed hitter (though he threw righty), from the Baltimore Elite Giants, also played center or any other outfield position. Alberto (Sagüita) Hernández, a black Cuban who was a .300 hitter in the Mexican League, played left. He was a right-handed hitter. René Monteagudo, one of the many Cubans signed by the Washington Senators in the thirties and forties, a lefty, also played the outfield (he was the property of the Phillies, however, when he left for Mexico). Behind the plate Habana had reliable Salvador Hernández, who had caught eighty-four games for the Chicago Cubs in 1943–44 before going to Mexico. His backup was Raúl Navarro, also a Cuban, who played for San Luis in the Mexican League the year before. Both hit right-handed. Habana's pitching staff was arguably the best in the league when the season opened. It was led by a short, portly, veteran left-hander, a standout of the Cuban Stars in the early history of the Negro National League, by the name of Manuel García but known as "Cocaína," "Coca," or "La Droga" because of his ability to daze hitters with his slow stuff; also because his is one of the most common names in the language, and worse yet, that of the most notorious nineteenth-century bandit in Cuba. He won seven straight games in the 1946–47 season before he lost. Cocaína was also a powerful hitter, capable of playing the outfield. Habana's premier right-hander was Fred Martin, a Cardinal who had gone to Mexico with Lanier, followed by Lázaro Medina, a Cuban with the Cincinnati-Indianapolis Clowns in the Negro Leagues and Tampico in the Mexican League. Habana was loaded with pitchers. It also had Natilla Jiménez, a Cuban star from the amateur leagues; James (Jim) Lamarque, a stately left-hander from the Kansas City Monarchs; and eccentric Terris McDuffie, a veteran right-hander from the Negro Leagues. As a kid, I liked the sound of his name so much that I named my dog after him.

Luque's Almendares was strong at every position, and then some. The Blues had John (Buck) O'Neil, from the Kansas City Monarchs, at first base, and backing him up Lázaro "El Príncipe de Belén" (The Prince from Belén, a Havana neighborhood) Salazar, an aging Cuban superstar who was also a superb pitcher. Both were lefties. At second was peppery George "La Ardilla" (The Squirrel) Hausmann, from the New York Giants and Torreón in the Mexican League. At third Almendares had the best Cuban third baseman of all time, Héctor Rodríguez, who was playing in Mexico during the summer but who would eventually play for the Chicago White Sox. At short Luque had Avelino Cañizares, a black Cuban who played for the Cleveland Buckeyes in the Negro Leagues and alongside Hausmann at Torreón. The catcher was Andrés Fleitas, of the Jersey City Giants and later

Monterrey, in the Mexican League, who had a distinguished career as an amateur in Cuba playing for Hershey and the Cuban national team. He was a strong right-handed hitter who came close to winning the batting title in 1946–47. In left Almendares had Santos "El Canguro" (The Kangaroo) Amaro, a strong hitter possessed of a cannon for an arm. He was a star with more than ten years in the league and a great career in Mexico (where he settled and had a son, Rubén, who went on to play with the Yankees, and he in turn a son named Rubén, who plays with the Phillies). Amaro was a large man with superstar abilities, but at this point was a veteran in decline. Center field was in the capable hands of Lloyd (Pops) Davenport, who played for several teams in the Negro Leagues and who was known for his bat and flashy defense, although he was barely five-feet-five. Right field was patrolled by one of the favorites of Cuban baseball, Roberto "El Gigante del Central Senado" (The Giant from Senado Sugarmill) Ortiz, a six-foot-three, right-handed slugger with such a strong arm that the Washington Senators tried to make him a pitcher. Ortiz also played in Mexico, where his tape-measure shots became the stuff of legend and where he is still remembered fondly. In addition to Lanier, Mayor, and Salazar, Almendares had an impressive staff that included two standouts from the Negro Leagues: Jonas Donald Gaines, of the Baltimore Elite Giants, and Gentry Jessup, a tall fastballer from the Chicago American Giants. As if this were not enough, Luque also had Tomás de la Cruz, who had won nine for the Cincinnati Reds in 1944, had more than ten years of experience in the league, and was carving himself a niche in Mexico with the Mexico City Reds; and he had Jorge (El Curveador) Comellas, another veteran of more than ten years in the league, known as "The Curveballer" for obvious reasons. Finally, as we saw, Almendares had, for the last month of the season, Conrado "El Guajiro de Laberinto" (The Peasant from Laberinto) Marrero. With Lanier, Mayor, de la Cruz, Salazar, Jessup, Comellas, Marrero, and Gaines, Luque had a staff that could have won in any league.

Cienfuegos and Marianao had impressive teams also. Under Luque Cienfuegos had won the year before, in the last championship played at La Tropical. In 1946–47 Cienfuegos lost two of its outstanding players to the rival league playing in the old stadium: shortstop Silvio García, reputed to be the best Cuban ever at that position, and Regino (Reggie) Otero, the most elegant and effective first baseman of all time in Cuba. Otero had a substantial career in the Pacific Coast League and a long and outstanding career as manager and coach in Cuba as well as in the major leagues. But Cienfuegos still had outfielder Alejandro Crespo, whose career in the Negro Leagues stretched back to the Cuban Stars. He was a man of great power and defensive skills, considered by some as one of the best Cuban players ever. Another outfielder was Pedro (El Gamo) Pagés, known as "The Hare" for his speed on the bases and the field. In the outfield Cienfuegos also had Roy Zimmerman, from the New York Giants and the Mexican

League, and Danny Gardella, a former Giant and "jumper" to Mexico. At first or third Dihigo had Napoleón (Nap) Reyes, of the New York Giants, who had an outstanding career as an amateur playing for the University of Havana and who had also gone to Mexico. Conrado Pérez shared third with Napoleón Heredia, who had played for the Cuban Stars and the New York Cubans, but more recently with Puebla, in Mexico. Mexican Vinicio García was at second. Behind the plate was the sturdy Rafael Noble, catcher for the New York Cubans and eventually the New York Giants. But Cienfuegos had imported catcher Myron (Red) Hayworth, too, who was also in Mexico, worried about Noble's defense. On the mound, other than himself, Dihigo had Luis (Lefty) Tiant, one of the greatest Cuban pitchers ever, who was already, like his manager, a veteran in his midforties (his son and namesake, of course, became a star in the majors). But he also had Max Manning and Sal Maglie. The first was a front-line pitcher with the Newark Eagles, while the second was one of the "jumpers" to the Mexican League. Maglie had pitched the year before for Cienfuegos under Luque, who taught him his intimidating style of pitching. The staff was rounded off by the likes of Adrián Zabala, a fast Cuban lefty who pitched some for the Giants and had a good career in Mexico, as well as Alejandro (Patón) Carrasquel, the Venezuelan who had a fairly distinguished career with the Washington Senators. "Big Foot" was the first South American to play in the major leagues in the modern era (Colombian Luis Castro played 42 games in 1902).

Marsans' Marianao had a strong resemblance to his Alijadores de Tampico in the Mexican League. Second was covered by Roberto "Beto" (Bobby) Avila, who would win the American League batting championship in 1954 playing for the Cleveland Indians; short by Murray Franklin, another American who went to Mexico; first by the powerful Mexican Angel Castro; third by Orestes Miñoso, a star in the Negro Leagues and later in the majors. In the outfield Marsans had Antonio (Tony) Castaño, who had a long career as player and manager in Cuba and had been a batting champion in the Cuban League; Roberto "El Tarzán" (or Bobby) Estalella, who played for Washington, the St. Louis Browns, and the Philadelphia Athletics, who was short and stocky, and was known for his great strength and build, hence his nickname; and Jesús (Chanquilón) Díaz, another Mexican with power and a long career back home. Among his reserves Marsans had Lorenzo (Chiquitín) Cabrera, a husky Cuban black who played first for the New York Cubans, and Francisco (Frank) Campos, very young then, who would make the Washington Senators. The catcher was Gilberto (Chino) Valdivia. Among the pitchers Marsans had Jesús (Cochihuila) Valenzuela, a star from Mexico; Sandalio (Potrerillo) Consuegra, a favorite as an amateur playing for Deportivo Matanzas, and a man who would lead the American League in pitching while with the Chicago White Sox; Oliverio (Baby) Ortiz, Roberto's brother, who had pitched briefly for the Washington Senators in 1944; Booker McDaniels, a standout for the Kansas City Monarchs and in Mexico; and Aristónico Correoso, who would have a modest career in Cuba and Mexico. Marsans also had, at the beginning of the season, Max Lanier, who pitched ineffectively and was traded to Almendares in December for veteran Negro Leagues catcher Lloyd Basset.

The Cuban League's strong ties with the Mexican League in 1946–47 are clear: Dihigo, Marsans, and Luque all managed in Mexico, as did Salazar, who also played, of course. Almendares had, in Hausmann and Cañizares, Torreón's double-play combination intact, and Marianao had in Carrasquel, Chanquilón Díaz, Cochihuila Valenzuela, Angel Castro, and Beto Avila a great part of Tampico. Fleitas, Almendares' catcher, caught for Monterrey. In addition, some of the most notorious American "jumpers" were in Cuba: Lanier, Gardella, Maglie, Hausmann, Martin, and Klein. As we saw, the Cuban League's association with Mexico had led to the founding of the Liga de la Federación. But on the whole the Cuban League retained most quality players from Cuba, Mexico, the Negro Leagues, and Organized Baseball. It had tradition and much more money behind it than the Liga de la Federación, not to mention a larger, brand-new stadium.

But the doings of other leagues, in Cuba or elsewhere, were far from the minds of frenzied Cuban fans as the deciding game of the season approached that Tuesday, February 25. What was in the air was Almendares' sudden surge in the last weeks of the championship, putting them within striking range of Habana, who had dominated the season practically from the beginning behind the pitching of Cocaína García, Lamarque, and Martin, and the hitting of Klein, Thompson, Pearson, Sagüita Hernández, and Formental. The season's unfolding, Habana's decline, seemed perfect for the enjoyment of that deepest of satisfactions: the conquest of haughty victors, the fall of the mighty after great toil and repeated setbacks. Habana's season-long reign had been savored with great delight by its partisans. But the last week of the championship had turned into sheer agony for the legions of Habanistas, who had within their grasp a decisive defeat of their bitter enemies. Almendares fans, on the other hand, had become used to winning in the early forties to midforties (as recently as 1944–45). Purchased by a group of wealthy sportsmen representing the prestigious Vedado Tennis Club and led by Dr. July Sanguily, scion of a patrician family, the Blues thought of themselves as the class of the Cuban League. So their resurgence in the waning weeks of the 1946–47 season seemed like a restoration of order. Habana's one-man operation under Miguel Angel could not prevail.

The season opened with a clash between Cienfuegos and Almendares on Saturday, October 26, 1946, before an overflow crowd of more than thirty thousand. Why not Habana and Almendares for the premiere? Clearly because Cienfuegos had won the championship the year before in a race with Almendares, and to save the clash between the "eternal rivals" for Sunday and ensure another full house. Recent bad weather had delayed construction and the Gran Stadium was not even finished, with parts of the roof over the grandstand still to go up and the light towers not ready.

Almendares won behind Curveador Comellas, supported by a huge home run by Roberto Ortiz, the first ever at the stadium. Other firsts duly recorded by the journalists that day were: Comellas, first winning pitcher; Alejandro Carrasquel, first loser; Cañizares, first out; Reyes, first strikeout; Gardella, first error; Heredia, first hit, and so on. Ortiz's winning shot was hit off veteran Luis Tiant, whom Dihigo had sent in to relieve Carrasquel. The homer perhaps signaled a transition from players whose careers had blossomed at La Tropical to those who would shine in El Cerro.

The next day, before an even larger crowd, Almendares blanked Habana behind Tanner and Mayor, although the Reds' hurler, Jim Lamarque, pitched a beautiful game. Cienfuegos, looking for its first win, was pummeled by Marianao, who rained hits on Dihigo's staff, including the manager himself, who pitched in relief. Cochihuila Valenzuela won for the Frailes. Meanwhile, the owners of Marianao received a cablegram from Max Lanier saying that he would be arriving soon. The crowds at the Gran Stadium continued to be enormous, better than in some major-league cities whose stadiums were of comparable size (such as Braves' Field in Boston).

In the early weeks of the season Almendares and Habana kept on winning, while Cienfuegos could not get out of its slump. But the first weeks of the season for the Cuban League could be deceiving because often a good number of the imported players had not arrived, and once they did, it could take them a while to round into shape and fit in with their new teammates. Habana is a case in point. The Leones began the season without two of their pillars, Hank Thompson and Lou Klein. When Klein arrived, having played the summer in Mexico, it was announced that he was underweight and needed time to build up. It was reported, on the other hand, that Agapito Mayor had returned from Mexico *overweight*, and Luque was making him run off the excess pounds. Marianao had Miñoso playing second base while waiting for Beto Avila to arrive, and Dihigo was anxiously awaiting the arrival of Hayworth, unhappy as he was with Noble. It was at this point, early in the season, that Marianao imported Ray Dandridge and Booker McDaniels, but both bolted to the Liga de la Federación after only a few games. Once in Havana, Lanier could not find himself. He showed flashes of brilliance, but lost several games with Marianao early in the season.

What seemed clear from the start was that veteran left-hander Cocaína García was at the top of his form, although he turned (at least) forty-one during the season. The chubby García, a black with a very round face and a cheerful disposition, was five-eight. Cocaína's career in the Cuban League had begun with Almendares in the 1926–27 season. He played with the Cuban Stars in the Negro Leagues as well as in Venezuela and Mexico. In 1945 he won eighteen for Tampico and in 1946 fourteen for the same team. Cocaína, who was a dangerous power hitter, too (he also hit lefty), had played for the fabulous Santa Clara teams of the thirties in the Cuban League, alongside stars such as Joshua Gibson. In 1942–43 Cocaína was champion pitcher in the Cuban League, winning ten and losing only three for Habana. During November and December 1946 Cocaína kept on winning, helped by the hitting of Thompson, Pearson, Klein (who got into shape quickly), and the surprising Sagüita Hernández. Backed by the pitching of Cocaína, Fred Martin, and Lázaro Medina, Habana forged ahead in December.

After its early successes, Luque's Almendares went into a slump in December. Comellas, de la Cruz, and Jessup pitched well, but Tanner, Mayor, and Salazar slacked off. Catcher Andrés Fleitas was scorching the ball, as were Hausmann and Amaro, but Cañizares was not producing, and Roberto Ortiz, though hitting for power, was averaging about .260 and playing erratically in the outfield. The "Gigante del Central Senado" was edgy, and in one game, late in November, got into a fistfight with the Cienfuegos battery of Hayworth and Gibson. He had been hit by pitches in successive at-bats after clouting a homer. Did "El Inmortal" Dihigo order this? Probably.

Habana, on the other hand, was winning without much help from Formental, who was mired in a slump. A left-handed hitter for average and power, "Perico .300," as he came to be known, was a charismatic, outgoing man from Báguanos, in Oriente, the same region as Batista, whose loyal supporter he always was. A dark mulatto with a pencil-thin mustache, Formental was a flashy dresser, and a devotee of cock fighting, which endeared him to the *macho* crowd in Cuba. In fact, Formental seemed to be the quintessential *criollo* man. Brave, a lady-killer, and reputed to carry a gun, he played with flair, often making spectacular catches in center field (but also prone to dropping an easy one). Though he began with Cienfuegos (1942–45), Formental became a fixture with Habana. He was a stocky five-ten, nearly two hundred pounds, and could hit the ball a long way. But in the fall of 1946 Formental was slumping.

Fortunately for Miguel Angel, Habana had Sagüita Hernández, Kimbro, Jimmy Bell, and Monteagudo. But Miguel Angel was really most fortunate in having Cocaína, Martin, Medina, and Lamarque. Martin and Medina, along with McDuffie when he was not injured, were crucial, being right-handed, to contain the right-handed power of Almendares (Amaro, Fleitas, Ortiz, Héctor Rodríguez). In fact, it is obvious that Almendares brought in veteran Buck O'Neil to shore up the left side, once it was clear that Lázaro Salazar was really finished as a hitter and would mostly pitch.

On November 6 the newspapers reported the death, on the day before, of Alejandro "El Caballero" (The Gentleman) Oms, a beloved former star outfielder. Sick and destitute, Oms had just returned from abroad, perhaps from Venezuela, where he was probably still trying to play. He must have been only in his fifties when he died. Out of pity, Luque had him in the Cienfuegos roster the year before, and Oms had struck out against Fred Martin in his last at-bat in the Cuban League. A slender black from Las Villas Province, Oms was known for his exquisite manners and for never raising his voice (a truly rare virtue among Cubans), hence his nickname. Oms was one of the stars of the golden age of Cuban baseball in the twenties. In 1928–29 and 1929–30 Oms led the Cuban League with averages of .432 and .380, respectively. He was a member of the Cuban Stars, with whom he toured the United States. Oms threw and hit left-handed and seems to have been a line-drive hitter somewhat in the mold of Rod Carew, though Oms had much more power. He was also a superb outfielder who roamed the vast expanses of Almendares Park and La Tropical. His only weakness was a mediocre arm. Oms' death during the 1946–47 season was another sign that this championship marked the end of an era and the beginning of another. His end in poverty and neglect was probably one of the factors that spurred the players to organize a union.

Oms' was not the only death relevant to Cuban baseball during the 1946–47 season. On January 20, 1947, Josh Gibson died in Pittsburgh. He was only in his forties. The great black home-run hitter and catcher was a favorite in Cuba, where he had smashed the longest shot ever seen on the island. Oms and Gibson died broke and broken in the very years when the color line was being erased in organized baseball. What careers would they have had if they had been born even fifteen years later? What kinds of salaries would Oms and Gibson command today? In a season full of significant events, these two deaths were sharp reminders of the brevity and frailty of baseball greatness and of the irreparable damage that racism did to talented black players in Cuba and the United States.

Habana surged into first place as November turned to December. The Leones were playing with good luck as the fans of the other three teams, particularly Almendaristas, did not fail to proclaim. For example, Sagüita Hernández, a consistent .300 hitter with Puebla in the Mexican League, hit a number of dramatic home runs to bring about Habana victories. In Cuba, except for the 1939–40 season, when he hit .347, Sagüita had been a modest player. In 1946–47 he was dubbed "La Vaca Lechera" (The Milk Cow) because "milk" is associated with good luck in Cuba, by fans hostile to Habana. By mid-December, with the holidays approaching, Habana pulled away to a 3½-game lead. Cocaína was 4 and 0, Martin 3 and 2, Natilla Jiménez 4 and 1, and Medina 4 and 2. Thompson was hitting .337, Klein .325, and Sagüita .319. Meanwhile, Lanier was only 1 and 2 with Marianao.

On December 19 the newspapers announced that Lanier had been traded from Marianao to Almendares for Lloyd Basset, a catcher. Marianao's catcher, Chino Valdivia, had been injured and the team even had to resort to putting pitcher Aristónico Correoso behind the plate for a few innings. But the trade seems enormously one-sided, particularly in view of what transpired later, and makes one wonder. Couldn't Marianao have imported another catcher? Probably not one who could get into shape to play soon enough to be of help.

Yet it is difficult to suppress the thought that the league needed Almendares to be more competitive, now that Habana seemed to be ready to run away with the pennant, and that Lanier needed a better cast to showcase his talents. On the other hand, two of Lanier's defeats were against Habana. But one's suspicions are further aroused by Armando Marsans' resignation as manager of Marianao. Was he protesting the trade? He was replaced by a respected manager from the amateur league, Tomás (Pipo) de la Noval. Lanier, in any case, lost his first game with Almendares, though he gave Cienfuegos only one run on five hits. On Christmas Eve, the traditional "Nochebuena" celebration in Cuba, Habana was four games ahead, and Cocaína was undefeated at 6 and 0. The pork roast and black beans with rice must have tasted good to all Habanistas that night.

By the end of December the individual series between Habana and Almendares stood at six wins for the Reds and four for the Blues. Martin was four and one against Almendares. Mayor was 2 and 2 against Habana, and Jessup was 2 and 1. Curiously, Cocaína had no decisions against the Alacranes, being held back by Miguel Angel because of the predominantly right-handed attack of Almendares. The Blues' effectiveness against lefties was proven, perhaps, by Lamarque's 0 and 2 record against them. All of this, as will be seen soon, clarifies the end of the season somewhat, particularly if we add that Habana's left-handed power (Thompson, Kimbro, Formental) was vulnerable to lefties.

By January the teams in the Cuban League were settled, and the business of winning the championship became more strategic and intense. By this time weaknesses and strengths had been evaluated, the imported players had panned out or not and had been kept or shipped back. The veteran Cuban players had also demonstrated whether they were still capable of producing as before. It was becoming clear, for instance, that Dihigo and Tiant, glorious warriors of yore, were in their final season as active players. Among the crop of native rookies, Miñoso continued to display his class. (The merciless Cuban public rarely allowed rookies to develop during the winter season, unless they were truly exceptional.) This year, because the Liga de la Federación ended play in early January, teams in the Cuban League did pick up a few players in the second half. Almendares, as we saw, signed Marrero, although he did not become a factor, and Habana José "Cocoliso" (Smooth Coconut or Baldy) Torres. Other than these changes, and but for the inevitable injuries and sore arms, by January the teams were set.

During December Almendares had played at a paltry .312 clip, while Habana had romped at .705. But there was time, the Almendaristas kept saying; almost two months of competition in which, because of the reduced number of teams, the contenders would have to face each other often. The Almendaristas had certainly not given up hope, although Cocaína started the year by winning again to reach a record of 7 and 0. Whatever he was throwing was certainly a powerful drug.

In January Habana continued its winning ways, but Almendares began to pick up some steam with the help of Lanier, and a revitalized Salazar and Mayor. On January 5, for instance, Lanier beat Habana, 6–1, with Natilla Jiménez as his opponent. Six days later Lanier beat Cienfuegos by the same score. But on January 15 Cocaína raised his record to 9 and 1 (he had finally lost one) by also beating Cienfuegos on four hits. By this time Almendares was closing the gap, and Sergio Varona, a rabid Almendarista writing for *El Mundo,* remarked that nine games remained between Habana and Almendares, so there was still plenty of time. Varona was probably hoping to turn the tide with his very words. On the seventeenth Lanier again beat Habana, this time 9–1, on six hits. It was his third consecutive victory.

Habana's luck seemed to hit a low when Cocaína came down with pneumonia (it was first reported that he had died) and would be out for a long time. But, as if to balance things out, Almendares' third baseman Héctor Rodríguez suffered a deep cut, and the first report was that he would be out for at least a month. The gravity of both players' condition had been seriously exaggerated, however. Cocaína recovered quickly, having missed only one turn, and Rodríguez came back within two weeks, prompting a formal protest from Habana, which claimed that according to league rules, once a man went on the disabled list, he could not be reinstated for a month. The league threw out the protest, which seemed like a desperation move by Miguel Angel, and Rodríguez continued to play. Cocaína came back, but only went 1 and 2 the rest of the way, to finish with a league-leading 10 and 3. Perhaps the pneumonia did take something out of him, or, more likely, it was that he had been pitching all year without a break.

By the end of January, Almendares had inched to within 2½ games of Habana, which seemed to be reeling for lack of pitching. A serious test was at hand on a Friday night game, on January 24, pitting the "eternal rivals" once again. Lanier was chosen by Luque on the strength of his three victories that month, two against the Reds. Miguel Angel was faced with a weakening staff (Medina was having arm trouble), and vexed by his own reluctance to pitch lefties against the Almendares lineup. He had Martin, but he couldn't use him every day, and he did not like to pit him against Lanier, diminishing his chances of winning. He followed the old baseball saw not to throw your best pitcher against theirs, to improve the chances of your best winning. Agapito Mayor attributes the outcome of the season to Miguel Angel's stubbornness on this count, and to the fact that he beat Martin every time, foiling the strategy. So in this case Miguel Angel turned to Terris McDuffie, a bit clownish and temperamental, not to mention long in the tooth. But McDuffie had been improving lately, and beat Lanier, 4–2, in a game that featured a beanball war between the two pitchers that almost provoked a riot. Almendares suddenly found itself 3½ games behind, again. Habana, with Martin pitching masterfully and McDuffie refocused on winning, began to look once more like sure victors. McDuffie's victory on January 24, almost a month to the day before the decisive game of the season, loomed large throughout February. By Varona's anxious count, there remained now seven games between the Leones and the Alacranes, not to mention a number of crucial games with Cienfuegos and Marianao, whose genuine effort to win each contest was closely gauged by everyone.

Habana's vulnerability to lefties, not just to Lanier and Mayor, was evidenced on the last day of January, when Cienfuegos's strong southpaw Adrián Zabala beat them for the fifth time during the season. But Habana was far from dead, and on February 2 they battered Almendares' Lázaro Salazar, which complicated matters for Luque. This was a game that Lanier could have pitched, but the lefty had flown to be with his family in St. Petersburg, Florida. Varona and other Almendaristas wailed, criticizing Lanier for his frequent trips home during the season, but Almendares explained that the pitcher's wife was gravely ill. Lanier told me that he often flew to Florida to shop, for instance, for supplies to make proper American breakfasts. He lived next to the Martins, in the same apartment building, often ate with them, and would go grocery shopping in Miami for Mrs. Martin and other American wives! He told me that the custom agents at the Havana airport got to know him so well that they would just wave him by: "After I pitched a ball game—it's hard to get bacon, ham, or anything like that—they let me fly back to St. Pete and I'd bring back enough stuff for four or five other families, and they'd tell me at the airport customs, 'Well, you'd better win today.' They wouldn't even check it. Sometimes I went to Miami, and sometimes I went to St. Pete. I didn't even stay overnight. I'd go and sometimes come back the same day." Some in Cuba began calling Lanier "The Pilot" for his frequent flying. I am sure that, in spite of the team's explanations, the fiery Luque was none too happy with Lanier's absences, and Salazar's loss to Habana must have left a bitter taste in his mouth. Then on 4 February Marianao beat Comellas, and Almendares fell back again to six games behind Habana, with about twenty days left in the season.

Almendares' march to the pennant began the next day, by winning a doubleheader behind Cuban veterans Agapito Mayor and Tomás de la Cruz. Mayor was at his best, giving up only one run in spite of Cienfuegos' eight hits. The most dangerous hit was a long blast by Noble with men on base late in the game, which made Luque bolt out of the dugout to berate his veteran hurler. Papá Montero thought Mayor had loafed on the pitch to the dangerous Noble, and he was neither strapped to the bench nor lacking a tongue. Agapito bore down and finished. In the second game, de la Cruz, with the help of Gaines, defeated Dihigo's Elephants, 7–2, on a homer by Roberto Ortiz, who would lead the league and set a record for a season with eleven. Cienfuegos also fell to Habana on February 7, on doubles by Pearson and Heberto Blanco, a triple by Formental, and the pitching of Lamarque and Cocaína. Formental was coming back. But February was Almendares' month.

From February 5 to 22 Almendares won ten and lost only one, to Marianao's Sandalio Consuegra on the sixteenth. As we have seen, Mayor and de la Cruz beat Cienfuegos on the fifth. Salazar then beat them on the eighth. Lanier and Mayor beat Habana on the ninth and the twelfth, and Salazar beat Cienfuegos again on the thirteenth. On the fifteenth Max Lanier beat Habana, 6–2, on two hits. Then Mayor beat Cienfuegos twice, on the eighteenth and the twenty-first. On the eighteenth Mayor blanked them, aided by outstanding fielding plays by Cañizares and Héctor Rodríguez. Manning pitched superbly for Dihigo, giving up only two runs, but Almendares was hot and Mayor unbeatable. Going back to February 2 Mayor had won four crucial games in a row, allowing only two hits in thirty-six innings. After the shutout on the eighteenth, he had pitched twenty scoreless innings in succession. As he told me: "This fool you see sitting here won seven of the last twelve games." On the twenty-first Salazar started but was reached for four runs. Comellas put an end to the rally, but Mayor came in, pitched the last three innings, and picked up the win when Almendares came from behind to finish the 6–4 win. It was Mayor's ninth win overall.

The next day, on the twenty-second, de la Cruz defeated Marianao easily, 12–2. Amaro homered, Ortiz tripled, Hausmann doubled, and Héctor Rodríguez had three of the twelve hits the Blues sprayed to all fields. This was on Saturday. Almendares had three games left with Habana, now only 1½ games ahead. The first two would be second games of doubleheaders on Sunday the twenty-third and Monday the twenty-fourth (a holiday in Cuba celebrating the beginning of the War of Independence in 1895). To make it to a deciding game on Tuesday the twenty-fifth, Almendares had to win the games on Sunday and Monday, which meant, of course, that to be champions they had to win all three games in a row. If Habana won on Sunday, climbing to 2½ games ahead, Almendares would have to win Monday and Tuesday, and depend on Cienfuegos beating Habana in the last game of the season Wednesday, which would bring about a playoff. The same situation would arise if Habana lost on Sunday but won on Monday. Even by winning on Tuesday Almendares would have to wait for the Cienfuegos game, and then also win the playoff. But if Almendares won on Sunday and Monday, they would reach Tuesday half a game in the lead, with the championship up for grabs.

By pitching de la Cruz against Marianao, Luque had managed to save his lefties, Mayor, Lanier, and Salazar, for the crucial series. Salazar and Mayor had pitched only four and three innings, respectively, on the twenty-first. Lanier was well rested, having beaten Habana on the fifteenth. Papá Montero also had his righties: Jessup, Gaines, and Comellas. However, by now Luque and probably everybody else knew that what hurt Habana were the lefties, because they neutralized Kimbro, Formental, and Thompson.

Klein and Pearson were Habana's only right-handed threats, though second baseman Heberto Blanco, Cocoliso Torres, and Jimmy Bell provided some protection from the right side, not to mention Sagüita and Salvador Hernández.

Miguel Angel's pitching was a problem because Almendares was essentially a team of right-handers, as we have seen. Habana's leading pitcher throughout the season had been, without question, Cocaína García, already at 10 and 3, and Miguel Angel was reluctant to throw a lefty at Almendares. Habana had four right-handers, however: Natilla Jiménez, Fred Martin, Lázaro Medina, and Terris McDuffie. It seems that Medina had recovered from some arm miseries, and also that, in spite of his recent successes, Miguel Angel did not have confidence in McDuffie. Martin, at 9 and 7, was his workhorse and trump card, and Natilla had pitched well and was 6 and 2. Almendares had momentum, but also had the law of averages against them. How long could they keep playing at such a pace? Habana had been on a slide, but it had two of the leading hitters in Klein and Thompson, as well as front-line pitchers Cocaína and Martin.

Miguel Angel opened on Sunday with Natilla Jiménez, probably thinking he should save Martin for a more crucial game, if he lost, on Sunday. Having an advantage of 1½ games allowed him such a luxury. Besides, for reasons already mentioned, he did not want to use Martin against Lanier, who was in his view Almendares' best. (Of course, there are those who say, use your best pitcher today because tomorrow's game could be rained out.) Lanier was masterful and beat Habana 4–2, scattering nine hits, all singles, and getting two hits himself (Lanier hit right-handed). Habana's best hitters, Klein and Thompson, got two hits each, but Lanier, who only walked one, dominated Sagüita, who had no hits in four times, while Pearson, Heberto Blanco, and Formental had one each. Habana lost on errors (five). Almendares got eight hits, and Pearson made fifteen outs at first, which shows that Natilla and those who came after him were making the Blues hit the ball on the ground. There was no question about who would pitch the next day for both teams. It would be Martin for Habana and Mayor for Almendares. I wonder if Lanier had dinner at the Martins' that evening.

The twenty-fourth was rainy. But it would have taken a hurricane to postpone the crucial game between Habana and Almendares that afternoon, which would turn out to be the most fiercely contested, and the one in which Luque and Miguel Angel would have difficult tactical decisions to make. The first important one for Luque was about his catcher. On this damp, rainy day, Fleitas showed up with a cold, perhaps running a fever. He told me that the trainer gave him a shot of brandy, and the tough Luque stuck him in the lineup without a word.

Mayor was at his best, giving Habana only one run on four hits, while Martin only gave up two runs on seven hits. But one run was manufactured by Luque's cunning, and the other scored as a result of a poor decision by

Miguel Angel. Almendares' first run came in the fourth, after several wasted opportunities. Davenport walked, and Luque tried to bunt him over to second with Ortiz. Cuban baseball was (and is) played by the book, harking back to the dead-ball era and parks of imposing dimensions. Even a slugger was expected to bunt. Ortiz, however, failed, and when allowed to swing, hit one to deepest center field, where Formental made a circus catch. Davenport was still at first. Up came Amaro, and Davenport stole second when Martin threw a change of pace, making it more difficult for Salvador Hernández's throw to beat the runner. Varona and other sportswriters figured that either Luque had stolen the signs or his experience told him what was coming. In any case, Amaro then singled to left, scoring Davenport for the first Almendares run. Why was Davenport, a little fellow, hitting cleanup? some writers had wondered. Here was the answer. Luque wanted a second leadoff hitter in the middle of the lineup to bring about precisely this kind of play. With a lumbering slugger hitting ahead of Amaro, a slow man by this time, this play would not have been possible.

Almendares scored the decisive run in the seventh on a play that would hound Miguel Angel and keep fans arguing until today. In his obsession to send right-handed power against the Blues' tormenting left-handers, Miguel Angel sent Carlos Blanco to hit for Bell in the seventh. He failed, but the Habana manager decided to leave Carlos in Bell's position, right field, although he was an infielder by trade. After all, since Almendares' hitters were mostly right-handed, it was unlikely that Carlos would get a chance. In the very bottom of the inning the Reds would pay for this. Hausmann opened with an infield hit behind second and up came catcher Andrés Fleitas, who was having a sensational season at the plate (he finished at .315). I have been told that Fleitas was a pull hitter and Miguel Angel could not have anticipated what happened. Others have told me that Fleitas was a line-drive hitter who hit to all fields. Fleitas himself told me that he just went with Martin's pitch, which was a bit high and outside. He hit it on a line toward Carlos Blanco in right. Blanco, who was playing too short to begin with, came in on the ball, and when he tried to backtrack it was too late. The ball rolled all the way to the fence for a triple, scoring Hausmann. Mayor had yet to give up a run, so Habana was suddenly down by two with only two innings left to play.

Why did Miguel Angel keep Kimbro and Monteagudo, two experienced outfielders, on the bench and send instead Carlos Blanco to right? Monteagudo and Kimbro hit left, and Miguel Angel stubbornly wanted to give Blanco, a righty, another chance against Mayor. Besides, if a right-handed pitcher were to come in later, he needed his lefties to pinch-hit. Each team carried twenty-two men, so there were some limitations. But Luque's more aggressive style of managing was carrying the day against Miguel Angel's very conservative, plodding strategy.

This was made painfully evident once more in the ninth. In the eighth Habana came to within a run when Heberto Blanco hit a triple to left-center, and Pablo García, a righty hitting for Formental, lofted a long fly to Davenport for the score. Then, in the last inning, Pearson opened with his second hit, and Thompson came to the plate. It is true that Thompson had slacked off somewhat, but he was still hitting .320, with four home runs. But Miguel Angel had him try to bunt the runner over. Mayor pounced on the ball and calmly threw to second to force the lumbering Pearson! The attempted sacrifice is inconceivable unless Miguel Angel thought that Thompson was helpless against Mayor, in which case he should have yanked him. With Pearson at first being held by O'Neil, even if perfunctorily, Thompson had a hole in the right of the infield to shoot for, though, of course, there was also the chance of a double play. But why was Miguel Angel playing for a tie when Habana was the visitor for this game? On the road one plays to win, the book says. Kimbro, finally in the game (in place of Formental), hit a difficult roller to O'Neill, who was only able to get the out at first, while Thompson reached second with the potential tying run. Mayor pitched carefully to Salvador Hernández, and walked him to set up the force (Salvador was no speedster). But he had also put on base the go-ahead run. Still, Almendares could have that luxury because it had last ups. It didn't matter; Mayor induced pinch-hitter Cocoliso Torres to hit a foul fly that Fleitas caught near the boxes for the last out. It was Agapito Mayor's tenth victory, and it put Almendares in first place by half a game. Fans stormed the field, and Almendaristas all over Cuba celebrated wildly. There would be a significant game tomorrow if the rains did not persist. The forecast was encouraging.

But who would pitch tomorrow? There were rumors that Lanier would come back for Almendares on forty-eight hours of rest and that Miguel Angel would turn to his ace Cocaína García, who was rested and ready. Sunday and Monday the stadium had been filled beyond capacity, but the crowds were somewhat distracted by the first games staged by Cienfuegos and Marianao. But tomorrow's was a single game for all the marbles, unless Almendares lost, in which case it was still possible for Habana to lose the next day with Cienfuegos and force a playoff.

The most dramatic thing about the game on Tuesday the twenty-fifth was the choice of pitchers. Luque had all his righties fresh (Comellas, de la Cruz, Gaines, Jessup, and Marrero), as did Miguel Angel (McDuffie, Medina, even Natilla), not to mention his ace lefty, Cocaína. Agapito Mayor, true to his feistiness, offered to pitch without rest. But Luque had another idea. At first it was rumored that Tomás de la Cruz would pitch, but he was not Luque's choice, and the pitcher never forgave Luque for it. Then, Fausto Miranda who was present related to me, Dr. July Sanguily told Luque that he was concerned about a report he had heard to the effect that Lanier was starting on only one day of rest. The Pride of Havana bristled, said Miranda: "Doctor, you may well be a big fucker when it comes to medicine, but in baseball you are an asshole." The Almendares owners were persuaded by Luque's conviction and offered Lanier a $1,000 bonus to pitch. Lanier accepted, on the condition that Agapito Mayor be first to relieve if the need arose, and that he get the money win or lose. The announcement that morning that Lanier, now being admiringly called "El Monstruo" (The Freak, for his unusual resilience), would take the mound for Almendares again sent ripples of nervous chatter through the gathering crowd, and stirred the bettors, who shouted their odds throughout the stands. Miguel Angel stuck to his theory and chose right-hander Medina over Cocaína. Medina must have been highly regarded then, for I have not found surprise at his choice by the participants I have interviewed, though in hindsight I still find the choice perplexing. Granted, he was 5 and 2 in the season and had won fifteen for Tampico in the Mexican League. But what about Lamarque, or Cocaína, even if they were lefties? The fact is that Almendares had not hit much in the previous two games, and perhaps Miguel Angel thought that his theory was correct: that Habana's problem was hitting. He made one baffling change in the lineup, putting Kimbro in center instead of Formental. Both were left-handed batters, with Kimbro having the edge on defense. Formental had only one hit in four turns on Sunday against Lanier and none in three turns against Mayor on Monday. But Miguel Angel did nothing about Sagüita, a right-handed hitter, who was zero for eight in the two games. Why didn't Miguel Angel put Kimbro in left and keep Formental in center? Almendares, home team again for this final confrontation, took the field with the same players in the same positions, and batting in the same order as in the last two games. Why tinker with success? must have been Luque's thought.

The two forces, the two traditions, the red and the blue, were about to collide, blue Almendares tradition reaching back to the 1860s, red Habanista history also stretching back to the origins of the Cuban League. Had these colors also come to be associated with two syncretic Afro-Cuban deities? Red, fiery Santa Barbara or Changó, of the long sword at its side, against blue Ochún, Virgen de la Caridad del Cobre, mulatto virgin and patron saint of the island. Were the devotees of these powerful figures aligned by ritual color, or were all the color lines being crossed, as it were, with prayers and even sacrifices being offered randomly to one or the other? Afro-Cuban syncretic faith and liturgy, like music, had slowly been bonding Cuban society in a movement that went from the bottom up, from the descendants of former slaves to the descendants of former masters. Many of the players I talked to, white and black, had contacts with *santería*, the overall mantle of popular beliefs in Cuba, combining Catholic and African doctrines. Some players were reputed to be *santeros*, or officiants of some sort, and many had been initiated. White, Canary Island descendant Fermín Guerra, a major leaguer, was a *santero*, according to his longtime teammate Agapito Mayor, and Guerra himself told me that he *se había hecho el santo* (had been initiated). Was this last game a mock war of saints, a ritual to purge out the many conflicts in Cuban society? Was the loser going to be the sacrificial lamb?

With the crowd on the field roped in, Lanier strolled to the mound. A veteran of major-league pennant races and World Series competition, he still must have been impressed by the fervor and frenzy in the stands and around the stadium. But Lanier was and is a calm, poised individual, and in 1946–47 he was at the top of his game. He toyed with Habana, striking out every man who came to bat after a hit, as if he were only extending himself when he needed to. The Leones had only six hits, and scored their two runs in the eighth, on a bad-bounce single by Klein that went over Cañizares' head and rolled ever so slowly to Davenport in center. But by that time the game was virtually decided. Almendares struck with one in the second, three in the third, and a demoralizing five in the eighth. Hausmann had four hits, Fleitas two, and veteran Amaro another two. Davenport hit a double that drove in two. By the eighth Medina was long gone, so Almendares got the five against his successors, Natilla Jiménez and Lamarque. Armando Roche mopped up. In the ninth, Habana, still fighting, got two on base with two outs, and Miguel Angel sent Cocoliso again as a pinch hitter. With the crowd on its feet and beginning to hurl objects in the air, Lanier fanned him on a called third strike to end the proceedings.

The crowd surged onto the field, while the police, alerted by Luque, tried to escort Lanier to the dugout. He barely made it, engulfed by adoring Almendaristas and bettors who had made a killing on his feat. El Monstruo was to tell me nearly fifty years later that grateful bettors had stuck $1,500 in his pockets by the time he reached the clubhouse. Later, as he left the stadium, other excited fans tried to rip off parts of his clothing as relics or souvenirs: "When I came down to get a taxi they tore my coat off. They wanted a part of it, you know. I just let them take it. I ran back in and they brought the taxi underneath the grandstand. I got in and then three big trucks followed me all the way to the apartment where I was staying."

A throng chanted and screamed in and out of the stadium. A fan dressed as a blue butterfly pranced frenetically around the infield, as if trying to take to the air. A group of Almendaristas ran to the center-field pole, lowered the Cienfuegos pennant, and hoisted a huge Almendares flag. Out in the street *comparsas,* quadrilles of dancers, carried around big, stuffed scorpions, while blue banners unfolded from windows and balconies. A mock funeral of the lion was staged, and a few fistfights broke out. Ernesto Azúa, writing for *Avance,* reported that a group of fans were seen running toward El Prado boulevard to put an enormous bucket on the head of one of the marble lions that adorn that elegant avenue. Miguel Angel weaved around among the fans as he ran toward the dugout and the safety of the clubhouse, dodging those who accosted him with questions and muttering, "That's baseball, that's sports. . . ."[6]

The man from Santos Suárez, an Habanista, had to walk almost half-way home. Buses and trolley cars were overflowing with excited and exhausted fans. Fireworks were going off in and around the stadium, he was to remember, and chaos seemed to have erupted in the city. Carmelo Mesa

Lago, now a distinguished economist at the University of Pittsburgh and also an Habanista, told me that he heard the last out on the front step of his porch. He turned around, ran through the house, jumped over the back fence, and disappeared so as not to have to face the Almendarista kid next door. Carmelo returned only at dusk.

That night, the celebration continued in the capital and all over Cuba. The Caibarién city council, in Las Villas Province, issued an official statement honoring favorite son Agapito Mayor and set the date for a celebration.

The next day Cienfuegos beat Habana, 8–3, though Klein homered and Formental tripled. By that time Lanier was already at home in peaceful St. Petersburg, Florida, a retirement community that must have seemed like another planet to the tired pitcher. Lanier had settled in St. Petersburg because it was the spring home of the St. Louis Cardinals, the team he had abandoned to go to Mexico. He would not be training with them this year or in the immediate future. Lanier had accomplished his most memorable feat in Cuba, where he would be forever remembered. But in his own country he was a pariah, the victim of the baseball wars of 1946–47.

On the morning of the twenty-sixth, before the last Cuban League game, and before mostly vacant seats, the Dodgers had a workout at the Gran Stadium. The sound of ball meeting bat echoed loudly through the quiet, empty park.

From a House Divided to a Full House

The outcome of The Game, when Max Lanier beat Habana at the end of the 1946–47 season, was an escalation of hostilities between Latin American and Organized Baseball, with Cuba as the focus. The frenzy created by the race between Almendares and Habana, the attendance records set in the Gran Stadium, and the obvious availability of Latin American talent and money did nothing but whet the appetite of U.S. baseball, and harden its resolve to control the Latin American market and solidify its claim to primacy. Mexico had not only drawn an alarming number of American players, but even more Latin players, mostly from Cuba, though also from Puerto Rico, Panama, and Venezuela. The Mexican League had, in 1946–47, a dangerously intimate relationship with the Cuban League, then the premier winter circuit in Latin America. The sense of alarm among U.S. baseball magnates must have been heightened also by labor problems at home. American players formed a players' union and then initiated a pension fund. The Mexican League's tempting offers, moreover, started rumblings among U.S. players about the legality of the reserve clause, which bound them for life to the major-league team that signed him.

The atmosphere was ripe for conflict. In the spring of 1947 two American figures deeply involved in the struggle traveled to Havana to win over to their side the owners of teams in the Cuban League: Clark Griffith, owner of the Washington Senators, who, through scout Joe Cambria, had signed scores of Cuban players and who also partially owned the Havana Cubans of the Florida International League, and Commissioner A. B. (Happy) Chandler, who had succeeded Judge Kenesaw Mountain Landis upon his death in 1945. Luis Orlando Rodríguez, the dapper Cuban minister of sports, arranged for a meeting between Griffith and Jorge Pasquel's brother Bernardo, who was in the Cuban capital to look after the interests of the Mexican League. The occasion was a lunch held for the Washington magnate by the Cuban press. Rodríguez was interested in bringing about a truce that would benefit Cuban baseball players. But the event was awkward and stiff, and one can see in the newspaper pictures that the puritanical, straight-backed Mr. Griffith did not quite know what to do with the debonair and cosmopolitan Mr. Pasquel, who was impeccably dressed, like his brother Jorge. The visit by Mr. Chandler was even less felicitous.

In spite of having been the one to give the go-ahead to sign Jackie Robinson and thereby formally end discrimination against blacks in U.S. baseball, Chandler was no favorite in Havana, and neither was Branch Rickey. Influential Cuban sportswriters such as Jess Losada could see the bad faith behind the rhetoric of integration, when, for instance, though signed by the Dodgers, Robinson was put on the Montreal Royals' roster, and many black players remained unsigned. Also, while in Havana for spring training in 1947, Robinson and the other black American players (Roy Campanella, Don Newcombe, and Roy Partlow) did not lodge with the Canadian team at Havana Military Academy, a fancy prep school, or with the Dodgers at the plush Hotel Nacional, but in rickety hotels downtown (bowing to racism in Cuba).[1] Moreover, the Cubans, who had seen black American players for decades, knew that though good, Robinson was certainly not the best of them, nor the only one worthy of a major-league contract. Why not sign all the other blacks who were better than the whites occupying roster spots? The admittance of blacks into professional baseball did not appear as such a great "experiment" to Cubans because blacks, though banned from the island's Amateur League, had played and managed in professional baseball there since 1900. Cubans knew, too, that Roberto (El Tarzán) Estalella and Tomás de la Cruz, both of African descent, had already played in the majors in the thirties and forties, protected by the American confusion over race, color, and nationality. There was something about Rickey's paternalism and sanctimoniousness that rankled many Cubans, whose Catholic background did not endear them to his Sunday school Protestant rhetoric. Happy Chandler's pasted-on smile (which provoked his nickname) fared no better. Losada referred to him as "Feliciano," a tendentious mistranslation of his nickname that means something like "fool." To make matters worse, Chandler arrived in Havana riding the tall horse of U.S. arrogance in Latin American affairs, acting as if he had the moral and political stature of a Lincoln. When the owners of the Cuban teams declined to bow to his pressure tactics, he condescendingly proclaimed that baseball, after all, was an American sport that had to be played by American rules, and furthermore that American baseball was the only clean baseball. Such pronouncements did not make many friends for Chandler, who left Havana without an agreement.

But the owners of Cuban teams were in a very tight spot. It was true, as Chandler intimated, that there was a certain anarchy in "independent" baseball; players had a tendency not to honor their contracts with Latin American teams. Mickey Owen's case in Mexico was one example. The Dodger catcher, after accepting bonus money from Pasquel, had caved in to pressure from the United States and left Mexico without returning the substantial amount he had been given to sign. Vern Stephens did the same. In Cuba, during the 1946–47 season, taking advantage of the rivalry between the leagues in La Tropical and the Gran Stadium, Ray Dandridge and Booker McDaniels had not honored their contracts with Marianao. There had been many similar cases in the Negro Leagues, with Satchel Paige being the most notorious among those who jumped teams with cavalier disregard for written and verbal agreements. Organized Baseball offered an end to these practices by making players accountable for their actions also during the winter season. Cuban owners also feared that the best young Cuban players were already pledged to Organized Baseball, particularly to the Washington Senators via Cambria. If the Cuban League remained independent from Organized Baseball, it could have stars such as Agapito Mayor or Santos Amaro, who were at their peak, or just past their peak. But it would have no up-and-coming younger players, who constituted the league's future. Cambria's near mass signings of prospects had depleted the amateur ranks, and now that organized baseball was signing blacks, black Cuban ballplayers from the semipro ranks would also go with major-league organizations.

Organized Baseball offered the Cuban League much more, of course, in both tangible and intangible terms. On the tangible side there would be the continued availability of players and the economic support that accrued directly or indirectly from cooperation with powerful major-league systems. Miguel Angel González's relationship with the Cardinals was a good example of the benefits of such collaboration. In the postwar era American baseball was becoming the large, corporate-style business it is today, with a network of technical know-how that involved the media and other promotional practices. The cores of the most profitable and modern Cuban business ventures were intimately intertwined with American corporations, of which they were often subsidiaries. It is not surprising that such a model would appeal to the Cuban League. On the less tangible side there was the aura of efficiency and profitability that American business and industry had in the postwar era, not unlike the one the Japanese enjoy today. Added to it was the fact that many of the younger Cuban magnates had been educated in the United States, spoke English well, and had been schooled early in American business practices. Bobby Maduro and Miguelito Suárez, who owned large shares of the Gran Stadium, are good examples, but there were many others.

As the forties gave way to the fifties, the relationship between American and Cuban business would become even closer. Contributing to the superior aura of American products was popular culture, which in the Cuba of the forties and fifties was strongly influenced by the United States. Cuban movie houses showed mostly American movies, which in the postwar era continued to boast, through war films, about the invincibility of the U.S. Army and the virtues of the American way of life. Cuba's automobiles were overwhelmingly American, as were radios, telephones, trucks, and heavy equipment. Every day the ferry *City of Havana,* sailing from Key West, deposited at the docks American tourists with their own cars, and since World War II Cuba had become a hub for several American airlines, and for the Compañía Cubana de Aviación, which started as a branch of Pan American World Airways. By the early fifties it was easy and relatively cheap to fly from Havana to Miami or New York. There were more flights to the United States than domestic ones to Santiago de Cuba or Camagüey within the island.

Mexican popular culture, through its films and particularly its music, was also a strong presence in Cuba. Great Mexican movie stars such as Jorge Negrete, María Félix, Mario Moreno (Cantinflas), and Pedro Vargas were favorites throughout the island. But Mexican products and businesses could not compete in the Cuban mind or market with American ones. Few if any Cuban families sent their children to study in Mexico, while perhaps thousands sent theirs to American institutions, ranging from summer camps and military academies to the Ivy League. In fact, one could perhaps say that Mexican popular culture appealed to the Cuban lower classes, whereas American popular culture was consumed by the upper classes and those upward bound. That is, at least, the way I remember it.

In this economic and cultural climate it is not surprising that the Cuban League eventually caved in to pressure from Organized Baseball. In that spring of 1947 Dr. July Sanguily, one of the ten owners of Almendares, traveled to a meeting of baseball owners and the commissioner in Cincinnati to hammer out an agreement. Sanguily and the other owners of Almendares were, it should be remembered, associated with the exclusive Vedado Tennis Club, whose members were mainly upper-class Cuban families with strong ties to the United States and American business interests. Sanguily became one of the principal promoters of the pact signed between the Cuban League and Organized Baseball. This pact took the form of an agreement with the National Association of Professional Baseball Leagues, the organization that regulated the minor leagues in Organized Baseball. It was signed on June 10, 1947.

The National Association of Professional Baseball Leagues had been founded in Chicago in 1901 to end the divisive bickering among various professional leagues and to regulate the acquisition of players. When the

Cuban League signed its agreement, the National Association of Professional Baseball Leagues comprised 58 leagues, which included approximately 450 teams ranging in classification from Triple A to Class D. Its president at the time was George M. Trautman, who ruled over the minors for many years, and his director of public relations was Robert Finch, who visited Cuba often in the late forties and fifties.

The purpose of the agreement was, according to the Cuban League's propaganda, "to establish friendly and sporting relations with Organized Baseball in the United States." The agreement was for one year, but it was ratified every year, the Liga claimed in 1950, "owing to the undeniable benefits that it has brought to both parties."[2] From the point of view of Organized Baseball the agreement regulated the activities of players, both American and Cuban, during the winter season, turning the Cuban League into a minor circuit intended to develop talent for major-league teams. Following its agreement with Cuban baseball, the National Association was able to sign similar ones with baseball in Puerto Rico, Panama, and Venezuela, and eventually, following an initiative of the Cuban League, founded the Confederación de Baseball Profesional del Caribe in 1948, and organized the Caribbean Series. The champions of the winter leagues in the four countries involved (Cuba, Puerto Rico, Venezuela, and Panama) would compete in this Series.

The potential negative consequences of the pact for Cuban baseball were considerable. The most dangerous one was losing control of the composition of its teams, which would depend on rules determined by Organized Baseball as to which players could or could not play winter ball (only players with limited or no major-league experience were allowed). In addition, because the agreement forced American players to abide by their contracts, their own development within the American baseball ladder was more important than winning or losing in Cuba. In other words, a player could be sent to Cuba to learn a new position, and he would have to play that position regardless of the needs of his team in the Cuban pennant race. This had happened before, as in the case of Dick Sisler, who told me that he was sent to Havana by the Cardinals in the 1945–46 season to learn to play first base. After the pact this practice of sending players to hone a skill in Cuba regardless of its Cuban team's needs could become rampant. Moreover, under the pressure of scrutiny in Havana by the scouts and coaches of his own American team, a player might play a certain way in Cuba regardless of the needs of his Cuban team. A pitcher, for instance, might favor a certain kind of pitch, or a batter might try to hit for power and strike out more. Worst of all, a major-league team could ask a player to return home at some crucial moment in the Cuban season if it felt that his health was endangered or that he required rest.

Another negative consideration was lack of continuity of Cuban League teams. If major-league organizations only sent to Cuba players on their way up to the big team, but those players could not return once on the major-league roster for more than forty-five days (which was initially the agreement), then the cast would change nearly every winter for the Cuban teams, unless they only hired players without hope of making the majors. Could fans continue to support teams with so much turnover? All these restrictions and regulations did have negative consequences for Cuban baseball. The most disturbing one was that Cuban stars such as Orestes Miñoso, once he was signed by Cleveland in 1948, were not allowed to play in their own country. By the early fifties changes to the agreement had to be made, and Cuban major-league stars were allowed to play every year in the Cuban League.

There was also at issue, of course, the question of nationalism and pride. A large influx of American players could leave Cubans without jobs. Embarrassingly, Miguel Angel González, as already seen in the previous chapter, was reprimanded by Organized Baseball for managing his Habana in the Cuban League, which at the time harbored some of the "outlaws" who had jumped to Mexico. As a result, this revered figure of Cuban baseball lost his job as coach of the Cardinals, which provoked protests among his many fans and friends in Cuba. Signing the pact with Organized Baseball now meant separating from the Cuban League the other patriarch of Cuban baseball, Adolfo Luque, the Pride of Havana, who was managing in the Mexican League, not to mention a great number of venerated Cuban players, such as Agapito Mayor, Santos Amaro, Tomás de la Cruz, Lázaro Salazar, Napoleón Reyes, Roberto Ortiz, Sandalio Consuegra, and many others. All these Cuban players, as well as the American "jumpers," were declared "ineligible" to play in Cuba. The price of admission to Organized Baseball was not only accepting rules for the future conduct of business in Cuban baseball but also a pledge of allegiance in the form of punitive action against Cuba's own for past "misdeeds"—that is, having played for Pasquel in Mexico. This was too bitter a pill to take for many, who declared themselves against the pact, and to the players, who, led by Tomás de la Cruz, organized the Asociación Nacional de Peloteros Profesionales de Cuba and threatened to form a league of their own.

When the pact with Organized Baseball was finally signed in June 1947 it became clear that the only option the "ineligible" players had was to do just that: Create an alternative Cuban League. Thus the Liga Nacional was born, in a sense continuing the Liga de la Federación, which had played the year before at La Tropical, as well as in Matanzas and other cities. The new league would play its games at Don Julio Blanco Herrera's old stadium (the old man provided some of the funds for the league). It was an ironic reversal. The year before, the Liga de la Federación was the refuge for Cuban major leaguers such as Fermín Guerra and Gilberto Torres who did not want to risk their jobs by playing in the Cuban League, as well as others who did not make the grade at the Gran Stadium. But now its successor was conceived to give refuge to the "outlaws" from Organized Baseball, who were the stars of the game in Cuba. The fat was in the fire. The Cuban

League, with its new stadium, the support of Organized Baseball, the support of the "big ten" owners of Almendares, and Miguel Angel González was pitted against the Liga Nacional, which had Luque and most players known to the Cuban public.

Emilio de Armas, who, as adviser to the Cuban League, was one of the pact's engineers and whose experience as baseball promoter and team owner in Cuba reaches back to the early twenties, defends the agreement to this day. To him the crucial thing was that with the pact, play in Cuba became more meaningful to an American ballplayer, whose performance on the island now counted in his career development toward the major leagues. De Armas maintains that Cuban teams always had the right to ship back whoever was not putting out or producing. In addition, once the other countries also signed, the competition for players among the winter leagues was regulated. The ninety-year-old promoter is still bitter over "those Puerto Rican pirates" who "stole" Satchel Paige from him when the pitcher, with a $500 advance of his money pocketed, took a flight from Miami to San Juan instead of to Havana, lured by a better offer.[3] De Armas also maintains that the pact brought a financial bonanza to players, who could count on $1,000 a month salary, with $350 added for expenses if the player were married, and $250 if he were single. But the most important benefit was that each player now felt that his fate in Organized Baseball was at stake also in Cuba. De Armas had paid many a malingerer for a winter vacation in Cuba filled with booze and broads instead of balls and strikes. From a strictly business point of view de Armas is correct that the agreement financially benefited some players and certainly the owners of Cuban teams. But things did not go well right away for the Cuban League.

The Cuban League had some early disappointments. To counteract the fame of the Cuban players at La Tropical, some owners, most notably those of Almendares, decided to try to hire the best known among American major leaguers. This could be done under a rule that allowed major leaguers to barnstorm for thirty days during the off-season. Almendares had Bob Feller ready to come to Havana to pitch five or six games for them. Others, such as Stan Musial, Harry (The Cat) Breechen, and Dick Sisler, all with the Cardinals, were apparently willing to do the same for Habana, and Ewell Blackwell for Marianao. But to the annoyance of many, Chandler nixed the plan. The reasons behind his refusal are clear. Organized Baseball could not afford to have its stars do poorly in Cuba and tarnish the mystique of major-league baseball as a unique and superior product. This fear, provoked, as we saw, by repeated losses on the island by major-league teams, had led Commissioner Landis to forbid clubs to barnstorm under their own names. Younger, untried players could train in Cuba, and if they failed, the reputation of major-league baseball was not compromised. But if Feller were to be shelled by Cienfuegos, or if Musial did not hit well for Habana, the majors' claim to undisputed superiority would be questioned.

Chandler's decision was not a decisive blow to the Cuban League, but it added to the general turmoil.

To say that the situation was confusing is an understatement. Mexicans who had played in their country and had not, therefore, "jumped" an Organized Baseball contract, were eligible to play in the Cuban League (hence Chanquilón Díaz and Cochihuila Valenzuela played for Marianao at the Gran Stadium). Technically, black American players in the Negro Leagues were also eligible, because most of them had no contract with major- or minor-league organizations. Black players, however, were under pressure not to play in the independent Liga Nacional at La Tropical because many Negro Leagues teams rented major-league stadiums and were coerced to adhere to Organized Baseball's ban. For example, Alejandro Pompez's New York Cubans played many of their home games at the Polo Grounds when the Giants were on the road. Already weakened by the signing of young stars such as Robinson and Larry Doby, the owners of Negro Leagues baseball could not face the further harm that not being able to use major-league stadiums would surely cause them. As a result, most of the New York Cubans, including Panamanian Pat Scantlebury, played with teams in the Cuban League at the Gran Stadium, and Pompez drew closer to the Giants and to their owner, Horace Stoneham. Some Negro Leagues players who had gone to Mexico, such as Ed Stone, did play at La Tropical. To offset the power of the Cuban League, backed by the might of Organized Baseball and the fears and vulnerability of Negro Leagues baseball, the Liga Nacional counted on the prestige of its established Cuban players, as well as that of the banned Americans, such as Sal Maglie, Fred Martin, Max Lanier, Danny Gardella, Lou Klein, and favorites from the Negro Leagues who had gone to Mexico.

The Cuban League had other advantages over its rival. It had rights on the names of the teams, hence on the potential loyalty of the fans. This was a major stumbling block for the Liga Nacional, particularly in the case of the "eternal rivals" Habana and Almendares, who had by far the largest following. But, while the teams of the Cuban League had the rights to the names of the teams, the Liga Nacional could appropriate their emblems and colors, as the Liga de la Federación had done the year before. There were other names and cities that could be used as substitutes for the Marianao and Cienfuegos franchises, which did not have a deep-rooted fan base anyway. So the Liga Nacional fielded four teams. The Alacranes, or Scorpions, who wore blue, were managed by Luque and had most of the traditional Almendares players, such as Agapito Mayor, Roberto Ortiz, George Hausmann, Tomás de la Cruz, Héctor Rodríguez, Avelino Cañizares, Santos Amaro, and Lloyd Davenport. The Leones, or Lions, wore red, and had many of the players who were associated with Habana, such as Fred Martin, Alberto (Sagüita) Hernández, Lázaro Medina, and Carlos Blanco. The third team was Santiago, which drew on the distinct identity that Oriente Province has always had in Cuban history. Oriente had proven its viability by supporting the team named after it in the Liga de La Federación the year before. Santiago had Puerto Rican star Luis Rodríguez Olmo, Murray Franklin, and Booker McDaniels, among others. The fourth team was shrewdly named Cuba, a name on which no one could make any claim and that could draw fans from the entire country. This was also the name of a team that had played in the Cuban League years before (the last time in 1939), and could be associated with the national teams that represented the island in the amateur World Series of the early forties. Cuba not only had the popular Napoleón Reyes as player-manager but also boasted slugger Tarzán Estalella; Tony Castaño, a former batting champion; Roland Gladu, a Canadian who was a favorite of Cuban fans; Danny Gardella, the notorious "jumper" and former Giant; powerful Alejandro Crespo; Stan Breard at short; "Red" Hayworth behind the plate; and Jean Roy (another Canadian) on the mound. In addition to all these well-known players, the Liga Nacional also had the "traditional" umpires, who sided with the established players. These umpires were Amado Maestri, Bernardino Rodríguez, Raúl (Chino) Atán, Kiko Magriñat, and others. The Cuban League, on the other hand, had to import Patrick Padden, from the American Association, and Walter Ryan from the International League. Padden became a fixture in the Cuban League.

The Asociación de Peloteros and the Liga Nacional counted on the power of tradition. After all, La Tropical had been the shrine where most established Cuban players had become famous, where Cuban squads made up of native stars had scored stunning victories against major-league teams, and where several amateur World Series had been played. Its beautiful green expanses had seen feats such as Dick Sisler's three home runs in one game, Claro Duany's mammoth shot over everything in right, Alejandro Crespo's circus catch off a Pee Wee Reese line drive in an exhibition against the Dodgers, and Estalella's blast to deep left field, which allowed Crespi to tag up and score from second, ahead of Oms's throw. The Gran Stadium had been the site of The Game in 1947, but it was still just that: new. Cuban fans could remember scores of games where the likes of Alejandro Oms, Silvio García, Lázaro Salazar, Napoleón Reyes, Martín Dihigo, Luis Tiant, and so many others had starred at La Tropical. La Tropical's history bonded fans, teams, and players.

The managers that were selected to guide the eight professional teams in Havana during the winter of 1947–48 reflected what was at stake in the rivalry between the Cuban and National Leagues. At the Gran Stadium, former Yankee standout Vernon (Lefty) Gómez was imported to lead the Cienfuegos team; Miguel Angel González, contrite after his brush with Organized Baseball, continued to manage his Habana Lions and to stay close to the big money; Fermín Guerra, eager to preserve his eligibility in the United States, took over for the outlawed Luque at the helm of Almendares; and Tomás "Pipo" de la Noval was picked to manage Marianao. Meanwhile, at La Tropical, Luque led the Alacranes, Salvador Hernández took over the Leones, Lázaro Salazar headed Santiago, and Napoleón Reyes was given the reins of Cuba.

While it is true that the teams in La Tropical had the most famous Cuban players, and the Gran Stadium had many unknown American minor leaguers, the Cuban League had great Cubans from the Negro Leagues, particularly from the New York Cubans. Silvio García, a superb shortstop, was back with Cienfuegos; Pedro (Perucho) Formental was still with Habana, as was Manuel (Chino) Hidalgo. The Cuban League also had great black stars such as Sam Jethroe, who had signed with a major-league team.[4] But the stadium in El Cerro had above all Conrado Marrero, of Almendares, the "Premier," who was one of the most popular players in Cuba and who had gone from great prominence in the amateurs to a splendid career with the Havana Cubans of the Florida International League, where he was obviously too much for Class C competition. Rodolfo Fernández, a coach for Almendares that year, told me that what filled the Gran Stadium to capacity and saved the Cuban League were Marrero's duels with Alex Patterson of Habana and Dave Barnhill of Marianao.

The Asociación de Peloteros claimed that the Liga Nacional gave a chance to the local players, accusing the Cuban League of having sold out to foreign interests. This was no doubt true to some extent, but at La Tropical, in part with money made available by the Dirección General de Deportes and Luis Orlando Rodríguez, many non-Cuban players were also participating. Cuba, for instance, fielded at one point a lineup that had Myron (Red) Hayworth catching, Napoleón Reyes at first, Beto Avila at second, Ray Dandridge at third, Stan Breard at short, Roland Gladu in left, Ed Stone in center, and Danny Gardella in right: one Cuban, a Mexican, two Canadians, and four Americans. The Leones had Jean Roy, Fred Martin, and Lou Klein, who were very popular in *habanista* circles, and Santiago had Puerto Rican Rodríguez Olmo, considered by many in Cuba to be the best Latin American player of the moment. The issue was, of course, not so much a matter of nationality as of allegiance to Organized Baseball. The clear fact is that many of the white American ballplayers who performed in El Cerro only qualified because they belonged to major-league organizations, but were really not otherwise ready for the level of competition expected in the Cuban League.

But the competition was still keen, close, and acrimonious. For instance, on the night of November 2 both stadiums featured duels between Almendares and Habana, except that at La Tropical they were called Alacranes and Leones. Twenty thousand people went to the Gran Stadium, while twenty-two thousand overflowed La Tropical's capacity. The battle for players continued. Having fulfilled his contract with Monterrey, Andrés Fleitas forsook Mexico to sign a three-year contract with Almendares worth $10,000, and a one-year, $9,000 one with Organized Baseball. This meant, of course, that he was reneging on his pledge to the Liga Nacional and the Asociación de Peloteros, who criticized the catcher viciously in the press.

Fleitas has told me that the pledge made by de la Cruz to pay everybody the same was soon broken, with some American and Cuban stars getting more than others. This is what led him to jump from La Tropical to the Gran Stadium. But to this day Agapito Mayor is bitter about those who "sold themselves" to the Cuban League.

A popularity contest run by the weekly magazine *Carteles* during this 1947–48 season showed that Roberto Ortiz and Conrado Marrero, playing for their respective Blues, were in the lead, and that the two leagues were in a nip-and-tuck race in attendance. The contest also showed that adding the fans of the Alacranes at both stadiums, Almendares was the team with the largest following all over the island, and a substantial one in the entire Caribbean basin, Mexico, Central America, and Venezuela. Letters sent by Cubans living in the United Sates showed that there were many fans of the Blues among them. Habana and Leones together placed second in popularity.

In the Liga Nacional the Leones won. Roland Gladu, playing for Cuba, which came in second, was the champion batter with an average of .330, followed by Rodríguez Olmo, who hit .313. The Puerto Rican star was declared the best player in the Liga Nacional, and many thought he was the best ballplayer in Cuba that winter. Gardella led in homers with ten, Adrián Zabala was the champion pitcher, while Roberto Ortiz led in runs batted in and Cañizares in runs scored. Sal Maglie had the most complete games with twenty and the most wins with fourteen. By December 15, however, Santiago was withdrawn from the championship because the team was losing money. Rodríguez Olmo was moved to the Leones, as were Roberto Estalella, Sandalio Consuegra, and Amado Ibáñez, while Gardella went to Cuba. The season ended on a very sour note. The Liga Nacional sponsors, who had put up the money, pulled back when they saw that the struggle was being lost to the Cuban League, and the last payroll was not met. Rodríguez Olmo did not get paid for his last month of work. Soon accusations of mismanagement (or worse) by Tomás de la Cruz and the Asociación de Peloteros filled the air, and when the former Cincinnati pitcher returned to Mexico for the summer season he was spurned by his compatriots, who made public their accusations.[5]

At the Gran Stadium Habana also won, helped by its trio of Negro Leagues standouts: Lennox Pearson, Henry Kimbro, and Hank (Machine Gun) Thompson. Kimbro led the league with a .346 average; Thompson led in runs batted in with 50. Kimbro also set a record with 104 hits in a season. Alex Patterson, too, had a great campaign on the mound, as did Rufus Lewis, of the Newark Eagles. Almendares finished only one game behind. Marrero went 12 and 2 with 7 shutouts, and Sam Jethroe had an outstanding season, leading in runs scored, with 53, and in stolen bases, with 22. Cienfuegos came in third, behind the pitching of Max Manning, who finished at 10 and 8, and Carl Erskine, of future Dodger fame, who finished with 9 and 7. Noble had a good season, batting a solid .292 with

5 home runs. Silvio García also batted .292. Marianao had the support of David Barnhill, who led in strikeouts with 122, and Chanquilón Díaz, who was champion home-run hitter with 7. Miñoso led in triples with 13, and Duany also had a fine season, leading in doubles with 12.

Habana won because its team was not as weakened by defections to La Tropical as others, particularly Almendares, which lost Mayor, de la Cruz, Cañizares, Héctor Rodríguez, Roberto Ortiz, Max Lanier, and Luque. Meanwhile, Habana had, in addition to Pearson, Thompson, and Kimbro, Formental, Hidalgo, Lamarque, Rufus Lewis, and Patterson, who may have never made the grade in the major leagues but who more than held his own that winter in Cuba.

Several things stand out in the final records of the double 1947–48 season. First, while Miguel Angel González gained a measure of revenge in beating Almendares, the victory was tainted because the core of the Blues played at La Tropical under Luque. Second, very few of the American rookies from Organized Baseball did very well in El Cerro, with the exception of Patterson and Erskine. Players such as Dee Fondy, Hal Rice, Steve Gerkin, and Dick Younger had ephemeral major-league careers or none at all, and did not do that well in Cuba. Jethroe, although under contract with Organized Baseball, was really a product of the Negro Leagues, as were Kimbro, Pearson, Barnhill, and Thompson, not to mention Cubans Miñoso, Silvio García, Noble, and Duany. Yet the unavoidable conclusion is that the season at El Cerro was a financial and organizational success that spelled the doom of the rival Liga Nacional, now in disarray and with the Asociación de Peloteros beset by fierce bickering and ugly recriminations.

It is truly a shame that the two Habanas did not meet in a playoff to determine the overall champion, or even better, that they did not join the two Almendares in a four-team tournament to settle the dispute on the field. But the bitterness was too great for that.

Opportunities for Cuban players whose careers were peaking in the forties were diminishing with the encroachment of Organized Baseball. In the Negro Leagues the New York Cubans had a last hurrah as they won the 1947 championship of the Negro National League, with a team that included Miñoso, Noble, and manager José María Fernández. But black baseball as an independent venture was declining, and Pompez became more involved with the New York Giants, for whom he eventually became a scout. Meanwhile, in Mexico, the Pasquels could no longer afford to go on losing money and decreed a radical salary reduction in 1947. By 1948 Pasquel's dream had smashed against hard realities and the results of his own high-handedness. The Mexican League had lived out its brief moment of splendor. During the 1947 summer season players began to leave Mexico. In Cuba a summer league was quickly organized by 1948 to take up the slack, but it was not very successful. Eligible Cuban players fanned out through the minor leagues, even though the pay was low, playing and living conditions were atrocious, and discrimination against them was rampant.

Agapito Mayor wound up for a while at Sherman-Denison, of the Class B Big State League (Texas), which was managed by Cuban Joseíto Rodríguez, brother of Oscar Rodríguez, who was managing the Havana Cubans. The most attractive option by far was to play for the Havana Cubans, which, though merely Class C, were at least based in Cuba. Another possibility was to play for any other team in the Florida International League, which visited Havana regularly and were close to the island. Among these teams the Tampa Smokers and both Miami teams (the Flamingos and the Tourists) were the favorites. Tampa in particular had (and still has) a large Hispanic population, with thousands of Cubans still employed by the cigar industry in the forties, hence the team's improbable name. My great-uncle Aurelio, established in Tampa since the thirties, was the Smokers' team doctor. Miami was an hour from Havana by plane. Playing in the Florida International League the Cuban players could be part of Organized Baseball yet still be at home.

Another opportunity that opened up in 1947 both for Cuban players (particularly for those declared ineligible by Organized Baseball and who were fleeing Mexico) and for American blacks, was Venezuela, due to the oil boom in the Maracaibo region, which made possible the creation of a league. Black American players seeking better pay and playing conditions, along with ineligible Cubans, Puerto Ricans, and other Latin Americans, joined Venezuelans in a season played in one stadium in Maracaibo. The Liga Marabina (really called Liga del Estado de Zulia) had three teams: Gavilanes, Pastora, and Orange Victoria. Ernesto Aparicio, a Venezuelan impresario who owned the Gavilanes, started to turn up regularly in Havana, as had Pasquel before, to lure Cubans away. The league in Maracaibo survived a few years as the last bastion of independent baseball. Players such as Agapito Mayor, Pedro (Natilla) Jiménez, Pedro (El Gamo) Pagés, Roberto Ortiz, Héctor Rodríguez, Alejandro Crespo, and many others went directly from Mexico to Maracaibo. Others, such as Cocaína García, who were known already in the Venezuelan winter league, simply stayed on in the summer. The Cuban presence in Maracaibo was such that it extended to the umpires, with Atán and Vidal, and to the broadcast booth, where popular Felo Ramírez was imported to broadcast the games. American blacks also flocked to Maracaibo, among them Raymond Brown, of Santa Clara fame in the Cuban League, who came out of retirement, lured by the $1,500 monthly salary. Orange Victoria, the team for which he played, had a payroll of $20,000 per month.

As with all of the expansion of baseball in the Caribbean, the development of aviation made the Venezuelan venture possible. In the late forties and early fifties the Compañía Aeropostal Venezolana expanded its routes, with frequent flights to New York in luxurious Lockheed Constellations. These flights had a stopover in Havana in both directions. Ties between Venezuelan and Cuban businesses were strengthened as a result, as were cultural contacts. During these years the great Cuban novelist Alejo

Carpentier was living in Caracas and working for Publicidad Ars, an advertising agency, where he contributed to the development of Venezuelan
radio and television through the fifties. The Cuban players who went to
the Liga Marabina were the advance guard of many others who would play
or manage in the Venezuelan winter league in the late forties, fifties, and
even after the Cuban revolution, when the likes of José Tartabull and Luis
Tiant, Jr., without a native country in which to play winter ball, went there.

But, on the whole, the game was over for independent baseball by the
late forties: The Mexican League was in sharp decline and would eventually
be absorbed by Organized Baseball; the Negro Leagues were on borrowed
time, since their best young players were being signed by major-league
teams and even younger ones would go directly into Organized Baseball
(there were exceptions, such as Ernie Banks, Hank Aaron, and Cuban Francisco—Panchón—Herrera). Cuban blacks continued to play for the remaining Negro teams, particularly the Kansas City Monarchs, the Newark
Eagles, and the Memphis Red Sox, but eventually they, too, would be
signed directly by major-league organizations. In Cuba the Cuban League,
with the backing of Organized Baseball, was clearly victorious. It was time
to settle accounts after the bitter war. And the accounts were settled, often
in subtle but cruel ways over a long period that extended to the fifties.

When Lanier beat Habana in 1947 Cuba was, as we saw, in the midst of
an optimistic political and economic period created by World War II, which
(as with all major wars) increased the demand and the price for sugar. By
the time the 1948–49 season rolled around there was chaos in the midst
of plenty. Dr. Grau San Martín, the man who had beaten Batista in 1944,
had turned out to be ineffectual, corrupt, and diffident. This was a major
disappointment, for he had won a clean election and had been hailed as a
sort of messiah who would finally bring about the reforms for which the
1933 revolutionaries had fought. Grau, a professor of medicine at the University of Havana and belonging to a well-heeled family, had no need to
acquire wealth from politics. However, his underlings assaulted the national
treasury with a vengeance while he looked the other way. The Marshall
Plan had extended the sugar boom created by the war by buying Cuba's
entire production, so there was a great deal of money circulating in Cuba.
Havana was chock full of cars, creating enormous traffic jams; bus systems
renewed their equipment, and there were plans to find a modern substitute
for the trolley cars; construction of hotels and casinos continued. Prosperity
and political laxity attracted, as in previous eras, a number of undesirables,
such as New York mobster Lucky Luciano, who was, nevertheless, sum-
marily expelled from the country. But, needless to say, the local gangsters
were bad and plentiful enough. Warring groups of former revolutionaries
were in a feeding frenzy, vying for power and money. Gangsterism was
rampant around the university, and political infighting deteriorated into

full-scale battles, with many *atentados* (attacks on a single individual by gunmen). Among those felled in this fashion was Manolo Castro (no relation to Fidel, who was alleged to be one of his assassins), who had succeeded Luis Orlando Rodríguez as director of sports.

Grau gave way in 1948 to Carlos Prío Socarrás, another leader from 1933, whose administration was even more venal and who could not control the political anarchy. Among the unscrupulous politicians of the period, none was perhaps as notorious as José Manuel Alemán, minister of state under Grau and later minister of education under Prío. Alemán stole millions (his friends said ten, his enemies fifty), some of which he sent to Miami, where he built Key Biscayne, among other business ventures. He also bought one of the Miami teams in the Florida International League and built what came to be known as Bobby Maduro Stadium in that city. Alemán also purchased, through Alfredo Pequeño, who acted as his intermediary, Marianao, in the Cuban League.

Radio broadcasting was enjoying a moment of great splendor in Cuba during the late forties. The most popular soap opera ever, *El derecho de nacer,* drew the attention of millions throughout Cuba and the entire Caribbean basin. Written by Félix B. Caignet, from Santiago de Cuba, the program would establish records in various reincarnations throughout Latin America over many years. The original Cuban version had Carlos Badías as Alberto Limonta, Lupe Suárez as Mamá Dolores, and María Valero as Isabel Cristina. Only stars of their magnitude could compete for popularity with ballplayers and radio announcers. Another popular show, with the comedy team of "Chicharito y Sopeira" ("Garrido y Piñero"), one portraying a Galician who pulled for Almendares, the other a black who favored Habana, stoked the fires of fandom throughout the island. The *negrito* and the *gallego* were stock figures in Cuban theater and vaudeville, who in "Garrido y Piñero" were absorbed into the orbit of baseball.

The hold that baseball had on the Cuban public is shown by the fact that four radio stations competed in broadcasting the Havana Cubans' games from the Gran Stadium. No Class C ballclub had ever, or would ever, receive such attention in the history of the game. But then no Class C team had the kind of talent the Cubans had. Several Cuban players went directly from the Havana Cubans to the Washington Senators, their parent team. The most successful example was Conrado Marrero, who won twenty-five games for the Cubans in 1947, twenty in 1948, and again twenty-five in 1949. Julio Moreno, who went up to the Senators as well, also had effective seasons for the Cubans in the late forties, as the team won five championships in a row. Cambria's plan was working fine for him and for the Senators. By this time the shrewd scout had already bought a café in Havana, as well as some rental properties; he practically lived in Cuba. He would eventually own a string of bars and a small restaurant attached to the Gran Stadium, behind the center-field scoreboard, where he could lodge young players who were in the reserves (taxi squad) of the teams in the Cuban League. The interests of the Havana Cubans and the Cuban League were converging under the tutelage of Organized Baseball. In September, by the end of the 1948 season, the Cubans had won their third championship in a row, aided by Marrero and Moreno as well as by Chino Hidalgo, Tony Zardón, and Gilberto Torres, who had been sent down from the Senators to the Cubans. As the 1948–49 season of the Cuban League approached, all of these players, as well as others in the minor leagues, Mexico, and Venezuela, waited anxiously to learn the composition of the teams, in the aftermath of the Liga Nacional's demise and the pact sealed with Organized Baseball. Cuban talent would certainly be plentiful, and competition for spots on the rosters fierce.

The purchase of Marianao is as good an indication as any of the new level of finance to which professional baseball had risen in postwar Cuba. Alemán, through his intermediary Pequeño (a representative in the lower chamber of the Cuban congress), arranged to purchase two things from the owners of Marianao, Eloy García and Baldomero (Merito) Acosta: the franchise in the Cuban League and the trademark or registered name. Since all the teams played at the Gran Stadium, which belonged essentially to Bobby Maduro (who was in turn one of the owners of Cienfuegos) and Miguelito Suárez, the franchises did not include physical assets other than the baseball equipment. Alemán paid Eloy García $120,000 for the franchise, and Merito Acosta $40,000 for the trademark, with $30,000 also going to the shrewd Emilio de Armas for "unspecified services." In total the team cost Alemán almost $200,000, a fabulous sum in Cuban baseball, particularly when one remembers that the ten owners of Almendares had paid $17,500 in 1941 for the most recognizable franchise in the league and all of Latin America. In view of this, Miguel Angel González, notoriously frugal and cunning in business, had made a killing with Habana, which he had purchased for a song from Abel Linares's widow. If Marianao was worth $200,000 in September 1948 and was the *fourth* franchise in the Cuban League, then Habana could very well be worth $500,000, and Almendares even more. This is astonishing when one also realizes that a major-league franchise—not the Yankees, Dodgers, or Cardinals, to be sure, but the Browns or the Athletics—may have cost $1 million at that time, and some real estate and other physical assets would have been included in the price. With the following that Almendares had in the Caribbean basin as well as Central and South America, the team could have earned very substantial amounts of money barnstorming (as it did in the fifties, when it went to Colombia), or even more if the Cuban League had expanded to other countries, as the development of aviation could have made possible.

The way Marianao was purchased is also a good indication of the progressive encroachment of political corruption in the Cuban League. Eloy García, who was essentially the owner of the club, had no intention of selling Marianao, which was a legitimizing venture that covered up for his real source of income, which was the *bolita* or numbers game (according

to some he was the second biggest *bolitero* in Havana, the first being someone called Campanario). When Alemán, through Pequeño, expressed interest in the club, García showed no desire to sell, according to Emilio de
Armas. The Cuban League did not want to be ostensibly connected to
politics and wanted the club to remain in García's hands. But Alemán and
Pequeño had a powerful argument. If Alemán, who had the ear of President
Grau, removed the police protection García enjoyed for his illegal *bolita,*
he would be out of business in a day. He had no choice but to give in. All
García could do was raise the price of the club. This not only benefited
García but also provided de Armas with a powerful selling point before the
squeamish Cuban league officials. For, if Marianao could be sold for such
a sum, what would this do to the value of the other teams, particularly
Habana and Almendares?

In any case, Marianao, considered until then *ripieras* (riffraff), now
became *millonarios,* millionaires, in reference to its wealthy owner Alemán,
who died of cancer in March 1950, very soon after purchasing Marianao
and Miami in the Florida International League. Alfredo Pequeño stayed
with the club, and arranged for the Marianao city hall to issue a proclamation stating that the team represented that city, thus becoming the only
team to be so designated in the Cuban League. By 1950 Marianao had a
$27,800 monthly payroll. The team changed its colors to orange and black,
becoming the Tigres after an amateur team called Club Atlético de Cuba,
and tried to sign Luque as manager for the 1948–49 season. But The Pride
of Havana had not suffered enough in the eyes of Organized Baseball for
going to Mexico and challenging the Cuban League at La Tropical. He
was and was declared to be still ineligible to be signed in his own country;
hence Marianao had to make a trade with Almendares to obtain Gilberto
Torres to manage (and play). Marianao relinquished Francisco Campos,
who had just been "rehabilitated" after having jumped the Senators' organization to play in Mexico some years before. Luque would eventually
manage Marianao, but not before suffering the humiliation of being coach
under Miguel Angel González in the 1949–50 championship. (Marianao
had to endure other absences in 1949–50, most notably Miñoso and Beto
Avila, who had signed with the Cleveland Indians, and Al Rosen, who was
supposed to play, too, but was also put on the roster of the same team.)
Bolstering the third and fourth franchises became one of the plans of the
Cuban League, and though it would take some years before it won a championship, Marianao was on its way.

The 1948–49 season brought about a consolidation of the Cuban League
in another significant way. The Gran Stadium in El Cerro, "El Gran Stadium de La Habana," finally became the legitimate house, the temple of
Cuban baseball, superseding La Tropical, which would never again recapture its splendor (though professional and amateur baseball continued to
be played there for some time). The Gran Stadium's anointment, however,

was not a fresh start, but a continuation: The park in El Cerro inherited from La Tropical many of the permanent figures who performed the various rituals surrounding the game. Because all games were played on the same field, the Gran Stadium had a peculiarly intense aura of sacredness about it, one that could be felt throughout the country by way of radio and later television. Everybody knew where everything was located at the stadium, or imagined they did, from the advertisements on the fences that offered prizes to the players who hit a home run over them, to the ballboy's position behind home plate. The stadium's geography and people were a common space and cast of characters in the national mind's eye.

The stadium was conventional in shape, with a roofed grandstand that stretched from one foul pole to the other, much like Wrigley Field in Chicago. The distances were also rather conventional, and the field was symmetrical: 340 down each line, 375 in the power alleys, and 450 to center field, where a large and quite high, hand-operated scoreboard stood. At the bottom, the scoreboard had a large ad for Hatuey Beer, and at the top one for the beer's parent company, Bacardí Rum. There were no bleachers in left, but instead a second fence covered with advertisements, a few feet behind the one setting off the field's boundary. Beyond that fence there was a warehouse, and farther back, a street. There were two famous ads in left. One was for Sastrería El Sol ("Sastres anatómicos y fotométricos"), a haberdashery that offered $100 suits to players who hit the ball over it. Another was for Guayaberas Comodoro, which offered a similar prize. The light towers in the outfield—two in left and two in right—had signs, one for Casino Socks, another for Kresto, a chocolate drink for children.

The bullpens, as in Wrigley or Ebbets Field, were down the foul lines, along the box seats. They were moved to center field in the later fifties, when the distance was shortened to 400 feet by erecting a metal fence. The dugouts were of the sunken type, with some tubular columns. The stadium had four clubhouses under the grandstand, each with its own attendant. The press boxes were hanging from the roof, toward the back of the grandstand. They were reached by very high and precarious catwalks. (I once saw a whole side of the mostly male crowd stand to ogle Gladys Siscay as she rhythmically climbed the steps of one of these catwalks; she was a voluptuous mulatto vedette who starred in a cigarette commercial done live from the Gran Stadium between innings.) These boxes included the radio booths and eventually the television booths and studios. Since the games were broadcast by several stations and there were reporters from as many as a dozen newspapers, these boxes were crowded and lively. The official scorer and the official statistician of the league shared this space, as did the park's public-address announcer. There were high platforms attached to some of the steel columns of the stadium for still photographers, and later for television cameras.

Underneath the grandstand there was a whole world of concessions, and even a branch of Casa Vasallo, one of the better-known sporting goods stores in Havana. Another sporting goods store, from which I once bought a pair of spikes, was owned by a black man known as "Malayo," who was related to the ballboy Zulueta (more about him later in this chapter).[6] There was a bar, and the fare in the various concessions included hotdogs but was more inclined to Cuban popular cuisine, such as delicious pork and ham sandwiches and *medianoches,* a hot sandwich in slightly sweet bread containing ham, cheese, and butter. Monteagudo's shop was a favorite for these. Coffee, aromatic and as strong as any in the world, was sold in the traditional demitasses as well as in tiny paper cups. Coffee vendors hawked their product from long thermoses in the stands with a cry in which the first syllable was stretched for a long time, and the second shortened: *"Caaaaaaaafé."* To this they added, *"Acabadito de colar"* (just brewed). The stadium smelled of strong coffee and good cigar smoke, not of beer, as in the United States, though beer was also sold in great quantities by vendors who added to the din with their cries. They competed with the calls of the bettors, who changed the odds as the game progressed. Conspicuous among these was "Chicho Pan de Gloria," short, fat, and a vocal follower of President Carlos Prío Socarrás. Another bettor was known simply as "Alejandro." Others sold *quinielas,* rafflelike tickets that, when opened, contained the name of a position. If the first run of the game was scored by the player on either team currently playing that position, the owner of the ticket won. Needless to say, if people noticed that a certain vendor's tickets were heavy on "pitcher" and "catcher," he would not sell very many. As I remember, the *quinielas* cost about 25 cents, and one could win as much as $2.00. In the fifties and in Havana $2.00 was not a trivial sum. *"Preferencia"*—grandstand seats right behind the field boxes—cost about $1.25.

Other hawkers added to the carnival atmosphere. Those who did not have concessions within the stadium sold their food or souvenirs on the sidewalks around it. On Sundays, particularly, when the four-team doubleheader started at one in the afternoon, many fans had their lunch inside the stadium, or just outside. Pork was roasted on open fires for succulent sandwiches called *pan con lechón,* heavy with garlic and dripping fat. The souvenirs spanned the gamut of trinkets, flags, pennants, pictures, scarfs, and every imaginable representation of scorpions, lions, elephants, and tigers. Because all four teams played their home games at the stadium, business was brisk, and vendors had no loyalties. There were also, to be sure, scalpers, particularly when the stadium was full or nearly full. Beyond right field, in the gap between the grandstand and the beginning of the bleachers, there were apartments from whose balconies the games could be seen, as in Wrigley Field in Chicago or old Shibe Park in Philadelphia. Vacancies in this building were advertised emphasizing that tenants could see the games free. It is safe to assume that they could also hear the roar of the crowd.

Around the stadium were bars that catered to the baseball public and sometimes to the ballplayers, the press, and their many hangers-on. One such was Bar Primavera, down Carlos III Boulevard, in front of the Cuban Electric Company, and which was frequented by players from the Marianao team. As can be imagined, women also gravitated toward these bars, some in search of business, others just in search of fun.

There is nothing comparable in today's baseball, especially in the United States, to the atmosphere at the Gran Stadium. Except for the Sunday doubleheaders, baseball was not a spectacle for children, but part of the nightly entertainment of a very cosmopolitan city. This does not mean that children did not go to the stadium, but it was not in shorts, with a glove in one hand and a soda in the other. A visit to the stadium, as a child, was a serious outing, and one dressed in the better clothes reserved for wear after the daily afternoon bath. Moreover, night games began at nine o'clock, to allow for the Cuban family dinner hour, which was at about eight o'clock. Because it was winter, people, particularly women, dressed well, and it was not unusual to see furs in the more expensive box seats. In fact, it was quite common for people to go to the game and later catch the second show at one of the nightclubs, such as Montmartre, Tropicana, or Sans Souci. Cuban winter ball coincided with the tourist season and therefore the height of the casino and nightclub seasons. The Gran Stadium was a place to be seen if you were in show business or politics. Social chronicles would be written about who among the rich and famous was at the stadium, underscoring their affiliations to the various social clubs. Ballplayers were celebrities with whom to mingle. The popular Sonora Matancera, one of the better popular orchestras in the forties and fifties, would do a live radio show at eight and then go see the game. Cab Calloway and his Cavaliers, in town to play at the Montmartre, would show up regularly at the stadium during the 1949–50 season. Ballplayers had many friends among the musicians. Many ballplayers, Agapito Mayor boasted as he suddenly got up to show me a few fancy steps in his Tampa living room, were fabulous dancers.

A prominent member of this gallery of celebrities and would-be celebrities who gravitated toward the stadium for night games was Miguel Angel Blanco, who was the master of ceremonies at the famous Tropicana Nightclub. Blanco was known as "Güenpá," a corruption of *buen palo* (good fuck), because he was said to bed many of the starlets and aspiring starlets who hovered around the nightclub looking for jobs. This character gained a sort of immortality because popular composer "Bebo" Valdés wrote a piece about him called "Güenpá," and Cuban writer Guillermo Cabrera Infante has him appear in the opening scene of his award-winning novel *Three Trapped Tigers*. Blanco, whom I met at the stadium several times, was an obnoxious showoff who claimed that he had played minor-league ball in the United States.

If one arrived very early for the game, or if it rained, then one got to see one of the more venerable officiants at the temple, the head groundskeeper, Alfredo (Pájaro) Cabrera. Cabrera, a former shortstop, had begun his professional career in 1902, the year Cuba was declared independent. He played until the 1917–18 season, stealing forty-four bases in 1909, and leading Almendares to the pennant as a player-manager in the 1915–16 season. In the United States, Cabrera, who was white, played with New Britain, Waterbury, and Springfield between 1908 and 1915. In Almendares Park Cabrera had played against American major-league teams, as well as Negro Leagues teams, and distinguished himself as a courageous infielder who even pitched on occasion. Apparently Cabrera always showed an interest in how ballfields were groomed and carefully observed how it was done in the various parks in which he played, particularly in the United States. This avocation led him to the role in which most younger Cuban fans remember him: a tallish, gaunt figure in a denim uniform, with a cigar stuck in the middle of his mouth and a rake in his gnarled hands. He was such a fixture at the stadium that he was featured in Hatuey beer adds in national magazines. Pájaro Cabrera was the true guardian of the sacred turf.

If Pájaro Cabrera projected a benevolent air, the opposite was true of the keeper of baseballs, or ballboy, the fierce-looking Faustino Zulueta, known simply as "Zulueta," or mockingly as "Bicicleta," for the "speed" with which he pursued errant balls in spite of his portly build. Zulueta, an ebony black man dressed in a blue worker's uniform and a red cap (he was, like me, *habanista*), protected baseballs as if he were defending consecrated objects. Balls that went into the stands could be kept by the fans, but any deviation from the unspoken rules (such as jumping onto the field, or even leaning in too far) in obtaining one of those cherished articles brought about Zulueta's wrath, which was expressed by exaggerated, aggressive gestures, threatening looks, and sinister faces reminiscent of the silent movies. Such displays were usually answered with derision by the crowd, which loved to taunt Zulueta and did it often.

The only ball I ever caught at the stadium provoked Zulueta's ire. This was after the revolution, in the spring of 1959, when the Los Angeles Dodgers and the Cincinnati Reds were playing a series of exhibitions in Havana. I was in the first box seat to the right of the net, surrounded by bearded rebels from Fidel Castro's army who were boasting about their baseball prowess. Dick Gray of the Dodgers hit a foul high on the screen, which came off the edge of it and headed straight down for our box. One of the *barbudos,* taller than I, reached for the ball, but only deflected it onto my chest. I crossed my arms and bent over to protect my prey. When I looked up, victorious, I met Zulueta's angry stare a few feet away. He gave out a loud, stage grunt and stalked off in disgust, probably because he thought that any ball hitting the net was his. I still have this ball, which the two clubs signed the next day. It sits on one of my shelves as I write this.

Zulueta's station was behind home plate, where he kept a supply of balls in a wooden chestlike contraption under the base of the screen. When not chasing balls, Zulueta could be observed lovingly rubbing the new ones, or carefully restoring to good appearance those scuffed or soiled during the game. At the umpire's request, Zulueta would give him a fresh batch and then go back to his chores. Zulueta's position was so well known that whenever an outfielder threw home over the catcher's head, all an announcer had to say was that he had thrown the ball to Zulueta, as in "Ortiz threw the ball to Zulueta."

In spite of his gruff appearance and theatrics, Zulueta was a well-spoken, intelligent man. He was a true expert on baseballs and knew first-hand the history of Cuban baseball going back to Almendares Park. When during the 1949–50 season a reporter intimated that the balls were livelier than before, Zulueta answered with a learned disquisition about how when baseballs arrived from the United States they were quite hard, but would lose their resiliency over time because of Cuba's humidity. Zulueta began as a kind of secretary or right-hand man to Martín Dihigo, back in Almendares Park. Zulueta would collect Dihigo's and Oms's salaries from empresario Abel Linares, who eventually gave him the job as ballboy, replacing a man named Socarrás, who had been the Zulueta of his time. Ballplayers liked and appreciated Zulueta, and those who went to Mexico took him there in 1946 to compare the Mexican and Cuban games and to have a good time. But at the Gran Stadium, with his histrionics and his often frantic and futile attempts to capture errant baseballs, he was part of the show, and through the radio a known figure throughout Cuba, the Caribbean, and Central America.

Another fixture at the stadium, going back to La Tropical, was Luis González Moré, the public-address announcer, known as "El Conde Moré." Conde (Count) Moré had a rich, deep voice and flawless diction. His booth was connected by telephone to the scoreboard, manned by Amado (Loco) Ruiz, a less visible figure to be sure, but known by all the regulars. Moré's voice and elocution gave the proceedings a solemn tone. For a young ballplayer it was a kind of investiture to have his name echo throughout the park in Moré's authoritative voice. Not too far from Moré was the official scorer and statistician for the league, Julio Fránquiz, and his staff. A man of serious, even a bit lugubrious appearance, Fránquiz also harkened back to La Tropical and to Almendares Park. He took his job very seriously and seemed impervious to criticism, which he often had to endure when making decisions. The joke in the press booth among those keeping score often was: "Who made the error?" "Fránquiz," somebody would inevitably answer.

The radio booths and press boxes, teeming with announcers and reporters, were arranged in two tiers. A lower, frontal tier contained, on each corner, microphones for COCO and CMBZ (Radio Salas). On the higher one were the booths for three other stations: Unión Radio, RHC, and Cadena Oriental. The principal announcers were, for Unión Radio, Felo Ramírez and René Molina; for Cadena Oriental, Orlando Sánchez Diago and Pedro Bonetti; for RHC, Manolo de la Reguera, with Jorge Luis Nieto,

Ibrahim Urbino, and others. COCO had Cuco Conde, whose faulty pronunciation of English names would make us know-it-all teens in the fifties howl with laughter. Sánchez Diago was the dean of announcers, but the most popular team was the one made up of Felo Ramírez and René Molina. Soon these announcers were joined by the "Inmortal" Martín Dihigo, retired from playing and managing. Dihigo was a well-spoken, intelligent man whose reputation was such as to dwarf that of any mere mortal. The radio announcers' guild protested the intrusion of a ballplayer in its ranks, but to no avail. In Cuba, Dihigo was above everything.

Among the sportswriters in the booth were Raúl and Fausto Miranda (brothers of Almendares' and Orioles' shortstop Willie Miranda), Pedro Galiana, Sergio Varona, Eladio Secades, Rafael Secades, Rafael Galiana, and Pedro Martínez Bauzá. Other writers preferred to cover the games from the field boxes or the stands; among these were "Llillo" Jiménez, Rai García, and Jess Losada. Bilingual in English and Spanish, Losada was one of the more knowledgeable and cultured sportswriters. The press boxes and radio booths also had a fellow called Lopito, who was a sort of gofer and attendant.

A conspicuous group at the Gran Stadium were the press photographers, who stood on the field, sometimes perilously close to the plays. Among these were Bernardo Iglesias for *Diario de la Marina,* Charles Seigle for *El Mundo,* Pepe Agraz for *Avance,* Aldo Díaz for *Información,* and Ramoncito Fernández, who was the stadium's official photographer. Eventually they would be joined by TV cameramen in 1951, and by "El Caballo" Miranda, a CMQ producer who became a regular.

Going into the Gran Stadium, one could have one's ticket taken by Juanito Decall, the former amateur pitcher who years before had defeated the Boston Red Sox, 2–1, in an exhibition game. Once in the stands one would surely find some of the notorious fans who, as in Ebbets Field, became a part of the show. One was "Chocolatico Habanero," a black fellow in outlandish dress who was conspicuously *habanista* and showed it by blowing a loud whistle. Another was an older lady who blew hundreds of soap bubbles into the air after each hit by Almendares. But no fan was as well known as *el hombre de la sirena,* the man with the siren. His name was Benito Menéndez Zorrilla, and he was in his early thirties by 1950. As a child he had been taken to Almendares Park, and later to La Tropical, where he became a fan of the great shortstop Silvio García. But he was fiercely *habanista,* and began expressing his joy by banging a stadium girder at El Cerro with a sledgehammer to show his allegiance. Reinaldo Cordeiro, who was then stadium manager, reprimanded him, so he switched to the siren, which another *habanista* gave him. The contraption had belonged to a yacht at the Miramar Yacht Club, where it was originally a foghorn. The siren had a sound that rose in pitch as the man cranked harder, something he did to celebrate great feats by Habana players. Needless to say, the siren could be heard plainly through the radio, so the "siren man" also became well known not only in Cuba but around the Caribbean basin as well.

Though not as loud, another well-known character in the stands was "Mocho," a mongrel dog who had appeared when the stadium was being built. He was adopted by the workers, and later made the park his home. ("Mocho," which means shorn, was a name commonly given dogs whose tails had been cut off.) He lived under the stands, but would come out for games and learned to chase only foul balls, which, like "Bicicleta," he tried to rescue from the avid fans. "Mocho" never ran onto the field of play during the game. Most of the time he just rummaged for food, an activity at which he must have been quite successful, to judge by his healthy and rather plump appearance in press pictures of the times.

Such was the geography and cast of the stadium in the late forties, and so it would remain more or less unchanged until the demise of professional baseball in Cuba with the coming of the revolution. And such was the scene for the much-anticipated 1948–49 season, which marked the consolidation of the Cuban League after the pact with Organized Baseball.

How Almendares would reconstitute itself was perhaps the most interesting question, since all Habana really had to do was to bring back last year's team from La Tropical to the Gran Stadium, add the few significant players who had remained in the Cuban League, and put them under the direction of Miguel Angel González. Almendares had to show that the pact with Organized Baseball was more beneficial than had been apparent from the previous year's crop of American ballplayers.

As Luque was still banned, Fermín Guerra was brought back as manager. Almendares did its best to shore up its pitching staff by bringing in Clyde King, Don Newcombe, Clarence Podbielan, and Morris Martin. All four, along with outfielder Al Gionfriddo and first baseman Kevin (Chuck) Connors (later of TV fame in the title role in *The Rifleman*), belonged to the Dodgers, with Connors, Gionfriddo, Podbielan, Newcombe, and King having played that summer with the Montreal Royals, while Martin pitched for St. Paul, another Dodger farm team. This started a trend of cooperation between the Dodgers and Almendares that lasted through the fifties, and was in part due to Dr. July Sanguily's friendly relations with executives of the Brooklyn team. Of course, Almendares still had Marrero, and Mayor was back, along with three Cuban rookies who had started their careers the year before at the Gran Stadium: Octavio Rubert, Vicente López, and René (Tata) Solís. Hausmann did not return to play second, which wound up in the hands of Wesley Hamner (brother of the more famous "Granny" Hamner, of the Phillies), though Jimmy Bloodworth, the Montreal second baseman, was originally hired. Avelino Cañizares returned to short, with Willie Miranda waiting in the wings. René González and Sojito Gallardo were reserve infielders, the first a powerful first baseman, the second a middle infielder. Sam Jethroe came back, after his .308 season in 1947–48 and league-leading twenty-two stolen bases. He was in center, flanked by Gionfriddo and future Hall of Famer Monte Irvin, who had finished a brilliant career with the Newark Eagles of the Negro National League and was about to begin his notable one with the Giants. Veterans Santos Amaro and René (Villa) Cabrera were more than capable backups. Behind the plate Almendares had Andrés Fleitas and Gilberto (Chino) Valdivia, but because of injuries to both players, Almendares had to import veteran Mike Sandlock (also in the Dodger chain), who was in turn hurt and had to be replaced with still-injured Valdivia. Of course, the team also had Fermín Guerra, but he chose not to play that year, or was paid by the Athletics to rest in the winter.

The all-out effort to excel and show the benefits of the new relationship with Organized Baseball is evident in the amount of turnover that Almendares experienced during the season. King was sent back because he was hurt, and Podbielan was released because he did not pitch well. Newcombe pitched most of the season but never got along with Guerra, who told him to pack his bags after a confrontation in which the manager felt his authority was being questioned. (This incident led to a famous fistfight under the stands between the two during 1949 spring training in Florida, when Newcombe claimed Almendares owed him money.) Ed Wright, a veteran knuckleballer, was brought in and had a fine second half, scoring a number of victories over Habana.

In spite of the problems with the catching, this was a fine team. There is nothing wrong with an outfield made up of Irvin, Jethroe, and Gionfriddo, or an infield with Héctor Rodríguez at third, Cañizares at short (with Miranda as backup), and Connors and Hamner on the right side. When Hamner and Rodríguez went down during the season, Gallardo filled in with distinction. While it is true that Connors failed in two tries to make the majors (probably because he could not hit the curve), he was a very good defensive first baseman, who at six-five provided an excellent target for the other infielders and who was a reliable RBI man for Almendares in the 1948–49 season. The pitching, with Wright, Marrero, Mayor, Rubert, and Solís, was strong. Rubert won eight and lost only one, Marrero had another great season, and Mayor enjoyed a revival, making several memorable relief appearances at decisive moments toward the end of the season.

There was still a conspicuous absence in the Almendares roster: Roberto Ortiz. Ortiz had a very good season at La Tropical playing for the Alacranes, finishing with a .308 average and leading in RBIs. And in Maracaibo, where he also went with other ineligibles, he had become a great favorite with the Venezuelan fans. But, along with Luque, Estalella, and Zabala, Ortiz was still banned by the Cuban League, obeying the edicts of Organized Baseball. During the winter season, Eloy García, who (as we saw) had just sold Marianao, organized a brief championship in Camagüey, Ortiz's province of origin, to capitalize on his popularity and to provide

him with a livelihood. Throughout the Cuban League season, Ortiz's banishment continued to hang over the Gran Stadium, which he had helped
inaugurate in 1946 by hitting the first home run. If Ortiz, rather than
Gionfriddo, had played in the 1948–49 Almendares outfield with Jethroe
and Irvin, Guerra's team would have waltzed to the pennant.

Miguel Angel González may have stood pat too much in preparing
for the 1948–49 season, and it cost him. But Habana still had a formidable
team, with an outfield of Kimbro, Pearson, Formental, and Thompson
(playing left field this year), and with Sagüita Hernández and José (Calampio) León as backups. Miguel Angel imported Ferrell Anderson, a hefty
catcher who was dubbed "Trucutú" by the fans after a cartoon character
of a caveman. Anderson could hit, and liked to put on a show belting balls
over the warehouse in left field during batting practice, but Miguel Angel
soon grew disenchanted with his inability to call a game, and to catch in
general. As backup Habana had reliable Emilio Cabrera, who had a modest
career in that role in the Cuban League. The infield still had Chino Hidalgo, with Carlos Blanco, and rookie Pablo García, who played the year
before at El Cerro. Veteran Bill Schuster was imported to bolster the infield,
though he was already in his middle thirties and a career minor leaguer
after a spotty stint with the Cubs during the war. The Habana pitching
staff had Oliverio Ortiz (Roberto's brother), Cuban rookie Tony Lorenzo,
imports George Stanceau and Jack Yochin, who were both from Columbus
(at the time a Cardinal farm), along with huge Bill Reeder, who also belonged to St. Louis, and a favorite in Cuba, the Canadian Paul Calvert.
Habana also had a notable absence: Fred Martin, popular among
habanistas, who was still ineligible, along with Danny Gardella and Max
Lanier.

The Cienfuegos trio of owners—de Armas, Parga, and Maduro—hired
Salvador Hernández to manage and catch, on the strength of his victory
with the Leones at La Tropical.[7] So Cienfuegos was set behind the plate,
with Hernández and Noble. Around the infield the Elefantes, so newly
named, had fixture Regino Otero at first, with Silvio García at short or
third, and Stan Breard, Angel Fleitas (brother of Andrés), and Armando
Gallart filling in at the other positions, along with some imports, such as
Pete Coscarat. The outfield was strong, with Alejandro Crespo, Don Richmond, El Gamo Pagés, José Luis Colás, Pedro Duñabeitia, and Conrado
Pérez. The pitching staff again had Max Manning, Jean Roy (the Canadian
who played for Cuba at La Tropical the year before), Max Surkont, and
Witto Alomá, who had had a good season with the team the year before
and who was about to move up to the majors.

Marianao, in its first year under new management, had Louis Kahn, a
career minor leaguer from the Pacific Coast, behind the plate, with Cuban
Mario Díaz backing him up (he had hit .300 the year before, for Almendares and Marianao). Lorenzo (Chiquitín) Cabrera was at first. He was
a consistent .300 hitter with the New York Cubans. Harrington was at

second, Miñoso at third, and Damon Phillips at short, with rookies Pedro Ballester and Amado Ibáñez in reserve. Given a chance the previous year because of the split league, Ballester had hit .253 in ninety-nine times at bat for Marianao, while Ibáñez hit .256 for the Leones at La Tropical. Claro Duany was still a mainstay in the outfield, with Tony Castaño, import Ray Howerton, Cuban rookie Mario Arencibia, and Francisco Campos, who was traded to Almendares to obtain the services of Gilberto Torres when Luque could not be hired to manage the team due to his ineligibility. Torres managed the Tigres.

Almendares ran away with the pennant, finishing eight games ahead of Habana. The Alacranes, in spite of Roberto Ortiz's absence, just had too much depth, and then, toward the end of the season, Mayor made two demoralizing relief appearances against the Reds. The first was on Sunday, January 30, in the traditional second game of the doubleheader pitting the "eternal rivals." If Habana won, it would move to within 1½ games of Almendares. If it lost, the distance would be 2½, with very little time left. The game was a crucial one for Fermín Guerra's team. Rubert had opened the game for Almendares and Calvert for Habana, but the Canadian had nothing on the ball that day, and the Alacranes took a four-run lead into the eighth after Habana scored three in the seventh. Knuckleballer Wright came in to put out the fire. But in the eighth inning Habana, still pressing, filled the bases with none out, and Fermín ran to the mound and called Mayor to the fray. The next three hitters were Formental, Thompson, and Pearson, the meat of the order. The first two were lefties. Miguel Angel called Formental back to the dugout and sent in righty Carlos Blanco to face the veteran southpaw. Blanco lifted a foul fly behind third that was caught by Héctor Rodríguez for the first out. Thompson, leading the league in hitting, was next, and Mayor reached back and struck him out. Pearson, number one in RBIs, stepped up with a chance to add to his total and possibly tie the game, but Mayor induced him to hit a harmless fly to center to close the door. Almendaristas all over the stadium and the island rejoiced. Mayor still remembers this inning in detail. On another occasion, Newcombe left a game while in the lead, but after having given up many bases on balls. As he walked off the field to a chorus of whistles (the equivalent of boos in Cuba), Mayor waddled to the mound with his patented look of determination and shut Habana out for the rest of the afternoon.

Almendares' triumph was not only due to the superior team the owners put on the field, but also to Fermín Guerra's shrewd managerial mind. Aware that American pitchers often slacked off toward the end of the Cuban season to reach spring training fresh, Guerra saved his native pitchers for the end of the campaign, because they would be more involved in the emotions of the championship. He decided, moreover, to play an aggressive game (hit-and-runs, bunts, steals), because his team did not have that much power. Guerra was also saddled with a severe catching problem, and even considered at some point using Héctor Rodríguez or Jethroe behind the plate. Valdivia and Fleitas were injured, and newcomer Sandlock, probably because he was playing before getting into shape, was also injured. Valdivia had to play hurt, with a torn leg muscle, which made throwing very difficult if not almost impossible.

Veteran Alejandro Crespo, of Cienfuegos, won a second batting championship (he had won back in 1942–43), with an average of .326, followed by two players for Habana: Hank Thompson, at .321, and Chino Hidalgo, at .318. Chiquitín Cabrera, Marianao's first baseman, hit .314, and Al Gionfriddo of Almendares hit .308. Pearson won the RBI title again, this time with fifty-four, and Jethroe also repeated in stolen bases, this time with thirty-two. Octavio Rubert had the best won-lost percentage with .889, having won eight while losing only one. Agapito Mayor, by the way, finished at 4 and 2, but with a sparkling 1.84 earned-run average. And he was saving the best for last.[8]

The season had been a success, in spite of the fact that as many as fourteen American players had to be shipped back home for one reason or another. The teams, united now in one stadium, played in front of many full houses, and interest generated by the radio around the island was at a fever pitch. But the end of the 1948–49 season was not the end of winter professional baseball in Havana. The first Caribbean Series was about to be played, and Havana was, naturally, the site. All the Cuban fans—the followers of Habana grudgingly—could now be united behind Almendares.

At the beginning of 1948, the winter leagues of Cuba, Puerto Rico, Panama, and Venezuela had a meeting in Miami in which the Cuban representatives suggested to the Confederación de Baseball Profesional del Caribe the idea of having a final series among the winners from each country to determine an overall champion. At a meeting in Havana in August of that year, it was agreed to hold such a series annually, the first to be played in Cuba, with the site rotating each year. The teams would play each other twice in a series of six consecutive two-team doubleheaders. The agreement was signed by the following representatives: for Cuba, Miguel Angel González, Florentino Pardo, and Emilio de Armas; for Panama, Eric del Valle; for Puerto Rico, Jorge Córdoba and Eduardo Santiago; and for Venezuela, Sebastián Ardiles and Felipe Huizi. The agreement was ratified by George Trautman, president of the National Association of Baseball Leagues, and by his head of public relations, Robert Finch.

Trautman was in Havana on February 20 to throw out the first ball at the ceremonies in the Gran Stadium, in which national anthems were played, flags displayed, and teams lined up along the foul lines. Besides Almendares, representing Cuba, the other three teams were Indios de Mayagüez (Puerto Rico), Cervecería Caracas (Venezuela), and Spur Cola (Panama). Even before the first real pitch was thrown there were several interesting things to note about the teams. The most visible was the fact that, as opposed to Almendares and all other teams in the Cuban League, the teams from the three other countries either had commercial announcements on their jerseys or actually had the name of a commercial product. I remember, a few years later, when the Caribbean Series returned to Havana, what a bad impression this made on me. Only semipro teams in Cuba used the names of products; in this Series Almendares was going to oppose the likes of Spur Cola and Cervecería Caracas. Another interesting fact, which revealed much behind the idea of holding the Series, was that Cervecería Caracas carried on its roster a full ten players from the team that had defeated Cuba in the Amateur World Series of 1941, among them none other than Daniel (Chino) Canónico, who, earlier in the decade, had conquered the Cuban team in the most memorable amateur game ever played in Cuba. There is no question that the Caribbean Series was yet another outgrowth of the Amateur World Series of the early forties. The Venezuelan team had another, even more striking feature, which harked back to the Amateur World Series: it consisted only of Venezuelan players. Because it had not yet signed an agreement like Cuba's with Organized Baseball, Venezuela decided to go to the Series with no American players. This made them the most interesting team in Havana that February, and the one everyone expected to finish last. Another revealing fact, which would be repeated many times in the future, is that other countries—in this case, Panama—brought Cuban players to the Caribbean Series to play against Cuba. Spur Cola had among its players infielder Orlando Moreno, and left-handed pitcher Leonardo Goicochea, known in Panama as "Guillotina." As far as I know, no player from another Latin American country ever played for a Cuban team in the Caribbean Series.

From the Cubans' point of view, Puerto Rico seemed like the team to beat. The Indios de Mayagüez, led by player-manager Artie Wilson of the Birmingham Black Barons, had a roster that read like a combined Puerto Rican–Negro Leagues all-star team, with Lorenzo Piper Davis, Carlos Bernier, Luscious Luke Easter, Wilmer Fields, Cefo Conde, Alonso Perry, Carlos Manuel Santiago, Quincy Trouppe, and Bill Powell. A most notable absence from the Puerto Rican roster was Luis Rodríguez Olmo, still banned from competition by Organized Baseball because of his play in the Mexican League. Spur Cola, which was managed by Negro Leagues notable Leon Treadway, had, in addition to Moreno and Goicochea, a number of Negro Leagues stars of their own in Sam Bankhead, Sam Jones, and Cuban favorite Pat (Lord) Scantlebury, who not only pitched for the New York Cubans in the summer, but also had played in the Cuban League, and would in later years resurface in Havana with the Sugar Kings. Many of these players, particularly the American and Caribbean blacks, knew each other well from various other competitions. Cervecería Caracas, on the other hand, with its all-Venezuelan roster, had players known mostly to Cubans, because of the Amateur World Series, or because of their participation in the Mexican League. In addition to Canónico, Cervecería Caracas had a bright rookie shortstop named Alfonso (Chico) Carrasquel, who would go on to have a great career in the major leagues. There was legendary Venezuelan slugger (and pitcher) Ascanio Vidal López, who had played in the Cuban League and was currently in Mexico, and the Bracho brothers, José (Carrao) and Julio, the first of whom would become a Caribbean Series fixture and who later played for the Cuban Sugar Kings. Finally, Venezuela had hard-hitting Dalmiro Finol, Guillermo Vento, and Félix (Tirahuequitos—Hole Thrower) Machado.

The Gran Stadium was in a carnival mood for the premiere, with radio celebrities involved in the proceedings. "Sopeira," a rabid Almendares fan and foil of "Chicharito," was named "honorary manager" of Almendares. Sporting a uniform with the number 88, he accompanied Fermín Guerra to meet the umpires and Cervecería Caracas counterpart José Antonio Casanova. (The number 8 means "death" in the Cuban kabbala, so the Galician was sporting "double death" on his back.) This was the second game of the first doubleheader. In the opener Spur Cola beat Mayagüez, 13–9, in a slugfest won by Pat Scantlebury. But this was nothing like Almendares' feats against Cervecería Caracas, won by Marrero, 16–1. The Cuban team had twenty-one hits against Julio Bracho, Domingo Barboza, and Enrique Fonseca. It must have seemed uncanny to the Venezuelan players to come to Havana eight years after the Amateur World Series and find themselves facing Marrero again. Canónico, on the other hand, was handily defeated by Cuba in the fourth game.

Cuba's victory over Venezuela and Panama's defeat of Puerto Rico were prophetic beginnings. Cuba won the Series undefeated, and Puerto Rico, so highly regarded, finished last. The only thing that could not have been anticipated was that Venezuela would finish second, with an even 3 and 3 record, without American reinforcements. Carrao Bracho beat Panama in the third game, Luis Zuloaga took care of Puerto Rico in the fifth, and Carrao came back and beat Puerto Rico in the eleventh. In this game Cervecería Caracas scored fourteen times, and Carrasquel hit a homer. Cuba captured all the honors, however. Al Gionfriddo won the batting title with a .533 average, Monte Irvin the home-run title with two and the RBI crown with eleven, and none other than Agapito Mayor finished as the champion pitcher, with three victories: two in relief and one as a starter. (Cuban Leonardo Goicochea, on the other hand, lost three games for Panama.) Guerra, faithful to his theories, opened only two games with American pitchers (Wright and Martin), and the rest with Marrero, Rubert, Solís, Vicente López, and Mayor. Other than Mayor, only Marrero, Solís, and Wright won games.

The first Caribbean Series capped off Organized Baseball's attempts to extend its control to Latin America and put an end to Mexico's threat. There was no final truce to be celebrated yet, with Luque, Roberto Ortiz, and Rodríguez Olmo, among others, still considered ineligible. But that would come. In Cuba the new owners who had taken control from the likes of Don Julio Blanco Herrera, and the heirs of Abel Linares, had managed to move baseball within the more profitable orbit of U.S. hegemony. They established at the Gran Stadium a plaza that not only was second to none in Latin America but also superior to many in the United States, including some in the major leagues. Their victory led to just over one decade of successful professional baseball operations in Cuba, during which it was fully expected that eventually the major leagues would expand to the island. But it was not to be, and the next ten years would be the last of professional baseball in Cuba, a period that would close with the demise of the Cuban League.

In chapter eight of the *Quijote,* Cervantes freezes the action with the mad gentleman and the gallant Basque in the midst of battle, to recount how he got ahold of the story he is narrating. I am going to ask the indulgence of the reader here and leave the more recent history of Cuban baseball for later in order to trace its origins and more remote history. Why was baseball such an integral part of Cuban culture? How could it bring together, through common lore and rituals, Cubans of all races and classes? In reaching back to the beginnings of Cuban baseball we retreat to an era of heroes, where legend and fact, history and myth are difficult to separate. After telling that story, which will bring us back to The Game on February 25, 1947, we will let the first pitch of the 1949–50 season sail, and pick up the narrative of the more recent and familiar past.

1 2 3 4 5 6 7 8 9 R H E

A Cuban *Belle Époque*

Ask a Cuban fan about the origins of baseball on the island and he will tell you that the first game was played in Matanzas, at Palmar del Junco between a team from that city and the visiting Habana Base Ball Club, in 1874. Pressed as to how there could have been a game without previous developments, he will answer that the crew of an American ship, forced to remain in Matanzas Harbor for repairs, taught Cubans the rules of the sport. The young men from Havana had learned baseball in the United States, where they had been students. If the fan is somewhat knowledgeable, he will add that many baseball players in the early years fought in the War of Independence against Spain (1895–98) and that some gave their lives for the fatherland. A few fans may even know that one of those pioneers of Cuban baseball, Emilio Sabourín, was arrested by the Spanish authorities for conspiring against the colonial regime and sent to the feared political prison in Ceuta, northern Africa, where he died.

Like all lore, particularly stories about origins, this account blends facts with errors, inaccuracies, and distortions. Precisely because of this, stories of beginnings have a significance that is disproportionate to the value of their factual content. Their truth lies beyond corroboration or correction. Myths of origins, therefore, have a weight and influence of their own as documents of a people's or a culture's collective bonding. The origins of

Cuban baseball coincided with independence from Spain and with the consolidation of a national identity. Baseball in Cuba is part of the constitution of what Benedict Anderson has called an "imagined community," a group of individuals who, though they have never met, believe they share a common set of values and customs. This founding role of the sport accounts for the depth and durability of baseball as a part of modern Cuban culture. Baseball is so ingrained in Cuba that it has thrived as the "national sport" through forty years of a bitterly anti-American revolution. The coincidence of the birth of the nation and the inception of the game is a key in understanding that resiliency.

The force of Cuba's baseball mythology is such that sometimes Cubans have tried to usurp from the United States the honor of having invented the game. If that Cuban fan were to be questioned even further he might remember from history classes that the original inhabitants of the island, the Taínos, played some sort of a ball game. The game was supposed to be called *batos,* which is close enough to *bate,* the Spanish word for baseball bat. Could the Taínos have been brandishing their Louisville Sluggers centuries before Abner Doubleday and Alexander Cartwright? We were not told this in school. But the suggestion was there. In fact, Batos is the brand name given to Cuban-made sporting goods since the revolution, a not-too-subtle way of erasing the United States from early baseball history.

As we know from Irving Rouse's authoritative book on the Taínos, the game the Indians played was closer to tennis than to baseball. Besides, the Taínos were virtually exterminated by the Spanish during the sixteenth century. They bequeathed Cuban and world culture the use of tobacco and a host of words but little else. When baseball made its way to Cuba in the nineteenth century, the Taínos were an archaeological curiosity. Thus Cubans do not really take too seriously the Taíno origin of baseball. It is the game at the Palmar del Junco that still has currency and is monumentalized against all factual obstacles.

Errors and distortions are most revealing in mythic stories because the shaping force of common belief overpowers fact at the most interesting junctures. The 1874 game in Matanzas, which was without doubt an important one in the history of baseball in Cuba, was played at the Palmar *de* Junco, not "del Junco"—the possessive "de" would make it "Junco's," while "del" turns it into "of the." This is no mere professorial quibble. The more common "Palmar del Junco"—Palm Grove of the Reed—gives the place an emblematic and patriotic aura. The palm tree, particularly the royal palm, is an emblem of Cuban nationality. If to "palm grove" one adds "of the reed," or "the palm grove with the reed," one is adding a poetic, even biblical resonance to the name. Moses' mother saved her infant son by putting him in the river in a *cestilla de juncos,* a basket of reeds. "Palmar del Junco" sounds poetic and scans better than "Palmar de Junco." "Palmar del Junco" conjures up an image that is heraldic. But the name of the field where the famous game was played was really "Palmar de Junco," meaning, more prosaically, "Junco's Palm Grove," after the man who owned the field. Be that as it may, most Cubans know it as "Palmar del Junco," which is how I will continue to refer to it here, in deference to usage. A stadium was rebuilt on the site in 1940 with as much enthusiasm and historical inaccuracy as the one in Cooperstown, New York. (On the archway over the entrance of the still-standing, if dilapidated field, it reads "Palmar de Junco," whereas on a plaque placed there in 1974 to commemorate the hundreth anniversary of the legendary game it reads "Palmar del Junco.") However, the game at the Palmar del Junco was far from being the first played in Cuba. By the time the traveling Habana Base Ball Club boarded the train for the journey to Matanzas, many games had been played on the island, particularly in the capital. If not, how could there already be two clubs? Misconceptions about the nature of baseball clubs in the nineteenth century can lead to attaching too much importance to that one game, as does our modern view of how leagues and competition are organized. Baseball is still played at the Palmar, however, and the Matanzas area became one of the richest purveyors of great Cuban ballplayers throughout the years, although not for any mythic reasons.

The Palmar had no palm trees, anyway, according to Wenceslao Gálvez, first historian of Cuban baseball and a prominent player in the 1880s. In *El baseball en Cuba: Historia del Base-Ball en la Isla de Cuba* (1889), Gálvez says that it was a level, clear field, in Pueblo Nuevo, a neighborhood of Matanzas that still exists. But in the Cuban imagination the Palmar certainly had palm trees, at least as words that evoke patriot and poet José Martí's self-identification: *Yo soy un hombre sincero/de donde crece la palma* (I am a sincere man/from the land of the palm tree). Matanzas itself, with its beautiful Yumurí Valley, rivers, and streams, and with the city's magnificent bay, is at least poetically an appropriate landscape for the birth of Cuban baseball.[1] Matanzas is so appropriate a scene that the whole construct obscures the reasons why there should have been a baseball game in that city on Sunday, December 27, 1874, and why the region should have continued to produce so many great Cuban ballplayers. Why would the Habana Base Ball Club travel to Matanzas to play a local club on that date? Myth replaces historical fact, or deflects it, but only by probing both can one get at the depths of culture.

It is a suggestive coincidence that another fabulous first occurred in Matanzas during the 1870s: the composition of the first *danzón*, "Las Alturas de Simpson" ("Simpson Heights"). This dance piece was the first mature product of what would become known as Cuban music. The composition, by mulatto composer Miguel de Faílde, was played and danced at the aristocratic Liceo de Matanzas on January 1, 1879. That danzón is the first link in a chain that can be easily followed all the way to salsa. Like baseball, and perhaps even more so, Cuban music and the appearance of this danzón played a crucial role in the constitution of a national consciousness. The history of the danzón, as Alejo Carpentier has shown in his beautiful book *La música en Cuba* (1946), contains, in a nutshell, the history of Cuba. It is a history that seems truer than the conventional one found in textbooks because it involves major components of Cuban popular culture. Music and baseball cut across social and racial boundaries.

"Las Alturas de Simpson" was the result of a musical evolution that reached back to the French *contredance,* originally the English "country dance," brought by the colonists who fled to Cuba during the Haitian revolution at the end of the eighteenth century. The melody, and particularly the rhythm of the contredance, hence of the danzón, were powerfully influenced by African music. Their symbiosis in the danzón, composed and played in Matanzas by free black musicians, was soon danced by whites at their parties. It was a ballroom dance, sometimes performed in quadrilles. It is still danced in Cuba, where new dances never completely eliminate the old. By our standards today it was chaste, but in the 1870s and '80s the older generations considered it sensual and provocative. In fact, it became confrontational, a protest against old-fashioned Spanish mores. Some of the titles of the pieces, such as "Amarillo, suénamelo pintón" and "Mulata, dame tu amor," were suggestive in a playful manner. The African component was evident in the movements of the body, particularly the hips, and the swaying of the couples. All this was highly alluring in a society where a woman had to be careful not to show her ankles, though she was surely wearing stockings and high-top shoes. The danzón became the rage across social classes, invading middle- and upper-class parties, where it shared time and space with other such modern dances as waltzes, polkas, and mazurkas, in which bodies were beginning to be liberated in ways that are already modern. There was a public controversy about the dance, but to no avail. The danzón was the first instance of a major influence running from the bottom up through Cuba's society, a bonding beyond race and class that would also be reflected, simultaneously, in the game of baseball.

The Haitian revolution, at the end of the eighteenth century, had a decisive impact on Cuban culture at even more basic levels. Haiti's demise as the world's chief provider of sugar pushed Cuba to become a principal producer in the world market. This sealed Cuba's fate until the present, determining its economic, political, social, and even ecological history. Modern Cuban popular culture, among whose best-known products are music and baseball, is the result of this historical turn of events, as Manuel Moreno Fraginals has shown in his dramatic and precise *The Sugarmill* (1978).

Moreno Fraginals has demonstrated how the Cuban elite, once it decided to compete in the world market, embraced the latest modern trends in finance and production, casting its lot with the progressive European nations that were experiencing the effects of the industrial revolution. In its quest for the modern, this group, which Moreno Fraginals called "saccharocrats," forged ahead of Spain and the rest of its colonies and former colonies to be on a par with the new powers, including the United States. For instance, the Cuban sugar elite enjoyed the benefits of the "water closet" before it was known in the peninsula. More important, Cuba had a railroad before Spain, and its rail network was the most advanced in Latin America by midcentury. Although Cuba had not become politically independent, like Mexico or Argentina, it was pulling ahead of Spain and its former colonies economically and culturally. The Cuban wars of liberation (1868–78, known as the Ten Years' War, and the already mentioned 1895–98, known as the War of Independence) were, among other things, conflicts between the modern spirit guiding the creole elite, which reflected that of the North, and the backward spirit of the mother country. (This is a crude generalization, of course, for the modern spirit was alive and fighting within Spain itself.)

In Cuba the die was cast. Havana and environs had been in British hands for nearly a year in 1762. During this occupation the Cubans had a firsthand taste of the modern. It lingered. Then there was the opening of Cuban ports to foreign trade in 1817, which meant increased commercial and cultural relations with the United States. As the case of Matanzas shows, the American presence in Cuba during the nineteenth century was considerable: Major towns had American consuls; American firms bid and won contracts for various projects (gas lights for Havana); Americans bought and operated sugarmills; and some cities, such as Santiago, even had American clubs. American businessmen crowded the lobby of the Hotel Inglaterra in Havana and bellied up loudly to its famous bar. When the battleship *Maine* was sent to the Cuban capital in early 1898, it was to protect real and substantial American interests, not simply to provoke the Spaniards or to make an empty threat.

Cubans traveled often to the United States, and many immigrated there after the Truce of Zanjón, which ended the Ten Years' War in 1878. Key West, Tampa, Jacksonville, and New York received a considerable number of Cuban families, some of whom eventually returned to the island. The immigration to Florida of Cubans fleeing political persecution came to be known in Cuban history as "La Emigración." It was among these people that José Martí campaigned to bring war and freedom to Cuba. In spite of the political boundary, Tampa, Havana, Key West, and to some degree Matanzas became part of the same cultural system. The transfer of cigar factories to Tampa and Key West to bypass the Spanish monopoly tightened a bond between these areas that remains today. These close contacts with the United States also put Cuba ahead of Latin American regions that were politically independent in terms of modern industrial techniques and ideas.

Why would the Cuban elite, which at the turn of the eighteenth to the nineteenth century meant mostly the Havana elite, be so receptive to the new? The factors mentioned (English occupation, the sugar market) played important roles, but Havana was a cosmopolitan city almost from the moment it was founded in the sixteenth century. Because of its geographical location, Cuba was considered the "key" to the Gulf of Mexico, and the gateway to Spain's empire in the Americas and the Far East. As a result, Havana became the most important way point between Europe and the New World. In fact, Havana became the meeting place (coming and going) of the two yearly fleets through which Spain communicated with the New World and the Philippines. These huge convoys, organized to repel the frequent attacks by primarily the French and the British, carried everything from the Old World to the New: ideas, foodstuffs, laws, goods, and, most important, people. They brought back everything, including chinoiserie shipped to Mexico via the Manila galleon, which connected the Philippines to the New World, and, again, ideas and people. Havana had been at the center of this traffic since the sixteenth century, years before Plymouth Rock. Everything went through Havana before it reached Lima or Manila, and everything went through Havana before it reached Cadiz, Seville, or Madrid.

Fleets sometimes remained in Havana Harbor for a considerable time, creating a market for everything both good and bad. Meats and other foodstuffs for the return voyage had to be secured, entertainment for the restless crews of the ships had to be provided, as well as lodging for people whose social station covered the entire range. The wealth of Havana, both the transient one afloat in the ships (all that gold and silver) and the permanent one of the city, had to be protected, so huge and beautiful fortifications were built through the eighteenth century. Havana was no Mexico City or Lima in terms of architectural splendor or size, but it was a cosmopolitan city open to the world.

Another reason why Cuba was so receptive to the new was smuggling. It is an island with thousands of miles of coast, much of it protected by rows of keys where ships can easily hide. Cuba was thus impossible to seal off in order to comply with Spain's pre-1817 ban of commerce with other nations. Havana and other Cuban coastal towns were regularly sacked by French and British buccaneers. Many Cubans, in fact, were quite willing to trade with the enemy. Such willingness was aided by another peculiarity: Cuba was not as much under the sway of the Catholic Church as other regions of the Spanish Empire. In Mexico and Peru the church had built imposing cathedrals to compete with powerful and elaborate native religions, and the religious orders as well as the Inquisition had inordinate powers. But this had not been necessary in the Caribbean, where native cultures were not as advanced. In Cuba the church was not strong enough to stem the tide of modern trends brought in often by people whose religious beliefs were inimical to Spain's. The weakness of Cuban Catholicism, compared to Colombia's or Argentina's, for instance, is a constant throughout its history. The Cuban Catholic Church collapsed before the Communist revolution.

It should not be surprising, then, that when a new American game like baseball appeared, it would be embraced by the sons of the Cuban elite, eager to adopt the latest trends and fashions, particularly those that differed sharply from Spanish ones. Baseball would become a modern recreational activity as opposed to barbarous bullfighting.

Matanzas also grew as a result of the boom in the sugar market, becoming the "Athens of Cuba," in the nationalistic parlance, as well as the "Rome" of fast-developing Afro-Cuban religions and the Bayreuth of emerging Cuban music (distinctions it retains). It did have a thriving artistic life, and was the city where major nineteenth-century Cuban poets José Jacinto Milanés, José María de Heredia, and Gabriel de la Concepción Valdés (Plácido) were active in literature and revolutionary politics. The economic forces behind Matanzas' development have been meticulously laid out by Laird W. Bergard. Broadly speaking, this development can be described as follows. As the sugar boom sparked by the demise of Haiti began, the Havana elite, impelled by the need for virgin lands with plenty of wood for fuel, pushed eastward and southeastward, toward Matanzas and Colón. They bought land, built mills, and began importing slaves at an unprecedented rate. They also built railroads to connect the region to Havana, and the sugarmills to the ports of Matanzas and Cárdenas. Improvements in steam-driven machinery for the mills and the railroads, and the fortuitous richness of the land, made the Matanzas area the principal sugar producer of Cuba (driving tobacco west, to Pinar del Río). The upward trend of sugar prices in the world market through the first three quarters of the century propelled the industry forward at a rapid pace, making the Havana saccharocrats fabulously rich. These absentee owners did not change their place of residence to Matanzas and rural areas adjacent to Havana but instead built seasonal homes at their mills, which they could reach within a day by railroad. They also erected palatial residences in the capital, and traveled to Europe and the United States in regal splendor. Eventually they began to send their sons to be educated in the United States, where they learned, among other things, the game of baseball. According to Gálvez's *El béisbol en Cuba,* "Mssrs. Tolón, Hernández, Amieva and Delgado, having received their education in the United States, organized the first baseball nine in Matanzas" (p. 85). The city's prosperity continued through the Ten Years' War because the conflict was circumscribed to the eastern part of the island until nearly the end.

By that time control of the sugar industry was passing from the old aristocracy to immigrant entrepreneurs, who had direct dealings with the United States. The significance of all this for the history of Cuban baseball is clear. There was a substantial American presence not only in Havana but also in the Matanzas region. Who was the Simpson in the title of the first danzón? An American who originally owned the land in Matanzas that became the neighborhood "Simpson Heights." There were American merchants, mechanics, machinists, and even sugarmill owners. Matanzas' beautiful port and bay harbored many ships that sailed directly to New York or Boston. Matanzas, along with Havana, became part of the web of nautical commerce that included major cities of North America. The development of steam navigation brought these cities closer, and the exchange of products and people brought about in turn the exchange of cultural artifacts and practices.

The development and expansion of baseball in the nineteenth century are closely related to commerce among port cities. Not all were seaports, to be sure, but they were part of the extensive system of waterways that played a decisive role in the economic growth of the United States. Baseball took hold first in American ports such as New York, Brooklyn, Boston, Providence, Baltimore, Cincinnati, Cleveland, and Detroit. Havana and Matanzas soon became a part of that system because of the sugar trade, so it was natural that Cuban baseball would develop first in these two cities, and that their respective teams meet in that mythic first game in 1874.

Because of the intense development of sugar in the Matanzas region and the dramatic increase in the slave population, the city turned into a hotbed of Afro-Cuban culture. Matanzas had the highest density of blacks in Cuba, and continued to have it through the years of the republic (1902–59). Afro-Cuban cultural practices in Matanzas were nurtured by many free blacks who worked in various small trades, including that of musician, which is the reason for Matanzas's importance in the history of Cuban music. The density of the slave population and the proliferation of sugar-mills account for the number of great black Cuban ballplayers who came and continue to come from the region. Reading Bergad's lists of sugarmill owners, one finds names that became famous later through the feats of black Cuban players whose ancestors toiled in their fields and boiler houses: Torriente, Arrieta, Baró, as in Cristóbal Torriente, Orestes Saturnino Arrieta Miñoso, Bernardo and Asdrúbal Baró. In Cuban history, as with all history, the slightest probing brings out the fundamental role of pain and cruelty in forging the elements of a nation's culture.

By 1899, during the U.S. occupation that followed what is known as the Spanish-American War, Brigadier General James H. Wilson, commanding the departments of Matanzas and Santa Clara, was able to write in a report that "the higher classes of white people [in Matanzas] are generally fairly well educated. The doctors, pharmacists, engineers and planters are the most intelligent, and many of them were educated in the States or in Europe" (p. 242). He also noted that "the sugar-mills in these two provinces are owned as follows: 50 by Cubans, 21 by Spaniards, 11 by Americans, 2 by Germans, 1 English and 1 French, from which will appear that the popular idea that the sugar business and plantations of the island are controlled by Spaniards and foreigners, has but little foundation in fact" (p. 12). Though his point is well taken, and Bergard also insists that the sugar boom in Matanzas was a Cuban phenomenon, eleven sugarmills in American hands is no small number. If to the Americans in those mills one adds others in various trades, it is easy to see that the American presence in Matanzas was considerable at precisely the time when baseball was in a period of expansion in the United States.

But the key group here, as in Havana, were those U.S.-educated professionals. Cuban families of means began sending their sons to study in the United States because it became clear that an American education was more relevant to the economic needs and future of the island. The trend seems to have increased sharply after 1871, when seven medical students at the University of Havana were executed by the Spanish government. They had been charged with desecrating the tomb of a firebrand pro-Spanish journalist who had died in a duel against a Cuban. This event, which still lives in Cuban memory (the date November 27 is a national day of mourning), made everyone fear for the safety of young people who were out of sorts with the decaying Spanish regime. The feared "volunteers," thugs recruited to do the government's bidding, killed and maimed at will. Young men, among them future patriot José Martí, were routinely arrested and sent to appalling prisons in Cuba itself or Ceuta, while others were deported to Spain.

If baseball and music seemed to have matured in Matanzas in the 1870s, it was because, in the aftermath of the frustrating Ten Years' War, Cuban nationality and polity were forging a fledgling identity. One component of that identity was American. Martí himself spent fifteen crucial years of his life in the United States, and it was from New York, Tampa, and Key West that he launched the War of Independence. Martí never mentioned baseball in his writings as far as I know, but proceeds from games in Havana and Key West went to the revolutionary cause. In fact, one of the most influential figures in the history of Cuban baseball, Agustín (Tinti) Molina, a native of Key West, once hit a decisive homer in a game against an American squad with Martí in attendance. The revolutionary asked to meet the triumphant athlete, and Molina says that Martí told him that the victory in baseball was a good omen for the cause of independence.[2] Support for the cause came from owners of cigar factories, who probably sponsored the baseball teams. Among them were Fernando Figueredo Socarrás, who "had probably arranged for a visit with Teodoro Pérez and José González Pompez, who had just opened separate West Tampa factories. They were longtime Key West manufacturers and financial supporters of Martí's efforts since early 1892, when Martí was first invited to Key West following his great success in Ybor City."[3] González Pompez was the father of Alejandro Pompez, who became an important entrepreneur in the Negro Leagues, was owner of the New York Cubans, and gave many Cuban players (black and white) a chance to play in the United States.

But if Martí did not write about baseball, others did. Cuban baseball origins are closely bound to Cuban literature. Diego Vicente Tejera, a well-known writer at the time, gave a lecture in 1897 decrying the baseball craze among the Cubans in Key West.[4] Julián del Casal, a Cuban poet who achieved continental fame, wrote about the sport, as did Enrique José

Varona, an influential Cuban thinker and essayist. On March 8, 1891, *El Score* published a letter by the revered black patriot Juan Gualberto Gómez, written from prison, a situation that the magazine protests. Gómez was in favor of baseball and other sports to strengthen the physical and moral fiber of youth. Moreover, *El Fígaro,* a leading cultural journal in Cuba in the late nineteenth century, proclaimed itself in its first issue (July 23, 1885) "the organ of baseball," as did quite a few others in Havana, Matanzas, and elsewhere. *El Fígaro*'s blend of baseball and literature was not an isolated instance, but an entire trend that lasted until the early years of the twentieth century.[5]

As if that were not enough, Wenceslao Gálvez y Delmonte, the aforementioned mentioned first historian of Cuban baseball, a great shortstop and later manager who is enshrined in the Cuban Baseball Hall of Fame, was also a novelist and journalist. His *El baseball en Cuba* may very well be the first history of the game ever written anywhere. It is an excellent description of the origins of the game on the island at all levels, from the social and the political to the aesthetic. My narrative of this early period of Cuban baseball follows Gálvez's book closely, as well as the second history of Cuban baseball, Raúl Díaz Muro's *Historia del baseball profesional en Cuba* (1907). I also draw on the detailed chronicles and writings that appeared in *El Fígaro* and other journals, and reminiscences published elsewhere by some of baseball's participants.

By the last third of the nineteenth century the Spanish fleets had been replaced in Havana Harbor by the steamships of various lines connecting Cuba with the United States and Europe. *Mascotte, Olivette,* and *Juniata,* which combined steam and sail, plied the waters among Mobile, Tampa, Key West, and Havana weekly or semiweekly, depending on the season. They belonged to the Plant Steamship Line, which linked up with the South Florida Railroad, by which passengers could reach all points in the United States. These ships made the Tampa-to-Havana journey in thirty hours, with a two-hour layover in Key West. The Morgan Mail Steamship Line boasted the *Hutchinson* and the *Whitney,* which covered the New Orleans, Punta Gorda (Florida), Key West, and Havana route. The Ward Line, among others, had "palatial steamers" on the New York-to-Havana run, a trip that generally took "only" four and a half days. All these handsome crafts, with their tall masts and shapely stacks, crowded Havana Bay, bringing to the city American businessmen and tourists avid for the pleasures of a European capital that Havana offered so near to home. It should be remembered that though the countries do not share a land frontier, Cuba is much closer to the populated parts of the United States than Mexico and many areas of Canada.

A measure of Cuba's relations with the United States in these years may be gained by leafing through the *Illustrated Book of Havana and the*

Island of Cuba (5th ed., 1892). Compiled by one J. C. Prince, this guide not only details the tourist attractions of Havana and other Cuban cities such as Matanzas and Cienfuegos but also includes information on hotels in Key West and Tampa that were part of the usual tour, as well as railroad timetables for American trains that connected with the steamships cruising the waters between those cities. Information on Cuba, particularly Havana, is thorough, and includes many advertisements for shops, cafés, bookstores, and hotels catering to tourists. "Every year the number of tourists increases from all parts of the United States," it boasts. The guide's centerpiece is Havana, "essentially cosmopolitan," with a population of more than two hundred thousand and "one of the finest and most important cities in West India and South America" (p. 27).

Havana had evolved during the nineteenth century into a city with broad boulevards such as the Prado, ample public spaces such as Central Park, flanked by the famous Hotel Inglaterra, and open areas such as the Plaza de Armas. Carriages belonging to well-off Havana families cruised the Prado at appointed hours with their tops down, the better to exhibit their distinguished passengers, who waved to each other or to passersby. The Teatro Tacón and lesser houses had good seasons with European actors and singers, and the Havana Bullring hosted some of the best "swords" (bullfighters) from the motherland. There were numerous hotels and cafés, with broad terraces where people gathered to display their fineries and exercise their wit. One café, the Louvre, was the meeting point for Havana's literati and baseball players. At the Acera del Louvre, the Louvre Terrace, or Portals, one was sure to find Wenceslao Gálvez and his friends in animated discussion about the latest game or the brightest European luminary. Baudelaire and baseball could very well be the topics of conversation on a given day, to judge by Gálvez's accounts.

Over the years, sportswriters looking back at what records there are of Cuban baseball in the nineteenth century have been puzzled by how short seasons were. They find it difficult to compare ballplayers from that era with those of today because the performances then seemed too brief to provide an indication of their quality. But the problem stems from a misconception of the notion of "season," and ultimately of the nature of nineteenth-century baseball teams.

In the Cuba of the 1870s and 1880s, as was the case earlier in the United States, baseball teams were truly "clubs," a term that remains in today's vocabulary but has lost its original meaning. A baseball club was a social organization made up of people interested in the game, who met not only to play the sport but also for many other activities, such as dances, dinners, and the like. A baseball club had several teams, arranged according to skill, and named "first," "second," "third," and so forth. Hence *el primer Almendares* meant "Almendares's first team." In the 1880s some of the clubs even had a *juvenil,* made up of children or adolescents. The more powerful clubs had their own fields, whose centerpiece was the *glorieta,* a sort of large gazebo from which women and other spectators watched games protected from the sun and in which dances, dinners, and literary soirees were held. The purpose of the club, then, was not exclusively to compete against other clubs but to also promote games, practices, and other activities within its ranks. Of course, games with other clubs, involving the "first team," were arranged, and eventually entire tournaments, called *premios*—that is to say, "prizes" or "cups." Often a club split into two or more teams that played each other under a given banner or color and were called *bando azul* and *bando punzó* the blue and scarlet camps (the origin of the blue-red rivalry of Habana and Almendares). This practice, together with the relatively small number of clubs and the fact that games against other clubs took place only once a week, is why "seasons" appear to have been so short. In the beginning, the social part of club activity was as important, if not more so, than the competitive one.

The game at the Palmar del Junco on December 27, 1874, is as good an example as any of the kind of baseball first played in Cuba, and of the close relation the sport then had to literature. The game may not have been the first in Cuba, but it was probably the first about which an article was written. This is how Gálvez presents it in *El béisbol en Cuba.* The story was written, appropriately, by Enrique Fontanils, an aspiring author like Gálvez, and appeared four days later in *El Artista,* an irreverent journal devoted to the theater. Fontanils signs the piece "Henry." The match had all the characteristics of the sport at the time, including an amateurish uncertainty about the rules. The clubs flipped to see who would be *in,* meaning who would be home. Habana won the toss. They took their positions and the game started, but a dispute soon arose: The Matanzas pitcher was "throwing" the ball instead of "pitching" it. The umpire ruled against Matanzas at first, but the club refused to take out their pitcher, who obviously could not hurl any other way. It was finally decided to allow both pitchers to throw with the same motion. This still turned out to favor Habana, for their pitcher, Ricardo Mora, threw so hard that the Matanzas players could hardly see the ball and "only" scored nine runs in the seven innings that the game lasted (it was called because of darkness at 5:35 P.M.). Habana, on the other hand, scored fifty-one runs, partly on the strength of two home runs by Esteban Bellán and one by pitcher Mora. The visitors had players who were already well known, such as Emilio Sabourín, or who would become so, such as home-run hitter Esteban Bellán, identified as a member of the New York Mutuals. He was the first Latin American player in what could be considered the major leagues. Fontanils reports that a large crowd at the game enjoyed the novelty of the spectacle. He adds, laconically, that in a couple of months the two teams would probably meet again at the Habana field in El Vedado. The pace of "seasons" was quite slow. No big issue was made of the lopsided score.

Another reason why relatively few games were played against other clubs is that baseball was essentially a Sunday activity. Matches against other clubs were in the beginning substantial social events that filled a Sunday afternoon, sometimes stretching until evening if the game was followed by a dance, as was often the case. As clubs became more competitive and as professionalism began to enter the sport, baseball became a Sunday spectacle that competed against bullfights, the theater, and other public entertainments. The American occupation of Cuba following the war of 1898 tilted the balance in favor of baseball, particularly when the administration of General Leonard Wood banned bullfighting the following year (military order 187 of October 10, 1899). But in the 1880s the Havana Ring still posed a threat to baseball games.

In the Cuba of the 1880s, particularly in Havana and cities such as Matanzas, baseball was part of a host of social activities for mostly young middle- to upper-class men and women. These activities were part of the "decadent" spirit of the *belle époque,* decadent here meaning something useless and frivolous, the opposite of work or worship. Decadent activities involved primarily the body as a means of obtaining both pleasure and health.[6] They were leisurely, collective, ludic activities, often taking place outdoors. They were also occasions to wear colorful attire, including, in this case, the baseball uniforms, to exchange presents and prizes, and to indulge in vaguely explicit erotic play, such as dancing the danzón. These rituals were animated by an artistic spirit that celebrated the exotic, the foreign, the artificial, and the erotic, and were intimately related to the Latin American literature of the times, which came to be known as *modernista*. In fact, Cuban baseball appears to have been born under the aegis of modernista literature and to be part of its cosmopolitan, aesthetic spirit, as was the danzón.

Modernismo, as a literary movement, valued what was foreign, particularly French, and was opposed to Spanish traditions, which were viewed as retrograde and repressive. It was a literature motivated by an aesthetic spirit that searched for beauty in dynamic shapes and by a languorous sexuality devoid of the sentimentality of romanticism. Modernista poets such as Julián del Casal and José Martí were enthralled by the beauty of the body in motion and by the allure, perversity, and danger of sex. Baseball and the danzón shared all of these qualities. The danzón, French and African in origin, was sensuous in its movements but not explicitly so, favoring the indirection of rhythmical feints, advances, and retreats. In the danzón the bodies attain a freedom of expression unheard of in previous Hispanic dance forms. Baseball was of American, not Spanish origin, and also afforded a liberation of the body through graceful, regulated movement. Baseball uniforms were in scandalous contrast with the austere black suits and bowlers men wore at the time in sweltering Cuban cities: bright bandannas tied at the neck, shirts with removable front panels displaying the club's emblem in ornate, Gothic letters, gaudy caps, and knickers above long, colorful socks. But baseball was mostly modernista by the indirection and complexity of its metaphors. There was no crass, warlike occupation of terrain, as in rugby or soccer, but instead runs were scored by running in a circle around a square and avoiding being touched by an object that would render one "out." The erotics of baseball are sublimated by movements and gestures, by touching and being touched, by chasing, and by throwing, though Gálvez asks himself at one point if the game is not too overtly masculine with all the business of bats and balls. Baseball, like the danzón and the poems of Rubén Darío, is decadent in spirit. As with the sad and bored princess in Darío's *Sonatina,* spectacle and play are needed to boost life with temporary meaning.

Though the parallel with Europe should not be extended too far, Cuba in the late nineteenth century provided political and social conditions similar to those that produced what came to be called the belle époque in France. A general feeling of melancholia and skepticism prevailed in France as a result of its defeat at the hands of the Austrians. But this malaise was encouraged by the gloomy scientific theories of the times. The biological conception of life led to a nihilism that found its highest exponent in figures such as Nietzsche, and in France writers such as Renan and particularly Zola. Gaiety, frivolity, and the pursuit of pleasure were ways of combating these feelings. In Cuba, the first war of independence had ended in 1878 with the defeat of Cuban forces. Spain made many concessions, granting Cuba—its last major colony—great autonomy. But the result was, at best, inconclusive and frustrating. The war had unleashed epidemics and famine through the eastern part of the island, and many families had lost their sons in the struggle. It was a climate similar enough to that of France to provoke an equally frivolous and frenzied pursuit of pleasure among some, particularly the young. To this one must add the prestige of French culture at the time, to which backward Spain always compared unfavorably. Havana's cafés were called Louvre, restaurants Las Tullerías, publications *El Fígaro,* and writers avidly followed all literary innovations from Paris. French plays were performed in the original at Havana theaters, indicating that quite a few Cubans were fluent in French.

The Ten Years' War had also brought about an increased leveling of social classes, a spirit of democracy that was also part of the belle époque. With emancipation in 1886, all blacks became free, and their assimilation into society was an urgent issue, particularly in the urban areas. People of all classes had opposed the Spanish regime; hence the new society to which progressive writers, thinkers, and patriots aspired was a less rigidly stratified one. The model here, as in much else, was the United States. Since the nineteenth century, Cubans and Latin Americans in general have seen American culture as a social leveler. American things and customs tend to be practical and informal, not ostentatious, and American culture tends to be secular. So baseball appeared as an activity that brought together individuals of different social classes, and the matches constituted a lay ritual distinct from church ceremonies and holidays. Baseball was a powerful force in the democratization and secularization of Cuban culture, at least as an ideal, if not quite so in practice. The tendency to combine people of all classes, much exaggerated at first, became part of the ideology of the sport throughout modern Cuban history. By the 1890s, with the increasing professionalization of baseball, it is true that a young man's skill as a ballplayer often opened doors normally closed to others of his social class. Gálvez makes this claim in his book, and it was repeated throughout the twentieth century by many apologists of baseball.

The presence of ballplayers among the revolutionaries was no doubt a result of this political component of baseball. But it is also part of a more general movement toward entrusting the political future of countries to men who engaged in activities typical of the belle époque, particularly literature and the arts, but also sports. As noted earlier, the second Cuban war of independence—the one finished or aborted (depending on one's point of view) by the American intervention in 1898—was planned by José Martí, a leading modernista poet. Many Cuban patriots were men of letters. The secular conception of society that these men had was shaped by an artistic view of political and social activity. There was no break between Martí's political activism and his poetry. The society that was trying to emerge from the war of 1895 was shaped by beliefs and customs of the belle époque, including sports. Fidel Castro already loomed in the future of Cuba.

Baseball, in particular, together with dancing, was a collective, erotic ritual in which the young, whether as participants or spectators, gathered to engage in flirtations. All of this would change after independence, and indeed was already changing as the century came to a close. But in the beginning the social nature of baseball clubs was the predominant quality of baseball.

The picture Wenceslao Gálvez paints of his first years in the game during the 1860s and 1870s is one of carefree afternoons in Havana, playing ball after school with boys of diverse racial and class origins. Some of the white, middle-class boys would take off their heavy black coats and ties and play in shirtsleeves until the sun and exertion showed so much on their faces that they feared punishment at home. They would play pickup games in empty lots, from which they were often chased by irate owners. As they grew older and were freer to roam, they would cross the bay to play in empty lots next to the Cabaña Fortress or go west or south to El Vedado and Almendares in search of open spaces. In hilly areas surrounding the bay they would compete for space with kite enthusiasts taking advantage of the sea breezes to fly their colorful contraptions (no doubt made more so by the Chinese presence in the city). Baseball was a sport played in defiance of Spanish authorities, who viewed this American invention as vaguely secessionist and dangerously violent because of the use of sticks. A ban was issued in 1869, just as the Ten Years' War was starting. The boys occasionally had to run from the police or from sentries around the fortresses that surround Havana. These teenagers would flaunt the modernity of their game and its exoticism. Their enthusiastic adoption of the danzón, with its obvious African component and erotic movements, was part of the same defiant attitude. According to Díez Muro, the Habana Base Ball Club—which was the first—was established in about 1868, when "various distinguished sportsmen, among whom were Messrs. Alfredo Maruri, Ernesto Guilló, Lavotal, Bulnes, Enrique Canals, Ricardo Mora and Emilio Sabourín . . . lay the foundations of that organization, bringing together under the name Habana two teams, that is to say, a group of twenty players divided into two squads of ten, which, by practicing and playing each other, adapted to our milieu Base-Ball, or the American Ball Game, which, though opposed by the colonial elements, gained the sympathy of Cuban youth" (p. 19).

We are extremely fortunate in that there are published interviews with two of the originators of Cuban baseball: Nemesio Guilló and Teodoro Zaldo. Guilló was one of three boys sent in 1858 to Mobile, Alabama, to study at Springhill College. The other two were Ernesto, Nemesio's brother, and Enrique Porto; they ranged in age from eleven to fifteen. Nemesio was the youngest. Six years later, in 1864, the three returned as fully grown young men. Nemesio brought in his trunk a bat and a baseball, the first to be seen in Cuba, and little known even in the United States, where the game was just then catching on. The very next day after their arrival, the three were playing ball in El Vedado, in front of some public baths owned by a certain Don Ramón Miguel. At first the game consisted in hitting fungoes, which became a hit, or a double according to where it struck, and an out could be made by waiting for a ball to drop after hitting a tree. In that area groups of players began to be organized with other boys returning from the United States. They wore drill pants, white shirts, and a tie that was red or blue according to the "camp." By 1868 they formed the Habana Base Ball Club, whose founders were Leopoldo de Sola, Ernesto Guilló, Alfredo Maruri, Enrique Canal, Emilio Sabourín, Ricardo Mora, Esteban Bellán, Francisco Saavedra, Rafael Saavedra, Roberto Lawton, Octavio Hernández, Manuel Lorenzo Bridat, Lavotal, Bulnes, and Nemesio Guilló.[7] It was in that year that the club first traveled to Matanzas, where Guilló remembers they played and defeated the crew of an American schooner anchored at that port for repairs. In 1869 the Spanish authorities issued their ban on the game. It resurfaced in 1878, at the end of the war, when Habana was reorganized, and the Almendares Base Ball Club was founded. Progreso and Matanzas were the new clubs in the "Athens of Cuba." Guilló provided all this information to *Diario de la Marina* in 1924 (January 6). In October 1922 Nemesio, fat but apparently still spry, appears in a *Carteles* picture throwing out the first ball in a benefit game.

On January 20, 1924—the same month and year as the article on Guilló—*Diario de la Marina* published an interview with another baseball pioneer: Teodoro de Zaldo. In 1924 Cuba was in a baseball fever and eager to discover the origins of the game on the island. Teodoro de Zaldo was involved in the organization of the Almendares Base Ball Club.[8] He and his brother Carlos are typical of the young men who started the game in Cuba, in social background as well as in their various activities and business enterprises. They were born in Sagua la Grande, Las Villas Province. Carlos, the more important of the two brothers from the point of view of the origins of Cuban baseball, was born on December 22, 1860. From 1875 to 1877 they attended Fordham College, in New York's Bronx, then a pastoral area, where they learned to play baseball. Upon returning to Cuba they were among the founders of the Almendares B.B.C. in 1878, a team that Carlos captained while playing shortstop. Some of the other early players for Almendares were the Franke brothers, Leonardo Ovies, the Basque Antonio Arzola, Zacarías Barrios, Fernando Zayas, Alfredo Lacazette, Adolfo Nuño, and Alejandro Reed. Teodoro, a pitcher, is credited with having thrown the first curveball in Cuba (Teodoro explains that umpire Leopoldo de Sola, who sat under an umbrella about twelve feet from the catcher, could not appreciate that the ball was going over the plate and refused to call it a strike). Upon his graduation from law school, Carlos quit playing but remained on the club's board of directors. More importantly, he and Teodoro purchased the land opposite the Quinta de los Molinos, on Carlos III Boulevard, and had the original Almendares Park built there. It was designed and constructed by Nicolás Navarrete y Romay, a well-known engineer from a prominent Havana family. The Cuban League was to play there for thirty-five years, and through Carlos' efforts, several visiting American clubs played in the field. In 1910, in association with José María Barraqué, Arturo Mañas, Ricardo Martínez, Eloy and Aquiles Martínez, and others, he instituted the *sistema de empresas* to run the league. In other words, each club, not the league, would be an independent corporation. The Zaldo brothers became leading bankers, and Carlos was the first secretary of state of the Cuban Republic under its first president Tomás Estrada Palma. There is a plaque to his memory at the Gran Stadium in Havana.

According to Teodoro Zaldo, Almendares' following was aristocratic: "Its board of directors included Esperanza Navarrete, the Aguirre sisters, Finlay, Countess Fernandina, Chacón, Calvo, the most distinguished and genteel families of Havana's society, the well-to-do, as one would say today. . . . All the elegant society wore the blue emblem." They would, he said, board the little steam train on Sundays, at about noon, and travel from La Punta to El Vedado to play against Habana, and "the entire neighborhood of San Lázaro district came to their windows and doors until that whole colorful and gay convoy of beautiful women and enthusiastic players who fought for the sky-colored team left." The Zaldos were friends of Don

Santiago Aguirre, a wealthy patrician who owned the sugarmills Cabañas, Mercedita, Manuelita, and San Claudio, and were regulars at the Payret and Tacón theaters, not to mention the Louvre Portals. Teodoro says that Habana had more followers among the people because it was not as aristocratic in its composition.

Another team founded at this time was Fe. Its organization shows to what degree the game had taken hold in Havana. At the beginning of 1879 a team called Alerta was organized in the Jesús del Monte neighborhood, with the intention of playing in the *segundo premio*, meaning a league a notch below the Cuban League, against Progreso, América, and Esperanza. Progreso (not to be confused with the Matanzas team of the same name) was a nearby club, with players from the same neighborhood as Alerta. A man named Florentino Ayala decided to amalgamate both clubs and created the Fe Base Ball Club, which would donate proceeds of its games to the founding of a school for poor children. A Dr. Manuel Fernández de Castro brought about the plan. Like its predecessors, this team competed in the second championship, which it won, and then decided to issue a challenge to the Habana B.B.C., given that Almendares had dissolved. Fe beat Habana in three of five games. In 1881, under the leadership of General Manuel Sanguily, Fe again defeated the champion Habana. The team traveled to Key West, where it played for the patriots who were then plotting Cuban independence. The Fe team dissolved as a result of disputes arising from the trend to professionalism in Cuban baseball as the century closed, but reappeared for the 1900 season. They were then called the Browns (*El Fígaro*, December 9, 1900, p. 561).

By 1889, when Gálvez published his book, baseball had spread throughout Cuba like an epidemic. According to him and to chronicles in *El Fígaro* there were hundreds of clubs throughout Cuba and dozens of publications devoted to the sport in Havana and the provinces. There was much activity in Las Villas Province, just east of Matanzas. Since 1887 there were baseball clubs in Santa Clara, Cienfuegos, Sagua la Grande, and Remedios. In 1889 the province was in a baseball fever because of a championship being played among Bélico, Villaclara, and Niágara. Bélico, which wore red, won with a team of players all under twenty years of age. The star was outfielder Manuel Ramos, a great runner, batter, and fielder who for fifteen years was the star of the region. In 1890 the first provincial championship was played, with teams from Sagua la Grande, Cienfuegos, and Santa Clara, which managed to draw attention away from the passionate struggles between Habana and Almendares in the capital. There were some great players, later national stars, who first became known in this provincial season: the notable Matanzas catcher Román Calzadilla; Emilio Ruiz, who later starred at short for Matanzas; and Esteban Prats, who shone with Almendares. An internal struggle within the Santa Clara team led to their losing the championship on technicalities, and the fans set fire to the baseball park. Sagua la Grande was declared champion.

Another provincial championship was played at the end of 1899 and early 1900, right after the Spanish-American War, with the same Sagua la Grande, Cienfuegos, and Santa Clara clubs. Baseball championships continued to be played in the province in the early years of this century. In 1903 the Villaclara team defeated clubs such as Fe, Clío, and Almendares, from the Havana region. In that same year, Cienfuegos' Yara defeated Habana, which had won the Cuban League championship. Among the notable players were pitchers Inocencio Pérez, who played for Almendares and the Cuban Stars, and Julián (Fallanca) Pérez, who pitched successfully for Habana.

A good example of how baseball started in Las Villas Province is the case of Sancti Spíritus, a beautiful colonial town to the south. While in many respects typical, Sancti Spíritus is significant because it is not a port city like Matanzas. Baseball arrived in Sancti Spíritus in 1888, brought by a young man named Juan Cañizares Gómez. Cañizares, like Guilló and the Zaldo brothers, had been educated in the United States. He was also a man of letters, like Gálvez, and a translator from English. He and his father had been deported to the United States by the Spanish government at the start of the 1868 Ten Years' War. In baseball he made it all the way to the Fe club in the Cuban League, and in 1893 he published a book titled *Manual de Base Ball para uso de principiantes (Baseball Manual for Beginners)*, with the rules of the game and instruction on how to play each position. On January 29, 1888, two teams, Libertad and Yayabo, played the first game in Sancti Spiritus (*El Fénix del Yayabo*, January 1979, p. 4), from which not a few distinguished players would soon emerge.

In Havana the baseball fad had turned into a furor. Photography studios in Havana displayed the pictures of winning teams, which ran the risk of being defaced by fans of other clubs, and there were several memorable disputes and even fights. One led to the dissolution of the Almendares club and to polemics about the sport in which leading intellectuals participated. Around Havana there were fields, with pavilions or *glorietas,* in El Cerro, to the south and west of the city, where Almendares played, and to the west, in El Vedado, where Habana played. There were also important clubs across the bay in Guanabacoa, Regla, and Casablanca.

The location and structure of the playing fields reveal the nature and function of the sport at the time. Baseball clubs generally moved to the outskirts of the city, to areas that had once been devoted to the pastoral leisure of Havana's elite. Walled and fortified, Havana lay on a broad peninsula on the west side of the bay, which, like most Cuban bays, has the shape of a bag, broadening inland, with a narrow passage to the sea. The part of the peninsula attached to the mainland was closed off by a wall. But this wall was torn down in about 1863, when the railroad connected Havana with such bucolic areas as Almendares and El Vedado. The latter's name (which means off-limits) is due to its original wildness, which the Spanish authorities believed provided a natural defense of the coastline west of Havana. The railroad also reached along the coast to Marianao and its nearby beaches west of the city. In these areas, particularly Almendares, the Havana sacarocrats had built *quintas de recreo,* summer or weekend homes, where they could entertain in cool surroundings and devote themselves to country pleasures. The sugar boom and its aftershocks, particularly the new rail lines that led out of the city, made areas such as Almendares almost part of Havana. Across the bay, Guanabacoa and Regla also grew nearer— quaint little steamers made crossing the bay a popular amusement. In short, the beaches to the west, the sylvan recreation areas to the south and west, and the small towns on the other shore of Havana Bay were incorporated into the expanding metropolis.

The leisure-oriented parks, boulevards, and sidewalks of Havana proper had now expanded to the periphery. The city had incorporated recreation into its domains, creating a buffer zone between the urban landscape and the countryside, which was the domain of toil, where sugar was produced. Work and recreation began to share a liminal space similar to the French *faubourg* (*faux bourg,* false or fake city), masterfully studied by John M. Merriman. Reading Gálvez and others gives the impression of Havana as a city that migrated every Sunday across the bay in chugging steamers or to the countryside in open railroad cars and horse-drawn carriages. It is a pity that we have no Impressionist paintings of these crowds of happy young people releasing the energy acquired from sugar (in every sense) on these Sunday outings. Baseball, with its sprawling lawns and *glorietas,* was at the heart of these activities.

The crowds retreat not to the countryside but to a domesticated, artistically rearranged rural zone. What had been the countryside was now a modernista landscape. The borderline region where baseball thrived was neither totally urban nor entirely rural but a combination. The rural had been remade to fit a certain urban sense of pastoral leisure and recreation. Baseball fields are more like gardens than open fields, particularly in the tropics, where closely cropped grass and open meadows are uncommon. The paths connecting the bases, bulging around second to accommodate wide turns, the circle around the pitching rubber (originally a square or rectangle), and the one around home plate all bespeak the gardener's cropping and hedging tools following a designer's precise blueprint. Though it gives the impression of openness, particularly in its fenceless early baseball, the baseball diamond is, as its name implies, a rigorous and closed geometrical design. The lines in the perimeter separate two areas, fair and foul, indicating a separation between the good, regulated space where the game is played, and the wild, untamed area around it. If fair, the ball is playable; if foul, the batter is penalized for sending the ball there. Everything in baseball involves the regulation of space and the control of geometrical figures, such as the ball, a perfect sphere. Catching a fly ball within the confines of the field is an exacting operation involving space in three dimensions. The same dialectic between nature and art is present in the construction of the glorieta and in the very location of baseball fields within rural recreational areas, already subjected to the gardener's shears and hoe.

If any structure is typical of the Cuban belle époque it is the pavilion erected by the clubs at their baseball grounds—the glorieta. It is a structure that endured, perhaps even today, in vestiges of stadiums and in customs surrounding the game. The name is itself revealing: glorieta, according to eminent etymologist Joan Corominas, has existed in Spanish since the twelfth century, when it was derived from the French. It has always been associated with a construction built for pleasure, preferably in a garden. The name derives from *gloire,* as being *en la gloria,* "in heaven," because of the pleasure found there. A glorieta, then, is a building erected in a garden, employed mostly for holding dinners. It is also called a *cenador,* a place to dine. It is essentially a large gazebo, roofed in zinc, with trellislike or latticed walls to admit the breeze, where dinners, poetic readings, and dances were held and from which the members of the clubs, particularly the ladies, watched baseball games and practices. A drawing in *El Fígaro* shows a merry building with pennants flowing from the top, resembling the kind of structure one finds at Churchill Downs in Kentucky and other old-fashioned horse-racing venues.

The glorieta is a space mediating between the city and the countryside, between art and nature. Its roof protects people within it from the sun and the rain, but its walls are trellises through which the breeze, the scents of the grass and flowers, and the sounds of crowds and players could penetrate and invade its inner space. They are false walls, marking a boundary but not impeding the free flow from one realm to the other. Brightly painted and adorned, one can imagine these glorietas as spaces where the sort of activity one sees in a Renoir painting takes place: spirited dancing, drinking, eating, and flirting. It was in these structures that Cuban youth danced the danzón to the sound of bands like that of the great composer-musician Raimundo Valenzuela, a mulatto from Matanzas. An 1885 piece in *El Fígaro* informed its readers that after one particular game there had been much dancing due to "the presence of many Eves, many Adams, and of Valenzuela, who played the part of the serpent" (October 29, p. 7). It was also in these glorietas that the culminating activity of the elaborate ritual of a baseball game took place: a sumptuous dinner and dance at which the players celebrated each other with toasts and bantered about the game just played, often reading poems and other literary texts.

The glorieta also established a social distinction. Members of the club and their guests watched the game protected from the elements and near food and drink. In the glorieta one found beautiful young ladies of good social standing dressed in their Sunday best. The rest of the crowd sat at the *gradería,* or stands, out in the punishing tropical sun. Following bullring terminology this section was also called *sol,* or *tendidos de sol,* meaning unroofed bleachers exposed to the sun, a distinction that prevailed until at least the 1950s in Cuba and whose origin I did not discover until I visited Seville, cradle of bullfighting.[9] In his well-known novel *Generales y doctores* (1920), Carlos Loveira (1881–1928) offers the following description of a baseball game in the Matanzas of the 1880s that captures the distinction between the two structures and between a bullfight and the new game:

That afternoon, besides the game of baseball—civilized, manly, healthy—there was a bullfight, that savage entertainment that never took hold in the noble and progressive Antillean milieu. In the glorietas and stands of the baseball stadium there swarmed a creole [native Cuban] crowd made up of members of "both sexes." In the barbaric ring there thronged an imported crowd [Spaniards], and among them, naturally, the city's entire police force, among whose members, also naturally, there wasn't a single native of the nation. In the glorietas of the baseball game, with no other incentive than the noble American game, or the stimulus provided by belonging to one or another camp, be it Matanzas or Habana, people clapped, cheered, and argued heatedly. In the stands, out in the sun, betting was starting, an evil that later corrupted baseball and scared away from the game the ladies, who were the ones to ennoble the spectacle by their presence [pp. 36–37].

No doubt Loveira saw many such games as a child, so his description, though part of the fiction of his novel, is probably very authentic.

In Havana the games followed an elaborate ritual. The field, home of the Almendares Base Ball Club and owned originally by a certain Narciso Barbier, was first erected near Quinta de Palatinos and later moved closer to the city, to Calzada de Carlos III, a boulevard leading southwest from the city after the wall enclosing Havana was demolished. This field was in the Cerro district, or Barrio de Tulipán, and underwent several transformations, such as the addition of the stand brought from the horse track in Marianao in the late 1880s. As Cerro indicates, this was one of the hilly sections surrounding Havana where summer homes were built by the rich plantation owners. The previously quoted *Guide* describes this area as "dotted with beautiful summer residences . . . the rendezvous of the fashionable society of Havana" (p. 55). Carlos III Boulevard made this outlying region part of Havana, particularly on Sundays, when games were played at the new field. Down the boulevard came the carriages bringing beautifully dressed young ladies, who were escorted to the glorieta. Larger, initially horse-drawn buses, later trams, brought the rest of the crowd. The teams dressed in Havana proper, some at well-known gyms along the Prado, and rode in "breaks" down the boulevard sporting colorful uniforms and waving banners. Crowds cheered their arrival and watched the stylized ritual of the warm-ups, already an integral part of the spectacle. During the match, players who made spectacular plays were rewarded with *moñas,* ornamental ribbons, by the ladies. At game's end—after teams gave each other a collective cheer—the glorieta became first a dining hall and later a dance floor. The teams left the grounds in their respective "breaks" waving their flags according to the outcome of the game.

The preceding description follows a text by Aurelio Miranda, who was known by his *nom de plume* "Charivari." Written in 1907, it is full of nostalgia for the good old times of amateurism in the sport. But baseball was such an established part of Havana by the early 1890s that the *Guide* lists it among the city's attractions, providing this description of clubs and their activities:

BASEBALL CLUBS. The spacious and commodious building of the Almendares Club is situated opposite the Quinta de los Molinos, or Captain-General's summer residence. The Havana Base Ball Club is at the Vedado, up the north shore. Games are played every Sunday afternoon, and many spectators are attracted to the sport on account of American clubs coming every season to play with the Cubans, who are great lovers of athletic sport. The main floors of both club houses are also especially arranged for dancing. Very fine balls are given here during the season [p. 60].

After the game players and spectators might wind up at the Louvre Portals to discuss the game until late in the evening or attend a performance at the nearby Teatro Tacón by famous French actress Sarah Bernhardt. To judge by chronicles in *El Fígaro*, theatrical activity was intense in Havana at the time, ranging from serious plays in Spanish or French and operas sung by French and Italian companies to light, Spanish-style musical theater. Some of this light theater bordered on burlesque, though by today's standards it was as risqué as American situation comedies for television. Other diversions were more typical of the belle époque.

One such establishment was a skating rink opened in Virtudes Street, near the Prado. In winter roller-skating competitions were held for young men and women. A peculiar sport of the time was also held here: exhibitions by *andarines,* men who could walk great distances in a very short time. American andarines were imported to set records at the skating rink, and a Spanish andarín did so well that he was booked for several races in the United States. A circus named Pubillones was also active, with the usual fare of high-wire acts and displays of strength by men who lifted enormous weights. But these strong men often found competition among the locals who had taken to weight lifting, as well as other forms of physical culture, in the various gyms that opened their doors in late nineteenth-century Havana. Fencing clubs and matches were also common.

Among the public "spectacles" against which baseball competed and was at the same time allied, none was more widespread than literature. I have spoken of the presence of literature in gatherings that included baseball players and aficionados. It was no coincidence that *El Fígaro* was published by a group of literati who were also baseball enthusiasts. Modernista literature was a social affair that took place in salons, cafés, and theaters. A peculiar form of literary venture in the Havana of the 1880s and 1890s, for example, was the *velada,* or literary soiree, held not only in private homes and cafés but also in theaters rented out by literary clubs. Poets and orators would take the stage to read their work or improvise on a given topic.

In *El Fígaro* literature and baseball coexisted, manifesting their common source in the decadent spirit of the time. Though the magazine boasted of being "the organ of baseball," it contained much more. The best-known writers published their work in this journal, most of it on matters unrelated to the game. But it did carry articles about the various baseball clubs and reported the games in detail, including box scores. It furnished statistics and gossip about the players' comings and goings and about the parties and dinners given in conjunction with the games. It also contained information about other spectacles, such as skating, and tidbits about fashion and fads. A section called "Peloteras" was directed to young women. "Peloteras" means both female baseball players and a melee. The young women in question, of course, were not baseball players but baseball fans whose presence at ball games and subsequent celebrations was very much a part of the game. The joke typified *El Fígaro*'s comic spirit. The presence of women marked the modern spirit that animated the sport, as opposed to the cloistered activities allowed women in traditional Spanish culture. *El Fígaro* published poems, essays, serialized novels, and the like. Some poems dealt with baseball, and occasionally "Peloteras," or accounts of a game, were written in rhyme. The confluence of baseball and literature was complete, and no one incarnated it better than Wenceslao Gálvez, writer, historian, man about town, and shortstop.

Though Gálvez was a minor writer, his older brother José María Gálvez was a noted one at the time, as well as a lawyer and orator. José María was deeply involved in the struggle for independence. The older Gálvez also played baseball and became a respected umpire. He was obviously one of the first players in Cuba, already a retired veteran by the 1880s. The brothers were born in Matanzas to a prominent family. Their second surname, Del Monte, may indicate that they belonged to the family of Domingo del Monte, a key figure in the origins of Cuban literature in the 1830s. Little is known of Wenceslao Gálvez as a writer. He was obviously enthralled by American culture, calling himself "Wen," but it is unclear whether he studied in the United States or spent part of his childhood in Florida (during "La Emigración"). He did spend years of his later life in Tampa, perhaps during the 1895–98 War of Independence, and wrote a book called *Tampa–Ybor City* (Tampa, 1897). He received a law degree from the University of Havana.

Gálvez's other works consist mainly of collections of articles written in a frivolous, irreverent spirit typical of the times. He was a *costumbrista,* a reporter and critic of social mores. But Gálvez also wrote literary and theatrical criticism, and collections such as his *Esto, lo otro y lo de más allá (mosaico literario)* demonstrate his up-to-date knowledge of French, Spanish, and Spanish-American literature. He is as familiar with the works of Emilia Pardo Bazán as he is with those of Baudelaire, and he kept up with journals from Paris and Madrid. Readers of his decadently titled and soporific novel *Nicotina* will look in vain for traces of Gálvez's baseball addiction.[10]

☺

But what kind of baseball did these well-read dandies play, and how did the game fit within evolving Cuban culture? The baseball played in Cuba during the 1870s showed some of the same trends as the game played in the United States, with variations that are hard to explain. Baseball's beginnings were essentially amateur, restricted in the cities to the social clubs. As the sport gained in popularity the quality of play improved and the club rivalry, particularly between Habana and Almendares, deepened. Championships were organized, and the games took on more and more of the features of a spectacle. By the mid-1880s Sunday games were one more show, competing with old-fashioned ones such as bullfighting, and new ones such as roller skating or the circus. Although the atmosphere at games retained many of the qualities of the social event it originally was, now play became a specialized skill, and the best-known players, such as the veteran Emilio Sabourín, Pablo Ronquillo, and Carlos Maciá became celebrities. Baseball was becoming professionalized, with players "jumping" from one club to another, with visiting professional American teams, American players imported to reinforce Cuban teams, and with heavy betting on the contests.

A clear indication of this trend is what transpired in 1890, which also shows how the game's strategy was evolving under the pressure of changes brought about by professionalization. In the fall of that year Habana, Almendares, Fe, Matanzas, Cárdenas, and Progreso were readying themselves for the 1890–91 season. A young man, Oscar Conill, was named president of Almendares B.B.C. to try to shake the spell of bad luck that team had lately been suffering. Conill offered money and gifts to a number of Almendares players to get them to defect to Habana. He managed to lure Moisés Quintana, Miguel Prats, and others. When the Reds took the field at Almendares Park they were greeted with jeers by the crowd, who began to call them "pirates." Emilio Sabourín, the Habana manager, brought players from Columbia, a team from the Pilar neighborhood that played in a lower classification, to replace the defectors. Among these were future stars Valentín (Sirique) González, Martín Aróstegui, Carlos (Bebé) Royer, Alfredo Arcaño, Francisco (Pancho) Alday, and Juan Antigas. Given the chance to play, these youngsters acquitted themselves quite well. Their first surprising win was against Progreso, in Matanzas, which had veterans such as Calzadilla, Castañer, Padrón, and the Matos brothers. Sabourín won the game by the application of a strategy unheard of before in Cuba. With the game tied in the tenth, Habana came to bat last (the game was being played in Matanzas, but the Reds were the home team because teams flipped to determine who was "in"). The first batter got on and Sabourín called for a bunt, which the shocked Progreso players could not handle, thus putting runners on first and second with no outs. The next batter also bunted, but the opposition, alerted to the possibility, threw him out at first, with the runners moving to second and third. A perfect sacrifice. The next batter also bunted, squeezing in the winning run. Neither Habana nor Almendares won that year, but the Reds managed to hold their own in spite of the raid, which revealed to what degree the game had been commercialized by the last decade of the nineteenth century.

Another indication of the trend toward professionalism was the emergence of marquee players. Pitchers Carlos Maciá and Adolfo Luján were among these, but the most coveted one was a Matanzan known as "El Inglés" (The Englishman). He was so called because he spoke English, had an exquisite education, dressed like a gentleman, and was a regular at the Louvre Portals. His name was Antonio María García, and veterans of the era considered him to be the best Cuban player of all time. He was a great catcher, first baseman, and outfielder, not to mention a fleet runner and tremendous hitter. When John McGraw visited Cuba in 1889 he wanted to sign El Inglés, but the Cuban was making good money at home and declined. He starred for ten years in the Cuban League, making his debut with Habana in 1884. In 1900 El Inglés played for Almendarista under manager Evaristo Plá. El Inglés was later an umpire.

According to Gálvez, Habana was the first club to import American "catchers," a move rivals criticized. They recruited for catchers because it was the most specialized position and the one for which it took longer to get into shape. One such catcher, Billy Taylor, was fat as a barrel and a heavy drinker—the first in a long line of professional American ballplayers who became notorious in Cuba for their drinking. In the 1879–80 season Colón Base Ball Club hired two Americans—Carpenter and McCuller, a pitcher and a catcher—who so dominated the games that other teams refused to take the field against them. There were Americans who were hired to work on the gaslight system of Havana but who really came to play for baseball teams. According to "Charivari," a team named Progreso, which played in the Havana neighborhood of La Víbora, was led by an American player named Wilson. In 1878 Hops Bitter, a squad sponsored by the beverage company, was the first American team to visit Cuba. They beat Almendares decisively on December 25. Carlos de Zaldo, who bunted his way on, came around to score the only run by the home team; he is credited with having been the first player to bunt in Cuba. In 1885 a "gentlemanly manager" named Scott, according to Gálvez, brought two teams that he baptized Providence and Athletic, with players called Nash, Fogarty, Crane, Striker, and Robinson. Athletic beat both Habana and Almendares. Crane hit a mammoth home run that reached the racetrack at Almendares Park.

Many of these Americans played in major-league teams in the American Association. Though the Americans taught the Cubans much about the game, this particular visit was a financial bust—the bulls outdrew baseball!

By the eighties, then, the players were no longer middle- to upper-class Cuban young men who had learned the game in the United States, but seasoned veterans and a few Americans playing for glory and gain. The game continued to grow at the amateur level, however, throughout the rest of the island, far beyond the Havana–Matanzas region. As a result, a summer league had to be organized to accommodate all the teams. This league briefly fulfilled a wish that was to haunt Cuban baseball until the revolution of 1959: to have a truly national league of baseball, including teams from the entire country. This summer league was inferior to the winter championship, which pitted the by now well-known rivals Habana, Almendares, and Fe, among others, and did not succeed for very long. But its existence attests to the fact that a great deal of baseball was being played in the rest of Cuba, much of it, I suspect, in the new, larger sugarmills called *centrales*. Wenceslao Gálvez and other recognizable players did participate in the summer league, but the circuit succumbed, probably to transportation problems and the increasing political tensions leading to the war of 1895. One of the more interesting and revealing features of the summer league was the names of the teams. The Boccaccio and the Fattinitza were named after operettas; others, such as the Tinima and Undoso (in Sagua la Grande), took the names of rivers; while others, such as Bacardí, were sponsored by the rum company. This last association anticipated a long relation, throughout the history of baseball everywhere between companies making alcoholic beverages and the sport. It also reveals the sport's origins in the decadent atmosphere of the belle époque.

I am not suggesting that by the mid-1880s Cuban baseball was mostly professional, but simply recognizing a trend. In the mideighties baseball clubs were still being organized, such as the one in Guanabacoa, which began playing its games in the town square, but soon built a new ballfield with all the amenities of those in the capital. And the games at Habana's Vedado Field, or at the by now famous Almendares Park, retained some of the genteel aura of earlier years. As the decade of the eighties wore on, however, the spread of the baseball frenzy to all social classes became evident by the rowdiness of the crowd at the games. The fierceness of the competition between Habana and Almendares culminated in a melee that led to the temporary disbandment of the latter in 1887, and a thoughtful article by philosopher Enrique José Varona on the evils and benefits of baseball. Aside from its obvious benefits in terms of health, Varona thought that baseball would teach Cubans how to compete with dignity and equanimity. Noting the widespread popularity of dancing, Varona wrote in lapidary style that "Our progress will be real and beyond dispute the day when the accomplished sportsman dethrones the good dancer" (p. 87). The philosopher saw in the lasciviousness of the danzón a greater moral danger to the emerging Cuban society than the unruliness that baseball could foster. Varona's comments, and the decision of the members of Almendares to dissolve the club, reveal to what degree baseball had changed in Cuba.

One of the leitmotifs of Gálvez's 1889 book is the democratization that baseball promoted. This was an essential element of the modern component of the game; like all American products it was seen as inimical to inherited social privilege, and an antidote against obsolete barriers among classes. It was this belief that made baseball part of the ideology of the independence movement from Spain. Everything Spanish reeked of old-fashioned, outmoded trends, from religion to public spectacles, while everything American bespoke a popular, democratic spirit. However, as the sport began to attract the baser elements of Cuban society, the class divisions on the island began to generate strife. An example of this is evident in the scene from *Generales y doctores,* where the fracas breaks out in the *gradería,* the stands, not in the *glorieta,* or pavilion. Descriptions of games at Almendares Park in the eighties reveal the same friction among the classes. Reporters from *El Fígaro* were jostled about in standing-room-only crowds, and the heckling of players had already begun in earnest. Loud arguments and even fights provoked by betting broke out regularly. Eventually the presence of women at games, the strongest vestige of the social ritual the game had once been, diminished and almost disappeared because of the rowdiness and coarseness of the language.

If he became a great ballplayer, skill and dedication could bring a young man out of humble living conditions to mingle with the upper classes, but to his kind, loyalty to a club was measured in money. In addition, the presence of his brethren at games in the stands or as large groups of restless, standing men changed the nature of the spectacle. Winning became not a question of bragging rights, a few ribbons, or a lovely decorated pennant. One's livelihood was now at issue. Tensions and clashes ensued as those committed to the "old" ways attempted to retain the "purity" of the sport, while those who could not afford it as a leisurely pastime took it in another direction. The democratic quality of baseball became part of a nationalist ideology, remnants of which still survive among Cubans, but the facts were other, as will become evident in later chapters.

A salient inequality was the absence of blacks among the clubs competing in the Cuban championship. Ironically, blacks were allowed in the glorieta, but only as members of the bands that played for the dances that often took place after games. Raimundo Valenzuela blended the danzón with baseball on these occasions. But there were no black ballplayers in Almendares, Habana, Fe, or any of the teams in the capital, nor in Matanzas and other cities. Cuban blacks did play, however, as Gálvez attests, first with white kids in the sandlots, and later on clubs of their own, often organized by various businesses. In his chapter devoted to blacks in baseball, Gálvez jokes sardonically that white entrepreneurs exploited talented blacks. Black teams were from the beginning more professional in nature, no doubt because blacks could not afford to be amateurs. They would eventually become the "semipro," an institutional venue for black players during the Republic.

It is also likely that blacks played on sugarmill teams. Evidence of this comes in an indirect fashion. In the period between the Ten-Year War and the War of 1895, Cuban black players were coveted by emerging Mexican teams in the Yucatán area. Cuban families who emigrated from Cuba to that region—La Emigración, which, as we saw, also included Florida and New York—took baseball to Mexico. Cuban blacks such as the famed Quince y Medio, so known for his having gone around the bases in fifteen and a half seconds, were stars in the early stages of Mexican baseball. This began a trend that would be repeated throughout the century: Cuba was the center from which baseball spread to other parts of the Caribbean, such as Venezuela, Puerto Rico, and the Dominican Republic. But early Cuban baseball practiced an apartheid that would be perpetuated by Cuban amateur baseball during the years of the Republic. The leveling influence of baseball was real, as with many of the spectacles of the belle époque, but its actual results were slow and not without huge contradictions and inequities.

After the Spanish-American War, the professionalization of the game eventually brought down racial barriers, both in the professional championships and in the sugarmills. Baseball became more democratic as the economic motive behind the spectacle became more explicit. This movement toward equality probably began in the sugarmills and reflects a well-known piece of Cuban economic history. After the Ten Years' War, and owing to political, technological, and economic factors, Cuban sugarmills diminished in number but increased in size. The early sugarmills were family-owned, plantationlike ventures. The owner ground his own sugarcane in his small mill, and his workforce was made up of slaves. However, after the devastation of the war, many families were forced to sell their mills, or were foreclosed by American banking firms. These *colonos* now sold the sugarcane from their plantations to the huge mills built by American firms and some other foreign and Cuban entrepreneurs. With a substantially larger workforce, these mills were appropriately called *centrales* and became like factory towns in the United States. Everything revolved around the *central,* which ground the crop every year during the winter months. It is easy to see how these company towns could have baseball teams to provide the Sunday entertainment and exercise their rivalry against neighboring *centrales.* It was here that gifted blacks began to play alongside whites, in teams that were professional by most standards and that would continue to be so during the years of the Republic.

A curious feature of nineteenth-century Cuban baseball is that it was played with ten men to a side, a fact that left its mark in Cuban baseball jargon.

As kids we referred to sandlot games where sides were chosen on the spot as a *pitén,* as in *echar un pitén,* to play a casual, pickup game. The expression, I know now, comes from a "picked ten," a selected team of ten players. I have been unable to ascertain why early Cuban teams were made up of ten, not nine players. It is known that ten men to a side was common in early baseball in the United States, so it is likely that the game was brought to Cuba at a point when this was the practice. The tenth man was a short right fielder who played, much as in softball today, somewhere behind the infield, or between second and first, with the second baseman behind the bag. The short right fielder was the symmetrical opposite of the shortstop. In all other aspects the game was the same as in the United States, and when in 1885 the Athletic played Havana, the Cuban teams had ten men while the visitors used the now conventional nine. Infuriatingly, reports in *El Fígaro* of these games (in which the Americans crushed the Cubans) say nothing about this glaring discrepancy.

The first championship or league in Cuba was organized in December 1878, a full ten years after the game had begun to be played on the island, and right after the conclusion of the Ten Years' War. On the twenty-second of that month representatives from the Habana Base Ball Club and the Almendares Base Ball Club met at 17 Obrapía Street, in Havana, to discuss terms and sign the binding documents, having in their possession a letter from the Matanzas Base Ball Club stating that it would abide by whatever was decided at the meeting. Beltrán Senarens, Ricardo Mora, and Manuel Landa represented Habana, while Adolfo Nuño, Carlos de Zaldo, and Joaquín Franke represented Almendares. After some deliberations they reached these accords: (1) that each club would play three games against the others, the winner being the team that defeated each of the other two twice; (2) that the prize would be a white silken flag, adorned with fillets in the colors of the winning club, inscribed with the word CHAMPIONSHIP, to be paid for by the two losers; (3) that each of the players would receive a silver medal, with the inscription, ISLAND OF CUBA, BASE-BALL CHAMPIONSHIP 1878, to be paid for by all three clubs, with the Habana club in charge of having them made[11] (it is not clear if only the players in the winning team would be given the medals); (4) that games would be played on Sundays or holidays, beginning with the twenty-ninth of the current month of December; and (5) that the rules and general conditions of play be those set forth in the 1878 *Spalding Baseball Guide.*

The league officers were Leopoldo de Sola, president, Alfredo Maruri, treasurer, and Antonio Pérez Utrera, secretary. The rosters were as follows: Habana B.B.C.: Francisco Saavedra, E. Cadaval, Manuel Landa, Emilio Sabourín, Roberto Lawton, Ricardo Mora, Nemesio Guilló, Esteban Bellán, B. Senarens, Enrique Canals, and Rodrigo Saavedra; Almendares B.B.C.: Adolfo Nuño, Leonardo Ovies, Carlos de Zaldo, Teodoro de Zaldo, Antonio Alzola, Alfredo Lazazette, Alejandro Reed, Standhope, Zacarías Barrios, Fernando Zayas, Joaquín Franke, and N. Barbón; Matanzas B.B.C.:

F. Delgado, R. Amieva, A. Hernández, Samuel Tolón, J. Sands, M. Amieva, C. Pujand, F. Domínguez, J. Amieva, and Ricardo Martínez. Games would be played at Almendares Park, Habana's field in El Vedado, and Palmar del Junco in Matanzas. The Habana B.B.C. won undefeated (it was tied once) what should have been called the 1878–79 championship. Lore has it that this was the first season of the Cuban winter league, which continued uninterrupted until the 1960–61 season. While the continuity of Cuban baseball is real, the fact is that several championships or *premios* were sometimes played in a single winter during the nineteenth century, and there were interruptions throughout the entire history of the "league." But the importance of lore cannot be denied, and the 1878–79 season stands as the inaugural one in Cuban baseball history.

As can be seen from the prizes won by the winning team and players, in 1878–79 Cuban baseball was still largely amateur, though some of the players were already being paid. Habana's third baseman, Esteban Bellán, was a full-fledged professional, even a major leaguer, having played in the United States for the New York Mutuals and the Troy Haymakers. As the seasons continued, and as various championships were awarded to the teams, particularly Habana, the nature of the spectacle changed, with a more professional element taking over. By the mid-1890s teams were organized both as cooperatives (with players sharing the profits) or as professional outfits (with players paid salaries). As spectacles the games became increasingly lucrative affairs, with the sale of drinks, scorecards, and baseball magazines. The fledgling transportation industry also made some profits, as did businesses that sponsored teams, such as the Bacardí Rum Company.

The Sunday games between Habana and Almendares gradually changed from a genteel social ritual into a major confrontation, mobilizing a great segment of the population. By the late eighties these teams had acquired the character they would have for the first sixty years of the Republic. I can do no better here than simply translate the last section of Wenceslao Gálvez's 1889 history of Cuban baseball. This is what the Almendares shortstop wrote:

Habana and Almendares

Since early morning some of the field's employees have busied themselves climbing on top of the Almendares pavilion to hoist various flags announcing the game. Others raise the national flags at the entrances to the park, and yet others groom the field and arrange the chairs in the stand, which had been moved to and fro during the days of practices.

Starting at eleven the little cars from the Príncipe [site of a fortress in Havana] start regurgitating passengers who, each getting his ticket, begin to arrange themselves in the stands and bleachers, while the poorer fans climb on the sickly branches of the rickety laurel trees along Carlos III boulevard, in spite of the impresario's perverse measure of shrouding them with thorns. Some curious people peer from the high windows and high walls of the houses next to the field, far away, beyond the racetrack, enduring the sun the entire day and unable to clap because they cannot let go with their hands from jutting bricks and railings.

As if by agreement, the *habanistas* place themselves on the extreme right side of the pavilion, yielding the left to the *almendaristas*.

The common people, who have crowded the bleachers since the earliest hours of the day, talk loudly about baseball, arguing heatedly over the most trivial issues or the most insignificant player. Cabs, passing in front of the bleachers like an endless string, let off ladies and gentlemen at the foot of the stairway leading up to the pavilion. Privately owned carriages do the same, except that these park themselves in the shade while the cabs return looking for another fare. But, facing back, already empty, the cabbies confront an angry mob, impatient because the game has not started at one o'clock. So they begin shouting and whistling, riling up those bellicose in nature who think that they can fight everybody at the same time. Humbled by their predicament, the cabbies rain lashes on the backs of the poor horses who, with their ears down and panting, resume their painful trot.

The pavilion is overflowing with an enthusiastic crowd. Some ladies who have lingered too long in their toilette cannot find seats, nor even gallant young men willing to give one up to them, and have to return home sad and pensive, as one usually returns from a funeral.

Those who just had their lunch and wish to ease their digestions promenade themselves back and forth behind the chairs, inside the pavilion proper, with their hands clasped on their back. While others, with hurried step, anxious looks and contorted faces search avidly for their friends on the opposing side to arrange for a bet of several coins.

They carry pieces of ten in their hands, playing with them, flinging them up and down in the air a short distance so that they will clash with each other and jingle.

"Ten pieces of ten on Habana, even money!"

"Well, let's put them up."

"As you like, but I'm betting on the team that scores the most runs, even if the game is called."

"You're on."

The most impatient ones look at their watches constantly.

"Why haven't the players arrived yet? We are going to lose for being late. . . ."

One by one we, the Almendares players, arrive at the Aurelio Granados Gymnastic Club. We put on our uniforms and swing from the trapeze while the ten was completed. The most enthusiastic or bold fans come in to see us get dressed, witnessing it all—a bit indecorous to a certain point. And in their delirious partisanship they might praise the beauty mark that so and so had on the right thigh. They would help us with our toilette, tying the string on our undershirts and the brand new silken blue scarf, which was just purchased at the Chinese boutique, around the neck.

"How about dedicating a hit to me today. I have already seen the *habanistas* at the gym on Consulado Street. Don't strike out. Have you had too much wine?"

They went on with these and other impertinent remarks until it was time to leave.

"I'll go with you. Can I carry your bat?"

"No, man, I can carry my own bat."

No sooner have we stuck our noses out the gym door than the curious began to stop in their tracks and stand brazenly in front of us, and those who recognized us, to point us out to their friends as if we were some sort of monument.

"The one over there is Carlitos Maciá," would say one, pointing his finger at my teammate.

"Look, this one is Alfredo Arango."

"So fat? I would have expected him to be thinner."

"Well, so that you have no doubt about it, pst, pst, hey, aren't you Alfredo Arango? Of course it is him, it's just that he doesn't feel like answering."

We finally arrived at the park by three in cabs with their tops down (the cabs' not the cabbies'). We went through Prado, the Campo de Marte, Reina Street and Carlos III Boulevard.

We were first seen by those atop the laurel trees and they broadcast the news that we had arrived.

From the stands there came twenty thousand shouts, greetings, a fluttering blue flag that could make one dizzy, applause, whistles and boos. . . .

Our partisans in the pavilion would raise from their seats to clap with their hands, their fans stumping their canes on the floor. . . .

A few moments later, when one could not expect more spectators to show up, the *habanistas* would appear with their pennants, and then one could hear the same uproar in the stands, louder on the left side of the pavilion, with cheers for Habana that would intimidate us, even against our wills.

And then the big struggle to find an umpire would begin.

"Who is the umpire?"

"So-and-so."

"But he is an *habanista*! You'll see how we lose. . . ."

"Hey, listen, if so-and-so is not the umpire our bet is off."

Finally, the victim would come onto the field, accompanied by the two captains.

"You'd better have a sharp eye," they would shout at him from the stands. "Don't you dare cheat!"

Before this, the respective tens had gone through their preliminary warm-ups and the players had been applauded or booed by the opposing parties.

Once the game began, conversations ceased in the pavilion. Only the screeching voice of the hawkers could be heard: "Buy *El Pítcher*! *El Habanista*! *El Pelotero*!" "Eat candy, drink water!" "Scores!" "Buy *El Cátcher,* with a picture of Tehuma!"

"Play ball," the umpire would say, once the players had taken their positions, and no sooner had the first ball been thrown than people began to get excited.

The batter had not yet swung and missed and needed only two more balls to get first base.

"Throw another ball," would growl someone from the stands, while others shouted, "Strike him out."

"What was that?" says the pitcher.

"A ball," replies the umpire, and a partisan protest can be heard from the pavilion, the stands and bleachers.

"That was a strike! . . . a strike. . . . !" "Down with the umpire!" "Throw him out!" "That's no way to win, that's cheating!"

The young ladies become alarmed, not quite fainting, and an opportune hit changes everyone's focus of attention. Then the applause begins, the cheers, the hurrahs, and the cane blows on the venetian blinds of one of the rooms on the corner of the pavilion.

If the player has been called out, the fans rooting for the other team, who had been silent when the play had been cheered by the player's fans, imitate the applause, the passive voice becoming active.

The game is constantly interrupted by complaints, generally out of place, to the umpire, who is perplexed, not knowing what to do, stunned by the protests of the players, who are all shouting at the same time, while the public screams, taking an active part in the discussion from their seats, each trying to impose his own point of view.

The most excited ones, believing that the umpire's decision is damaging to their club, ask the players to leave the field, because to go on playing is a humiliation. The uproar finally dies down, hope is rekindled, and the game continues.

Victory is at hand for one or the other team. The nervous fans bite the tip of their fingers, grow excited, yell, grab their neighbor by the arms, shake him, pummel him, pleased or proud of this or that play.

Suddenly the sharp crack of the bat is heard and the ball soars far and away from the fielders' reach, the pitcher hangs his head in shame, and the batter runs with increasing speed, prompted by his fans, like the jockey spurring on his mount. He is already close to home, his goal, but the ball has arrived in time and good-bye effort, good-bye all. Then one has to watch the fans of the team at the field shout, make gestures, clap and cheer.

Midway through the game one player makes a masterly play. Exceptionally, all the fans applaud, creating an impressive scene. Thousands of hats fly through the air, the public rises to its feet in the pavilion, and there are hundreds of hankies and blue and red pennants. A total standing ovation. Now it is not the partisans of this or that club who cheer, now it is the sport that triumphs, controlling passions, imposing itself. But this is momentary. With new plays, partisanship is renewed and praise is again divided.

There has been a good hit, a batter has clubbed a home run, and there is pandemonium. A generous soul throws a half-ounce gold piece to a player, the other hurls a ten piece, they call his name, acclaim him, kiss him, grab his hand, pat him on the back, a young lady fan pins a ribbon on his chest, another gives him a bouquet of fresh flowers.

And when the game is over the losers' fans make themselves scarce to avoid those who make fun of them. They leave, muttering oaths against the players, who lost because they are a bunch of pampered little boys without pride, who let themselves be beaten. . . . Those with cooler heads remain and listen to their rivals who, with smiles on their faces, come to pay their condolences, but what condolences, the most insincere in the world!

The exit from the field looks like a parade. There are few carriages, so the vast majority decide not to wait and beat a retreat on foot. They now look like battalions out of uniform.

The losing players who found cabs are chased by young boys mocking them.

Later, one must go to the Louvre Café Portals to watch the groups that gather to discuss the game played that afternoon. One must not only go on Sunday, but during the entire week, sure to hear talk about nothing else.

In the late afternoon of February 25, 1947, the crowds leaving the Gran Stadium after the epic championship confrontation between Habana and Almendares would not look much different.

☺

What remains of nineteenth-century Cuban baseball? The division between amateur and professional along racial lines resurfaced after the American occupation. The pavilion or glorieta and the gradería or stands left vestiges in provincial ballparks, along with some of the rituals, such as meals after games. Former great amateur shortstop Quilla Valdés told me recently in Miami that opposing teams liked to play his club Hershey (which represented a sugarmill owned by the chocolate company) because of the splendid lunches served at a local hotel for the players from both teams. The connection between baseball and sugarmill towns continues. I remember that in the fifties, the nineteenth-century custom that the player who made

the last out got to keep the ball was observed in Cuban professional baseball. A few terms also remain. Besides pitén there is *escón*, a scoreless inning,
which derives from "skunk," the name given such an occurrence in the
United States in the nineteenth century (alluding to the animal's odor, I
presume). Yet another is the verb *ponchar*, "to strike out," derived from
the English "to punch out," a term that has made a comeback recently in
the United States.

To us the players of the belle époque are blurry, mostly just names.
They look stiff and remote in their studio pictures. It is hard to envision
them in action and nearly impossible really to imagine their style of play.
This does not mean, however, that we should be condescending about their
ability and courage. These were agile, strong young men who hit, threw,
and ran hard with barely any protection. Accounts of games in *El Fígaro*
often mention injured players, particularly catchers with swollen hands, and
Gálvez writes about balls striking players in the stomach and knocking the
wind out of them. Yet today the players who started the game in Cuba are
mere bronze letters on plaques and lines in history books. Those who went
to war have an added dimension, but mostly in the rhetoric of official proc-
lamations. Theirs is not a living legacy, like that of the players who came
to be known after independence in 1902.

The two most important legacies of nineteenth-century Cuban baseball were the association of the game with Cuban nationality and the bitter
and enduring rivalry of Habana and Almendares. The link between baseball
and Cuban identity has had its ups and downs throughout the twentieth
century—at times soccer seemed to have the upper hand, at least in Havana.
But, on the whole, growing up Cuban meant growing up with baseball
as an integral part of one's life. Baseball was played since the beginning of
the nation; hence it was part of the nation. In the countryside, playing
baseball was as quotidian as eating black beans and rice and roasting a pig
on Christmas Eve. And more often than not, one's identity was tied up
with being for Habana or Almendares, an affiliation that had little to do
with where you lived, but rather, I suspect, with one's family ties (whether
your father was *habanista* or *almendarista*). Also, though a true apartheid
undeniably existed in the Amateur League, soon there appeared great professional black baseball players who were revered by all segments of the
Cuban population.

The Habana-Almendares rivalry had been developing since the early
1870s, perhaps since the late 1860s. As the game became more professionalized and as an increasing number of publications, some attached to each
team, began to make the rivalry more widely known, it became one of the
facts of sporting life in Cuba. It was also, and would continue to be, a
source of hard cash for entrepreneurs and players. The tally of winners of
the early seasons favors Habana heavily and tilts in its favor the final count
of pennants won in the history of the Cuban League. But intellectual hon-
esty compels this *habanista* to confess that the advantage is illusory and fit

only for idle arguments and speculation. The fact is that one can hardly consider some of the early *premios* seasons, and that some remain unaccounted for in extant histories. The rivalry flourished, in any case, and would make possible the Golden Age of Cuban Baseball, which began with the first years of the Republic and is closely intertwined with the development of black baseball in the United States.

Nineteenth-century Cuban baseball is a fabulous beginning, more myth than history. But when it comes to national identities, myths are often more important than history itself.

1 2 3 4 **5** 6 7 8 9 R H E

The Golden Age

President McKinley was eloquent, if perhaps disingenuous, when he declared that ties "of singular intimacy" bound Cuba and the United States. This could not be truer than during the years of U.S. military rule following the Spanish-American War (1898–1902), and other occupations of the island until the thirties, particularly the one between 1906 and 1909, when Cuba was again under U.S. control, a mere four years after having been declared independent. Intimacy does not necessarily mean love, of course, but familiarity; it can breed hatred, affection, competition, and the whole gamut of tensions prevalent in any family group. From a Cuban point of view, McKinley's statement could be countered with a variation on Porfirio Díaz's famous quip about Mexico: "Poor Cuba, so far from God, yet so close to the United States!" In the twentieth century, baseball was perhaps as good an index as any of the complicated relationship between Cuba and its mighty neighbor to the north, whose game it had adopted in the process of rejecting the Spanish motherland and of developing a sense of nationality.

In the first third of the twentieth century, Cuban baseball, particularly the professional kind, was deeply affected by the close political, economic, and cultural relations between the island and the United States (close is something of a misnomer, since the politics and business of the United

States and Cuba were sometimes really one and the same). The first thirty years of the twentieth century were the Golden Age of the sport in Cuba, an era when Cuban baseball evolved in ways that would influence its history to the present. Nineteenth-century Cuban baseball was becoming then a receding and increasingly romanticized origin, whose impact on what followed took various forms. Players who began their careers in the teens and twenties of the twentieth century, on the other hand, were present and active as managers, coaches, and in a couple of cases even as players, in the pivotal 1946–47 season that culminated with the duel between Habana and Almendares chronicled in chapter 2. That game, in turn, was pivotal in the contemporary, even current history of baseball in Cuba.

But I call the years between 1898 and the early 1930s the Golden Age of Cuban Baseball for several other reasons. First, it was the era that my elders—my grandfathers and uncles in particular—evoked when they waxed nostalgic for the great heroes of the past: José de la Caridad (El Diamante Negro) Méndez, Adolfo (Papá Montero) Luque, Miguel Angel (Pan de Flauta) González, Eustaquio (Bombín) Pedroso, Cristóbal Torriente, Gervasio (Strike) González, Oscar Charleston, Alejandro (El Caballero) Oms, John (Bemba de Cuchara) Lloyd, Cool Papa (El Guineo) Bell, John (Mono Amarillo) McGraw, who straddled the nineteenth and twentieth centuries, and the incomparable Martín (El Inmortal) Dihigo.[1] It is also the period that produced, again in the recollections of my elders and in journalistic lore, the greatest team in the history of Cuban baseball, the equivalent of the '27 Yankees in the United States: the 1923 Leopardos of Santa Clara. This was an era when Cuban baseball players competed regularly with and against the best in the world, be they major leaguers or stars from the Negro Leagues. Finally, it was the era that saw the emergence of the three promoters who shaped the early history of professional Cuban baseball and beyond: Abel Linares, Agustín (Tinti) Molina, and Alejandro Pompez. Out of their relationship with the fledgling Negro Leagues in the United States and with their founder, Rube Foster, would be born the two Cuban Stars teams and eventually the New York Cubans. Linares' control of Cuban professional baseball continued even after his death in 1930, since his widow retained ownership of and leased out the "eternal rivals" Habana and Almendares until the late thirties.

I remember that when I was a child, in the late forties and fifties, to praise a current ballplayer—for example, my favorite, Pedro (Perico or Perucho) Formental—would bring a condescending smile to the lips of Inocencio, my maternal grandfather. He would then proceed to state categorically that Perico was good, but not on the same level as the incomparable Oscar Charleston or Alejandro Oms. Besides, Oms was known as The Gentleman because he never raised his voice or showed off, whereas Perico was a *postalita,* a hot dog. As for shortstops, he would make an elegant gesture of pity (for the current players and my hopeless ignorance) by bringing his hands together as if in prayer, lower his head, and pronounce in a low, reverent tone that Lloyd was capable of making plays that were beyond the reach of mere mortals. And could he hit! And what could anyone say about Dihigo, known as The Immortal while still very much alive, who was a star at *every* position, including pitcher?

My grandfather had seen them all at Almendares Park, in our own hometown of Sagua la Grande, and in nearby Santa Clara's La Boulanger Park. No argument was possible, given that I had never witnessed those demigods play, and besides, it was understood that the present was a fallen time, never to equal the grandeur of the past, with its larger-than-life titans and epic deeds. The Golden Age was the Age of Heroes, shrouded in a luminous aura that magnified it and put it beyond the reach of mere reason. Méndez had beaten major-league teams repeatedly, often shutting them out for good measure, and Pedroso had no-hit the Detroit Tigers! Luque had won twenty-seven games in 1923 for the Cincinnati Reds, and Miguel Angel, who had caught in the majors for many years, could throw out runners at second without rising from his crouch. This was the lore passed on to me.[2] To the Cuban fans, and to Cubans aspiring to be ballplayers, this was the heavy burden of tradition.

But these were golden years also because they saw the development of Cuba, particularly Havana and environs, into a major tourist area, which in turn brought about the worldwide dissemination of Cuban music and dance at a time when jazz and other U.S. musical forms were also reaching their peak. The popularity of Cuban music helped to promote professional Cuban baseball. Both increasingly became spectacles, entertainment, a so-cial zone, and practices in which men of modest social standing, particularly but not exclusively nonwhites, could earn money and sometimes fame. The pervasiveness of music and sports transcended social class and race, though this did not mean that barriers in all spheres disappeared—a Cuban musi-cian's only access to a high-class party would be to play in the band, and a black ballplayer would never be invited. But Cuban music and Cuban base-ball were activities where a sense of commonality existed and in whose pleasures all could rejoice. Because they were physical activities that ap-pealed to or satisfied basic urges, they tended to extend the limits of social decorum and prejudice.

This golden era encompasses the Roaring Twenties, Prohibition, the Harlem Renaissance, and the rise of the Afro-Cuban Movement in the arts. During Prohibition Cuba became a purveyor of bootleg liquor, carried across the Florida Straits in boats and later airplanes. Meanwhile, Havana became a city to visit and indulge in pleasures difficult to obtain in the United States, including alcohol. Perhaps more importantly, during these years radio and the movies attained a level of development that turned entertainers and athletic figures into celebrities in a way unheard of before (although baseball games were not broadcast in Cuba until the thirties). Jack Dempsey, Ty Cobb, Babe Ruth, Christy Mathewson, Jess Willard, and Jack Johnson, as well as countless movie stars, came to Havana. The era culminated with the first Cuban revolution, which toppled the government of Gerardo Machado (1925–33) and brought onto the scene Fulgencio Batista, who would play a commanding role in Cuban politics until 1959, when he was defeated by the next strongman, Fidel Castro.

Cuban literature and the arts, already a major force in nineteenth-century Latin American culture, began to attain worldwide recognition in the first three decades of the century. In sports, too, the island started to produce world-class figures, such as Ramón Fonst, world fencing champion; José Raúl Capablanca, chess grand master; Alfredo de Oro, world champion in pool; and Kid Chocolate (Eligio Sardiñas), professional world featherweight boxing champion. Baseball was intertwined in all these activities, helping to consolidate, by the late twenties and early thirties, a sense of national identity and pride that was to prevail until today. Major- and minor-league teams and top-notch Negro-Leagues teams played in Cuba, while Cubans began to star in the United States at all levels, including the majors. Excelling at the American game and defeating major-league teams were important factors in these developments and continues until the present, when the Cuban national team relishes its victories over American amateur squads, even if they are made up of college boys.

From the Spanish-American War to the Depression in the early thirties Cuban baseball developed at four discernible levels. The first was the professional game, which centered in Havana (though not exclusively). The second was semipro ball, with teams sponsored by companies of various sorts and open to everyone, particularly to blacks, including former professionals winding down their careers. The third was sugarmill baseball, the kind with the broadest national dissemination because it spread through the provinces and was directly tied to Cuba's main industry. It was perhaps strongest in the East, where tournaments were for all intents and purposes professional. Finally, there was amateur baseball, played by the social clubs, which flourished in Havana, but that soon expanded to other parts of the island and that excluded blacks until 1959. Amateur baseball was the most direct heir to the original game played by the upper- and middle-class Cubans who brought the sport to the island. I will only deal with the professional game in this chapter.

The era also seems to neatly fall into three periods: the first from independence (1902) to the second American intervention (1906–9), when there was a great influx of American professional players, particularly black ones. The year 1907 was one of self-reflection in the sport, for it saw the publication of the second and third histories of Cuban baseball: Raúl Diez Muro's *Historia del Base Ball Profesional de Cuba* and *El Base-Ball en Cuba y en América* by Ramón S. Mendoza, José María Herrero, and Manuel F. Calcines. The second period starts during the years 1909–11, when the first Cubans in the century began to play in the majors and when the Cuban Stars were founded, to 1920, a time of dizzying wealth brought about by skyrocketing sugar prices and the beginning of Prohibition in the United

States. The culmination of this stage was the visit to Havana of Babe Ruth, wearing the uniform of John McGraw's New York Giants. The third phase began after the Dance of the Millions in 1919 and is marked by a steady decline in sugar prices, which brought about the political unrest that toppled Machado. This phase ends in about 1933. The twenties, until the latter part of the decade, were baseball-rich, and in 1923 a peak was attained with the performance of the Santa Clara team, stocked with many American Negro Leaguers. In the waning years of the twenties the Cuban League divided as a result of internal strife, seasons were canceled, and, symptomatically, in 1934 the three Cuban League teams were defeated by a semipro squad sponsored by Rum Havana Club, a business that had flourished during Prohibition. Five deaths at the end of the decade seem to bring the era to a close. José de la Caridad Méndez died in 1928 of tuberculosis. He was followed by stellar outfielders Bernardo Baró, Valentín Dreke, and Esteban (Mayarí) Montalvo (they had all played for Almendares). Finally, Abel Linares, who was the chief promoter of professional baseball during these years, succumbed in 1930.

The clash of extremes seems to be a dominant feature of Cuban culture and history. While in the early part of this century the U.S. presence was pervasive and could have led to a thorough and definitive Americanization of the island, at the same time the influx of immigration from Spain was greater than in the four centuries of Spain's colonial domination. Hugh Thomas writes that between "1902 and 1907 almost 200,000 Spaniards, mostly Gallegos or Asturians, emigrated to Cuba, attracted by opportunities of high wages. Spanish emigration in these years was ironically higher than at any time when she herself owned the colonies."[3] The social impact of this immigration to Cuba was enormous, particularly if one considers that in 1899 there were only 1.5 million Cubans, with 250,000 crowded in and around the capital. In addition, the growth of the sugar industry, which at some points in this period was frenzied, brought to Cuba thousands of blacks from the neighboring countries of Jamaica, Haiti, the Dominican Republic, and even Puerto Rico and Panama. A demographic development studied with alarm in 1927 by Ramiro Guerra Sánchez in his classic *Sugar and Population in the Antilles*, the influx, made up mostly of Haitians and Jamaicans, was a yearly phenomenon stimulated by the sugar harvest, and the advantage of bringing ever-renewed cheap labor each season. Those displaced by the newcomers moved to the cities and swelled a marginal but culturally rich neo-African population. This was to have a direct impact on Cuban life at all levels, including religion, music, and sports.

Spanish immigration continued at a very high rate in the twenties and thirties, until protectionist labor policies were passed by the government. In the meantime, powerful Asturian, Galician, Basque, and other clubs and associations, supported by salesclerks' unions that were made up almost exclusively of Spaniards, gathered economic strength, erected impressive buildings, and promoted soccer to the point where it came to rival professional baseball in popularity during the twenties and thirties. Spain was making a comeback in Cuba with an army of poor, illiterate workers, some of whom did not even speak Spanish. Canary Islanders came in great numbers, too, brought to toil at the most brutal jobs, such as laying railroad tracks. Chinese, who had begun to arrive in Cuba since 1848 to cut sugarcane, continued to disembark at Havana's docks in considerable numbers during this era. Jews from central and eastern Europe also came, particularly after 1923. There was a sense of alarm in the predominant white majority of the Cuban population, which led to the protectionist labor laws mentioned before.

All of these social, ethnic and economic factors played decisive roles in the development of baseball. As with Italians and Irish in the United States, the sons and grandsons of Spanish (and other) immigrants found in professional sports a way to move up quickly on the socioeconomic ladder. Galician surnames such as Almeida soon became well known, as well as Catalan ones, such as Marsans.[4] Galician last names, in particular, still resonate among Cuban ballplayers, from Pascual to Palmeiro, while Haitians such as Leroux and Noble or Jamaicans such as Dreke and Taylor also abound. Among the descendants of Canary Islanders are Conrado Marrero and Fermín Guerra, though their names do not give away their origin. The Chinese would eventually contribute one respected umpire, Raúl (Chino) Atán, and several ballplayers, also inevitably called, "Chino": Armando Cabañas, Gilberto Valdivia, and Manuel Hidalgo, who were the best known, but also Carlos Morán and Lázaro Bernal. Cuban blacks, of course, carried the names of former slaveowners, mostly Castilian in origin, such as Dihigo, Méndez, González, or Fernández, but also Galician, such as Miñoso, or Catalan, such as Oms. Their nicknames, as in the case of other ethnic groups, were often crudely racist.

Whereas Cuban society was predominantly white, particularly as one moved up the economic scale, professional baseball was more of a melting pot of races and cultures. Upper-class Cubans, particularly the *nouveaux riches* sugar barons who replaced the saccharocrats of the nineteenth century who had been impoverished and decimated by war, erected palatial mansions in El Vedado, west of Havana, and hobnobbed with their counterparts from the United States. These Cubans lived above the fray. Ordinary Cubans, meanwhile, were dealing with the thorny issue of the variegated racial composition of their world, now that the island was supposed to be a democratic republic with equal opportunity for all.

Appropriately enough, then, the professional Cuban League was ushered into the twentieth century by a conflict involving black players. Baseball had languished during the War of Independence (1895–98), but had picked up again with American intervention and with the economic recovery this brought about. José Antonio (Jess) Losada, one of the best sportswriters in the history of Cuba, claims in a *Carteles* article that American troops played a series of exhibition games that had an impact on the development of Cuban baseball, but I have not been able to corroborate this. We know that baseball had been played in Cuba for about thirty years by the time the *Maine* was blown up in Havana Harbor. American soldiers had been playing baseball since the Civil War, so it is likely, too, that games were played by them in Cuba. It is also likely that most of those games involved blacks, given that American authorities, reflecting nineteenth-century racialist theories, had sent mostly black troops in the occupation army, believing that they were better at withstanding the tropical heat. While these may have been factors leading to the conflict of the Cuban League in 1900, the more important elements had to do with internal developments of the professional game in Cuba itself.

War is a leveler of social barriers. World War II led to the integration of American baseball because of pressure brought about by the fact that so many blacks had fought and died for "democracy." In Cuba the War of Independence had brought many whites and blacks together in the common cause of liberating the island from Spain. It was difficult to deny them access to public venues and activities in a "free" Cuba. Greed and need are also levelers of social barriers. The increasing professionalism of Cuban baseball in the 1880s and 1890s, which turned the sport into a potentially lucrative spectacle, together with the reality that blacks played mostly in what could be called semiprofessional teams because they could not afford to be amateur nor join the social clubs that comprised the Cuban League, led to their admittance to the main teams. The blacks wanted to play and the impresarios saw the advantage of including them in the teams, a combination that could only lead to the integration of the Cuban League.

Raúl Díez Muro writes, in his 1907 history of professional baseball in Cuba: "1900. For reasons of a social nature, the Liga Nacional de Base-Ball was dissolved, despite having convened the 1899–1900 Championship, hence the latter would not have been held but for the organization of the Liga Cubana, which convened its own Championship for 1900, which was entered by the clubs Habana, Almendarista, Cubano, and San Francisco, the last two having been recently established" (p. 61). What Muro evasively calls "reasons of a social nature" simply meant that some opposed the inclusion of the two new teams because San Francisco was a squad made up almost entirely of blacks, while Cubano had both blacks and whites.[5] This must be the reason why Almendares does not play under its own name, but as Almendarista (meaning followers of Almendares), to avoid legal problems with the club, which probably still existed as such, and it did not admit blacks. It is clear that during the early years of the century, the Cuban League changed radically from teams made up of remnants of the social clubs, to squads that included professional black players as well as whites of low social standing. Middle- to upper-middle and high class Cubans fled the Cuban League to play in their clubs as amateurs.

El Fígaro, now a lavishly printed and illustrated weekly without much baseball coverage (the game was not chic anymore), devoted most of one issue to the trials of the 1900 season, the culmination of a series of conflicts, which included threats, forfeited games, anonymous letters, and pressures of all sorts to prevent teams with black players from participating. During the last championships before American intervention in 1898, Habana had been called Habanista, Fe was Feísta, and Almendares was Almendarista, clear indications of legal wrangling with the clubs and disputes probably involving the issue of professionalism, which removed the cloak of genteel amateurism from the game and opened it to blacks. In an article on the history of Almendares, Juan Francisco Prieto, a veteran baseball writer, goes out of his way to make clear that Almendarista is not really Almendares, which has been out of the league since 1895. The team pictured has at least two blacks. San Francisco's picture apparently needed no comment, since all the players were black. But a story about Cubano by Luis F. Crespo, another veteran sportswriter, is more explicit about the existence of a controversy. This team was originally owned by one Severino T. Solloso, with the support of none other than Abel Linares, soon to become the virtual owner of Cuban professional baseball. Cuba was the name of the team, but Solloso made a present of it to Agustín (Tinti) Molina and José Poyo rather than allow it to play, under his direction, in a championship that included blacks.[6] Poyo was the son of José Dolores Poyo, who had been José Martí's secretary in Tampa and Key West and who had played with the Cuban team that raised funds in Key West for the cause of independence. Molina, with Linares, would be a dominant figure in Cuban baseball, particularly in dealings with the American Negro Leagues. These two apparently had no qualms about playing in an integrated league. Crespo explains that Solloso turned over the uniforms to the new managers, who proceeded to add the *no* to make up Cubano because Solloso did not want the team to play under its original name, Cuba. It is clear, by the way the suffix is added to the jerseys, that the new owners are punning to embarrass Solloso: the name now reads "Cuba no." Written this way it means, "This is not the team Cuba." But they obviously meant to say also that the white Cuba Solloso envisioned was no Cuba at all. Tomás Chapotten writes, in a brief history of San Francisco included in *El Base Ball en Cuba y en América*, that to bring about the change that allowed blacks to play in the league "it was necessary to put forth very weighty reasons of a moral order to convince those who were adamant in their effort to put obstacles in the way of democratic truth that the times are demanding." The wordplay with team Cuba's name, however, was significant beyond what Crespo, Molina, and Linares envisioned, for the "Cubanness" of the league would come up soon again as the influx of American players, a trickle before, became a torrent.

The 1900 season, the first played during the American occupation that followed the end of the Spanish-American War, is a crucial one in the history of professional baseball in Cuba and shows to what extent the Cuban League is connected with the development of black baseball in the United States. In fact, the American Negro Leagues and the Cuban League are each an important chapter in the history of the other. As shall be seen, a team from the Negro Leagues will play in the Cuban League, and several Cuban teams, most notably the Cuban Stars and the New York Cubans, actually played in the Negro Leagues.

Moreover, it is a well-known though curious fact that the first professional black team in the United States was the Cuban Giants, organized in 1885 by Frank P. Thompson, headwaiter at the Argyle Hotel in Babylon, Long Island. As James A. Riley writes in his broad-ranging *The Biographical Encyclopedia of the Negro Baseball Leagues,* Thompson "recruited players from the Philadelphia Keystones to work at the hotel as waiters and form a baseball team to play for the entertainment of the summer guests. At the end of the tourist season he added more players, from the Philadelphia Orions and the Manhattans of Washington, D.C., to form the Cuban Giants, [and toured as] the first black professional [baseball] team." According to *Sol White Official Base Ball Guide* (1907)—the first "book" on black baseball in the United States—the Cuban Giants really gained prominence once they moved to Trenton, New Jersey, under the management of S. K. Govern and the sponsorship of "capitalist" (entrepreneur) Walter Cook. This team was so successful that it was imitated by other squads, who adopted variations on the name "Giants." By 1900 the Cuban X-Giants (a pun, meaning ex-Giants, or former Giants), made up mostly of defectors from the original teams, were the most successful among these, claiming several "championships" under the direction of manager and financier E. B. Lamar, Jr. This team visited Havana in the spring of 1900.

Not a player among the Cuban Giants or later the Cuban X-Giants had anything to do with Cuba directly. Lore has it that the original Giants called themselves Cuban to pass as Latins and thus avoid some of the more virulent forms of discrimination prevalent in the United States. It is said that they jived in gibberish among themselves while on the field to make people believe they were speaking Spanish. But no one asks why these American blacks called themselves Cuban to begin with. Besides, is it really credible that anyone would take them for Cubans or be gullible enough to believe that their jabber was Spanish? They were still black and eventually would have to speak English to each other to communicate. In baseball there are too many intimate pauses during the game in which words are exchanged with the opposition not to know if another player understands what one says or not. It seems to me that the waiters of the Argyle Hotel and their successors called themselves Cuban Giants because there must have been Cuban teams already active in the New York area, as they were in Key West, during "La Emigración" (the period of Cuban influx to the United States after the end of the 1868–78 first War of Independence). The Giants' move to Trenton suggests that they took advantage of the existence of teams of genuine Cubans, made up of players drawn from the substantial Cuban populations in Manhattan, Brooklyn, and other boroughs of New York City. These Cuban teams must have been seen in action against white American teams by the blacks who then called themselves Cuban Giants, probably tongue-in-cheek. Furthermore, the guests they originally entertained during the summers on Long Island probably went south to Cuba in the winter, where they may have seen Cubans play baseball. The point is that the association between the term "Cuban" and the game of baseball must already have been strong when the black team decided to call itself the Cuban Giants. The relationship between Cuban and U.S. baseball has never been one-sided, and this is one of the most significant and early instances of Cuban influence on the game's originator.

But the irony of the Cuban X-Giants' visit to Havana in 1900 could not be greater (in the Cuban press they are always called the Cuban Giants, without the X, which would have increased the bewilderment). How uncanny it must have seemed to Cubans when the *Diario de la Marina* announced on Tuesday, February 6, that "According to a cablegram sent to this city by Mr. E. B. Lamar, manager of the famous nine Cuban Giants, we learn that the latter will sail to Havana from New York next Saturday. The team is coming to play a series of ten matches against the nines of Habana, San Francisco, Almendares, and Cuba." The brief article goes on to state, no doubt quoting from Lamar's advance publicity, that "The Cuban Giants are the strongest nine outside of the National League, as is demonstrated by the following record of the last three years. . . . Out of 449 games, they won 333, losing only 96." The Cuban Giants played a series of games in Havana, some against the regular teams of the new league, and others against what must be called all-stars made of up of players drawn from several teams. On February 26 they won the first game against Habana, 6–5, after having the first match with Cuba (which must be Cubano) rained out. The Americans did not bat well, but the (real) Cubans made many errors behind pitcher José Romero. The Giants continued to win, also playing independent teams such as Libertad, in Regla, which gave them a good fight but lost, 15–11. Finally, an all-star team named Criollo, managed by the popular Valentín (Sirique) González, beat the Cuban Giants twice. This racially mixed team (with the original affiliation of each player) had future entrepreneur Agustín (Tinti) Molina (Cubano) behind the plate; Carlos (Bebé) Royer (Cubano) on the mound; Esteban Prats (Cubano) at first; Sirique (Habana) at second; Carlos (Chino) Morán (San Francisco) at third; José María (Kiko) Magriñat (Cubano) at short; Rafael (Felo) Rodríguez (Cubano) in right; Alfredo Arcaño (Habana) in left; and Manuel Martínez (San Francisco) in center. Cuban baseball had come a long way since Habana and Almendares had been crushed by the visiting American team called Athletic in the 1880s. Even if it took an all-star to beat them, the Cuban X-Giants were after all the dominant team in "colored baseball" in the United States.

These victories were the first in a long line of cheerfully savored Cuban triumphs over U.S. teams. Contact with the circuit of barnstorming black teams also whetted the appetite of Cuban impresarios, who found that there was a potential public for Cuban teams in the United States, indeed, that the very word "Cuban" was now associated with baseball and could turn a profit. In three or four years teams made up of real Cubans from the island would be touring the Northeast of the United States.

The 1900 championship of the Cuban League per se did not begin until May 17 and ran until December 23, with teams playing a total of only twenty-seven games each. San Francisco won with seventeen victories, and Esteban Prats, of Cubano, won the batting championship. A number of important things stand out in this first season of the twentieth century. The first is that so few games were still played among the members of a league. Newspaper accounts show that each of these teams played games outside the league, not only against the Cuban Giants but also against independent Cuban teams from around the capital. This means that the league did not control baseball or consider itself to be the only first-class set of teams. Second, there were no American players yet on any of the teams. And finally, the season was not scheduled to accommodate the calendar of American baseball, as would be the case later, when, with both American and Cuban players in organized baseball and the Negro Leagues, seasons had to end in time for them to report to spring training in March. In fact, soon the Cuban baseball calendar would even include an "American season," which at first involved independent American teams (i.e., black teams) and would be played before or after the Cuban season. Beginning in 1908 the American season would take place between the end of major-league baseball in September and the beginning of the Cuban winter league, anytime from October to December or even January. During this period Cuban teams played against U.S. squads from the major, minor, and independent Negro circuits. But that was still in the future. Games against the Cuban X-Giants in 1900 were a taste of things to come.

Between 1900 and 1906 the number of teams in the Cuban League fluctuated between three and five, play went on through the summer or parts of it, and most games took place at old Almendares Park, which was leased by Eugenio Jiménez, the first important baseball impresario of the century. On November 20, 1904, *El Fígaro* reports that on Sundays ten thousand to twelve thousand people regularly gathered at the field on Carlos III Boulevard to watch the games. This is said in the context of an article discussing the construction of a new baseball park in Santiago de Cuba, with a sumptuous glorieta (which could also serve as dance hall and theater) and capacity for more than six thousand spectators. It is clear that the economic recovery brought about by the end of the war and American intervention (during which health conditions improved drastically) had re-kindled interest in the sport.

The leading players of the era were Alfredo (Pájaro) Cabrera, Almen-dares shortstop, who was elected (with 940 votes) the best baseball player in Cuba in a survey conducted by *El Fígaro* in March of 1903, and whom we met as groundskeeper at the Gran Stadium in the forties and fifties; Agustín (Tinti) Molina, a catcher, who, as we saw, played for several teams but would be best known later as team owner; a hefty black first baseman, Julián Castillo, who was batting champion in 1901 playing for San Fran-cisco (.454) and in hits (37) playing for Habana in 1903; Valentín (Sirique) González, a second baseman for Habana, who led the league in batting twice before the turn of the century and in hits in 1902 (twenty-four) and 1905 (thirty-three); catcher Regino García, who won four consecutive bat-ting championships from 1903 to 1907 playing for San Francisco, Habana, and Fe; catcher Gervasio (Strike) González, considered the first great Cu-ban receiver of this century, who would gain fame later as Méndez's battery mate; Habana pitcher Carlos (Bebé) Royer, who went 12 and 3 in 1901, 17 and 0 in 1902, and 13 and 3 in 1904; and Agustín Parpetti, reputed to be the best defensive first baseman of the era and who played for Almen-dares. The best center fielder was Heliodoro (Jabuco) Hidalgo, known for his circus catches, which would bring a hail of coins from the stands as he ran back to the bench at the end of an inning. "Jabuco," meaning "satchel" or "bag," meant that anything hit his way would be caught. There was also Luis Bustamante, known as "Anguila," a great shortstop and among the first Cubans to play independent ball in the United States and acquire a measure of fame. Anguila means eel, and presumably alluded to the way Bustamante maneuvered at short. In 1905 Almendares won under the direction of Abel Linares and the help of two promising young-sters, Rafael Almeida, a third baseman, and Armando Marsans, an outfielder who could play other positions and who was touted as "the Cuban answer to Ty Cobb." Marsans mastered all nine positions. These two would be the first Cubans in this century to play in the majors (Bellán had played before, as we know), when the Cincinnati Reds signed them in 1911. An interesting note is that Evaristo Cachurro, a veteran of nineteenth-century Cuban baseball, is now an umpire, which shows how some men remained in the game after they retired as players, creating a living link with the past.

In the 1901 season the league was called Liga Cubana de Base-Ball, and there were five teams: Fe, Almendares, Cubano, San Francisco, and Habana. Molina played with Cubano, Julián Castillo with San Francisco, and Valentín González with Habana. Play began on February 3, at Almen-dares Park. There were blacks and whites on these teams, and it is clear that players moved from team to team without much compunction. Castillo won the batting championship. Each team played only nineteen league games, and the season went through the year. In 1902 the league was still called Liga Cubana de Base-Ball and had the same five teams. Strike González caught for San Francisco, while Tinti Molina moved to Habana. Habana won undefeated, reeling off seventeen victories in as many games. In 1903 it was still the Liga Cubana de Base-Ball, but it was down to three teams: Almendares, Fe, and Habana. Habana now had Julián Castillo, and still had Bebé Royer and Sirique. Play extended from January 1 to a playoff in June between Habana and Fe. Counting the playoff, Habana and Fe played thirty-four games each, almost twice as many as teams had played the previous year. The league changed its name again in 1904. It was now the Liga Habanera de Base-Ball. Was that because there was another league in the provinces? Games were still held at Almendares Park and there were only three teams, but San Francisco took the place of Fe. Habana had the best-known players: Castillo, Sirique, and Strike González. Molina played for San Francisco. Games began the first week of February, and Habana won again. (Habana won the first of four championships in a row.) Teams played twenty games each. In 1905 the league retained the name Liga Habanera de Base-Ball, and the three teams went back to being Almendares, Habana, and Fe. Almendares now boasted the likes of Almeida and Marsans. Habana still had the two Gonzálezes and Royer. Games continued to be held at Almendares Park, and play began in late January. Almendares won, with the teams playing thirty games.

The next championship was for the 1905–6 season, so called because play began on December 31. The name of the league changed again, to Liga General de Base-Ball de la *República* de Cuba (my emphasis). The change was significant, given that the political situation was deteriorating and, with American intervention, Cuba would soon cease to be a "republic." Three teams competed: the very familiar Almendares, Habana, and Fe. Play was still at Almendares Park. Fe now had Strike González and Julián Castillo. Almendares still had Marsans, Almeida, and Parpetti. Habana retained Sirique and now had Esteban Prats. Teams played twenty-four games. This season was the end of a phase of Cuban professional baseball.

As the baseball season of 1905–6 progressed, opposition to don Tomás Estrada Palma, first elected president of Cuba, had been mounting, escalating finally into armed conflict. In September, citing the Platt Amendment, appended to the 1902 Cuban constitution, the American government occupied the island. First William H. Taft was named provisional governor of Cuba, but he was soon replaced by Charles E. Magoon. Thus began three years of U.S. occupation that brought major changes to Cuban baseball, as it did to all Cuban life.

Professional baseball during the "first republic" had been a relatively minor operation, with Cuban players and games still held at old Almendares Park. This stadium preserved the genteel appearance it had during the previous century. It was wooden, had intricate latticework, trellislike construction, and picket fences. The Cuban press in later years liked to refer to this

stadium as the "primitive Almendares Park," but there was nothing primitive about it. On the contrary, it was still a *fin-de-siècle* structure, ornate
rather than functional, with long outfield expanses bordered by the beautiful palm trees of the nearby Quinta de los Molinos. But it was a nineteenth-century baseball ground. In the press of the times it is often referred
to as *los terrenos de Zaldo,* meaning that the park was owned by the family
of the Zaldo brothers, who were among the founders of baseball in Cuba,
as we saw. But reference is also made to Eugenio Jiménez as the *arren-
datario,* meaning that he leased the park to put on shows, baseball among
them. The league itself was, as far as I have been able to ascertain, run as
a cooperative venture, with individuals leasing franchises from their owners.
It is likely that by this time Abel Linares owned at least Almendares (he
would not be able to purchase Habana until 1914). Emilio de Armas, today
a sharp-witted nonagenarian with a deep memory and who worked closely
with Linares, explained to me that the shrewd impresario had managed to
claim rights to the names of the teams with the help of his son-in-law, a
wily lawyer who got around the ban against the registration of geographical
names. (This led de Armas, no dunce either, to put under his name for
future use so many Cuban towns that he came to be known as *mapa
mundi*). Linares had really started, according to de Armas, by "embedding
himself" in the Zaldo brothers' business.

Be that as it may, this cooperative system, which lasted until the thirties, was to come under attack periodically because it seemed that the championship was a staged struggle among teams owned in common, the suggestion being that deals were made to spice up the championships, by, for
instance, moving players around from team to team. The problem was com-
pounded by a larger one, which the league tried to solve many times until
the 1950s: Profitable fan interest was centered only on the rivalry between
Habana and Almendares, the Red and the Blue. Finding a third or a fourth
team to expand and diversify loyalty and increase revenues was difficult. It
is easy to observe that players changed teams often and that the composition of the league varied, with the exception of the continued presence of
Habana and Almendares. These were difficulties typical of a spectacle struggling to stay economically viable, and competing with other forms of show
business.

A harbinger of things to come is that, once alerted to the commercial
value of the word "Cuban," real Cubans decided to capitalize on this in
the U.S. market for independent baseball. This meant, for the most part,
black baseball, though not exclusively. Several teams, the Havana Reds, the
All Cubans, and others lost in the mists of time, were formed and traveled
mostly to the East Coast of the United States, where booking agents found
them dates in the New York, New Jersey, and Philadelphia areas. Julián
Castillo was among the Cuban players who first participated in these ventures, as was Anguila Bustamente, who was one of the best shortstops of
all time in the Negro Leagues and in Cuba, and is enshrined in the Cuban

Baseball Hall of Fame. According to Sol White, "Of the many Cuban teams that have visited America, the strongest was the Cuban Stars of Santiago de Cuba. They were organized in 1905 and composed of all Cuban players. Their American manager is Manuel Camps, of Brooklyn, N.Y. This team is the only Cuban team in the National Association of Colored Base Ball Club [sic] of the United States and Cuba" (p. 99). The *Guide,* from which this quote is taken, displays an advertisement for cigars called La Flor de Manuel Camps, so it seems safe to assume that this businessman was either a Cuban or a Spaniard, clearly of Catalan origin because of his last name, who had taken American citizenship and residence in Brooklyn. Was the team in any way connected with Santiago de Cuba, or was it banking on the fact that, because the city had become so well known in the United States during the Spanish-American War, it would enjoy a recognition factor? The cigars, according to the ad, were from Havana.[7] The Havana magazine *El Score,* in its issue of May 22, 1908 (Año 12, no. 21, p. 4), reports that Abel Linares bought from Camps the rights to his All Cubans and turned them into the Cuban Stars. But Linares did barnstorm first with the All Cubans, and *El Score* informed its readers on May 22, 1903 (Año 7, no. 21, p. 5), that Linares's team had run into trouble in Florida with the team because he was carrying three black players. It seems clear that both of these teams' names were an answer to the spurious Cuban Giants, who continued to visit the island, and that they moved in the sphere of independent baseball where blacks were allowed to play. In any case, the links between American Negro baseball and Cuban baseball were strengthening. Hence that "National Association" that included Cuba!

What happened during the next season of the Cuban League appears to corroborate that, once the United States occupied Cuba again, the booking agents in control of the black game set their sights on the island. Thus H. Walter (Slick) Schlichter is featured in Sol White's *Guide* as "President of The National Association of Colored Baseball Clubs of the United States and Cuba," while Nat. S. Strong is listed as secretary. Slick, a sportswriter, was also "President and Manager of the Philadelphia Giants B.B. and A.A., Inc." With Cuba in U.S. hands, these impresarios must have felt that they had the right to extend their territory to the island. Rube Foster, who was then pitching for the Philadelphia Giants, and who must have already had designs of his own, would come to Cuba that winter to pitch for Fe. Cuban impresarios such as Linares and Molina were primed for a counterinvasion in a larger scale than Camps's inaugural foray with a team called All Cubans. And, in a year or so, veteran pitcher Bebé Royer would discover in Las Villas province a young phenom by the name of Méndez.

The 1907 league retained the title Liga General de Base-Ball de la República de Cuba and fielded the three teams that by now were traditional: Almendares, Habana, and Fe. The season began on January 1 and lasted until April 14, with teams playing thirty contests. Games were still at Almendares Park. But the great difference was that now Habana and Fe were loaded with American players. Habana has George Johnson, who played for the Philadelphia Giants in 1906, Dan McClellan, George Wilson (who could be George Prentiss, who pitched in eleven games for Boston of the American League in 1901–2), and George Mack. Fe, on the other hand, had the cream of American black baseball, nearly all of the players coming from Schlichter's and Strong's Philadelphia Giants: Pete (J. Preston) Hill, Rube Foster, Charlie (Chief Tokahoma) Grant, Grant (Home Run) Johnson, and Bill Monroe. Almendares' only player with an American name is a man called Hope, whom I cannot identify. But they had the best and most popular Cuban players in Pájaro Cabrera, Marsans, and Almeida, with Strike González as their catcher and veteran Bebé Royer among the pitchers. The Blues were clearly making a political statement, which they backed up by winning the pennant in a close race with Fe, decided on the last game of the season. *El Fígaro* notes that a most remarkable phenomenon occurred during the last few games pitting Almendares and Fe: The bulk of Habana's followers, traditionally bitter enemies of Almendares, became rabid supporters of the nearly all-Cuban Blues in their struggle against the nearly all-American Fe. Pictures of the last game show a packed Almendares Park, with fans encircling the outfield fence and many sitting on the outside wall, beyond the park's boundary. Nationalism overcame the Almendares-Habana rivalry and showed the depths of Cuban resentment against the American occupation. The local press referred to Fe mockingly as the *intervencionistas,* the "interventionists." Almendares' triumph over Fe (and their ace pitcher Foster) was really over Schlichter's and Strong's Philadelphia Giants. The outcome of the 1907 season and the large crowds also showed that the Americans vs. Cubans match was a good moneymaker that surpassed the clashes between the "eternal rivals." This was a lesson not lost on the Cuban and American promoters and players, whom I am sure were not bothered by their roles as heavies as long as the pay was good. The obvious next step was to bring major-league teams to play the Cubans, which was promptly done in 1908.

In 1907, black American players and their booking agents discovered the bonanza that Cuba, particularly Havana winter baseball, could be for them. Since the trip by the Cuban X-Giants, other teams, such as the Philadelphia Giants, had come to play on the island. But in 1907, by actually playing in, not against the Cuban League, players remained in Cuba longer and probably made a greater profit. These players knew, as many others would in years to come, the advantages of a league that played all its games in one stadium, located in a large, cosmopolitan city, where many of the restrictions blacks suffered back home did not exist. By playing for a Cuban team a black American player did not have to endure traveling, which in the United States often meant tiresome journeys with stops in very small towns, with awful accommodations and worse food. In addition, the Cuban League did not play every day, but at most four or five days a week, and there were seldom doubleheaders (or if there were, they would be four-team doubleheaders). These advantages made Havana at once a favorite spot for the best American black players, virtually all of whom came to Cuba during these years.

The 1908 season—with Cuba still occupied by the United States— was again played under the name Liga General de Base Ball de la República de Cuba, with a significant addition: Matanzas fielded a team that joined the traditional three of Habana, Almendares, and Fe. It is significant, too, that the representative for Fe before the league is Abel Linares, who stocked the team again with black American players, such as Ashby Dunbar, Bruce Petway, George Walter Ball, Sam Mongin, and Nate Harris. According to *El Fígaro,* most of these players were known to the Cuban fans because they played on the island with the Cuban Giants. This is true for Petway, an outstanding catcher; Ball, a great pitcher; and standout pitcher-outfielder Harris. *El Fígaro* adds, facetiously, but making a sharp political statement, that to the simpleminded the team would look like part of an offensive by *anexionismo,* the political movement dating to the previous century that favored the annexation of Cuba by the United States. But Fe also had in Eustaquio (Bombín) Pedroso and Agustín Parpetti a couple of strong Cuban players. Linares was obviously already doing business with the American impresarios, and the storm brewing in Negro baseball around the Philadelphia Giants and agents Schlichter, Strong, and soon Foster was reflected in Cuba.[8] Habana fielded a mixed team with Americans Clarence Wilson, Preston Hill, George Johnson, and Rube Foster, in addition to Cubans Julián Castillo, Anguila Bustamante, Luis Padrón, and Regino García. Almendares won again, with an all-Cuban squad that still had Almeida, Marsans, and Strike González. But they also had a rookie pitcher named José de la Caridad Méndez, who finished the season undefeated, at 7 and 0. Matanzas did not have any Americans either, but its Cuban players were not among the best, so they finished with five wins and twenty-seven losses. The season was played at Almendares Park and in Matanzas, probably at the Palmar del Junco. The first game was on January 1, 1908, and Emilio Palomino was the batting champion.

Schlichter and other entrepreneurs of Negro baseball were not the only ones to take advantage of having Cuba under U.S. rule between 1906 and 1909. Albert G. Spalding, who had sold his equipment in Cuba since the nineteenth century and whose *Spalding Guide* was used on the island as a source of information and authority on the rules of the game, began to publish a Spanish edition of the *Guide* in 1906.[9] It contains the rules of baseball in Spanish, glossaries of baseball terms in that language, records of the Cuban League, and histories of the game in Cuba, Mexico, Venezuela, and Panama. There are also invaluable photographs, mostly of Cuban baseball. American intervention in Cuba and elsewhere in the Caribbean basin had clearly whetted the appetite of Spalding, who had been the foremost proponent of baseball as a means to spread American influence and had even organized a world tour by two teams in 1888–89. In fact, his

America's National Game, published in 1911, contains a chapter titled "1894–1910. Base Ball in American Colonies—Story of League Games in the Land of the Midnight Sun—Base Ball Popular in Alaska, Hawaii, Porto Rico and the Philippines." In it he states: "As a result of the introduction of Base Ball into our island colonies, many American professionals are finding winter employment, both as coaches and players, while here and there the appearance of a Spanish name on the published score card of games played at home shows that first-class professionals are being developed in the islands."[10]

The 1907 and 1908 Almendares victories over teams made up for the most part of American Negro Leaguers are crucial in the incorporation of baseball as a national game in Cuba. These games showed that Cubans felt baseball was as much theirs as the United States' and that not only could they compete, they could also win against the best American players. An essential element in this development was the rise of José de la Caridad Méndez as a star of the first magnitude. Méndez would become the first Cuban baseball star with nationwide recognition, consolidating feelings of nationhood and general solidarity that went beyond race, class, or politics.

José de la Caridad was born in Cárdenas, Matanzas Province, on March 18, 1887, in the area east of Havana where baseball developed along with sugar production in the nineteenth century. It was a region, as seen in the previous chapter, with a high density of blacks and a hotbed of Afro-Cuban music and religion. As a boy, the future star went to the San Luis school in his native city. Trained as a carpenter and musician, Méndez must have come from an urban, petit bourgeois black family of artisans; he was not a sugarcane cutter, as some have written. Méndez learned the clarinet and later mastered the guitar. In nineteenth-century Cuba and later, many blacks played in the municipal bands and had a formal education in music. The young José must have excelled in baseball early because Charles Monfort, a most meticulous historian of Cuban baseball, says that the boy was playing in men's teams by age thirteen. By 1905 he was in Sagua la Grande, farther east of Havana, playing for a club significantly named Patria (Fatherland). Patria was involved in a championship that included Remedios and Caibarién, towns, like Sagua la Grande, on the northern coast of the old Las Villas Province. Méndez also played for a team called Vesubio, and for Majagua in Cienfuegos, on the southern coast of the same province. In 1907 Bebé Royer, Marsans, Armando Cabañas, Jabuco Hidalgo, and other Almendares players went to earn a few extra dollars by playing in that provincial championship (professionals continued to do this throughout the forties and fifties). Royer was charged with looking at a Remedios pitcher who was being touted by people in the region as a phenom. Bebé reported back to Pájaro Cabrera, who was then managing Almendares, that there was a scrawny black kid playing short (he was apparently 5 feet, 9 inches and 150 pounds) who, when he pitched in relief, showed speed, uncanny control, and a snapping curve. Méndez was signed at once by Almendares and thrown in against Matanzas in nonleague game only a few weeks later. This Matanzas team was no less professional than Almendares and would enter the league again the next season. Young José de la Caridad shut them out, whiffing many batters and becoming an instant success.

Méndez was an unmixed black, with unmistakable African features. While his first nickname was "El Cardenense," or "The Man from Cárdenas," he was also called at the beginning "Congo" or "Congolese." This is a common (if tasteless) Cuban way of referring to someone who is very black. Cuban blacks themselves apply it to each other to distinguish people from diverse African origins and of various hues. Congos are reputed to be short but tough, like Méndez. Congo might also have alluded to a religious affiliation, for Congo is one of the three major *palos* or religious creeds of African origin. In any case, Congo refers to a certain essential Africanness, and blacks of Congolese origin abounded on the northern coast of Cuba from Matanzas to Sagua la Grande. Méndez was from the interior, not from Havana, and he came from a humble if proud background of modest but honest city dwellers. Uncompromisingly black, a musician and a ballplayer, he could not be a more typical offspring of the sugar-producing region east of Havana. If the patriotic doctrines of the Republic were sincere, then Méndez embodied qualities that Cubans had to accept as valid elements of Cuban nationality.

But José de la Caridad also reflected the Matanzas region in an even more fundamental way: religion. Méndez had the good fortune of having a name that was an emblem of Cuban cultural unity—one obviously given to him by pious parents. (For the record, his complete name was José de la Caridad Méndez Arco de Tejada.) "De la Caridad" means someone entrusted at birth to the Virgen de la Caridad del Cobre, the patron saint of Cuba. She is a syncretic Catholic deity represented as a richly clad mulatto figure to whom three men on a boat, caught in a storm, desperately pray for their lives. The three men are a white, a black, and an Indian, the supposed ethnic components of Cuban nationality (the Indian was by now little more than a romantic myth because they had been virtually exterminated by disease and by the Spaniards in the sixteenth century). The Virgen de la Caridad had been transformed in Afro-Cuban syncretic doctrine into the *orisha* (deity) Ochún, one of the most powerful gods of the Yoruba pantheon. Méndez was the very embodiment of the Cuban nation as represented by the ideals that led Cubans to fight for independence during his childhood. He was born in 1887, when José Martí was organizing the War of Independence that broke out in 1895 and culminated with the first American "intervention," the Spanish-American War. When Méndez triumphed, "Congo" was transformed by the adoring public into "El Diamante Negro," "The Black Diamond," the reverential epic epithet by which he came to be known.

One has to add to this fortunate mixture of ethnic and cultural traits several more influential factors to explain Méndez's generalized embrace by the Cuban populace. One is that Méndez was a relatively small man. This not only put him in the sentimentally advantageous role of David against Goliath when facing bigger players, but it struck a chord in Cubans whose stereotype of Americans of whatever color was that of hulking, insensitive, if powerful clods devoid of finesse (this was perhaps underscored by all those baseball teams called Giants who visited the island). Méndez was a man ordinary Cubans could identify with, not a behemoth who smothered opponents by brute force. He had a superlative arm, to be sure, but he was also a smart, cunning pitcher.

Méndez was also well-spoken, intelligent, had good manners, and was a gentleman not given to vulgar self-promotion. He had class. All of these qualities made him a celebrity and an enduring icon. His rise to fame was such and his later enshrinement so thorough that Cubans in general do not even know (or care) that Méndez had a significant career in the Negro Leagues, where he managed the famed Kansas City Monarchs and had some rousing successes in celebrated championship games through the 1920s. Just as most Americans know little about Méndez's exploits in Cuba, except perhaps for his victories against U.S. teams, so Cubans draw a blank about his career in the United States. Fausto Miranda, arguably the leading Cuban sportswriter, and a man in his seventies possessing vast knowledge about Cuban players of all ages, was surprised when I mentioned that Méndez had been the manager of the Monarchs. Some Cubans have even told me that Méndez, whom they claim was a cigarmaker in the off-season, stayed in Cuba during the winter to practice that trade. It is possible that he may have worked in a cigar factory in the years when his arm was hurt.

With Cuba under American rule, Méndez emerged at a propitious moment to capitalize on nationalist passions and deep-seated resentments. His greatest triumphs came during the 1906–9 American occupation. Méndez's first Cuban League appearance was on February 2, 1908, against Habana, in relief. His debut as a starter came on February 19, facing Matanzas, a game he won, 8–3, blanking his opponents for eight innings before tiring in the ninth and giving up the runs. He would not lose a single game and led the Blues to the pennant. But his most resounding victories were still to come. It is good to note that, in Almendares, Méndez paired with Gervasio (Strike) González, who would become his favorite catcher in years to come, in both Cuba and the United States. Gervasio was a modest to good hitter but a superb receiver with a cannon for an arm, and he and Méndez must have had a great rapport and friendship. In February 1908 their greatest victories and acclaim lay just around the corner.

Nothing seemed more logical, after the surge of nationalism during the regular Cuban League season, than to import American teams with marquee value to play against Almendares and Habana. This is precisely what Eugenio Jiménez did by inviting the Cincinnati Reds in the fall of 1908. The Reds' visit was to have many consequences, such as the signing of Marsans and Almeida and eventually Luque, but its first effect was to enshrine forever in Cuban baseball memory the name of José de la Caridad Méndez.

The Reds came to Havana in the late fall of 1908 to participate in the *temporada americana* or American season, together with the Brooklyn Royal Giants, a superb team from the independent Negro circuits. Habana and Almendares would play these teams, and the Americans would also play each other. The Reds had finished fifth in the National League and sported a lineup of John Kane in center, Miller Huggins at second, Hans Lobert at third, Mike Mitchell in left, Dick Hoblitzell at first, Larry McLean behind the plate, Rudy Hulwitt at short, and Bob Spade, a pitcher, in right. The Reds' Jean Dubuc opposed Méndez's Blues on November 13 before an overflow crowd at Almendares Park. Strike González drove Marsans in for the first and only run of the game in the first inning. Meanwhile, Méndez no-hit the Reds until the last inning, when Huggins got an infield hit on a slow grounder between the pitcher and the second baseman. Cuban fans exulted, but there was more to come. On November 15 the Reds defeated their Habana counterparts, 8–0. Habana had three American blacks in the lineup: Pete Hill, Frank Earle, and Grant Johnson. But Almendares came back to torment the big leaguers. With Provisional Governor Magoon in the stands at Almendares Park, the Blues defeated the Reds again on November 20 behind the pitching of Andrés Ortega and Strike González's brilliant catching. The score was again low, 2–1, and the Cubans made many impressive plays. Mr. Magoon called Strike to his box after the game to congratulate him.

The next day Cincinnati was trounced by the Brooklyn Royal Giants, a team that included some of the blacks who had played for Habana the previous day. The Giants had Pete Hill in left, Frank Earle in right, Grant (Home Run) Johnson at short, Bill Monroe at third, Ashby Dunbar in center, Phil Bradley behind the plate, Harry Buckner on the mound, Al Robinson at first, and Sam Mongin at second. The score was 9–1, and according to *Diario de la Marina* the infield was turned into a merry-go-round in the fifth and sixth innings. Hill homered, Buckner and Dunbar tripled, and Bradley doubled. Cincinnati gained a measure of revenge the next day, November 22, by defeating the Habana Reds one more time, by the lopsided score of 11–4. Habana reclaimed its black Americans from the Royals, but to no avail. On the twenty-third, Almendares came back to save Cuba's pride by defeating Cincinnati by the narrow score of 4–3, with Joseíto Muñoz on the mound and Méndez, who got a hit, at short in place of Pájaro Cabrera. After a break of almost a week, Almendares and Cincinnati took the field one more time. The Blues handed the ball to veteran Bebé Royer, but he was wild, issued four bases on balls, and left the game down, 3–0. Almendares lost, although it made a valiant comeback by scoring runs in the sixth and seventh innings. But the remarkable thing about this game was that "The Black Diamond" relieved Royer in the third and blanked the Reds the rest of the way. Méndez had shut out the National League team sixteen innings in a row. On December 1 Habana finally defeated the other Reds, 6–4, but the game everyone was waiting for was the next Almendares-Cincinnati contest, which would bring Méndez again to the mound. On December 3 Méndez shut out Cincinnati once more, this time on five hits, with Almendares winning, 3–0. He had not been scored upon by the big leaguers in twenty-five consecutive innings of hotly contested baseball!

Méndez became a hero, a celebrity, not only because he had trounced the major leaguers, proving that Cuban baseball was as good as any, but also because he had done it during the American occupation of the island. Other players, such as Pájaro Cabrera and Strike González, distinguished themselves, but none attained Méndez's fame. And he was not finished.

Ten days after Méndez's last shutout of Cincinnati, on December 13, Almendares played the visiting Key West club. To judge by the names of the players, this was a team made up of Cubans of any color and Americans. They competed regularly against teams in the Cuban League. (At a time when communications with the provincial ports were mostly by water, Key West was closer to Havana than many Cuban cities.) Méndez shut them out, too, winning, 4–0. On the seventeenth Almendares sailed to Key West, and Méndez not only repeated his feat, but pitched a no-hitter for good measure. Back in Cuba, Méndez took the mound against Habana on Christmas Eve, and after two shutout innings, the Reds broke the string at forty-five scoreless innings by pushing through a run. Méndez's fall heroics in 1908 stand as one of the greatest achievements in the history of Cuban baseball and a key story in its lore.

The irony of the situation should not be missed, for it provides a glimpse into the nature of sports, spectacle, and nationalism in the modern era. Baseball, an American game, established itself as the national sport of Cuba during an American occupation of the island because Cuban teams defeated American ones. The conqueror's mantle of superiority in economic and military power could not be denied, but it was removed in the mock battlefield of sports. At the same time, once Americans left their native shores, they were able to shed racial prejudices long enough to risk baseball hegemony not only before the Cubans but also with their own black compatriots. In Havana, during the fall of 1908, a space was being created where pleasure and sport displayed all of their evil lures but where certain divisions and animosities could be put aside temporarily.

But what exactly did Méndez have as a pitcher? How could he compete favorably with the big leaguers? We are fortunate that a visiting American who played against him, not precisely in 1908, but a few years later, left an account. Ira Thomas, a catcher for Connie Mack's Philadelphia

Athletics, wrote an exceptionally revealing article for *Baseball Magazine* in March 1913 titled "How They Play Our National Game in Cuba: The Remarkable Progress of Baseball at Havana and Its Important Place in the Sports of the Tropics."[11] Thomas visited Havana twice with the Athletics. The first time was in 1911, after they had won the World Series, and the second was in 1912. Their first set of games in Havana turned out to be a disaster, for they were crushed by Cuban teams. The second time they won ten of twelve games. Their defeat as "world champions" had been particularly embarrassing to American baseball and a source of great pride to Cuba. Thomas writes the article to reassure Americans about their superiority, but at the same time makes fair judgments about Cuban stars and about Cuba in general. He was most impressed with Méndez, whom he calls "one of the greatest twirlers the game ever knew," and continues:

Méndez is a remarkable man. More than one big leaguer from the states has faced him and left the plate with a wholesome respect for the great Cuban star. It is not alone my opinion but the opinion of many others who have seen Méndez pitch that he ranks with the best in the game. I do not think he is Walter Johnson's equal, but he is not far behind. He has terrific speed, great control and uses excellent judgment. He is a natural ballplayer if there ever was one and with his pitching it is no wonder that the Cubans win games. And not only is he a phenomenal slab man, he is a most excellent fielder as well and his hitting is hard and timely. Méndez is still great, though it seemed to me on my last visit, that he had slowed up a little since the first time I became acquainted with his fast, straight ones. He has seen years of service, has worked uncommonly hard and no doubt the effect of it all has begun to tell. At that, he is a remarkable pitcher, and if he were a white man would command a good position on any Major League club in the circuits. Méndez, with all his terrific speed, has not what would seem a good build for such a wearing delivery. He is rather slight, does not appear muscular enough to stand such a strenuous pace as he sets himself. But he can pitch with the best, and no mistake.[12]

Méndez's performances against visiting major-league teams in the next few years were outstanding. In a total of eighteen games he won eight, lost seven, and tied one. On November 5, 1911, he blanked the Philadelphia Phillies, and in 1913 he no-hit Birmingham, of the Southern Association. One of Méndez's finest games, however, was a loss to the New York Giants and Christy Mathewson, in which his team was shut out, 4–0. According to John B. Holway, it was one of three shutouts among his defeats.[13] Méndez demonstrated once again, at a time when Cuba's baseball pride was at stake, that baseball on the island, as well as the baseball played by American blacks both in the United States and Havana, was as good as the game played in the major leagues. Baseball was an important component in the development of Cuban national pride, and it continued to help build a sense of self-assurance for Cubans in their relations with the powerful neighbor to the north. It would have an effect on future political developments.

Méndez won fifteen and lost six in the 1909 season of the Cuban League. It was again called Liga General de Base Ball de la *República* de Cuba, a significant change because with the end of American occupation, the Republic was "restored." Abel Linares appears, for the first time, as Fe's representative before the league. This was the team with the most connections to American black baseball, a clear indication of Linares' influence in that world, which would lead to the formation of the Cuban Stars, a touring team run by his associate Tinti Molina.[14] The 1909 Cuban League fielded the same four teams as the year before: Almendares, Habana, Fe, and Matanzas. There seems to have been fewer black American players, though some very significant ones appear for the first time. Habana had Preston Hill, Frank Earle, Emilio Palomino, and Parpetti. Fe featured Julián Castillo, Harry Buckner, Bruce Petway, Sam Mongin, Jules (Home Run) Thomas, and Pelayo Chacón, a future star and a manager who was making his debut in the league. Matanzas had Phil Bradley, Jude Gans, a difficult-to-identify Anderson, Al Robinson, Billy Francis, and John Henry Lloyd (for the first time). Almendares boasted Marsans, Almeida, Strike González, and, of course, Méndez, but apparently still no Americans. Games were played at Almendares Park and Palmar del Junco in Matanzas. On February 2 a press release stated, "The league decided to drop Matanzas from the championship and forfeit all of its pending games in favor of the other clubs." Habana won, and Julián Castillo was batting champion. The teams that finished played forty-six games.

The year 1909 brought another thrill to Cuban baseball as Eustaquio (Bombín) Pedroso, a powerful right-handed pitcher who usually played for Fe, no-hit the Detroit Tigers on November 18 for eleven innings, defeating them, 2–1. A strong fireballer who could hit, play first, the outfield, and catch, Pedroso had a long and distinguished career in the Negro Leagues (with the Cuban Stars) as well as in the Cuban League. But in Cuba Pedroso is remembered for his gem against Detroit, which had just won the American League pennant and then lost the World Series to the Pittsburgh Pirates in seven games. The only run against Pedroso came on an error in the seventh. Almendares scored in the first on a double by Armando (Chino) Cabañas and a triple by catcher Strike González. In the riotous seventh, second baseman Cabañas made a wild throw to first, allowing Matty McIntyre to circle the bases when umpire "Silk" O'Loughlin ruled that the fans had helped catcher Strike González retrieve the ball. There was a prolonged protest by Almendares and the fans howled, but to no avail. Order was finally restored, and Almendares won the game in the eleventh. Bill Lelivelt walked left fielder Rogelio Valdés, and Marsans laid down a perfect bunt, inducing Detroit first baseman Heinz Beckendorf to throw wide to second when there was no chance to get the runner. Valdés scooted around to third. Cabañas then made up for his seventh-inning error by executing a perfect squeeze play, leaving the Tigers on the field. Several well-heeled followers of Almendares started a collection to make a gift to Bombín for his prodigious feat. President José Miguel Gómez and his son Miguel Mariano made contributions, as did several Detroit players, such as second baseman Charley O'Leary. Pedroso received nearly $300, quite a sum in those days. A notable feature of the Detroit-Almendares game is the classic, "inside baseball" kind of ending, with two perfect bunts, the last a squeeze play. This was still the dead-ball era, to be sure, but Cuban baseball would retain this style of play much longer than in the majors.

All in all, the American season was a success. The gates were large, and both Habana and Almendares won their individual series against the Tigers, 4–2. It is true that neither Ty Cobb nor Sam Crawford made the trip, the former because of his notorious racism. But Detroit also faced a burgeoning Cuban baseball power. Anguila Bustamente, playing for Habana, led the series with an average of .415; also for Habana, Agustín Parpetti hit .336 and Carlos (Chino) Morán hit .333. Almendares did not hit well, with José de la Caridad Méndez having the best batting average at .300.

Once the Detroit series was over, a major-league "all-star" team disembarked in Havana to continue the American season at Almendares Park. This club had Jimmy Archer (Cubs) behind the plate, Fred Merkle (Giants) at first, Germany Schaefer (Detroit) at second, Danny Hoffman (Browns) at third, Tommy McMillan (Dodgers) at short, Sherry Magee (Phillies) in left, Jack Lelivelt (Senators) in center, and Mike Simon (Pirates) in right. The pitchers were Addie Joss (Indians), Nap Rucker (Dodgers), Mordecai (Three-Finger) Brown (Cubs), and Howie Camnitz (Pirates). While this may not have really been an all-star club, it was stronger than most regular major-league teams. Luis (Chicho) González, pitching for Habana, welcomed the Americans by beating Joss, 2–1, in the first game, which was decided by Luis (Mulo) Padrón's homer in the fifth. Rucker defeated Almendares and Joseíto Muñoz in the second game, although the Blues connected nine hits. Pastor Pareda blanked the visitors in the next game. The fourth game saw "The Black Diamond" sparkle again. Méndez allowed only two hits and one run while Castillo doubled and tripled to lead the attack for victorious Almendares. In the last game of the series the Americans won handily, though they had to use Joss, Brown, and Camnitz against the Almendares onslaught. The series ended in controversy when most of the American players returned home claiming that promoter McAllister had not lived up to his monetary promises.

Next came Indianapolis, a double-A team, the highest classification in the minors at that time. They were defeated by Joseíto Muñoz and Chicho González, and once by Méndez. But what is truly most remarkable about this visit is that Indianapolis lost, 2–1, against the Vedado Tennis Club Marqueses, a team in the Amateur League, with Armando Castellanos in the box! It is clear that the quality of Cuban baseball was already very high at all levels. The Marqueses fielded only white players. A counterinvasion of the North by both white and black Cuban players was already beginning.

The 1910 season was very brief, eighteen games per team, and no American players appeared. One can only wonder if the departure of the Americans had a negative impact on professional baseball, or if, perhaps, the American season was proving to be more lucrative than the Cuban League season. The league was still called Liga General de Base Ball de la República de Cuba, and Abel Linares was treasurer. With Matanzas out again, the circuit was back to the traditional Almendares, Habana, and Fe, and play was at Almendares Park. Méndez won seven, lost none, and Almendares was crowned champion. The season only lasted from February to April. The 1910–11 season was more of the same. The traditional three teams again competed, but the games were held at Oriental Park (the racetrack) instead of at the traditional Almendares Park. It is difficult to figure out why. The baseball season coincided with the racing season, so there could have been an effort to link the two, though these spectacles probably drew different kinds of crowds. Abel Linares was still treasurer and appears to have squeezed Jiménez out of the picture completely, so there could have been some turmoil. Almendares does not appear to have fielded any Americans, but they had Castillo, Pedroso, Méndez, and Strike González, a formidable foursome. Habana had Hill, Johnson, and for a time, Lloyd. Petway was the catcher. Fe, still the team with the most connections to American Negro baseball, had Spot Poles in left, Pelayo Chacón at short, catcher Clarence Williams, William (Bill) Pierce, who played for the Chicago American Giants, at first, and George Walter Ball, a famous pitcher from the Negro leagues. The first game, Habana vs. Almendares, was played on Christmas Day. Méndez lost. On March 5, upon beginning the third round, all three teams were tied. However, in March Fe was disbanded and all its games awarded by forfeit to its opponents. Again only Habana and Almendares played. Preston Hill was the batting champion, and Almendares won again. Its victory proved so bitter to Habanistas that it led to one of the most interesting experiments in Cuban baseball history.

Víctor Muñoz, chief editor of *El Mundo,* a prominent newspaper, and a rabid Habana fan, claimed in print with undisguised bitterness that Méndez, not Almendares, had really won the championship. Rafael Conte, a distinguished sportswriter for *La Prensa* and a notorious Almendarista, countered that the Blues could win with or without Méndez. Other sportswriters, among them Abel Du-Breuil, of *La Lucha,* Alfonso E. Amenábar of *El Triunfo,* Antonio Martín Lamy of *El Comercio,* José Camilo Pérez of *La Discusión,* and José Pettari of *Diario Español,* joined in the polemic. There was but one way to find out who was right. A match was arranged between the "eternal rivals," but switching batteries: Méndez would pitch for Habana to his catcher Strike González, while Habana's Luis (Lico)

Mederos would take the mound for Almendares with the Reds' Bruce Petway catching. The game was played on April 3 to an overflow crowd and, no doubt, with all kinds of wagers being made. Almendares had a superb club, with Pájaro Cabrera at short, Jabuco Hidalgo in center, powerful Julián Castillo at first, and Rafael Almeida at third. Nonetheless, Méndez shut out his own mates on four hits, and Habana won, 4–0! Perhaps the game was a publicity stunt—it was surely a moneymaker—but it led to another consecration for Méndez.

Méndez and Pedroso ushered in a new period for the Golden Age, one in which Cuban baseball reached new heights as the country basked in the wealth derived from rising sugar prices. With the outbreak of World War I sugar profits began to reach unheard-of levels. According to Hugh Thomas, "In 1914 the harvest brought in $M163; in 1915, $M202; in 1916, $M308—almost three times more than the prices under Gómez. With the collapse of the European beet production, Cuba was once again the greatest sugar producer in the world, as she had been between 1830 and 1880. War brought back plenty" (p. 526). In 1916 and 1917 Cuba was the main sugar producer for the Allies, and the 1918 sugar harvest was "entirely bought by the allies" (p. 532). In terms of the development of baseball during the Golden Age, the most important statistic is that "By 1913 U.S. investment in Cuba, mostly in sugar, was reckoned as being worth $M200 or 18% of all U.S. investments in twenty-two countries of Latin America" (p. 536).

This second period of the Golden Age, encompassing the teens, saw the development of Cuban teams that entered the burgeoning Negro circuits and that culminated with the foundation of the Negro National League in 1920 under the stewardship of Rube Foster. Almeida and Marsans were signed by Cincinnati, of the National League, and many other Cuban players found spots on major- and minor-league teams during the summer. The American season continued to boom in the teens, with John McGraw's Giants becoming a fixture, as was their manager, who lived in Havana during the winter and became a member of the "smart set."[15] A Cuban magazine of the period published a caricature of McGraw with a caption declaring him 100% Cuban. In 1919 he bought a share of Oriental Park together with Charles Stoneham, the new owner of the New York Giants. In 1920, just after the passage of the Volstead Act, Babe Ruth himself came to Havana as a New York Giant to play exhibition games against Cuban teams. With Prohibition, the rise of tourism increased the spectacle nature of baseball. The sport commingled with new forms of Cuban music, such as the rumba, in an effort to profit as much as possible from the pleasures available in Cuba yet forbidden in the United States.

The flavor of the period is perhaps given by an event in another sport held at Oriental Park on April 4, 1915: the Jess Willard–Jack Johnson heavyweight championship fight. Major-league teams competed in Havana against Cuban squads and black teams from the United States because the island had become a neutral zone dominated by pleasurable activities where prejudices could be suspended. A boxing match between a white such as Willard and a black such as Johnson was illegal in many states of the Union. Johnson, in addition, had taken advantage of his status as a celebrity to disregard the restrictions of American racism, particularly as they pertained to amorous relationships with white women. In Cuba such liberties could be overlooked, and legal discrimination was nonexistent. Willard trained in a Havana gym on Prado Boulevard, astonishing the locals with his size, particularly his enormous feet. This was a period when it was fashionable among Cuban men to have small feet. Willard, known as "The Cowboy," was practically a circus freak in this regard. Johnson was the 7–5 favorite as he climbed into the ring before a crowd of twelve thousand people that hot afternoon. Members of the most prominent *nouveaux riches* Cuban families were in attendance, including President Mario García Menocal, a graduate of Cornell University who had made a fortune in sugar working with the United Fruit Company, after a distinguished career during the War of Independence. The 242-pound Cowboy defeated Johnson in twenty-six boring rounds of a fight that many consider to this day to have been fixed. Pictures show the overweight Johnson (230 pounds) flat on the canvas, shielding his eyes from the sun as the referee counts him out. How hurt could he have been? Fifty thousand dollars in bets exchanged hands at Oriental Park that afternoon.

After the emergence of players of the stature of Rafael Almeida, Julián Castillo, Pájaro Cabrera, Strike González, Armando Marsans, Bombín Pedroso, and, above all, José de la Caridad Méndez, quite a few new players reached stardom in the teens. During this period sugarmills produced both sugar and baseball players in record quantities, owners and entrepreneurs had money to pay top-notch performers, and ordinary Cubans had cash to buy the tickets to see them in action. The leading players who emerge in the 1910–20 period are, in alphabetical order: Baldomero (Merito) Acosta, José Acosta, Angel Aragón, Jacinto Calvo, Pelayo Chacón, Manuel Cueto, José María Fernández, Eusebio González, Miguel Angel González, Adolfo Luque, Emilio Palmero, Bartolo Portuondo, José (Joseíto) Rodríguez, Tomás Romañach (a slick-fielding shortstop considered to be one of the best of the era), Ricardo Torres, and Cristóbal Torriente. These stars, in addition to the superb talent imported from U.S. Negro baseball, raised the level of play in the Cuban League to major-league status.

In fact, after the signing in 1910 of Almeida and Marsans by Cincinnati, many other Cubans reached the majors during this decade. Adolfo Luque attained stardom and Miguel Angel González became an established figure. But, in addition, Merito Acosta played with the Senators and the Athletics. When he was sold to the Louisville Colonels later, he not only thrived but also married the owner's daughter and settled in Kentucky. José (Acostica) Acosta, a diminutive hurler, played with the Senators and White Sox; Angel Aragón saw some action with the Yankees; Jacinto Calvo, with the Senators; Manuel Cueto with St. Louis (Federal League) and Cincinnati; Emilio Palmero, with the Giants, Browns, Braves, and Senators; and Ricardo Torres, with the Senators (his son Gilberto played for the same team in the forties). There were many others who had been playing on minor-league teams since the turn of the century. The 1917 *Spalding Guide* lists twenty-three Cubans in organized baseball during the 1914 season, including those in the majors. In addition to Méndez, who went on to star in the Negro circuits with the All Nations team and later with the Monarchs, there emerged another black star of the highest magnitude: left-handed slugger Cristóbal Torriente, who linked up with Rube Foster's Chicago American Giants, the dominant black team of the period. Others, such as Almendares infielder Bartolo Portuondo, went on to have brilliant careers in independent Negro baseball and later was a star with the Kansas City Monarchs after the Negro National League was founded in 1920. There he teamed up with Méndez, who eventually became manager of this powerhouse.

During this time the road to major-league baseball as well as to high-caliber minor-league ball was widened for Cubans, the American season in Havana continued its success in the fall, and two Cuban teams were organized to enter the circuit of barnstorming independent Negro baseball. These two teams were the Cuban Stars (West), run by Tinti Molina, a white entrepreneur whom we have seen as a professional catcher and team league official in Cuba and who was Linares' right-hand man; and the Cuban Stars (East), run by Alejando Pompez, a mulatto entrepreneur from Key West and Tampa, where he moved among the cigar workers and became a numbers man. Pompez's father, as we remember, had been an acquaintance of José Martí's in Key West. Cuban players such as Méndez, Torriente, Portuondo, and others had played in the shadowy All Nations, a barnstorming team of multiracial composition. This team had visited Havana in November 1904 (there is a picture in *El Fígaro,* November 27, 1904, p. 615). With the formation of the Cuban Stars teams, empresarios were exploiting the marquee value of the name "Cuban" among fans of Negro baseball and others. These teams did reasonably well financially, giving Cuban black stars a way to earn a living during the summer and to sharpen and maintain their skills. Otherwise they would have had to return to the sugarmills, or join the semipro circuits around the island. The American season and the Cuban League were for these players probably the chief source of income and satisfaction. In fact, until the fifties, winter professional baseball was *the* season for Cuban professional ballplayers.

An interesting development in this counterinvasion of the North by Cuban players was the organization of the Long Branch Cubans. A series of touring, independent teams had been organized, such as the All Cubans,

Stars of Cuba, and New Jersey Cubans. Cuban players such as Méndez had played on the All Nations team. The first All Cubans toured the East of the United States in 1901, while Cuba was under American rule, clearly in response to the visits by the black, non-Cuban, Cuban Giants. All of these teams had been independent teams, except for those affiliated with the Philadelphia entrepreneurs mentioned before. But according to Peter C. Bjarkman, the Long Branch Cubans, organized by Dr. Antonio Hernández Henríquez, a Cuban entrepreneur residing in New Jersey, played in the New Jersey–New York State League. Proximity to New York, and the fact that professional baseball was not played there on the Sabbath, allowed the Cuban players to showcase their talents before major-league teams, who "often supplemented sparse travel money by scheduling exhibition contests with the conveniently located Long Branch team on the available Sunday afternoon dates." A chief beneficiary was Adolfo Luque, who was signed by the Boston Braves.[16] Luque, in fact, went 22 and five with Long Branch in 1913, a year in which they received some coverage in Havana's *Baseball Magazine*, where on August 9, 1913 (p. 11), the team, a picture of which was printed, was called an "academy" for Cubans with major-league ambitions. Long Branch won the championship of the New York–New Jersey League in 1913, with Juan Violá leading the league in hits with 131 and Luque in winning percentage with .815. As far as I have been able to ascertain, the following players performed in Long Branch during the two years in which the team seems to have been active: José Acosta (1914), Angel Aragón (1913–14), Tomás del Calvo (1913–14), Miguel Angel González (1913), José María Gutiérrez (1913), Fidel Hungo (1914), Adolfo Luque (1913–14), Luis (Mulo) Padrón (1913–14), Tomás Romañach (1914), Ricardo Torres (1914), and Juan Violá (1913). This is a squad made up of stars, quite a few of them bound for the majors. Another common denominator is that they are all white. It would seem that the Long Branch Cubans were taking advantage of the association between Cuba and baseball prevalent in the New York–New Jersey area since before Cuban independence. It is also likely that they played barnstorming Negro circuit teams in the area. Were the Long Branch Cubans organized because the white Cubans were not allowed on the Cuban Stars? Or was it perhaps that they themselves did not want to play on all-black teams? Since the Cuban Stars, not to mention their successor New York Cubans of the Negro National League, did occasionally field a white Cuban, the second is most probably true. Located in a famous New Jersey beach resort, this team is a throwback to the original Cuban Giants, who were made up of employees of the Argyle Hotel on Long Island. As such, and given the fame of Long Branch as a tourist attraction—and having been also a resort of presidents— it seems apparent that the Cubans were part of the entertainment bustle around the area.[17] In this the Long Branch Cubans were typical of the continuing trend in professional baseball toward entertainment and spectacle. This was so during this period, not only of teams in the Negro barnstorming circuit and of these Cubans, but also of major leaguers who sought to make a buck in the off-season. A bit later, Babe Ruth and other major leaguers would not only play in exhibition games but actually join vaudeville acts and tour the United States.

The 1912 season of the Liga General de Base Ball de la República de Cuba was a memorable one, in part because Miguel Angel González and Adolfo Luque performed for the first time in Cuban winter ball. As mentioned before, the "República" in the league's name may have been added to underline that the American occupation had ended and that Cuba was again an "independent" republic. Play returned to Almendares Park, which had probably been refurbished. The president of the league was Dr. Federico Mora, and the treasurer was Abel Linares. The three traditional teams played again: Almendares, Habana, and Fe. Habana won, having played thirty-three games, of which it won twenty-two. The season began on January 14 and ended on April 29, which shows that its schedule was not yet wholly determined by the American one, but that it was moving in that direction. Almendares had Rafael Almeida, now a major leaguer; Emilio Palomino, a white Cuban who won the batting championship; Armando Marsans, also a major leaguer; Rogelio Valdés; Strike González; Tomás Romañach; Bombín Pedroso; and, of course, Méndez. They also had major leaguer Matty McIntyre, playing in Cuba near the end of a career in which he played with Detroit and Chicago (he had scored the only run against Bombín Pedroso in the eleven-inning no-hitter). Fe had Rube Foster, not to mention Luque and Miguel Angel. The shortstop was budding star Pelayo Chacón. Fe also fielded Kiko Magriñat and veterans Julián Castillo and Armando Cabañas. Among the Negro Leaguers, in addition to Foster, Fe had powerful Louis Santop, fleet-footed Spotswood (Spot) Poles, James (Jimmie) Lyons, and Leroy Grant. As if this were not enough, Fe also had Cannonball Redding. This was a very strong team influenced by Foster, who by this time had moved from Philadelphia to Chicago and founded his Chicago American Giants. The winning Habana Reds were led by hard-hitting Grant Johnson, Sam Lloyd, Preston Hill, Bruce Petway, Smokey Joe (Cyclone) Williams, and José Acosta, a Washington Senator. These teams were clearly of major-league quality, combining the cream of Negro baseball with the best Cuba had to offer, and a few white major leaguers to boot. Competition must have been keen, with only these three teams, all concentrated in the same stadium.

Three of the stars who emerged between 1910 and 1920 became superstars of Cuban baseball, and two of them veritable patriarchs of the game. Miguel Angel González, Adolfo Luque, and Cristóbal Torriente, with Marsans and Almeida, were the Méndez, Pájaro Cabrera, and Julián Castillo of this period, but because of the increase in press coverage their fame in later eras has actually outstripped that of the earlier stars. In terms of baseball ability Torriente may have been the best of the three: a left-handed power hitter who won two batting championships in the Cuban League and one in the Negro National League, he was also an accomplished outfielder and pitcher. When Foster brought him to the Chicago American Giants, he moved Oscar Charleston from center to left to make room for the Cuban. Torriente had outstanding careers in both Cuba and U.S. Negro baseball, where he became one of the mainstays of Foster's team. He later played for the Kansas City Monarchs. But because Torriente was black he was not allowed to perform in the major leagues, and even though by the twenties there were black managers in Cuban baseball—Pelayo Chacón, for instance, who also managed the Cuban Stars (East)—Torriente was not the type to follow up his playing career in that capacity. With a fatal penchant for alcohol and nightlife, he drank himself to death when he was only in his early forties. Having the good fortune of being white in a racist world, Luque and Miguel Angel had long careers in the major leagues, and in Cuba they played with or against each other for decades, and later managed the rival Habana and Almendares in that fateful 1946–47 season with which this book begins.

Miguel Angel's life is a rags-to-riches story. He was born (on September 24, 1890) and raised in Regla, across Havana Bay, in modest circumstances. He soon grew to six-one, but without much flesh on such a large frame (for the period). Miguel Angel, as we saw, came to be known as "Baguette" or "Pan de Flauta," but accounts of the reason for the nicknames differ. Some say that he was so called because of his elongated, gaunt appearance, which brought to mind a loaf of Cuban bread. Others thought it was because as a young man he earned a living delivering bread. Miguel Angel did deliver bread in his native Regla and he was skinny and tall, so we will never know which of the two gave him his moniker. It was probably both. At the start of his career there was something comical about Miguel Angel, with his lean body, protruding ears, and vacant smile. His early appearance was deceiving, however, and he filled out later. Miguel Angel had a prodigious arm, great fielder's hands, and could hit well enough. By 1912 he was Fe's shortstop and also pitched. In 1913 he was traded to Habana, and when Abel Linares bought the club in 1914 from Manuel Azoy, the first thing he did was to name Miguel Angel González manager. He was only twenty-four, but already a major leaguer. Linares must have seen leadership qualities in the boy from Regla, who was to control the Reds until the demise of the Cuban League in 1960. As we saw in an earlier chapter, Miguel Angel bought the team from Linares' widow in the early forties and built it into a franchise worth $500,000. In later years he was often criticized for acting like a czar of Cuban baseball, but most of it was probably due to envy.

Miguel Angel's career as a player was modest in the major leagues. At that level he was a career .253 hitter in seventeen years, all in the National

League, with Boston, Cincinnati, New York, Chicago, and above all the St. Louis Cardinals. For many of those years Miguel Angel was a second-string catcher with exquisite defensive abilities and a good baseball head. In 1934, his playing days over, he was named a coach of the Cardinals, a position he held until 1946, when he was dismissed as a result of the controversy involving the Pasquel brothers and Mexican baseball. In 1938 he was interim manager of the Cardinals, becoming the first Latin American manager ever in the major leagues. He will forever be remembered in the United States as the third-base coach who gave the green light or the red light—depending on one's sources—to Enos Slaughter in the deciding game of the 1946 World Series. But he is also remembered for a telegram that revealed both his broken English and his notorious frugality. Legend has it that the Cardinals sent him to Princeton to scout a promising catcher named Moe Berg, who would eventually make the majors and become famous for his linguistic prowess and activities as a spy rather than for his baseball exploits. Miguel Angel wired back what has become a standard phrase to describe a certain type of player: "Good field, no hit."

Miguel Angel was steady, smart, conservative, and loyal, and came to be regarded as the most knowledgeable baseball man in Cuba. He ran the Habana Reds efficiently, doing the scouting himself in the United States for potential players, running the team on the field, and taking care of business. The delivery boy from Regla became a wealthy, respected grand old man. What Miguel Angel always lacked was charisma. He got the job done and made progress surely but slowly. In this, as in so many other things, he was the opposite of his rival, the other patriarch of Cuban baseball, Adolfo Luque.

Luque was born in Havana on August 4, 1890, the same year as Miguel Angel. He was also of modest extraction, so when the republican army was organized, he enlisted and became an artilleryman. He also became a baseball star as a hard-hitting third baseman on an army team. The Marqueses of the Vedado Tennis Club, the exclusive society that fielded one of the best amateur teams in Cuba, recruited him. But Adolfo had such an arm that he became a pitcher, soon signed by Fe, where he joined Miguel Angel for the first of many times during their parallel careers. In the 1912–13 season Luque finished with only one victory and four defeats. By 1914 after having played for Long Branch and competed against major leaguers in exhibition games, he was pitching for the Boston Braves himself. In Cuba he pitched first for Habana, but by 1914–15 he was with Almendares, the team with which he became largely identified, though he pitched again for Habana from 1922 to 1924.

In the majors Luque had a brilliant career, particularly with Cincinnati, where he played from 1918 to 1929. He won in double digits in every season with the Reds, and in 1923 he had an astonishing 27 and 8 record, with a 1.93 ERA, one of the best seasons ever enjoyed by a pitcher in the majors. Luque became the toast of Cuba, where he was also having great

Fidel Castro was no pitcher, as can be seen from the way he amateurishly shows his grip to the batter in this staged 1959 game.

"Fidel Castro que por su amor al Colegio y el entusiasmo con que defendió el Pabellón Belemita en casi todos los deportes oficiales del Colegio, ha sido proclamado el mejor atleta colegial del curso".

The future Maximum Leader in the basketball uniform of Jesuit school Belén, from his 1945 graduation yearbook. The caption reads: "Fidel Castro who, because of his love for the School and the enthusiasm with which he defended Belén's colors in nearly all the sports in which the school competed officially, has been proclaimed the best collegiate athlete of his class." Another picture shows him delivering the valedictorian address, but none has him in a baseball outfit.

The Gran Stadium de La Habana in October of 1946, when it opened.

Max Lanier and Agapito Mayor, pillars of the champion Almendares Blues in the 1946–47 season and winners of the last two games of the season.

Agapito Mayor in the uniform of
the Mexican League Puebla
Pericos, with whom he played in
1942–44 and again in 1947.

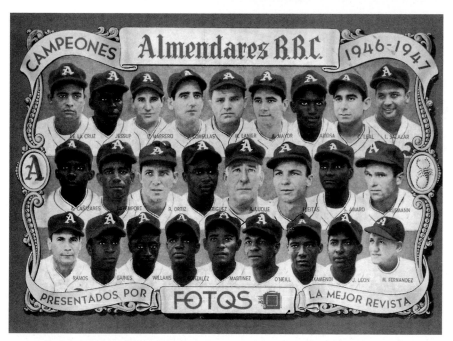

The 1946–47 champion Almendares Blues, with Lanier and Marrero at the top,
center, and Adolfo Luque in the center of the middle row, flanked by third-
baseman Héctor Rodríguez and catcher Andrés Fleitas.

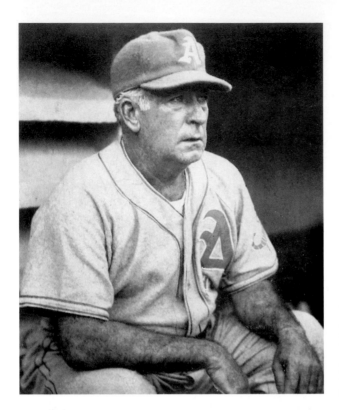

Adolfo Luque, "The Pride of Havana," with the uniform of the Alacranes of the Liga Nacional 1947–48 season.

Left to right: Bernardo Pasquel, Jorge Pasquel, Cardinals infield prospect Lou Klein, and Mario Pasquel. Klein, who signed with Jorge's Veracruz Blues, became a favorite in Cuba with the Habana Reds. Credit: Frank Scherschel/*Life* Magazine © Time Inc.

Napoleón Reyes in
the uniform of
Cuba, the team in
the 1947–48 Liga
Nacional.

Lázaro Salazar (El
Príncipe de Belén) with
Santiago, the team in the
1947–48 Liga de la
Federación.

Emilio Sabourín, among the founders of the Habana Baseball Club, outfielder and patriot in the struggle for independence from Spain. The picture, from the cover of *El Score. Organo Oficial de la Liga Cubana de Base Ball* (año 6, no. 30, July 25, 1902), is an homage to Sabourín right after the American occupation was lifted and Cuba declared independent on May 20, 1902.

Ramón Hernández, Antonio María (El Inglés) García, and Adolfo Luján, on the cover of *El Score. Semanario de Sport, Arte y Literatura* (August 3, 1890).

Wenceslao Gálvez, first historian of Cuban baseball, Almendares shortstop, and novelist, on the cover of *El Pitcher. Semanario de Sports y Literatura* (March 15, 1891).

Carlos D. Maciá, Almendares' celebrity pitcher and infielder in an 1886 picture from *El Sport*.

The Acera del Louvre boys, baseball players, literati, and danzón dancers, pose for a picture in the 1880s.

A typical *glorieta*. This one is from the park El Campo Rojo, in Santiago de Cuba, and appears in an October 7, 1904, issue (año 8, no. 41) of *El Score. Organo Oficial de la Liga Cubana de Base Ball.*

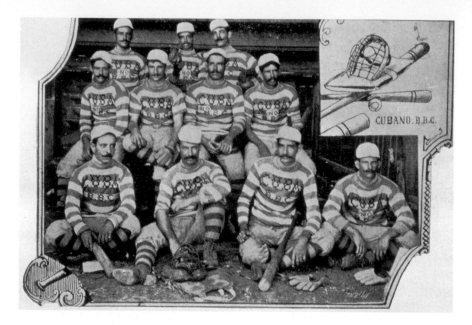

Cubano or Cuba-no, formerly Cuba, as they appeared in the 1900–01 season, after Severino T. Solloso gave the team up so as not to participate in a racially integrated league.

Almendarista, the name Almendares took to play in a racially integrated league in 1900–01.

Catcher Regino García, who won four consecutive batting championships from 1903 to 1907 playing for several teams, here with the Almendares uniform.

El Fígaro devoted a special issue to baseball on September 9, 1900.

Manuel Camps' All Cubans pose for the cover of *El Score* on August 15, 1902. The first American occupation of Cuba had just ended in May.

The 1908 Cuban Stars, pictured in the *Spalding Guide* of that year. They still have white players. The numbers correspond to 1. Gervasio (Strike) González, 2. Carlos (Bebé) Royer, 3. Borges, 5. Agustín Parpetti, 6. Govantes, 7. José de la Caridad Méndez, 8. Manager Ben Kinney, 9. Santa Cruz, 10. José Figarola, 11. Ricardo Hernández. Luis (Anguila) Bustamante, Emilio Palomino, and José María (Kiko) Magriñat do not appear in the picture but were on the team.

The 1907 champion Almendares team featured in the *Spalding Guide*. Standing, left to right: first, Heliodoro (Jabuco) Hidalgo, fourth, Carlos (Bebé) Royer, and on the far right, Gervasio (Strike) González. Crouching, left to right, future major-leaguers Armando Marsans and Rafael Almeida, and popular shortstop Alfredo (Pájaro) Cabrera.

The Cuban Stars at a dinner in San Juan, Puerto Rico. Left to right: Juan Pablo Armenteros, José María Fernández, José Sánchez, Bartolo Portuondo, Julián (Recurbón) Terán, P. Miranda, Julio Rojo, Alejandro Pompez, Aurelio Valdez, Marcelino Guerra, Bernardo Baró, Julián Fabelo, Agapito Lazaga, and Ramiro Ramírez. The patriotic iconography in the background suggests that the dinner took place at some sort of Cuban club.

Rogelio Valdés, Armando Marsans, and Emilio Palomino, 1907 Almendares stars, pose for a picture in the *Spalding Guide* of that year.

A young José de la Caridad (El Diamante Negro) Méndez, in a 1908 picture after his outstanding pitching against the Cincinnati Reds.

John Hummell has just hit a double for Brooklyn sending George Cutshaw and Otto Miller home in a game against Almendares at Almendares Park on November 29, 1913.

Miguel Angel González, top right, the young manager of the 1915 Habana Reds, as pictured in the 1917 *Spalding Guide*. The others are: top left, pitcher Emilio Palmero; center, catcher Crescencio Ferrer; below, left to right, pitchers José Valdez Pérez and Oscar Fernández.

Abel Linares, the most important entrepreneur of professional baseball in Cuba
during the Golden Age, as pictured in the
1910–11 *Spalding Guide*.

The all-star outfield of the 1923 Santa Clara Leopards: Pablo (Champion) Mesa,
Oscar Charleston, and Alejandro (El Caballero) Oms. There is a Casa Tarín ad on
the fence in right of what appears to be La Boulanger Park.

The staff of the 1929–30 Santa Clara Leopards: Ramón (El Profesor) Bragaña and Satchel Paige on top, and Basilio (Brujo) Rossell at bottom left. From *Carteles*, January 5, 1930.

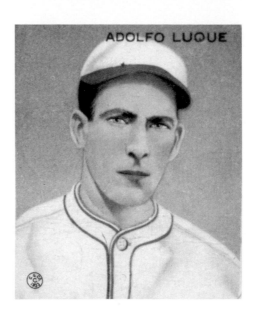

Luque's 1933 baseball card
showed him in a New York Giant
uniform.

Miguel Angel González, on the left, as a coach of the Gas House Gang St. Louis
Cardinals, with manager Frankie Frisch and coach Buzzie Wares, in the mid thirties.

Pitchers Juanelo Mirabal, left, and Martín (El Inmortal) Dihigo, right, at the town-square park in Holguín, during the early thirties.

seasons during the winters. Luque became the new Méndez but was as different from "The Black Diamond" as he was from Miguel Angel. Méndez was a polite, unassuming man. Luque was the opposite. He was a snarling, vulgar, cursing, aggressive pug, who, though small at five-seven, was always ready to fight. He was known as a headhunter, who mastered the art of pitching close to the batter (something he taught later to others of his ilk, such as Sal Maglie). In the majors Luque endured being the butt of many racial epithets, including being called a "Cuban nigger," to which he responded with murderous beanballs. Once, while pitching for Cincinnati, Luque charged the Giants' bench and punched Casey Stengel on the jaw because he had heard invectives coming from this direction. Later, in his long career as manager in Cuba and Mexico, Luque was reputed to carry a gun even while in uniform, and there are at least two anecdotes involving the weapon. One happened in the thirties, at La Tropical Stadium. Luque had removed Negro Leagues standout Ted (Double Duty) Radcliffe from a game in the Cuban League. A loud bang was heard in the locker room to which both had retreated. Rodolfo Fernández, who was present in the locker room, told me that he was the one who pushed Luque's arm away as he tried to shoot the pitcher, whom the enraged manager claimed was not giving his all. It was stated in court that Luque had slammed a door hard in anger, and the episode came to be known as *el portazo de Luque* (Luque's door slam). Radcliff left Cuba the next day. The other story involves Terris McDuffie, a pitcher in another team managed by Luque (Marianao in the early fifties). Though talented, McDuffie was a character, given to insubordination and who also had a taste for liquor and the ladies. Apparently McDuffie (probably with a hangover) told Luque that he did not feel like pitching on that particular day, whereupon the manager returned from his office waving his gun. McDuffie changed his mind on the spot, went out, and won the game. Stories about Luque berating and threatening players who did not perform to his own level of fiendish aggressiveness abound. But by the fifties he had mellowed somewhat, and Francisco (Panchón) Herrera told me in Miami that Luque was just a *viejo cascarrabias* (cantankerous old man).

In the United States Luque was inevitably known as the "Havana Perfecto" or "The Pride of Havana," after cigars. But in Cuba his nickname was "Papá Montero," after a legendary Afro-Cuban rumba dancer and pimp originally from Sagua la Grande and celebrated in songs and poems. A popular rumba from the twenties sings of this legend's wake, after a not so peaceful death, one assumes.[18] It is Eliseo Grenet's "Papá Montero," whose refrain is:

> *A llorar a Papá Montero, zumba,*
> *canalla rumbero.*
> *Ese negro no llega al cielo, zumba,*
> *canalla, rumbero.*

> Let's all weep for Big Daddy Montero, zumba,
> what a carousing bad dude.
> That bad nigger won't go to heaven, zumba,
> what a carousing bad dude.

Luque was white, but it did not matter. Like Papá Montero he had *zumba,* an Afro-Cuban concept of Yoruba origin that is a kind of life force, including sexual prowess, aggressiveness, and charisma. Montero is not without depth in Afro-Cuban lore. Though it is not an uncommon last name in Spanish, it means someone from the "Monte," the hills or bush, abode of the gods in Afro-Cuban mythology. So Luque was incorporated into a lore that, though African in origin, was permeating, through music and popular religion, all of Cuban society from the bottom up. This shows how baseball, particularly the professional kind, dropped in social class only to become more widely accepted and ingrained in the fabric of Cuban society, with few racial restrictions.

The connection of Luque with the rumba is very revealing in this respect. According to Emilio Grenet (Eliseo's brother), the rumba is the most popular of Cuban musical genres, close to its African origin, and expressing "the joy of the lower classes which take their themes from the most puerile occurrences as easily as from the most important event. . . . The *Papá Montero* type . . . incarnates the popular negro who is preoccupied only with satisfying a most vivid sensuality. . . ."[19] Nicolás Guillén, the leading poet of the Afro-Cuban movement, saw the pathos in Papá Montero's figure and wrote a poem, "Velorio de Papá Montero" (Papá Montero's Wake), which he published in his widely acclaimed 1931 *Sóngoro cosongo.* Baseball as spectacle, together with music and avant-garde literature, were moving toward a cultural synthesis in the twenties that was quite different from that of the *fin-de-siècle,* when it involved anti-Spanish feelings among Cuba's patriotic elite. Literature and baseball in the "belle époque" started as activities proper to that elite; now baseball was associated with cultural practices, such as Afro-Cuban music and dance, that had a much broader appeal.

In a twenty-year career Luque won 194 games in the National League, the most by a Cuban pitcher in the majors until Luis Tiant, Jr. In Cuba Luque's record was 93 and 62 in twenty-two years. But this includes only Cuban League games. Luque barnstormed through the island and hired himself out to pitch in sugarmill games. My paternal grandfather Oscar, general manager of Central Amistad at the time, once employed Papá Montero to pitch for the mill's team in the twenties. Luque showed up in his cups and demanded a higher fee than what had been agreed upon, refusing to dress unless he was paid in advance. My grandfather and others put together the money and Luque won, but not without giving up a few hits. He also pitched in the American season against major- and minor-league American teams, as well as teams from the Negro Leagues. If, in addition to his accomplishments as a player, one considers Luque's impact as a manager in Cuba and Mexico, it is an injustice that he is not in the Hall of Fame in Cooperstown (he is, needless to say, in Cuba's). There are worse ballplayers and characters enshrined in that American temple.

Torriente may have been a truer Papá Montero, with his penchant for nightlife and tragic ending. He was born in Cienfuegos in 1895, but little else is known about his early life. He had, by all accounts, shocking power at the plate. Torriente was built like Hack Wilson, but a little taller. Torriente was a muscular, tough-looking mulatto who could fly in the outfield and had a powerful arm. Stories about his prodigious clouts in Cuba and the Negro Leagues are plentiful. His home-run prowess came at the same time that Babe Ruth was establishing the four-base hit as the most exciting play in the game.

Torriente often did not return to Cuba in the winter, remaining in the United States, perhaps barnstorming through the West with Foster's American Giants. After Torriente's playing abilities had eroded he remained in Tampa and New York, where it is said that he lived in destitution, a hopeless alcoholic, until his death in 1938. There are accounts that a Cuban politician managed to get his body sent to the island in a flag-draped coffin. Torriente towers in Cuban memory as one of the best hitters and outfielders ever. As a slugger in the Negro Leagues he was the precursor of Josh Gibson, another tragic figure.

Stability continued for the next few years after 1912, when Miguel Angel and Luque made their debut in the Cuban League. The same three teams—Almendares, Habana, and Fe—went on competing at Almendares Park, and the American season thrived every year. In 1913 the Cuban League was still called Liga General de Base Ball de la República de Cuba. The president was now Dr. Carlos M. Alzugaray, but Abel Linares was no longer treasurer. Play began on January 1 and ended on March 23, obviously accommodating the American baseball calendar. Each team played thirty-two games. Fe won, with Almendares's (and Cincinnati's) Armando Marsans as batting champion. Players continued to move from one team to another, though each retained a fairly stable core. Fe had Lloyd now (he had been with Habana the previous year); Jude Gans, of the New York Lincoln Giants; Spot Poles; pitcher and slugger Mulo Padrón, who played many years in the Negro Leagues; Kiko Magriñat; Marcelino Guerra, a first baseman who played for Pompez on the Cuban Stars; Smokey Joe Williams; Pelayo Chacón; Cannonball Redding; Luque; and Joseíto Rodríguez, a slick first baseman considered then to be the best Cuban at that position. Almendares had Bombín Pedroso, Julián Castillo, Pájaro Cabrera, Tomás del Calvo, Tomás Romañach, Marsans, Jacinto Calvo, Strike González, Méndez, Julio LeBlanc (a pitcher who was later killed with a bat in a fight), Emilio Palomino, and Jabuco Hidalgo. Habana had the fewest, if any, American ballplayers, featuring Cubans Agapito Lazaga; Almeida; Torriente; Agustín Parpetti; Roberto Villa; Chino Morán; Bienvenido (Pata Jorobá) Jiménez, a great second baseman with bowed legs, hence his nickname (he was known in the United States as "Hooks"); Juan Violá; and Joseíto Muñoz.

In 1913–14 the league became the Liga Nacional de Base Ball de la República de Cuba. The change from "General" to "Nacional" may reflect the absence of American ballplayers, white or black. Was this due to World War I? Was it a nationalistic impulse provoked by García Menocal's election with American backing? Or was it simply a way of distinguishing the Cuban League from the American season? The president was still Dr. Carlos Alzugaray, but Linares did not appear as league officer. Play began on December 6 and ended on March 3, so the schedule seems to have been tailored to the American one, giving the Cuban players already in the majors a chance to report to spring training. The batting champion was Torriente, now playing for Almendares, who won the championship after playing thirty-two games. Habana had Octavio González, Juan Violá, Almeida, Padrón, Miguel Angel, Luque, Jacinto Calvo, Merito Acosta, Tomás del Calvo, Ricardo Torres, Emilio Palmero, and Manuel Baranda. Habana also had Fidel Hungo, a first baseman in 1916 with the Long Branch Cubans, and one of the best at that position during these years. As should be obvious, Habana was the winter version of the Long Branch Cubans. Almendares had Marsans, Strike González, Torriente, Manuel Cueto, Pájaro Cabrera, Tomás Romañach, Ramón Herrera, Bombín Pedroso, Jabuco Hidalgo, José de la Caridad Méndez, and Pata Jorobá Jiménez. Fe had Pelayo Chacón, Chino Morán, Roberto Villa, Ricardo Hernández, Pastor (Monk) Pareda, Joseíto Muñoz, and Kiko Magriñat, as well as catchers José Figarola; Marcelino Guerra, another catcher; and José Junco, a pitcher.

The 1914–15 season had three anomalies: Miguel Angel González played second base for Habana, José de la Caridad Méndez shortstop for Almendares, and Almendares' famous pitcher Bombín Pedroso won the batting championship. The league was still called the Liga Nacional de Base Ball de la República de Cuba, but now it had American players again. Almendares won with a lineup that consisted of Manuel Cueto, left field; Strike González, catcher; Rafael Almeida, third base; Cristóbal Torriente, right field; Heliodoro Hidalgo, center field; Juan Violá, first base; José de la Caridad Méndez, short stop; Fidel Hungo, second base; and Bombín Pedroso, José López, and Adolfo Luque, pitchers. Habana countered with Baldomero Acosta, right field; Jacinto Calvo, center field; Armando Marsans, first base; Angel Aragón, third base; Miguel Angel González, second base; Tomás del Calvo, right field; Tomás Romañach, short stop; Ramiro Seigle, short stop; and Ballesteros (who played with Long Branch) and Emilio Palmero, pitchers. Fe fielded Pelayo Chacón, short stop; William (Speck) Webster, catcher; Spot Poles, center field; Roberto Villa, left field; Marcelino Guerra, right field; William Oscar (Bill) Handy, second base; Ramón Herrera, third base; Manuel Baranda, first base; Crescencio Ferrer, catcher; Joseíto Rodríguez, first base; Inocente Mendieta, no position given; Orgazón, third base; and pitchers William (Dizzy) Dismukes, Cannonball Redding, and Valdés Pérez. Fe was still the team with the closest relations with American Negro baseball.

The facts that Miguel Angel was playing second for Habana, that Pedroso won the batting championship, that Méndez played at short, and that Torriente was not only a great slugger but also a remarkable pitcher show the versatility of these players but also reflect the economic constraints of independent baseball. Barnstorming teams, whether black or white, could not afford to carry many players because of transportation, lodging, and meal costs. Each player received a cut of the profits, so the more players, the smaller the cut. Although travel costs did not usually apply in Cuba because most of the time games were held in the same city, it was still expensive to dress too many players. Switching positions was more common back then. For instance, toward the end of the decade the Boston Red Sox would allow their star left-handed pitcher Babe Ruth to play the outfield.

Through the first half of the 1915–16 season, as in 1913–14 and for reasons that are difficult to fathom, no Americans appeared in the Cuban League. The president of the League was now Juan L. Sánchez, with journalist Víctor Muñoz as secretary and Abel Linares as treasurer. Curiously the teams were called Almendares Park, Habana Park, and San Francisco Park, suggesting that some legal wrangling was again going on. This is the year when Linares purchased Habana, so the dispute may have involved his gradual takeover of the league. Almendares Park won that first half with a roster that included Chacón, Villa, Strike González, Torriente, Almeida, Ramón (Paíto) Herrera, Cueto, Joseíto Rodríguez, Padrón, Pareda, Méndez, Luque, and Pájaro Cabrera. Habana Park came in second, with Merito Acosta, Jacinto Calvo, Eusebio González, Miguel Angel González, Aragón, Tomás del Calvo, Torres, Romañach, Palmero, and Marsans. San Francisco Park won only one game and lost twenty-one with a team that consisted of Bernardo Baró, Guerra, Parpetti, Pedroso, Pata Jorobá Jiménez, Chino Morán, Jabuco Hidalgo, Rafael Figarola, and Benito Marrero. This was not a bad club. For the second half San Francisco imported a bunch of black American players: Hill, Petway, Lloyd, Gans, Williams, Barbour, and Frank Duncan (an outstanding black catcher who became a much-admired player in Cuba), but to no avail, and on March 20 the club dropped out of the championship. Two games between Habana Park and Almendares Park decided the championship on March 26, with Almendares finishing first after having played forty games. Torriente was the batting champion again. The change in the name of the teams and the disarray at the end of the season signal that the league was in some sort of crisis.

The crisis was not financial, for the American season had continued unabated, with regular visits by McGraw's Giants as well as others, such as the Brooklyn Dodgers, the Pittsburgh Pirates, both Philadelphia teams (the Phillies and the Athletics), as well as minor-league and Negro-circuit teams.

In the fall of 1911, for instance, the Giants played in Havana, with Christy Mathewson baffling Cuban hitters (but the local teams trounced their other pitchers, crowed *El Fígaro* of December 3). In October of 1913 the Birmingham Barons, of the Southern Association, entered a three-team tournament with Habana and Almendares. This series featured a no-hitter by Méndez, who was recovering from "muscular atrophy." In a curious reversal of racial stereotypes, Guillermo Pi, a reporter for *El Fígaro,* refers to the Barons as *los rubios* (the blond ones). They more than held their own against two Cuban squads of very high caliber that included not only Méndez, Torriente, and Pedroso, but also major leaguers Almeida, Marsans, Miguel Angel, and others. The Barons finished with eight victories and five defeats plus two ties. But Pi reports that they did not fare as well in a tour of the provinces, a tantalizing indication of the caliber of baseball being played outside the Cuban capital, particularly in the sugarmills. Some of those games, however, were played against Fe, the Cuban League team left out of the Havana tournament.[20]

Next came the Dodgers (still called the Superbas by the Cuban press), who spent the month of November 1913 in Havana engaged in the same kind of tournament as the Barons had played in October. The Brooklyn team sported a lineup of Herbie Moran in left, Jake Daubert at first, Casey Stengel in center, George Cutshaw at second, Red Smith at third, John Hummel in right, Bob Fisher at short, and Bill Fischer behind the plate. Fisher was by this time the property of the Cubs but had played earlier for the Superbas. One of their pitchers, Bull Wagner, had seen little action during the season. Another, Earl Yingling, had a .500 record during the season, at 8 and 8. Their best pitcher in Havana was Pat Ragan, who had a laborious 15 and 18 record that year in the National League. Bombín Pedroso had a four-hit shutout against the visitors, and Miguel Angel, Luque, and Marsans also had a good series. Torriente and Strike González did not do as well this time. Stengel put on a show at Almendares Park with his steals, one of which resulted in his pants being ripped by infielder Baranda's spikes, thus "showing the public his gluteus flesh, as white as scouring soap" (*El Fígaro,* November 30, 1913). The Dodgers finished with ten victories and five defeats, Habana at three and four, and Almendares at two and six. The Blues were already being managed by Marsans, who was considered the Cuban star of the moment.

The 1915–16 season was the last played at the old Almendares Park, a relic by now with its trellised glorieta and grandstand. Besides, it was obviously too small for the volume of business expected by the new magnates of Cuban baseball, particularly Abel Linares. With money flowing from sugar sales as a consequence of the war in Europe, with the process of modernization begun during the first American occupation, and with the growing influx of tourists, Havana was ready for a new baseball stadium. Land was cleared to build the new one, only a few blocks from the old Almendares

Park. The new park would retain the name of its predecessor to profit from the memories of so many feats accomplished on the old field.

The new Almendares Park was erected at the end of Pozos Dulces Street, at a spot now occupied by the Havana Bus Terminal. Like the old one, it was still near Quinta de los Molinos, in a knoll near the hill where the Príncipe Fortress sits, guarding the western flank of the city. By this time the Havana Electric Company had built an extensive web of trolley car lines, and the new Almendares Park could be reached by three of these: Príncipe-San Juan de Dios, Principe-Muelle Luz, and Marianao-Parque Central. These lines converged on the Príncipe Fortress, where there had been a station for the little steam trains used in the nineteenth century and where fans would get off to go to the old Almendares Park. Leaving the trolley car at this spot, the fan would now walk five blocks down Pozos Dulces and come face to face with the park's pale blue portals, on whose façade he could read the name of the stadium painted in white letters.

I never visited Almendares Park, which only lasted until 1926, when it was destroyed by one of the most brutal hurricanes ever to hit the city of Havana. I am following here the loving description by Eduardo Robreño in his *Cualquier tiempo pasado fue. . . .* On the right of the portal there were the ticket windows: glorieta (fifty cents) or "sol" or bleachers (twenty-five cents). According to Robreño, there were two ample, two-tiered glorietas in the style of Ebbets Field, but to me the construction, seen only in pictures, is more reminiscent of the original Polo Grounds. Given the influence McGraw and his Giants had on Cuban baseball, it is likely that the model for this stadium would have been that of the park in Manhattan. Behind home plate there was also a small, two-tiered glorieta called the Grand Stand, with the scorer's box next to it. The benches for both teams were along the first-base line, divided by a wooden partition. While this may seem a bit too intimate, one must consider that rosters at the time were very small and the coaching staff, beyond the manager, was almost nonexistent. When one team was out in the field, very few players of the other would be left behind to annoy the team at bat. Unlike modern dugouts, which are sunk into the ground so as not to impede the view of spectators, these benches were at ground level, with the press box built on top of them.

The baseball field was of very generous dimensions. The left-field fence was well over five hundred feet away, and according to Robreño no batter ever clouted one over it. At a later point a glorieta was built, closer to home and slanting away from it. The low fence in right field was four hundred feet away, and only the great left-handed sluggers, like Torriente, Alejandro Oms, Oscar Charleston, Jud (Jorocón) Wilson, and Esteban (Mayarí) Montalvo were able to hit one past it. The infield was in pretty good shape, says Robreño, though there was a slight slope behind the diamond that made catching pop-ups treacherous.

The dimensions of this Almendares Park, like those of the previous one, reveal that Cuban baseball thrived on the play of fleet outfielders making circus catches, rather than sluggers hitting balls over the fences. This was typical of baseball in the dead-ball era, but this kind of play remained on the island until much later, to judge by the dimensions of the stadiums built after Almendares Park. A great catch by Heliodoro Hidalgo or Alejandro Oms after a long run over a vast expanse of grass was more exciting than a home-run blast, though when there was a homer, it had to be a monstrous one. In stadiums such as Almendares Park, baserunning was also at a premium, as was the defense against it. Triples and inside-the-park home runs must have been common. As mentioned before, Jabuco Hidalgo would sometimes run back to the bench, after a breathtaking grab in deep center, to a shower of coins from the glorieta.

Almendares Park had its own atmosphere, created as much by the beauty of the field as by the expectation of seeing high-caliber performers and of being entertained by a host of characters. One such character was Perico el Mono, a monkey that served as the Habana mascot for many years. Valentín González, the great Sirique of yesteryear, was now the umpire for most games. He was known for lighting a long cigar of his own making at the conclusion of each game, and strolling back to the grandstand to chat with the fans. Villamil was the official announcer. A tall, gaunt fellow, he would walk through the glorietas and bleachers, megaphone in hand, announcing the game's batteries, but sometimes, by the time he reached "sol," the pitcher whose name he was shouting had blown up and been replaced. There was also Socarrás, the first in a line of ballboys—all black—that reaches to the present day. And, in the reminiscences of Robreño, there was a short, plump man who sold almond cheese bits in the bleachers and would urge customers to buy his product by yelling, "I'm leaving and won't come back until the sixth inning!" On one occasion they waited for him to come back in vain. A heart attack had killed him in the stadium's offices.

If there is a symbol of Cuban baseball's golden age it is this Almendares Park—memories of the "primitive" one are dim, and there are few if any alive who set foot in it. But the second Almendares Park—though short-lived—saw the greatest Cuban and Negro Leaguers compete and has bequeathed a living lore that reached me through the voice of my elders. My uncle Oscar, as a boy in Belén, the renowned Jesuit prep school in Havana, used to sneak into Almendares Park on Sunday afternoons. Until his death my uncle had engraved in his memory the figure of Oscar Charleston, the greatest player he had ever seen, sprinting through the outfield of that stadium. And Alejo Carpentier, the great Cuban novelist, once told me that he would be better schooled in philosophy had his professor at the University of Havana not often appeared in class only to announce, wearing an air of resignation, that Méndez was pitching at Almendares Park. The professor would then lead the whole class to the stadium instead of discoursing on Aristotle or Plato. He was probably an Epicurean.

A very odd season was played in 1917, while the new Almendares Park was being built. Instead of the traditional teams, three clubs, called Orientals, White Sox, and Red Sox, participated in a league called Liga Cubano-Americana de Base Ball, even though no Americans performed. The Orientals had nothing to do with Cuba's substantial Chinese population, nor with Cuba's Oriente Province. The team was named after Oriental Park, the horse-racing track in Marianao where the league played its games.

The reason for these changes was due to the revolt against President García Menocal known as "La Chambelona," the song the Liberals sang mocking the conservative, U.S.-propped leader. Though there was no "formal" intervention by the United States, marines were stationed in various parts of eastern Cuba to "protect U.S. property." The Liberals claimed, not without merit, that García Menocal's reelection in November 1916 had been rigged. García Menocal's second term, and the term of his successor, Alfredo Zayas, were marked by unabashed interference by the United States, at first under the pretext of protecting interests and areas of strategic significance during World War I. The rise in sugar prices and general wealth increased government graft as well as legitimate business. As a result, a new generation of *nouveaux riches* built palatial mansions in El Vedado, west of Havana, and in other cities throughout the island. Baseball would profit from all this wealth.

The Orientals, who won the championship led by batting champion (.355) and star pitcher Luque, played fourteen games, whereas the other two teams played only thirteen. It was a closely contested if brief season that only lasted from January to the end of February. The teams were strong. The winning Orientals had Marsans, Romañach, Torres, Luque, Calvo, and the two Acostas; the White Sox had Pata Jorobá Jiménez, Portuondo, Pedroso, Chacón, and Junco; and the Red Sox had Miguel Angel, Aragón, Cueto, Herrera, Pájaro Cabrera, Palmero and Dibut.

An added attraction, conceived to profit from the Habana-Almendares rivalry, was a brief fall tournament involving only the "eternal rivals." It was played before the American season and was called the Copa (Cup) *El Mundo,* because it was sponsored by that newspaper. This championship, which began in the fall of 1917, did away with the annoyance of the third team, an endemic problem of the Cuban League throughout its history. It is clear from this development that Fe, which would eventually disappear and be replaced by the Cuban Stars, Marianao, Santa Clara, and others, was not holding its own. The very name of the tournament is a throwback to the amateur beginnings of the Cuban League, but these teams were certainly professional.

The Cuban League returned in 1918–19, under the name Liga General de Base Ball de la República de Cuba, with Abel Linares as treasurer and with games held at brand-new Almendares Park. This championship also offered another novelty: the Cuban Stars, who during the summer participated in the U.S. Negro circuits of independent baseball, joined the league under their own name, replacing traditional team Fe. This was a memorable season in which the winning Habana team played forty-seven games, while the other two played forty-five. The discrepancy stems from the fact that the second half of the season ended with all three teams tied at eleven games won and eleven games lost (Habana had won the first half). A double elimination tournament decided the season, with Habana winning its last two after dropping the first, 4–3, to the Stars.

No Americans participated in this championship. Almendares fielded a team made up of Rogelio Valdés, Antonio Susini (the infielder who killed teammate pitcher Julio LeBlanc with a bat), Ramiro Ramírez, T. Rivero, Strike González, F. Fernández, Oscar Rodríguez, Lorenzo Alfonso, Benito Marrero, and others. The significant absence is Adolfo Luque, who did not play that winter in Cuba. The Cuban Stars had Pata Jorobá Jiménez, Pelayo Chacón, Isidro Fabré, Roberto Villa, Marcelino Guerra, Bombín Pedroso, Tatica Campos, Mayarí Montalvo, Eufemio Abreu, Benito Calderón, José Junco, and Pasquel Martínez. This was Tinti Molina's powerhouse, which, according to a *Diario de la Marina* story of October 5, 1919, had a *tournée* of seven months through Mexico and the United States. Habana's team was made up of Tomás Romañach, Ramón (Kakín) González, Rogelio Crespo, Miguel Angel González, Eusebio (Papo) González, José (Cheo) Ramos, Ricardo Torres, Joseíto Acosta, Fidel Hungo, Abrahám Tolosa (who had played with the Cuban Stars during the summer), and Pedro Dibut.

Habana ran away with the championship, winning twenty-eight and losing nineteen. The Cuban Stars came in second and Almendares last. The teams played between forty-five and forty-seven games, and the season ended on March 23, giving the players time to report back to their teams in the United States. It is remarkable that this season could have been played without American players, yet it appears to have been quite a success. The Americans were returning from World War I, the Cuban economy was booming, and professional baseball was thriving. In addition to the Cuban League, there was a "Campeonato Oriental" in Oriente Province, pitting teams from Delicias, a sugarmill, and the towns of Holguín and Gibara. This season, which took place in September 1919, saw many front-line players perform: Francisco (Paco) Luján, José (Acostica) Acosta, Eusebio (Papo) González, Joseíto Rodríguez, Andrés Hernández, and Isidro Fabré. In addition, the American season was a huge success, with a visit from the Pittsburgh Pirates.

Habana and Almendares, as well as the team from the University of Havana, faced the Pirates. It was one of these games that Robreño remem-

bers as the first he ever saw at the new Almendares Park. Fortunately and
quite fortuitously, one of the games against Pittsburgh was witnessed and
described by Harry A. Franck, a famous travel writer of the period, known
for his *A Vagabond Journey Around the World.* In his 1920 *Roaming
Through the West Indies,* Franck wrote this superb vignette about his visit
to Almendares Park, the best account I know of activity at that stadium:

A constant procession of Fords, their mufflers wide open, were hiccough-
ing out the Carlos III Boulevard toward the Havana ball-park. The
entrance-gate, at which they brought up with a snort and a sudden bronco-
like halt that all but jerked their passengers to their feet, was a seething
hubbub. Ticket-speculators, renters of cushions, vendees of everything
that can be consumed on a summer afternoon, were bellowing their
wares into the ears of the *fanáticos* who scrimmaged about the ticket-
window. Men a trifle seedy in appearance wandered back and forth holding up a dozen tiny envelopes, arranged in fan-shape, which they were
evidently trying to sell or rent. The pink *entradas* I finally succeeded in
snatching were not, of course, the only tickets needed. . . . They carried
us as far as the grand-stand, where another maelstrom was surging about
the chicken wire wicket behind which a hen-minded youth was dispens-
ing permissions to sit down. . . . We certainly could not complain, however, of the front-row places we obtained except that, in the free-for-all
Spanish fashion, all the riffraff of vendees crowded the foot-rests that
were supposedly reserved for front-row occupants. Nine nimble Cubans
were scattered about the flat expanse of Almendares Park, backed by the
Príncipe Hill, with its crown of university buildings. Royal palms waved
their plumes languidly in the ocean breeze; a huge Cuban flag undulated
beyond the outfielders; a score of vultures circled lazily overhead, as if
awaiting a chance to pounce upon the "dead ones" which the wrathful
"fans" announced every time a player failed to live up to their hopes. On
a bench in the shade sat all but one of the invading team, our own "Pirates" from the Smoky City. The missing one was swinging his club al-
ertly at the home plate, his eyes glued on the Cuban *zurdo,* or "southpaw," who had just begun his contortions in the middle of the mound.
The scene itself was familiar enough, yet it seemed strangely out of place
in this tropical setting. It was like coming upon a picture one had known
since childhood, to find it enclosed in a brand new frame.

    I reached for my kodak, then restrained the impulse. A camera is of
little use at a Cuban ball game. Only a recording phonograph could
catch its chief novelties. An uproar as incessant as that of a rolling-mill
drowned every individual sound. It was not merely the vendees of *"El es-
cor oficial,"* of sandwiches, lottery-tickets, cigars, cigarettes, of bottled
beer by the basketful, who created the hubbub; the spectators themselves
made most of it. The long, two-story grand-stand behind us was packed
with Cubans of every shade from ebony black to the pasty white of the

tropics, and every man of them seemed to be shouting at the top of his well-trained lungs. I say "man" advisedly, for with the exception of my wife there were just three women present, and they had the hangdog air of culprits. An uninformed observer would have supposed that the entire throng was on the verge of a free-for-all fight, instead of enjoying themselves in the Cuban's chief pastime. . . . But baseball, strictly speaking, is not what the Cuban enjoys most. It is rather the gambling that goes with it [pp. 25–26].

He goes on to describe the betting, particularly the *quinielas,* sold in the familiar little envelopes. They paid $8.00 to the winners. Franck liked to exaggerate for effect, as one could surely note from the above quotation. He adds:

The game itself was little different from one at home. The Cuban players varied widely in color, from the jet-black third baseman to a shortstop of rice-powder complexion. Their playing of high order, quite as "fast" as the average teams of our big leagues. Cubans hold several championships in sports requiring high degree of skill and swiftness. The umpire in his protective paraphernalia looked quite like his fellows on the North, yet behind his mask he was a rich mahogany brown. His official speech was English, but when a dispute arose he changed quickly to voluble Spanish. The "bucaneros," as the present-day pirates who had descended upon the Cuban coast were best known locally, won the game on this occasion; but the day before they had not scored a run [p. 28].

He goes on to comment on the baseball slang used by Havana newspapers. It is clearly a game between Habana and the Pirates, with Miguel Angel catching for the Reds, Acostica on the mound, and Sirique umpiring behind the plate. But what is most evident about Franck's descriptions is the wealth (all those Fords) and enthusiasm at the height of what is called in Cuba *la danza de los millones* (the dance of the millions), when skyrocketing sugar prices pumped fabulous sums of money into the island's economy.

The empresario who made all this possible was Abel Linares. He now owned the two best-known Cuban teams, leased Almendares Park, and was the one with contacts in American baseball. In *Carteles* the games against Pittsburgh were advertised in the section called *cartelera* (hence the magazine's name), or billboard: "ALMENDARES PARK: Empresa Abel Linares. Tel. M-2108. Temporada Americana de base ball, jugando el *Pittsburgh* de la Liga Nacional. Juegos, lunes, jueves, sábados y domingos."

The next season of the Cuban League saw yet more changes involving the third club. Habana and Almendares seemed fairly set. The Blues had Torriente, Herrera, Baró, Chacón, Fabré, Abreu, Almeida, Marsans, Luque, Jiménez, Portuondo, Ramón González, and Palmero. The Reds had brothers Oscar and Joseíto Rodríguez, Cueto, Joseíto Acosta, Hungo, Miguel

Angel, Aragón, Jacinto Calvo, Ricardo Torres, and H. P. Holden. The third team this year was América, whose delegate was Tinti Molina. Given that many of its players performed for him in the summer, it is clear that América is a winter version of the Cuban Stars. It had José María Fernández, a great catcher destined for a long career as player and manager in the Negro Leagues, Strike González, Bombín Pedroso, Pájaro Cabrera, Susini, Le-Blanc, Lucas Boada, José (Cheo) Hernández, Rogelio Crespo, Roberto Villa, Julián (Recurbón) Terán, and José (Cheo) Ramos.

But there were problems. Almendares finished the first half ahead, having won ten of thirteen games, with Habana second, at 9 and 4. América, however, had only one victory and thirteen defeats. By February 9, having lost several games in a row, América was crushed by Almendares, 21–7. It appears that during this game the América players gave up and clowned around. According to Díez Muro: "The league agreed to separate the América Club from the championship because of its lack of seriousness and respect for the public, forfeiting the games it had pending in favor of its opponents" (p. 195). Almendares and Habana finished the season with the Blues running away at a total of 22 and 5, while Habana finished at 16 and 10. Cristóbal Torriente, who hit a mammoth homer on February 14, was batting champion again. The reduction of games played and the troubles with the third team seem to indicate that by this time the American season, which was played in the fall, was encroaching on the popularity of the Cuban League. The old rivalry of Cubans against Americans drew more than the one of Habana against Almendares. This development was not lost on the promoters, who decided to add a team from the United States to the Cuban League, turning it into an extension of the American season, but not before Abel Linares attempted the greatest promotional coup, up until this time, in the history of Cuban baseball: to have Babe Ruth play in Havana.

In 1920, a year of plenty and promise, fall baseball was abundant in Cuba. Not only was there an American season, but even a *pre*-American season, pitting the by now quite established Cuban Stars against the All Leagues, who were an assortment of white Cubans who played in both the major and minor leagues in the United States during the summer. The best two of three would be played beginning on October 9, and the Giants would arrive on the fifteenth. In a sense, the pre-American season was a series between Cuban blacks and Cuban whites who were eligible to play in Organized Baseball. McGraw's New York Giants would enter a three-team tournament with Habana and Almendares, as had become the custom in recent fall competition. But this year the American season would have the additional attraction of Babe Ruth's visit. The Babe had revolutionized baseball by socking fifty-four home runs in a single season for the New York Yankees in 1920. His twenty-nine the year before had already set a record, but fifty-four home runs in one season was inconceivable. It was the kind of individual feat that would characterize the Roaring Twenties, like Lindbergh's solo crossing of the Atlantic. Ruth was turning into a celebrity the likes of which had never been seen before anywhere. With money to spare and ambitions that knew no limits, Cuban impresarios wanted to cash in on the new phenomenon and invited the Babe to display his talents as a Giant at Almendares Park.

The All Leagues had players such as Ricardo Torres, Joseíto Rodríguez, Fidel Hungo, Andrés Hernández, Rafael Almeida, Jacinto Calvo, Ramón (Paíto) Herrera, and an American named Ted Easterly (who played with Cleveland and Chicago in the American League, and Kansas City in the Federal). The Stars had Valentín Dreke, Bernardo Baró, Pata Jorobá Jiménez, Bombín Pedroso, Julio LeBlanc, Marcelino Guerra, Pelayo Chacón, and Portuondo—their usual powerhouse. The games were closely contested, played in and between torrents of rain. The weather would mar many of the plans of the pre-American season and spoil some of the American season itself, though it would be a memorable campaign nonetheless. The Stars won the three-game championship, two games to one, thus setting the stage for the three-team American season, when most of the Cuban players would be shuffled around to make up Almendares and Habana, with the addition of others, such as Cristóbal Torriente, who was performing for Rube Foster in the United States, not for the Cuban Stars.

McGraw and his Giants arrived by steamer from Key West on October 15 and were met with much fanfare at the dock by Abel Linares and a large contingent of fans. They were taken to the plush Hotel Plaza. With them arrived Miguel Angel González, a Giant backup catcher then in the summer but, more importantly, Habana's manager during the winter. (McGraw's acquisition of Miguel Angel showed how much he valued his connection to Cuba.) That very afternoon the Giants went to Almendares Park for a practice. McGraw brought with him the following roster: George Burns, Ross Young, Vern Spencer, George Kelly, Larry Doyle, Dave Bancroft, Frankie Frisch, Jesse Barnes, Lee King, Pol Perritt, Rosy Ryan, Frank Snyder, Earl Smith, and Johnny Evers as coach (of Tinkers to Evers to Chance fame). No Babe yet, however, and the squad seemed a bit short of pitchers, with twenty-game winners Fred Toney and Art Nehf missing. Barnes, the third twenty-game winner, did make the trip. He was the best hurler on the team that took up residence at Havana's Hotel Plaza that fall morning. Perritt, for instance, was a veteran who had seen his better days and had been used very little during the 1920 season.

The Giants won a close game against Almendares to open the season on October 17. Barnes pitched for McGraw and lefty Palmero for the Blues. Almendares had quite a team, with Abreu behind the plate, Chacón at short, Baró in center, Torriente in right, Merito Acosta in left, Paíto Herrera at second, Bartolo Portuondo at third, and Marsans at first. Fans flooded the field and had to be restrained with ropes. Chacón put on a show on defense, and the Giant infield of Kelly, Doyle, Bancroft, and Frisch impressed the Cuban fans with their agility and teamwork. According to *Diario de la Marina* the take was 10,000 pesos, a princely sum back then (each peso was worth a dollar). The paper not only congratulated Linares for the success of the event but also opined that Almendares was the team to beat the major leaguers.

They did on October 18, a rainy day that saw Cheo Hernández take the mound against Perritt. The score was 7–4, but a sour note was introduced when the fans and the press detected that the Giant players were performing with some indifference. *Diario de la Marina* suggested that the Americans were not taking care of themselves well (i.e., that they were drinking too much), and not playing with the same dedication and intensity that led them to nearly defeat Brooklyn for the National League pennant: "It is well known to all that players in American clubs who visit us, do so with the purpose of taking a trip and enjoying certain freedoms that are forbidden back home, and that for that reason it is not possible for them to conduct themselves with the same earnestness as when they are competing for their league championship" (October 20, 1920). It might be well to remember that Prohibition had been in force in the United States since January 29, 1919, and that the complaint about American players imbibing too much in Cuba goes back to the nineteenth century. This complaint continued for as long as there was professional baseball on the island.

On the nineteenth, Habana's Oscar Tuero (also a St. Louis Cardinal) blanked the Giants, 1–0, though the Reds had only one hit against Barnes. The Giant hurler walked three in the seventh, which together with an error by shortstop Bancroft produced the run. Habana had Cueto at third, Joseíto Rodríguez at second, Almeida in right, Calvo in center, Aragón in left, Horace (Hod) Ford at short (he played for the Boston Braves), Hungo at first, Torres behind the plate, and Easterly, who took over first for the last few innings. The *Diario de la Marina* editorialized that the games played so far showed that the Cuban teams were as good as any in the major leagues. Nevertheless, little-heralded Perritt shut out Habana, 2–0, in the next game, defeating Washington Senator José Acosta.

On October 24, still without Babe Ruth, the Giants tied Almendares at seven in a spectacular game before a huge crowd, the biggest so far in the series. The Giants played aggressively, arguing umpires' calls, stealing bases, bench-jockeying, and carrying on as advertised, which made sportswriters happy and the fans delirious, because Almendares responded in kind. Darkness intervened, and the game had to be called a draw after twelve innings. Tuero came back for Habana the next day and lost a heartbreaker to Ryan, 3–2, on a wild throw by Cueto from third (a *laboratorio* in the current slang because Wood Pharmaceutical Laboratory was behind the first-base stands and the ball was presumed to be heading in that direction). Ruth's impending debut "next Saturday" was announced in the *Diario de la Marina* of October 26, which added facetiously that he would play for the New York team. The schedule called for Habana to be the Giants' opponent that day. (Given the independent status of this American season, the Babe could just as well have played for Almendares or Habana, not the Giants, which was not his team in the majors anyway, a daunting proposition that probably would have overjoyed the fans.) On the twenty-eighth Almendares' (and the Cuban Stars') Isidro Fabré shut out the Giants, 5–0, on three hits, reducing them to midgets, according to *Diario de la Marina*. Fabré, a lefty of Catalan-black ancestry, was becoming a superb pitcher, and he could also hit. Not a single Giant reached third. Portuondo, having a tremendous series, got three of Almendares' eleven hits against Barnes. While everyone awaited the Babe, Almendares took the first half of the American season.

Ruth arrived on October 30, accompanied by his wife. He was virtually taken straight from the dock to Almendares Park, where he was received tumultuously by fans and photographers. Kids ran up to touch him, and all were awed by his corpulence. The Babe, in his Giant uniform, came up to the plate against Habana in the first inning with two on base. He lined a savage drive past Hungo at first that cleared the bases. He got a triple, but actually scored on an error on the throw. Joseíto Acosta was on the mound for the Reds. As a Senator he had given up Ruth's fiftieth homer during the summer, so he knew what he was up against. In the third, the Babe hit another screamer, for a double—not bad for a man who still probably had his sea legs. The Giants won, 4–3, though Habana, particularly Calvo and Hungo, roughed up Perritt. The Babe's debut was a success, but the crowd was not as large as for previous games because the ticket prices had been raised. The reason for this was that Ruth was being paid $2,000 a game!

On the thirty-first the Giants defeated Almendares and Emilio Palmero, 3–0, behind the pitching of Ryan, who was aided by four double plays. The Cuban lefty struck out the Babe twice, but Ruth got a single and a triple. The triple hit the fence in right, four hundred feet away. The next batter, Frankie Frisch, hit a fly ball to right and the Babe tried to tag up and score, but Baró threw him out at the plate. Palmero got great ovations each time he struck out Ruth, to whom he pitched without fear—challenging him with strikes. On November 3 Joseíto Acosta, pitching again for Habana, struck out Babe Ruth three times, also to great ovations. New York, however, defeated Habana on a home run and a double by Young and a triple by Burns. Perritt beat the Habana Reds for the third time.

On November 4 Ryan and Perritt beat Almendares, 10–8, though they were roughed up by Portuondo, Marsans, Torriente and Abreu. Torriente, had a triple and two singles. But Cheo Hernández and Palmero were not at their best, giving up fourteen hits, one a double by Ruth. On the following day, November 5, 1920, one of the most memorable games in

Cuban baseball lore took place, not just because Almendares blasted the Giants, 11–4, but also because of Cristóbal Torriente's performance. I was genuinely sad to discover that the facts did not quite square with the myth, however. There are relatively accurate accounts of this game (box score included), by Monfort, Figueredo and Holway. Yet even in these, hyperbole prevails.[21] The story goes that on this day Torriente outdueled Ruth by blasting three home runs, while the American idol could muster only one. The facts are as follows: Babe Ruth did not get a hit that day, and while Torriente got three homers and a double, the homers were against High-pockets Kelly, the Giant first baseman, who had pitched one game in relief three seasons earlier. The double was against the Babe himself, who had taken the mound for an inning as a stunt. Why did McGraw use Kelly? As observed before, the Giant squad that came to Havana that fall was short on pitchers. But the inescapable truth is that Torriente's feat was accomplished against a first baseman and a former pitcher and in a kind of holiday spirit—almost a carnival atmosphere. Furthermore, it is not clear from contemporary accounts if Torriente's homers actually went over the far-flung fences of Almendares Park. All three went to left or left center, where the dimensions reached six hundred feet, but the only thing the newspaper story says is that the balls went over the fielders' head, one reaching just below a Partagás sign. With such dimensions, most homers in Almendares Park were inside the park. But there are other reasons why Torriente's burst was a bit tarnished.

Ramón S. Mendoza, whose story in *Diario de la Marina* of November 6 I am following, wrote that the game was like a batting practice session for Almendares because the Giants did not seem to be too focused on winning. Besides, he alleges, some of the Giant players showed up in no condition to compete (*descompuestos* is the word he delicately used to mean drunk). Smith, the catcher, for instance, committed four passed balls. Mendoza concludes: "We admire the extraordinary power of the blasts by the great Almendares slugger and we recognize the merit of having placed the ball where he did yesterday, but that does not mean that we should not admit also that he took advantage of the opportunity offered him when he was opposed by someone who may very well be a pitcher but does not play that position for his club." Nonetheless, the fans, overjoyed by Torriente's accomplishments, which did eclipse Ruth's on this day, showered him with coins, as in olden times, writes Mendoza. Needless to say, some enthusiasm that greeted the 1907 all-Cuban Almendares team that defeated the nearly all-American Fe surfaced on this occasion. Regardless of the facts, Torriente was a hero because he bested the biggest American hero of all. Damn the facts.

On the seventh, Habana was beaten again by the Giants, who were probably bouncing back from their hangovers. Kelly hit a homer that rolled to the scoreboard in center field, and Ruth hit a triple to right. Mendoza opined that they were playing the Babe so far back that he would never be able to hit a homer, which underscores that most, if not all, homers at

Almendares were inside the park. But on November 8 Ruth finally did hit a homer, in a game won by Almendares, 6–5. The Babe's blast went to the corner between the end of "sol" and the center-field wall or scoreboard. Mendoza says that it may very well have been the longest homer ever hit in Almendares Park; a rough estimate would be about 550 feet. But Torriente got two singles, as did Baró, and the Blues prevailed.

On the twelfth the Giants and the Reds tied at 3, in a game that Habana could have won but somehow fell short. Ruth did not get a hit in four trips to the plate. The American series ended as pure circus and on a sour note. It was announced that for the last game Ruth and the Giants would face an all-star team made up of Cuban players from Almendares and Habana. But Ruth refused to play because he had upped his fee and it was not met by Linares. The Giants started with a pitcher, Perritt, in left, and the Cubans with five Almendares players (Portuondo, Torriente, Paíto Herrera, Papo, and Abreu) and four Habana players (Joseíto Rodríguez, Jacinto Calvo, Cueto, and Acostica). The fun began when Torriente, after tripling, let himself be picked off third on purpose. But it reached the level of slapstick when the Cubans fielded three jai alai players from Havana's famous Frontón. They were deployed at first, center, and right and used their wicker *cestas* to catch and throw the ball. When they came to the plate equally equipped, Ryan served them lobs, and Young and Evers tried to catch their "hits" with *cestas,* too. It was a very funny act, writes Mendoza, "worthy of a circus." It was said that Linares had lost a bundle with his experiment because of Ruth's extravagant fee, and that the Babe lost most of it gambling at jai alai and other games.

The Babe's visit was a harbinger of things to come, as Cuban and American impresarios sought to cash in on the frivolous spirit of the Roaring Twenties and as baseball increasingly became intertwined with Cuban life and further incorporated into the mythology of the nation. During this decade there emerged what in Cuban lore is the greatest team ever to take the field on the island, the 1923 Leopardos of Santa Clara, and the greatest Cuban baseball player of all time, Martín Dihigo. In that same year, 1923, Luque won twenty-seven for the Cincinnati Reds, the best season that a Cuban pitcher has ever had in the majors. Other stars to appear or to come into their own in this period were Luis Tiant, Lázaro Salazar, Ramón Bragaña, José María Fernández, Rodolfo Fernández, Pelayo Chacón, Valentín Dreke, Isidro Fabré, Alejandro Oms, Manuel (Cocaína) García, and Pablo (Champion) Mesa. Rube Foster's founding of the Negro National League in 1920, which included the Cuban Stars as charter members, enhanced the availability of black talent from the United States. Practically all the stars from the Negro National League played in Cuba during this period, whether it be in the Cuban League or on sugarmill teams, particularly in the eastern part of the island. Lloyd, Charleston, Holland, Marcelle, Duncan, Bell, and many others became household names throughout Cuba.

This period, like life itself and historical eras in general, has a rise and a fall, going from the peak of the midtwenties to the valley at the decade's end, when the Wall Street crash of 1929 brought down the Cuban economy and Cuban baseball along with it. The economic crisis was accompanied by political turmoil, revolution, and the toppling of Gerardo Machado's government. In baseball it brought dissension, splits in the Cuban League, canceled seasons, and the ultimate humiliation of having the three professional teams defeated by Havana Club, a semipro squad sponsored by a rum manufacturer that had flourished because of Prohibition. Players such as Dihigo, Chacón, Fabré, Tiant, Salazar, Bragaña, and others who made their debut in the twenties had the misfortune of peaking during the thirties, lean years of the Cuban League. They had to make a name for themselves abroad, many in the Negro circuits, as well as in Mexico, Venezuela, the Dominican Republic, Panama, and Puerto Rico, countries where Cubans were often the first or most significant disseminators of the sport.

The twenties saw a great boom in public works, particularly in the second half of the decade, under Machado's administration (1925–33). A central highway was built linking all six provinces; an impressive capitol building, an exact replica of the one in Washington, was erected; avenues were widened in Havana and other cities; and urban as well as interprovince transportation was expanded. Huge sugar centrales churned out their products and became small cities of their own, and mining operations in the eastern end of Cuba brought in American capital. But the most visible change was the transformation of Cuba, particularly Havana, into a tourist paradise of a scale not seen before.

Basil Woon wrote in his delightful *When It's Cocktail Time in Cuba* (1928) that "Havana is becoming a second home for that section of the smart set which formerly spent its winters on the Riviera" (p. 28). Many factors contributed to the rise of Cuba, and of Havana in particular, as a choice tourist attraction for rich Americans. American tourism in the first decades of the twentieth century went well beyond what it had been in the late nineteenth century. The first factor was World War I, which made Europe inaccessible for a long time and also made the Cuban economy boom and become even more tightly bound with the economy of the United States. The second was Prohibition, which did not curb the fondness for spirits in the Roaring Twenties, but drove it underground or abroad—notice the title of Woon's book. Yet a third, more permanent factor was the glorious winter weather. Havana, Woon intoned, was "the closest thing to Paris in a season when Paris is not available" (p. 31). It was mostly during the winter that Americans came to Cuba, though there were many who lived on the island, employed by the sugar industry. Woon observes that the "season is lengthening year by year and in time to come will probably last from November to April, for during these six months the weather is dry and well-nigh perfect. The snobbery of society, with its restless insistence on change, will always have a 'high' season, however, and this begins shortly after the New Year and culminates at the end of March" (p. 27). Tourists came to Havana, in other words, during the professional baseball season, though most came to indulge in other forms of amusement: drinking, gambling at the National Casino, and betting on the horses at lavish Oriental Park. John McGraw was a regular among them, as were Charles Stoneham, owner of the Giants, and Tillinghast L'Hommedieu Houston, who owned the Yankees. McGraw and Stoneham had bought Oriental Park in 1919. Houston got into some shady business with President García Menocal in a deal to dredge Cuban ports. But most Americans came to have fun and escape the cold and dreary northern winters. The Vanderbilts, Astors, Whitneys, Paynes, Morrows, Lindberghs, and Hersheys commingled with Cuban high society at fancy hotels, the track, bars, and restaurants. They danced under a canopy of stars on roof gardens along Prado Boulevard, built homes in developments such as the Biltmore, and played golf in beautiful courses west of Havana. Woon lists President Gerardo Machado, former presidents García Menocal and Zayas, the Mendozas, Julio Blanco Herrera, Conrado, editor, and Joe Massaguer, caricaturist, the Agramontes, Zayas Bazáns, and others among the Cuban social elite.

For the Cuban economy the tourist season became a *segunda zafra* (second harvest) (sugar, of course, being the first). Tourist guides were printed with pictures and maps of the capital and other cities. Glossy magazines and newspapers were published in English, such as *Havana: The Magazine of Cuba,* run by Joe Massaguer, who was sports editor of the widely circulating newspaper *El Mundo* and the *Havana Post.* These glossy publications recorded the comings and goings of the smart set and kept them informed of news back home. While baseball was not likely to be high on the agenda of these visitors to Havana, known already according to George Manington as the "Paris of the West" (*The West Indies,* p. 138), all the wealth they brought to the island during the professional baseball season helped advance the game. Cubans earned money to pay for tickets for the Cuban League in the myriad jobs created by tourism. Musicians had gigs at hotels, roof gardens, dance halls, and private parties. Others worked in famous bars such as "Sloppy Joe's," yet others cared for houses and golf courses at the Country Club. Many became expert croupiers, waiters, barmen, the whole gamut of professions good and bad that tourism fosters. The upper crust delved into banking, real estate, and, needless to say, the sugar market. Many made money in bootleg liquor. Cuba was described in a tourist pamphlet of the times as "Seven hundred miles of Playground."

In Havana the Sevilla Hotel was rebuilt as the Sevilla-Biltmore by Charles F. Flynn and John M. Bowman in 1919. Its Moorish arches resembled buildings in the city whose name it bore, for Americans were fond of making Cuba into an ersatz Andalusia. The Sevilla-Biltmore looked like a stage set for *Carmen,* a projection of the bad taste of the American *nou-*

veaux riches. By 1926 another tourist pamphlet published pictures of twenty-four Havana hotels, ranging from the old, staid Inglaterra in the center of town to the newer Almendares, to the west. Others had names such as Ritz, Saratoga, or Maison Royale. If Havana was like Paris, it was also like Monte Carlo.

Cubans riding the crest of the sugar prices built themselves palatial homes in El Vedado, to the immediate west of Havana, where the Habana Baseball Club had had its glorieta in the nineteenth century. Some of the mansions had Roman baths with sand actually brought from the Nile. The most exquisite Italian marbles were imported. Artists were brought from Spain and other European countries for the stained-glass windows. There were columns, domes, elaborate gardens, terraces, ballrooms, libraries, billiard rooms, and majestic staircases. In the frenzy, styles were mingled and mangled, always in an effort to make the residences look like movie sets. Liveried chauffeurs polished the grillwork of gleaming Packards and Cadillacs in driveways and garages. It was an explosion of high kitsch made possible by money, American know-how, and the Cuban elite's lingering ties to Europe.

The social clubs also erected (or refurbished) elaborate houses on the shore, also to the west of Havana, with baseball fields, tennis courts, swimming pools, gymnasiums, reading rooms, stately dance halls, and dining rooms. The Vedado Tennis Club not only boasted all of these and a famous baseball nine but also fielded a team of American football played by young men who attended schools such as Harvard, Princeton, and Yale. Rowing was all the rage, and regattas became high points of the Cuban sports calendar until the 1959 revolution.

Once again, theater thrived in Havana. María Barrientos, the famous Spanish opera singer who had been to the city twice during 1912, returned in 1920. On this occasion she appeared with Enrico Caruso and other stars, such as Gabriela Benssanzoni, Flora Perini, and Ricardo Stacciari. The Cuban elite's ambitions were, and have always been, of the highest order, going invariably for the best in all realms. If Babe Ruth could be enticed to Cuba, why not Caruso? Until about 1930 opera was the preferred spectacle of the Cuban moneyed classes, and Havana competed with the most famous U.S., Latin American, and European opera centers. But popular Cuban music was also evolving and still finding its way up the social ladder. Danzones were still being played and danced, but faster, more sensual rhythms, such as the rumba and the conga, filtered into high society at parties and balls on the roofs of fancy hotels such as the Sevilla-Biltmore. Jazz invaded Cuba by way of the most famous and accomplished musicians whose Cuban counterparts gave the music a special flavor. Cuban music bands and ensembles proliferated. Some, like the "Lecuona Cuban Boys," traveled to Europe, others to the United States, where they began to cut records and appear in movies. As in the case of baseball, the dissemination of Cuban music owed much to the proximity of the United States and with it accessibility to powerful mass media capable and quite willing to exploit it.

Cuban music became fashionable in Paris. Cuban poets, novelists, musicians, and painters began to see in the syncretic forms of Cuban music an example of artistic originality that was peculiarly Cuban. Popular music turned into something worth studying and imitating by "serious" artists. By middecade this trend had developed into what came to be known as the Afro-Cuban Movement, a program that combined the avant-garde with popular forms of Afro-Cuban expression. Alejo Carpentier and Nicolás Guillén, novelist and poet, respectively, gained international fame with works of Afro-Cuban inspiration. Amadeo Roldán and Alejandro García Caturla composed symphonic music based on Cuban popular melodies and rhythms. Ernesto Lecuona wrote pieces for the masses and the stage that have endured in the Cuban popular tradition. Fernando Ortiz, a criminologist by training, turned to the study of Afro-Cuban culture, particularly religion. He was the first to point out the crucial role that those who were brought to Cuba in chains, and their descendants, played in shaping Cuban art, society, and politics.

Popular Cuban music became a way for blacks to express their culture and to earn a living. The two did not necessarily go together. Certain forms of sacred music and dance were discreetly revised for the general public so as not to desecrate them. Concessions were also made in shows and balls for the taste and expectations of the audience. These changes were unthinkable in private religious rituals, where Afro-Cuban music and dance were essentially liturgical. Playing musical instruments became a trade poor blacks passed down from generation to generation as a way to survive and even thrive. Baseball, too, became such a craft. Like music, the game was a way to advance in society, but one demanding very specific skills and knowledge. This wisdom was passed down as a sort of cryptic art involving certain reserved techniques for doing things in the proper way. Steps and moves, not unlike those required by the rumba and other dances, had to be mastered. Though it may appear so to the untrained eye, there is nothing frenzied or improvised in real Afro-Cuban dance, some of which is like an elaborate form of gymnastics or even a martial art. Those who know the game are aware that footwork is a crucial component of baseball, too, particularly around second base, at first, behind the plate, and at bat. As in dance, these moves need to be taught. This link between dance and baseball is another reason why Adolfo Luque's association with rumba dancer Papá Montero is hardly casual. Like the dancer, Luque had mastered a set of moves that raised him to a special status that one may say held a certain religious aura.

Perhaps because of its direct link to religious ritual, there is no myth of "the natural" in Cuban physical activities such as dance and sport, though native gifts are, of course recognized. The body has to be tamed, seasoned, controlled, made to respond to received tradition. This attitude carried—and carries—over to baseball, as well as to boxing and other popular games. Talented young blacks were sedulously taught by their elders how to do things the right way, in both individual skills and team play. No nonsense was allowed. Teachers were stern because on one level physical action was related to the sacred, and on the other because making a living depended on it. In this teacher-student relationship the game reached back to the sacred source of all ludic activity even when it appeared as most profane.

Recently, in Miami, Panchón Herrera told me that when the Philadelphia Phillies tried to make a second baseman out of him in the fifties, he had great difficulty adjusting at first—he was a hulking first baseman by trade. But on a trip back to Cuba during a religious holiday (he had an agreement with the club that he could return to Havana for the high Afro-Catholic holidays), Panchón went back to an old man in his neighborhood who straightened him out, showing him ways of pivoting, avoiding the runner, and making the throws. He had more confidence in this teacher than in the major-league coaches who were working with him in Philadelphia. When I was a child catcher in the fifties, "Corcho," a young black young man accomplished at that position and reputed to be on the taxi squad of Marianao in the Cuban League, taught me subtle ways of holding the mitt to deceive the umpire into calling a strike on marginal pitches. This was the wisdom of generations passed down to me like the ceremonial gestures of a sacred dance. It was with this kind of wisdom that blacks (as well as many poor whites) triumphed in baseball, in the same way that they excelled at the various spectacles that entertained the tourists who came to Cuba.

Music and sports, especially boxing and baseball, were spectacles for the masses. Performers and athletes were admired for their skills, character, deportment, courage, and success. But they occupied a social rank of no significant consequence. While what they did was remarkable and praiseworthy, it was not serious business. It was a trade closer to the circus or to vaudeville than to a profession, close to that of the performers at the famous burlesque theater the Alhambra, which was thriving then in Havana. Only a few musicians and athletes transcended this marginalization. The first was Méndez during the teens. In the Cuba of the twenties only Kid Chocolate, the black professional world featherweight boxing champion, reached such heights, along with white ballplayers Adolfo Luque and Miguel Angel González. Later Martín Dihigo would also reach such recognition and fame. Interest in athletes by artists and intellectuals did not bring them out of the realm of spectacle, but on the contrary was dependent on their remaining there. Athletes and musicians dwelled in a longed-for world of physical and psychic release not available to the rest of the population. Their feats were admired as artistic phenomena that depended in no small measure precisely on the players' superficial qualities. By superficial qualities I mean quite literally their garments and the skin: the gaudiness of the baseball uniforms with their bright colors, the outlandish gestures, the apparent liberation of the body (apparent in that the gestures are part of a rigorous code). This made Cuban baseball of the twenties a total spectacle, with a clear separation between spectators and performers. It was unlike Cuban baseball of the previous century in which spectators, some of them women, participated by awarding ribbons and prizes to the players, and everyone got together after the game to dance the danzón. Athletes were now thoroughly professionalized, paid to perform and entertain.

Because the sport appealed now to a broader spectrum of the population, its incorporation into nationalistic mythology was more complete. There was no contradiction with the fact that the origin of the game was American, or that the activity, per se, was of no particular value and carried little social prestige. To begin with, there was already such historical depth to Cuban baseball—fifty years—that it was easy to construct a mythology leading from Palmar del Junco and the early ballplayers to recent, still current heroes such as Méndez, Luque, and Miguel Angel. There were frequent veterans' games in the twenties, involving players who had performed in the previous century and who were charmingly, and significantly, called "Habana's Relics" and "Almendares' Relics." Newspapers such as *Diario de la Marina* also had features on nineteenth-century baseball and the origins of the game in the island.

In matters of modern games and music the question of origins is rendered moot or ignored altogether at the level of everyday practice. The English origins of baseball in rounders or cricket present no problem to Americans, for instance, as they mythologize about baseball and their nation. In Cuba the same situation obtained, though the analogy is somewhat strained because the relationship between the United States and England is different from that between the United States and Cuba. To Cubans in the twenties, Americans had their baseball and Cubans theirs, and while the American game was superior because of the disparity in population size between the two countries, it was not necessarily so in quality of play or in the kind of spectacle it had become. Like Cuban music, Cuban baseball had a brand of its own, which, while partly supported by American money, remained independent. This theory became populist cant exploited by politicians and ideologues, who extolled the social leveling of the game, as well as its affirmation of Cuba's modernity and ability to compete with the best the United States had to offer.

The mythical quality of the game's influence as a social leveler, which harks back to the previous century, is evident in that a magazine such as *Social,* aimed at the rich and with contributors such as Alejo Carpentier, chronicled the arrival of Luque and Miguel Angel González from the United States, but never Torriente's or Méndez's. Luque looks uncomfortable in his suit and fedora; Miguel Angel, even with his big ears protruding, appears more comfortable in his conservative ensemble. Joe Massaguer, publisher of *Havana: The Magazine of Cuba*, crows in the January 1, 1929, inaugural issue that "In the realm of sports our little island has produced some great athletes, well known in all sporting circles. Every fan of our 'national game' knows the names of Acosta, Calvo, González, Marsans, and Luque, the 'deliverer' of the Cincinnati Reds. Sportswriters remember the Sola brothers of Yale. . . ." (p. 40).[22] Every single ballplayer in this list was a white Cuban major leaguer. The memory of the "national game" at this level, at least, did not include Strike, Bombín, or The Black Diamond, not to mention black stars of the day such as Chacón, Mesa, Oms, or Dihigo.

And yet they all continued to play together at Almendares Park and elsewhere in Cuba, in contrast to the United States, where apartheid not only prevailed in the social sphere but also on the field of play. There was in Cuba, after all, a kind of leveling, for in some realms there was a place where those players who ascended converged in the national mythology regardless of color. Cuban baseball was different from the American game and had a distinctive Cuban inflection, like Cuban music. Part of that inflection was a greater tolerance of racial differences, a tolerance that spread to the white Americans who participated as players or spectators, even if bracketed in time and space by their stay in Cuba. But like all nationalisms, fables about the pan-Cubanness of baseball hid many contradictions, the most flagrant being the exclusion of blacks from amateur competition and therefore from national teams, which will be seen in the next chapter.

As if to emphasize the blend as well as the distinctiveness of Cuban and American baseball, but mostly to capitalize on the appeal of games pitting teams from the two countries, the Cuban League decided to include an American team in the 1920–21 season. Once McGraw's Giants were gone, the Bacharach Giants, a team from the Negro circuits, disembarked in Havana to play in the Cuban League. It was like importing a whole jazz band (which was done), and it showed the wealthy status of the Cuban League when an entire team could be brought to Havana for a whole season. But, as in the case of the Babe's visit, things did not quite work out as planned.

The Giants were a top independent team from the East. They were based in Atlantic City, New Jersey, and had taken their name from the city's mayor. Their opponents in Cuba would be the "eternal rivals" Habana and Almendares. This year the Giants would be the solution to the problem of finding a third team to captivate the fans' interest. The league magnates hoped that their presence would bring fans to Almendares Park even when the "eternal rivals" were not playing each other, if only because of the nationalistic appeal of a contest involving an American and a Cuban team. These Giants came loaded with American talent from the Negro circuits: Harry Clark, Red Ryan, Oscar Charleston, Joe Hewitt, Louis

Santop, Charles Blackwell, Dick Lundy, Phil Cockrell, Jesse (Pud) Flournoy, and Cannonball Redding. They also added some Cuban players, such as Agustín Parpetti, Rogelio Valdés, and Tatica Campos. The Blues and the Reds were ready, too. Almendares fielded Bernardo Baró, Bartolo Portuondo, Baldomero (Merito) Acosta, Pelayo Chacón, Cristóbal Torriente, Ramón (Papo) Herrera, Marcelino Guerra, Eufemio Abreu, Emilio Palmero, Cheo Hernández, José de la Caridad Méndez, back after arm miseries that had kept him out of the league, Adolfo Luque at the top of his form, and Julián (Recurbón) Terán. This was a formidable squad. Habana had Miguel Angel, Oscar Tuero, Pata Jorobá Jiménez, Jacinto Calvo, Manuel Cueto, Rafael Almeida, Joseíto Rodríguez, Ricardo Torres, José (Acostica) Acosta, José López, Fidel Hungo, and Roy Ford. The Reds were no patsies either.

The Bacharach Giants did not fare well. They won only four games and lost eleven in the first round, finishing last. Almendares came in first at 9 and 2 and Habana second at 6 and 5. The famous Redding lost four and won only two. Almendares bombed him on December 12. Habana had blasted Ryan on the fourth. On December 26 an altercation in a game between Habana and Almendares led to the game being called after "the public became scandalized by the disrespectful attitude assumed by the Blues' players" (Díez Muro, 196). Worse trouble came on January 13, when the league dropped the Giants because their representative informed them that most of their players had returned to the United States, and the team was left without pitchers. The championship would have to be finished by Habana and Almendares once again.

While these developments must have been a setback for the league, in truth the absence of the Giants cleared the way for a protracted series of dramatic games between the "eternal rivals." Habana won the second round, and a three-game playoff between the two teams was set for February 12–14. Almendares won the first but lost the last two, giving Habana the flag. Almendares' Pelayo Chacón was the batting champion. Luque won six and lost four, while The Black Diamond won three and lost none. He was obviously not capable of pitching in as many games as before but could still win.

In 1921 the baseball season was again the victim of economics and politics. The price of sugar dropped precipitously after reaching unheard-of heights the previous year, causing several banks to go under. The bank crash was accompanied by the election of Alfredo Zayas, García Menocal's handpicked successor, in hotly contested voting of questionable fairness. All this led to a de facto intervention by the United States, when General Enoch Crowder was sent to Cuba to dictate policy from the battleship *Minnesota,* moored in the port of Havana. The Cuban League fielded only two teams in the fall of 1921—Habana and Almendares—and the season lasted only five games. Habana won, at 4 and 1. But baseball would make a comeback, as the sugar prices stabilized and American tourists, protected by their navy, continued to flock to Cuba.

What follows shows to what degree baseball had spread to the provinces and the need perceived by Cuban baseball entrepreneurs to cash in on that popularity. In 1922–23 the league added one more Havana-area team, Marianao, representing the municipality west of the city where Oriental Park stood, and one from Santa Clara, the capital of Las Villas Province, in the center of the island. Marianao would appear, disappear, and reappear several times in the Cuban League and was part of it at its demise after the 1959 revolution. Santa Clara had an intermittent life, but one punctuated by moments of great splendor.

By this time Abel Linares controlled the league because he owned the Reds and the Blues, so he sent his right-hand man, former player Tinti Molina, who ran the Cuban Stars (West), to organize the Santa Clara team. With his contacts with Negro Leagues baseball in the United States, Molina was able to assemble quite a squad, which would play at La Boulanger Park, named apparently after the original owner of the land (at one point the field was also named after Trinidad y Hermanos, a tobacco company that may have owned it). It was a small stadium of limited capacity, probably fewer than three thousand (*Diario de la Marina,* on October 5, 1923, reports a near-capacity crowd at 2,343), but then Santa Clara, a quaint provincial capital, was no Havana. Molina and the league, aware of this, scheduled home games only during the weekends, hoping to draw fans from the entire province of Las Villas, also known as Santa Clara, after its capital city. This was an effort to bank on a regional loyalty, as teams in California, Minnesota, and Florida were to do years later in the United States.

From the States, Molina hired pitchers Bill Holland, Dave Brown, and J. Branahan, infielders Jack Marshall, Frank Warfield, and Oliver Marcelle, and outfielder Oscar Charleston. With Charleston, Gentleman Oms, and Champion Mesa, Molina put together an outfield the likes of which had never been seen in Cuba. There is a magnificent photo of all three wearing the Santa Clara pinstripes. Molina also had veteran Bombín Pedroso to add to his staff; capable Julio Rojo, a budding leader behind the plate; and Manolo Parrado, Kakín González, and Matías Ríos in the infield. Charleston was a favorite in Cuba and a superstar in the United States, and Holland, Brown, Warfield, and Marcelle were star-quality players from the Negro Leagues. Holland would also become a Cuban favorite, pitching for four years on the island.

The league magnates were also banking on the depth of baseball activity in Las Villas Province, and the Santa Clara team had a hometown flavor thanks to local heroes Alejandro Oms, a native of Santa Clara itself, Champion Mesa, who was from nearby Caibarién, and Julio Rojo, from neighboring Sagua la Grande. The impresarios had engaged the support of local dignitaries and the well-to-do, such as Isidro Clua, Pedro Bermúdez, Dr. Ramón Lorenzo, and Dr. Eudaldo Gómez. Linares and Molina hoped that the team would benefit from provincial pride as well as anticapital (Havana) sentiment. This is probably the reason why Santa Clara, in addition to the Leopardos, also came to be known as Los Pilongos, meaning The Townies or The Locals. Pilongos are those who have been baptized in the same baptismal font, meaning in the same parish church (*pilongo* is derived from *pila*, as in *pila bautismal*). There is no small amount of irony in all this, given that at its best the Santa Clara team often fielded only two Cubans: Oms and Mesa.

Still, there had been in the 1920–21 winter a Santa Clara team that had won a regional championship, obviously professional with players drawn from sugarmill clubs as well as amateur. Towns in the vicinity, Camajuaní, Caibarién, and Esperanza, participated. This early Santa Clara team won with three Oms brothers in the lineup: Tito, who played first, Alejandro in right, and Eleuterio on the mound (there was also Pedro, a team mascot, obviously too young to play). By 1920 Alejandro was an accomplished professional who toured the United States in the summer with the Cuban Stars, as did the team's shortstop, Julián Fabelo. Many of the players on the 1920–21 Santa Clara team had performed even earlier with a local team named Tosca, a throwback to the belle époque, when some baseball clubs had the names of operas. A local candymaker known as "Libis" sold baseball cards of this Santa Clara team, offering prizes to those who completed their albums. The team also had its own *charanga* (musical cheering group), a custom that was to linger well into the fifties. The city of Santa Clara boasted the best batmaker in Cuba, a lathe operator named Noel Pegudo, who was much sought after by all baseball players, according to Emilio de Armas. It was with these favorable circumstances in mind that Linares and Molina planned to exploit the Santa Clara market in the 1922–23 season.

Marianao, which eventually won the championship, was loaded with Cuban talent, including their player-manager, Merito Acosta (who, conveniently, was the son and namesake of Marianao's mayor), Pelayo Chacón, who hit over .300, at short, and José María Fernández, who also reached that mark, behind the plate, with Lucas Boada, Juanelo Mirabal, and Emilio Palmero on the mound. Miguel Angel had procured Luque for his Habana Reds this year, along with Torriente, Jacinto Calvo, Eusebio González, rookies Armando López, Rafael Quintana, and H. Pareda. Almendares fielded a team with recognized native stars such as Marsans, Baró, Valentín Dreke, Oscar Levis (a Panamanian by birth), Eugenio Morín, José (Cheo) Ramos, Portuondo, José and Oscar Rodríguez, and Isidro Fabré. A glaring dearth of Americans on teams other than Santa Clara invites speculation that the league was still banking on the nationalistic angle. However, as was then already common, imports such as Lloyd (Habana) were added once the season was in progress to shore up weak spots on a team. By January the Leopardos were leading the league, but only 2½ games separated them from the fourth-place team. Then a dispute over a forfeited game, in which Molina's team was declared the loser, led to the decision to drop Santa Clara from the championship. It is difficult to fathom how this came about or the real reason behind it. Was it disappointing attendance in the provincial park, together with travel and lodging costs? The result was that the three Havana-based teams finished the season, with Marianao winning the flag in its first year in the league in a dramatic victory (by Lucas Boada) over Habana on the last day of the season.

Before the 1923–24 season began, two important events took place. One was the Copa *El Mundo*, in which only the three Havana-based teams participated and that was played during the early days of October. Some Santa Clara players, such as Oms, played for these teams because the provincial squad was not ready and the series was too brief to have it travel to the capital. The other event was more telling: the reception of Luque and the public celebration of his remarkable season in the National League. This was an elaborate affair, a pageant of nationalism, and a striking example of how baseball was fast becoming a crucial component in the constitution of the nation as a set of beliefs and practices (almost a liturgy).

Guillermo Pi, writing in the *Diario de la Marina* of October 1, 1923, intones a paean to the pitcher who, representing the entire Cuban nation and fighting for its mere 3 million, bested all the athletes of the United States, who represented 110 million. His feat, according to Pi, made the American throngs in major-league parks aware that the island of Cuba was on the map of baseball and "on the first row" (giddy with emotion, Pi mixed metaphors). He goes on to liken Luque's lofty position to those of chess grandmaster Raúl Capablanca and world fencing champion Ramón Fonst. This is the reason why the multitudes should congregate to receive this true *criollo*, this humble representative of the Cuban people, upon his return in triumph from Cincinnati. But this reception would not be a disorderly mob, but unfold according to strict rules and be perfectly choreographed. The first rule to be observed was that no political banners would be allowed, as this was a celebration above the fray of politics (this shows, of course, to what degree it was not). Pi's nationalistic nirvana, an ideal that would bind all Cubans beyond all differences, must be quoted:

We shall depart tomorrow from in front of the offices of the DIARIO in the strictest order, each in the place corresponding to his association: the army, the police, plain citizens, from the highest to the lowest ranked, from the most distinguished to the most humble, from the richest to the poorest, all equals, all embraced by the same feelings of affection, by the same purpose: to glorify a Cuban before his glory can fade; to show our gratitude for the noble, imponderable achievement that he has made in the powerful and fraternal Yankeeland.

Among those marching would be Luque's old artillery division, the navy's band, popular music ensembles, groups of professional, semipro, and amateur baseball players, a float with a playing organ advertising Candado soap, members of the Havana fire department, and fans in general. Dr. Ramón Zaydín, a member of the House of Representatives, famous for his oratory, who had just obtained credit to build the University of Havana Stadium, would deliver a speech. Abel Linares would be among the dignitaries marching at the head of the parade as it proceeded from Prado Boulevard to the docks. Thirty thousand people attended, and all went according to plan.

This was an exceptional display of the interaction between nationalism and sports. It was almost as if Luque were being celebrated for having created Cuba in the consciousness of the United States, and feted for defending the fatherland, as if he had been a soldier in battle. The sense of nationality in modern Cuba was built in contrast and opposition to the United States. The presence of the army and police at this pageant could not be more telling: The state's forces that preserved order honored Luque as one of their own. His physical and moral sacrifice was akin to theirs and legitimized their mission. Luque embodied the order of the state, which is above all forces and privileges. Over the years, and up to the present, when Omar Linares, a slugger on the Cuban national team, was regaled with a similar ceremony in his native province of Pinar del Río for his exploits in the 1996 Olympics, baseball would provide the occasion for pageants of national solidarity transcending and abolishing all discord and strife. Luque was hardly an angel, as we know: He was an ill-tempered, combative professional who went with the money and was likely to throw one in your ear or even to shoot you. Papá Montero drank, enjoyed cock fighting, and was a ladies' man. But none of that mattered. He was a hero of the nation for having attained glory in the United States, surpassing its greatest athletes. He was The Pride of Havana.

The next day, as if to show the true feelings behind the pageant, and in a more appropriate space, a show featured Luque at the Martí Theater performing in a skit that reenacted his attack on Casey Stengel, who had yelled racial slurs at him in Cincinnati. The incident was dramatized and made more intelligible to the public by making the insult be about Luque's mother (*pace* Roberto Alomar), by featuring Stengel as a giant (he *was* a member of the Giants), and by incorporating a popular actor from the burlesque Alahambra Theater, "El Negrito Acebal," who played the role of the umpire in the faked fracas.[23] This burlesque display of popular Cuban nationalism showed that its deepest sources were in areas of the national soul closer to more elemental drives than Pi's high-flown appeals to patriotic ideals. The contrast between the pageant and the show also highlights the split between the true nature of sport as an activity fostering solidarity, and its translation into political ideology. Luque was a macho Cuban who beat the hell out of an American who insulted him (probably by calling him a Cuban nigger), and the whole thing was celebrated with laughter and merriment in a carnival atmosphere in which racial strife was trivialized by the mediating "black" umpire, who obviously upheld no rules of proper conduct. Here was Papá Montero, a white Cuban with the nickname of an Afro-Cuban rumba dancer and pimp, beating an American white, while the "authority" to stop him is invested in a white Cuban disguised as a black. Only in this carnivalesque sphere, where greed, lust, and other appetites prevailed, could social and racial distinctions really be abandoned, not in the vapid speeches of dignitaries or the regimented patriotic parade staged on the streets of Havana. As if to make this event even more emblematic and at the same time more deeply ironic, it took place in a theater named after the hero of Cuban independence, José Martí.

The enthusiasm spilled over to Almendares Park, where the Copa *El Mundo* was played before what were then record gates. On Saturday, October 6, Habana and Almendares played in front of 12,500 people, and on Sunday, 14,000. The take was $3,656 for the first game and $4,431 for the second. Tickets were 50 cents for a glorieta seat, $2.00 for a box with four chairs, and the bleachers (sol) 20 cents. Fans were on the field, with mounted police on the premises to maintain order and ropes to keep them out of the action. Abel Linares promised to build new bleachers at once. Almendares was managed by first baseman Joseíto Rodríguez, while Luque himself, taking over for Miguel Angel, who had gone to Matanzas to organize another championship, managed and pitched for the Reds.

The 1923–24 season has gone down in Cuban baseball lore because of the prowess of the Santa Clara Leopardos. Despite this fact, the season would prove again that it was difficult to make professional baseball of the highest caliber pay beyond the capital area. This in spite of the increasing popularity of sports and the willingness of Cubans to invest in them. In *The Cuba Review* of June 1923 (vol. 21, no. 7, p. 53) it is reported that "The demand for American sporting goods was on the increase. Baseball, tennis, football, and basketball supplies are the chief articles called for." But the cost of having professional teams travel to the center of the island and be lodged there for a weekend series in a very small park was too much, even when that team proved to be a runaway winner, or precisely because of it. Another factor was the predominance of soccer in the capital, with many teams supported by Spanish regional clubs (the soccer squads had names such as Juventud Asturiana, Vigo, and Iberia, with Cuban social clubs such as Fortuna thrown in). Soccer, with imported players being paid as much as or more than those in baseball, got the better time slots for Almendares Park, forcing the Cuban League to schedule its Sunday games at ten in the morning, clearly not a good time anywhere. Even in Santa Clara, where presumably there would not be pressure from soccer, the league scheduled split doubleheaders on Sunday, clearly to charge two separate admissions. The Sunday games in both Havana and Santa Clara were disastrous from a financial point of view and again doomed the experiment of Cuban League provincial baseball.

In a fit of nationalism and xenophobia, soccer came to be known derisively in Cuba at the time as *la patada gallega* (the Galician kick). The term underscores what to a Cuban seemed typical of the uncouth Spaniards who continued to pour onto the island: a kick, a brutish, gross gesture compared to the stylized moves of baseball. There must also have been resentment against these immigrants who had the economic clout to rent Almendares Park during the choice hour of Sunday afternoon. Soccer was a competitive spectacle that posed a challenge to baseball's hegemony. This situation continued during the thirties at La Tropical stadium.

Given the 1922–23 debacle, Linares and Molina decided to load up Santa Clara to such an extent that the season would not wind up again as a contest between the "eternal rivals." The Leopardos were a Negro Leagues all-star team with a few Cuban luminaries, also from the Negro Leagues, added for good measure. Tinti Molina managed this team, which would have won in any league. Some players returned from the previous season. His pitching staff was anchored by lefty Dave Brown; Reuben Currie, a right-hander; Jesse Winters, a lefty with control problems; Bill Holland, a superb right-hander; and fading Cuban stars Méndez and Pedroso (both could play other positions, and Bombín was a feared hitter). Santa Clara also had right-hander Pedro Dibut, who had played in the Negro circuits with the Cuban Stars (West), and later with the Cincinnati Reds of the National League (one of several white Cubans who played in the Negro circuits and Organized Baseball). The infield had Frank Warfield at second, Oliver Marcelle at third, and Dobie Moore at short. These were all frontline Negro Leagues players, particularly Marcelle, a sensation in Cuba. First base was played by three different men: Oscar Johnson, of the Kansas City Monarchs, who did not pan out; later Eddie Douglass, of the Brooklyn Royal Giants, who was spectacular; and occasionally Julio Rojo, the switch-hitting backup catcher. The outfield again had Oscar Charleston flanked by Champion Mesa and Gentleman Oms. The regular catcher was Frank Duncan, one of the greatest receivers in Negro Leagues history. On the bench were powerful Mayarí Montalvo and useful Matías Ríos. Santa Clara had power, defense, pitching, and speed. Champion Mesa, a .300 hitter, was the fastest man from home to first in Cuba.

Because of its winning performance in the Copa *El Mundo*, Almendares was the favorite for the 1923–24 season, even though, on paper, sportswriters could tell that Santa Clara was tough. Managed by Joseíto Rodríguez, the Blues had José María Fernández and Eugenio Morín behind the plate. Morín was a veteran already and could play other positions. Joseíto played first himself. He was considered the best defensive first baseman in Cuba. His brother Oscar, Papo and Kakín González, Papo Herrera, and Manuel Cueto were the other infielders. In the outfield he had Dreke, Baró and Ramos, plus the now veterans Almeida and Marsans. The pitchers were

Cubans Boada, hero of the previous season with Marianao, Fabré, Tuero, Americans major leaguers Oscar Fuhr and Frank (Jakie) May, minor-leaguer Eddy (Musiú) Lepard, and Negro Leagues standout Jess Hubbard. Almendares had a steady nucleus of players who returned to the club, with Joseíto several years in a row.

Luque, now managing Habana, had with him on the staff Levis, Mirabal, and Acostica, pitching to veteran receiver Abreu and American import John Bischoff (whose name sounded like *bicho* to Cubans, which means bug, but also someone who is clever). The Reds' infield had veteran Lloyd, already probably in his fifties, playing at first, with Chacón, Portuondo, and rookie Rafael Quintana. Once the season started, however, Habana imported slugging left-handed first baseman Edgar Wesley and sent aging Lloyd back to his position at short. Chacón had to play second. The outfield was anchored by Torriente, with outstanding Clint Thomas of the Detroit Stars in the Negro circuits, admired in Cuba for his hitting and great agility in center. There was also Marcelino Guerra, and veteran catcher-outfielder Mack Eggleston, whose name gave fits to the Cuban press and headaches to me trying to identify him: Eggleton, Ennglington, etc. Merito Acosta, looking to repeat, had hardly any Cubans on his Marianao squad (called the Elephants at the time) other than himself. They were Jacinto Calvo, José (Pepín) Pérez, Rogelio Crespo, Emilio Palmero, Cristóbal Torriente, and Luis (Lico) Mederos. The white Americans could be from the Louisville team, where Merito had found his niche. A Ryan who could be right-hander Patrick (Rosy) Ryan, a middling major leaguer. There also were Joe DeBerry, another right-hander and former major leaguer; Jesse Petty, a lefty who would have three or four good years with Brooklyn in the National League; another lefty, Elmer (Slim) Love, who had a lackluster career in the American League; and right-hander Walter (Ed) Morris, who had a few mediocre seasons with the Boston Braves. John (Bull) Henry, a former major leaguer, was at first. Another infielder was an E. Brown, who is anybody's guess, but mine is that he was Eddie Brown, a somewhat marginal major leaguer though a good hitter, because he fits the profile of several Marianao imports who were modest major leaguers on the way up or down, probably with Louisville, or in the American Association, where Merito had scouted them. Art Phelan, another former veteran major leaguer, was in the infield, with Calvo, Crespo, and Pérez. Once the season began, Marianao added Charles (Chuck) Dressen, of major-league fame, then an infielder with the Cincinnati Reds but whose accomplishments were mostly as a manager, and future outstanding major-league pitcher Freddie Fitzsimmons. The catcher was veteran major leaguer Ernie Krueger, of modest accomplishments mostly in the National League. Marianao, with the exception of Crespo, Torriente, and utility Pérez, was made up mostly of white Cuban and American players.

These teams were not cannon fodder for the Leopardos, and once the season started, other players were brought in to beef them up. But to no avail. Santa Clara won the first five games; by November 29 they were 13 and 5, by December 14, 21 and 7, and a week later, 23 and 8, leading the league in hitting with a collective .324. On Christmas Day they got twenty hits against Marianao, prevailing, 11–7, in a slugfest. By year's end they were 29 and 10, for a .744 average, and every regular (even Rojo) but Warfield, who was at .286, was over .300. The most interesting competition was against Habana, 21–20 on January 3, 1924, and led by Luque, who was having a great season on the mound and at the plate. The brash Papá Montero would not hit ninth when he was pitching, occasionally played third base, and pinch hit often. On November 28 he had been at .395 and by January 3 had seven victories and two defeats as a pitcher. Two of his victories had been against Santa Clara, a team that also had defeated him. When Papá Montero showed up in Santa Clara with his Reds, La Boulanger Park filled beyond capacity, and the authorities had to prohibit crowds above a certain number (to the irritation of fans who had traveled to the provincial capital for the game). But such crowds did not materialize often and particularly on Sunday mornings the attendance was low. Santa Clara was not drawing as much as was hoped in the nation's capital either, where the Almendares-Habana rivalry still prevailed, and was dampened only by the Leopardos' massacre of the Havana teams. This in spite of the fact that glorious veteran Méndez had a couple of superb outings, relying on guile, while favorites Oms and Mesa were burning up the league. Other favored players, such as Charleston, Marcelle, Holland, and Moore, were also shining bright. However, as there was no real contest, the fans began to stay away from the parks, and the league decided to take measures.

They simply declared the season over on January 16, with Santa Clara (36–11) the winner, divided the spoils, and decided to call for a new, brief championship, to be called Gran Premio (Grand Prix). The reason given, which became part of the mythology of Santa Clara's prowess, was that a humanitarian halt had to be called to the carnage; a technical knockout in favor of the titans from the provinces was declared. It is more likely that the reason for ending the season abruptly was, of course, money. The smaller crowds called for a drastic solution, and it was found. The new championship would be played with only three clubs: Habana and Almendares, reinforced with the best of Marianao, which would dissolve, and Santa Clara. All games would take place in Havana, at Almendares Park. When the mayor of the champions' city begged to have some contests of the new tournament played at La Boulanger Park, he was politely told that with a three-team league it would be impossible. What would the idle team do while the other two traveled to the provinces? It is clear that if La Boulanger Park's capacity had been larger, and had there been huge crowds as expected, the answer would have been different. The Santa Clara fans and authorities had to be content with a banquet to celebrate the achievements of their superb team, immortalized in another set of baseball cards put out by the Compañía Cigarrera Díaz, a Havana tobacco company.[24]

Oliver Marcelle was the batting champion, and Luque's performance was truly remarkable. He managed his team to a second-place finish, had a 7 and 6 record as a pitcher, and hit .390. He only had forty-one times at bat, but it was still quite a feat. With twenty-seven wins in the summer, Luque's seven in the winter added up to an incredible thirty-four for the year. He had also hit a respectable (for a pitcher) .209 in 104 times at bat in the National League.

The Gran Premio was a success, although Santa Clara won that, too, but by just one game, against 11½ in the "regular" season. Luque and Joscíto bickered over the terms of player reshuffling; both wanted Dressen. "Chiquitico" (Tiny) was finally awarded to the Blues, along with pitchers Petty and Palmero and catcher Krueger, while Luque got Fitzsimmons, Baró, and Cueto. Fans streamed back to Almendares Park as they had in the fall. Torriente, now playing for Almendares, won the batting championship, but the hero of the Gran Premio was Valentín Dreke, who played an inspired center field for the Blues and who scored the most runs and tied for the lead in stolen bases.

Yet the irregular ending of the season, the merciless disbandment of Marianao, and the abandonment of Santa Clara as a site for games showed that the Cuban League was having trouble. The criticisms leveled earlier about how the whole thing seemed like a prearranged contest, not a real competition, surfaced again. Players continued to be switched from one team to another, with an overriding concern for profit that pushed aside any notion of fairness. Linares was hailed by some but criticized by others. One such critic was Alberto Barreras, governor of Havana Province and president of the amateur baseball league (Unión Atlética), who wrote to Guillermo Pi, sportswriter for *Diario de la Marina* (November 25, 1923), complaining about the overwhelming number of American players in the Cuban League. Such uneasiness is not surprising coming from a politician who already understood baseball to be the Cuban national game. If the pageant orchestrated to receive Luque was to have any meaning, then the players in the Cuban League must be predominantly Cuban. Pi printed Barreras' comments, but answered that he felt Cuban fans wanted to see the best baseball possible, regardless of where the players came from, adding that when they went to the opera they would not care for the nationality of the diva Tetrazzini, but for how well she sang. By making this connection, Pi showed that he understood baseball to be a spectacle. But opera was no national game, one could have countered, underlining the contradiction between nationalistic mythologizing and the show-business nature of baseball.

But the negative consequences of having a high number of American players were real for many Cubans who found themselves left out of the top-ranked teams. Some, led by Miguel Angel González, went to Matanzas and organized an all-Cuban professional tournament at the Palmar del Junco. It was a dissident league that protested Linares' monopoly of the spectacle. Miguel Angel's defection was no small matter, though the reason for his absence may have also been because of a larger, burgeoning monopoly: the majors. Commissioner Landis had forbidden players from "barnstorming" after the first week of November, and Cuban baseball could fall under the ban. In fact, toward the end of the regular Cuban League season there had been stories to the effect that Landis had been apprised that Luque was playing in Cuba and intended to reprimand or suspend him. Nothing came of this in part because the judge was apparently unable to obtain hard information on the matter. But the stage was set for a confrontation. It seems to me, however, that Miguel Angel went to Matanzas mostly because he was uncomfortable with the way Linares was running the league. The magnate owned Habana, Almendares, *and* Santa Clara.

The Matanzas championship, which was made up of many Cuban minor leaguers, had one unique distinction. It featured none other than Martín Dihigo, who had played third briefly the year before with Habana in the Cuban League under Miguel Angel but who was not picked up in 1923. Was the youngster in Matanzas in solidarity with his manager, or was his manager trying to protect the phenom from Linares' reach? Dihigo was already playing for Alejandro Pompez's Cuban Stars (East), managed by Pelayo Chacón. With Dihigo's being black, there was only so much Miguel Angel could do to hold him; he could not take him with him to the Giants. Be that as it may, Dihigo, a native son, was the drawing card in Matanzas, where his precocious abilities must have been very well known. In one memorable game, on November 7, 1923, against nearby Cárdenas, the eighteen-year-old Dihigo pitched to major-league veteran Miguel Angel González, quite a battery. They won, 5–2, with Miguel Angel batting third and his child prodigy fifth. Cárdenas scored on only two hits because the youngster was wild and gave up a few bases on balls. Dihigo would mature into what many consider to have been the greatest baseball player of all time, regardless of nationality.[25] He is the only Cuban to date in Cooperstown.

Martín Magdaleno Dihigo Llanos was born in the sugarmill Jesús María (town of Cidra), in the province of Matanzas (where else?), on May 25, 1906. When he was around three the family moved to the Pueblo Nuevo neighborhood, in Matanzas proper, a couple of blocks away from the Palmar del Junco. Little is known about his childhood and adolescence, but it is clear that he began playing baseball very early, for by the time he was sixteen he had been signed by the professionals. Dihigo was a tall man for the period, about six-three, and played at around two hundred pounds when he filled out. He was relatively slender when he was young, but very powerful. Those who played with Dihigo or who saw him play say that he had it all: coordination, speed, power, arm, good hands, batting eye, intelligence, and poise. But he had something else difficult to describe, an intangible trait associated more with bullfighting, a sport in which there are no numerical records to evaluate an individual: He had grace. His blend of style, dignity, and elegance was apparently unique. Fausto Miranda told me that once he took a friend to see Dihigo at La Tropical stadium for the first time and the friend asked him to point out Dihigo to him when they got there. But Miranda said no, that his friend would be able to spot him just by the way he moved. And his friend did. Dihigo's demeanor and style, which I imagine to have been like Roberto Clemente's, are qualities much appreciated by Latin American fans.

Dihigo also had leadership qualities, was personable, well-spoken, and had a sense of humor. With the years Dihigo developed into a sharp dresser who wore his suits well. In short, like his fellow *matancero* Méndez, he had class. He eventually became a successful manager and the first Cuban ballplayer to become a sportscaster after retiring. Dihigo was also endowed with a social and political conscience: He supported and aided his fellow players, and took a position favorable to the Cuban Revolution in its early years. He was rewarded with a position in the ministry of sports and was buried a hero when he passed away in Cienfuegos, on May 20 1971. His son, a sportswriter, is still in Cuba.

But the most remarkable trait Dihigo had as a baseball player was his uncanny versatility. This was a quality developed by economic necessity in independent baseball, particularly the Negro Leagues, as noted. It was costly to carry a large roster, so players, especially pitchers, could usually play first or the outfield. Some of them were feared hitters. And there were some outstanding cases, such as Ted (Double Duty) Radcliffe, who could catch and pitch. In Dihigo's case, however, the wisdom is that he could play *every* position like a star. Apparently such was his coordination and intelligence that he learned to pivot with the best at second base (his initial position on the Cuban Stars), call games from behind the plate with Miguel Angel's shrewdness, and make all the plays in center field. He could also hum it from the mound and threw a vicious curve from a three-quarters angle that gave jelly legs to right-handed hitters. Eventually, as he grew older, Dihigo concentrated on pitching and had outstanding seasons in Cuba, the Negro Leagues, and Mexico. He was batting champion and leading pitcher in the same season twice, once in Cuba and another in Mexico. In 1935–36, with Santa Clara, he hit .357 while posting a 12 and 4 record as a pitcher. He also managed this team, which actually won the pennant. The next year he moved to Marianao, hit .323, and was 14 and 10 on the mound. He again managed and won. In the summer of 1938, in Mexico, he was 18 and 2 on the mound, was champion pitcher and won the batting championship with an average of .387. The tenth edition of *The Baseball Encyclopedia,* which contains what records could be gathered from the Negro Leagues, gives Dihigo a lifetime average as a hitter of .319, with 62 home runs in twelve years of play in the United States. As a pitcher, it credits him with a 27 and 21 overall record. The *Enciclopedia del béisbol mexicano* indicate a .317 average and 55 homers in eleven years, and a 119 and 57 pitching record, with a 2.84 ERA. In Cuba, according to Alfredo Santana Alonso's *El Inmortal del Béisbol,* he was 106 and 57 as a pitcher in twenty-three years and finished with a .295 batting average with twenty homers. But the Negro League records are most probably incomplete. Santana Alonso writes about early seasons with the Cuban Stars when Dihigo won fifteen games that do not appear in the reference works mentioned. Whereas the record, as it stands, yields 252 victories and 135 defeats as a pitcher, Santana Alonso speculates that the total victories surpass 350. These are approximate figures, which do not include Dihigo's records in Venezuela, the Dominican Republic, Puerto Rico, and independent professional baseball in Cuba, including sugarmill tournaments that sometimes featured stars from the Negro Leagues and the Cuban League. It does not matter. Dihigo's consummate mastery of the game was something that could not be quantified. He seemed to belong in a league of his own in everything he did.

The following year Miguel Angel was back in the Cuban League with his pupil Dihigo. But the 1924–25 season was another failure, this time because Almendares, with Luque back pitching (and Joseíto Rodríguez as manager), raced 8½ games ahead of its nearest competitor in early January. Santa Clara again proved a financial disappointment, so the league moved the team to Matanzas' Palmar del Junco on January 11. By the end of the month the league declared Almendares champion and canceled the remaining games. Marianao was back in the league, with Palmero, Merito, Krueger, pitcher Ben Tincup, a marginal major leaguer, and Dressen again. Habana had Miguel Angel, Dihigo, Chacón, Torriente, and Levis. Santa Clara still had Oms, but Charleston had moved to Almendares, who also had Lloyd this time around. Dihigo hit only.276. The batting champion was Almendares' Manuel Cueto. The quest for a third team and for expansion to the provinces continued to vex Linares. In 1925–26 the third team was called San José, but on December 22 it folded, and by the end of January the league had to terminate the season early once again. The reason given this time was excess rain. Manuel Cueto, batting champion the year before, had left earlier for a championship in Oriente Province, where he was reported to be earning good money without regard for "dividends" (*Carteles,* December 20, 1925), a dig at Linares' league and its cooperative system.[26] In 1926–27 the third team was called Cuba and was loaded with Dihigo, Crespo, Portuondo, Oms, Mesa, and Fabré, while Cienfuegos, The Pearl of the South in Santa Clara Province, entered the league for the first time. All the teams played at Almendares Park in Havana.

Both natural and man-made disasters beset the league this time. Trouble arose when Miguel Angel and Luque moved to the new University of Havana Stadium to form a league of their own, called Campeonato Triangular. Just built, the Stadium Universitario had a large grandstand of steel and cement sitting against the side of the hill where the University of Havana stands (the *colina universitaria*). The grandstand ran along one side of the running track, which had inside a soccer or American football field and the baseball diamond. The grandstand was (and is) parallel to the first base line. Both dugouts were on the same side, as in old Almendares Park. Temporary bleachers could be built along the third-base line. Outfield dimensions were enormous. The three teams were called Marianao (managed by Chacón), Alacranes, and Leones, the last two using the colors and symbols of the "eternal rivals" but not their city affiliation (Habana and Almendares).[27] Some called the Red Miguel Angel's Leones and the Blue Luque's Alacranes. But the Reds were also sometimes called Havana Reds (in English because Linares had the rights to Habana), and other times Havana Red Sox, and they did have an RS on their caps. Everybody knew that these were the "eternal rivals" in disguise, even if the traditional teams were performing in Almendares Park. Teams under the names of Leones and Alacranes had played for the Copa *El Mundo* in early October, before the seasons at Almendares Park and the University Stadium began. The Leones in that championship were managed by Ricardo Torres, with Pelayo Chacón as captain, and the Alacranes were managed by Pájaro Cabrera and captained by Bartolo Portuondo. The Leones won that series.

I suspect that 1925 was the year when Linares, aided by his son-in-law lawyer, had finagled to obtain exclusive rights to the names of the cities of Havana and Almendares. The rival league, Campeonato Triangular, dipped into the amateur ranks for talent, banking on the popularity of some of those players who performed during the summer in Cuba and had a substantial following. The abundance of talent, as in the case of the Matanzas tournament, was undermining the Cuban League. The Campeonato Triangular was a success and was won by Luque, who was hailed in *Carteles* as "exterminator of the baseball monopoly that Abel Linares attempted to perpetuate in Almendares Park" (February 13, 1927).

To make matters worse for Linares, a vicious hurricane pounded Havana in late October, virtually destroying the new Almendares Park (it would never be the same, though several more seasons were played there). It was quickly rebuilt, on a much smaller scale (with a single deck), and the season continued, but only until January 3. Habana, which won, played only thirty-four games (forty according to another source), while Cienfuegos managed only twelve, having withdrawn from the league.

The end of the decade saw several seasons canceled midway through. There were continued efforts to expand the number of teams and the territorial reach of the Cuban League. Miguel Angel returned to Habana and Luque to Almendares, but they had to play under pseudonyms to evade the vigilance of Commissioner Landis, who had issued an order prohibiting the participation of the two major leaguers in winter baseball. Luque pitched under the name of his chauffeur and crony J. Cabada. He won six and lost one. Miguel Angel played as Alfredo Suárez, a longtime friend and Habana's delegate before the league. He hit .297 and had an outstanding season defensively. It is a greatly savored bit of Cuban baseball lore that several major-league scouts expressed interest in those two outstanding yet unknown players. But the most interesting development was the creation (or better, the revival) of a team named Cuba, which played in 1927–28 and 1928–29. It was clearly a move to profit, again, from the nationalistic angle: How could anyone root against a team named after his or her country? It was understood, of course, that it was not a national team, but a "club" with the name Cuba. The motive was still obvious: to find that elusive third team. Cuba, which was managed by former major leaguer Marsans, was loaded, fielding Chacón (who was captain), Charleston, newcomer Cando López, a fleet outfielder, and Negro Leagues star Willie Foster, a great left-handed pitcher who was a half brother of Rube. This team had a very beautiful and distinctive logo on their jerseys, depicting the Cuban flag in the form of a pennant inside the letter C. There are several pictures of Charleston and Foster in this uniform, which was recently copied by the 1996 Cuban national team. In 1927–28 Cuba, alas, finished last, while Habana won, with Dihigo playing center field and pitching (4 and 2) for the first time in the Cuban League. The next year the team was managed by Luque, with Marsans switching to the helm of Almendares. This time the league again included Cienfuegos, with the team playing home games in that city, at Aída Park (another echo of the belle époque). Cienfuegos had a powerful team, with up-and-coming left-hander Luis Tiant and Negro Leagues stars Mule Suttles, Willie Wells, Cool Papa Bell, and the Kansas City Monarchs' catcher Frank Duncan, of Santa Clara fame, who managed the team. The speedy Cool Papa was known in Cuba as "Guineo." [28] But Habana, led by Oms, who won the batting championship with a .432 average, and Dihigo, who posted a 10–4 record as a pitcher and hit .300, won the championship. Oms had a thirty-game hitting streak broken on December 26, 1928, by lefty Sam Streeter, a star pitcher for the Homestead Grays, playing for Habana. Cuba and Cienfuegos, however, did not make it to the end of the season.

This was probably due to the inadequacy of Aída Park, but also to the market crash and the deteriorating political situation. Machado, who had tampered with the Constitution to remain in power, was opposed by a determined coalition that resorted to terrorism, particularly bombings and attempted assassinations of government officials. There were demonstrations, strife at the university, and an unstable climate in which the army and the police were often guilty of atrocities. Revolutionary fervor gripped the country. The conflict would escalate until August 1933, when Machado was finally toppled. A compromise government was installed, instead of the revolutionaries, due to pressures by the United States through the shrewd diplomacy of Sumner Welles, who was able to dictate policy from the American embassy.

Undeterred, the Cuban League organized a 1929–30 championship that brought back Santa Clara to join nearby Cienfuegos and the "eternal rivals" in competition. The addition of Santa Clara was obviously dictated by the need to make road trips from the capital more profitable for Almendares and Habana and to stir a rivalry between the two cities in Las Villas Province. Santa Clara was the capital, but Cienfuegos was and is a superb and a beautiful port, with a character very much its own. Almendares now had the sensational Dihigo, while Habana again had Luque. Meanwhile, the Leopardos brought back some of the luminaries from the 1923 team: Marcelle, Warfield, and, of course, Oms. Cienfuegos had Wells, Bell, Streeter, Chacón, now managing the team, and Duncan behind the plate, backed up by Sungo Pedroso. But their star turned out to be a black fireballer from Puerto Padre in Oriente Province, Heliodoro (Yoyo) Díaz. The right-hander won thirteen games while losing only three, and was tops in complete games with eleven. Santa Clara added Ramón Bragaña, a youngster destined to have a brilliant career, and the Negro Leagues sensation, Leroy (Satchel) Paige, who did not finish the season. An amorous incident involving a young lady from the provincial mulatto bourgeoisie resulted in charges brought against the pitcher. He quit the island in haste, and remained ever wary of returning, even when the case was dropped.[29] A more public stir was created by Cool Papa, who socked three homers in one game at Aída Park. Cienfuegos won the championship by a good margin, though Santa Clara's Oms again won the batting championship, at .380.

This was the last good season of the Cuban League in some time and, with Cienfuegos' victory, they accomplished the plan of extending interest to the provinces, particularly to the sugar-rich central part of the island. The next season, which began with the same four teams, ended on the last week of October. A *campeonato único* was called with reshuffled teams, including one called Almendarista and a resuscitated Marianao. With Linares' death and the turbulent political situation, the next few seasons reveal a Cuban League in disarray. A team named Regla played in an abbreviated season in 1931–32; the 1932–33 season was played at the Vedado Tennis Club grounds. New stars such as Ramón Bragaña, Rodolfo Fernández, Roberto Estalella, Cocaína García, Luis Tiant, Lázaro Salazar, Silvio García, and the incomparable Dihigo continued to shine. They would make their mark as professional baseball was revived toward the end of the decade. There were also new leaders who emerged: Chacón, who managed the Cuban Stars and in the Cuban League; José María Fernández, who did the same; Julio Rojo; and also, of course, Dihigo. They all would return to play significant roles along with Luque and Miguel Angel. No season could be played in 1933–34 in the wake of the final collapse of Machado's government.

The 1934–35 season saw the Cuban League reach its nadir: Marianao and the "eternal rivals" were crushed by Havana Club, a semipro team from Cárdenas led by new slugging star and future major leaguer Roberto

Estalella, a light mulatto.[30] Rum Havana Club was made by the Arrechabala Company in Cárdenas, which named Ramón Iturrioz its "sports director." Iturrioz, in turn, called on Ramón Couto, a former professional player, to manage the team. Couto assembled the club, which was a typical semipro squad sponsored by a business as part of its advertising campaign. But Couto put together a powerhouse "to the alarm of the patriarchs of Cuban baseball, Miguel Angel González, Adolfo Luque, and Joseíto Rodríguez," wrote Jess Losada in *Carteles* (December 16, 1934). After running through the local opposition, the Havana Club defeated other semipro, sugarmill, and amateur clubs in the provinces. Games against the professional teams in Havana were the only tests left. Marianao, Almendares, and Habana traveled to Cárdenas and lost by scores of 16–2, 11–2, and 16–5! It is true that these Cuban League teams were not those of the Golden Era anymore, and they fielded no American players. But these crushing defeats marked the end of an era.[31]

The Black Diamond had been dead since 1930, as well as Baró, Torriente, Dreke, and Mayarí. Linares' widow leased out the well-known franchises to those who were willing to risk operating them, but with the Depression, business was not good. A new entrepreneur had emerged, Don Julio Blanco Herrera. He owned the Fábrica de Hielo La Tropical, which made beer. He had "donated" to Cuba a stadium in Marianao, built hastily in 1930 for the Second Central American Games and called La Tropical. This became the new venue of the Cuban League, which had finally given up Almendares Park. The park closed in 1932. The grounds filled up with weeds and were eventually reclaimed by the wild until the current bus terminal was built there in the fifties. Baseball would no longer be played with the swaying palm fronds of the Quinta de los Molinos as a backdrop beyond the outfield fence.

Baseball had become completely woven into the fabric of Cuban nationalism as part of a complicated relationship with the United States. On the one hand Cuba had adopted the American penchant for sports as an entertainment and leisure activity. No other Latin American country embraced these practices with as much conviction as Cuba, a factor that would determine the island's disproportionate prowess in sports both before and after the revolution. Cuban players and coaches took the game to neighboring countries such as Mexico and Venezuela from the beginning of the century, in the same way that Cuban instructors would be sent many years later to the Soviet Union, Italy, Spain, and Japan. Belief in the health benefits of sports and their salutary societal and political effects was intertwined with the national mythology in spite of the fact that, as in the United States, games always retained an aura of vice, and the professional games were often sponsored by businesses selling alcoholic beverages and tobacco. Just as brewer barons ran American franchises such as the St. Louis Cardinals (and the Milwaukee team is actually called the Brewers), Cuban teams were sponsored by companies that made rum and beer. Leisure and pleasure commingled in Cuban professional sports, the only significant area where the national ideal of equality came closest to being achieved. Vice and the communal impulse commingled joyfully in the field of play, closest to primal battle.

Cuba rejected the U.S. influence and defined itself by absorbing it. A factor that made this possible was that the game lost its original upper-class affiliation, and was embraced by people throughout the social spectrum. In fact it had competition from other sports only in the upper classes, with the exception of soccer, whose sudden popularity was due to the Spanish immigration already mentioned, and which as a result served to make baseball even more of a nationalist cause. The increasingly popular nature of baseball is evident not only in the mixing of races but even in the players' nicknames, which are typically peasant or low-class in flavor: Papo, Yoyo, Cheo, Paíto, Kiko, Kakín, Chicho, Lico, and so forth.[32] Another factor that made the game become so deeply embedded in the national consciousness is that baseball was intertwined with other forms of physical activity, chiefly music and dance, that sink their roots into ancestral beliefs and practices. These roots were mostly Afro-Cuban, but had invaded white society, particularly at the levels from which ballplayers were drawn. Moreover, the game became a part of collective leisure activities, as it was played above all on weekends and holidays. This was particularly true in the sugarmills, as we shall see. Baseball was associated with physical pleasure such as drinking (liquor and coffee were often sold at the parks), and was profoundly affected by the culture that sugar created. Sugar and tobacco, as Fernando Ortiz famously demonstrated, were the sensual foundations of Cuban culture, and baseball was deeply ingrained in both.

Baseball was associated with these pleasures, or these vices, which, together with betting, gave the game the allure of the forbidden. The carnival atmosphere of a sporting event involves a release from the law, from societal strictures, and an abandonment to pleasure untrammeled by morality or ideology. The consumption of mind-altering substances, the reveling in bodily activity, or the ogling of physical prowess lower or abolish the artificial barriers erected by social and political conventions. The collective nature of the spectacle, its ritualistic core, ground the game farther into the national consciousness and into the infrastructure of daily life. It is this connection of professional baseball with immorality that has vexed, but not deterred, ideologues everywhere in their attempt to integrate the game into national mythmaking.

Though to the historian, the decline of the Cuban League in the late twenties and early thirties is evident, it may not have been perceived as being so catastrophic by the average fan. Nor is it probably viewed as such by those who remember it. The expectation of completed, protracted seasons is more recent and part of the mystique of organized baseball. In the Cuban League during this period, as was the case with the Negro Leagues, each game was a unit sufficient unto itself, a festival, a ritual confrontation in the here-and-now that need not necessarily be seen in the context of a long season. The only comparable example I can think of is the Harvard-Yale yearly showdown in football, whose importance is independent of Ivy League standings. So each game of the Cuban League, particularly between the "eternal rivals," had an aura of its own and left a definite and unique imprint in a fan's memory.

I believe that this also explains why the Habana-Almendares rivalry endured even while the teams' rosters varied and players wearing the blue this year could be in red the next. As Roland Barthes shrewdly perceived in his beautiful *Mythologiques* about professional wrestling, who wins a match is not particularly important. It is the ritual of confrontation and the production of victory and defeat, with their attendant emotions, which, as in Greek tragedy, give the spectator pleasure. Games in the Cuban League were not fixed, to be sure. The Blue or the Red would win, but the important thing was that they remained the "eternal rivals," poised for another match on another day that they would consecrate with their timelessness, their hint of immortality. This is what made the rebirth of the Cuban League possible once political and economic conditions allowed it.

1 2 3 4 5 6 7 8 9 R H E

The Great Amateur Era

Where did all those baseball players who swelled the Cuban League come from? How and where did they develop? Baseball cannot be learned quickly because it demands finesse instead of brute force. Catching a fly ball, let alone a grounder, and throwing accurately are difficult skills to master. Some have claimed that hitting a moving ball with a round bat is the hardest thing to do in sports. So these players had to have been nurtured in practice and competition through a process that took years. It is a measure of how ingrained baseball was in Cuban life by the beginning of this century that little kids of all races learned to throw, catch, and hit early. There were organized teams and leagues for boys and adolescents, and both private and public schools sometimes had teams or intramural competition. But most of the baseball played by boys was unstructured. The immediate sources of talent for the Cuban League were the semiprofessional teams and leagues, sugarmill baseball, and the amateur leagues (which also included teams and tournaments in the armed forces).

Although I will cover all three in this chapter, when I write "amateur" I mean specifically the game played by social clubs who played in the Amateur League. The original teams represented the exclusive social clubs in the Havana area, such as the Vedado Tennis Club. But this league eventually included teams sponsored by business concerns and even a sugarmill

(Hershey), but organized as sports' clubs not as representatives of the companies. I will write "Amateur League" when referring to the various organizations in which these clubs played, specifying when necessary which league I mean. This usage attempts to approximate what Cubans meant when they said *los amateurs*. Sugarmill baseball, on the other hand, was loosely organized, often regionally, and each team represented a sugarmill. The players were originally workers at the sugarmill, but increasingly they were hired from elsewhere to play for the baseball team. Sugarmill baseball saw many professionals, both Cuban and American, in its ranks, and some of the tournaments were essentially professional. Semiprofessional baseball leagues, with teams representing companies and bus routes, included marginal or up-and-coming professional players as well as other highly skilled players. The players received compensation.

In Cuba's amateur baseball tradition one finds some of the greatest moments and players the sport has ever produced on the island, but also the most blatant and sustained iniquity: Blacks were excluded until 1959.[1] Segregation can be traced back to the turn of the century, when the disagreements brought about by the professionalization of the game led to a split. The amateur game, which was the origin of it all, remained a sport played among private, exclusive social clubs. Membership in these clubs was restricted to whites; hence blacks were excluded from amateur baseball. They had to play on semiprofessional teams or in the sugarmills. By the forties they also participated in the Liga Pedro Betancourt and the Liga de Quivicán, two leagues in the Matanzas and Havana areas respectively, that were specifically created to counter the racism of the Amateur League. There was no state discrimination in prerevolutionary Cuba, so blacks could not be discriminated against in public institutions (although the team of the University of Havana, with students of all races, played in the Amateur League and did not field blacks). Private clubs, however, had the right to determine their own composition. Whether the whites-only policy was a retention from colonial times or a consequence of American influence on upper-class Cubans is difficult to ascertain. It was probably a combination of both. Membership in a club would have meant that the individual in question had the right to participate in all the social functions, such as dances and dinners, where the presence of nonwhites would have been a more sensitive issue than on the field of play. The separation between the public and the private in these matters could not have been more dramatically drawn than when President Batista, a light mulatto, was blackballed from one of the more exclusive clubs while he was in power during the fifties.

In terms of baseball the split between the two spheres became most revealing and unjust at the time of selecting amateur national teams. Discrimination here brought out the contradictions in nationalist doctrine during the Republic. These were resolved in the professional leagues more readily because in activities ruled by greed and the pursuit of pleasure, ideology loses its grip more easily. National teams occasionally included a black or two in the forties. But the fact that most blacks played in semiprofessional leagues also rendered them ineligible for amateur international competition, in which players who had received compensation were banned. It was a blatant double bind. Blacks were not allowed in the Amateur League; thus they could only play on semiprofessional or sugarmill clubs. They could not have been amateurs even if they had wanted to. Most blacks could not *afford* to be amateurs, anyway; being poor, they had to have compensation for playing. There are older Cubans who can rattle off the names of several men of African descent who played on amateur teams (Charles Pérez, Roberto Estalella, and so on), but these were very light mulattoes who could "pass," and they mostly played on teams from the provinces, not in Havana.

Ironically, very few of the clubs in the Amateur League were genuinely exclusive or high-class anyway. The "reason" for the policy of discrimination was that the teams from the high-class societies would not have played teams with blacks on the roster, that the University team could not have competed at the Vedado Tennis Club grounds, for instance. However, the irrefutable fact remains that, with a few exceptions that confirm the rule, blacks were systematically excluded from amateur baseball before 1959, a custom tolerated because the Cuban population was and is overwhelmingly white and because there was (and is) no small measure of racism in Cuba. No justification or revisionism can erase this shameful legacy, nor should it be forgotten.

Having said this, it is also indisputable that amateur baseball was immensely popular in prerevolutionary Cuba, sometimes much more so than the professional game. It is also evident that the amateur game saved the professional Cuban League from oblivion and financial ruin. Until the mid-forties, many amateur players refused to go into the professional ranks because it was not seen as a very lucrative career, and in some cases because of class prejudices. Professional baseball was seen as a spectacle, somewhere above the circus or vaudeville in terms of prestige, put on by people from the lower classes, many of whom were black. Amateur baseball was not seen as significantly lesser in quality, and amateur teams regularly played visiting major-league teams and professional Cuban teams, with mixed results. Moreover, particularly in the provinces, amateur teams had a genuine local composition, which made them more appealing than professional squads, often made up of Americans. Some men, such as Reinaldo Cordeiro, never played professional baseball, yet later in their careers coached or managed in the professionals. Players of modest means, on clubs that did not belong to the elite, received some form of compensation, while others were given cushy jobs by club members or in businesses connected to some of the members. A few of these men lived better than many professionals, played fewer games, and did not have to pursue uncertain careers in the United States, where they would be the object of discrimination and vexed by a language barrier. Disputes about the definition of amateurism (as every-where else) were frequent, acrimonious, and remained unsettled.

But before I turn to the amateur game per se, I will deal with sugarmill and semiprofessional baseball, which—though rich sources of talent and meaningful manifestations of the game throughout Cuba—are the least documented. During the Golden Age of the Cuban League, sugarmill and semipro baseball were the most important producers of talent, and the for-mer often involved tournaments that included players from the Cuban League as well as the American Negro circuits. In chronicling that Golden Age of the Cuban League we have already seen that players often left for the provinces to participate in professional championships; some of these teams represented sugarmills, particularly in the East, around Santiago de Cuba and Holguín. The semipro was also a league in which blacks (and whites) could develop their talents and also wind down professional careers, or find spots when the Cuban League teams were already set. Given the scarcity of documentary information about baseball outside the Cuban League, in this chapter I will have to be less historically precise and depend more on my own memory as well as on those of others I have been privi-leged to interview: sportswriter Fausto Miranda; Agapito Mayor, who pitched for Fortuna; Conrado Marrero, who pitched for Cienfuegos; An-tonio (Quilla) Valdés, shortstop for Hershey; Andrés Fleitas, catcher for Hershey; and Napoleón Reyes, infielder for the University of Havana Ca-ribes. Although only by telephone, I also learned a great deal from Preston Gómez, former player in the sugarmills, the Amateur League, and the ma-jors, where he also had a long career as a manager of teams such as the Padres, the Astros, and the Cubs. Gómez also managed in Mexico and the Cuban Sugar Kings of the International League.

The sugarmill nearest my hometown of Sagua la Grande—there were thir-teen sugarmills in the area—was called Central Resulta. It was not a very large or important one. I remember its baseball stadium, where I occasion-ally played pickup games as a child. It was fenced in, with a small grandstand that went from behind home plate to about third base. The net was chicken wire. Perhaps about three hundred could have sat to watch a game, a num-ber that on a special day would have swelled, with people standing behind the first-base line. The playing field itself never seemed to be in very good shape in my time, and I do not remember the sugarmill actually having a team in the fifties. Home plate was made of wood, something I saw in many Cuban fields at the time. Everything, in fact, was wooden and un-painted. The right-field fence ran parallel to a railroad track that connected Central Resulta to my town and to the barges that transported the sugar to the port of Isabela. The track—which ran across the road from my house—also served to carry sugarcane to the central.

The baseball park in Central Washington, of which my paternal grandfather was the general manager in the fifties, was smaller than the one at Central Resulta. It had some bleachers behind home plate and modest dugouts in the form of sheds protected by chicken wire. But for an important game I am sure that for prominent people better seating was improvised, and many spectators would watch standing behind the low fences. The sugarmill field on which I played was at Central Constancia, in Mata, a small town about an hour away from Sagua la Grande. I was taken there by Corcho, who as we saw was a local player reputed to be in the taxi squad of Marianao, in the Cuban League, and who organized games among various town teams. I was about fourteen, and Corcho had to obtain permission from my parents to take me along. This was a team made up of men and older adolescents, so I was not a starter, and when I did play it was in the outfield, not at my normal position behind the plate.

The field at Central Constancia was better than the one at Central Resulta. The grandstand, which also ran parallel to the third-base line, was larger and painted white. Most of it was protected by chicken wire. The players sat in shedlike enclosures, like the one in Central Washington, and the one we had, along the first-base line, had a "dressing room" in the form of a hut where the groundskeeper stored his tools. It was there that Corcho taught me how to make the "uniform roll," something I later learned was used in the Negro Leagues: One rolled up everything inside the pants, which were laid flat on the bench, and tied it up with the belt. Home plate, also made of wood, was completely enclosed by the backstop. This game I am remembering must have been in 1956, for the opposing pitcher, a white man in his early twenties, was nicknamed "Vinagre Mizell," after "Vinegar Bend" Mizell, the Habana Reds (and Cardinal) pitcher who had set a strikeout record in the Cuban League that winter. Vinagre Mizell was fast and pitched in his bare torso. The umpire stood behind him with a revolver at his hip, as many men did carry guns in sugarmill towns. I remember my elation when I made solid contact on a fastball. But I did not get around on it and it went foul, wide of first. Trino Morales, who was at second, yelled encouragement, clapping his hands and trying to distract Vinagre. I regret to say that I swung right through a hissing curve ball on the next pitch and struck out.

There were better sugarmill baseball fields throughout the country. Preston Gómez remembers the field at the central from which he took his name (he was named Pedro but became Preston after the sugarmill in Oriente Province, where he was born) as having a substantial grandstand. It was next to the golf course, and golf balls would often land on the field while they were practicing. Preston was one of several huge centrales owned by the United Fruit Company on the northeastern Cuban coast. Games against nearby Boston, another of these centrales (its team was called Ferroviario, for unfathomable reasons), were fairly elaborate affairs, though

Gómez says that the field only had a mound with no diamond. Other centrales, such as Chaparra, Delicias, and San Germán, played Preston, and local tournaments were organized. He says that a team in the 1926–27 season included Frank Duncan behind the plate, Pepín Pérez at first, Cuco Correa at second, Dick Lundy at short, and Oliver Marcelle at third, with Oscar Charleston and Mauricio Funes in the outfield. This was a powerhouse that could have challenged any team in the Cuban League. While tickets for sugarmill games were normally 5 cents, games in this tournament cost 20 cents. Gómez believes that Charleston was getting $180 a month plus expenses. A sugarcane cutter probably made less than $1.00 a day, so it is unlikely that crowds at these games included the entire population of the sugarmill area.

Sugarmill teams like those described by Preston Gómez also played teams like Casa Bacardí, the Cuban Mining Company Team, the Nicaro Nickel Company, and, in Camagüey Province, Cromo Mining, a copper mining enterprise. Gómez believes that these teams, in the baseball- and sugar-rich Oriente Province, were stronger than teams in the Amateur League. It is easy to see that to compete with professional talent such as Marcelle, Charleston, Lundy, and Duncan, the Cuban players had to be of the highest quality. Cuban blacks were allowed on these teams, and Gómez remembers some of Jamaican origin as well.

Hugh Thomas writes that due to "the increase [in sugarmills] since 1907 Oriente had seen the biggest surge forward. . . ." (p. 539). As a result, Oriente began to produce stellar players in the way that Matanzas had done before (and would continue to do so): Other than Preston Gómez, there would be Antonio (Tony) Castaño from Palma Soriano, Heliodoro (Yoyo) Díaz from Puerto Padre, Carlos and Heberto Blanco from Bayamo, Napoleón Reyes from Santiago, and Pedro Formental from Báguanos, among others. Championships around cities such as Holguín and Santiago, home of the Bacardí Rum Company, were professional, and the stadiums were far more elaborate than those I described before. Distinguished poet José Rodríguez Feo, whose family owned sugarmills in Oriente, wrote in 1945 to his friend and even more distinguished writer José Lezama Lima about a game in which he witnessed a home run by a large mulatto, "strong as a horse," playing for Central Contramaestre.[2] Far from Havana and the hub of professional and amateur baseball, Oriente competition was keen and sometimes self-contained.

Great baseball players also emerged from sugarmill teams outside Oriente Province. Orestes Miñoso, for instance, played at Central España, in Matanzas, as did Antonio (Quilla) Valdés, who would later distinguish himself playing for Central Hershey, in the Amateur League; Roberto Ortiz began his career at Central Senado, in Camagüey; Andrés Fleitas at Central Constancia, in Las Villas Province. How many sugarmill teams were there? It is hard to say, but according to Thomas, in 1909 there were 170 mills grinding: "34% of the sugar came from U.S.-owned mills, 34% from Spanish or other European, 31% from Cuban: some of the Spanish group among the Europeans were really Cuban, but then some Cuban mills had U.S.-guaranteed mortgages" (p. 501). He adds that "twenty-one new mills were constructed in the period 1907–19" (p. 539). Even if one assumes that only the American and Cuban sugarmills had baseball teams, a conservative estimate would be that during the good years at least one hundred of these sugarmills had them.

My colleague from Vanderbilt University, Enrique Pupo-Walker, who is from the vicinity of Holguín, in the sugar-producing region Preston Gómez evokes, remembers that barnstorming teams of professional players would come "in caravans" to play in the local field. They also played in nearby Gibara. These parks were dilapidated affairs, he says, with primitive grandstands. People would sit on the ground along the sides of the field and consume local beverages such as *champola de guanábana* and *pru santiaguero* as well as more conventional ones, such as Hatuey beer and Bacardí rum. Vendors with wooden trays would sell sweets such as *polvorones* and *coquitos*. Some of these visiting professional teams would play sugarmill teams or simply play each other. Games would take place on Sundays or holidays in a carnival atmosphere and with, I assume, a good deal of betting going on. On occasion local players would join the visiting teams and were allowed to display their talents before their friends and relatives. While all this baseball has the peculiar flavor of independent baseball as it was played in the United States by company and town teams as well as by touring black squads, sugarmill baseball had a peculiar quality given by the unique nature of the central and its site, the *batey*.[3]

The transition from the small ingenios to the centrales in the latter part of the nineteenth century brought about a change in the structure of the sugarmill, although traces of the old ways remained. The centrales were large factories that ground the sugar of the *colonos*, landowners who originally ground their own sugar in small mills on their properties. An *ingenio* was a patriarchal rural town commanded by the owner of the land, the machinery, and the slaves. It was a plantation with traces of a barony. The central, on the other hand, took on the characteristics of a company town. The company, an abstract, all-controlling entity, often had its seat in Boston, New York, or New Orleans. The central's organization was more modern and systemic than patriarchal and was aimed at maximizing production and profit, though it retained much of the traditional social structure. Part of the plan to increase the yield involved providing recreation for the staff and the workers. The *administrador* or general manager was the town's boss, responsible for both production and order. He came to replace the owner as the patriarchal figure of authority and lived in the *casa de vivienda*, usually a mansion larger than other residences and equipped with servants, chauffeurs, bodyguards, and cooks. This house was the center of the batey or urban complex, which was, as the name "central" given to the factory itself suggests, at the center of a whole sugarcane-producing region. Roads and rails converged in the hub, the sugarmill itself.

In U.S.-owned sugarmills, the management, office staff, and administrators would often consist mostly of Americans, so recreation for them included everything from tennis to golf. These bateys were almost independent enclaves, with unusual legal ties to local, provincial, and national politics. In many cases they were like boomtowns, founded where there was no previous municipality. Others, of course, were old ingenios that had been expanded, as in the case in Canasí of the San Juan Bautista sugarmill, bought in 1916 by Milton Hershey and named after his company. Part of the entertainment in the bateys was, of course, baseball. Quilla Valdés recalls that, at Central España, in Matanzas Province, there were box seats for the Americans who owned the central. But baseball was not just a spectator sport for the higher-ups. It also involved the staff and the workers, with one of the staff sometimes acting as manager. Some of the workers were hired just to play ball and were given easy jobs at the central. Sugarmill teams were not squeamish about the issue of professionalism. They wanted to win and entertain, and would pay both Cuban and black American players to perform in one game or for an entire season. Some of these teams were professional powerhouses—American Negro circuits all-stars with a few prominent Cuban players added. A general manager or owner who happened to be interested in baseball would be as proud of his team as of a good stable of fighting cocks. Given the nature of the batey, which encompassed both the workplace and the town, one can see how there could be the kind of loyalty needed for a team to have a following.

Centrales were often relatively far from towns, so entertainment for the workers had to be provided within the batey and its environs. Socializing among the management was easy, as they usually had cars or could afford other means of transportation. On the other hand, the workers, who consisted of sugarcane cutters, those who toiled in the sugarmills, and even railroad personnel, had very limited opportunities for diversion. Other than traditional pastimes such as cock-fighting and dances, there was very little to do. At the Central España, Quilla Valdés remembers that a screen would be erected on the infield of the baseball park, where people watched movies from the grandstand.

Baseball was the main form of recreation. Centrales had their own railroads, so on occasion, when there was a game against a neighboring central, the owners and administrators provided trains to transport fans to the place of the action. *Carteles* reports on November 17, 1929 (p. 19), that in a game between the teams from Central Stewart and Central Baraguá, "there was even an excursion train provided by the administrator of the winner [Central Baraguá] to allow fans to travel to the game." A picture of both teams shows black and white players. Fierce rivalries were developed, and the lust for victory led many an owner or administrator to spend good money to import a ringer of the quality of major leaguer Adolfo Luque or standout Martín Dihigo.

In some sugarmills, such as Central Hershey, the baseball team was organized as a tennis club, following the model of the Amateur League squads. Some of these sugarmills, presumably those owned by Americans, included baseball in an array of sports activities designed to provide exercise and recreation. The Central Senado team, where slugger Roberto Ortiz developed, was called Senado Tennis Club. According to a *Carteles* report of February 1, 1942, at Central Manatí there was a wide-ranging sports complex, including basketball, tennis, softball, soccer, and baseball teams. We already saw that at Central Preston there was even a golf course. Hershey occasionally fielded a team in the amateur basketball league in Havana.

Fernando Ortiz describes the batey and environs in his beautiful *Cuban Counterpoint: Tobacco and Sugar* as "that complicated social-economic institution which is the *ingenio* or central, consisting of a vast cane plantation, a huge factory with all its apparatus for grinding, evaporating, crystallizing, separating, and shipping the sugar, and the urban center, village or city, which is the *batey* with its sheds, dwellings, and machine shops, stores, stables, and other services" (p. 81). What Ortiz did not see is that the batey was also a company town in the American sense, such as the ones that emerged in Pennsylvania's coal country. Centrales created towns of their own, relatively independent of the Cuban state and, because they were new, they were free from certain traditions and even laws. As we saw, they had their own railroad systems. They also had their own police force, electricity (often only during the grinding season), and other services. In some ways the bateys were also self-enclosed economies thanks to the oppressive system of paying workers with *vales* that could be redeemed only at the company store. Lowry Nelson has provided a superb analysis of life in the centrales in his *Rural Cuba*.

In a lighter vein, but with an American eye that focuses on the elements that make the batey a company town, travel writer Harry A. Franck offers this vivid description of the batey in his 1920 book *Roaming Through the West Indies:*

The *batey* is the headquarters of the entire *central,* as the sugar estate is called in Cuba. It clusters about the *ingenio,* the mammoth sugar-mill, which stands smokeless and silent through all the "dead season," its towering chimneys looming forth against the cane-green background for miles in every direction. Here the manager has his sumptuous dwelling, his heads of departments their commodious residences, the host of lesser American employees their comfortable screened houses shading away in size and location in the exact gradations of the local social scale. Usually there are company schools, tennis courts, clubs, stores, hospital, company gardeners to beautify the surrounding landscape. Outside this American town, often with a park or a flower-blooming plaza in its center, there are scores of smaller houses, little more than huts as one nears the outskirts, in which live the rank and file of employees of a dozen nationalities. In the olden days, when many slaves were of necessity kept the year round, the *batey* was a scene of activity at all seasons. But the patriarchal plantation life, the enchantment of the old family sugar-mill where each planter ground his own cane, has almost wholly disappeared before these giants of modern industry which swallow in a day the cane that the old-fashioned mill spent a season in reducing to sugar (p. 80).

Baseball took root in Cuba's countryside because of the development of this urban and socioeconomic phenomenon. The bateys of the new cen-trales were created for the express purpose of capitalist exploitation, with hierarchies that combined both the old feudal-like order and the new business-oriented organization. They were self-contained and sprawled around the heraldic phallic symbol of the sugarmill's stack, reaching high into the air, with the name emblazoned vertically, often in ornate script or gothic letters. As opposed to the semipros, sugarmill teams enjoyed more of a community feeling, despite the transient nature of the boomtownlike batey and the itinerant life of many of the workers at the lowest echelons. This loyalty centered on the owner or general manager, the lord of the realm.

Little baseball could be played during the frenzied *zafra* or grinding season, when the sugarmills worked in shifts around the clock. The litur-gical year of sugar is divided into two periods: the zafra, lasting from about December to the end of February or early March, and the *tiempo muerto,* or dead season, when other chores such as clearing, planting, repairs, and so forth are carried out. As the name implies, it was a bad season because there was little work, which meant that the poorer workers had to mortgage next season's wages to make ends meet. As far as I can tell, sugarmill base-ball was mostly played right after the zafra, when people still had money to spend on entertainment. But tournaments would be organized during other times of the year, depending on the fluctuations of the economy. There were probably quite a few of these during the months of October and November, just before the Cuban League season and the zafra.

Fernando Ortiz showed in "La antigua fiesta afrocubana del 'Día de Reyes'" how leisure was ritualized in the sugarmills and inserted into the Christian calendar. The Feast of the Epiphany, on January 6, was the cul-mination of the Christmas season. It was a feast on which slaves were al-lowed to play at being free. On that day they dressed up, elected kings, and went in carnival-style quadrilles to demand bonuses in front of the owner's house. In *The Sugarmill* Manuel Moreno Fraginals has detailed how leisure was allotted with a view to maximize the exploitation of the slaves, often extending the week to make it ten days long, so as to further space out days free of work. The exacting sugar calendar, driven by the demand of the plant to be harvested and ground without delay once it is mature, and by the fluctuations of the international market, set the yearly rhythms of leisure in Cuban culture. Professional baseball coincided with the grinding and tourist seasons, times of the year when people had money to spend on leisure. This is another reason why professional baseball was played mostly in Havana, where no grinding of sugar was taking place, only the expenditure of the profits from its harvest. Sugarmill baseball, on the other hand, came at the end of the frantic zafra as a sort of celebration of the conclusion of work, a free time that was not quite yet a dead season. It was also after Lent, Holy Week, and the Easter holy days in spring. I surmise that the length of sugarmill baseball play depended every year on the success of the harvest and particularly on the price of sugar.[4]

As in the case of professional baseball, each sugarmill game, even when part of an organized championship or tournament, had an independent quality of its own. Each game was like a performance, to be valued in itself. Hence, as we saw, it was common practice to import a talented player for a given game. My father, who played for Central San Agustín, where my grandfather was general manager in the thirties and early forties, used to tell me that there was always speculation about which luminary would show up with the opposition. This made the competition cutthroat because there were no age limitations, or any categorization or classification of players. A local talent, barely in his teens, would suddenly find himself facing a star like Oscar Charleston or Martín Dihigo. Teams carried no more than ten or twelve players, so substitutions were unlikely. The show of talent, effort, and boldness was right now, right here, with everyone watching, and with no excuses. If you were good you should be able to play with the best, professional, amateur, semipro, Cuban, or American.

It is consistent with the ephemeral nature of each game that there is no documentation concerning sugarmill baseball, except in the case of teams that joined the Amateur League, such as Central Hershey. It is impossible to know who won the regional tournaments or who finished as batting champion or top pitcher. No records remain of sugarmill baseball, and I have no idea if after the revolutionary takeover the archives of sugarmills were kept or disposed of. There are only the memories of those who saw Charleston make a circus catch in center field, Dihigo or Luque pitch a great game, or Alejandro Oms stroke hit after hit. Word of mouth magnified these feats as they entered local lore. In the provinces sugarmill was often the best baseball available. The other kind was what Cubans called *pelota de manigua,* or *pelota manigüera,* or baseball *en la manigua redentora. Manigua* is a Cubanism for "bush," the wild, so it seems to me that the term is an adaptation of the English "bushes," used to refer to the minor leagues. But in the mocking *manigua redentora* the term is parodically combined with patriotic rhetoric. *Irse a la manigua* meant, during the Wars of Independence, to take to the hills to join the rebel forces—hence the "redeeming bush" is where freedom was obtained through much sacrifice. Some of this baseball was truly primitive, played on unkept fields, with hardly any equipment. For example, I once heard that Ultus Alvarez, a real hick who made it to the Cuban League, actually began playing in games where the ball was struck with a clenched fist. An unpolished baseball player was often called *manigüero,* and dumb play was called to *jugar pelota manigüera.* Nonetheless, the sugarmills' source for players was often the *manigua.*

Intertwined with Cuba's main industry, sugarmill baseball was one of the themes of the counterpoint of sugar and tobacco that made up Cuban culture, according to Ortiz's felicitous formulation in his 1940 book *Cuban Counterpoint: Tobacco and Sugar.* Like sugar, it was coarse, rural, and dependent on foreign interests. The other theme was the semipro, which, appropriately enough, was urban rather than rural, and was initially sponsored by the tobacco industry. The semipro was less determined by the calendar of sugar. It was played, in the summer, during the "dead season," mostly in the Havana region.

The lines dividing amateur, sugarmill, and semipro baseball were not sharply drawn. White players moved from one to the other, as did some teams, most notably Central Hershey. Blacks moved from the semipro to the sugarmills and back, and from there to the Cuban League and also back. Some sugarmill teams were sponsored not by the mill itself, but by another business, like the one at Central Cunagua, which, to judge by a team picture in *Carteles* (April 13, 1941), was supported by Cigarros El Jefe. Orestes Miñoso played sugarmill ball in his native province of Matanzas, moved to the Partagás (a tobacco company) team in the Havana semipro league, later to Ambrosía in the same league, from there to the Cuban Mining team in Oriente Province, and eventually to the Cuban League, the Negro Leagues, and the majors. The Central Hershey team, winner of several championships in the Amateur League, was among the better-known in that circuit. It began as a sugarmill team and retained some of the characteristics of that brand of baseball. According to Quilla Valdés, their most famous player, the team practiced three times a week and played nonleague games sometimes on Saturdays and the league game on Sunday. The players had jobs at the sugarmill "that would not kill us," he says, and they were given other perks. In his case—he is reputed to have been the best shortstop in Cuban history, amateur or professional—the job was to dole out tools from a large shed or warehouse to the workers, keeping track of who took what. Quilla had a comfortable house for which he paid the Central $13 a month in rent. Hershey's batey, which I once visited in the fifties, was clean as a whistle and organized like a small American town. There were roads lined by neat palm trees, with the first few feet of their trunks painted white to discourage insects, yards with Page fences, and pine orchards that swayed and whistled with the wind. Quilla was often approached by the professionals, but he saw no advantage to it. Once he actually did sign with Merito Acosta, who, as we remember, had married the daughter of the owner of the Louisville team in the American Association. Merito's wife was to take the contract back to Kentucky, but when she arrived there she died suddenly, and the matter of Quilla's contract was never brought up again. An alumnus of the Hershey team, Tarzán Estalella, signed with the Habana Reds in the late twenties (he went on to play in the American League), and told Quilla that after his first professional game he was given only $6.00. Players were then being paid on the basis of a percentage of the gate. Agapito Mayor told me that once, after a game in Santa Clara, Almendares paid him less than $1.00 for the game. The thirties were hard times. With a secure job at Central Hershey, and at a time when amateur baseball was enormously popular in Cuba, one can understand Quilla's reluctance to turn professional. He went on to have a very long and distinguished career and was still playing in his fifties. But Central Hershey was one of the exceptions in that its team had continuity, played in the Amateur League, and rewarded its players well. Most accomplished sugarmill players, white or black, wound up in the Cuban League or the semipros.

Alejo Carpentier captured the essence of sugarmill baseball with the character Antonio in his 1933 Afro-Cuban novel ¡*Ecue-Yamba-O!* Antonio is a black man from the sugarmill San Lucio who has moved to Havana, where he lives in a typically marginal neighborhood. He is a ballplayer, a musician *(marimbulero),* and a pimp who rents out his services to politicians during electoral campaigns. In the novel he first appears as the shortstop of Panteras de la Loma, the team that has defeated San Lucio's. Antonio gets the winning hit, having rounded the bases in twelve seconds and having slid home with great élan. In the afterglow of his triumph he impresses the young protagonist Menegildo, whom he will usher into the criminal underworld of Havana. In Antonio, music and baseball meet as restricted practices where craft and craftiness coalesce to produce profitable spectacles. It is in this fringe that sugarmill, semipro, and professional baseball converge.

Ligas azucareras (sugarmill leagues) were formed in the central and eastern regions of Cuba, from Las Villas to Oriente. Teams from mining companies, the Casa Bacardí Company, and its subsidiary Hatuey Beer, were often involved. The most famous of these teams was the Cuban Mining, which had its seat in Cristo, Oriente Province. In a *Carteles* article of February 7, 1943, Jess Losada writes about these teams from mining companies, particularly the Cuban Mining one. Losada complains that 80 percent of the athletes who competed in Havana were from the provinces and that the provinces supplied talent to the capital but could hardly enjoy it themselves. He also complains about the poor state of Laguna Park in Santiago, the second Cuban city, which, he says, did not even have half of 1 percent of the sports facilities of the capital. Losada speaks of the fabulous teams fielded by Cuban Mining, Nicaro Nickel, and Cromo Mining, the first two from Oriente Province, the last from Camagüey Province, and reports on how Cuban Mining had just defeated the Orbay y Cerrato team, champions of the Havana-based semipro league. The Cuban Mining team was managed by one Alfred Zent, who was at that time trying to organize an entire amateur league in Oriente Province. With players such as Yoyo

Acosta, Gallego Núñez, Chago Salazar, Calampio León, and Fidel Lora (regarded as the Conrado Marrero of the East), the Cuban Mining squad was indeed a formidable team. In February 1943 it traveled to Havana and was undefeated in competition against amateur teams. They enjoyed a tumultuous reception back in Santiago. In the article cited above, Losada mentions how bitter people in Oriente Province were about their petition to have Benjamín Lowry, a local black slugger, try out for the national team, which petition had gone unheard.

Semiprofessional baseball in the Havana area goes back to the nineteenth century when, as Wenceslao Gálvez explains in his *El baseball en Cuba,* business owners began to pay athletes, mostly black, to play on teams sponsored by their firms. In the early part of the century semipro baseball was centered in Havana and called *Liga de los Torcedores* (Tobaccomakers' League). At times it was also called "Liga Inter-Fábricas," with *fábricas* understood to be cigar factories. Tobacco firms had a significant role in Cuban popular culture in the nineteenth century, particularly in the area of graphics. Cigar boxes were (and are) adorned with elaborate vignettes that proclaimed the hedonistic nature of their product, which often carried poetic names such as "Romeo y Julieta." In fact, there is a close connection between the Parnassian aesthetics of the *modernista* movement under which baseball developed in Cuba and the names of and illustrations on cigar boxes. (There is also a deeper connection between the sensual pleasure provided by the sport and the leaf.) Cigarette wrappers were emblazoned with comic-booklike vignettes, often depicting popular street life, musical activity, and a generally picaresque atmosphere in which blacks and mulattoes were protagonists. These *marquillas* often included pictures of famous musicians and dancers, making explicit the sensual bond between smoking and physical activity. It is therefore not surprising that tobacco companies turned to the decadent, chic sport of the time—baseball—as an advertising venue.

In the early part of this century the cigarmakers' league became one of the chief sources of black talent for professional baseball, although working-class whites also played. By the 1920s the league even got some sporadic coverage in the press, and games were played before large crowds at Almendares Park. The league even had a kind of offshoot in the cigarmaking community of Tampa, Florida, where the great Al López learned his baseball from Cuban *tabaqueros.* The picture (*Carteles,* October 9, 1927) of a veterans' game pitting former Almendares and Habana players shows many of them wearing semipro uniforms. Most of the Almendares veterans appear in Partagás suits, while those of Habana are in El Crédito and Gener flannels. These were two famous tobacco companies. It seems clear to me that at this time, and through the thirties and forties, the semipro was a kind of minor-leaguelike operation that may have actually rivaled the Cuban League in popularity because it fielded only Cuban players, some with marquee value. Alejandro Oms wound up his career with Partagás, though he did make a brief final appearance in the Cuban League before his miserable, pauper's death. Old and semiretired, Bombín Pedroso no-hit an independent professional team called Toros de Paredes. Julio Rojo managed Norton in the semipros in the early forties, and so forth.

Eventually the Liga Inter-Fábricas included teams from many other kinds of businesses and similar organizations spread through the island. Toward the east, where sugar and mining prevailed, the teams, as we saw, represented sugarmills, mining companies, and the Bacardí company and its subsidiaries. But there were many other teams. For example, El Globo, which was sponsored by a store in Camagüey, evoked with its name the belle époque and its colorful balloons. A picture of this team in 1930 shows that it is nearly all composed of blacks, and a note indicates that it often played against sugarmill teams. On June 14, 1931, *Carteles* shows a nine from Cienfuegos called B. B. Siglo, obviously a store, which is taking part in a local championship. Its name exudes nostalgia for the *fin de siècle*. A browse through *Carteles* turns up semipro teams with equally quaint names and provides a glimpse of how the sport, at this level, reflected Cuban politics.

On May 30, 1926, under a picture of a team called Punch, representing a well-known cigar factory, it is said that thousands attend games of the Liga Inter-Fábricas. This team has fourteen players of all colors dressed in handsome, pinstriped uniforms.[5] They appear again on August 1, after having defeated Romeo y Julieta, 10–3. The next year, on September 19, the inauguration of the championship is covered, with a picture of Dr. López del Valle, described as an avid fan, throwing the ceremonial first pitch. In April Partagás had defeated a team named Billiken, which, according to Quilla Valdés, was an independent professional team. El Crédito is another team that appears frequently in *Carteles*. On May 8, 1927, they are pictured, also in pinstriped uniforms, a fashion probably copied from the New York Yankees and Babe Ruth (it was instituted to make the slugger look slimmer). In 1928 there is a picture of El Cuño, another tobacco label, a team from Guantánamo, which demonstrates that the practice of fielding teams associated with tobacco was expanding, even to Oriente Province (tobacco is associated with western Cuba). On January 27, 1929, a Cárdenas team named Estrella defeated the champions of the Amateur League in that city, an indication that, as in the case of sugarmill teams, the semipro squads played against amateurs. The Estrella team was at least half black, so the apartheid of the amateurs did not include playing against mixed teams, as long as it was not on the fields of the exclusive societies. On April 29, 1928, another pinstriped squad, this one from La Gloria de Cuba (the name of another cigar), is pictured with its twelve uniformed members. At the time, as in the Amateur League and even the Cuban League, rosters seemed to hover between twelve and fourteen players.

It seems clear that the semipro league was made up of players from humble backgrounds, black or white. Fermín Guerra, who went on to have a major-league career, as well as a distinguished one as player and manager in the Cuban League, began playing in the semipro league. The impoverished and illiterate son of an *isleño* (a Canary Islander), Guerra, a native of Havana, began as a batboy at Almendares Park and was recruited by Acción Cubana, a team in the semipro league. He was paid for playing, or, as he put it, "we got something." As a boy he sold fruit and vegetables from a basket in the Plaza del Vapor, the huge Havana market. Though white, because he was so poor, Guerra could not afford to be amateur and would not have been taken by any social club. Very poor whites suffered restrictions akin to those that applied to blacks.

Another player who began in the semipro league was Rodolfo Fernández, who went on to pitch for Almendares and Habana in the Cuban League and for the New York Cubans in the Negro circuits. He coached and managed in Cuba, Venezuela, and the Dominican Republic. A native of Guanabacoa, the young Rodolfo had to go make a name for himself in nearby Güira de Melena because there was a glut of ballplayers in his hometown. In Güira de Melena, Fernández beat the Círculo de Artesanos from the Amateur League, and many semipro clubs who came by for games. This was the late twenties and early thirties, hard times, and Fernández says that he often played for a cold drink and the bus fare. He came to be known as "La Maravilla Güireña" before he signed with Almendares in 1932.

Claro Duany, a black left-handed slugger who led the Cuban League and the Mexican League in batting, played for the New York Cubans, and became a stalwart of the Marianao Tigers, straddled sugarmill and semipro league baseball at the beginning of his career. Born in Caibarién, Las Villas Province, in 1917, Duany first played for a stevedore union in his native town. He was given a job on the docks carrying sugar sacks, which no doubt added muscle to his large frame. He did so well that he was hired to work and play at Central Pino, in Camagüey, and later at Central Violeta, in the same province. At that sugarmill he played with professionals such as Fermín Guerra, already a major leaguer, Regino Otero, Salazar Cubillas, and Antonio (Pollo) Rodríguez. After a year at the Central, Duany went to Havana, where he played for the Fifth Regiment in the armed forces championship and eventually La Ambrosía in the semipro league. At La Ambrosía, a cracker, chocolate, and candy factory, he was given a job to support himself. Then he was called to Santiago de Cuba, to play for a team called Central in another semipro league. From there he went to the Cuban League.

The presence of politics in the semipro game, which will increase by the middle to late thirties, is evident in the fact that on October 5, 1930, a *Carteles* picture from Matanzas shows Dr. Mario Haedo, secretary of the municipal government, throwing out the ceremonial first ball at a baseball game played at General Machado Stadium between the teams Tropical and

Casa Cueto. By this date Machado had become a hated dictator, but with a tenacious following among certain groups (many blacks and mulattoes), particularly toward the center of Cuba and his home province of Las Villas. On January 4, 1931, Las Villas governor Juan A. Vázquez Bello is shown throwing the ceremonial first ball at an interprovince championship game between Cienfuegos and Santa Clara at La Boulanger Park. The Vázquez Bellos were strong Machado followers. There are blacks on both teams.

On April 23, 1933, *Carteles* reports, "To the delight of baseball fans— deprived of the good fortune of witnessing big-league baseball, or even Cuban-made professional games—the semiprofessional matches taking place at La Tropical stadium have all the zip of a *petite* big league. Team Cuba, depicted here, is a fighting squad that knows how to manufacture emotions on the diamond. It recently staged a hard-fought game against Cienfuegos" (p. 36). The script on the Cienfuegos uniform reads, allur- ingly, "Venus Soap." "Manufacturing emotions" is a pun alluding to the team's provenance from the tobaccomakers' league, because their players presumably "manufactured" cigars. We are at the nadir of the Cuban League at this point, so clearly the semipro league is filling the vacuum.

Eventually the semipro league included teams from other kinds of businesses, such as the already mentioned Orbay y Cerrato, a furniture com- pany, and La Pasiega, a cracker-making factory, as well as many others, some supported by American firms, car dealerships, Cinzano, Chocolate Ambrosía, Club Norton, and bus routes. The bus-routes squads were prob- ably composed of and followed by the humblest Cubans. Each route of the Compañía de Omnibus Aliados de Cuba had its distinct character, and the shed where the buses were stored and maintained functioned as a kind of modest clubhouse. Workers of each route were fiercely loyal to these in- formal clubs, which were on the opposite end of the social spectrum from the exclusive social clubs that sponsored the Amateur League. Some of these bus-routes teams were superb, and the Ruta 23 boasted of an alumnus of the stature of Alejandro Crespo, one of the best Cuban ballplayers in the thirties, forties, and early fifties. *Carteles* reports on September 26, 1943, that the Cuban national team, getting ready for the Amateur World Series, played and lost to Ruta 16, the second-place team from the semipro league. As would often be the case then and now, the Cuban national team faced the stiffest competition at home.

By 1943, semiprofessional baseball had been officially incorporated into the Cuban government's sports program for some time. The season opened on March 21, 1943, at La Tropical stadium, with General Ignacio Galíndez, a close associate of Batista, raising the flag. Dr. Arturo Bengo- chea, adviser on professional baseball before the Dirección General Na- cional de Deportes, was present. The DGND (later DGD, or Dirección General de Deportes) had been founded on June 9, 1938, in an attempt to bring some order to sports activities in Cuba, including professional baseball, which, as we saw, was in a state of decadence and disarray. (Actually, General Galíndez, then a colonel, had been named commissioner for professional baseball in 1936 and brought about important reforms in the Cuban League.) The founding of the DGND was also an effort to counteract the discriminatory policy of the Amateur League. At the time, Federico Laredo Bru was the figurehead president of Cuba, but power was in the hands of Batista. Hence the first director of the DGND was Colonel Jaime Mariné, another Batista associate. Mariné, in fact, accomplished a good deal. He set in motion the organization of the Juveniles, an amateur league for boys under twenty that was open to all races (the Amateur League occasionally had a tournament for *novicios,* organized under the same rules of racial exclusion). Mariné opened facilities for other sports, created free health organizations for athletes, and even had a *cocina deportiva,* a cafeteria where amateur athletes could eat for free. He was also instrumental in bringing the Amateur World Series to Cuba.

Another development brought about by Batista's influence and Mariné's agency was the development of the armed forces championship, which was racially integrated and virtually professional, since the players were paid as soldiers but were recruited for their baseball skills. This league became a stepping-stone to the Cuban League, and its teams potent rivals to semipro, amateur, and national selections preparing themselves for international competition. In the late thirties, Luque and his assistant "Pindongo" Solís were involved in the armed forces league, with Papá Montero actually managing the Sixth Regiment team. In these championships the symbolic link between war and sports was made even stronger: Soldiers and players were one under the authority of the all-powerful military leader.

Batista's and Mariné's ventures into sports were part of a worldwide movement, culminating in the 1936 Berlin Olympics, that associated sports and national states. It was fueled by the intense nationalism prevalent in the thirties that led to World War II and that had strong if unspoken ties to the rise of fascism. National teams presumably represented the nation, and fought for its honor like the armed forces, of which it seemed to be an extension. The armed forces were in turn led by strong military figures who were the ultimate embodiment of the fatherland. Cuba, which had done very well in the 1926, 1930, 1935, and 1938 Central American Games in general (winning every time in baseball), was swept along by this trend, which peaked in the early forties in Cuban baseball, and again after the 1959 revolution. It is not by chance that we see colonels such as Mariné and generals such as Galíndez involved in the DGND. Cuban sports after the revolution are a direct heir of this kind of involvement. Commander in Chief Fidel Castro follows the footsteps of Colonel Mariné and General Galíndez. Germany's and the Soviet Union's investments in wide-ranging sports organizations to promote health, provide recreation, build character and a martial spirit, as well as to cull the best athletes to represent the nation, became models followed by many countries, but particularly postrevolutionary Cuba. The pomp and circumstance of military pageant were now reserved for victorious athletes, disciplined like soldiers, who would proudly carry national flags and occasionally wear native garb. Medals, anthems, parades, and the presence of dictators in full military garb were and still are featured at these extravaganzas.

When on September 22, 1942, *Carteles* ran an article about how a selection from the semipro league had defeated the national team being prepared for the Amateur World Series, Jess Losada, always a gadfly, referred to the semipro league as "our most humble" baseball and complained about the nearly total absence of blacks from the Cuban national team, because this modest game was producing black stars who were products of that peculiar dynamic of older players passing down the tricks of the trade to the younger generation. Two such stars of this new generation were shortstop Avelino Cañizares and Héctor Rodríguez, who would shine behind Max Lanier when Almendares beat Habana in that decisive game on February 25, 1947. Others, such as Alejandro Crespo, Pedro Formental, Napoleón Heredia, Conrado Pérez, Santiago Colás, and Orestes Miñoso, would feed the Cuban League with first-rate talent, invade the Mexican League, and stock the New York Cubans of the Negro Leagues as well as other independent teams in the United States and Latin America.

As in the case of the sugarmill teams, there are no records left of semiprofessional baseball in Cuba, but that does not mean that the game played by these men was in any way inferior, or not worthy of remembrance. On the contrary, semiprofessional baseball, as witnessed by those victories against "national" teams, was probably some of the strongest baseball played in Cuba, just a step below the Cuban League. Sometimes, in fact, as with the series lost by Cuban League teams to Havana Club, or the 1926 Central Preston powerhouse, this baseball was better than the Cuban League. And, in terms of the players, it was more Cuban.

Amateur baseball in Cuba until 1959 was a continuation of the nineteenth-century game played by exclusive clubs, though, naturally, it evolved considerably over the years, incorporating many teams from organizations of lesser social standing. But in the beginning, after independence, amateur teams were created expressly in contrast to the professional ones, which were increasingly spectacles competing for entertainment money. For instance, *El Fígaro* of August 11, 1901 (año 17, no. 30, p. 354) prints the picture of a team named Clío sitting on the steps of what appears to be a rambling clubhouse, with the following caption: "CLIO B.B.C. A group of young men from Havana's high society who are enthusiasts of the game of baseball, have organized this brilliant club whose number of games played equal their number of victories. Profit is not what these players seek, but the practice of the noble sport of baseball, which in the past had a substantial following in Havana's social circles. May the example of Clío's young men be imitated by our youth!" The creation of this team was a deliberate effort to bring back a time when baseball was a chic sport for the elite and when the game had much in common with modernista aesthetics. Clío is, significantly, the muse of history and epic poetry, no less. The team's classical name harks back to that time of Parnassian pleasures of the fin de siècle when players and poets assembled at the Café Louvre portals. The team's picture appears under a poem by Diego Vicente Tejera that does not allude to it, but provides an appropriate frame in the layout of the page.

Clío's roster boasts a figure from the past, former great Carlos Maciá, a grizzled veteran by this time, who obviously eschewed professionalism. There is also an Emilio Power listed as president, and a figure that is a throwback to the nineteenth century but who would endure in the twentieth: a black *fongueador* named Evaristo Plá. The fongueador was a special trainer who would hit fungoes to the infield and outfield during practice. Some became much sought-after because they had special techniques for training players and developing teamwork. (I saw one working what must have been a semipro team in the fifties; he kept a rhythm going by emitting guttural sounds and nonverbal commands as the players scooped up grounders and repeated over and over a choreography of infield maneuvers, such as the doubleplay.) Blacks would appear in that role for years to come, and also as *masajistas,* masseurs, or trainers. Some were reputed to possess private potions, secret liniments, and magic unguents derived from Afro-Cuban cults. These were skills and jobs akin to those of stableboy and trainer in horse racing. But the significant thing is that Clío, which played for a number of years, was a deliberately amateur squad that aligned itself with the original strand of Cuban baseball. It was an origin seeking an origin.

The Asociación Atlética, an amateur league, was organized in 1905 essentially by the Vedado Tennis Club and the University of Havana. Besides these, the league had a club named Columbia and eventually also Clío. By the time this league was assembled, Clío and other clubs had been playing in the Havana area, and probably elsewhere, too. In any case, the key team here is the Vedado Tennis Club, which should be considered the foundation team of Cuban amateur baseball in the twentieth century. Its organization became the model for all such clubs and baseball teams through the years, even when more modest associations joined the league.

The Vedado Tennis Club was founded on June 11, 1902. Its founding members were José Agustín Ariosa, Antonio Suárez, Luis Rabell, Pedro Fantony, Julio Rabell, Alonso Franca, Gabriel García Echarte, Juan F. Morales, Miguel Franca, Edgardo Rabell, Juan Arellano, Julio Blanco Herrera, Miguel Morales, Alberto Rabell, and Ramiro Cabrera. A picture from 1903 shows them in front of a modest bathhouse on Paseo and Third in El Vedado, holding tennis rackets. Several are sporting their tennis whites. A 1905 picture of their first baseball nine includes many of them. The original idea for the club was José Agustín (Chicho) Ariosa's, who had distinguished himself as a tennis player in the courts at Sandy Hill, New York. But in the early years, Porfirio Franca, who played on the original baseball team, was the most active promoter of the club and its president. In 1912 the club built a palatial house near the mouth of the Almendares River, facing the sea. There were five tennis courts, a basketball court, a field for polo, squash, and a pool. There was no baseball field yet. The building cost $75,000, a huge sum then. The monthly membership fee of the Vedado Tennis Club was, at that time, $4.24.

The Vedado Tennis Club won several "cups" in tennis, polo, and crew, and captured the championship in the first Amateur League season of 1905, and again in 1909 and 1910. They also won in 1914, 1915 and 1916. In 1914 and 1915, they were managed by Guillermo E. de Zaldo, of the family that produced the Zaldo brothers during the early years of baseball in Cuba, and owners of the land where the first Almendares Park stood. The Vedado Tennis Club put together another string of pennants from 1925 to 1928, managed by Rafael Almeida, a former major leaguer. In 1909, as we saw in the previous chapter, they defeated, with Armando Castellanos in the box, the Indianapolis professional team that belonged to what was then the highest minor-league classification. Although the articles from *Carteles* and *El Fígaro* that I am following here speak of the club's exclusivity, it was not so stringent as to prevent them from recruiting Adolfo Luque to play, when this soldier from a modest background showed promise. It was with the Marqueses of Vedado Tennis Club that the future Papá Montero began his pitching career. They nurtured many great amateur players, most of whom chose not to turn professional, as was often the case with young men from middle-class or well-to-do families. In the early years the Vedado Tennis Club had champion pitchers in 1914 (G. Portela), 1915 (R. Goizueta), 1916 (again Portela), 1926 (A. Casuso), and 1928 (J. Ravena); and batting champions in 1916 (G. Villalba), 1917 (Ciro Seigle), 1924 (P. Palmero), 1926 (Gustavo Alfonso), 1928 (Ramiro Seigle), and 1930 (Alfonso again).

A 1910 chronicle in *El Fígaro* gives an excellent account of the atmosphere of amateur baseball in Cuba during the teens. In this case (September 11), the Vedado Tennis Club defeated Marianao, 9–1, behind their "idol," Armando Castellanos. The Marqueses peppered Marianao pitchers for twenty-three hits. But the most significant thing is how the reporter evokes nineteenth-century baseball, emphasizing that these players, from the best Havana society, "only participate to fight, with legitimate pride, for the victory of their club's emblem." The spectacle itself was a pageant that evoked bygone eras. The Vedado and Marianao fans, in different sections of the stands, gave "yells," meaning cheers (but the word is in English), a practice they had probably learned in American prep schools and Ivy League universities. A horse-drawn carriage arrived carrying a group of distinguished ladies, among whom were Nena Ariosa de Cárdenas, Teté de Cárdenas de Guilló, Amalia Hierro de González del Valle, Otilia Crusellas, and among the gentlemen General Monteagudo, González del Valle, Guilló, Cárdenas, and the "charming young man" Chicho Ariosa. This man named Guilló must be Nemesio, who brought baseball to Cuba, and Crusellas was a family who owned an important soap factory. There were several founders of the Vedado Tennis Club in this carriage. The victory secured the championship, or "trophy," for the club; hence a sumptuous lunch, to be presided over by Porfirio Franca, was announced.

In the teens, the Vedado Tennis Club's keenest competition came from Atlético de Cuba, which had its clubhouse on Prado Boulevard. They wore orange piping on their uniforms and were often called "the orange men" (the Marianao Tigers, of the Cuban League, adopted the color of this team). Besides Castellanos, the Marqueses had a pitcher named Francisco López, known as Mullin, who received a good deal of coverage. Atlético de Cuba won in 1917 and 1919. In that last year they faced strong competition from the Cienfuegos Federales (Federales de Heredia was their name at that time) and their star pitcher, Pedro Esquivel. This team won the next year—1920—behind Pedro Dibut, who would make it to the majors briefly, with Cincinnati.

But as with the Cuban League and professional baseball in general, Cuban amateur baseball cannot be circumscribed to the one official circuit, or to a series of consecutive seasons. In 1919 "El Recluta" (The Rookie), a sharp critic of sports in general, complained in *Carteles* about the fragmentation of amateur baseball. This fragmentation was due to the very nature of the amateurs, which emphasized the ritual celebrations of games against other clubs, each of which was independent, not bound to or reliant on a league for its activities. As in sugarmill ball and some professional independent tournaments, each game was a performance unto itself. Hence there abounded "trophies," "cups," "interclub series," and the like, organized or sponsored ad hoc. The results of most of these are lost, the games having already fulfilled their ritualistic purpose. One such competition was the "Copa Teixidor," donated by Leopoldo Teixidor, vice president of the Teixidor Trading Company. This was won by the Fortuna Sports Club, which was about to win the Amateur League in 1921 and 1922 and which would have a brilliant history in the next twenty years.

The practice of playing brief tournaments of an independent nature continued during the twenties. For instance, following a *Memorias* published by Club Teléfonos in 1962, the origins of its baseball team, which was to have a splendid history, is as follows.[6] In July 1924, in Víbora Park, a tournament for the PWX Trophy Cup was played. PWX, the first radio station in Cuba, belonged to the telephone company. Three teams participated: the Cuban Telephone Club, Vilaplana, and Pan American. Vilaplana won. Adolfo Febles was the star pitcher for Teléfonos. Toward the end of that same year a Trophy Cup Teléfonos was contested with the same teams plus Sociedad Deportiva de Empleados de Seguros (insurance company employees), won again by Vilaplana. In January of 1925 an O'Nathen Cup was disputed among Teléfonos, Vilaplana, and La Prensa, which was again won by Vilaplana, with Teléfonos in second place. In August 1925 the Royal Bank of Canada convened a championship with teams Teléfonos, Royal Bank, and La Prensa, which finished first. Toward the end of the year an "Inter-Clubs" championship was held, which included Teléfonos, Royal Bank, and Empleados de Seguros, which Teléfonos won. In November 1926 a Morales and Co. Trophy was disputed, with the participation of Teléfonos, San Carlos, Hermanos Maristas, Havana Central, and Deportivo Seguros Whitner. Teléfonos won, with their future ace, Narciso Picazo, on the mound for the first time.

Another amateur team from this period whose history has been written and is indicative of how clubs were formed is Santiago de las Vegas. The town club was organized as part of the Centro de Instrucción y Recreo (CIR) in 1882. This was in the period between the Wars of Independence when, as we saw in an earlier chapter, baseball was adopted by the Cubans. Cuba was still, of course, under Spanish rule, so the Spaniards in the area organized a rival team with the belligerent name of Numancia, which was soundly defeated (Numancia was the Spanish town that committed mass suicide rather than surrender to Scipio Africanus). Baseball in Santiago de las Vegas continued in the early part of this century, with teams inevitably called Habana and Almendares. Later, at a newly built though very modest Acuña Park, teams with the names of Venus and Liverpool played very strong baseball, with professional reinforcements occasionally imported from Havana. These teams were merged to form La Unión, which established a bitter rivalry with nearby Quivicán, a town that brought none other than Bombín Pedroso, along with the Calvo brothers and Ricardo Torres as ringers. La Unión countered a week later with Hungo, Paíto Herrera, and Baranda. Eventually the CIR constituted an amateur club, which entered the Amateur League in 1921. In its three years in the league (1921, 1922, and 1923), Santiago de las Vegas came in fifth, second, and ninth, respectively. In 1921 the town hired twelve railroad cars and a locomotive to travel all the way to Cienfuegos, where they were defeated in a close contest by Pedro Esquivel. The next year Deportivo Cárdenas traveled to Santiago on a similar train, where they were beaten by a CIR that boasted Octavio Diviñó, already a famous amateur manager who would gain national fame with Teléfonos.

As the Amateur League expanded and included teams from much more modest backgrounds, the Vedado Tennis Club stopped winning, though it still had great teams through the thirties and early forties. The Vedado Tennis Club, however, was to play a crucial role in the revival of professional baseball in Cuba when ten of its members bought the Almendares franchise from Abel Linares' widow in 1940, an event that will be discussed in the next chapter. But in the dawn of the Amateur League the Vedado Tennis Club was the powerhouse and the model that the rest of the country followed.

The Liga Nacional de Baseball Amateur (what I have been calling here the Amateur League) was founded in 1914 with the following teams: Vedado Tennis Club, Instituto de La Habana, Sociedad de Marianao, and Club Atlético de Cuba. It was an unofficial organization until 1917, when it was registered in the Registro Especial de Asociaciones del Gobierno, La Habana Province, on April 26, making it the first official athletic organization in Cuba. These early championships consisted of few games, ranging from eleven in 1917 to twenty the previous year. This was dictated, obviously, by the scarcity of clubs. Of all of those seasons the most memorable one was in 1917, when Atlético de Cuba managed to dislodge the Vedado Tennis Club from the championship in a closely contested race. Expansion came soon. Teams called Bellamar, Lawton, Víbora Social, Aduana, and Federales de Heredia competed in 1919, and in 1920 there were provincial teams from Sagua la Grande and Matanzas, which joined newly formed Fortuna and Universidad, clubs that in future years would be among the leaders. Cienfuegos won, as we saw, with a 19 and 4 record, and the batting champion was an L. García, who hit .409. Their star pitcher, Pedro Dibut, went on to play for the Cincinati Reds of the National League, where he won three games without a defeat in 1924, and had a solid career in the Cuban League.

The economic bonanza of the late teens, brought on by World War I and rising sugar prices, also boosted the Amateur League, which came under the jurisdiction of the Unión Atlética Amateur de Cuba in 1922. Under this agreement, the Liga Nacional retained the right to select its governing board, made up by the representatives of the participating clubs. A Liga Social was formed that included even more social clubs of modest standing, and in 1927 there appeared a Liga Intersocial, led by team Teléfonos, representing the Cuban Telephone Company, and their ace left-hander, the diminutive Narciso Picazo. During the four years the league existed, a Serie Co-Criolla, between the champions of the Liga Nacional and the Liga Intersocial, was played. We will return to this high point of amateur baseball shortly.

A look at the teams that comprised the Amateur League from 1914 to 1944 shows that only the Havana Yacht Club, among the really exclusive clubs, fielded a team. Círculo Militar y Naval (the Army-Navy Club), Casino Español, and Casino Deportivo were not really that elite, nor was Fortuna. The others became progressively more working-class in nature. Círculo de Artesanos de San Antonio de los Baños, a town near Havana, for instance, presumably represented a guild of artisans or craftsmen. The Santiago de las Vegas team, Artemisa and Regla, two towns in the environs of Havana, were of modest social composition at best. The Matanzas and Cárdenas sports clubs were barely middle class. Policía and Aduana were clubs formed by the police and the customs workers.[7] Dependientes was the clerks' society, dominated by immigrant Spaniards (they were mocked in the press by being called Dipindientes, the way a Galician would mispronounce the word). Cubaneleco, or Cuban Electric Company, was supposedly made up of workers from that company, as was the Teléfonos team from that company. Universidad fielded a socially mixed team of players who had four or five years of eligibility and then usually went on to other teams. Because students arrived at the University after a five-year *bachillerato* (the equivalent of at least two years of college in the United States), players at the university were in their twenties. There was, of course, no age restriction in the Amateur League, and men sometimes played until they were in their fifties, because the physical demands of the sparse schedule were light.

Though the Golden Age of the Amateur League runs from the midthirties to the midforties, the twenties were also a period of splendor, highlighted by two victories in the Central American Games and the construction of La Tropical in 1930, the field most generally associated with amateur baseball in Cuba during the Republican era. The first half of the decade was dominated by Fortuna, the second by Vedado Tennis Club and Teléfonos.

The Fortuna Sports Club was founded in March 1917, mostly as a soccer club, though it also competed in regattas held before Havana's bayshore boulevard, the famous *malecón,* where it erected its clubhouse. It was a modest one if compared to the one built by the Vedado Tennis Club, but it was well located in San Lázaro and Malecón. It had no tennis courts but a splendid trophy room, bar, library, handball courts, gym, fencing room, billiards room, but no gambling rooms. It seems that this was mostly a middle-class men's club made up largely of Spaniards or first-generation Cubans. Fortuna's soccer and baseball teams worked out at the University Stadium.

If Armando Castellanos of the Vedado Tennis Club was the star amateur pitcher of the teens, in the twenties there were many new ones. First and foremost was Silvino Ruiz, a Fortuna curveballer. In the first years of the decade Juanillo Albear managed Fortuna. He led them to the 1921 championship, but then went to the Havana Yacht Club. He was succeeded the next year by first baseman Alfonso Peña, who brought Fortuna another pennant. Known for the black piping on their uniform and their gothic F, Fortuna was the class of the Amateur League, along with Vedado Tennis Club and the University of Havana. Vedado Tennis Club, probably tired of being upstaged, hired Rafael Almeida of major-league fame, as manager, and won in 1925, the first of three pennants in a row. Their star players were René Gallardo, Rogelio Tavío, Julio López, Antonio Casuso, Jorge Consuegra, Gustavo Gómez Calvo, Ramiro Seigle, Raúl del Monte, Gustavo Consuegra, Manuel (Remache) Sotolongo, Chichi Bruzón, and Joaquín del Calvo. Silvino Ruiz was still winning, and Ramiro Seigle, mentioned as *tutankámico* (meaning he was old as a mummy), was not only still active but also would soon win a batting championship. There is a picture from September 27, 1927, in *Carteles* of the Vedado Tennis Club, which defeated the University of Havana Caribes in a game at "the spacious University Stadium, where an attendance record was set" (p. 18). These were halcyon days of amateur baseball, no longer a Sunday ritual for the elite, but a spectacle followed avidly by a substantial portion of the population. The professionals would have wished to have done so well. In fact, as we saw in the previous chapter, when the Cuban League split in 1928, and an independent championship was held at the University Stadium, quite a few amateurs were recruited for this professional event because of their fame. The team called Red Sox signed Echarri, Fortuna's third baseman, and Roberto Puig, who was with Policía in the amateurs. This would not be the last time that the Amateur League helped the Cuban League.

In 1927 there began a Campeonato Inter-Social, which included Dependientes, Maristas, and teams called Vasallo, Barinaga, and Bárcena. There was also a Santos Suárez Tennis Club. Teléfonos dominated this league, with Narciso Picazo, Pages, Lugo, Palencia, R. Uriza, and M. Flores. Club Atlético de Marianao entered in 1928. The Liga Intersocial now included Teléfonos, Círculo de Artesanos de San Antonio de los Baños, and Víbora Tennis Club. *Carteles* shows, on September 23, 1928 (p. 34), a picture of the Cuban Telephone team, champions of the Liga Inter-Social Amateur de Cuba. Octavio (Divi) Diviñó is the manager, Oscar Reyes is the first baseman, Romero Mujica is listed as outfielder, Matías Flores, left field, Francisco Espineira, catcher, Roberto Uriza, second base, Adolfo Febles, right field, Conrado Lugo, center field, Narciso Picazo, pitcher, José Ventura, catcher, Ramón Pajares, third base, Antonio Palencia, short stop, Salvador Costa, second base. Febles could also pitch. But Picazo pitched most of the time, going 19 and 1 in 1929. This was a superb team and a worthy rival of the Vedado Tennis Club veteran powerhouse.

The first Co-Criolla series was in 1928 and pitted Teléfonos against the Vedado Tennis Club. Teléfonos won the first game but was dominated by Rocamora in the second. In the deciding contest Picazo pitched a shutout for the victory. *Carteles* of November 25, 1928, intones: "His [Picazo's] shutout against Vedado last Sunday gave the Teléfonos Club the National Amateur championship. It was a double triumph, both a victory for the Telefonistas, and another for the Liga Intersocial de Amateurs de Cuba, presided by René Gálvez." Jess Losada wrote, in a summary of sports activities for 1928: "The baseball season offers a very favorable balance. The amateurs held their national series between Vedado Tennis Club, winners of the season organized by the Unión Atlética de Amateurs and the Cuban Telephone Club, winners of the Liga Inter-Social tourney. The Telephone Club won the series by one game, the hero being Narciso Picazo, the diminutive pitcher-revelation." Teléfonos continued its mastery of the Co-Criolla series in the next two years, defeating the University of Havana in 1929 and the Círculo de Artesanos de San Antonio de los Baños in 1930. Picazo continued to shine, dominating the Co-Criolla series. These series brought a fitting end to a remarkable decade of growth in

Cuban amateur baseball, which had become the predominant form of the sport in the Havana area.

In 1926 Cuba participated in its first international amateur competition when it sent a baseball team to the first Central American Games, held in Mexico City. Only Mexico, Cuba, and Guatemala participated in these games, and Guatemala did not send a baseball team. Mexico was recovering from its revolution and eager to assert its renewed sense of national identity. In Cuba, Gerardo Machado had just come to power in 1925 and was riding a crest of popularity and spasmodic prosperity. Sending a delegation to these games was a way to legitimize Cuba's independence and boast of its progress. The Cuban baseball team had a strong Vedado Tennis Club flavor. Porfirio Franca, the club's president, was named commissioner of the Cuban delegation. He was in charge of overseeing the selection process. Team Cuba had from the Vedado Tennis Club veteran Antonio Casuso as pitcher, the two Consuegras as catcher (Gustavo) and shortstop (Jorge), and Joaquín del Calvo as outfielder. Havana Yacht Club's Silvio (Chino) O'Farrill was another pitcher, while Rafael Inclán was an infielder, and Porfirio Espinosa (a medical doctor) was a slugging outfielder from the University of Havana. Chino O'Farrill, by the way, was also on the swimming team.[8] Echarri, Fortuna's third baseman, was selected, along with Antonio Castro, as a catcher from the Police Club and Miguel Aguilera as a first baseman-catcher from the Loma Tennis Club. The team was under the direction of Horacio Alonso, the Police Club manager, with Vedado Tennis Club's Ramiro González as "trainer," meaning *fongueador*. This was a magnificent team that blanked a professional selection in Cuba, behind Casuso, in preparation for the Central American Games. They easily swept Mexico in three straight. Lalo Rodríguez of the Police Club beat Mexico in the first game 12–0.

By 1930, when the Second Central American Games were organized, the political and economic situation had changed drastically in Cuba and the world. Before the end of his first term, Machado changed the constitution to prolong his tenure in office. The opposition took to arms and terrorism. The 1929 market crash sent the Cuban economy reeling, contributing to the unrest. Machado needed legitimation now much more than in 1926. Nothing diverts attention from domestic trouble and fosters nationalism above the fray of politics like international athletic competition. So Machado named a delegation that traveled through Central America attempting to organize the second Central American Games, to be held in Havana in 1930. The lavish program published at the conclusion of the games, with an opening picture of the "Honorable President of the Republic, General Gerardo Machado y Morales," is an invaluable document to recapture the atmosphere of the event. These were lean years in many of the countries to be invited, and Cuba lacked the proper facilities for some sports. The program affords a glimpse into the inaugural competition held at Stadium Cerveza Tropical, built for the occasion, which was to become a baseball shrine in Cuban baseball lore, linking the era of Almendares Park to that of the Gran Stadium.

The committee named by Machado to organize the games was headed by Porfirio Franca, of the Vedado Tennis Club, and the construction of the stadium was in the hands of Julio Blanco Herrera, who was among the founding members of that association. The Cuban government sent a committee of two—Miguel Angel Moenck and Ibrahim Consuegra y Anchia—to promote interest in the games among Central American countries. It was hoped that Colombia, Venezuela, and Mexico would also participate, as well as Jamaica, Puerto Rico, and the Dominican Republic. Consuegra and Moenck made an arduous trip through Central America via steamer and railroad in the early fall of 1929, during the rainy season, but met with only partial success, given the poor state of sports organizations in most of those countries. The committee organizing the games asked Machado to make available two cruisers of the Cuban Navy to transport Central American teams to Cuba. They were provided along with lodging at Tiscornia, across Havana Bay, in facilities built by the Immigration Department to temporarily house the avalanche of Spaniards arriving in Cuba. In spite of all these efforts, only nine countries participated: Costa Rica, Cuba, El Salvador, Guatemala, Honduras, Jamaica, Mexico, Panama, and Puerto Rico. Cuba, El Salvador, Guatemala, Mexico, and Panama were the only participants in baseball. It is baffling that Nicaragua and Puerto Rico, countries where baseball was popular, did not play.

Cuba, as would continue to be the pattern in years to come, did very well, winning, of course, in baseball. An indication of the sudden importance of soccer, due to Spanish immigration, is that Cuba also won, undefeated, in that sport. This must have come as a surprise, given that soccer was strongest in Central America and Mexico. But the games appear to have been a bust. Very few of the pictures of La Tropical Stadium show a good attendance, though there are no pictures of baseball or soccer games. Basketball, volleyball, and all water sports were played at the Vedado Tennis Club and the Havana Yacht Club, which presented a problem because of the discriminatory policies in their facilities and the presence of blacks on several teams, particularly Jamaica and Panama. Jess Losada, in a very critical article, chastised the government and the organizing committee for this situation, though it is difficult to ascertain if black athletes did swim in the forbidden waters of the clubs' pools.

Despite the presence of Porfirio Franca as president of the Cuban National Committee for the games, and the fact that Rafael Almeida was the baseball team's manager, the Vedado Tennis Club's influence had diminished considerably by 1930. The Cuban squad still had the Consuegra brothers, but five of its members came from Teléfonos, which had become the dominant amateur team. The most important, of course, was Narciso Picazo, responsible for two of Cuba's five victories. Manuel Domínguez, also of Teléfonos, was the winner of another game, and lost a heartbreaker to Mexico, 2–1, in Cuba's only loss. Teléfonos also contributed infielders Luis Romero and Oscar Reyes, as well as their star catcher, Francisco Espineira. But the tournament was very lopsided, with Mexico and Panama being the only competition for Cuba. Cuba beat the Panamanians in their last meeting, 15–4 (but only 2–1 in their first). Routs were in fact the rule. Cuba crushed Guatemala, 15–1, in the first game of the series, while Panama rolled over El Salvador, 25–0. Mexico was trouncing El Salvador 26–0 when Joaquín Aguilar, El Salvador's only catcher, was bowled over at the plate, breaking his collarbone. By this time the Salvadoreans had no players left (the roster was eighteen, but there are only twelve players in their team picture), and the game was declared a forfeit. El Salvador withdrew from the competition. The University of Havana's Porfirio Espinosa hit .429, with nine hits in twenty-one at-bats (he also won the javelin throw, while pitcher Juan Mendizabal, from the University of Havana, won the shotput competition). Seven Cuban players finished above .300. Mexico came in second, at 4 and 2 to Cuba's 5 and 1, and Panama had a 3 and 3 record.

Baseball may not have been an artistic success at the Central American Games, but the stadium built for them was—Stadium Cerveza Tropical, known to Cubans simply as La Tropical. As I walked around last year what is today called Stadium Pedro Marrero (after a young man who died in the July 26, 1953, attack on the Moncada Barracks), I could still see, through its present squalor, the beauty of the site and the charm of its layout. Near the west bank of the Almendares River, La Tropical is built in a sylvan setting: a green, lush area that comprised the beer gardens, which included the brewery and the ice factory (the Compañía Nueva Fábrica de Hielo owned the Tropical beer factory). Through the fifties the beer gardens were famous for their popular dances, which attracted a large crowd of people of all races, mostly from the lower middle class. By the thirties this area, even though considerably farther from the city of Havana than Almendares Park or the Gran Stadium, was easily accessible by trolley car and bus. Its location is a throwback to early Cuban baseball, and it bespeaks the purpose of its construction for Olympic-style games. The brewery had been founded by Don Cosme Blanco Herrera, a shipping magnate who eventually willed it to his son Julio. The stands take advantage of the sharp slope of a knoll, with the playing field proper in a flat valley below. Made of steel and concrete, like its near-contemporary Stadium Universitario, La Tropical encased principally a running track, and within that a soccer field. The stand ran along the third-base and left-field foul line, angling behind home plate toward right field, but not going as far as it does to left. The baseball field did not fit comfortably in La Tropical's plan and now has completely disappeared, to give way to track and soccer. The park had a seating capacity of about sixteen thousand, but many more gathered there in the heyday of amateur baseball. The park is surrounded by thick vegetation, swaying palm trees, and a forestlike area toward left field. The ice factory's chimney loomed in center field (now obstructed by ghastly cement stands).

As a baseball stadium La Tropical was known for the excellence of the playing field itself, which I have been told was built on top of a deep bed of crushed beer bottles to facilitate drainage. But La Tropical was notorious mostly for the monstrous distances of its outfield fences—a ball hit over a fence was an event. A program for the 1942–43 season of the Cuban League announces the new distances at La Tropical as 359 feet to left, 495 to center, and 350 to right, but the old as 498 to left, 505 to center, and 398 to right. Like its predecessor Almendares Park, this was not a stadium built for home-run hitters—it was a heaven for pitchers and fleet-footed outfielders. Pitchers were further aided by the ample foul areas all around. Because of its generous expanses, La Tropical became an excellent spring-training site. Teams could conduct, simultaneously, several conditioning drills while the infield was in use. In fact, the Dodgers trained there in the thirties and early forties.

Julio Blanco Herrera became the successor of Abel Linares as the principal entrepreneur of Cuban baseball. He would not own teams, but by promoting visits by American teams, and by leasing his stadium to the Cuban League, the Amateur League, and various independent baseball ventures, the game was centered around his brewery until 1945–46, when the professionals fled to the newly built Gran Stadium. The Habana-Almendares confrontation on February 25, 1947, signaled the end of La Tropical as the fulcrum of Cuban baseball activity. But in the intervening years—1930–46—the beautiful park on the banks of the Almendares saw the most spectacular rise in Cuban amateur baseball, the revival of the Cuban League, and Cuba's entry into the ranks of organized baseball with the Havana Cubans of the Florida International League in 1946. To the generation preceding mine, that of my father and father-in-law, La Tropical was Cuban baseball.

After the success of the Co-Criolla series of the late twenties and early thirties, the Amateur League suffered the same decline as the Cuban League, due to the unrest and the eventual toppling of Machado in the summer of 1933. Central Hershey, really the Hershey Sports Club, along with Regla, Cienfuegos, and Fortuna, became the dominant teams by the middle thirties. Hershey won championships in 1932, 1934, 1935, and three straight from 1938 to 1940. Fortuna won in 1936 and 1937. Regla won in 1932 and had several second-place finishes. Cienfuegos, which would shine in the early forties, finished second in 1939 and third in 1940. By this time the Amateur League in the Havana area (including Matanzas, Cárdenas, and Cienfuegos) had as many as eighteen teams. There were quite a few games every Sunday in stadiums such as La Tropical, Vedado Tennis Club, Galbán Lobo (in Regla), and Stadium Universitario. This was truly the heyday of Cuban amateur baseball, unrivaled by any other sport except soccer.

In this period, teams usually had a star with some marquee value, a few of whom jumped early to the professionals in Cuba, Mexico, or the United States. One of the first to do so was Roberto Estalella, whom we saw playing for Rum Havana Club, but who left his mark in the Amateur League playing for Deportivo Cárdenas and Central Hershey. He signed with Habana in 1931 and began his career in organized baseball with Albany in 1934. He made it to the majors with the Washington Senators in 1935, played for a couple of years, bounced around the minors, and returned to the Senators in 1939. He also eventually played for the St. Louis Browns and the Philadelphia Athletics, never quite living up to his promise as a slugger. A fireplug at five-six, Estalella was known in Cuba as El Tarzán because of his impressive build. Another who made the jump was Fermín Guerra, who had a long and distinguished career in Cuba both as a player and as a manager, and who moved to the professionals in Cuba and the United States in the midthirties. Guerra, who would be associated mostly with Almendares in the Cuban League, signed with Habana in 1934 after a career in the Amateur League (Liga Social) with Acción Cubana and Havana Electric. Yet another was Regla's Gilberto Torres, whose father, Ricardo Torres, had caught and played first base in a few games for the Washington Senators in the twenties (the first father-son Cuban combination in major-league baseball). Gilberto, known as Gil in the United States, was a versatile player who had success both as an infielder and a pitcher. Some in Cuba considered him a "white Martín Dihigo" because of this versatility. He signed with Habana in 1934 and began his career in organized baseball with Milwaukee the next year. Another product of Central Hershey was Tomás de la Cruz, who signed with Marianao in the Cuban League in 1934 and with Albany, in Organized Baseball, in 1936. A pitcher of star status in Cuba and Mexico, he made it to the majors with Cincinnati in 1944 after a brilliant 21 and 11 record with Syracuse. All of these were exceptional players and also exceptions in that they turned professional after a stint in the Amateur League. Most of the amateur stars of the early to midthirties, such as Narciso Picazo and Quilla Valdés, did not sign with the professionals, ensuring the continuity and strength of the Amateur League. But this trickle of signees, mostly with the Washington Senators and their indefatigable scout Joe Cambria, was a harbinger of things to come.

Two others who did not turn professional were Reinaldo Cordeiro and Juan Ealo. Cordeiro began his amateur career with the Police Club in 1929. In 1931 and 1932 he played with the Círculo de Artesanos de San Antonio de los Baños, and from 1933 through 1937 he was with Fortuna. A tall, peppery, and spindly catcher, Cordeiro managed Fortuna and the Vedado Tennis Club, as well as the Cuban selection in the Amateur World Series of 1940 and 1942. In 1944 he went from the amateur ranks to manage Almendares in the Cuban League, where he won the championship. His career as manager and coach spanned the forties and fifties. Ealo, known as "Espinacas" because his forearms were like Popeye's, was a slugging first baseman for Fortuna. He eventually did play a few games in a Class C minor league, but he became famous in the Amateur League and in international competition, including the Amateur World Series. After his retirement as a player he managed the Nicaraguan team in one of those tournaments.

A significant development in the thirties and forties was the emergence of players, mostly pitchers, from the provinces, who represented ideal types of the Cuban Republic. These were all white *guajiros*—country bumpkins from the provinces, not from corrupt Havana—who presumably embodied innocence, candor, and strength. They all had notable nicknames. Marrero was called El Guajiro de Laberinto (also El Premier); Julio Moreno was dubbed "Jiquí," after a native hardwood; Rogelio Martínez was known as "Limonar," after the modest little town in Matanzas Province where he began to play; Sandalio Consuegra, who already had a typically backwoods first name found who knows where by his parents, was called "Potrerillo," after the village where he was born in Las Villas Province. The name means little pasture land. Pedro Jiménez, a Central Hershey stalwart, answered to "Natilla," after a sugary Cuban dessert. All five, particularly Marrero and Moreno, became revered amateurs and later famous professionals. These players hailed from a fairyland in the Cuban Republic's mythology situated in the countryside, the *manigua* or the bush, where the Wars of Independence had been waged against Spain, a privileged location in the national imagination. In that pastoral setting, with swaying palm trees in the background and sugarcane stalks bent by breezes in the foreground, the candid guajiros lived in tune with nature and beauty, devoid of guile or greed. Festooned with the emblems of the nation on their uniforms, or quite simply with CUBA across their breast, Marrero, Moreno, Martínez, and Consuegra often appeared in magazines, sometimes even on the covers. Quilla Valdés, a gifted Central Hershey shortstop from Matanzas, Roberto Ortiz, a gigantic slugger from Camagüey, Napoleón Reyes, a superb athlete from Santiago de Cuba who played for the University of Havana, complete, with a few others this gallery of patriotic icons—all white. They were the rural aristocracy of the Amateur League, which, in the thirties and forties, fed on the nationalism of the period, fanned by the likes of Batista and his coterie of recently minted officers, who had ousted the army brass in the September 4, 1933, coup of enlisted men led by the then stenographer sergeant. The sports pageants of the Amateur World Series gave this entire assemblage a fascist tinge from which red was not absent, for the Communists had backed Batista in his 1939 democratic election.

The Amateur World Series coincided exactly with Batista's tenure in power as elected president and with his common front democratic administration. He was elected president in 1939, backed by a broad coalition, assumed power in 1940, and relinquished it in 1944, at the end of his term when his chosen successor was defeated at the polls. The Series were played in Havana from 1939 to 1944 and were brought about by the DGND, its director, Colonel Jaime Mariné, and the various functionaries he appointed. Their enormous success cannot be denied. They not only brought thousands of fans to La Tropical but also focused attention on the amateurs to such an extent that Amateur League games began to set records in attendance. The yearly competition for spots in the Cuban selection was keen and was followed eagerly by fans across the nation. The series also drew attention to the fact that Cuba was and had always been the center of Latin American baseball.

The success of the series was possible because of the political stability of Cuba under Batista's pluralistic rule, and also because of the rise in the economy brought about by World War II. This boost was not as dramatic as that experienced during World War I but still was quite significant. Moreover, with the outbreak of war and with Cuba's strategic position for the defense of the Americas, the United States built military airports in various parts of the country (for instance, San Antonio de los Baños, near Havana) and stationed troops in areas such as Nicaro, where the Nicaro Nickel Company extracted that strategically important metal. During World War II, although not in the nature of previous occupations, Cuba was, again, in a slightly different sense, under U.S. intervention.

Paradoxically, part of the propaganda surrounding the series centered on a Latin Americanism or New Worldism, which proclaimed that, while the European powers waged war, Latin American countries competed only in the field of sport. Machado, under siege in the late twenties, had sponsored the Central American Games to profit from the sense of shared nationality they would foster. Batista, riding a crest of popularity and a nationalism sparked by the crises of the thirties, made the Amateur World Series a showcase for Cuba's progress, stability, and achievements in sports. Politics and baseball continued to be intertwined until today, when the triumphs of the Cuban national team enjoy the support of their number one fan, Maximum Leader Fidel Castro. But given Cuba's dire economic situation today, a cynic in Cuba reminded me not long ago that "people cannot eat medals."

In the chapter on the origins of Cuban baseball I transcribed a chapter from Wenceslao Gálvez's 1889 book *El béisbol en Cuba,* a precious document written by a participant. The oral self-portraits that follow by Agapito Mayor, Andrés Fleitas, Conrado Marrero, and Napoleón Reyes interspersed in the narrative were assembled by me from my interviews with those players. I follow in these the techniques of the *novela de testimonio,* which derived from anthropological practice and had its greatest development in postrevolutionary Cuba. The greatest writer in this trend, Miguel Barnet, author of *Biografía de un cimarrón,* is my model here. Since he is also my dear friend, I have had the unusual privilege of having him actually revise for me these first-person accounts. Mayor, Fleitas, Marrero, and Reyes were protagonists in some of the pivotal games recounted in my narrative, and they are all inscribed in my childhood memories. In giving them a voice, I have attempted to multiply and enrich the perspectives from which this history is told.

On February 24, 1947, Agapito Mayor pitched Almendares into first place and gave them the chance to win the pennant of the Cuban League. But Mayor's triumphs with the professionals, which were many, pale when compared to those he enjoyed as an amateur. He is, with Quilla Valdés, the most representative amateur of the thirties, and the successor of Narciso Picazo as the premier left-handed Cuban pitcher then outside of the Cuban League (Luis Tiant, Lázaro Salazar, and René Monteagudo were the top pro lefties then).

AGAPITO MAYOR: I was born in Sagua la Grande, the eighteenth of August, 1915, on Luz y Caballero Street. Max Lanier and I were born on the same day, the same month, and the same year. I was raised in Caibarién. Caridad Valenzuela and Agustín Mayor were my parents. When I was a month and a half or two months old they took me to Caibarién. I began to play ball in Caibarién, naturally. It was at the Marist Brothers' School. I was a very bad first-baseman, and one day we were being clobbered and Brother Plácido, a priest who was something else, told me: "We have no pitchers." So he put me in to pitch. And I became a pitcher. I was a boy of twelve, but I did well, I was lucky. That's when I began to play ball. It may not be nice to say it, but I didn't like school. I liked baseball. In Las Villas Province I pitched with Santa Clara and in the sugarmills. The first time I pitched a whole doubleheader was with Santa Clara in 1930. I have the records right there in that box. Champion Mesa, Alejandro Oms, all those people, took me with them. I pitched two shutouts that day. I went to the sugarmills from there. How many games did I pitch in the sugarmills? Lots of them. I beat everybody. It may not be nice for me to say it, but I beat everybody. I left for Havana when I was fifteen, recommended by Cesítar Sánchez, who was then Cuban consul in Panama and thought I had the talent. That's something I will never forget. I left with great dreams. My father gave me a silver *peso macho,* which is what we called those in 1930, and a bus ticket.

I arrived in Havana, where I hardly knew anyone. I went to see a gentleman from Caibarién, a little black guy who was a tailor, and he said, "I can't put you up here, Mayor." So I went to sleep in the upstairs of a pool hall, over in Neptuno Street. The next day I showed up at the old Almendares Park, you know, behind the bus terminal, to work out with the Universidad team. Leo Ruiz, a great pitcher then with Universidad, one of the main teams in the Amateur League, was there. Do you think that he was going to let me pitch? He said, "Go over and practice at second base." You know what he meant, he was telling me to leave. All right, I said, damn it. . . . I didn't have a penny by then and I ran into Chino Valdivia, who was my buddy, and I told him: "Chino, I am not going back home to Caibarién." He said: "I have a friend from Placetas who can get you a job selling coffee around Havana out of a little thermos bottle." So I began selling penny-a-shot coffee around Havana. Yes, sir, there was nothing else that I could do. So Chino told me: "I am leaving for Central Algodones, Mayor, if there is a chance I'll send for you to go pitch there." And that's exactly what happened. A week later he sent word: "Hey, come on over here."

Can you imagine what it would have been to raise the fare to go all the way from Havana to Central Algodones? It would have cost me a bundle. Central Algodones is next to Ciego de Avila, in Camagüey Province. So, since I sold coffee around the Plaza del Vapor [Havana's central market then], I got them to take me in a vegetable truck all the way to Santa Clara. When I got there I went to see my uncle Medardo, who was one of the greatest accountants in Cuba and a professor at the university, may God rest his soul, and I said: "Medardo, please . . ." But he said: "No, you are going back home to Caibarién." He refused to give me the money. So I went to see Fallanca [Julián (Fallanca) Pérez, the local nineteenth-century pitcher], who was around the corner, and I told him: "Fallanca, I have to pitch tomorrow in Algodones and I have no money." He said, "Don't worry" and put me to work unloading a truck, which then took me all the way to the Majagua Junction. That's just before Ciego de Avila. I got off there, with the little shirt and pants I had on and nothing else. It was about nine in the evening. Do you remember those little cars with handlebar gear levers? Those *très patá*, Model T Fords? It cost 20 cents to go in one to Central Algodones and I didn't have a penny. But I got there and I found that they had Regino Otero, Chino Valdivia, René Monteagudo, Tito Isla, Juan Decall, Tata Alonso, Estalella, Sungo Carreras, a great team. But Santa Clara was coming with Alejandro Oms. So I said, "Wow!" And Chino told me: "If you don't win you are going to have to leave." I said, "Fine." I went to bed, but before that I wolfed down twenty fried eggs with rice. I was hungry as hell. It was past nine and that's all they had at the company store. So I went to bed, and Gallego Estévez, who was there, too, told me: "Mayor, if you don't win you are going to have to go." "Fine," I said.

They had to lend me spikes because I had none. The ones they gave me didn't fit well. But I thank God that I went out and in one hour and ten minutes I shut out Santa Clara. So they said: "You have a job here." And I stayed.

I could throw everything. It may not be nice for me to say it, but it was hard to beat me. And the proof is that I was selected, from the provinces of Camagüey and Oriente, to go play against Rum Havana Club in

Cárdenas. Rum Havana Club was a professional team but we were from the sugarmills. So we went there and I pitched on Saturday, I pitched Sunday morning, and I pitched Sunday afternoon. Then they signed me to pitch for Deportivo Cárdenas to play a series against Central Hershey. This was in 1935. You were not born then, I think. I was very lucky. We lost the series but I struck out sixty-six in five games. I lost the last game at the Vedado Tennis Park because the catcher could not hold on to my pitches. So I went back to the sugarmill.

The next year they took Juan Decall to Vedado Tennis. Tata Alonso left. Monteagudo left. They didn't take me because I was a little rowdy. I liked to fight and things like that. I was a brawler. But then Central Hershey signed me. So I get to Hershey and the following week we were working out, and I am walking back from the field, when the police come and handcuff me and Mario Díaz. So I said, "But sir, I haven't. . . ." I wanted to call somebody. But they put me in a car. Things were awful in Cuba then. I called out "Mario!" I said to myself: "I'm nothing but a little hick who came here just to play ball, and look at the mess I'm in!" When we crossed from Matanzas to Havana I told myself: "It's over, I won't play ball ever again!" But when we got to Havana they headed to the Fortuna Sports Club, where Laureano Prado was behind a table from here to there, and I realized "This is going to be different." He said: "Here is your application to play for Central Hershey, but you cannot play for Hershey, you have to play for Fortuna." So I answered: "Look, I may be nothing but a poor little peasant, but at Hershey they offered me three hundred dollars and they gave my brother a job." So he said: "Here are the three hundred, and your brother can begin to work tomorrow in Jaruco, with Orúe." He is the one who was mayor of Marianao later.

I was fortunate. In 1936 I won the championship pitching for Fortuna, and I won the Co-Criolla series undefeated. This was the play-off between the champions of the Liga Social and the Liga Nacional. They—the Escuela de Comercio—had eight batters who hit .300, and we had my pitching. I won the four games. In 1936 I went to Mexico with Fortuna, and I established a record that no one in the world can beat. I pitched on Thursday against Martín Dihigo and a professional team from Veracruz. I have the records stored somewhere. I pitched on Saturday. I pitched on Sunday. I pitched Monday. And they didn't let me pitch on Tuesday because they said that my arm would fall off. I won four games in a week. In 1937 I again won the championship with Fortuna. In 1938 I went to Panama, to the Pan American games, and I set a record for games won that still stands. I got four gold medals. Mexico was there, Cuba, Venezuela, Panama. I was champion pitcher, lucky that I was, and most valuable player. I came in second athlete for the Games, behind Juan Luyanda. And second in the Cuban delegation behind a great swimmer, Olga Luque, Luque's daughter, a phenomenal athlete.

When I played for Fortuna I worked in a paper factory. One had to have a job. You could not play for nothing in the amateurs. After Panama I was signed by Luque for the Sixth Regiment, because I went into the military then. I was signed up for training by General Ignacio Galíndez. So I played for the Sixth and I started with Almendares. I played in the armed forces during the summer. I was in the military and already made one hundred pesos a month. In 1939 Luque and Al López signed me for the Boston Braves. I began with Almendares in the 1939–40 season. My debut was against the famous Santa Clara team and I shut them out. Until today I believe that I am the pitcher who has pitched the most games in Cuba. And the one who has won the most.

Perusing the publications of the period, one can easily notice the gradually rising curve of economic recovery in Cuba during the midthirties, which is reflected in the growth of amateur baseball. From a low of six teams in 1933 and 1934, the Amateur League increased to seven in 1935, eight in 1936, eleven in 1937, thirteen in 1938, back to twelve in 1939, but up to eighteen in 1940. Colonel Mariné was obviously restructuring and trying to expand the Amateur League toward the end of the decade. The rise in nonprofessional baseball during the thirties was highlighted by two more Cuban victories in Central American Games that paved the way for the sequence of World Series begun in 1939 that constitute the high mark of Cuba's amateur baseball history to this day.

At the end of the second Central American Games it was decided that the third games would be played in El Salvador, in 1934. A devastating hurricane delayed the construction of facilities for the competition, and the games were not held until March 1935. Engineer Miguel Angel Moenck was put in charge of running the "Olympic" delegation, with Porfirio Franca still presiding, and Cuba sent the largest delegation, with Mexico's being the second in size. There was great anticipation for the meeting of these two sports powers in a neutral site (given that Mexico and Cuba had each prevailed at home in 1926 and 1930, respectively). But in baseball the clash was not to be. Contacts between the Mexican League and Cuban professional baseball were frequent by this time, with Cuban blacks (and some whites) playing in Mexico during the summer. Rosell, Dihigo, Bragaña, Tiant, and many others went to Mexico with the decline in Negro circuit baseball in the United States. Horacio (Lechón) Hernández, a Cuban, managed a professional team in Mexico called Azteca organized by Homobono Márquez, which featured many of these players. Thus, it was not difficult for the representatives of the Cuban delegation to discover that the baseball team Mexico sent to the games was made up of professionals. Romo Chávez, Zenón Ochoa, Pancho Torrijos, and Cocuite Barradas were known to be pros. Cuba protested and the Mexicans withdrew their team, not only because of the putative advantages of professionals, but also because playing against professionals would compromise the amateur status of the Cuban players. Meanwhile, back in El Salvador, there was nearly a brawl at a dining hall when members of the Cuban baseball team taunted their Panamanian counterparts by flinging banana peels at them and calling them professionals. The fight was averted, and Cuba's allegations about the Panamanians' status (particularly about pitcher "Criatura" Karamañitis) were disallowed. Panama and Nicaragua—teams that were clearly professional—would be Cuba's main competitors. El Salvador, Guatemala, and Honduras were no match for these teams.

Cuba's team, managed by Club Atlético de Cuba's manager, León Rojas, had Ricardo Morales in center, from the Marqueses of the Vedado Tennis Club, and Narciso Picazo, the Teléfonos' hero of the 1930 games, along with Manuel Fortes and Felo Suárez as pitchers. Antonio Palencia, from the Police Club, was at short, with Hershey's Jorge Santacruz at third and Deportivo Cárdenas' Esteban Maciques in the outfield. Nicaragua had J. M. Vallecillo and Stanley Cayasso, players who would continue to play for them in international competition for years. Panama, in addition to Karamañitis, featured veterans Applewhite and Mahoney. A picture of the Nicaraguan team that appeared in a Havana newspaper revealed that they also had in their ranks Ramón Méndez, a Cuban professional pitcher who had played in the tobacco semipro circuit and with Almendares in the Cuban League. He was obviously playing under an assumed name. Cuba, led by Fortes' pitching and hitting, finished first at 8 and 1, Panama second at 5 and 3, and Nicaragua third at 4 and 4. Cuba's amateurs were used to playing against professionals back home.

The fourth Central American Games, played in Panama during February 1938, raised the level of expectations and had more attention from the public, partly because the 1936 Olympics in Berlin had strengthened the bond between athletics and nationalism as never before. The stage was set for a confrontation in baseball, this time with Mexico and its professionals in the competition. The presence of professionals was so troubling to the Cuban Olympic Committee (which supervised all Cuba's international amateur teams) that it was asked to declare that the amateur status of its baseball players would not be jeopardized by playing in the games. It did so based on the fact that the amateur federation of each competing country in the games had certified that its athletes were amateur. By this time Miguel Angel Moenck had replaced Porfirio Franca as president of the Cuban Olympic Committee. But little could be done about professionalism. The games' ruling body took at face value the statements made by each country's committee concerning the status of its players. In Mexico, players could shuttle back and forth between amateur and professional teams under existing rules. Legendary Mexican manager Ernesto Carmona brought to Panama a team that included four players I found in the box score of a game in which Agrarios, a professional Mexican team, defeated the Philadelphia Athletics in an exhibition game on March 7, 1937. The pitcher, Romo Chávez, who gave up only five hits and one run to the Athletics, was in the 1938 Mexican selection, as were Torrijos, Ochoa, and Cabal.[9] There were others who played in the Mexican League. Nicaragua added J. A. (Chino) Meléndez, a superb pitcher and hitter who would become a feature in international competition. Venezuela and Puerto Rico were added this time to the baseball competition, and much was expected of them. Cuba brought a formidable team, again under the direction of León Rojas, aided by Reinaldo Cordeiro and Narciso Picazo as coaches. Cuba's pitching included Fortuna's Agapito Mayor, Vedado Tennis Club's Juan Decall, and Hershey's Natilla Jiménez. The catcher was Hershey's Andrés Flcitas, with his teammate Jorge Santacruz at second, Fortuna's Segundo (Guajiro) Rodríguez in center, Deportivo Cárdenas' Esteban Maciques in right, José Luis (Cocoliso) Torres in center field and Antonio Palencia back at short, with Remigio Vega at third and David (El Caballero) Pérez also in the outfield. They need only have brought rubber-armed Agapito Mayor, who won four of the games as a starter and reliever to set a record that still stands in Central and Pan American Games. In a game against powerful Panama, with twenty-five thousand in attendance, Natilla Jiménez opened and Mayor came in after four innings to pick up the win, 6–2. In another, Mayor went the route to beat Mexico, 7–2, on eight hits, with the Mexican runs being scored on errors by Santacruz and Pérez. In yet another, Mayor blanked Nicaragua and Chino Meléndez, 2–0, with the runs coming on errors—each pitcher allowed only five hits. In the deciding game, Natilla Jiménez shut out El Salvador, 4–0, and hit a mammoth homer to boot. Cuba's only loss was to Puerto Rico, when Juanito Decall tired in the ninth and gave up four runs (it was said that Puerto Rico was using *maestros* [professional players]).

Agapito Mayor came back triumphantly to Cuba, where he was bombarded by professional offers, and by Luque's enticement to play for the Sixth Regiment in the armed forces championship, which was virtually professional. First he went home to Caibarién, where he pitched for a powerful Liceo de Caibarién against a Selección de Morón that included major leaguer Roberto Estalella. Mayor defeated them, 5–3, giving up only six hits.

The success of the baseball competition in the 1938 Central American Games brought about the transference of the Amateur World Series to Havana, which was clearly the capital of the sport in Latin America as well as the logical hub now that developments in aviation made the Caribbean a privileged area. Cuba also had an advantage because the city of Havana was accustomed since colonial times to be at the center of the world.

The first Amateur World Series was a five-game tournament played in London, England, from August 13 to 19, 1938. It was organized by an

American businessman named Leslie Mann, who called the tournament "The John Moore Trophy" in honor of the founder of the English Baseball Association. The two teams, supposedly representing England and the United States, were really squads of American soldiers on duty at European bases. As baseball players they had no particular distinction. The team from "England" won, four games to one.

The second Amateur World Series, really the first of any consequence, took place in Havana, at La Tropical, from August 12 to 26, 1939. On June 11, 1939, *Carteles* ran an article announcing the organization of the Series for August of that year. The article stated that the Unión Atlética Amateur de Cuba was in charge of the tournament. The following countries had been invited: Venezuela, Panama, Nicaragua, El Salvador, Jamaica, Mexico, Peru, Puerto Rico, Colombia, Honduras, Haiti, Guatemala, and England. The article says that in England the baseball season began in August, so it was unlikely the defending champions would attend. I very much doubt that there was a baseball season in England, so this seems like a pretext to justify England's absence while claiming continuity. It is amazing that anyone would have thought of inviting the likes of Peru, Jamaica, Haiti, and Honduras, where baseball was hardly played. The fact is that only Cuba, Nicaragua, and the United States competed, the latter with a very weak team not sanctioned by any organization.

Cuba won undefeated, with Nicaragua second at 3 and 3 and the United States last, with six defeats. Nicaragua, managed by Cuban Ramoncito Méndez, brought a strong team led by J. A. (Chino) Meléndez, a veteran pitcher who could also hit, Jonathan Robinson, another hard-hitting pitcher, slugger Stanley Cayasso, and Sam Garth, who was the Series' batting champion with nine hits in eighteen at-bats. Robinson and Cayasso hit the only homers of the tournament. Meléndez, most likely a professional, held Cuba without hits in the first game until the fifth inning, only to lose, 4–3, in ten against Pedro (Natilla) Jiménez. Cocoliso Torres got the deciding hit. Cuba's team, whose makeup appeared somewhat arbitrary, was strong: The catchers were Andrés Fleitas and P. (Kiko) Gutiérrez. The pitchers were M. Tamayo Saco (also an outfielder), Natilla Jiménez, Eliecer Alvarez, Conrado Marrero, Wenceslao González, and N.Corbo. The infielders were Bernardo Cuervo, first base; Ernesto Estévez, second base; Mario Fajo, second base; Clemente González, shortstop; L. Minsal, third base, and A. González, a reserve; the outfielders were D. Pérez, G. Toyo, José Luis (Cocoliso) Torres, and Esteban Maciques. The manager was León Rojas. One wonders why Quilla Valdés was not at short, given that the Hershey battery of Jiménez and Fleitas was included. The remaining players came from clubs such as Regla, Fortuna, Círculo Militar, Cienfuegos, and Deportivo Cárdenas. However, there was none from the elite clubs, thus continuing a trend that had begun in the Central American Games of 1935 and 1938. There was definitely a more egalitarian cast to the Cuban selection.

Colonel Jaime Mariné threw the ceremonial first ball before a crowd of sixteen thousand people at La Tropical. The tight game against Nicaragua was a fan's feast, with good pitching, good fielding, and timely hitting. The Cuban crowd apparently rose to its feet to applaud the Nicaraguans, who later lost yet another heartbreaker to Cuba, 3–2, with Wenceslao González on the mound for the locals. Cayasso, a strong Nicaraguan black, won the admiration of the fans with a mammoth blast. Garth and Robinson, by the way, were also black, while Chino Meléndez looks Indian in the pictures. The eighteen-man Cuban squad had two blacks. The government's effort, even though very modest, to break through the racism of the Amateur League was having some success.

The Series was a huge triumph for Mariné and the DGND, even though the American team was routinely routed and was the doormat of the competition. According to *Carteles* (September 10, 1939) the gate figures are eloquent of the Series' achievements. More than fifty thousand people attended the eight doubleheaders, with a balance of $19,000, the highest take ever for an amateur competition in Cuba. (This makes it about $2.50 per person, though grandstand tickets were 50 cents, a significant amount for average fans back then.) The DGND turned over $4,504.72 to the Nicaraguan team, $3,208.48 to the United States team, and gave the International Federation $3,015.35. The rest went to general expenses; publicity, including posters and signs put on highways throughout the country; transportation for players from outside Havana; and uniforms, equipment, and the like. But the greatest benefit was to the Unión Atlética and the Amateur League, because attendance at its games increased dramatically from then on through the first half of the forties. Marrero and Natilla Jiménez became greater drawing cards than any professional. In June 1940 a new stadium was opened in Matanzas (actually a refurbished Palmar del Junco), following the initiative of Colonel Manuel Benítez, a Batista man who had participated in the sergeants' revolt of 1933. The Vedado Tennis Club team played the powerful Deportivo Matanzas in the inaugural game. This was merely a portent of things to come, as amateur baseball became the game's centerpiece in Cuba.

The third Amateur World Series was played at La Tropical from September 14 to October 6, 1940. Probably encouraged by the success of the 1939 event, seven teams participated: Cuba, Nicaragua, the United States, Venezuela, Hawaii, Mexico, and Puerto Rico. The competition was much more balanced this time. The United States brought a strong squad, as did Nicaragua. The Hawaiian team had a good number of Japanese players, particularly Kunihisha, a lightning-fast runner who stole seven bases. The Americans were led by a left-handed pitcher, Frank (Stubby) Overmire, who went on to have a ten-year major-league career, mainly with the Detroit Tigers. Nicaragua again brought Meléndez, Robinson, and Cayasso, as well as J. M. Vallecillo, who hit four doubles; Carlos (Pichón) Navas, a hard-hitting shortstop; and star catcher Julio (Canana) Sandoval. Robinson was the batting champion, at .444. He hit the only homer and scored the most runs, Vallecillo led in runs batted in, Cayasso led in hits with nineteen, and Meléndez, who won three and lost none, was the champion pitcher. Venezuela came with a good team on whose coaching staff was Cuban Joseíto (Joe) Rodríguez, a star first baseman from the twenties. Cuba won again, but was not undefeated. They won ten and lost two, while the Nicaraguans and the Americans, each of whom beat Cuba once, were tied for second at 9 and 3, Venezuela and Hawaii tied for third at 5 and 7, and Mexico and Puerto Rico each finished at 2 and 10.

The Cuban team was managed this time by Fortuna's Reinaldo Cordeiro. Carlos Fleites, from the same club, and Vitico Muñoz, manager of the University of Havana team, were the coaches. There were significant changes in the roster. The first catcher was Carlos Colás, a black, with Kiko Gutiérrez again as backup (they actually split the duties). Conrado Marrero, Eliecer Alvarez, and Natilla Jiménez were back, but this time Fortuna's left-handed sensation Daniel Parra was added, along with Hershey's Antonio (Loco) Ruiz, who also played the outfield, and Tomás Hechevarría, from Círculo Militar y Naval. Ruiz had gone 12–0 in the Amateur League that year and hit over .300. The infield was boosted with the addition of Napoleón Reyes, from the University of Havana, who played first, short, and right field during the Series, and Manuel (Chino) Hidalgo, a sensational shortstop with Fortuna who hit over .300 in the Amateur League that year. Chino Hidalgo, who was indeed of Chinese ancestry, would go on to have a good career in the professionals and became one of my favorites with Habana. Pedro (Charolito) Orta, a black third baseman from Pinar del Río, was also added. Orta, whose distasteful nickname—Patent Leather—alluded to his color, played in the Cuban League later with Marianao, and also in the Mexican League (he moved to Mexico, where he married, and his son Jorge Orta reached the majors). Another infield addition was Virgilio Arteaga, from the Círculo Militar y Naval, a slugging first baseman. Mario Fajo was the only returning infielder from the previous year. Esteban Maciques returned in the outfield, but this time with Loco Ruiz (when he was not pitching), José Ramón López from Regla, Segundo (Guajiro) Rodríguez from Fortuna, and F. Sánchez. It is obvious that the team was loaded with players from the top teams in the Amateur League at that time: Hershey, Fortuna, University of Havana, Cienfuegos, Círculo Militar y Naval, and Regla.

Cuba's pitching was just too much. Marrero had three of the team's ten victories (and also its two defeats), while Hechevarría had two, and Alvarez, Ruiz, Jiménez, and Parra one each. Parra's 2.77 earned-run average was the *highest* among the Cuban pitchers; Marrero's was 1.15, Hechevarría's 1.16, Ruiz's 1.29. and Jiménez's 1.91! While Nicaragua's Robinson and Cayasso were the best hitters of the Series, Cuba's Rodríguez (.433), Ruiz (.372), Fajo (.341), Hidalgo (.316), and Reyes (.297) hit very well indeed. Although he hit only.156, Colás was deemed to have been the hero of the Series because of his defensive play (he is said to have had a tremendous arm), but the Most Valuable Player was Conrado Marrero.

The Series was a success beyond anyone's wildest dreams. An average of sixteen thousand people attended the games, and twenty-one thousand crowded into La Tropical the afternoon of September 29 for the game between Cuba and the United States, won by the home team, 3–2; Marrero had lost, 2–1, to the Americans the previous day. As if ordained by a higher power, Batista's inauguration as the democratically elected president of Cuba took place on October 10, a Cuban national holiday, four days after the conclusion of the 1940 Amateur World Series. There was a coalescing of politics, sports, and nationalism that would turn the next Series into the apotheosis of baseball in Cuba, perhaps its highest point ever.

Mariné's DGND was riding a historical crescendo. After the 1940 Series the Cuban team lost two tight games to a selection from the Cuban League managed by Luque (with Tomás de la Cruz, Gilberto Torres, Fermín Guerra, and others), and then accepted an invitation from Venezuela to travel to Caracas for a friendly series. The Cuban team won the seven-game tournament in Caracas, where the games were sold out and avidly followed by the Venezuelan fans.

The glow from Cuba's victory in the 1940 Amateur World Series continued to brighten the country's baseball fans in the spring of 1941. On March 27, 1941, Juan (Juanito) Decall pitched a Cuban selection to a 2–1, five-hit victory over the Boston Red Sox, in Havana for some spring-training games. Cuba's team had Guajiro Rodríguez, Quilla Valdés, Mario Fajo, Loco Ruiz, and Juan Ealo, and looked very much like the selection for the next Amateur World Series. This game became as much a part of Cuban lore as Bombín Pedroso's no-hitter against Detroit and José de la Caridad Méndez's one-hitter against Cincinnati. The Red Sox did not have Ted Williams with them, but had Bobby Doerr, Jimmie Foxx, Joe Cronin, Dom DiMaggio, Skeeter Newsome, and Tom Carey. It was common in the thirties for major-league teams to come to Havana to play against both amateur and professional selections. Rodolfo Fernández, Luis Tiant, Tomás de la Cruz, Ramón Bragaña, Agapito Mayor, and others had defeated the big-leaguers. But amateur Decall was masterful against the Red Sox, and his team, drawn from the Amateur League, seemed to belong on the same field with the American League team. Boosted by the Amateur World Series win the previous year, the fourth "classic," as it was already being called, loomed large on the horizon.

The 1941 Amateur League championship was one of the most hotly contested ones, followed by thousands both in person and via broadcasts. Cienfuegos, Hershey, Deportivo Matanzas, the University of Havana, Teléfonos, Círculo de Artesanos, and Fortuna struggled in one division, while Círculo Militar, Artemisa, and Atlético de Cuba competed in the other. Hershey had, in addition to Natilla Jiménez, another stellar pitcher, Ramón (Colorado) Roger, a powerful redhead. Club Deportivo Matanzas had come up with Rogelio (Limonar) Martínez and Catayo González, the first a righty and the second a lefty (soon they would add Sandalio Consuegra to make up the best amateur staff ever in Cuban amateur baseball). Círculo de Artesanos had discovered Julio Moreno, a fireballing right-hander who would have a meteoric career as an amateur, a distinguished one in the Cuban League, and a brief one in the majors. In 1941 Moreno, a slender, smallish man, struck out 160 batters. He was quickly dubbed "the Cuban Bob Feller." Meanwhile, Círculo Militar counted on its own right-handed phenomenon, Isidoro León. Cienfuegos continued to rely on Marrero, who won eighteen and lost six in 1941. The season ended in a tie between Cienfuegos and Círculo Militar. The deciding game, a duel between Marrero and León, was played on September 27, as the first game of the first doubleheader of the 1941 Amateur World Series. Marrero lost. The stage was set for a game that would rival Lanier's 1947 victory over Habana in the memory of Cuban baseball: the "Canónico game" against Venezuela.

Nine countries came to the fourth Amateur World Series: Cuba, Venezuela, Mexico, Panama, the Dominican Republic, the United States, Nicaragua, Puerto Rico, and El Salvador. The addition of Panama and the Dominican Republic, countries where baseball was developing fast, raised the level of competition. Led by their popular manager, José Luis (Chile) Gómez, Mexico arrived with a seasoned team that would be completely revamped the next year except for third baseman Víctor Manuel (Pingua) Canales. Nicaragua brought its usual group of powerful sluggers and veteran pitchers, including Cayasso, Robinson, Meléndez, and Vallecillo. El Salvador and Puerto Rico brought weak teams and were routed. (The reason why the Puerto Rican teams did not fare well in the Amateur World Series was that, as American citizens, Puerto Rican young men were subject to the military draft, in force since the fall of 1940. But the greatest expectations were the quality of the Panamanian and Dominican teams. Panama had among its players Patricio (Pat or Lord) Scantlebury, who would pitch for years in Cuba and the United States, for teams such as the New York Cubans, the Cuban Sugar Kings, and the Cincinnati Reds. He also could hit. They brought catcher Leon Kellman, who hit the only homer in the Series. The Dominicans, managed by the colorful Luis Ernesto (Burrolote) Rodríguez, came with a seasoned squad that featured catcher-first baseman Luis St. Clair and his brother José, a second-baseman, pitcher Luis Castro, who won two games, third baseman Tetelo Vargas, and pitchers Rafael Hereaux and José D. Pérez. Venezuela added suspense to the proceedings by not arriving in Havana until the Series had actually begun (some said they were waiting to see if Cuba would lose a game to the Dominican Republic before finally deciding to come). Venezuela came with a great team of veterans who had played the Cubans in the past Series and in the invitational tournament in Caracas. They were José Pérez Colmenares, Julio Bracho, Enrique Fonseca, Dalmiro Finol, Héctor R. Benítez,

José Casanova, and a man whose name would forever be remembered in Venezuelan and Cuban baseball: Daniel (Chino) Canónico.

The Cuban team had a tremendous pitching staff, composed of the best from the recently finished Amateur League championship (except for Isidoro León): Julio (Jiquí) Moreno of Círculo de Artesanos, Conrado Marrero of Cienfuegos, Rogelio (Limonar) Martínez of Matanzas, Pedro (Natilla) Jiménez of Hershey, Ramón (Colorado) Roger of Hershey, Daniel Parra of Fortuna, and Tomás Hechevarría of Círculo Militar y Naval. The catcher was again Andrés Fleitas, after a year's absence backed by Rouget Avalos. The infield was revamped, except for Camagüey's Bernardo Cuervo, who remained at first. Napoleón Reyes was at second, with his teammate from the University of Havana Antonio (Mosquito) Ordeñana at third, and Clemente González was at short. The outfield retained Segundo (Guajiro) Rodríguez (Fortuna) in center but had Cienfuegos' Charles Pérez in left and Rafael (Villa) Cabrera, a black from Oriente Province, in right. Cabrera had a great arm and also could pitch and play third. The team was managed by Hershey's Joaquín M. Viego, with Teléfonos' Narciso Picazo as coach.

The Series was tight, and at the end Cuba and Venezuela were even, at seven victories and one defeat each. Marrero had won three games and Limonar Martínez two; Martínez and Jiménez had not given up a single earned run. Moreno and Hechevarría had won the other two games, with Jiquí losing the only one to Venezuela's Canónico, who had won four and lost none with an ERA of 1.69 in thirty-two innings. Venezuela's shortstop Casanova hit .429, while for Cuba Bernardo Cuervo finished at .400, González at .395, and Fleitas at .378. Napoleón Reyes hit .344 and Guajiro Rodríguez .323, with two doubles. On October 17, Venezuela tied the Series by defeating Cuba 4–1 behind Canónico, who gave up only five hits. Cuba used Marrero, Moreno, and Martínez, who only allowed seven hits. Cuba and Venezuela would be co-champions. Then came the fateful decision. It is reported that Venezuela was content with the tie and would have happily gone home with it, while the Cubans wanted to play a deciding game. Venezuela stalled, claiming that they had no other hurler than Canónico, who, having pitched the entire last game was not ready. The Cuban authorities, probably confident of winning it all, agreed to give Venezuela a few days to allow Canónico to recover. To stay in trim, Venezuela played and won, 3–1, against a strong Club de Artesanos de Placetas that included Mario Díaz, Catayo González, Pancho Villa, and Esteban Maciques.

The die was cast on October 23, 1941, with La Tropical overflowing with fans, and the whole of Venezuela, Cuba, and probably the entire Caribbean basin hanging on every word of the broadcast. It was Marrero against Canónico for all the marbles. Venezuela scored three in the bottom of the first on two bases on balls, a hit to center that Guajiro Rodríguez muffed, and a bonehead play at third by Mosquito Ordeñana. Marrero was notorious for first-inning woes; some said because he did not warm up properly. He was also probably tired after the hectic finale of the Amateur

League and the three victories in the Series. Viego let Marrero get out of trouble and pitch another inning, but then brought in Natilla Jiménez, who shut out the Venezuelans the rest of the way. Meanwhile, the wily Chino Canónico was mowing down the Cuban team with his pinpoint control, wide assortment of junk, and with help by spectacular plays at third by Romero and at short by Casanova. In the ninth, Cuba finally scored one and seemed to be on the verge of coming back, but it was not to be. Venezuela had prevailed. The Cuban crowd, in a grand gesture of sportsmanship, surged onto the field and carried Canónico around in triumph. In Venezuela the country went berserk and gave the winners a riotous reception when they returned home. To this day Canónico's victory is the highest peak in the history of Venezuelan baseball. Cuba was numb. Colonel Mariné issued a magnanimous proclamation in a pamphlet published by Radio Cadena Azul, which broadcast the games, stating that the best team had won and congratulating the Venezuelans. Preparations for the next Series were started at once, however. But the 1941 Series would remain the greatest of all, for on December 7 the Japanese bombed Pearl Harbor, the world went to war, and travel restrictions and other impediments reduced the number of participants.

Cuba, nevertheless, was anxious to regain its Latin American baseball supremacy by defeating Venezuela and Canónico.

Conrado Marrero was the most successful amateur pitcher in Cuban history. He won 123 games in the Cuban Amateur League, led Cuba in several Amateur World Series, and was on the Almendares roster the afternoon Lanier beat Havana, having just turned professional at age thirty-five. He made it to the major leagues with the Washington Senators in 1950. In the fifties he also pitched in the Florida International League with the Havana Cubans, in the International League with the Cuban Sugar Kings, and beat Panama in a crucial game of the Caribbean Series, pitching for Marianao when in his midforties. He is a pleasant, placid, and small man of Canary Island descent, known for his late-breaking curves and his elephantine memory: Once he discovered a hitter's weakness, he would never forget it. Marrero was what Cubans call *un guajiro lépero* (a cagy, tricky, devious hick). He remained in Cuba after the Revolution, often working as a pitching coach. Someone once said that Marrero, in uniform, looked like someone disguised as a baseball player. But he won and won and won, and saved the Cuban League from ruin by deciding to stay at the Gran Stadium when others went to La Tropical in the late forties. Marrero, whose hometown is the same as mine, once gave me a Washington Senators hat, which someone promptly stole from me.

CONRADO MARRERO: I was born on a farm called El Laberinto, district of Sagua la Grande, on August 11, 19 . . . I mean April 25, 1911.[10] I began to play baseball right there in the country. On the very farm they played ball and that's where I began. So I grew and I played and I worked. We had a little business, a small sugarcane plantation my father owned, and we worked there. We played on Sundays right there at El Laberinto. And because little teams came from Sagua la Grande, and I would beat them, I came to be known as El Guajiro de Laberinto, the Hick from Laberinto. They would come to play us and the people would tell them: "El Guajiro from Laberinto is going to get you!" That's how I began to play ball. They used to take me to play in all the little ballfields around there. I also went to the port of La Isabela. I played for the Casino Español in Sagua la Grande, when they organized a little championship. Casa Blanco, Antiguos Alumnos, Casino Español, and ABC, those were the names of the four little clubs that were in it.

I beat Casa Stany, in La Isabela, when they came to give me a try-out. The Stany people, though they had pitchers, were about to join the Unión Atlética de Cuba, and wanted to get another one. The dredger from Cienfuegos was working at La Isabela and there was a fellow in it who had been a ballplayer in the twenties, a catcher. He would watch me pitch against the little teams that came by. Because I would go to Isabela and pitch against those nothing clubs and beat them. So this man kept going back to Cienfuegos to tell them: "There is this little hick over there who can really pitch; he beats everybody." He had said so much to them that they found a way of coming from Cienfuegos to try me out. I pitched against them and beat them. We only played seven innings because it got dark. We beat them, 2–0. The field was very little. I think that you must have seen it. A field they called La Punta. There was a little house behind first base and a little wooden fence. We used to play it so that any ball hit over it was only a double, not a home run, because it was too short. But the people from Cienfuegos, since they came with three left-handed hitters, insisted that it be left to chance. And we had to accept. But every time the left-handers came up, they struck out.

I threw them little curveballs, because I always threw a lot of little curveballs. Then it turned out that they were sliders, or what they call sliders today. Mine was a bit wider and shorter. I developed a lot of control, it seems that because I was always throwing since I was a boy. I became a pitcher in the Amateur League when I was already a hardened and seasoned peasant. I was already twenty-six or twenty-seven by the time of what I told you happened at La Isabela. I had pitched a lot around the countryside. I pitched quite a bit, you know.

Casa Stany was a men's clothing store. Peña de Armas, who was an employee there, became team representative when they got together a board of directors to organize the club for the Amateur League. That was at the time when they came to get me to take me to Cienfuegos. I went on living in El Laberinto for a long time until I moved to Sagua la Grande. We played on Sundays. The team practiced twice a week, but

since I was over there in El Laberinto or Sagua, I was the one who practiced the least. I only pitched for that team because it was forbidden to
play for any other. During the season I could only play for Cienfuegos.
The team had two or three pitchers. At first they pitched, but when I got
a chance and won more than they, they left. I pitched every Sunday.
There were seasons in which Cienfuegos finished with twenty-two wins
and five losses and I finished at 22 and 5. I pitched every game. Of
course, on a day when I didn't have it, there was a substitute pitcher who
would relieve me. If I was not on that day, couldn't hold them, they
were hitting me or whatnot, they would put another pitcher in. But I always started.

When I began pitching I stopped playing other positions, but I did
play others before. When I was a kid I was a shortstop or a third baseman. I played the infield and had a good arm. I didn't like to pitch.
What I liked was to play the infield and hit. Everybody likes to hit. In
the Amateur League I only hit so-so.

We played one-game home-and-away series in the Amateur League.
One game in Cienfuegos and another in Havana. We played against Hershey, Fortuna, Círculo Militar, Artemisa, Santiago de las Vegas. All that
was around Havana. Matanzas and Cárdenas were also in the league.
There were many clubs within Havana. Fortuna, Cubaneleco, Teléfonos,
Vedado Tennis, Círculo Militar, ABC, Yara. Yes, sir, there were many
clubs.

Blacks did not play in the Amateur League because these were social
clubs. Casa Stany changed its name to Cienfuegos Sports Club because
the league did not allow advertising the names of businesses. Hershey
was the name of the sugarmill town.

When our championship ended—it lasted about six months, playing
every Sunday—they would send for me to play in Camagüey, or in a sugarmill, or in Santiago de Cuba, or Caibarién, or a place like that. They
would pay me. Casa Stany subsidized me, they gave a monthly allowance,
because amateurism prohibits pay as if it were work. But, well, you know,
to be able to play, to be able to support myself and so forth, they gave
me money. They also gave me a job working for Almacenes Castaño in
Havana. They had a farm, and since I had farm experience and all that, I
would spend the week working on the farm.

From March to September, while the championship was on, I only
played for Cienfuegos. The grinding season began in January. There was
very little baseball during the grinding season. The sugarmills hardly
played during the grinding season. When I was not playing for Cienfuegos I would go out about twice a month to play elsewhere in different
places. I began to play in Cienfuegos in 1938 and moved from the farm
to Sagua la Grande in 1941 or 1942.

They took me to the first Amateur World Series in 1939. I only
pitched one game because there were very few teams. I think Nicaragua

sent a team, there was another from the United States, and Cuba. It was a Series with very few clubs. Later, in 1940, more came. The duel that I lost to Canónico was in 1941. I lost, 3–1. Canónico had good control. He moved the ball around, and he pitched very well that year, because Canónico won four games in that Series. He beat Cuba twice. And we were a good team. A good nine. Fleitas was the catcher. Venezuela came back in 1942 and I pitched the first game against Canónico and we beat them, 9–0, or something like that.

I was suspended in 1943 because I played elsewhere. The league did not allow playing for somebody else when the club was not playing. There were times when you did it and they didn't pay any attention. But that time I pitched in Camagüey, they paid attention, and suspended me, because it was understood that if I went to Camagüey it was because they were paying me. I wasn't allowed to pitch in the Series. I had to serve a six-month suspension, and I did. I served my suspension. In 1944 we went to Venezuela. It ended up in a brawl. All the teams withdrew. The Venezuelans went too far in having it their way with the umpiring. It was quite something. Then, in 1945, I pitched again for Cienfuegos, which was the last year I pitched. But I went to that little town called Santo Domingo, near Santa Clara, and pitched in a benefit game for the Colored Society, and they suspended me again. Indefinite suspension. So I said enough is enough, I'm going to turn pro.

☺

Andrés Fleitas was the Almendares catcher in the 1946–47 season, and behind the plate in the three decisive games of February 23, 24, and 25, 1947, when Agapito Mayor and Max Lanier disposed of Habana. Fleitas was also behind the plate on October 22, 1941, when Daniel Canónico defeated Conrado Marrero and Cuba for the championship in the fourth Amateur World Series. He was again Marrero's catcher when "The Premier" and the Cuban team trounced Canónico and Venezuela on October 4, 1942. A feared line-drive hitter and superb defensive catcher, Fleitas made it to the Triple-A Jersey City Little Giants, then jumped to the Mexican League, where he enjoyed great seasons with Monterrey. He played through the forties and fifties in the Cuban League with Almendares.

ANDRÉS FLEITAS: I was born at Central Constancia, Las Villas Province, on November 8, 1916. I was raised there. I began to play in the sugarmills, like you play in the semipro league. My position was catcher. Yes, sir, I always played catcher. At Constancia they were organizing a team, you know, boys sixteen, seventeen, eighteen, and there was no catcher. I was a third baseman. So I told the manager: "All right, I'll be the catcher." And he said: "Have you ever caught?" And I answered: "Yeah,

I've caught, and I like the position." From then on I began to play catcher. From Constancia I went to Casa Stany in Cienfuegos.

I played there with Marrero. That's when, precisely in 1937, they made a selection to go to the Central American Games in Panama. I don't know if you remember. A selection from Camagüey, Casa Stany, Camagüey, and Unión Atlética. They went around Camagüey and Las Villas picking up independent players, you know, players outside the Unión. But it turned out that the only one they took, not in the Unión, was David Pérez, Charles Pérez's brother, a great athlete and a great hitter. He was the only one to go. Agapito was the hero. Juanito Decall and Natilla Jiménez were also heroes in that Series. Agapito won three or four games. He participated in every game in the games.

Marrero stayed behind in Cienfuegos and I went to Hershey. I left Constancia in 1938 to go there, because they wouldn't give me work in Cienfuegos. At Hershey they gave us jobs, food—you know, everything needed for us to stay there at the sugarmill. The truth is that Hershey was for me like my own sugarmill, because I had a good time there. I loved it very much. And they loved me very much, and continue to love me, because many of my teammates are still alive. Others, like my comrade Natilla Jiménez, died a few years ago. I played for five years at Central Hershey in the Amateur League. As a matter of fact, we won three pennants in a row, and then came in second and third.

Hershey was a team without too many ballplayers. In the Amateur League you played every Sunday. Once a week. Sometimes on Saturday, too, but most of the time only on Sundays. At Hershey we always had the same team, we had no substitutes like Círculo Militar y Naval, a powerhouse; but they had forty players, forty stars. That's the reason they beat us. They were too many. We had, by position, let's begin with me: I was the catcher, there was no other catcher. Cheo Nápoles was at first, Jorge Santacruz at second, and Quilla Valdés at short. He is the greatest amateur shortstop ever. Fusil [Rifle] González was at third. In left we had Loco Ruiz, in center Enrique del Sol, and Pedro Echevarría in right. Roberto Ortiz left in 1937. He played for a year or two at Hershey. There was only one substitute. The one who could catch and play several positions was Loco Ruiz, who was a great athlete. But there was no other catcher than me. I never missed a game in the five years I played at Hershey. Natilla didn't either. It was a matter of luck. Ballón was the utility, but he never played. José Ballón. As pitchers we had Natilla, Ramón Roger, and a boy named Padrón, from Matanzas. Three pitchers and we almost always used Natilla or Roger. So Padrón, a young boy, pitched only once in a while, but just an inning or two.

I mean that we won three championships at Hershey with the same team. And in the five years I was there it was always almost the same team. When Santacruz retired, about 1940, a guy named Pelayo, from El Perico, came to play second. There were a few changes, you know, but the team that won the three consecutive championships was the same.

From there I went on to the Amateur World Series. I played for two years in the Amateur World Series. The first was in 1941, when we lost against Canónico. And the last was in 1942, when we got back the pennant by beating Canónico and everybody else. We had a great team. I was the catcher, with Tatica Hernández as second catcher. Ealo was at first, Fajo at second, and Vega at third. No, it was Luis Suárez, Luis Suárez. Quilla was at short. Loco Ruiz in left, Félix del Cristo in center, and Echevarría in right. Ah, and Charles Pérez was also a left fielder. The pitchers were Natilla, Moreno, León, Limonar, Consuegra. A tremendous team.

Daniel Canónico pitched a great game, you cannot take that away from him. He threw a knuckleball and a slow pitch that he sometimes put a little more on. He was a pretty good pitcher. But I attribute Venezuela's victory not exactly to Canónico, but to the team they had. Because they had an infield that played incredible ball. You know, they had Casanova at short, Finol at second, Romero at third, and a player who was later killed in an accident called Pérez Colmenares. Chucho Ramos was in left, Benítez in center, and Bracho in right. They tied the Series and didn't want to play the next day to decide. So they gave them three days of rest so Canónico would be able to pitch. That was another advantage they had. Well, of course, they won because they played better than we did. Their third baseman played like a major leaguer. There was a play when we had two on, I remember. We had a man at third, no, men at second and first, and Villa Cabrera hit a sizzler right over the bag and this guy leaped, stepped on the base, and threw to first for a double play. That was just one of the many great plays they made. Then came Casanova's turn. He did the same on my hit, and with another by Ealo, and so on. Well, it was tremendous. They played fantastic ball. So I think they deserved it because they played better than we did.

Napoleón Reyes had a long and distinguished career in Cuba as both a player and a manager. As an amateur for the University of Havana he led a strong team managed by legendary coach Víctor (Vitico) Muñoz. Reyes' signing with Almendares in 1941 was instrumental in restoring the prestige of the Cuban League. Napoleón, known as Nap Reyes in the United States, played one year for the Jersey City Little Giants in Triple A, and three years during the war with the New York Giants, 1943 to 1945. He worked those winters in shipyards instead of returning to Cuba, and he acquired American citizenship. In 1945 he signed with Pasquel and had a four-year career in the Mexican League, returning to Cuba to play with Cienfuegos in the winter. In 1950 he played one game for the Giants. In the fifties Napoleón became a sought-after manager, leading Marianao in the Cuban League to two pennants, and earlier a Venezuelan team that he took to the Caribbean Series. He also managed the Cuban Sugar Kings in the International League at that time. He was known as a combative manager in the mold of Leo Durocher. Napoleón Reyes passed away in 1994, a little over two years after I spoke with him.

NAPOLEÓN REYES: Well, I was born on November 24, 1919, in Santiago de Cuba. When my father died—he died very young—my mother was left pregnant with my sister. My father was twenty-four when he died. We moved to Central Santa Ana, in Oriente Province. My mother remarried there a man with our same last name, Reyes, a coincidence. We were raised there until we were adolescents, and it was there that I began to play baseball, in the sandlots of the central. But by then I was already attending secondary school in Santiago de Cuba. At first, since the distance was so short between the Central and Santiago, I played a little in Santiago and also, when I had the time, in the sugarmill. I was about sixteen or seventeen years old then.

It was a very strong league the sugarmills played in. There was the Cuban Navy team, which had great ballplayers, and Central Palma. Many great ballplayers came from there. There was also our sugarmill, Central Santa Ana. Central Palma, which was in Palma Soriano, had a good stadium. The fourth team was Casa Bacardí, Bacardí Rum. So there were: Ron Bacardí, the Navy, Central Santa Ana, and Central Palma. The four were very, but very strong. We played once a week, and perhaps a few other games, but nearly all of us worked during the grinding season. I began to work from midnight to noon when shifts were twelve hours long. I was a sugar chemist. That is to say, I began as an assistant sugar chemist at the Central. We were not paid much for playing because at that time there was no money for that sort of thing. The Navy players had everything they needed issued to them. Casa Bacardí's had its players that worked at the Bacardí plant. Central Palma's players nearly all worked at the Central, and we were workers of Central Santa Ana. There were white and colored players.

This was a very strong league, a very, very strong league, because we even brought players from Havana as reinforcements. Adrián Zavala pitched there, Angel Cordeiro, Reinaldo's brother, pitched there. Dihigo pitched in that league. We brought them in because the professionals were nobody in Cuba. They played their championship and nobody went to see them. People didn't follow the Cuban League at that time. So we, who played on Sundays, who had excellent players—because the Navy had tremendous players—brought in the professionals. Charolito Orta played there, Zabala pitched for Central Palma, and the Casa Bacardí had great colored players. Harry Wilson was a fantastic colored player. He was our shortstop. His name was English because he was Jamaican, but he was a Cuban. Sometimes we played at Central Palma, others we played at our sugarmill. Central Santa Ana was also powerful because we sometimes also brought somebody from Havana, a ringer. You know what I mean. But the whole league was very strong because at that time the players in Cuba did not turn professional. They stayed and worked in the sugarmills, or at Casa Barcardí. These were magnificent players who could have easily gone to the pros.

I used to play first then. I was tall, but I was a man who could run fast. I can't run now because of the arthritis. My legs are hurt. But I was a 195-pound man who could run at great speed. I made it to the pros playing shortstop. But at the Central I played first because we had others who played the infield.

I came to Havana in 1936. I came to study. I had graduated from secondary school in Oriente and went to Havana to study. Since I was already working as a sugar chemist, I came to Havana because they offered a two-year course to become a certified sugar chemist. They had passed a law in Cuba to replace all the foreigners who were sugar chemists. In all the Cuban sugarmills the sugar chemists were foreign nationals. They provided two years of study in Havana for any Cuban who wanted to become certified and return to the sugarmills as chief sugar chemist. That's the reason I went to the University of Havana. I had no intention to go on later, but I did and graduated as an agronomist. That's the time when I turned professional.

I began playing for Club Fortuna, because when I arrived in Havana there was a man, a friend of my father's, who was the chief of police of the sugarmill, who told him: "When your son gets to Havana I'm going to get him into a club." He was then on Fortuna's board of directors, so when I made it to Havana, not knowing anybody or anything, he took me to Club Fortuna. Agapito was already there. So I would be studying and going back to the Central to work during the grinding season those two years.

In the middle of all that there came a coach, who died already, a friend of mine from the University, who was about to take charge of various coaches at the University. He was Víctor, Vitico Muñoz. In Cuba the amateurs played only on Sundays because everybody worked the famous Cuban twelve hours a day, and on Saturdays even more; now it's eight hours, four hours, even three hours, but not then. So there was a makeup game against Regla on a Saturday, and Cordeiro, who was the manager, came over and told me: "Hey, Big One," which is what he always called me, "I want you to play shortstop tomorrow . . . Saturday." Our shortstop was a boy named Cubells who worked all week at a store lugging sacks of rice. He could only come on Sundays to play for us, for Fortuna. So I said, "All right, I'll play." I had been working out at short, and Cordeiro had noticed me. So I started and, bang, I made my debut with a homer. Bang! Bang! Vitico was watching because he was going to take over at the University, so he turns to this boy who was a classmate of mine at the agricultural school near Boyeros and says: "Listen, what's that hick there doing playing with Fortuna?" And my friend said: "Don't you know that he is a student at the University?" "What do you mean, 'He is a student at the University'?" "Yes," my friend said, "he's been at the University for a year. Why don't you take him to the University team?" Can you believe how things turn out? The game was over and I had really cleaned up. I had been playing better baseball in Oriente. So Vitico stops me and says: "Hey, listen, are you a student at the University?" And the boy from the University who knew me said: "Yes, he is the one, he is a student at the University." At that time you could transfer without any problems from another team to the University. To move to any other team you had to wait a year. But not to the University. That was a right you had by being at the University. So Vitico said: "Look, I'm going to manage the University, and I want you to play for the University next year." I answered: "Well, let's see what happens." But he said: "No, nothing is going to happen, you'll play for me." There were a few games left in the season and I went on playing short because Cordeiro just left me in there. The next year, when I returned for my second year, when I would graduate as a sugar chemist, then I played for the University. I played three years for the University, because once I finished as sugar chemist I needed two more years to graduate as agronomist. I then, immediately, jumped to the professionals. So that's how I played in the amateurs, beginning with Fortuna and changing to the University. It was one of those things; if not, I could have stayed playing for Fortuna because I had been recommended by the chief of police.

I played in international competition abroad once, in Venezuela. After we won the Amateur World Series in 1940 Venezuela invited us and we spent a month playing in Venezuela. It was a very beautiful seven-game series. And we won. Then we returned to Cuba for the 1941 season. That summer I graduated, and afterward jumped to the professionals.

We lost against Canónico in 1941 because of a confusion in our infield. And you have to realize that the Venezuelan team was very good. It was a mistake by our third baseman, who got confused. He caught the ball right next to the bag and, instead of throwing to our catcher, who was Andrés Fleitas, he ran the runner all the way to home plate and the guy scored. That was the key to the game between us and Venezuela, because I hit Canónico and Fleitas hit Canónico. We were the two best hitters on the team. But Venezuela had good players, and a concession was made to them. They had tied the Series and had to play the deciding game against Cuba. Then Venezuela started saying that they wanted to decide on another day, to give them a break. So they were given three days for Canónico to rest. When things are going to happen, they happen. But no one took notice of that play I just mentioned until the other day, when Fleitas, who is here in Miami, told me: "Napoleón, do you remember how we lost the Series?" And he added: "Do you remember that Mosquito ran with the ball after the runner?"

La Tropical was full. That last year of mine in the amateurs I was named captain in the World Series. That means that in that World Series I had to deliver the opening speech before the assembled nations. That was a tremendous Series in Cuba, because the fans all followed the amateurs. The professionals did not matter.

It so happens that Adolfo Luque, who was then a coach for the Giants, had been after me for two years. The Giants came that winter for some training, and Luque brought me to Bill Terry, who was the manager, so that he would have a look at me. I was not expecting money or anything, what I wanted was to play ball. They gave me a thousand-dollar bonus to report to Jersey City, which was the Giants' Triple-A team. I had signed with Almendares in the Cuban League and finished second in batting [1941–42]. There is an anecdote that people don't know about. Eloy García was, with Armitas [Emilio de Armas], the owner of Almendares at the time, and both were hounding me to sign. I remember that they offered me forty dollars a month. But I said: "No, I'm not going to play for forty dollars. I have a family here to live with, though I am not a rich boy, so if you offer me sixty I'll sign." I started arguing with Armitas, and Eloy García finally said: "Listen, I'll put in the extra twenty dollars, let's have the boy sign." And that's what I signed for. I was not well off, but I wasn't poor either. My father worked at the sugarmill. We were a humble family but we were lacking for nothing. I wasn't as desperate as to sign for forty dollars, although my desire to play was such that I really didn't care for those extra twenty dollars.

The jump to the professionals was not that hard. First of all, I was a great hitter and I could run and had tremendous desire. I didn't have much of a problem playing professional. The first time I came to bat I hit a double off Max Macon, of Marianao. And I went on from there. I finished fighting for the batting championship with Silvio García. That first year of mine Almendares won. We won. And that's when I reported to Jacksonville, where Jersey City was training.

I came over in a Pan American seaplane that took off from Havana Bay and landed here, in Miami. And from here, I didn't know much English or anything, I don't know who put me on a train to get to Jacksonville. I slept in the train that night. That was right before the war. When I got there, the manager told Tomás de la Cruz, who was training nearby with Syracuse: "Tell this boy that when we get to Jersey City, which is next to New York where there are many Latins, I'm not going to allow him to speak any language but mine. So the best thing he can do is to learn English." There was a young woman there who was hostess of the hotel who heard this and began to work with me, even at breakfast. She began to speak to me in English and I to pick up words.

We became friends. I was the only one the manager allowed to hang out with her. When I got to New York I could speak English. She went to England with all those women and aviators who went as volunteers to defend England. I used to write to her at home. Then I got a letter from her mother one day saying that she regretted to tell me that she had been killed in an air raid. I will always remember her. Always, always. Her name was Laura Wilkenson.

⊖

The fifth Amateur World Series, held again at La Tropical, from September 26 to October 20, 1942, saw only five teams, and the Americans withdrew before the end of the competition. This was after Pearl Harbor, so Colonel Mariné had to put pressure on the U.S. government to ease wartime travel restrictions. But regardless of who else came to play, Cuba and Venezuela had serious business pending. Cuba won with a record of 10 and 2, followed by the Dominican Republic, which finished at 9 and 3, and by Venezuela, which came in third, with 7 and 5. Mexico and the United States finished in a tie at 2 and 10, though after withdrawing from the tournament the Americans lost four of those by forfeit.

The selection of the Cuban team had become such a hot item of controversy by this time that *Carteles* ran a survey to have the fans choose the players. The Amateur League season in 1942 had again been a rousing success, with Círculo Militar y Naval, led by their star pitcher Isidoro León, edging out Círculo de Artesanos and their stellar hurler Jiquí Moreno. León had finished with a 19 and 4 record and an ERA of 1.75. Marrero was 22 and 5 with an astonishing 1.22 ERA. Moreno, with a 20 and 5 record, had struck out 213 and ended up with a 1.76 ERA. Deportivo Matanzas, with its three front-line pitchers, Limonar Martínez, Catayo González, and Sandalio Consuegra, had spread the work. Limonar and Catayo finished with seven victories each and Consuegra with five. The leading batters had been Pedro Echevarría (Hershey), Mario Fajo (Círculo Militar y Naval), Francisco (Chito) Quicutis (Artemisa), who also pitched, Andrés Fleitas (Hershey), and Quilla Valdés (Hershey). Fortuna's Ealo finished at .388. Part of the problem in making the selection came from the suspension of Ealo and Valdés on a technicality about their amateur status provoked by turf wars among the various leagues and the overarching Unión Atlética Amateur de Cuba. This was eventually resolved, and both were chosen for the Cuban team. Ealo barely beat out Regla's Bernardo Cuervo at first. Marrero was the top vote-getter, with 7,615. He, along with Moreno, León, Parra, and Erasmo (Coco) del Monte (University of Havana), made up the pitching staff, from which, inexplicably, Natilla Jiménez was absent. Another absence was Napoleón Reyes, who had turned professional. Ealo was at first, Fajo at second, Remigio Vega at third, and Quilla at short, with Charles Pérez in left, Quicutis in center, and Villa Cabrera in right. Fleitas was the catcher. Luis Suárez, Pedro Echevarría, José Luis García, Pla Sánchez (a catcher from Círculo Militar y Naval), and José R. Hernández rounded out the roster. In a tune-up game, the team beat by one run a selection from the semipro league that included Avelino Cañizares and Héctor Rodríguez.

Venezuela came back with their championship team, led by Canónico, Romero, Pérez Colmenares, Casanova, Fonseca, Benítez, and Bracho. They had added a sensational shortstop, Luis Aparicio, whose son would make the Hall of Fame in Cooperstown, and who dazzled the fans with his defense and hit a respectable .279. But Cuba would not be denied this time. An incredible 29,300 crowded into La Tropical for the inevitable duel between Marrero and Canónico. Cuba crushed Venezuela, 8–0, and Quicutis sent one of Canónico's tosses over the scoreboard, a ball that must have carried more than five hundred feet. Venezuela would savor some victories, such as the one Plácido Delgado pitched against the Americans, that was won by Aparicio's hit. Meanwhile, the Cuban pitchers were dominating the opposition. León shut out Mexico and Coco del Monte the United States. Moreno pitched eight scoreless innings against the Americans before tiring. Marrero and del Monte were responsible for the only Cuban loses, one against the Dominican Republic. Both Moreno and León were champion pitchers, at 3 and 0, with ERAs of 1.36 and 1.93, respectively. Moreno whiffed thirty-one in thirty-three innings. The hitters were just as devastating, with Suárez, Hernández, Cabrera, and Fleitas over .400, and Ealo, Echevarría, Sánchez, and Valdés over .300. Fleitas, who was named Most Valuable Player, finished at .405 and shined behind the plate.

But the excitement in 1942 was provided by the Dominican delegation. They were led by their manager and organizer, Burrolote Rodríguez, one of the most important figures in the history of Dominican baseball. They had in Hereaux, Castro, and Báez a strong pitching staff, in Lantigua a professional catcher (he had played for the New York Cubans as far back as 1935), and three St. Clair brothers (there were also two Báezes and two Vargases). Luis Castro beat Venezuela, but the Americans, who had been beaten soundly by Cuba, 20–0 and 17–0, defeated the Dominicans, 3–1, behind Leonard Mayo in a game that turned out to be the most notorious of the Series. The Cuban crowd was behind the Americans because a victory by them would be to the benefit of the local team. Hecklers had been taunting Burrolote throughout the game by chanting his rather insulting sobriquet, which means "big donkey." A large, rotund man, Burrolote was easy prey for the pranksters from the stands. My father, in attendance, remembered and would recite to me the rhythmic refrain: "Bu-rro-lo-te, Bu-rro-lote, Bu-rro-lo-te." Given the score, the Dominican manager was not suffering the mockery well, and his shows of displeasure incited the crowd even more. At one point a ball trickled into the American dugout, from within which it was hurled back softly, striking Burrolote in the coaching box. He fired it back in anger, then picked up a bat, twirled it over his head, and flung it toward the crowd. The throng surged onto the field after Burrolote and the Dominican players. Police and soldiers tried to protect them, as did the Cuban players, who were in the stands. Order was finally restored, but there were some wounded by the hail of bottles and other objects, as well as by the pushing and shoving. In radio interviews and magazine articles, Burrolote, who would continue to promote Dominican baseball for years to come, comported himself as the opposite of the laughable buffoon he appeared to be. He became a favorite in Cuba, and the story of his tantrum a highlight of the island's baseball lore.

Another significant feature of the 1942 Amateur World Series was that the trophy was no longer called the Moore Cup, but the "Copa Presidente Batista," according to *Carteles* (August 16, 1942), though the *Guía Esso* that I am following and *Viva y en juego* do not mention this. But the presence of the government in these series was obvious because of the role played by the DGND. The pageant of sports and nationalism could not take place without the intervention of the state. With a strong economy, the jingoism of war (Cuba had declared war on Germany and Italy in December 1941), and a pluralistic administration, Batista was riding the crest of Cuba's baseball victories.

In fact, it was the DGND that provoked the greatest controversy about amateurism in Cuba, affecting not only the Amateur League championship of 1943 but also the Cuban selection for the sixth World Series, slated again for Havana. Mariné and the DGND went on a rampage to ensure the amateur status of baseball players, suspending Bernardo Cuervo for professionalism, and Marrero for accepting payment for a game. Jess Losada, from the pages of *Carteles,* attacked the Amateur League for its tangle of useless regulations and its hypocrisy. He accused the Amateur League of monopolizing amateur competition and concentrating it in the Havana area, allowing certain teams to recruit, with financial inducements, in other regions. The players were really workers unprotected by unions. In the meantime, amateur baseball continued to thrive, and the Juveniles' 1942 season included thirty-six teams and five hundred players. Throughout the spring *Carteles* ran a survey to determine who was the most popular amateur player. Marrero and Quilla Valdés ran neck and neck. New figures continued to appear: Félix (Lengüita) Fernández of the Círculo Militar y Naval, Pedro (Preston) Gómez of Fortuna, Bayito Dedric of Santiago de las Vegas, Alberto Fabregas of Cienfuegos, Miguelín López of Cubaneleco, and Gustavo Ubieta of the University. The amateurs were frequently on the radio, not only on broadcasts of the games but also in popular shows such as *Tribunal Deportivo,* in which Losada, Orlando Sánchez Diago, and Gabino Delgado talked about them.

But the sensation of the 1943 season was Deportivo Matanzas and its threesome of stellar pitchers: Limonar Martínez, Catayo González, and Sandalio Consuegra; all three were also feared batters. In fact, manager Tomás (Pipo) de la Noval led Matanzas to the flag that year in a close race with Círculo Militar y Naval. Matanzas was the best in what was a league dominated by star pitchers: Fortuna still had Daniel Parra, Cienfuegos had Marrero, Círculo Militar y Naval had Isidoro León, Círculo de Artesanos had Jiquí Moreno, Hershey still had Natilla Jiménez, Santiago de las Vegas had Antonio Estrella, Artemisa had Mario Rojas, and so on. The pitchers' dominance was surely due to the schedule of the Amateur League, with games being played only once a week. A starting pitcher can retain his edge pitching every seventh day by throwing some in between, but batters who do not see live pitching for that long have a hard time adjusting. Most of the great players in the Amateur League were pitchers, as were those who moved on to careers in professionalism, such as Mayor, Marrero, Natilla Jiménez, and Consuegra.

Such was the state of affairs in 1943 when September rolled around and the sixth Amateur World Series opened in Havana with only four teams due to the transportation obstacles created by the war. Venezuela did not come back, but Panama reappeared, and the Dominican Republic also sent a team. In Cuba a scandal brewed because of Marrero's suspension and absence from the team. Some said that he had not been chosen because, with a roster now limited to eighteen, the selectors (who included Mariné, the presidents of the Amateur League and the Unión Atlética Amateur, plus the team's manager, Reinaldo Cordeiro) wanted to add some punch to the outfield. Besides, with Isidoro León, Limonar Martínez, Sandalio Consuegra, Jiquí Moreno, and Natilla Jiménez, Cuba would not be lacking in pitching. Andrés Fleitas had turned professional, but his brother Angel, an infielder, made the team. Other infielders were Agustín Cordeiro, the manager's brother, and Quilla Valdés, who would be the shortstop. Veteran Ernesto Estévez was a utility man who could play the infield and back up Rouget Avalos, now the starting catcher. Félix del Cristo, Virgilio Arteaga, Leandro Pazos, and Luis Suárez made up the rest of the infield. Bautista Aristondo, Mario (Veneo) Morera, Francisco Quicutis, and Armando Báez were the outfielders. Del Cristo also played the outfield, as could Natilla Jiménez. It is true that Marrero was more of a one-dimensional player than other pitchers. Limonar Martínez and Consuegra were strong hitters who could pinch hit. Besides, the Guajiro de Laberinto was pushing thirty-two.

Mexico came determined to do better this time. They sent Ernesto Carmona, their renowned manager, at the head of a strong team that again included not a few professionals. Their greatest fear was having to face Jiquí Moreno, whose invincibility and reputation as a strikeout artist was at its peak. According to a Mexican account of Mexico's confrontation with Moreno on September 25 (in *Los grandes juegos*), people were wondering not whether Cuba would win, but how many Jiquí would whiff. Carmona harangued his troops at the hotel, telling them that anyone could be beaten. They went out and defeated Moreno in a fourteen-inning game that was truly one of the masterpieces of Latin American baseball. Mexico, which was the home team for this game, scored in the eighth on a rare error by

Quilla Valdés. Quilla himself opened Cuba's ninth with a single, was pushed to third by a sacrifice and a groundout, and scored when Pingua Canales, who would later make the final out, muffed a roller to third. Moreno went the fourteen innings, but lost it when Estévez could not hold Luna's hit to right, which rolled to the depths of La Tropical to allow Villarroel to score, with Carmona in happy pursuit from the coaching line. The play of the game was made by Mexico's Mosco Reyes in the second. With two on via bases on balls, Arteaga, a left-handed hitter, slapped a line drive to left that looked like a sure hit, but Reyes dove for the ball and caught it while horizontal to the ground; he tumbled, but held on and fired to second for a double play. After a moment of shocked silence, the Cuban crowd got to its feet and gave the Mexican a standing ovation.

Cuba won nine and lost three to take the Series. Moreno was the champion pitcher, with three wins, the one loss, and an incredible 0.70 ERA. Angel Fleitas hit .371 for the batting title. Luis Suárez led in RBIs and hit .354. Natilla Jiménez, who both started and pitched in relief, and gave up no earned runs in 30⅔ innings, was named Most Valuable Player. This was, obviously, a pitchers' Series. Ventura (Loro) Escalante, a Dominican pitcher, won two and lost one, with an earned-run average of 0.40! Limonar Martínez won three, lost none, and his ERA was 0.96. Panama's Scantlebury lost two, but his ERA was 2.05, and he impressed the Cuban fans. Not a single home run was hit. Mexico came in second, at an even 6 and 6. The Dominican Republic was third, at 5 and 7, and Panama last, at 4 and 8. Burrolote Rodríguez had brought a powerful team—Escalante and Luis Castro were excellent pitchers—but his batters could do nothing against Cuban pitchers. Víctor Greenidge got three of Panama's four victories (Pablo Mudarra won the other), but although Applewhite, Greenidge, and Mahoney hit reasonably well, Cuba's pitching was too strong.

The 1943 Amateur World Series was the last of that era played in Cuba. Given what transpired in the next one in Caracas, it was indeed the end of an era.

The Amateur League championship was again a tremendous success. Círculo de Artesanos won, followed closely by Círculo Militar y Naval, Deportivo Matanzas, Cienfuegos, and Santiago de las Vegas. José Ramón (Motorcito) Castañeda, manager of Círculo de Artesanos, had the biggest star in Jiquí Moreno, who won twenty-three games and lost only three. At Círculo Militar y Naval Isidoro León won twenty-two and lost five, while Marrero bounced back with a twenty-one-and-eight season. Fortuna's Juan Ealo hit .500, with thirty-five hits in seventy times at bat. Moreno was striking out an average of 13.44 batters per nine innings, and whiffed 21 in a game to establish a record. In a match that filled La Tropical beyond capacity in late August, Marrero beat Moreno, but Jiquí struck out fifteen. Sánchez Diago kept on announcing the games over the radio for the entire country, and enthusiasm was still on the rise. But there were some prob-

lems. One was the continued disputes about amateurism, which led to the
suspension of Daniel Parra and which pushed many amateurs into the professional ranks. Another was the elections. Batista guaranteed clean elections, and when this was held, his candidate lost. In a grand gesture of
democratic principle, Batista handed over power to his political enemy Dr.
Ramón Grau San Martín. Grau was diffident and ineffectual. With him
came a new administration to the DGND, where Luis Orlando Rodríguez,
a revolutionary from the thirties, took over from his nemesis Colonel Jaime
Mariné. As a result, the Series, which had been conceived and run under
Batista, would not be played at La Tropical for the first time since 1939.
Rodríguez's main task as director of the DGND would be to mediate in
the disputes concerning professional baseball.

Preparations for the Series did not go well, due to bitter controversies
about the composition of the team. Public workouts and exhibition games
were held to showcase the talent and make the selection, with more blacks
from the eastern region of the island involved. One was infielder Amado
Ibáñez, who played for Cromo Mining in Camagüey and who went on to
have a career in the Cuban League and the Negro circuits. Another was
Pablo García, a slugger. Managed by Deportivo Matanzas' Pipo de la
Noval, the Cuban team had Marrero back (he could not fail to appear in
Venezuela, where his duels with Canónico were the stuff of legend), Isidoro
León, Limonar Martínez, Antonio Estrella, and Sandalio Consuegra as
principal pitchers, with Rouget Avalos behind the plate, backed up by
Tango Suárez. Juan Ealo, Angel Fleitas, Quilla Valdés, and Ibáñez were
the infield, with Charles Pérez, Pablo García, Evelio Martínez, and Félix
del Cristo in the outfield. This was another strong squad, though it was
missing Andrés Fleitas, now a professional, not to mention Napoleón Reyes
and Chito Quicutis, who also had turned professional. Travel restrictions
forced them to go by train to Camagüey, where they played some exhibitions, to board KLM planes there to Venezuela (the Dutch airline, which
serviced the Caribbean, did not land in Havana).

Eight teams participated in the seventh Amateur World Series, but not
all of them finished. Mexico, with Beto Avila; Panama, with Mudarra, Mahoney, and Kellman; Puerto Rico, with Luis (Canena) Márquez; Nicaragua,
with Cayasso, Meléndez, Robinson, and Navas; and Burrolote's powerful
Dominican team were there. Venezuela assembled a stellar team but could
not include Canónico and Aparicio, who apparently had turned professional. Colombia fielded a team for the first time. With a three-way tie
among Mexico, Venezuela, and Cuba, a playoff for the title was set up, but
the problems that had been simmering during the Series came to a head.
These involved the umpiring, which was provided by the host country. In
a game between Venezuela and the Dominican Republic the Venezuelan
umpire ruled to suspend the game on account of darkness before the bottom of the ninth. The Dominicans were the home team and would not
bat, but Venezuela's runs at the top of the inning had to be erased, and

Burrolote won the game. The controversial umpire was nowhere to be seen when Cuba faced Venezuela the following day; he was replaced by a fellow who had been the first-base coach the previous day for the locals. This was the umpire who made the ruling that ended Cuba's participation.

With Cuba at bat and a man on first, there was a grounder to the first baseman, who threw to the pitcher covering. But the pitcher dropped the ball, which rolled into foul territory, where it was fielded by a photographer, who flipped it to the first baseman. He pivoted and threw to third to nail the runner coming from first. The umpire called him out. The entire Cuban team exploded from the dugout and mounted a loud protest, but the umpire, unmoved, answered blithely: "You gentlemen have not understood that the photographer is also a baseball person." Cuba pulled out of the Series and Mexico did the same later when a similar incident happened. The Series ended in disarray, but the Venezuelans claimed the championship anyway.

Cuba did not participate in these competitions again until 1950, but by then they had lost their luster, with many key players having turned professional. In 1947 Juan Ealo managed the Nicaraguan team in the Series played in Managua, but after losing a close game to Mexico, dictator Anastasio Somoza took over the team himself. They still finished next to last. In 1953, in Venezuela, Cuba's Luis (Lindo) Suárez gave up a double to Luis Aparicio, Jr., and walked two others in the same inning, but slammed the door and pitched a shutout. In other amateur international competition Cuba continued to do well, but the level of interest had dropped. In 1946 the Cuban team that played in the fifth Central American Games, held in Colombia, included future great Guillermo (Willie) Miranda, who was with Teléfonos in the Amateur League. In Guatemala in 1950, a product of the Juveniles, Edmundo (Sandy) Amorós, clouted six homers in seven games to lead the undefeated Cuban team to victory. Great moments awaited him in better arenas. National teams continued to carry two or three blacks, and Amorós was one of them that year (pitcher Justiniano Garay was another). Mariné's Juveniles program was paying dividends. International baseball competition reached a nadir for Cuba in 1959, however, when its team finished eighth in the Pan American Games, in Chicago. This defeat took place nine months after the revolutionary takeover. This kind of debacle would never happen again.

During the fifties the Amateur League staged a comeback, with games now played at the Gran Stadium (where I witnessed a few), as well as in the other traditional parks, such as La Tropical, Vedado Tennis, and Stadium Universitario. In the late fifties it was Cubaneleco that shone, winning three championships. Lindo Suárez, from Liceo de Regla, was the top pitcher of the period. But the Amateur League was never again what it had been from the late thirties to the midforties.

The decline of amateur baseball after 1944 was due to several factors. The most important were the extensive signings of players by the likes of scouts such as Joe Cambria, who depleted the Amateur League to stock the wartime Washington Senators. With the end of World War II and the revival of the minor leagues, many Cuban players signed professional contracts and fanned out over the United States. In Cuba itself, Cambria and Maduro founded the Havana Cubans in 1946 and practically created the Florida International League, which siphoned off countless players. By taking players right out of the Juveniles, as in the case of Washington Senator shortstop José Valdivielso, American baseball compromised the Amateur League's future. Another important factor was the rise of the Mexican League, which also took many Cuban amateur stars, whereas before the forties few Cuban players except blacks went there. Finally, the Cuban League, which the Amateur League had saved from oblivion, revived and began to attract interest with talent drawn from all the brands of nonprofessional baseball described in this chapter.

As I stroll through what was center field at La Tropical in December 1995, I try to imagine what those September and October afternoons were like in the forties, when the Amateur World Series were played before overflow crowds of fervent fans. The park is now in shambles, but the stands remain, as does the lush vegetation encircling them. The tattered building behind the outfield still has the sign NUEVA FABRICA DE HIELO on it. Because of World War II, which gave the economy such a boost and focused attention on a common foe, it was a time of national reconciliation after the turbulent thirties. It was an illusory unity, to be sure, a mirage embodied in those squads of Cuban rustics that time ravaged but could not condemn to oblivion. And so La Tropical is not really a ruin, but a relic to those of us who remember.

1 2 3 4 5 6 7 8 9 R H E

The Revival of the Cuban League

Abel Linares' death in October 1930 left a vacuum in the promotional area of professional Cuban baseball that was filled mainly by Julio Blanco Herrera and Alejandro Pompez, aided by the likes of Tinti Molina and Emilio de Armas. Their operations, together with Colonel Jaime Mariné's Dirección General Nacional de Deportes, aided by a recovery of the Cuban economy from the middle thirties to the early forties, brought the Cuban League out of the doldrums into which it had sunk during the last years of Machado's regime and the Depression. It was a very slow revival, culminating with wartime seasons that led to a revamping of the league, the move from La Tropical to the Gran Stadium, and the thrilling 1946–47 season.

Toward the end of this period of roughly fifteen years, from about 1930 to 1945, there emerged new entrepreneurs, such as Roberto (Bobby) Maduro, Miguel (Miguelito) Suárez, Dr. July Sanguily, Mario Mendoza, Eloy García, and Alfredo Pequeño, who bought franchises, brought about the construction of the new stadium, and ushered Cuba into Organized Baseball by creating the Havana Cubans of the Florida International League. They succeeded Blanco Herrera and Pompez, moving the Cuban League away from reliance on old Cuban money, close ties with the Negro circuits and the Mexican League, and into the protectorate of Organized

Baseball and an Age of Gold in the fifties. This phase also witnessed the advent and entrenchment of the Washington Senators' scout Joe Cambria. Cambria's presence and influence continued through the fifties until the demise of the Cuban League after the revolution. Also, during the thirties and until 1941, when the United States entered the war, Havana became a spring-training site, and many exhibition games were played between major-league clubs and various Cuban teams. But perhaps the most telling event of that era was the sale of Almendares and Habana by Linares' widow. This was the definitive break of the Cuban League with the Golden Age, which now became a romanticized past of titans and heroes, formalized as such by the foundation of the Cuban Baseball Hall of Fame in 1939.[1]

The thirties saw the rise of many stars of professional Cuban baseball who had the misfortune of having their careers peak in a time of economic want, lingering racial discrimination, and stiff competition from soccer as a spectacle. These professional baseball figures cannot be measured or perhaps even referred to in the same sentence with the greatest of them all, Martín Dihigo. Dihigo shone in the Mexican League, the Negro Leagues, and the Cuban League, not to mention countless independent games and transient tournaments. In the thirties he also became a successful manager. But along with him there appeared in this era men such as Lázaro (El Príncipe de Belén) Salazar, Ramón (El Profesor) Bragaña, Luis Tiant, Santos (El Canguro) Amaro, and Silvio García. Just a rung below them were Tomás de la Cruz, Fermín Guerra, José María Fernández, Rodolfo Fernández, Manuel (Cocaína) García, Basilio (Brujo) Rosell, Antonio (Tony) Castaño, Roberto (El Tarzán) Estalella, Regino Otero, Gilberto (El Jibarito) Torres, Clemente (Sungo) Carreras, and of course, Agapito Mayor. But Mayor's ascendancy as a professional was really in the forties. His star rose along with those of Adrián Zabala, Roberto (El Gigante del Central Senado) Ortiz, Claro Duany, Pedro (Perico) Formental, Alejandro Crespo, Orestes Miñoso, Rafael Noble, Manuel (Chino) Hidalgo, Andrés Fleitas, Héctor Rodríguez, and Avelino Cañizares. Many players from these two lists were active in that 1946–47 season with which this book opens, and not a few would still be playing in the fifties.

With the exception of Mayor, Otero, Torres, Zabala, Guerra, and Castaño, all of the players who arrived in the thirties were black or mulatto, including two who made it to the major leagues before Jackie Robinson: Roberto Estalella and Tomás de la Cruz. With all the opportunities in the Amateur League and even sugarmill and semipro baseball, turning professional was not very desirable for white Cubans at the time. Blacks who did turn pro, particularly the stars, had to cobble together a career by going abroad to different countries, particualarly the United States, where the Negro circuits were also in a state of crisis. Their compensation was meager in most cases. Dihigo, Tiant, and others played with the Cuban Stars and after 1935 with the New York Cubans. However, those teams, with their small rosters, could not accommodate so much talent; thus many players went to other Latin American countries. Mexico, Venezuela, Puerto Rico, and the Dominican Republic were the favorites, in that order. The black players often stayed permanently in those countries, particularly Mexico and Venezuela, because there were more opportunities for them and because racial discrimination was much less severe than in Cuba.

Pelayo Chacón moved to Venezuela in the early thirties after brilliant careers in the Cuban League and as playing manager of the Cuban Stars. In Venezuela he was instrumental in the development of professional baseball, and his Venezuelan son Elio made it to the major leagues with Cincinnati and the New York Mets. Others who went there in the thirties were Cocaína García (who eventually also stayed) and Sungo Carreras. They were also involved in the promotion and advancement of Venezuelan professional baseball. García became a Venezuelan citizen and had children in that country. He died at the ripe age of eighty-nine in La Guaira, where he was a beloved patriarch.

Dihigo, Cocaína García, Bragaña, Salazar, Rosell, and many others also played in Mexico during the thirties, and a few went to the Dominican Republic in the summer of 1937. Bragaña, Salazar, Rosell, Dihigo, and Roberto Ortiz are in the Mexican Hall of Fame. Brujo Rosell left for Mexico in the early thirties and settled there permanently. Rosell was a right-handed pitcher who started the trend of black Cuban players moving to Mexico to stay. He would be followed by Bragaña, Salazar, and Amaro in the thirties, and Pedro Orta, Héctor Rodríguez, and Avelino Cañizares in the forties. There is scant information about Rosell in Cuban publications because he spent most of his life and career abroad.

Rosell began playing with Almendares in 1923 and played with the Cuban Stars (West) from 1926 to 1928, and the Cuban Stars (East) in 1929. In 1926–27 he was 2 and 2 with Cienfuegos of the Cuban League, with four complete games. In 1929–30 he was 6 and 7 with Santa Clara, and in 1930 2 and 1 with Almendarista in the Campeonato Unico. These were lean years, so in 1933 Rosell went to Mexico and came back only sporadically. He never returned to the United States, disgusted with the racial discrimination he experienced there. While in Mexico, a friend once told him that if he won against a certain very strong American team, he would be considered a wizard. He did, and the name "Brujo" stuck. Rosell was also known to make a few incantatory gestures before a game and to talk to the ball. How much Afro-Cuban cult was behind this and how much of it was part of a show routine is difficult to ascertain. Rosell left very little imprint on Cuban baseball, though he beat the Cardinals and the Giants in exhibition games in Havana in the thirties.

But Rosell's life, told appropriately in a book of interviews with celebrities from the field of entertainment that includes vedettes Tongolele, Ninón Sevilla, and Toña la Negra and mambo king Pérez Prado, provides a touching glimpse of how close the worlds of popular music and professional sports were in the twenties and after.[2] While playing for the Cuban

Stars (West), which were based in Chicago, he traveled with the team to St. Louis. In that thriving hub of jazz Brujo met a delicious young dancer named Josephine, who was to become Josephine Baker. They liked each other and enjoyed a brief affair. Years later, when Josephine, a star, visited Mexico City, Brujo showed up, announced himself backstage, and was led to her dressing room, where he recalls: "We looked at each other, motionless, and I don't know why we simply began to cry. . . . It must have been because at the meeting we realized that the time had passed, at least the time for us. . . ."[3] Having found a niche in Mexico, Rosell's career did not depend on the fortunes of the Cuban League. For others, particularly Luque and Miguel Angel González, not to mention scores of active players, it was essential for their survival, so efforts continued to bring it back to life.

By the forties quite a few Cuban whites were again playing in the minors, and some in the majors (mostly with the Senators). Some, of course, such as Estalella and de la Cruz, were not white, taking advantage of the prevalent confusion about Cuban nationality and race in the United States. The gradual recovery of the Negro Leagues and the growing stability of the New York Cubans provided a steady venue for some Cuban blacks, and the dramatic rise of the Mexican League offered opportunities to both. Meanwhile, with the reorganization of the Cuban League and its rise in popularity due to the signings of many Amateur League stars such as Napoleón Reyes, Andrés Fleitas, Natilla Jiménez, Limonar Martínez, and Julio Moreno, winter-ball chances improved. Finally, the organization of the Havana Cubans in 1946 gave Cuban whites the luxury of being both at home and in Organized Baseball.

I will chronicle first the revival of the Cuban League through the main events mentioned, leading up to the 1945–46 season and the construction of the Gran Stadium in El Cerro. Because of the dearth of information and the fragmented nature of their careers, I will sketch brief biographies of the main stars of the thirties and forties. Those who made their debut in the thirties will appear here before the 1935–1936 season, when the recovery begins (I will have to wind back the chronology in their case). Those whose careers started in the early forties will come after, around my narrative of the 1941–42 season, which marked the restoration of the Cuban League with the signing of popular amateurs. I will then reconstruct, as best as possible, given the meager documentary resources available, the fate of Cuban teams in the Negro circuits, leading up to the 1947 Negro World Series victory by the New York Cubans. By then we will have reached the point where the first ball of the 1949–50 season can sail and we can resume the account of the recent past up to the present.

☺

Having built La Tropical for the second Central American Games held in the spring of 1930, Don Julio Blanco Herrera (as he was referred to in the press), seeing the sorry state of professional baseball in Cuba, decided to invite to his beautiful new park major-league teams that would revive fan interest. Don Julio imported a group of twenty-five men, divided into two squads called "Ens's Stars" and "Bancroft's Stars," after their respective managers, Jewel Ens and Dave Bancroft. Ens was the Pittsburgh Pirate manager, while Bancroft had been a Giant shortstop under John McGraw, so he was familiar with the Cuban scene. The seven-game series would be played during the second week in October, at the end of the major-league season. In fact, Don Julio, eager to exploit the growing alliance between baseball and nationalism, set the opener for October 10, a holiday in Cuba commemorating the outbreak of the first War of Independence, in 1868. It was reported that twenty thousand fans showed up for a duel between the Giants' Carl Hubbell and the Pirates' Larry French. The game, however, was at nine-thirty in the morning, probably because soccer had the field for the more desirable afternoon slot.

It was still a coup of self-promotion on Don Julio's part, not to mention a marketing bonanza for his brewery. He had a bronze plaque installed at La Tropical that is still there and reads: "STADIVM CERVEZA TROPICAL: Those whose signatures appear below, members of the American Major Leagues, wish to perpetuate our gratitude to the NUEVA FABRICA DE HIELO, S.A, which owns breweries *La Tropical* and *Tivoli*, for the exquisite hospitality that we have received; of our admiration for the altruistic and sporting character reflected in their unsurpassable STADIUM, in tune with the beauty of this country, and finally, our salute to all Cuban fans and lovers of baseball." It is signed, Havana, October 19, 1930, by Dave Bancroft, director, and the players on both teams. Given the benefits derived from this series, the "altruism" displayed by Don Julio is somewhat suspect. There are obviously no qualms about the nature of his product—beer—and all of these lofty ideals, including the patriotism suggested by playing the opener on an official holiday. It seems clear to me that Don Julio enjoyed the protection of Machado's regime, for whose benefit he had "donated" La Tropical for the 1930 Second Central American Games, which attempted to showcase Cuba's stability at a time of political unrest.

The teams' rosters appear to be a throwback to happier moments in Cuban sports. Bancroft's squad had a strong New York Giant component, no doubt a McGraw legacy, and reminiscent of those visits that included Babe Ruth's ten years before. It featured, in addition to Hubbell, star first baseman Bill Terry, who would become McGraw's successor as manager a few years later and hire Luque as a coach. The team also consisted of Giants Bob O'Farrell, Doc Marshall, and Bill Walker. Then there were the Phillies' Chuck Klein, the Reds' Clyde Sukeforth, and the Senators' Sam Rice. Ens's team, which won five of the seven games (French had three victories, including the opener over Hubbell), had four Pirates, including Pie Traynor and Paul Waner, and crowd favorites Rabbit Maranville from the Braves and Heinie Manush from the Senators. The Pirates, it may be recalled, also visited Havana in the teens and twenties. Ens had Brooklyn's young catcher Al López, too. As we saw earlier, López could have very easily been born a Cuban (in the Havana press he was referred to as "El Astur," alluding to the Asturian birth of his parents). He had played a few games in the split Cuban League season in 1926 at the University Stadium, so he was familiar with Cuba and knew Luque very well. I am sure that, besides his superb skills as a catcher, López's native Spanish and knowledge of the country got him onto the team.

The series was a financial success, according to *Carteles,* but did not revive the Cuban League, which was nearly defunct. So the next thing to do was to make La Tropical available for spring training to major-league teams. The Brooklyn club, now called the Robins, not the Dodgers, came in the spring of 1931 with thirty-nine players, Luque and López among them. Spring training became in the thirties what the American season had been in the teens and twenties, only that now, instead of playing in the months of October and November, before the Cuban League, games would take place in March, after the winter season. The Brooklyn team, as well as others who came later (such as the Giants, Yankees, and Cardinals), would find in the Cuban players, hardened by a winter of play, more than worthy opponents.[4] The major-league teams were routinely defeated by the likes of Agapito Mayor, Rodolfo Fernández, Brujo Rosell, Ramón Bragaña, Luis Tiant, and others. The Cuban athletes found a much-needed source of revenue in those games before they scattered through the Caribbean, Mexico, and the U.S. Negro circuits. A split squad of Robins, featuring Luque pitching for one side with López catching him, filled La Tropical. Luque won, 2–1, and López had a couple of hits.

The Cuban League was a very small operation at this time. Rodolfo Fernández remembers how little he was paid in his first season—$8.00 a week, which he hid in his protective cup for safekeeping. In 1931–32 games were still played at Almendares Park and at Regla's Galbán Lobo. This was because a Regla team had again been organized, probably counting on the lingering memory of teams from that town in the past. The teams played only thirty games in a season where no Americans participated. Alejandro Oms, playing for Habana, led in hits with forty-four and in homers with three. Rodolfo, pitching to brother José María Fernández, led Almendares to the pennant, winning eight games, with two shutouts. Luis Tiant, pitching for Regla, won seven but lost six. Cocaína García won four and lost none while hitting .364. The 1932–33 season was never finished because of the turmoil surrounding the fall of Machado, and there was no season in 1933–34.

The Cuban League resumed operations in 1934–35, playing at La Tropical for the first time (Almendares Park was abandoned to weeds and decay), but the three teams participated in only twenty-seven contests. The third team this time was Marianao, probably because of La Tropical's location in that municipality adjoining Havana, but also because of the success the Marianao team had enjoyed in the twenties. Almendares won behind Luque, who in spite of being already in his forties, won six and lost two. But the Blues' star was Lázaro Salazar, who was the champion pitcher at 6 and 1 and the batting champion with a .407 average. Although the left-hander had been a member of the Cuban Stars (West) since 1924 and had played in the Cuban League seasons of 1931–32 and 1932–33, this was the season when he became a superstar. Other players who distinguished themselves for the first time were Gilberto Torres, who had had a great season with Regla in the Amateur League and who became the mainstay of Habana's pitching staff. As has been mentioned earlier, his father, Ricardo, played twenty-two games with the Washington Senators from 1920 to 1922, so when Gilberto made the same team in 1940, they became the first Cuban father-son combo in the Majors.[5] Fermín Guerra made his debut as a catcher-first baseman, also with Habana, as did Tomás de la Cruz, pitching for Marianao. Meanwhile, Antonio (Pollo) Rodríguez began his career playing for Marianao and Tomás (Pipo) de la Noval for Habana. These were the players who did make the jump from the amateurs to the professionals during the early thirties.

The 1934–35 season was a poor one in which some games had to be played at the Vedado Tennis Club grounds because soccer held sway at La Tropical. This was also the year that saw the defeat of the three Cuban League teams by Rum Havana Club, the independent club from Cárdenas. But it was a season that did see the emergence of players of the caliber of Salazar, de la Cruz, Torres, and Guerra, who would have long and distinguished careers in Cuba and abroad. All four reached the fifties as active players or managers, and all four displayed leadership qualities, particularly Salazar, Bragaña, and Guerra. I will now briefly review the careers of some of the significant players who emerged in the early thirties and then continue with the narrative of the Cuban League, which was about to enjoy a series of memorable seasons as well as an organizational revamping.

The first three were black Cuban stars who followed Rosell to Mexico, where they settled permanently, even while returning to Cuba for winter seasons of the Cuban League.

Ramón (El Profesor) Bragaña, a six-foot, bronze-colored mulatto who weighed 195 pounds in his prime, was a pitcher with great velocity, a wicked curveball, and excellent control. Born in Havana on May 11, 1909, Bragaña participated in eleven winter seasons in Cuba, where he began playing in the late twenties and early thirties. His career in Cuba, however, really began with the 1936–37 season, when he won nine games. In the twenties and thirties he played with the Cuban Stars (1928–30) and later with the New York Cubans and the Cleveland Buckeyes (1947). But Bragaña played mostly in Mexico, where he is enshrined in the Mexican Hall of Fame. His plaque there reads: "The only pitcher with 30 wins in one season (1944 with Veracruz) and 200 or more in his admirable career (211). Other all-time records: 222 complete games and 3,375 innings pitched; ERA champion (2.58) in 1940. The great Cuban compiled for twelve years a winning percentage over .500 in wins and losses." Bragaña also managed successfully in Mexico with Jalisco, Veracruz, the Mexico City Reds, and Nuevo Laredo. His last season was in 1955 with Mexico City, when he was already forty-six. I have found 47 victories in Cuba, which give him a total of 258, not counting records in the Negro circuits and Venezuela. Bragaña died on his birthday in 1985, at age seventy-six. He was still in Mexico, where he had a family and had opened a restaurant in Las Choapas.

The high point of Bragaña's career in the Cuban League was reached in the 1941–42 season, when he won nine and lost six for Almendares, pitching four shutouts, all against the "eternal rival" Habana. From mid-December to mid-January Bragaña pitched 39⅔ scoreless innings in a row, 36 of them against the Reds. They called him "the Lion Tamer." Many of those victories came against Martín Dihigo, pitching then for Habana, in memorable duels that filled La Tropical beyond capacity. It was a clash of styles: the determined, serious-minded, and grim-faced Bragaña, with a professorial air about him; the gifted Dihigo, who liked to banter with the opposition and the fans, and flash his winning smile whenever he succeeded at something (which was most of the time). It was during these highly charged confrontations that betting reached a fever pitch at La Tropical, and insinuations were heard that Dihigo sometimes was holding back to accommodate bettors. Nothing came of this, but it is a rumor that is the only blemish on Dihigo's illustrious career, if indeed it is true. But the memory of those clashes of titans, when Cuban baseball was in a frenzy because of the Amateur World Series and the closely contested Amateur League, are part of the lore of the game on the island.

Bragaña's greatest triumph had come a few years earlier, in 1937, in a superb *mano a mano* with no less a figure than the New York Giants' Carl Hubbell. The Giants, who had won the National League pennant but lost the World Series to the Yankees, came to Havana for some games against a hastily assembled Cuban selection. It was still October, and Hubbell, who had won twenty-two games during the regular season, was at the top of his form. The Giants had Mel Ott, Dick Bartell, Gus Mancuso, Jo Jo Moore, and other luminaries. The game went twelve innings and ended in a 1–1 tie. Bragaña gave up a mere three hits and made only 128 pitches, of which 91 were strikes. Giant manager Bill Terry and his players raved about Bragaña's speed, curve, and control. They said that they had not faced better pitching in the majors and that Bragaña's curve was the best they had seen all year.

Lázaro Salazar was a favorite in Cuba, Mexico, and Venezuela. A well-proportioned, handsome mulatto of medium height, he was born in Havana on December 17, 1911. Salazar was known as "El Príncipe de Belén" not only for his looks but also because he was such a natty dresser; he had a gentlemanly demeanor, natural elegance, and obvious intelligence. The nickname, though affectionate and admiring, was somewhat mocking, given that Belén, Salazar's native neighborhood in Havana, was a rough, mostly black area of the city. It was the quintessential barrio where urban-bound blacks from the provinces settled, fleeing unemployment in the sugarmills. Belén was also a hotbed of Afro-Cuban culture, particularly for music and the syncretic cults. An indication of how this may have influenced The Prince through his brief life is that he always wore number 17, that of San Lázaro, after whom he had been named (Babalú-Ayé in the Afro-Cuban cult). Salazar was, then, a kind of pauper prince.

As a ballplayer Salazar was a left-handed Dihigo, though not as versatile precisely because a lefty could play fewer positions, and not as powerful. He was a superb pitcher and hitter, who played first base and the outfield with distinction. He soon became a manager and gained fame in that role in Cuba, Mexico, and Venezuela. His plaque in the Mexican Hall of Fame reads: "The greatest manager there has ever been in Mexico. The first to conquer seven pennants in a row. An extraordinary pitcher, first baseman, and outfielder. As a pitcher he won 113 games and lost 77. As a batter he had a career .333 average." In Cuba, as we saw, he was both the champion pitcher and the champion batter in 1934–35. He was again the champion batter in 1940–41. As a manager he won with Santa Clara in 1937–38 and 1938–39. In Venezuela he managed Magallanes' Navegantes in the fifties, and led the team to a Caribbean Series. He was on the Almendares team that, led by Lanier, beat Habana in 1947, having won four and lost three that season.

Salazar had a dramatic early death that added to his aura. He had moved to Mexico in 1938 after he established himself there as a manager and a player. He married a Mexican and had his children in Mexico, which became his home even when he returned to Cuba for winter ball or went to Venezuela toward the end of his life. His dream was to manage Almendares, the team where he had begun his career in the Cuban League. In 1957 the Almendares owners decided to give Salazar a two-year contract that would allow him to finally realize his dream. He was still a popular and respected figure in Cuba and the Blues were not faring too well, so it was no altruistic gesture. But on April 25 of that year, while managing the Mexico City Reds, Salazar collapsed in the dugout, gasping for air and muttering incoherently: "There are two outs!" "We win!" He was hurried to the dressing room and later to a hospital, where he died of a cerebral hemorrhage at age forty-six. Mexico's baseball world was stunned. The Mexico City Reds, in uniform, marched behind his casket. His widow rejected all suggestions to bury him in Cuba. Thus died "El Príncipe de Belén," a tragic hero whose name was that of a saint and an Afro-Cuban orisha, and his nickname that of a martyr.

Yet another star who became Mexican by choice was Santos Amaro, a large first baseman-outfielder who was 6 feet, 3 inches and weighed 225 pounds. Because of his size and ability to leap he came to be known as El

Canguro (The Kangaroo). A strikingly handsome black, Amaro could do it all, particularly hit. Fermín Guerra, who caught for years in the majors, told me that Amaro's arm was the strongest he had ever seen in an outfielder. Apparently Amaro, like Rosell, could not tolerate the racial discrimination in the United States, so he did not play in the Negro Leagues. In Mexico he hit .315 for Aguila in 1939, and .332, .349, .328, and .330 for Tampico from 1941 to 1945. In the Cuban League he hit over .300 three times with Santa Clara in the thirties, and had several outstanding seasons with Almendares in the early to middle forties, with a high of .326 in 1941–42 (the Cuban League was a pitchers' league). He was in left field and got two hits in the deciding game of the 1946–47 season when Lanier beat Habana, a year when Amaro finished at a solid .289. Like Bragaña and Salazar, Amaro started a family in Mexico, and his son Rubén (born in Veracruz in 1936) made it to the Yankees, and his grandson, named Rubén, too, is now playing with the Phillies. Neither one, by all accounts, comes close to grandfather Santos in ability.

Luis Tiant, a left-hander like Salazar, was rescued from oblivion by the success of his son, who became a major-league star. Tiant was a slender man who could throw hard when needed but who depended on guile, an assortment of pitches, and uncanny control. In Cuba his career spanned 1926–27 to 1947–48, playing for all the teams but Santa Clara. His best years came with Habana. Tiant was a pitcher who lost more than he won in Cuba but who had tremendous success against visiting major-league teams, and in championship games. In the Negro Leagues he played with the Cuban Stars and later the New York Cubans. Ironically, his best season was in 1947, when he was 10 and 0 in regular-season play and then excelled against the Cleveland Buckeyes in the Negro World Series. Tiant defeated the Cardinals and the Yankees in exhibition games in Havana. The most anticipated part of Tiant's routine was his unbelievably deceptive move to first base. He was fond, for example, of walking lightning-fast Cool Papa Bell on purpose, just to put on a show trying to keep him from stealing. The most famous anecdote in this regard is that once Tiant threw to first in such an unexpected way that the batter swung and the umpire called it a strike. The umpire is supposed to have said that if he were stupid enough to swing, then he deserved having a strike called against him. Older Cubans like to say that the older Tiant was the better of the two. With his talent and intelligence there is no doubt that the father would have had a great career in the majors had he been born later. But the younger Luis Tiant is the all-time leader in major-league victories among Cuban pitchers.

Another star with multiple talents to emerge in the early thirties was Silvio García, a rifle-arm infielder who began as a pitcher. García was a two-hundred-pound six-footer born in Limonar, Matanzas Province, on October 11, 1914. Before the Cuban League, he played in the armed forces and for the independent Toros de Paredes. In the Cuban League Silvio (as he was sometimes listed in box scores because of his very common last name) had one great season as a pitcher, in 1936–37, when he finished at 10 and 2, but he was too good a hitter and fielder not to be an everyday player. (I have heard it said that he was affected by his having killed a man with a pitch, and that he was himself hit in the arm; but he continued to pitch, though sporadically, in the Mexican League.) By 1940–41 he was with Cienfuegos, the team with which he would be mostly associated, and won the batting title, with a .351 average. Exactly ten years later, in 1950–1951, he won yet another batting title, with a .347 average (he also led the league in stolen bases and hit five homers). He was then in his late thirties. Many consider Silvio García to have been the greatest Cuban shortstop ever, and the competition is stiff, going back to Romañach, Bustamante, Cabrera, and the amateur Quilla Valdés. García was a stellar performer in Mexico, Puerto Rico (with Ponce in 1939–40), and a mainstay of Pompez's New York Cubans. His star shone brightest as the Cubans became a powerhouse right after the war and won the Negro World Series in 1947.

Legend has it that Silvio García was seriously considered by Branch Rickey to be the man to break the color barrier in the United States, but that when asked what he would do if a rival hurled racial slurs at him, the Cuban answered: "I would kill him." This ended his chances. The story is probably apocryphal, because by 1947 García was already in his thirties, and his not being an American would have detracted from the significance of signing him for the Dodgers. But in his prime he was probably a better player than Jackie Robinson. García had great years with Cienfuegos in the Cuban League during the early to midforties, playing for a winning team whose fortunes will be chronicled later. This was also his period of greatest success in the Mexican League.

Two brothers who emerged in the late twenties and early thirties as stars and leaders were José María and Rodolfo Fernández, the first a catcher and the second a pitcher, both born in Guanabacoa, a town that in this period also produced several greats of Cuban popular music: Bola de Nieve (Ignacio Villa), Rita Montaner, and Ernesto Lecuona. Both Fernándezes were smart and had leadership qualities. José María, born on July 6, 1896, actually began playing in the teens with the Cuban Stars. He was an accomplished defensive catcher with some power and much intelligence. José María had good seasons in the Negro Leagues with the Stars, and one outstanding season with the Chicago American Giants, but his most lasting contribution came as player-manager of Pompez's New York Cubans from 1938 until 1950, leading them to the pennant and the Negro World Series triumph of 1947. His greatest seasons in the Cuban League came mostly with Almendares in the mid- to late thirties and early forties. He was a coach with Marianao in the fifties, and their manager in the Cuban League's last season.

Rodolfo, born in Guanabacoa on June 27, 1911, was a strong right-hander with a sidewinding delivery, great velocity, a nasty drop, and control. His best years in the Cuban League were also in the mid- to late thirties, with Almendares, pitching to his brother, and had three years with Habana in the early forties. Rodolfo hurt his arm early, but remained a respected coach with Almendares through the fifties. He was with the 1937 Dominican team that represented Ciudad Trujillo, and played for two seasons in Venezuela, and also in Mexico. In 1952 he returned to the Dominican Republic, where he managed Aguilas Cibaeñas to a championship. In the thirties and early forties Fernández defeated several major-league teams in Cuba. In 1936 he shut out the Giants and Carl Hubbell. An intelligent, well-spoken man with an aura of wisdom and dignity about him, Rodolfo Fernández has lived long enough to be honored often as a star of the Negro Leagues.

One Cuban black star whose career blossomed in the thirties but actually began in the twenties and extended until the late forties was Cocaína García. He was the star of the Habana Reds team that eventually lost to Lanier in 1947, winning ten, as we saw. Cocaína, also known as La Droga, was born in Manacas, Las Villas Province, on December 28, 1905. Manacas is a very small town in the center of Cuba, not too far east of the Matanzas region from which so many black Cuban players came. It is, in fact, within the same sugar-producing plain. Very black, short, stocky, and strong, García was probably, like José de la Caridad Méndez before him and Edmundo Amorós later, a "Congo." A left-hander, García began playing ball at nearby Central Washington, where he was outstanding as a pitcher, hitter, and outfielder. He was taken to Santiago de Cuba, where he participated in a professional tournament. There, a promoter of professional baseball, boxing, political rallies, and beauty contests known as Miguelito "El Jabao" (the light mulatto) gave him his *nom de guerre* because of the way in which García anesthetized hitters.[6] Cocaína, Coca for short also, could actually throw hard, but learned early to pace himself and to mix his pitches. In 1947 Jess Losada provided the best description of García: " 'Cocaína' is the man without age. Not a wrinkle mars his face. His mouth is an ivory keyboard, suggesting a man in his first twenty years of life. His muscles are smooth, lacking sharp definition, his eyes have yet to be humbled by optic lenses. Everything in 'Cocaína' is the opposite of athleticism. His pitching technique improves with age like a wine. His anatomy, Buddha's or Falstaff's, is not the kind advocated by baseball sages for a pitcher. He is not a model in terms of diet, nor does he practice moderation. He eats whatever he wants, smokes huge cigars, living abundantly, never tiring. . . ." He never did, playing year-round in Cuba, the United States, Mexico, Venezuela, and Puerto Rico.

Cocaína played ten seasons of Negro Leagues baseball with the Cuban Stars (1926–31, 1933–34) and later the New York Cubans (1935–36). Because of the demise of the first Negro National League, García went to Venezuela in 1932, where in his debut with the Caribes he no-hit the Royal Criollos, went 2 for 4 at the plate, and beat them, 21–0. He spent several summer and winter seasons in Venezuela, where his last great game as a starter came on March 11, 1947, right after his hectic season in Cuba. Pitching for Magallanes and hitting fifth, Coca beat Hilton Smith and his Vargas team, 5–1, giving up only five hits and going 3 for 3 himself. In the forties he played in Mexico during the summer, having great seasons with Aguila, Puebla and Tampico. In 1942 he was 19 and 4, and in 1945 he was 19 and 11. In Mexico he often played the outfield, hitting .281 in 1944 and .270 in 1945. As a pitcher he won a total of 84 games there.

Cocaína began his career in the Cuban League in 1926, with Almendares, when he was 5 and 2, but hit only .222. He had good seasons both on the mound and at the plate in the twenties and early thirties, hitting .364 in 1931–32 and winning 6 in 1927–28, but his first outstanding season was in 1938–39, with Santa Clara, when he hit only .240, but was 11 and 4. His greatest string of winning seasons came with Habana in the forties, winning more than 10 three times, and 12 in 1944–45. He was the champion pitcher in 1942–43 and in 1946–47, and he no-hit Marianao on December 11, 1943. He threw seven no-hitters during his entire career in the various countries in which he played. In the Cuban League my figures give him a total of 89 victories and 60 defeats. In a touching letter from Venezuela shortly before he died, García told me that he knew he could have been a major leaguer, but for the color of his skin. Though I only remember him as a third-base coach for the Habana Reds, I have no doubt that the intelligent, multitalented García was right.

Roberto (El Tarzán) Estalella, Tomás de la Cruz, Fermín Guerra, Regino Otero, and Gilberto (El Jibarito) Torres, the other outstanding players who emerged in the early to midthirties, all played in the major leagues, although none of them was a star. All had substantial careers in the Cuban League, with Guerra becoming a respected manager.

Estalella—known in the United States as Bobby—was probably Joe Cambria's first signee in 1934, when he reported to the Albany Senators of the Class AA (the highest league classification then) International League. He had begun playing professionally in the Cuban League during 1931–32 season, but he was being paid so little that he left to play for Rum Havana Club, the independent, semiprofessional team in his native Cárdenas, Matanzas Province. Born there on April 25, 1911, Estalella had played in the Amateur League with Club Deportivo Cárdenas and later with Central Hershey. Estalella was a chunky five-seven who played at well over two hundred pounds. He was a very light mulatto, a *mulato capirro,* in the words of Rodolfo Fernández. He was white enough to play in the Amateur League and in Organized Baseball, including the majors as early as 1935. Estalella was a musclebound fireplug, hence his nickname "El Tarzán." Because he was so short, pitchers had to put the ball over the plate, where he could crush it. He hit the long ball consistently, with solid averages in the high .200s. In the majors he played a total of 680 games, many of them with the Senators, but he also had a number of games with the Browns and four years with the Philadelphia Athletics. He finished with an average of .282 and 44 homers, 33 triples, and 106 doubles. Many of his games were played at spacious Griffith Stadium in Washington, with the longest left-field fence in the majors (405 feet). In the minors he hit .316 at Harrisburg, .331 at Albany, .299 at Chattanooga, .349 and .378 at Charlotte, and .341 at Minneapolis. In the Cuban League he played mostly with Habana, but after 1945 he came to be associated with Marianao, with whom he had his best season in 1949–50, when he finished at an even .300, with 12 home runs. In 1943–44 he hit .336 for Habana but without the home-run production, perhaps because at that time the league still played at La Tropical, with its endless left field.

It was in that stadium that Estalella hit his most famous clout, which, although caught, has become part of Cuban mythology as proof of his incredible power. It was the afternoon of December 2, 1939, and Estalella was playing left field for Habana behind Luis Tiant. Frank (Creepy) Crespi, Habana's shortstop (he played for the Cardinals in the summer), opened the fifth with a walk from veteran Silvino Ruiz. Gilberto Torres sacrificed from pitcher to first, sending Crespi to second. Up came Estalella. Tarzán launched a colossal clout to left field, where venerable Alejandro Oms was patrolling the 498-foot prairie that sloped up toward the dressing rooms in foul territory. The ancient "Caballero" raced back and snared the ball at an estimated 460 feet from the plate, to the astonishment of the crowd and players. Crespi tagged up at second and cut around third toward home, scoring ahead of the relay from Oms to Willie Wells at shortstop to catcher Fermín Guerra. To this day old Cuban fans, many of whom claim to have been there, remember that Estalella smashed such a long fly ball that a runner tagged up and scored from second!

Estalella's problems were on the field, where he really lacked a position. The Senators tried him at third, but a history of the club says that it was finally decided to put him elsewhere for his own safety. He was way too short for first, though he did play six games there with Philadelphia. Estalella wound up an adequate left fielder, with a good arm. Although Tarzán did play with Washington and Philadelphia during the war, he was not merely a wartime player, as has been written. He played four years before and four years after the war. In between, he was one of the "jumpers" to the Mexican League, where he hit .306 for Veracruz and San Luis in 1946, and established a reputation as a dangerous slugger. Estalella's grandnephew, also named Bobby Estalella, is today a catcher in the Philadelphia Phillies' organization.

Fermín Guerra, who was born of Canary Island parents in Havana on October 11, 1912, began playing in the city's empty lots. He never went to school. *Isleños* (Islanders), as the immigrants from the Canaries were called, were among the poorest Spaniards who came looking for fortune in Cuba. They worked in the roughest jobs and were reputed to be strong and tough. Fermín, though relatively small at five-eight, was both. As a little kid he sold fruit at the Plaza del Vapor, the old Havana market, and went to Almendares Park to work as a batboy. He was a batboy for the Blues, for whom he would later play and manage for fifteen years. Though illiterate, Guerra was smart. He became a catcher and played in the semipro league. He could not afford the amateurs. He told me in Miami, in an interview a year before his death, that they were paid a little, which meant a lot to him. He was signed by Cambria in 1936 and played a game for the Senators in 1937. He did not return to the majors until 1944, playing through 1946 with Washington. He was then traded to the Philadelphia Athletics and in 1951 to the Boston Red Sox, where he played only ten games and returned to the Senators to wind up his nine-year major-league career. Guerra hit only .242, but he was valuable as a durable second catcher, with great defensive ability and brains. In the minors he hit over .300 with Springfield, of the Class A Eastern League, and Chattanooga, of the Class AA Southern Association. In the Cuban League he was mainly associated with Almendares, though he began in 1934–35 with Habana, and played with Marianao from 1935 to 1938 and again in the early fifties, when he managed the team. He also managed Habana at the end of the decade. After the revolution he managed Industriales, but was later sent to pick potatoes in Camagüey because of his resistance to the regime.

Guerra married the sister of another ballplayer from the era, Regino (Reggie) Otero, known in the United States mostly as a third-base coach for the winning Cincinnati Reds of the sixties and seventies. But in Cuba Otero was reputed to be the best and most stylish first baseman ever. He was a line-drive, not a home-run hitter, but he always finished with a high number of doubles and triples. He had only twenty-three at-bats in the majors, with the 1945 Cubs, filling in for first-baseman Phil Cavarretta, who was injured, at the end of the season. Otero was not put on the roster in time to play in the World Series. His greatest accomplishments came in the Pacific Coast League, where he hit very well and dazzled the crowds with his wizardry at first. Francisco Sánchez, a professor of Chicano studies at the University of California, Long Beach, and who grew up in Los Angeles, told me that many Mexicans and Mexican Americans went to Wrigley Field in Los Angeles to cheer Otero. And Joe Rosomondo, a coach at Yale for many years and a former player in the Pacific Coast League, has often reminisced with me about Otero's mastery of first base.

In Cuba, Otero was mostly known as a player for Cienfuegos, but he began with Habana in 1936–37, and played for Santa Clara in 1939–40. He moved to Cienfuegos in 1942–43 and played with them through part of 1945, when he was traded to Almendares for Napoleón Reyes, thus missing out on a championship season. Otero was back with Cienfuegos in 1947–48, playing out his career there in 1951–1952. Otero's best season at the plate was 1942–43, when he reached .295. In 1950–51 he hit .263 but had seven triples. He had six triples the next year, batting .246. After that Otero managed in the Cuban League, the Venezuelan League (against his brother-in-law Guerra, whom he beat out of a pennant), and in the

International League, where he managed the Cuban Sugar Kings. From there he went on to the coaching staff of the Cincinnati Reds.

Gilberto (El Jibarito) Torres turned professional for the 1934–35 season, turning down a spot on the Cuban team that played in the El Salvador Central American games. Known as "Gil" in the United States, Torres, who was from Regla, across Havana Bay, was called "El Jibarito" after a water bird that lives among the mangroves near his hometown. He was born on August 23, 1915. Like the bird, Torres had long, spindly legs—he was 6 feet, 2 inches and weighed only 160 pounds in the early years. Because of his versatility some thought of Torres as the white Cuban answer to Martín Dihigo. But El Jibarito, though good, was not quite in that league.

Torres played in the Amateur League with his hometown team of Regla, starring as a pitcher and infielder. In his first season in the Cuban League he pitched for Habana and had an auspicious beginning, winning 4 and losing 2. But before the next season he had a bout of yellow fever that weakened him considerably, sapping some of the strength from his arm for good. From then on he became essentially a smart junkballer, with a very good knuckler. He played eighteen years as a professional in Cuba, finishing with an average of .268 and 45 victories and 52 defeats as a pitcher. In 1940–41 he won 10, lost 3 and was the champion pitcher. He almost won the batting championship in 1943–44, finishing with a .333 average. Though he did play some for Almendares, Torres was mostly associated with the Habana Lions. His best season with the Senators was 1944, when he hit .267, playing mostly at third. The next year, when the Senators nearly won the pennant, Torres played short, hitting .237. This was the wartime Washington team, stocked with Cubans ineligible for army conscription (because they were not U.S. citizens) and with which Clark Griffith tried to steal the championship. Also on that team: Tony Zardón, Santiago Ullrich, Fermín Guerra, Roberto Ortiz, Armando Roche, and Venezuelan Alejandro Carrasquel. From 1948 to 1951 Torres played for the Havana Cubans, of the Florida International League. Traded to the Miami Sun Sox of the same circuit, El Jibarito had a last hurrah. In 1952 he pitched 273 innings, winning 22 games with 8 loses, with an earned-run average of 0.86, and with 13 shutouts! He finished his career in 1954 with West Palm Beach of the Florida International League as a playing manager. After the revolution Torres was among the former professionals who embraced the new regime, managing Occidentales in the new Cuban League, and the national teams that won in Central American Games in Jamaica and Puerto Rico, and the Pan American Games in Brazil. He died in 1983.

In the first chapters of this book we encountered another player whose career began in 1934–35: Pitcher Tomás de la Cruz was involved as a leader in the controversies surrounding the Mexican League, the Cuban League's pact with organized baseball, and the dissident season at La Tropical in

1946–47. We also saw his repeated good luck in the lottery at the end of his career in the early fifties, which was followed by an early death in 1958, twelve days before his forty-fourth birthday. De la Cruz was born in Havana on September 18, 1914, attended the prestigious Marist School, where he began playing baseball, and later played for a boys' team sponsored by the magazine *Carteles*. He was so successful that he was signed by Central Hershey, of the Amateur League, where he had an outstanding season in 1932. In 1933 he switched to Havana Electric, of the semipro league, where he again excelled. In 1934–35 he played for Joseíto Rodríguez's Marianao, in the Cuban League, with whom he won 5 and lost 4. He was then signed by Joe Cambria and the Senators, who sent him to Albany, where he was 6 and 10. He was traded to the Giants' organization and played for Jersey City, then back to the Senators, who sent him to Springfield. Finally he was bought by the Cincinnati Reds, who farmed him out to Syracuse, where he had a tremendous season in 1943, winning 25 games. The next year he played the entire season with the Reds, winning 9 and losing 9, including a one-hitter against Pittsburgh. It was then that he took an offer from Pasquel and went to the Mexico City Reds, where he won 17 games his first year. A very light, handsome mulatto over six feet tall, de la Cruz was a powerful and smart right-hander who expressed himself well. In Mexico, because of his looks and affectation as a celebrity, he was known as "María Félix," after the glamorous Mexican movie actress.

With so much talent milling around in Cuba it is not surprising that someone like Joe Cambria would emerge to recruit it. In doing so he gave something of a boost to the moribund Cuban League by improving the image of professionalism, but ultimately he brought about the downfall of the Amateur League by depleting its talent. But that came later. At the time Cambria came on the scene, the only Cubans in the majors were veterans Adolfo Luque and Miguel Angel González. González played for the last time in the majors in 1932 but was retained as a coach by the Cardinals, while Luque's activities trickled down to a few innings in 1935 with the Giants, for whom he eventually also coached. He spent some summers in Cuba during the late thirties managing in the armed forces league.

Born in Italy but brought to the United States when only a few months old, Cambria was a minor-league infielder who broke a leg in 1916, putting an end to his playing career. Eventually he became a successful businessman, owner of the Bugle Apron and Laundry Company in Baltimore. He bought the Baltimore Black Sox and entered the team in the new National Negro League in 1933, but the team, which he ran on a percentage of the gate basis, lost money, and he left it. Contact with Negro-circuit baseball must have alerted Cambria to the possibilities of Latin players for the majors. He must have seen some in the games his Baltimore team played, and heard from his own players and those on other teams about Cuban baseball. Having become a friend of Clark Griffith, and probably because with his Italian he could somehow communicate in Spanish, he became the Latin American scout for the Senators.

Cambria had from the start a penchant to search for talent in unusual places. In 1934 he had brought to the Senators Allen W. Benson, a bearded pitcher from the famed barnstorming House of David team. He was bombed. In 1935 he tried to sign Edwin (Alabama) Pitts, who had just been released, but from Sing Sing, not from another baseball club. Judge Landis intervened, suspicious that the whole thing was a publicity stunt that would demean baseball. Pitts was signed to a contract with Albany, a team in the Class AA International League that Cambria owned then. He did not make the grade. It is in this context, in addition to the fact that the Senators, after winning the American League pennant in 1933, had entered a period of decline, that Cambria's schemes can be better understood. He was on the lookout for cheap talent from sources not normally tapped by other teams, though he did eventually sign players who had significant careers, such as Mickey Vernon, Babe Phelps, George Myatt, Jake Powell, and Eddie Yost.

Cambria's activities in Cuba began with the signing of Estalella, Guerra, and de la Cruz, and continued with René Monteagudo, a left-handed pitcher who could also hit and play the outfield, and quite a few others. Morris A. Bealle, in his 1947 history of the Senators, describes Estalella as a "sawed-off Cuban" and refers to Cambria's "predilection for Cubanolas" (a reference to cigars again, as with Luque). In other words, the Cubans were part of Cambria's sideshow. Cambria was a cagey man who saw at once that much of the talent in Cuba was eventually funneled to Havana, but had its origins in the provinces, so he started a network of bird dogs who scouted for him in the Cuban bushes as well as Havana. By the forties he boasted quite a system—among them Merito Acosta and Cheo Ramos—and his operations had become notorious and controversial. Turning professional, as we saw, was not that desirable to young Cuban men, who risked their eligibility in the Amateur League if they signed and faced the daunting and uncertain future of the minor leagues. But to the poorest it was a risk worth taking, and Cambria had some success. He also soon had critics in Cuba and the United States.

One was Jess Losada, who mounted a campaign against the Senator scout in the pages of *Carteles,* accusing Cambria of signing players to a blank contract that he would then sell to the major-league club, without much concern about the prospect's ultimate chances of making the majors. In other words, his profit lay in quantity, not quality. Losada alerted the DGND to what he saw as a monopoly and made arrangements for other clubs, mainly the Cincinnati Reds, to try out promising Cubans. Cultured, bilingual, and probably educated in the United States, Losada was more than a match for Cambria. He mocked the scout, saying that being Italian, he aspired to be "the Christopher Columbus of baseball."[7] In that same 1945 *Carteles* article Losada puts the number of players signed by Cambria at seventy-three, all Cuban with the exception of Venezuelan Alejandro (Patón) Carrasquel. Knowing the United States well, the Cuban sportswriter was well aware of the conditions under which the young players would have to live, the taunts and insults they would have to endure, and the bewilderment and solitude to which the language barrier would condemn them. By the end of the decade he had found a kindred spirit in the American columnist Bob Considine. Writing in the popular U.S. magazine *Collier's,* Considine accused Cambria of going "ivory hunting" in Cuba, and reported how badly the Cuban players fared with the Senators, where they were paid meager salaries and were the victims of the sort of prejudice Jackie Robinson would have to endure a few years later.[8] Considine wrote that Estalella had to be farmed out because he was being constantly knocked down by pitchers. He, Roberto Ortiz, Monteagudo and Carrasquel—Cambria's first South American signee, recommended to him by Cuban Joseíto (Joe) Rodríguez—were also ostracized within their own team. Fermín Guerra told me in Miami that he was the object of quite a bit of bench-jockeying, much of it racial, but that he knew it was intended to make him lose his concentration and paid no attention to it. Except for the topic of the abuse, the taunting was no different from what other rookies then endured. Al López said the same thing in Tampa. In fact, in 1944, Bealle reports, a brawl broke out between the Senators and the Browns, who "had been feuding all season because St. Louis bench jockeys had insisted on expressing the opinion audibly and volubly that the Cuban players on the Washington roster were of African, rather than Latin, descent" (p. 173). What I have been able to gather from players such as Agapito Mayor suggests that the situation was much worse in the minors, particularly in the South. In short, Losada and Considine were right.

But Cambria prevailed, particularly in the forties, and wound up owning an apartment building in Havana and a bar called "Triple A" beyond the center-field fence at the Gran Stadium. He also owned the Havana Cubans of the Florida International League, which he eventually sold to Bobby Maduro. During World War II Cambria not only signed many players for the Senators but stocked their minor-league system, particularly the Chattanooga Lookouts of the Class AA Southern Association. In 1944 the Lookouts were heavily Cuban, with pitchers Witto Alomá, Armando Roche, Santiago Ullrich, Juvenil Gómez, Oliverio Ortiz (Roberto's brother), and Leonardo Goicochea; catchers Rogelio Valdés, Fernando Fuertes, and José López; infielders Héctor Aragó and Pedro (Preston) Gómez; and outfielders Chito Quicutis, René Monteagudo and Tony Zardón. Ullrich, Ortiz, Preston Gómez, Aragó, and Zardón had brief stints in the majors. Cambria continued to be criticized, however, and was often referred to in the press as *el lavandero* (the laundryman), as he was in the United States.

The other entrepreneur who culled talent available in Cuba was a more familiar figure: Alejandro Pompez. Pompez, a mulatto from Key West who centered his activities later in Tampa and New York, had been involved with Negro-circuit baseball since the twenties. He had sponsored and run the Cuban Stars (East), who, in their glory years in the late twenties, had been managed by Pelayo Chacón. With the collapse of the Negro National League, where the Cuban Stars (West) played (they were under the direction of Tinti Molina), there had been a vacuum, felt everywhere through the early thirties and the worst years of the Depression. Pompez picked up the pieces, reorganizing the Cuban Stars (East), and entering them in the new Negro National League in 1935. They won the second half of the season and went to the Negro World Series, which they lost to the Pittsburgh Crawfords. Pompez, who was a numbers man and heavily involved with the mob, was indicted by New York special prosecutor Thomas E. Dewey in 1936 and had to flee the country. But Pompez returned two years later and led the New York Cubans to pennants in 1941 and 1947, when they also won the Negro World Series.

A flashy dresser and a big spender, Pompez was bilingual, a rarity in the world of baseball, which gave him a tremendous advantage in both Cuba and the United States.[9] The old players with whom I have spoken skirted around his troubles with the law and unsavory reputation, still loyal and grateful for his having given them jobs when the economic situation was dismal and the chances for black players meager. In the sphere of professional sports and entertainment, contacts with the mob were not unusual. For black empresarios, the numbers game was a kind of alternative economy where they could thrive, being barred for the most part from mainstream business, much of which was not really much "cleaner." Pompez was respected by Cuban players of all races and was well received on the island, where, in the forties, there was no scarcity of homegrown gangsters and numbers men *(boliteros)*.

The New York Cubans became not just a team of Cubans but also of Latins (some of them white) from various countries as well as American black players. Other than the Cubans, the team fielded Dominicans Horacio Martínez and Tetelo Vargas (who had virtually become Puerto Rican), Panamanian Pat Scantlebury, and Puerto Ricans Pancho Coímbre and José (Pantalones) Santiago. The team developed or nurtured Cuban stars such as Martín Dihigo, Ramón Bragaña, Luis Tiant, Cocaína García, José María Fernández, Cando López, Rogelio (Mantecado) Linares, Rodolfo Fernández, Claro Duany, Silvio García, Pedro (El Gamo) Pagés, Orestes (Minnie) Miñoso, Rafael Noble, and Edmundo (Sandy) Amorós. A measure of Pompez's prestige is that when Agapito Mayor was suspended by his Eastern League club, Springfield, in 1939 for a whorehouse brawl, the pitcher sought out the mulatto entrepreneur to see if he could hook up with the New York Cubans. But it was not to be, for apparently Mayor had been declared *persona non grata* and had to leave the United States. Mayor is white, as is Pollo Rodríguez, who actually played for the New York Cubans. Pompez straddled two eras and two worlds of baseball, for he eventually became a scout for the New York Giants, whose Polo Grounds he had rented for his Cubans. His team also provided a link with the original Cuban Giants by keeping the word "Cuban" associated with baseball in the United States. Beginning in 1935 Pompez also improved the prospects of professional baseball in Cuba, and with them the Cuban League.

But the most significant development in Cuban professional baseball in the thirties was the reorganization of the league with the encouragement and assistance of the government. The creation of the Dirección General Nacional de Deportes on June 9, 1938, with Colonel Jaime Mariné as director, has already been mentioned in connection with amateur baseball and the Amateur World Series of the early forties. But before then, in 1936, the post of commissioner of professional baseball had been created, and Colonel Ignacio Galíndez held the position. Like Mariné, Galíndez was a close associate of Batista, who, though not president, controlled Cuban politics from his leadership position in the army, which position he had acquired in 1933 by ousting the aristocratic officer corps that had supported Machado. The populist thrust of Batista's political project was evident, and baseball, already incorporated as part of the national mythology, was an important component. So Galíndez was brought in to bring order to the sport. The Cuban League's disarray was considered a national disgrace.

A measure of that disarray and how scattered Cuban talent was back then is provided by a glimpse at some of the disjointed baseball activities of 1935, the year before the Cuban League began to regroup. On March 9, for instance, *Diario de la Marina* reports the organization in Mexico City of a team named Azteca that played the Mexican selection that was barred from the Central American Games that year because its players were considered professional.[10] Azteca, as we saw in the previous chapter, was assembled by Homobono Márquez, with Cuban Horacio (Lechón) Hernández as manager. Other Cubans on the team included Brujo Rosell, Profesor Bragaña, Alcibíades Palma, and Luis Entenza, who were apparently well known in Mexico, where they lived. Meanwhile, in Santiago de Cuba, capital of Oriente Province, a professional championship was organized by a Lieutenant Colonel Rodríguez, involving three teams called Palma (for Palma Soriano), Cuba, and Maceo. There were players of the caliber of Rodolfo and José María Fernández, Tomás de la Cruz, Isidro Fabré, René Monteagudo, Antonio (Pollo) Rodríguez, and Tony Castaño. Team Cuba, with the Fernández brothers, was made up mostly of Almendares players. The tournament could not be finished because of the political agitation and the frequent strikes. On March 19, 1935, Rum Havana Club issued a public challenge to all teams, particularly those in the semipro Liga Social. The Cárdenas-based club, which now calls itself the "Cangrejeros" or "Crabbers," after the prolific crustacean in that part of Cuba, also reported that it would play a series of three games against Central Stewart. Marianao, of the Cuban League, announced games against the Cuban Stars at La Tropical. The Stars would also play their counterpart, the New York Cubans of the new Negro National League. These games constituted spring training for these teams. The players, coming from Mexico, Venezuela, the Dominican Republic, and Puerto Rico, were convening in Havana on their way north. Anastasio Santaella, a brilliant infielder who had made his name in Mexico, came to join Pompez's team, as did Tiant, Dihigo, and others. The two black teams would be opposed, finally, by a selection of amateurs who had just turned professional, such as Fermín Guerra, Gilberto Torres, Pipo de la Noval, Tomás de la Cruz, and Pollo Rodríguez. In the most interesting game, the Cuban Stars, managed by their catcher José María Fernández and with Silvino Ruiz on the mound, defeated the New York Cubans, who featured Luis Tiant, Rodolfo Fernández, Martín Dihigo, Lázaro Salazar, and Cando López (a veritable all-star team). But all of these games formed an inchoate assemblage, not the orderly competition desired by the state.

The program for the 1941 Amateur World Series boasts that Cuban professional baseball was saved by Colonel Ignacio Galíndez—whose bemedaled figure appears in a picture—by bringing to it seriousness and orderliness:

The performance of Colonel Galíndez, no less brilliant for being brief, is well known to all. The 1936–37 championship, considered the Model Season by critics and fans in general, took place under his aegis. Four powerful, well-balanced teams competed that winter, and when the schedule was finished, there was a sensational tie between the Santa Clara and Marianao teams. In a three-game playoff, the Marianao team, managed by Martín Dihigo, won the championship, two games to one. The independent American players, an eternal problem for their managers and teammates because of their lack of discipline and penchant for breaking training rules, had in 1936–37 a clean, orderly behavior that impressed all. The direct cause of this was Colonel Galíndez's performance, as everyone recognized.

The complaint about the black American players was one that was heard for a long time, and would be one of the pretexts the Cuban League used to sign the pact with organized baseball in 1947. But the crucial thing to note is that professional baseball was taken back to Las Villas Province and that the government took an active part in restructuring the game.

The 1935–36 season had not been bad at all, however, with Martín Dihigo managing Santa Clara to the championship and winning both the batting (.358) and pitching (11 and 2) titles. He also led in triples, runs scored, and complete games. But this revival of Santa Clara did not translate into an economic recovery for the Cuban League for the same reasons that the fabled 1923 Leopardos had not brought about a bonanza to all teams: La Boulanger Park was small, purchasing power in the provinces was not like Havana's, and the fan following focused on Habana and Almendares. Entrepreneur Emilio de Armas told me that a crowd of two thousand fans at La Boulanger was a huge gate *(una entradaza)*. The winning bonus for Santa Clara was less than $50 per player. Though Americans came back for this season, there were only three or four: Bill Perkins, who caught for Santa Clara; Willie Wells, who played short for the same team; Barney (Brinquitos) Brown, a left-handed pitcher for Marianao; and Marvin Barker, an outfielder for the same club.[11] The only other import was Dominican infielder Horacio Martínez, Santa Clara's second baseman, who would go on to star with the New York Cubans.

But the 1936–37 season did see an improvement in the quality of the teams, and the finale was spectacular. American stars included Buck Leonard, David (Showboat) Thomas, Clyde Spearman, Harry Williams, Herman Andrews, Willie Wells, Thad Christopher, John (Schoolboy) Taylor, Bill Perkins, and Raymond (Jabao) Brown. With Tiant, Dihigo, Horacio Martínez, Silvio García, Mantecado Linares, and José María Fernández, the Cuban League showed a decided New York Cubans influence. Spearman, Taylor, Williams, and Andrews also played for Pompez's team at one time or another. This was a season whose highlights were provided by Jabao Brown, who amassed 21 victories for a team—Santa Clara—that played 69 games and won a total of 37. He also hit .311, playing the outfield often, and drove in 27 runs. But Dihigo, playing and managing Marianao this year (clearly to keep him in the capital), won 14 games and hit .323, with 4 home runs and driving in 34. He was backed by Silvio García, who won 10 and lost 2, and though he hit only .234, had 3 homers and drove in 23 runs. For Habana, Tiant and de la Cruz won six each, but lost twelve and eleven, respectively, while Brujo Rosell finished with a busy 9 and 5. Estalella and Andrews tied for the leadership in homers at 5 each for the Reds. Almendares did well, managed by Luque, who still pitched and had a record of 2 and 2. But their front-line pitchers were Rodolfo Fernández and Bragaña, each of whom won 9, and Salazar, who won 4 and hit .313.

But Jabao Brown's exploits in the 1936–37 season were truly epic. Brown was a strong right-hander and hit both ways with power. He was the premier pitcher of the Homestead Grays during their great seasons in the thirties, when they had Josh Gibson and Buck Leonard in their powerful lineup. In Cuba he had several outstanding seasons and was a favorite of the fans. Nothing did more for Brown's fame than his amazing accomplishments during the 1936 winter. On November 17 Brown no-hit Habana and Tomás de la Cruz at La Boulanger Park for his first victory of the year. But his most extraordinary deed came a month later, on December 16. Again at La Boulanger Park, pitching in the first game of a doubleheader against Habana, he was defeated, 1–0, by Luis Tiant in eleven innings. Tiant allowed only four hits in this masterpiece, but the deciding run against Jabao came after Leandro Forbes had dropped a harmless fly ball off the bat of Belito Alvarez. Brown fumed, stomped around, and demanded to pitch the second game, which would have to begin in ten minutes, given the length of the first. Santa Clara boss Emilio de Armas told me that manager Julio Rojo consulted with him, saying he was unwilling to risk his star pitcher's arm for just one game. But Brown threatened to jump the club if he did not have his way, and they were forced to give in. Brown faced off with Tomás de la Cruz. My maternal grandfather used to recount with relish the stir in the stands when it was announced that Brown would take the mound again, and the betting frenzy that ensued, with wagers made on everything, from the outcome of the game to how long he would last. Jabao proceeded to shut out Habana on five hits. He had pitched twenty innings in one day without giving up an earned run.

But the best was the season's finale. With Santa Clara leading by three games, Marianao came to La Boulanger Park for a three-game series and swept the locals at home. De Armas had pleaded with Rojo not to pit Brown against Dihigo in the first game, since all Santa Clara needed was one victory to clinch. They would reserve their winning card for the second game on the day after, when Dihigo would not be available, or if he risked pitching again, would be too tired. But Rojo would not listen, and the "Inmortal" rose to the occasion and beat Santa Clara. Demoralized, the Leopardos also lost the next two. That closed the schedule with a tie between the two teams. A three-game playoff was arranged, to begin on February 18, 1937, in Havana's La Tropical. Rojo again pitted Brown against Dihigo, but won this time, 6–1, to put Marianao on the verge of elimination. Jabao also got two hits and drove in a run. With the season in the balance, Marianao started Silvio García on February 20. García held Santa Clara to eight hits and two runs, tying the series at one win apiece and setting up the definitive confrontation between Brown and Dihigo for the next day. The great Dihigo came through one more time, holding Santa Clara hitless until the ninth, at which time they scored three on a homer by Perkins. But it was too late. Marianao won, 7–3, and Dihigo was carried around the field on the shoulders of the delirious fans.

But all this activity did not translate into profit, and the law and order desired by Mariné and Galíndez was frequently threatened by brawls on the field and disputes about money among players and entrepreneurs. In September 1938 Mariné named Dr. Arturo Bengochea *asesor de baseball*. Bengochea was a graduate of Columbia University, where he had been a friend of Lou Gehrig's and witnessed a legendary homer the Iron Horse hit playing for that school. Bengochea's task was to reorganize the league, which continued to function as a cooperative, with the important franchises (Almendares, Habana, and Santa Clara) leased from Linares' widow. Bengochea planned to limit the number of imported players to four per club and turn each team into a company or firm that would begin by depositing the payroll for a two-week period, plus severance pay, with the league. With this the players would be ensured of a salary even if the team folded. The plan was to eventually abandon the cooperative system and function as a group of corporations—the teams—under the protective umbrella of the DGND. De Armas told me that there was great dissatisfaction with the monopoly Linares' widow exercised, which impeded this plan. He said that at the end of one season he went to Luque's farm (called "El Pitcher") outside of Havana to settle the Almendares accounts, which they were leasing in partnership that year. When Luque signed the check for the 10 percent owed the widow, he told de Armas, with customary vulgarity, that he was through, and to tell her "to take the club and shove it up her ass."

De Armas, a born promoter, had better ideas.[12] He knew that the success of a spectacle depended on marketing and advertising. As *administrador* (business manager) of the Cuban League beginning in 1939, he decided to provide an incentive to the press by giving it a cut of 8%—later 10%—of the gross receipts, which was split according to each paper's circulation and doled out every fifteen days. Reporters were expected to provide *gacetilla* (advance publicity) for each contest as well as write a story about it and print a minimum of three pictures. This practice continued for the remainder of the league's history. Another idea was to sell the radio broadcasting rights. At first the magnates argued that the broadcasts would kill attendance, but de Armas correctly thought that the opposite would occur. He began by selling season rights for $300, with Miguel Angel González interjecting that he spent that much just on beer every month. But de Armas boasts that by 1959–60 the league was collecting $480,000 per season in radio and television rights. Radio made the Cuban League a truly national phenomenon beginning in 1940. By reaching fans in the provinces it became unnecessary to actually place teams away from the capital, where they would not generate sufficient revenue. Santa Clara disappeared after 1941 and Cienfuegos never played again in that city because it was not profitable. De Armas added, with a wink, that before acting on any of this he always demanded a *written* vote of confidence from the teams' representatives, "because you know how our compatriots are, they tell you one thing today and a different one tomorrow."

De Armas, or "Armitas," as he is known to his friends, assembled a powerful Santa Clara club for the 1938–39 season and won the pennant. This was a team that could have rivaled the 1923 Santa Clara powerhouse. Managed by Lázaro Salazar, who also pitched and played first base, this edition had Cocaína García, Jabao Brown, Armando (Indian) Torres, Leroy Matlock, Schoolboy Taylor, and Heliodoro (Yoyo) Díaz as pitchers. Josh Gibson was the catcher, with Salazar at first, Juan (Bragañita) García at second, Pollo Rodríguez at third, Sam Bankhead at short, and Tony Castaño, José (Huesito) Vargas, and Santos Amaro in the outfield, which was also played by Jabao and Cocaína. Although Habana contended, mostly because of Martín Dihigo's efforts (he won 14 games), the Leopardos prevailed. Gibson had a fantastic season, hitting 11 homers, while hitting .356 and scoring 50 runs. (With a mixture of awe and racism, Gibson became known in Cuba as "El Gorila," or "Trucutú," after a comic strip.[13]) Amaro hit .366 and led in hits with 78 and runs batted in with 49. Castaño won the batting championship at .371 and went 6 for 6 on Christmas Day against Almendares. Cocaína and Jabao each won 11, with García pitching 3 shutouts. De Armas says that he was paying Gibson $130 a month plus expenses, and Brown the same plus his wife's expenses (she was the daughter of Negro Leagues magnate Cum Posey).

This season was made memorable also by an enormous homer hit by Josh Gibson at La Boulanger Park in Santa Clara on October 22, 1938, against Manuel (Chino) Fortes, pitching for team Cuba. Lore passed on to me by my father, who was in the stands, claims that the ball cleared the cock-fighting pit beyond the fence (these are circular arenas with conical roofs). Charles Monfort Subirats, a very meticulous independent archivist of Cuban baseball, told me in Miami, in December 1990, that he surveyed that shot. Years after the feat, Monfort happened to have a layover at Santa Clara on a bus trip from Santiago de Cuba to Havana. He decided to pass the time by ascertaining once and for all the actual length of Gibson's already legendary blast. He bought a tape measure at a local hardware store, went to La Boulanger Park, and measured from the spot where the ball crossed the fence to a weather vane on the roof of a small grocery store where witnesses told him it had struck. Adding this distance to the distance from home plate to the fence, he came up with a figure of 704 feet! Wherever he went, Gibson hit the longest ball in that place's history, including Cuba.[14]

The decade closed with the inauguration of the Cuban Baseball Hall of Fame by the DGND on July 26, 1939, by placing a bronze plaque at La Tropical (the American Hall of Fame had been founded in Cooperstown in 1936). The first ten inductees, chosen by former and current baseball writers, as well as *asesores de baseball profesional en Cuba*, meaning Bengochea and his staff, were: Luis (Anguila) Bustamante, José de la Caridad Méndez, Antonio María (El Inglés) García, Gervasio (Strike) González, Armando Marsans, Valentín (Sirique) González, Rafael (El Marqués) Almeida, Cristóbal Torriente, Adolfo Luján, and Carlos (Bebé) Royer. By 1941 the following had been added: Alfredo Arcaño, Joseíto Muñoz, Regino García, and Emilio Sabourín.[15] The inclusion of Sabourín, Luján, and García shows to what extent Cuban baseball was writing its history with a view toward establishing the sport as part of the foundation of the nation. The presence of Marsans, Méndez, Almeida, and above all Torriente shows how the Golden Age had already become part of a legendary past, in spite of its relative temporal proximity. Finally, the inclusion of whites and blacks, of major leaguers and others who starred mainly in the Negro circuits and in Cuba, shows how much the inauguration of this modest Hall of Fame was a part of the populist, nationalistic impulse of the DGND, Mariné, and ultimately Bastista's rule. This was a Cuban Hall of Fame not controlled by American opinion. An average American fan would not have recognized a single name in the first listing of Cuban Hall of Famers.

⊖

The next few seasons of the Cuban League, from 1939–40 to 1945–46, have to be seen in the context provided by the tremendous popularity of amateur baseball, and the Amateur World Series played in Havana from 1939 to 1943. This phase culminates with the sale of Habana and Almendares by Linares' widow and leads to the abandonment of La Tropical for the Gran Stadium. These are years of recovery in which the Cuban League benefited from the same economic bonanza brought about by the war, the close tutelage of Cuba by the United States, and the stability of Batista's coalition government. These five years also coincided with the growth and improvement of the Mexican League, the return of the Dodgers to La Tropical for spring training in 1941 and 1942, and a new heyday of Negro circuits baseball in the United States. The decline of the majors and of Organized Baseball in general because of the conscription of many players into the U.S. Army created a vacuum that the Mexican, Cuban, and Negro Leagues filled. The abundance of amateur stars, who lent their prestige and popularity to the Cuban League when they signed professional contracts, was also a determining factor. Finally, there was the founding of the Havana Cubans in 1946, and with them Cuba's entry into Organized Baseball.

It is in this period of revival, which coincides with the heyday of amateur sports, and particularly with the Amateur World Series played in Havana from 1939 to 1943, that baseball was consolidated in Cuban ideology as the national sport. This occurred during the populist, coalition regime of Fulgencio Batista, when the symbolic connection between sports and the military was strengthened through the activities of the DGND. On March 9, 1941, *Carteles* refers to Colonel Mariné as the host of the Dodgers, and of major-league teams who came to La Tropical for exhibition games. But in all this, the overall bonding process was aided by the advancement of radio broadcasting, particularly of Amateur League games and the Amateur World Series. Following these contests fostered a sense of national solidarity allied with the game of baseball. The Cuban League also rode the coattails of the Amateur League's popularity through radio; legions of Almendares and Habana fans were created throughout the entire country. While actual games were again concentrated in the capital, broadcasts reached every corner of Cuba. Fans could get caught up in the emotion of the games as they happened, not after the fact through the cold medium of print. More people began to travel from the provinces to Havana for the express purpose of going to ball games. Professional players profited directly by becoming national figures as never before, and cashed in with postseason barnstorming tours. But the crucial development was the final bonding, the definitive alliance between baseball and national mythology at a time when patriotism and sport's lore could truly be shared by a majority of the population. The rise of modern totalitarian regimes in Europe and elsewhere was aided by the development of communications media, and Cuba was not an exception. The roar of the crowd at La Tropical could be heard throughout the island and promoted a feeling of patriotic fellowship that was tangible and truly emotive, not abstract and cerebral. An immediate Cuban "imagined community" became manifest, as never before, in the voices of broadcasters Orlando Sánchez Diago, Manolo de la Reguera, Felo Ramírez, and Cuco Conde.

Napoleón Reyes's signing with Almendares in 1941, and the signing of a host of other amateur stars in the years following, did pull the Cuban League out of the doldrums, but this process was made possible by the radio; otherwise it would have had no discernible effect. A few amateurs had already signed in the thirties, not just Guerra, Torres, and de la Cruz, but also Mayor, who had been a hero in the Central American Games. But they had all played in a very diminished Cuban League. It was only when amateurs with national exposure acquired through the radio, and who had starred in the Amateur World Series organized by Mariné, joined the league that the effect was fully felt. Baseball as the national sport of Cuba was Batista's doing, a fact emphasized by the president's frequent attendance at La Tropical, which was reported over the radio and in newspapers and magazines. Since all such bondings require a liturgy, various quasi-military rituals at the opening of Amateur World Series served that purpose, as well as the tradition of having Mariné throw out the ceremonial first pitch at the opening of Cuban League seasons. Another ritual was staged at the Polo Grounds, New York, in August 1945. Batista, who by this time had stepped down from the presidency, presided over a homage to Napoleón Reyes and Luque, who were then with the Giants, the latter as a coach. The former colonel presented Reyes with an expensive set of luggage as both populist hero and sports star smiled for the cameras.

Radio was not the only technological advancement influential in the process of reviving the Cuban League. These years also saw a change in Cuban tourism, aided in great measure by the development of the DC-3, which cheapened travel to the island and contributed to the foundation of Cubana de Aviación, which began as a subsidiary of Pan American. The DC-3 facilitated travel between Florida and Cuba, allowing teams to either train in Cuba or easily travel there for games. Without this airplane there would have been no Florida International League. By the late thirties and forties American tourism was not what it was during the Golden Age in the twenties. Fewer Americans now came by private yacht. The new Americans who came were middle-class and began to arrive in larger numbers as the political situation stabilized toward the late thirties. Their flow was curtailed during the war years, but was replaced by many American servicemen, who came with the U.S. Navy or to man the various airports and mines of strategic minerals such as nickel in Oriente Province that the United States had built on the island.

The seasons after 1938–39, when Santa Clara was dethroned by Almendares, saw the renaissance of the rivalry between the Blues and the

Reds. Almendares won in 1939–40, Habana in 1940–41, for the first time in many years, Almendares in 1941–42 and again in 1942–43, Habana in 1943–44, Almendares in 1944–45, and finally Cienfuegos in 1945–46, the last season at La Tropical.[16] It seems clear to me, following Jess Losada's view at the time, that the Cuban League could not do without the clash of the Scorpions and the Lions. The program for the 1942–43 season, which included only Habana, Almendares, and Cienfuegos, with all of the games played at La Tropical, is eloquent testimony of this: The A and the H are huge in comparison to the puny c, for Cienfuegos, sandwiched in between. Cienfuegos was no cannon fodder, though. Managed by Joseíto Rodríguez, they had a good team. But Almendares and Habana had most of the marquee players. Almendares had Bragaña, de la Cruz, and Mayor as pitchers, with Fleitas and Guerra as catchers; an infield of Héctor Rodríguez, Mexican José Luis (Chile) Gómez, Pollo Rodríguez, Napoleón Reyes, and Cocoliso Torres, and in the outfield Amaro, Ortiz, Duany, and Bejerano. The team was managed by Luque, featured on the program's cover. Miguel Angel, at the helm of the Reds, had Martín Dihigo, Rodolfo Fernández, Jibarito Torres, and Cocaína on the mound, with Salvador Hernández and Raúl Aragón behind the plate. In the infield he had the Blanco brothers (Carlos and Heberto), Dominican Horacio Martínez, Sungo Carreras, and former amateur Antonio (Mosquito) Ordeñana. In the outfield he had Sagüita Hernández, Rogelio Bolaños, Villa Cabrera, and Tetelo Vargas. Joseíto Rodríguez's Cienfuegos squad (referred to at this time occasionally as the Green Parrots) had pitchers Adrián Zabala, Julio (Yuyo) Acosta, Jorge (Curveador) Comellas, René Monteagudo, Max Macon, and Venezuelan star Ascanio Vidal López (who was also a strong hitter and played the outfield). Jorge Colás was the catcher. In the infield he had Silvio García, Manuel (Chino) Hidalgo, Napoléon Heredia, and Tony Castaño, while in the outfield he had Crespo, Pagés, and Formental. It was a closely contested season, with Almendares winning by four, with Habana second and Cienfuegos eight behind.

In 1943–44 Marianao, run by Emilio de Armas, Merito Acosta, and Eloy García, tried to steal the pennant by bringing in five Americans: Roy Campanella, Ralph H. McCabe, Eddie Popowski, Mickey Burnette, and Leon Treadway. They added three Mexicans, Epitacio (La Mala) Torres, Alberto (Coty) Leal, and Pedro (Charrascas) Ramírez, and two prestigious amateurs, Luis Suárez and Chito Quicutis. But to no avail; Habana prevailed. The four-team configuration of Almendares, Habana, Cienfuegos, and Marianao would remain intact until the end of the Cuban League's history in 1961.

The players who came to prominence during the first half of the decade of the forties played on through most of the fifties and are part of my own memories of the Cuban League. These were men profoundly affected by the changes in baseball after World War II. Some who were black made the majors; others played out the decline of the Negro Leagues. Among the white players a few had brief careers in the majors and in the minor leagues. Many from all groups went to the Mexican League until its decline in the late forties. Some wound up in Maracaibo, Venezuela, in the short-lived Liga Marabina. Most were able to enjoy the economic bonanza of the Cuban League in the early fifties.

Agapito Mayor, who had signed with the Braves, went to Springfield, in the Eastern League, where he had a good season until the fracas already mentioned. He later pitched in Greenville, South Carolina, where he made the all-star team and finished with thirteen victories and four defeats. In 1942, after having made the Senators, he decided to go to Mexico, where the pay was better, as well as the living conditions. In Washington, he told me, he had been put up in a dangerous neighborhood, yet the rent ate up most of his salary. In Mexico Mayor was 8 and 7 for Puebla in 1942, 16 and 15 in 1943 for Puebla and Mexico City, 14 and 13 for Puebla again in 1944, and a high of 23 and 14 in 1945 for Nuevo Laredo. He was 20 and 9 in his next and last season for the same team, the year he won 10 in Cuba during the winter, helping to vault Almendares over Habana.

Mayor had great success in the final years at La Tropical, always having busy records, with many wins and losses and always with numerous innings pitched. In 1941–42 he was the champion pitcher, tied with Max Macon, with a record of 6 and 2. The next four seasons he won 7, 6, 7, and 7, and lost 10 in 1945–46. Mayor continued to build his reputation as a courageous pitcher, not afraid to pitch to anybody in any situation, nor to pit his best pitch against the batter's strength. His name became synonymous with Almendares. He was at the very core of the Blues and when, at the end of his career, in the fifties, Miguel Angel González offered him a job as coach with Habana, he refused, unwilling to wear the Reds' uniform. A man of dignity, Mayor told me that he was always an amateur at heart. It cost him plenty.

Another pitcher whose career began in the thirties but extended through the forties to the fifties was lefthander Adrián Zabala. Like Mayor, Zabala had a great amateur career with Fortuna and turned professional with team Cuba in 1938–39. He had mediocre seasons with Almendares from 1939 to 1940, and was then traded to Cienfuegos, the team with which he would be associated in the Cuban League for the rest of the decade, before moving to Habana in 1950. A strong six-footer of Basque origin, Zabala was born in San Antonio de los Baños, near Havana, on August 26, 1916. From 1942 to 1945 Zabala pitched for Jersey City in the International League. He had good seasons with the Little Giants and in 1945 was called up to the New York Giants, where he was 2 and 4. But Zabala was among the "jumpers" to the Mexican League, pitching for Puebla, under Luque, and did not return to the Giants until 1949, when the ban was lifted. In 1946 he was 11 and 14 with the Puebla Pericos. He had outstanding seasons in the Cuban League in 1945–46, when he won

9 for Cienfuegos, and finished 11 and 10 in 1946–47 at the Gran Stadium. Zabala was a good overall athlete and also could hit. He was a favorite in Cuba and of mine in the fifties, when he was traded to the Habana Reds. He had speed and an elegant windup. The last part of his surname (bala) means "bullet" in Spanish, an auspicious linguistic association for a pitcher.

Andrés Fleitas, who would be Lanier's catcher in The Last Game, was with Zabala at Jersey City and Mexico. Fleitas was poised to move up to the Giants when he heeded Pasquel's call. "El Güero," or "The Blond," as he was known in Mexico, had a solid career with Almendares, particularly in the 1946–47 season, when he finished with a batting average of .316. The former Central Hershey standout hit .333 for Monterrey in 1945. He returned to organized baseball in 1948, hitting .281 in 1950 with Chattanooga of the Southern Association. He was a second-string catcher in the Cuban League during the fifties.

Roberto Ortiz was perhaps the most popular baseball player in Cuba in the forties and fifties, more so than others who had longer and more successful careers in the majors. If there is a version of "the natural" in Cuban baseball, Ortiz is it. He was a gifted athlete, 6 feet, 4 inches tall, weighing 220 pounds in his prime, with brown hair and blue eyes. He was known for his power as a hitter, but he had such a prodigious arm that when Joe Cambria signed him for the Senators, they tried to turn him into a pitcher. Ortiz was known as the "Giant from Central Senado," but that was probably a sportswriter's concoction. He was simply Roberto Ortiz— his name alone sufficed to stir the emotions of the crowd. He was famous for his enormous and frequent home runs, admired for his simplicity and candor; he was the very image of the *guajiro,* symbol of the fatherland.

Ortiz had been born at Central Senado, in Camagüey Province, on June 30, 1915, where he began his playing career. In 1937 and 1938 he played for Central Hershey as a catcher, under Joaquín Viego. In 1939 he signed with Cambria and went to Charlotte of the Class B Three States League, where he hit .301, and .307 the next year. Ortiz was a fierce, reckless competitor who sustained injuries in both of those seasons. First he suffered a fracture of the cranium, then he broke his arm. He split the season in 1941 between Charlotte and the Washington Senators. In the majors that year he hit .329 in twenty-two games, but was again injured. He failed to hit well the next two years in the American League but finished with a .360 average at Chattanooga. The Senators sold him to the Phillies, who in turn sold him to the Dodgers. They sent him to Montreal, where in 1943 he pounded International League pitching for an average of .304, fourth in that circuit, and led in runs batted in. The Dodgers sold him back to Washington in 1944, where he finished at .253 with five home runs in eighty-five games.

In that year Ortiz went, along with so many others, to Mexico, playing for the capital's Reds. Like Bragaña, Dihigo, and Salazar, he is in the Mexican Hall of Fame, where his plaque reads: "Roberto (El Guajiro) Ortiz: Sensational Cuban player. An outfielder with tremendous power at bat. He hit in thirty-five consecutive games (a record) in 1948 playing for Mexico. The only player to win the slugging crown four years in a row. He finished with an overall .317 batting average." Ortiz's career in Mexico extended to the fifties, playing with Nuevo Laredo in 1952 and Yucatán in 1955–56. Always a drawing card in his homeland, Ortiz also played with the Cuban Sugar Kings of the International League in the fifties.

A charismatic athlete, Ortiz had a flair for the dramatic. He hit the first home run ever at the Gran Stadium, off Luis Tiant. In 1949, after serving his suspension in the Cuban League for having gone to Mexico, which was lifted after clamorous protests from the fans, Ortiz came up to the plate against Jim Prendergast, a left-hander for Marianao. With the crowd on its feet at the Gran Stadium cheering for him, back in his Almendares uniform, Ortiz cracked a line drive over the fence for his most famous homer ever. That year Ortiz hit fifteen home runs, tying for the lead with Habana's Don Lenhardt, and finished with a .315 batting average. It was his best season in the Cuban League. Ortiz eventually also played for Marianao, but he was the quintessential Almendares Blue. He was such a popular figure that he is the only Cuban ballplayer I know of who had a movie of his life made, called, significantly, *Honor and Glory*.[17] In Ortiz the symbiosis of patriotism and baseball reached a crescendo.

It is a well-known story that in 1939, when the Senators tried to make Ortiz into a Cuban Bob Feller, in Cambria's words, they imported Al López to their training camp to work with the Cuban giant. López told me in Tampa that Ortiz had plenty of speed and good movement on the ball but that the Senators were not patient enough with him. Ortiz was a player whose career was hampered by the turmoil of the forties in baseball and who could have had a more illustrious career in the majors had he stayed with Washington instead of going to Mexico, when he was thirty years old and his career was beginning to peak. It is daunting to think what he could have accomplished in cozy Ebbets Field if the Brooklyn Dodgers had seen fit to keep him. Ortiz was also hampered by the various experiments to use his multiple talents. Viego had him catch for two years at Central Hershey, and Cambria had him pitch in the minors. Still, Ortiz's popularity in Cuba had few if any rivals in his time, and when he passed away in Miami on September 15, 1971, at age fifty-six, his funeral was attended by thousands of Cubans. His was not a tragic life, like Salazar's, and Ortiz had the advantage of being white in a racist world, but his brief existence was marked by the sadness of what could have been, and the injustice of a suspension, in his own country, dictated by the monopolistic reach of Organized Baseball.

Claro Duany, Pedro (Perico) Formental, Alejandro Crespo, Orestes Miñoso, Rafael Noble, and Héctor Rodríguez were the most prominent black Cuban players to arise in the early forties. Miñoso, of course, became the first Cuban major-league star since Luque, and both Noble and Rodríguez played briefly in the majors. But Crespo and Formental were stars in Cuba who enjoyed as much admiration as the others, at a time when making the majors was not the only measure of greatness.

Duany, a strapping outfielder from Caibarién, in Las Villas Province, was an excellent left-handed hitter with power, who, as we saw, made it into the Cuban League through the semipro league. Fausto Miranda has told me that the longest home run he saw at La Tropical was hit by Duany—it cleared the two fences in right-center and hit the trees behind them. Duany's first three seasons, from 1941–43 to 1944–45, saw him shuttle between Almendares and Habana. By 1945–46 he was with Marianao, the team with which he would be mostly associated through the 1951–52 season. Duany's most remarkable year had to have been 1945. He was the batting champion in the Cuban League 1944–45 season with an average of .340, and led the Mexican League that summer, playing for the Sultans of Monterrey, with an astronomic .375 (his closest rival, at .366, was Ray Dandridge, the Hall of Fame third baseman for the Mexico City Reds). In 1946–47 Duany led the Liga de la Federación, which challenged the Cuban League, with an average of .368. His greatest season in the Negro Leagues was in 1947, when he hit .304 for the champion New York Cubans. In 1947–48, with Marianao, he hit .300. He remained with that team, finishing the 1949–50 season at .274, with 7 home runs and 40 runs batted in; 1950–51 at .314, with only 2 home runs and 27 runs batted in; and 1951–52 at .275, with 6 home runs and 28 runs batted in. In 1952–53 he was traded to Cienfuegos.

A heavy, powerful man without much speed or range, Duany himself told me in Evanston, Illinois, with touching self-knowledge and humility, that he had not been a very good defensive outfielder. But in the Cuban League he was a feared hitter and slugger, the first left-handed power hitter of consequence since the times of Torriente, Oms, and Mayarí Montalvo. At spacious La Tropical and the Gran Stadium he was among a handful of batters who could clear the fences regularly. Had Duany been born a few years later (he was thirty in 1947), or had integration come a few years earlier, I have no doubt that he would have had a substantial major-league career. In the early forties he was among those who helped bring back the Cuban League.

Alejandro Crespo was an even greater ballplayer, the best Cuban outfielder ever, according to Fausto Miranda. Crespo had it all. A right-hander with speed, agility, and a great arm, he could hit with power and for average and also could catch. Crespo's career traces a sinuous itinerary through all the open venues for a Cuban black in the thirties, forties, and fifties. Born near Havana in Güira de Melena on February 26, 1915, he began playing in 1931 for Bus Route 23, in the semipro league. He remained with them until 1935, when he transferred to the Hotel Nacional club, in the same league. In 1937 he transferred to Alas de Oro, in Guanajay (also near Havana). Crespo then entered the Armed Forces League, playing for the Eighth Regiment, before turning professional in 1939–40 with Cienfuegos, the team with which he played until 1950, when he moved to Habana. He hit .339 his first year, was batting champion in 1942–43, and Most Valuable Player in 1945–46. Crespo was batting champion again in 1948–49, with a .326 average. In his declining years with Habana he hit in the mid-.200s. He retired in 1955.

Crespo played only two seasons in the Negro Leagues—1940 and 1946—both with the New York Cubans, finishing with averages of .344 and .326, respectively. But he preferred Mexico, where he played for Torreón, Nuevo Laredo, Puebla, and Veracruz and hit consistently over .300 (.320 lifetime). After the decline of the Mexican League he went to Venezuela, playing for the Gavilanes in the Liga de Maracaibo in the state of Zulia. But for all his accomplishments and the admiration he enjoyed in Cuba, Crespo is mostly remembered for a catch he made in a spring exhibition game against the Dodgers in 1942.

It was March 7 and the Dodgers, who were training at La Tropical, faced a Cuban selection whose lineup was Pedro (Gamo) Pagés, center field; Pollo Rodríguez, second base; Santos Amaro, right field; Silvio García, shortstop; Crespo, left field; Ramón Heredia, third base; Fermín Guerra, catcher; Regino Otero, first base, and Agapito Mayor on the mound. In the top of the third, Mayor tried to start Pee Wee Reese with a fastball over the plate and the Dodger shortstop hit it deep to left, where Crespo began to run after the ball with all he had. A portable fence had been erected at 345 feet to make La Tropical's dimensions more realistic. Crespo arrived at the fence together with the ball, which was about to go over much too high for the catch, but he leaped, stretched his left arm up, and caught it as he tumbled over on the other side. Bill Klem, the famous umpire who was working the game, said afterward that had it not been an exhibition game he would have had to call the hit a home run. Many people, including Charlie Dressen, a coach then for the Dodgers, said that it was the best catch they had ever seen. What stuck in people's minds, it seems, was that Crespo, at the top of the jump, appeared to hover for an instant, as if defying gravity. Mayor scattered nine hits and the Cubans won, 4–2. Fausto Miranda, who was there, has written that this game took place on a weekday, so there were very few fans present. But, as usual, thousands now claim to have been there and to have witnessed Crespo's feat.

Pedro (Perico, or Perucho) Formental was another black Cuban outfielder of great distinction who only played in Organized Baseball toward the end of his career, but who was outstanding in the Cuban League. He was my all-time favorite player, and to me and many others the quintessential Habana Red. A left-handed batter and thrower, Formental, who was five-eleven and weighed two hundred pounds in his prime, was a charismatic player with a flair for the flamboyant. As we saw in chapter 2, Formental was a flashy dresser and sported a thin mustache when no one else had facial hair in the Cuban League or elsewhere. He was born in Bágua-nos, Oriente Province, on April 19, 1919. This is the very same region where Batista was born and raised, and Formental was a loyal follower of his until the end. Fond of cock-fighting and reputed to carry a gun, For-mental once announced that he wanted to run for Congress. He had a large following in Cuba, rivaling that of Roberto Ortiz. Formental's life after baseball is the stuff of novels and will be told in a later chapter.

Formental played for Central Baguanos until 1941, when he was rec-ommended to Hoyo Castillo, owner of the La Pasiega team in the semipro league, one of the better clubs in that Havana circuit. But his stay there was very short because he was signed right away by Cienfuegos, of the Cuban League. For three seasons Formental played for Cienfuegos, on a strong team that included Crespo, Silvio García, Napoleón Heredia, Gamo Pagés, and other blacks. This team, which eventually won under Luque in 1945–46, was dubbed the "Petroleros" in 1941 by popular radio broad-caster Cuco Conde, in a moment of tasteless and racist inspiration (*petróleo* means crude oil, which is black; white men who like black women are called *petroleros* in Cuba). The name stuck in the tolerant and racist world of Cuba, and it has become part of the Cuban League's baseball lore. By the time they won, Formental, who had hit in the mid-.200s with them, had been traded to Habana, his team of destiny. By 1947–48 his average had climbed to .279, but the best was yet to come.

In 1949–50 Formental led the Cuban League with an average of .336, with 5 home runs and 40 runs batted in. He slumped to .250 in 1950–51 but had 8 homers, 6 triples, 7 doubles, and 38 runs batted in. He again had a relatively low average in 1951–52, finishing at .254, but with 9 hom-ers, 11 doubles, and 46 runs batted in. Formental's greatest season in the Cuban League was 1952–53, when he became my idol, finishing with an average of .337, with 57 runs batted in.

Formental pounded Mexican League pitching from 1943 to 1946, with averages of .312, .345, .362, and .384. During the middle years— 1944 and 1945—he was with the Veracruz Blues, which played in Mexico City and was, with the capital's Reds, one of the two most popular teams. In the United States Formental was the star of the Memphis Red Sox of the Negro American League from 1947 to 1950, where he hit .341 in 1949, with 101 hits in 296 times at bat. Twenty-nine of the hits were doubles, 22 triples, and 28 home runs, an incredible slugging performance. In a December 18, 1949, interview with Rai García in *Carteles,* Formental spoke of his desire to play in the majors, where he was sure he would excel. He tells García that scouts from the Cubs, the Pirates, and the Yankees had gone to see him play. Formental claims that the Yankees offered Mr. Mar-tin, owner of the Memphis Red Sox, $15,000 for him, but being a rich man, Martin was not interested in the money. (This Memphis team was one of the thriving franchises during the Negro League's period of decline.) With the short right-field porch in Yankee Stadium, I have no doubt that

Formental would have been a sensation in New York. But the Yankees did not field a black until 1955, by which time Formental was forty years old. Like many black players whose careers peaked at the time of Jackie Robinson (Formental was thirty-two in 1947), the slow-paced integration of Organized Baseball, and the damage done by it to the Negro Leagues, put a damper on their careers. In the fifties Formental played in the Dominican Republic, Venezuela, and for the Cuban Sugar Kings of the International League, for whom he hit a very respectable .293 in both 1954 and 1955.

Two other black Cuban players whose careers were profoundly affected by the integration of organized baseball were Héctor Rodríguez and Rafael (Sam) Noble. Rodríguez played a full season with the White Sox in 1952, hitting a decent .265 in 124 games. But he only hit one home run, and major-league third basemen are expected to have power. (The masterful first baseman, Regino Otero had an even briefer major-league career for a similar reason.) Héctor Rodríguez is considered to have been the best defensive third baseman Cuba ever produced. A slight man at 5 feet, 7 inches and 165 pounds, Rodríguez was a magician at third, with quick reflexes and a strong arm. He was as swift and graceful as a ballet dancer coming in on a bunt or a slow roller. Traded to Habana toward the end of his career, Rodríguez was an Almendares Blue from the beginning and became part of the core of that team (with Mayor, Ortiz, Cañizares, Amaro, Miranda, and later Rocky Nelson). Rodríguez was at third behind Lanier in the deciding game of the 1946–47 season. Though he reached a high of .301 in 1950–51, Rodríguez was a .260 to .280 hitter in the Cuban League, where he was revered more for his defensive excellence. But he led the second Caribbean Series, played in Puerto Rico, with a .474 average.

In Mexico Rodríguez played with Tampico, and with Pastora in Venezuela in 1946, 1947, 1948, and 1949. He spent the fifties in the International League, first with Montreal and later with Syracuse and Toronto. He was Rookie of the Year with Montreal in 1951, with an average of .302 and 95 runs batted in. That led to his promotion to the White Sox. He hit .302 again with Syracuse in 1953. Traded to Toronto, Rodríguez finished 1954 with a .307 average, followed by seasons of .290, .272, and .288. After 1954, with the Cuban Sugar Kings in the International League, he got to spend some time at home during the season and play before his admiring fans at the Gran Stadium. He was also a favorite with Toronto fans, whom he dazzled with his play at third, and once, in a pinch, played a brilliant center field for a week in 1958. The *Maple Leaf News* (vol. 3, no. 2, summer of 1958), Toronto's team magazine, claims, with good reason, that had Héctor Rodríguez devoted himself to being a shortstop he would have spent a longer period in the majors. Had he been white, or had there been no quotas in the majors in the fifties, he also could have made it as a third baseman. Eddie Yost, another defensive wizard in that spot, was not a much better hitter than Rodríguez. As it was, Rodríguez, who lives in Mexico, had a splendid career there and in Cuba, where he was not only idolized but also secure in his standing as the best defensive third baseman ever.

Noble, from Contramaestre, deep in Oriente Province, was in the game as a New York Giant when Bobby Thomson hit the shot that defeated the Dodgers in 1951. Noble was a second-string catcher behind Wes Westrum. Noble spent a total of three seasons with the Giants in that capacity, playing a total 107 games and finishing with an overall batting average of .218, with only 9 home runs in 243 at-bats. Born in 1920, the rugged Noble was nearly six feet tall and weighed more than two hundred pounds. He was a very powerful hitter who clouted some of the longest homers seen at the Gran Stadium. He began his professional career with Habana in the 1942–43 season, seeing little action. In 1946 and 1947 he caught for the New York Cubans, with batting averages of .404 and .342, respectively. Noble played at least two winters with Cervecería, in Panama, and returned to the Cuban League with Cienfuegos in 1946–47. He played with that team until the end of his career in 1959–60. In the fifties he had superb seasons as a home-run hitter and played for the Cuban Sugar Kings in the International League. He also played for Buffalo and Columbus in that league, hitting 20 home runs in 1957 and 21 in 1958 for Buffalo. In the early fifties, before he went up to the Giants, he had excellent seasons with Oakland, in the Pacific Coast League. Early in his career there were questions about Noble's defensive ability, but as the years progressed he improved and became a solid receiver with a strong arm. He was a rock blocking the plate. Noble was a fixture with Cienfuegos and a much respected player in Cuba.

I have saved for last the best-known of the black Cuban players whose careers began in the early to middle forties: Orestes Miñoso. Because Miñoso was a star in the majors, much more is known about him everywhere, and in the United States he even had an autobiography published, *Extra Innings* (1983). He and Luis Tiant, Jr., are the only Cuban players so far to merit such a distinction. In fact, a second biography of Miñoso (not much better) appeared in 1994 as *Just Call Me Minnie*. Like so many other black Cuban players, Miñoso was born in Matanzas Province, in the town of El Perico, on November 29, 1922.[18] He began playing ball in the sugarmills with Central España, was recruited by the Cuban Mining Team in Oriente Province, played some for Partagás and Ambrosía in the semipro league, and signed with Marianao in 1945, the team with which he played for his entire career.[19] My father, playing third for the Nicaro Nickel Company, stopped with his chest a hot grounder Miñoso hit while with the Cuban Mining. He scrambled after the ball and threw him out at first. On the way back across the infield Miñoso said to him: "Got a good arm there, whitey."

Miñoso's first professional at-bat came against none other than Bragaña, pitching for Almendares. Sent in by manager Marsans to play third after Tony Castaño hurt himself chasing a pop fly, Miñoso came up to the plate with the tie-breaking run at second and lined a single to right. He then made two assists in the bottom of the ninth on a bunt and a ground ball. That summer Miñoso signed with Pompez's New York Cubans and hit .293, reaching .331 in 1947, when the team won the Negro World Series. He was then signed by the Cleveland Indians, which had just broken the color barrier in the American League by signing and playing Larry Doby, of the Newark Eagles. Miñoso, who was twenty-four at the time, had been playing with major-league-caliber men for almost four years and could have stepped right into the Indians' lineup. Instead, he was sent to Dayton, where he burned the Class A Central League with a .525 batting average.

But he flopped in 1949 with Cleveland, hitting .188 in only nine games. He spent the balance of 1949 and 1950 with San Diego, of the Pacific Coast League, batting .297 and .339, respectively. In 1951 he was moved up to the majors, where he hit .326, with 10 homers. But most of Miñoso's great seasons were with the White Sox, who traded for him that very first year. Miñoso's career through the fifties will be dealt with in the next chapter. But it must be said here that he brought to the American League from the Negro National League an aggressive (not a reckless) running game, much like Jackie Robinson's, that electrified the crowds. They would chant "Go! Go! Go!" whenever Miñoso got on base, unnerving the opposition. In 1951 he stole 31 bases to lead a league in which such daring baserunning had not been seen since the time of Ty Cobb. Miñoso also had four seasons with more than 20 home runs and led the league in triples three times. In four seasons he drove in more than one hundred runs and had four others in which he scored more than one hundred. He was in eight all-star games. Shuttling back and forth between Cleveland and Chicago, he missed championship seasons with each in 1954 and 1959 when he happened to be with the other. In Cuba he finished with an overall average of .280 in thirteen seasons with Marianao (he missed two when the "parent team" did not allow him to play at home). He wound up his career in Mexico, where he played into his fifties. How could Joe Cambria have missed the plum of the Cuban baseball tree? Perhaps because, until the early fifties, he was intent on signing only white Cubans. It was his signee Carlos Paula who officially broke, in 1954, the Senators' color barrier (though, of course, Estalella had done so unofficially before). More urgent and correctable is this question: How can Miñoso not be in the Hall of Fame? Was Carl Yastrzemski a better or more significant player? Hardly.

Miñoso's aggressive, colorful style of play earned him in the United States the nickname "Minnie," with a somewhat condescending, if not racist tinge. It is difficult to fathom why, however, the feminizing slant, though the brevity of Minnie and the alliteration were probably the principal reasons. Like other Cubans, he was stereotyped in the role of the exciting, happy-go-lucky player seeking thrills in and out of the game. As

Miñoso says in *Extra Innings,* however, Cubans played and play a tight game of baseball, with steals always ordered by the manager. Stereotypes nearly always overcome facts. Among Cubans Miñoso is known by his proud name "Orestes Miñoso," which I can still hear resonating through the Gran Stadium in the voice of Conde Moré, or simply as "Miñoso." A natty but sober dresser, his image on the island was that of a serious-minded, generous, and honest man who gave everything he had. Crowding the plate fearlessly, Miñoso was hit by pitches in record numbers everywhere he played. He just dusted himself off, if he was conscious or not badly hurt, and headed for first base. Miñoso's most flamboyant indulgence was a Cadillac convertible, which he took back and forth to the United States on the ferry *City of Havana* and with which he was photographed with my uncle Oscar in Tampa, Florida, when the White Sox trained there. He was also the only Cuban player I know of about whom a song was recorded. It was a cha-cha-cha called "Cuando Miñoso batea" ("When Miñoso Is at the Plate"). The only factor that dampened Miñoso's popularity—not the respect and admiration he enjoyed in Cuba—was that he did not play for Almendares or Habana, and that, although exciting in style, he was not a *postalita,* a hot dog like Formental.

All of these players helped to bring the Cuban League back to financial health, aided by developments such as the radio and by policies such as those instituted by the DGND. But the leap forward could not be made while the long shadow of Abel Linares was still obscuring the financial horizon.

The sale of the "eternal rivals" by Linares' widow is one of the stories often told to highlight the differences between Luque and Miguel Angel. Lore has it that the widow wanted to sell Almendares to Luque and Habana to Miguel Angel, to make her husband's legacy more meaningful by having the franchises each in the hands of a patriarch of the game. But Papá Montero refused, saying he was not a businessman, but a ballplayer. Miguel Angel, on the other hand, bought Habana with a group of investors for about $25,000. By 1947 he was principal owner, and by the fifties the franchise was worth more than $500,000, while Luque died in relative poverty.

The details of the sale are sketchy and somewhat vague, as is the precise date of the transaction. Emilio de Armas told me that he tried to buy Almendares with Luis Parga, owner of the Casa Tarín, but that the widow turned them down because she had received an old bill of her late husband's from that sporting goods store and was still incensed. Eventually, in 1944, a group from the Vedado Tennis Club bought the Scorpions for $26,500 (Jess Losada, in the *Carteles* issue of December 17, 1950, claims it was $17,500). This group included members of very prominent and well-heeled Cuban families. The first ten were José (Pepe) Gómez Mena, Luis Aizcorbe,

Martín Menocal, July Sanguily, Juan Portela, Gene Castro, Raúl Perera, Neno Pertierra, Raúl del Monte, and Mario G. Mendoza. Later Raúl del Monte sold his share and Georgina Menocal, Baby Sardiñas, and Julio Pertierra bought into the club. It is clear that in the beginning this venture was something of a hobby for this group of "playboys," as Jess Losada calls them (and a "playgirl"), but soon Almendares became a profitable business, earning more than $200,000. By 1950 the club's monthly payroll was $25,000. Once Mendoza and Sanguily were the ones who ran Almendares, Raúl del Monte sold his stock.

The purchase of Almendares by a group from the Vedado Tennis Club was a kind of return to the origins of Cuban baseball, when the teams were owned by social organizations of the well-to-do. Seen in a broad historical context, it is as if the Amateur League had absorbed the Cuban League, which the Amateur League had originally contained but had strayed from because of professionalism. In reality, however, the purchase meant that the Cuban League was acquiring the prestige and ascendancy of the Amateur League. Significantly, the first move the new group of owners made was to name Reinaldo Cordeiro the team's manager. Cordeiro had never played as a professional, but had managed Fortuna, Cuban national teams, and the Vedado Tennis Club. Cordeiro's Almendares won going away, aided by the pitching of Oliverio Ortiz, who won 10, Tomás de la Cruz, who threw four shutouts and had a 2.30 ERA, and Agapito Mayor, who was 7 and 3. His infield was already that of Héctor Rodríguez at third, with Avelino Cañizares at short, both of whom were from the semipro league and pillars of the Blues through the forties. He also had former amateur standout Andrés Fleitas catching and at first, and Fermín Guerra, also behind the plate. In the outfield he had the great Santos Amaro, who hit .301 and led in runs scored and runs batted in. He also had the man who was proclaimed Rookie of the Year, Leovigildo Xiqués, a strong young black from Orbay y Cerrato in the semipro league. Almendares' and Cordeiro's triumph was the final consolidation of the Cuban League, which was now headed for its last season at La Tropical, an apotheosis that appropriately marked the beginning of the end for that beautiful and fabled park.

The last season at La Tropical—1945–46—of the Cuban League was won by Cienfuegos, led this time by Adolfo Luque, who had taken over the Petroleros in the game of managerial musical chairs that characterized this circuit. This is a season for which there is a precious source of information, itself a document of the times: the *Album Caramelo Deportivo*. Inside the album there were one hundred spaces upon which one could glue baseball cards. These came wrapped with candy and were obviously aimed at children. The value of the *Album* lies in the caption under each player (or umpire), which furnishes valuable information about where he played in the summer. This allows for a crude but revealing numerical juggling. The *Album* is a touchingly coarse printing and binding job, though the stickers are made up of good pictures of the men in their uniforms.

From now on marketing and advertising would leap forward as the Cuban League came under the tutelage of Organized Baseball and the new magnates who built the Gran Stadium established contacts with ad agencies in close connection with American ones. In this sense the *Album* is a relic of an age about to end. Empty, it cost five cents.

The *Album* opens with stickers for three of the umpires working the Cuban League: Amado Maestri, Bernardino Rodríguez, and Kiko (or Quico) Magriñat. The league, which shared its umpires with the Amateur League, had made these men, along with Raúl (Chino) Atán and Eulogio Peñalver, fixtures in the field. They provided not only a sense of authority but also continuity. The most famous and respected was Maestri, a former catcher in the amateurs with Cubaneleco (1928–30). He began umpiring in 1935 and soon became the chief umpire and the most sought-after arbiter in Cuban baseball. A square, stocky individual with a serious mien, Maestri was an admirer and emulator of the stern major-league umpire Bill Klem. Maestri was the umpire in the game during the Amateur World Series when Burrolote Rodríguez, the Dominican manager, provoked a riot. Maestri had also thrown out Durocher in an exhibition game the Dodgers were playing against a Cuban selection. He refused to resume play until Leo departed, escorted by the Cuban Rural Police, after a memorable protest. But Maestri's hour of glory came when he threw Pasquel out of a Mexican League game. The mogul had jumped onto the field to intervene in a dispute. Maestri, again, refused to restart the game until his orders were obeyed. As reported earlier, he drew his salary the next day and caught a plane to Cuba. Maestri was fearless. In Santa Clara he was ready to call a forfeit when an enraged Cocaína García threatened him with a bat. Maestri's career extended until the demise of the Cuban League after the revolution.

Magriñat, whom we have encountered before, began playing with Almendares (as a left-handed shortstop) before the turn of the century. He became an umpire in 1913 and was still active in the late forties, when he was nearly eighty years old. Like Maestri, he was stern, having once kicked out and fined the entire Santa Clara team after a violent protest by pitcher Pedro Dibut that almost caused a riot. Luckily Oscar Zayas, a judge, happened to be in the stands, and not only supported Magriñat's decision but also marched all the players to court in their uniforms. Like Maestri in Mexico a few years later, Kiko had acted against the wishes of a powerful magnate, in this case Abel Linares, who had jumped onto the Almendares Park turf to urge him to let the game continue. By the forties Magriñat worked the bases exclusively.

Bernardino Rodríguez had been an athlete with the Club Atlético de Cuba before becoming an umpire. He is the youngest of the three featured in the *Album,* and his moment of notoriety came under unfortunate circumstances. He was knocked out cold by a punch from Roberto Ortiz at a time when Rodríguez was weak from a recent operation. Ortiz, too, was marched to court in uniform.

Peñalver, who was black, had a long career umpiring in Cuba at every level and it is surprising that he does not appear in the *Album*. More surprising still is the absence of Atán, a former professional second baseman who played only a few games but who became a highly respected umpire. He also was lured to Mexico because of his reputation, and he was active until the end of the Cuban League. Atán was respected for his courage. A very slight man, he confronted much larger players fearlessly.

Although they did not appear in the *Album*, in order to round out the cast of men running the Cuban League I must mention two brothers who became synonymous with baseball in Cuba: Julio and Hilario Fránquiz, official scorers and statisticians in both the professional and the amateur leagues. Julio in particular scored Cuban League games and compiled statistics from the twenties to the fifties. We already met him in our description of the Gran Stadium. In Almendares Park, and I believe also in the early years of La Tropical, Julio sat in a separate, towerlike booth off the first-base line. Perched there he was the arbiter on errors, hits, and other decisions. Like Maestri, Fránquiz lent an aura of authority and justice to the proceedings.

The *Album* contains the rosters of the four teams—Habana, Almendares, Cienfuegos, and Marianao—that made up the Cuban League until it folded. Fortunately, it seems to have been produced toward the end of the season, after the teams were set and major changes could not have altered the rosters.

The 1945–46 season was the first important professional postwar season anywhere. World War II had ended after the atomic bombing of Japan in August 1945. The next season of organized baseball in the United States would not start until the spring of 1946. The same applies to the Negro Leagues and the Mexican League. So the Cuban League was chock-full of talent from all sources, including the substantial numbers of Cubans who had played in the majors and minors, many of whom were from the Amateur League; young major leaguers eager to make or stay with their clubs; returning American veterans, some of whom had "jumped" to the Mexican League; Negro Leaguers whose circuits had enjoyed a wartime bonanza; and numerous Cubans from the Mexican League, as well as substantial numbers of Cubans who also played and managed in that league.

These were four very strong teams. Managed by Armando Marsans, with José María Fernández (manager of the New York Cubans) as coach, Marianao had Orta, Duany, Castaño, Salazar, Moreno, Oliverio Ortiz, Consuegra, Estalella, Daniel Parra, a rookie named Miñoso, Chino Valdivia, Jabao Brown, Talúa Dandridge, Booker McDaniels, Red Adams, Barney Serrell, Lou Knerr, José Luis Colás, and Francisco Campos. This was a superb mix of ex-amateurs, major leaguers, and minor leaguers. Miguel

Angel, at the helm of the Reds and helped by coach Julio Rojo (who managed Puebla in Mexico), had the Blanco brothers, Salvador Hernández, Monteagudo, Formental, for the first time with Habana, Mantecado Linares, Mosquito Ordeñana, Chino Hidalgo, Natilla Jiménez, Sagüita Hernández, Cocaína García, Cecil Kaiser, Lou Klein, Dick Sisler, Fred Martin, Terris McDuffie, Yuyo Acosta, Pedro Medina, Art Rebel, and Raúl Navarro. Habana had been entrusted with three prominent Cardinal rookies—Klein, Martin, and Sisler—two of whom would go to Mexico. Luque's Cienfuegos had Roland Gladu, a Canadian outfielder belonging to the Dodgers but who went to Mexico, Jean Roy, another Canadian from the Dodgers, Tiant, Dihigo, Carlos Colás, Crespo, Silvio García, Zabala, Roger, Gallart, Zardón, Xiqués, Reyes, Chile Gómez, and New York Giants Ray Berres and Sal Maglie. With Reyes and Zabala, Luque had four Giants, and in Gladau and Roy he had two Dodgers, thus making clear his connection to New York teams. Almendares, the defending champions managed again by Cordeiro, had Roberto Ortiz, Héctor Rodríguez, Héctor Aragó, Gilberto Torres, Jacinto (Battling Siki) Roque, Guerra, Chifflan Clark, Regino Otero, Lloyd Davenport, Curveador Comellas, Witto Alomá, Mayor, Bragaña, Cañizares, Ulrich, Amaro, Fleitas, Beto Avila, and Limonar Martínez.

Though Luque's and Miguel Angel's connections with the Majors were evident in the composition of their teams, the predominance of the Mexican League is overwhelming. Doing some rough mathematics, I come up with the following percentages: forty-two percent of the players were from the Mexican League, 19 percent from the minors, 17 percent from the majors, and 16 percent from the Negro leagues. The *Album* does not record the provenance of 6 percent. To these totals the following must be added: Four managers from the Mexican League were managing, coaching, or playing in the Cuban League that winter, and Maglie, Roy, Gladu, Klein, and Berres eventually also signed with Pasquel. Cienfuegos won, with the highest percentage of major leaguers (28 percent): These were Zabala, Reyes, Berres, and Maglie, all Giants (with Luque himself, this makes five), and Zardón (Senators).

This season was a financial success and produced two great moments recorded in Cuban baseball lore, both with Dick Sisler as protagonist. Sisler hit .301 and hit an astonishing nine home runs in spite of the vast expanses of La Tropical (Gibson had hit eleven in fewer games, but many of his games were in cozy La Boulanger Park, even though it is true that he could hit the ball out of any park). Four of Sisler's homers were memorable. One, off Agapito Mayor on January 23, 1946, cleared the two fences in right-center—a mammoth blast that Sisler remembered better than his other feats. Mayor also remembers it with a dash of self-deprecating humor. It is said that the ball traveled 450 feet. The next day, Sisler hit three home runs off Cienfuegos' Sal Maglie, all of them prodigious blasts. Sisler also got a single. When he came up for a fifth time, now against reliever Colorao Roger, Luque decided to walk him intentionally—there was only one out, a runner was on second, and Cienfuegos was behind, 8–7. Papá Montero wanted to win, not to see records set. Habana eventually won, 9–7.

Cienfuegos, however, won the championship behind its superb staff of Maglie (nine wins), Zabala (also nine wins), Roger, Dihigo, and Roy with five each, and Tiant with four. Crespo and Silvio García also had a great season, and Napoleón Reyes had a solid season at .269 with six triples. Habana contended with the efforts of Natilla Jiménez. The former amateur star won thirteen games, completing nine. But Cienfuegos was too strong, and Papá Montero added this championship to his long list of triumphs. He even pitched in a game, and he was pushing fifty-five.

The season's financial outcome spelled the doom of La Tropical. Baseball had become too much of a profitable business to be played in this sylvan spot, clearly a paradisiacal garden too far from the city to be suitable, with too small a capacity for the ambitions of owners and players who no longer pretended that the game was a pastime, but looked beyond the box score to the bottom line. More importantly, World War II had brought Cuba closer into the orbit of American self-proclaimed Organized Baseball, and Organized Baseball was about to confront the most serious challenge to its hegemony since the foundation of the Federal League. The new battleground would be the Gran Stadium.

A battle of social and symbolic consequences nearly took place on the field in the fall of 1947 when plans were made, but never fulfilled, to have a series of games between the New York Cubans, champions of the Negro World Series, and the Havana Cubans, winners of the Florida International League. It seems clear that the Havana team had been named in response to Pompez's club, which had enjoyed a great deal of success through the forties, gathering the best Cuban and Latin American black players. Joe Cambria was the founder of the Havana Cubans, who had played their first season at La Tropical in the summer of 1946, but sold the team to Bobby Maduro, who moved it to the Gran Stadium. While at first such a series may have looked like a mismatch, given that the Florida International League was but a Class B circuit and the Negro National League was the top independent circuit, the fact is that the Havana Cubans fielded powerhouses drawn from the Amateur League and ran away with pennants four years in succession. Some of its players, such as Marrero, went directly to the Senators, while others shuttled between the Florida International League and the Mexican League.

There probably never was and never will be a Class B team quite like the Havana Cubans. Their home field, the Gran Stadium, had a capacity of thirty-five thousand spectators, it was located in a cosmopolitan capital whose metropolitan area had a population of nearly a million, it represented an entire country, and it was covered by several radio stations as well as by a host of major newspapers. For Cambria, Maduro, and the Washington Senators the team was a fantastic business. Cuban players could be developed within Organized Baseball, yet be really at home for home games and not have to suffer discrimination or problems with the language barrier. Living in Havana was cheaper than in the United States, so their salaries would go farther. There were even baseball cards of the Havana Cubans. The opposition, which also fielded quite a few Cubans, particularly in the Miami and Miami Beach franchises (the Sun Sox and the Tourists, respectively) and Tampa (the Smokers), used the training camp facilities of major-league teams. Attendance was quite respectable in Havana, and the team developed a national following. My great-uncle Aurelio, a physician in Tampa, was the Smokers' team doctor and would fly home to Havana for games. He witnessed Marrero's no-hitter against Tampa on July 12, 1947. The Havana Cubans, who were probably of Triple-A caliber, won four regular-season championships and two playoffs.

The team's and even the league's talent pool was the Amateur League. Besides Marrero and Moreno, the Havana Cubans also fielded stars such as Chino Hidalgo, who had outstanding seasons, and former major leaguers such as Tony Zardón and Moaín García as well as others on their way up to the majors, such as Witto Alomá. A veteran amateur star, left-hander Daniel Parra, pitched for the Havana Cubans, as did Octavio Rubert and Rafael Rivas. But the team was an extension of the Amateur League in another way: It was the only professional Cuban team without black players even after the Dodgers' signing of Jackie Robinson. This was because blacks could not play in Jim Crow Florida. It is said that in the early fifties (the team became the Cuban Sugar Kings in 1954, joining the integrated International League) they were on the verge of signing a black who would participate only in home games, but I have not been able to verify this. It is in this context that a series of games against the New York Cubans of the Negro Leagues would have been significant: Both teams were vestiges of practices that were about to wane.

Pompez's team was formidable in 1947: It had Noble behind the plate, backed up by manager José María Fernández, Lorenzo (Chiquitín) Cabrera at first, Fernando (Bicho) Pedroso at second,[20] Miñoso at third, Silvio García at short, and Crespo, Pagés, and Duany in the outfield. Their star pitcher that year was veteran Luis Tiant, with Lino Donoso and others behind him. This team received some press coverage in the New York Hispanic press, where they were sometimes still called the Cuban Stars. This, the last flash of the Negro National League, was a banner year, with teams such as the Memphis Red Sox, Chicago American Giants, Newark Eagles, Philadelphia Stars, Kansas City Monarchs, Homestead Grays and Cleveland Buckeyes appearing in New York for games against the Cubans and also the white semipro Bushwicks. In New York, fans enjoyed performances by visiting Luis (Canena) Márquez and José (Pantalones) Santiago, both of whom were Puerto Rican stars with the Red Sox and the Grays, respectively (Márquez won the batting championship). Black Cuban umpire Eulogio Peñalver was also working in the Negro National League (he also umpired in the Puerto Rican and the Cuban League). The World Series against the

Buckeyes, who had Cubans Avelino Cañizares and Ramón Bragaña, was not played solely in New York and Cleveland, but, as was the practice then, it barnstormed through several cities in search of revenue. The New York Cubans won, but Pompez claimed in *La Prensa* (September 16) that he had lost money. It was on the eighteenth of that month that the New York paper announced that his team would travel to Havana for a five-game series against the other Cubans, a meeting of champions in their respective leagues. It did not happen.

Having attempted to answer the question asked at the end of chapter 2 about the origins of Cuban baseball, the action frozen at the start of the 1949–50 season can now be resumed. Like Cervantes allowing the Biscayan and Don Quijote to follow through with their swings, we can now let the ball fly toward home plate.

1	2	3	4	5	6	7	**8**	9	R	H	E

The Age of Gold

The 1949–50 season marked the beginning of a decade of stability in the Cuban League that was like no other before in its long history but that led, ironically, to its demise with the advent of the revolution. The period is framed by two victories that rekindled the nationalism that had prevailed in Cuban baseball since the days of Almendares' victory over a Fe team made up of black Americans, since Méndez's shutouts of Cincinnati, Torriente's homers against the New York Giants, and since the triumphs in the Amateur World Series. The first was the already reported win in the inaugural Caribbean Series; the last, the Cuban Sugar Kings' capture of the 1959 Little World Series against the Minneapolis Millers. The Gran Stadium in Havana was the stage for both. The Little World Series, played to full houses that included a triumphant Fidel Castro, took place less than a year after the revolutionary takeover. The nationalist fervor brought such support to the Sugar Kings that it seemed to herald the coming of major-league baseball to Havana, the dream of Cuban entrepreneurs since the late forties. It was instead the last hurrah of Cuban professional baseball, in a reversal of epic dimensions and, for many players, tragic consequences.

The pact with Organized Baseball, together with postwar prosperity and the growth of Havana into a major, modern tourist center, secured the Cuban League's position as the premier circuit in Latin America. The fifties were like a new Golden Age, coming after another world war and leading to dictatorship and revolution. World War I had brought about an economic bonanza, a boost in the tourist trade, and the bustle of the Roaring Twenties; whereupon Machado took power, fierce opposition to him flared, the United States mediated with the threat of direct intervention, and eventually the 1933 revolt led to Batista's takeover. World War II also brought an economic boom and a dramatic rise in tourism; then Batista staged his 1952 coup d'état, opposition to his regime escalated to war, and eventually the 1959 revolution came about and Fidel Castro assumed power.

But these symmetries are deceiving. Prosperity in the fifties was more stable and durable, without the dizzying ups and downs of the teens and twenties; Batista's 1952 coup was a bloodless takeover from corrupt 1930s revolutionaries, not a pitched battle between terrorists and the police, and opposition to Batista was not as unsettling in Havana as was the opposition against Machado. As a result there was little disruption to the Cuban League. Moreover, the revolutionaries who took over in 1959 were determined to stay in power even if it meant taking measures that would completely change Cuban society. This inevitably meant a break with the United States, and, needless to say, with Organized Baseball. Furthermore, the tourist industry that flourished in the late forties and fifties was very different from that of the twenties. Following a trend already outlined, tourism now catered to middle-class Americans who were likely to come to Havana by plane or ferry instead of by yacht (though new marinas were built and yachts continued to cross the Florida Straits). Another novelty was the building of lavish nightclubs such as Tropicana, Montmartre, and Sans Souci, which, along with new hotels such as the Riviera, the Capri, and the Hilton, were also gambling casinos. Havana became, not the Monte Carlo of the Americas, as ads in the *New York Times* proclaimed (November 27, 1955), but more like the Las Vegas of the Caribbean. As in the case of the Nevada city, with gambling came organized crime and an increase in government corruption.

Americanization was the general trend in popular culture, noticeable mostly in marketing and the developing media, though there had been a gradual Cubanization in the ownership of sugar and other industries, such as banking. Advertising became an important business in a Cuba, where the purchasing power of the population made the country a desirable market. The modest programs of the Cuban League—flimsy pamphlets crudely printed on coarse paper during the years of La Tropical—now became glitzy magazines, with pictures of each player, statistical information, and plenty of advertising. Albums for baseball stickers, such as the one put out for the 1945–46 season at La Tropical, were replaced by much more expensively produced, glossier books. American baseball cards appeared in the stores, along with American baseball magazines, including the yearbooks of major-league teams. Devoted Cuban fans were knowledgeable and up to date.

Cuba was the first Latin American country to have television and the first where baseball games were telecast. An initial effort to show Cuban League games in the provinces was made with moving pictures during the 1949–50 season. Cameramen for an outfit called Cineplán shot the contests at the Gran Stadium; then the films were developed overnight and sent in canisters to the provinces, to be shown at theaters and movie houses. By 1950–51 games were being televised, and by middecade there were two different channels. Radio broadcasts continued, of course. Televised World Series games were beamed to Cuba at first by having a plane, serving as a relay antenna, circle over the Florida Straits. Later they were beamed directly. I watched Edmundo (Sandy) Amorós' catch in the 1955 World Series and Don Larsen's perfect game the next year live from Sagua la Grande. The Cuban Sugar Kings' home games were broadcast regularly. Sports shows on radio and television abounded. Comics Chicharito, an Habanista, and Sopeira, an Almendarista, entertained the public with their banter. The Cuban League became part of Havana showbiz, with TV stars frequenting the Gran Stadium as much to be seen as to watch the games. Players made appearances on shows and gave televised interviews.

The number of television sets per capita was such—as Fidel Castro discovered and used shrewdly to gain support—that the Cuban League became even more of a nationwide craze without moving games to the provinces. According to Hugh Thomas (p. 766) there were already 14,000 television sets in Cuba by February 1951, and 575,000 radio sets by 1949 (nearly one per family). Stars such as Orestes Miñoso, Pedro Formental, and later Camilo Pascual and Pedro Ramos were seen by many more people than the likes of Méndez or Torriente earlier, turning them into celebrities with broad national appeal. In this decade Cuba had a number of world-class professional boxers, such as Kid Gavilán, Niño Valdés, Isaac Logart, Urtiminio Ramos, Florentino Fernández, Benny Paret, José (Mantequilla) Nápoles, and Luis Manuel Rodríguez, who also became nationally famous because of television. Their championship fights in the United States were beamed to Cuba.

At the Gran Stadium the festive atmosphere described in chapter 3 continued and increased, particularly the commercial activity, with more shops and eateries. Beer, coffee, cigars, and baseball mingled with brisk betting to create merriment, made more exciting by the presence of celebrities, including the ballplayers and sometimes the boxers. Television commercials between innings were shot live at the park, so vedettes who played in them (such as curvaceous mulatta Gladys Siscay) were seen there. Well-known announcers and broadcasters, now more recognizable than ever because of TV, could also be seen in action. Musicians such as those with Sonora Matancera, a group that launched Celia Cruz, could also be spotted and recognized at the Gran Stadium because they appeared regularly on television. The Gran Stadium truly became a national stage.

Cha-cha-cha was the new rhythm. It was evidence of further cultural Americanization. Derived from the danzón, cha-cha-cha is a ballroom dance that is more athletic than sensuous. It is not difficult to teach to non-Cubans because it is somewhat removed from the matrix of African beats. Groups such as the Orquesta Aragón de Cienfuegos did wonders with it by accentuating its Cuban roots with *descargas* (solos) by famous flutist Richard Egües, and by accentuating its danzónlike capacity to incorporate melodies from varied sources. The lyrics tended to be silly, piquant rather than suggestive, and reflected the fascination of *pepillos* (middle-class teenagers who followed U.S. fads) with big cars and the new attractions of Havana. For all the success Orquesta Aragón de Cienfuegos and Sonora Matancera enjoyed, the competition in nightclubs and television shows from American stars was stiff. Sarah Vaughan, Nat (King) Cole, Frank Sinatra, all came to Havana, and soon Bill Haley and the Comets became the rage, particularly through Radio Cramer, a station that broadcast only American popular music. Cuban entertainment, including the Cuban League, was on the same playing field as the American kind, unbeatable if not by its quality then by its sheer quantity and capacity of dissemination.

The team's uniforms had been upgraded to major-league standards, and the practice of wearing visiting grays and home whites was introduced, though all games were played in the same park. Habana's home pinstripes and red, gothic lettering froze me in a fit of ecstasy the first time I saw the team on the field, and again, a few years later, when I stood next to a massive Wilmer (Vinegar Bend) Mizell at the Gran Stadium. Almendares' sober blue suits, with the A still modeled after the Philadelphia Athletics', were reminiscent of the Dodgers, with whom they had close relations in the fifties. Marianao took its colors from the amateur team Club Atlético de Cuba. Their flannels had black and orange piping with matching socks, a very pleasing color combination, perhaps recalling also those of its emblem, the tiger. Cienfuegos had the most elegant uniform in the league: black and green lettering and piping, with black socks and cap. Though television was not yet in color, these uniforms appeared enticingly in magazines and advertisements. Besides, their patterns and emblems were distinct enough even in black and white. They were surely part of the Cuban League's carefully orchestrated marketing campaign. Replicas of them could be bought in small sizes for children, as well as caps, jackets, and other paraphernalia such as drinking glasses with logos, pennants, and pins.

My fellow Sagua la Grande native and colleague at Swarthmore College, Enrique Sacerio Garí, still cherishes his Carnet de Almendarista, (Almendares Fan Identity Card). It is an elaborate affair, with a hard cover, his picture, and language stating that he is a fan in good standing for the 1950–51 season. To be validated, it reads, the document has to be signed by the Almendares manager or by a player. Enrique's is signed by, of course, Conrado Marrero (a native and resident of Sagua la Grande), then a

Washington Senator in addition to an Almendares Blue. My uncle Eduardo González, now a professor at Johns Hopkins University, appears in a family Christmas picture next to an American-style tree and clad in an Almendares cap and a satin blue jacket.

In 1949–1950 a booklet called *Autógrafos deportivos* was produced, one for each club, containing pictures and biographies of the players, with room for autographs. The one I have, for Almendares, states that it was distributed free as part of Antonio Prío's campaign for mayor of Havana. He was a brother of the president. A brand named "Junior" advertised socks with logos of each team, and in *Carteles* a beefy vedette appears scantily attired with four pennants in the right places. One can buy in the streets of Havana today many relics of the period that attest, forty years later, to the wide distribution of all this iconography. Curiously, the Cuban Sugar Kings, who were in Organized Baseball and affiliated with a major-league team (the Cincinnati Reds), did not carry out such a thorough marketing campaign.

The Cuba of the fifties was a paradoxical country: It was prosperous, even booming, and at the same time beset by political unrest. But because the worst part of the strife took place far to the east, in Oriente Province, the Cuban League, which played only in Havana, was not affected until the end of the decade. The decade began while Carlos Prío Socarrás, Grau's successor, was still president. A revolutionary from the struggle against Machado in the thirties, Prío outstripped Grau when it came to corruption in government. But Prío's sad claim to political fame is having been the victim of Batista's coup on March 10, 1952, shortly before the election in which both were vying for the presidency. Claiming that Prío was organizing a coup himself in case he did not win, and citing all the graft during Prío's administration, Batista called on his popularity in the armed forces to stage a bloodless coup. Prío, though urged to resist by university students and others, chose exile. Given the swiftness of the change in government and the relative smoothness of the transition, Cuban life went on, with many people breathing a sigh of relief and hoping for a better performance from Batista, whose administration in 1940–44 had been a success.

Batista's coup came after the Cuban League season had ended, so it did not affect it. Neither would Fidel Castro's attack on the Moncada barracks on July 26, 1953. This action took place on the other side of the island, Moncada was not an important garrison (like Camp Columbia in Havana), and the revolutionaries were defeated. Cuba was not much troubled, though the reaction against surviving attackers was brutal during the first few hours. Fidel Castro and other leaders were captured, jailed, and brought to trial. A more spectacular assault was made against the Presidential Palace on May 13, 1957, by the Directorio Estudiantil, a group other than Fidel Castro's, who was by this time in the Sierra Maestra. But again, this happened after the Cuban League season was over and was quickly repelled. The only major event that took place during the season was Batista's flight on New Year's Day 1959. However, it disrupted play only temporarily, as most of the population felt that the revolution would bring normalcy to Cuban politics by restoring the 1940 Constitution that Batista, who had enacted it during his first presidency, had violated in 1952.

Given what came later, no period in Cuban history has been the object of more mythmaking than the fifties. The urge to justify the revolution or to mitigate its failures has turned Batista's Cuba into a reign of terror and squalor, a kind of Dominican Republic under Trujillo, or Nicaragua under the Somozas, with an economy akin to that of Haiti. This is a mirage fabricated by political opportunism, crude and uninformed thinking, or (more often) the religious impulse to find a providential design in history— the urge to turn the passage of time into a theodicy leading inexorably to the coming of a messiah. Almost forty years of propaganda have turned Batista, a fairly ludicrous small-time populist dictator, into an evil monster of historic dimensions. The facts are quite different, and though they do not exonerate him, they do bring him down to more reasonable proportions. The booming economy during the fifties has already been mentioned. Experts agree, for instance, that 1957 was the greatest year ever in the Cuban economy. Sugar prices rose after World War II by the sale of sugar for the Marshall Plan, and the Korean conflict pushed prices and demand up again. New hotels and casinos were built, as well as a tunnel under Havana Bay to accommodate and further the city's spread to the east (as it had done to the west in the twenties). A four-lane highway—Vía Blanca—was built along the northern coast to link Havana to the beach resort of Varadero. Ferry service, in place for a long time between Havana and Key West, was extended to Cárdenas, next to Varadero.

There was much poverty in Cuba, some of it—such as the notorious slum Barrio de las Yaguas—in Havana itself. In the countryside there was even more, and in the backlands many peasants did live in squalor. There were prostitutes in Havana (though not as many as now), many of whom were young women drawn to the capital by economic necessity. But if poverty is the herald of revolution, then it should have erupted earlier in other Latin American countries infinitely poorer than Cuba, with larger masses of destitute people and victims of rampant abuse: the Dominican Republic, Brazil, or Mexico. If government corruption, of which there was plenty in Batista's Cuba, heralds revolution, then a second one should already have taken place in Mexico, or in Colombia. As for dictatorship, Batista was very unlike Trujillo and Somoza. These tyrants owned their counties. Somoza and his family were in possession of everything in Nicaragua, from the national airline on down. Trujillo ruled with an iron hand every aspect of Dominican life and owned most of the principal sources of wealth. Not Batista, who, for all the millions he misappropriated, owned very little in Cuba, and was far from being in control of the economic elite, who tolerated him as long as he was good for business, but who would not allow him in their clubs because of his African blood. Many supported Fidel

Castro, the brash upstart from their class and color, when he seemed to be the one who would help prolong the economic bonanza by restoring order. Batista's police force was run by his cronies from the thirties, along with a number of new thugs, and its crude tactics were aimed at those opposing the regime. Batista's repression was spasmodic, sporadic, and ultimately ineffectual. Censorship was episodic, as anyone who cares to look at the publications of the period can ascertain. Fidel Castro was brought to trial after the Moncada attack and allowed to defend himself. He did so by delivering the speech that later was published, under Batista's rule, as *History Will Absolve Me*. He was amnestied later and allowed to leave for Mexico to organize his landing in Oriente to begin his campaign in the Sierra Maestra. The Oriente Mountains were a sieve, with people going in and out to join the rebels, to serve as couriers, to transport weapons, and to interview Fidel Castro (to wit, Herbert Matthews and his famous reports in the *New York Times*). Batista was a dictator in that he took power by force and held it with the support of the army and the police, but his was not a totalitarian regime. Hence, except toward the end of the decade, when there was an increase in terrorism, and when bombs exploded with regularity in Havana, the Cuban League was hardly hampered by politics in the fifties.

For baseball players the fifties were an Age of Gold. Bert Haas, Rocky Nelson, and Bobby Bragan have all spoken or written to me in glowing terms about their seasons in Havana. American players made about $1,000 a month, plus a $250 allowance for married players. Bob Boyd told me that he was actually paid $1,800 a month. Cuban stars such as Miñoso made even more. Miñoso made $2,400 a month, according to Asdrúbal Baró, his teammate with Marianao. Baró himself made about $600 a month at first and later moved up to $850. My mother, a tenured teacher at the Instituto, made $215 a month, and many low-ranking public employees made about $100. So, for the Cuban players, these were fabulous salaries that the greatest luminaries from the thirties and forties could have never dreamed of. A $1,000 a month limit for Americans had been imposed to prevent bidding wars. Rocky Nelson told me, however, that when Dr. July Sanguily contacted him to play for Almendares for a second season he balked and demanded a raise. He was asked for his banking account number in Portsmouth, Ohio, where he lived, and told that he would find an extra $2,000 in it the next time he looked. Narciso Camejo, the last president of the Cuban League, told me that a great deal of money was paid under the table. The limit had also been set to avoid something that happened anyway: Marginal major leaguers preferred to stay in the minors so as not to exceed the time in the majors that would make them ineligible to play in Cuba (according to the agreement with the Cuban League), where they would make more in the winter than with the big club in the summer. Nelson told me that they were paid in cash every two weeks on the day the

The 1907 Vedado Tennis Club baseball team, the founding club in the Amateur League. Porfirio Franca is at the center, in a suit and tie.

Julio Moreno in full regalia of Cuban team that played in the 1944 Amateur World Series in Caracas, Venezuela. The picture is on the cover of the October 1, 1944, issue of *Bohemia*, one of the leading weekly Cuban magazines.

Pedro (Preston) Gómez, future major-league manager, with the flannels of Fortuna Sport Club, the fabled amateur team. This *Carteles* portrait is from September 19, 1943.

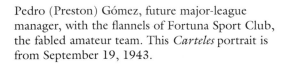

Carteles portrait (September 5, 1943) of Juan (Espinacas) Ealo, first-baseman of the Fortuna Sport Club.

August 1, 1943, *Carteles* portrait of Antonio (Quilla) Valdés, Hershey's shortstop, who never turned professional but many believe to have been the best Cuban at that position of all time.

November 17, 1929, *Carteles* picture of Central Baraguá's team, a racially integrated sugarmill team.

The Instituto de Remedios baseball team in the late thirties. Roberto M. González, the author's father, is standing second from right.

Front, left, Antonio (Tony) Zardón, in the uniform of Cuban Mining; right, in the uniform of Ambrosía, Orestes (Minnie) Miñoso.

The 1949 Pueblo Nuevo team from Matanzas, in the Juveniles of the Dirección General de Deportes. Front row, second from right, future 1955 World Series Dodger hero Edmundo (Sandy) Amorós.

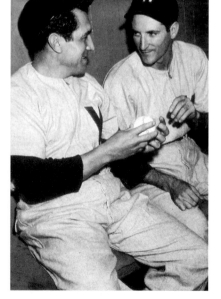

Former amateur stars Marrero and Consuegra in the uniform of the Washington Senators during the early fifties.

Powerful 1938–39 Santa Clara at La Boulanger Park. Back row left to right: Tony Castaño, Santos Amaro, general manager Emilio de Armas, Josh Gibson, Lázaro Salazar and Raymond (Jabao) Brown. Front row, left to right: Armando (Indian) Torres, Manuel (Cocaína) García, Rafael Ruiz, Sam Bankhead, Rafael (Sungo) Pedroso, and Antonio (Pollo) Rodríguez.

View of La Tropical in 1930 during the Second Pan American Games, when it was inaugurated. Visible are the enormous outfield dimensions as well as the location of the baseball diamond within the running track

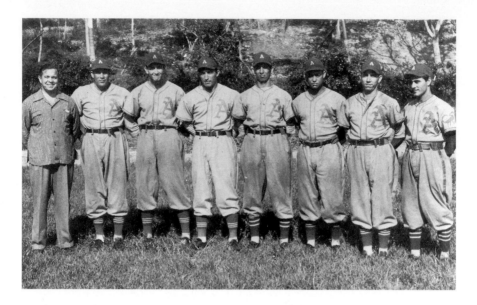

Dr. July Sanguily, who ran Almendares for the Vedado Tennis Club group that bought the club, with his 1945–46 staff. Left to right: Alejandro (Patón) Carrasquel, Witto Alomá, Oliverio Ortiz, Santiago Ulrich, Tomás de la Cruz, Agapito Mayor, and Daniel Parra.

On the right, Bert Haas, Habana's popular infielder, with Cuban Air Force officers at a New Year's party on December 31, 1950.

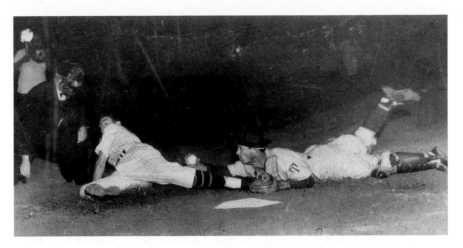

Almendares' tough Fermín Guerra catches Marianao's Wesley Hamner's foot with his mitt and applies the tag with his bare hand

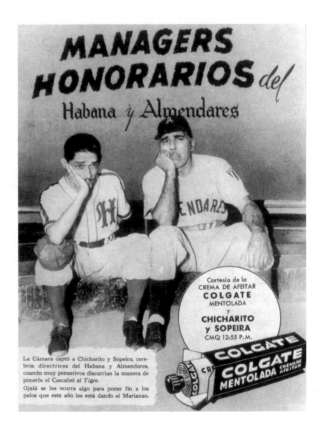

Chicharito and Sopeira (Garrido and Piñera), the comedy team of the Black and the Galician, as "honorary managers" of Habana and Almendares, from 1950–51 Cuban League program.

The Habana Reds celebrate a victory in the 1952 Caribbean Series in Caracas. Standing next to an unidentified Cervecería Caracas fan, from left to right: Vern Benson, Manuel (Chino) Hidalgo, Adrián Zabala, Orlando Varona, Gilberto (Chino) Valdivia, and Edmundo Amorós.

Miñoso outside Tampa's Al López Field, sitting in his famous Caddy convertible in the mid-fifties. Oscar J. González, the author's uncle, is on his right.

Pedro (Perico) Formental and Fermín Guerra with the Cuban Sugar Kings of the International League in 1954.

Wilmer (Vinagre) Mizell and Camilo Pascual pose for a picture during the 1955–56 season, when the Habana pitcher set a strikeout record. They flank Arthur Gardner, U.S. ambassador to Cuba.

Marianao's Asdrúbal Baró, Miguel Fornieles, and Orestes Miñoso confer before a day game at the Gran Stadium during 1956–57 championship season.

A dinner party at Rancho Luna, a renowned restaurant outside of Havana, during 1954–55 season. Rocky and Alberta Nelson are the first couple on right, facing camera. On the far right Bobby Bragan sticks his head up. George Munger, at the head of the table, turns to look to the camera. Third on his left, with bow tie, is Joe Cambria. Others in the picture are Joe Hatten and Gus Triandos.

It is January, 1959, Batista has fled, and Fidel Castro's followers celebrate at the Gran Stadium with their weapons. Joining in the revelry are Almendares' Rocky Nelson, on the left wearing the white cap, and Tom Lasorda, with rifle and cigarette.

The all-Cuban all-star team that faced its all-American counterpart in the 1956–57 season. Second from left, Orestes Miñoso; fifth, rookie Ultus Alvarez with Julio Bécquer to his left. The last three sitting on the right are Camilo Pascual, Miguel Fornieles, and Panchón Herrera. Sitting in the back row, far right, Humberto (Chico) Fernández, with Vicente Amor, Héctor Rodríguez, and Oscar (Barriguita) Rodríguez to his right. At the center, with jacket on, Pedro Ramos. On the far left, with hand on post, Gilberto Torres, and fourth and fifth to his left, Willy Miranda and Edmundo Amorós.

Captain of the Rebel Army Felipe Guerra Matos, the new head of the Dirección General de Deportes, shaking hands with Orestes Miñoso and Rocky Nelson.

Pulled from Havana on July 15, 1960, the Sugar Kings were hastily turned into
Jersey City. A patch with the new city's name has been sewn onto their jerseys.
Back row, left to right: Octavio (Cookie) Rojas, Miguel (Mike) Cuéllar, Félix
Torres, Daniel Morejón, Jim Pendleton, Ray Shearer, Brooks Lawrence, Zack
Monroe, and Elio Chacón. Middle row, left to right: Orlando Peña, Charles
Robert (Bob) Moorhead, Andrés Ayón, Napoleón (Nap) Reyes, manager, Enrique
(Hank) Izquierdo, Bob Miller, Henry John (Dutch) Dotterer, Howie Nunn, and
Zip Brooks, trainer. Front row, left to right: Pompeyo Davalillo, Rogelio (Borrego)
Alvarez, Paul Pinelli, batboy, Lou Jackson, and Raúl Sánchez.

Three-time batting champion Tony Oliva rounds third and is
congratulated by coach Floyd Baker after hitting a homer for
the Twins in the early sixties. Courtesy: Minnesota Twins.

The Oakland A's base-stealing and slick-fielding Dagoberto Campaneris, among the best Cuban shortstops of all time.

Luis Tiant with the Red Sox in the seventies.

José Canseco with the Toronto Blue Jays in 1998. His 1988 record with Oakland of 42 homers, 124 RBI's, .307 average, and 40 stolen bases is the greatest single season ever in the major leagues by a Cuban player. Courtesy: Toronto Blue Jays.

The Orioles' Rafael Palmeiro, perhaps the best Cuban-born first-baseman in the major leagues of all time. Courtesy: Baltimore Orioles.

A Cuban baseball card of Omar Linares, touted by the regime as the best baseball player in the world.

Orlando (El Duque) Hernández pitching for the Yankees. Courtesy: New York Yankees.

Asdrúbal Baró at the Latinoamericano in December 1996.

Fermín Guerra at home in Miami, August 8, 1991.

Heberto Blanco in Habana, on September 28, 1998.

Rodolfo Fernández, "La Maravilla Güireña," at home in New York City, on January 26, 1991.

The author with Conrado Marrero in Miami, December 10, 1993.

A boy infielder practicing at the baseball academy in the legendary Palmar del Junco, in Matanzas, on October 3, 1998.

team practiced because no games were scheduled. This was found money, I presume, as far as the U.S. Internal Revenue Service was concerned.

Besides the balmy, springlike weather, these players enjoyed Havana's booming entertainment scene. Amid Rocky Nelson's memorabilia there is a velvety program from Tropicana and pictures of banquets at Rancho Luna with all the wives. He speaks of his party of ballplayers getting special treatment at the opening of George Raft's casino at the Capri Hotel, where Spanish dancer José Greco was performing, because the actor was a friend of Bobby Bragan, the Blues' skipper, from his Pacific Coast days managing Hollywood. Players hopped to Havana from Key West by ferry, bringing their own cars. The Cubans did the same after their summer seasons, taking advantage of lower automobile prices in the United States. Money from endorsements was becoming significant for both natives and Americans. A winter season in Cuba could be very profitable and enjoyable for all concerned.

We now enter into a series of seasons that I experienced as a child and adolescent; hence the history in these pages becomes more directly drawn from my own recollections. Those memories are shrouded in sentiment and nostalgia, which I have tried to counter with as much hard information as possible, culled from printed and oral sources. It must have been in the 1949–50 season, when I was six or seven years old, that my father first took me to the Gran Stadium. We had come to Havana for some of his law school exams or courses, and I remember sharply the impression the capital's lights made on me as the rickety train approached the city at night. I was transfixed by the Jantzen billboard along the Malecón (bay shore drive), which displayed a diver plunging over and over into blue neon waves. But I was taken out of myself as we went into the stadium and entered a sphere of light that seemed like a huge diamond. We went up to the stands behind first base, midway to the top, with me clutching my father's hand. I lost all sense of reality and proportion and asked him what all those toy ballplayers were doing down there. They seemed so perfect in their bright uniforms, against the green grass and orange dirt of the infield! Years later, reading theology, I could not imagine resurrection or a timeless world beyond in any other way but like the Gran Stadium on that magic night. This was probably the time when I became a fan of the Habana Reds, not only because of my father's own predilection (though this was clearly the main reason), but also because of the beauty of their uniforms. I suspect that my allegiance was also reinforced by Habana winning several championships in the early fifties.

The 1948–49 season was the first successful one after the pact with Organized Baseball was signed, and Almendares' triumph as well as its decisive victory in the first Caribbean Series, staged in Havana, seemed to have sealed it. But there were still quite a few important adjustments to be made. The initial pact allowed the Cuban League to employ only players with two years or less of professional experience. This rule excluded established stars, some of them native Cubans. The fact that many mature Negro Leaguers would then be playing in Organized Baseball for the first time, and that a star such as Marrero had also turned pro recently, made the 1947–48 and 1948–49 seasons interesting enough. But many young Americans had to be shipped back because the Cuban fans were accustomed to a better quality of baseball. The 1949–50 season was a watershed as new arrangements were made.

The revised pact allowed players all the way up to Triple A, and major-leaguers with forty-five or fewer days of service, to be hired, and Cubans in the majors were allowed to participate (though teams reserved the right to refuse permission, as we shall see). The Cuban magnates continued to exercise their right to send back players who did not perform well, either because they were not up to the level of competition or because they took their sojourn in Havana as a vacation in the sun. "If you wasn't good you had to go home," Boyd told me. These changes placed the Cuban League, in terms of quality of play, where it would remain until its demise: between Triple A and the majors, given that the better Double-A and Triple-A players and promising major leaguers were picked, along with Cuban major leaguers. The high level is evident in that a major-league star such as Miñoso hit over .300 only three times in the Cuban League, and that rising stars such as Brooks Robinson, Jim Bunning, and Bob Shaw did very well but did not burn up the league. Some Cuban League teams were probably as good as or better than a few of the lower-division teams in the American and National Leagues, as was surely the case with the 1949 Almendares Caribbean champions. After the Blues' 1953 victory, Joe Cambria opined in the *Havana Post* that Almendares "could have trounced any 1953 Triple A team in the United States [and] finished well into the first division of the National League. It could have whaled the tar out of such teams as the Pittsburgh Pirates, St. Louis Browns, Chicago Cubs, or Cincinnati." This does not mean, however, that the Cuban League was as strong in the fifties as it was in the twenties. During the Golden Age superstars of the Negro Leagues played in Cuba, men such as Oscar Charleston, Cool Papa Bell, and Oliver Marcelle. Because of the ban on players—other than Cubans—with more than two years in the majors, no athletes of that caliber came to the island in the fifties. The equivalent to the twenties would have been to have a mature Frank Robinson or a Duke Snider at the peak of his career come to Havana. The Americans who did play at the Gran Stadium, such as Brooks Robinson, did so before they developed into superstars.

One of the deleterious effects of the pact was that teams' rosters tended to change more from year to year as players exceeded their time in the majors and could not return, and as new ones had to be found. This situation lengthened the period of adjustment at the beginning of each season as players were tried out and as each club developed teamwork. Baseball analysts such as Rai García and Jess Losada complained that it was not until early December that teams were really set. As players were sent back, those coming in, who had been inactive for some time, had to get into shape. As always, this was a particular problem with catchers and pitchers, who needed more time to get ready. Increasingly teams depended on a taxi squad of native players who practiced with each team and could be put in the roster to fill a gap. These were called *los gitanillos* ("the little gypsies") and included many young Cuban men who were in the lower minor-league classifications of organized baseball. The rule, according to Camejo, was that each team could carry twenty-two players and five rookies. These "reserves" could take infield and have batting practice with the team but had to be in street clothes and sit in the stands once the game began. They could be added to the roster if a player was dropped, but could not be on the bench otherwise. This taxi squad received minimal pay, and room and board if they were not from Havana. José Valdivielso told me that Cambria had rooms for these young players beyond the center-field fence at the Gran Stadium, where he also ran a restaurant, where they were fed. Occasionally the reserves played each other as teams in provincial cities, according to Asdrúbal Baró, who, like Valdivielso, was an Almendares *gitanillo* in the early 1950s. Some players who later starred in the Cuban League and elsewhere, such as Baró himself, Camilo Pascual, José Valdivielso, and Francisco (Panchón) Herrera, rose from these ranks.[1]

The increasing tendency for teams to change from year to year made the anticipation of who would be playing for whom all the greater during the months of September and October. In 1949–50 the biggest news was that Luque had been hired by Miguel Angel (again) as coach for the Habana Lions. Luque had played for the Reds before, and even managed them, but a very long time ago. He was associated, particularly since his great victory in 1947, with the Almendares Blues. Much was made of this in the press, with Habana fans crowing that they had the best two brains in Cuban baseball working for them. But there were other changes made, clearly to enhance the "other" franchises, namely Marianao and Cienfuegos.

Marianao dropped its nickname of Frailes Grises (Gray Monks) and became the Tigers, obviously in competition with the Habana Lions. Still under the leadership of Alfredo Pequeño, the team hired Reinaldo Cordeiro as its manager. He continued to be a respected figure and a winning manager in both the amateurs and the Cuban League. Cordeiro was assisted by veteran José María Fernández, manager of the New York Cubans in the summer. Cienfuegos, owned by Luis Parga and Bobby Maduro (owner of the Havana Cubans), dropped its unofficial (and racist) moniker of Petroleros in favor of its traditional one of Elephants. Perhaps they were recalling the Philadelphia team called the White Elephants, but more likely it was because the elephant (number nine in *charada*) is a symbol of good luck in Cuba, and many Cuban families display one made of brass or porcelain in their living rooms, always with its trunk held high in defiance. But choosing the elephant was also part of the jungle-book contest with lions and tigers. Cienfuegos' motto became: "The elephant's march may be slow, but it is crushing." Veteran Salvador Hernández was named manager. Meanwhile, Almendares continued under the direction of Fermín Guerra and the stewardship of Dr. July Sanguily, Mario G. Mendoza, and Monchy de Arcos, representing the Vedado Tennis group that owned the team. Sungo Carrera and Rodolfo Fernández continued as coaches, as they would throughout most of the decade. Miguel Angel was, of course, owner and manager of Habana, with popular Cocaína García an animated and sometimes humorous figure in the third-base box.

A significant change in player development was the tendency to sign young men right out of the Juveniles; another was the emergence of integrated amateur leagues such as Liga Pedro Betancourt and Liga de Quivicán, both in the talent-rich Matanzas–Havana region. The growth of these circuits was also a result of the admission of blacks to Organized Baseball. Now that Cuban blacks were of interest to major-league organizations, their progress could be better monitored in leagues such as these, rather than the semipro or the sugarmills. In fact, both the Pedro Betancourt and Quivicán leagues—both of which existed until the early sixties—incorporated sugarmill teams. As the Cuban League prepared for a new decade, now under the tutelage of Organized Baseball, the tendency was away from independent teams and leagues and more toward organization and centralization. These developments, ironically, reduced the importance of the Amateur League, given that the players on traditional teams such as Fortuna, Vedado Tennis, Hershey, or the University of Havana would be too old to be valuable to the professionals in search of fresh talent.

The opening game of the 1949–50 season—pitting Habana and Marianao—reflected some of the political struggles of the period. Nicolás Castellanos, mayor of Havana (an influential position then), threw the ceremonial first ball, but his rival Antonio Prío Socarrás, the president's brother and at the time minister of the treasury, was among the dignitaries present. González Orúe, mayor of Marianao along with his successor, with the redundant name of Manuel Alcalde (which means mayor), and Arturo Sueiras, Cienfuegos' mayor, were also there, with Robert L. Fynch representing George Trautman, commissioner of the minor leagues.[2] Emilio de Armas and Luis F. Parga are among the others in a *Carteles* picture of October 16, 1949.

Almendares won again in 1949–50, but in a very different manner. The season was full of drama for the Blues. They began without the services of Roberto Ortiz and Fermín Guerra, who was able only to manage because of the pact's interdiction against players on major-league rosters—even Cubans. But this rule was lifted during the season, and Ortiz homered dramatically before a full house on his very first at-bat. Meanwhile, Guerra was able to put himself behind the plate and move Fleitas over to first, once he gave up on Chuck Connors, who could not cope with the pitching this time. Ortiz went on to have a banner year, tying Habana's Don Lenhardt for the lead in homers with 15, a league record. Guerra hit a respectable .308, with 4 homers, while managing the club and anchoring it on the field as catcher. He was named Most Valuable Player. Guerra's most surprising and successful move was to bring Lester McCrabb in midseason when the team's pitching faltered. An unheralded and long-in-the-tooth knuckle-baller who was reported to have been a batting-practice pitcher with the Philadelphia Athletics, McCrabb proved to be a savior. Prematurely gray at thirty-six, he was the object of much derision in the press, who portrayed him as a kind of Methuselah. Guerra, who had been with the Athletics since 1947, must have known something. Though he had a high ERA of 5.03, McCrabb won 6 and lost only 1, mostly in relief.

What stands out in the 1949–50 season is the parity of the clubs. Almendares won with a 38 and 34 record, followed by Cienfuegos, which led most of the way, at an even 36 and 36, and by Habana and Marianao, tied for third with identical 35 and 37 records. Cienfuegos rode the arm of Thomas Fine, who had a very brief career in the majors with the Red Sox and the Browns, but who went 16 and 6 that winter in Cuba. Marianao enjoyed a tremendous season from Lorenzo (Chiquitín) Cabrera, who hit .330, and Amado Ibáñez, who finished at .303. The power was supplied by Roberto (Tarzán) Estalella, who clouted 12 homers, with 10 doubles and drove in 47 (Habana's Lennox Pearson led in this category with 55). Ray Dandridge only hit .264 but was his usual masterful self at third (and was "disciplined," wrote the press, perhaps alluding to his contract-jumping before). The Tiger's pitching depended on Ben Wade and Jim Prendergast (who gave up Ortiz's comeback homer). Habana was the top-hitting team. Pedro (Perico) Formental led the league in batting with a superb .336. He was first in hits with 93, had 11 doubles, and drove in 40 runs. Lenhardt had 15 homers and 51 runs batted, with 13 doubles, while he averaged a solid .314. Clearly brought to Cuba because of Miguel Angel González's St. Louis connections (Lenhardt was a Brown), this slugger never realized his promise, although he hit 22 home runs the summer of 1950, his rookie year. Lenhardt's tremendous season in Cuba made him a favorite of the many Habana fans and propelled him into the majors, although he was already twenty-seven, having lost several years because of the war. He and Formental were the great story for Habana that winter, though the Reds also had outstanding pitchers in Max Manning (8 and 5), Ford Smith (8 and 6), and Albert Gerheauser (10 and 11). The latter was a Browns' reclamation project who was already thirty-two and had last pitched in the majors in 1948.

Much was made of the fact that Almendares had to stitch together a club that was 80 percent Cuban after sending back American players who did not pan out. The downside of the pact with Organized Baseball was that the four teams were obliged to try out some of the talent sent by the major leagues before giving a chance to the local players. This affected not only the *gitanillos,* who were young and on the way up, but mostly the mature Cuban players, veterans of the league as well as the Negro and Mexican Leagues. Thus we see that Cienfuegos imported New York Giant catcher Sam Calderone, although they still had Rafael Noble, who also belonged to the Giants but was a former New York Cuban and older. Habana, meanwhile, played catcher Ferrel Anderson, a Dodger prospect with fearsome power in batting practice but able to hit only three homers in league play. Where was Gilberto (Chino) Valdivia? He had to play in Venezuela. There was a definite if subtle trend to phase out veteran Cuban players in favor of prospects—American or Cuban—on their way up to the majors. Agapito Mayor intimated to me that this was particularly so for those veterans who had played in Mexico and the Liga Nacional at La Tropical in 1947–48. It certainly did not apply to a drawing card such as Roberto Ortiz, but it seems to have been the case with Agapito, the Blanco brothers, Santos Amaro, and others. El Canguro played only ten games in 1949–50 and managed a meek .182 average. It is true that these players were getting old, but they lost their seniority and the right to wind down their careers in a more decorous manner.

Amateur heroes from the forties continued to enjoy success and to command a following. Marrero was just about to begin his major-league career at age forty. Julio Moreno and Sandalio Consuegra would join him in Washington, and Napoleón Reyes was briefly back with the New York Giants, with whom Adrián Zabala had spent much of 1949. Meanwhile, Limonar Martínez was with Marianao, for whom he pitched a no-hitter against Almendares on February 15 to cap a season in which he won 5 and lost 5. These amateur relics would continue to shine through the first part of the decade, but fade toward the end, to be replaced by a new crop of stars such as Tony Taylor, Camilo Pascual, Willie Miranda, and Pedro Ramos. Traded to the White Sox, Consuegra was the champion pitcher in the American League in 1954, posting a 16 and 3 record. Moreno hung on with Washington until 1953, with modest records adding up to 18 wins and 22 defeats, though it must be taken into account that these were poor Senator teams.[3] Consuegra lasted until 1957 in the majors, moving from team to team, and finished with a combined winning record of 51 and 32.

The second Caribbean Series was held at beautiful Sixto Escobar Park in San Juan, Puerto Rico, from February 21 to 27, 1950. Surrounded by pine trees and near the ocean, the stadium was flanked by the Normandy Hotel, an Art Deco jewel in the form of a ship, where showbiz stars and starlets stayed on their Puerto Rican *tournées.* As a boy, Carlos R. Hortas, now dean of the humanities at Hunter College in New York City, would watch the games from one of the windows of the Normandy, which was managed by his father. The hotel, still extant, runs along what was the first-base line (the Sixto Escobar is no longer used for baseball). Some of the visiting teams lodged at the Normandy during the Caribbean Series, giving it a festive atmosphere, particularly because in 1950 the gathering included some of the old luminaries of Caribbean baseball as well as some new stars.⁴ These men had been playing with and against each other since the thirties, including the famous Amateur World Series in Havana and Caracas. A few had been team mates in the majors, in their respective countries, and in the Mexican League.

Venezuela was represented by a team with one of the most beautiful names ever: the Magallanes Navegantes (Navigators). It was managed by slugger-pitcher Ascanio Vidal López, still active, and very familiar to Cubans because he had played in the Cuban League. His roster included veteran Alejandro (Patón) Carrasquel and his nephew Alfonso (Chico) Carrasquel, as well as soon-to-become-star Luis (Camaleón) García, a Caribbean favorite for years. The Venezuelan team sported two Cubans: catcher Gilberto (Chino) Valdivia and pitcher Santiago Ulrich, another of Cambria's signees.⁵ Puerto Rico's Caguas Criollos were managed by Luis Rodríguez Olmo, still referred to in the Cuban press as "the leading Latin American baseball figure." The "Jíbarito" was, like Vidal López, also on the active roster. His powerful squad included legendary Tetelo Vargas, future major-league pitching stars Luis (Tite) Arroyo and Rubén Gómez, plus fancy-fielding and hard-hitting first baseman Víctor Pellot Power. Panama was represented this time by Carta Vieja, a team sponsored by the rum company of that name, and was managed by Wayne Blackburn, who was, like all the other managers, on the active roster. Panama's only luminary was Pat (Lord) Scantlebury, well known in Cuba and a member of the New York Cubans. Almendares brought its own cluster of Cuban veterans, starting with catcher-manager Fermín Guerra, venerable Santos Amaro and Conrado Marrero, catcher-first baseman Andrés Fleitas, and the ever-popular Roberto Ortiz, as well as other seasoned athletes, such as Avelino Cañizares, Héctor Rodríguez, and René Monteagudo. Their budding star was Willie Miranda, a slick-fielding shortstop headed for the majors.

Caguas was reinforced by Wilmer Fields, a Negro Leagues standout pitcher and slugger who was the star of the fading Homestead Grays and who had good seasons in the minors in the early fifties. He got the most dramatic homer of the Series as he blasted one out of Sixto Escobar to give Caguas a victory over Magallanes in the bottom of the ninth of their first clash. But the favorites, Puerto Rico and Cuba and the solid Navegantes, could not contain Panama's Carta Vieja, which took the Series in a sensational extra game to break a tie with the home Puerto Rican team. Even though Héctor Rodríguez won the Series' batting title at .473 and Bob Hooper was the champion pitcher with two victories, Almendares did not play up to expectations, disappointing the many Cuban fans who traveled to San Juan for the games. Jess Losada opined in *Carteles* (March 12, 1950) that Guerra's team had been weakened by the indifferent performance of two Americans (Al Gionfriddo and Eddie Pellagrini). As he had done during the season, Guerra put Cuban players in their place to make the squad more combative and defeated Panama in one of the last games of the Series. But it came too late.

The 1950–51 season saw a reawakening of some of the labor problems brought about by the 1947 pact between the Cuban League and Organized Baseball, even though the pact had been amended to allow native major leaguers to play on the island in the winter. The pact had reduced the number of jobs available to professional Cuban players, some of whom went to play in other countries during the winter, preferably Venezuela, but also Panama, Puerto Rico, and the Dominican Republic (where the winter league was not as strong and not yet a part of the Confederación del Caribe). Some veterans went as managers to the Dominican Republic, where in 1954 every team was managed by a Cuban.[6] There were still many other mature ones who were of no interest to Organized Baseball and too old and proud to be part of the reserves. The players organized themselves, with the help of Martín Dihigo and Julio Blanco Herrera, Jr., and revived the Liga Nacional de Baseball, based in La Tropical Stadium. González Orúe, mayor of Marianao, where La Tropical stands, came out to throw the ceremonial first pitch. This league was like the "outlaw" Liga Nacional of 1947–48. However, this Liga Nacional did not style itself as a rival of the Cuban League but as a potential minor circuit that could supply players to the teams at the Gran Stadium.

The new league, made up exclusively of Cubans, revived some old names for its teams. One was Fe, with a glorious past in the Cuban League; another was Medias Rojas (Red Sox), a name used by a squad in the alternative circuit that played at University Stadium in the twenties. A Team Cuba was created, for the same motives as before (a team under that name had last played in the Cuban League in 1938): It could count on a broad nationalistic appeal, and it recalled Olympic teams of the past. Finally, there was Progreso, which harked back to the nineteenth century, when teams sported abstract names with positive connotations (such as Fe).

Among the veterans was Santos Amaro, player-manager for Fe, which had an outfield of seasoned players known to the fans: Calampio León, José Antonio (Tony) Zardón, and Tony Castaño. Zardón, one of Cambria's recruits, had played fifty-four games for the Senators in 1945. Castaño had won batting championships in the Cuban League. Julio (Yuyo) Acosta, another veteran, was the playing manager for Progreso, while the Medias Rojas boasted an outfield that included old Senator René Monteagudo and former standouts Chiflán Clark and José Luis Colás, both with Negro Leagues experience. Other highly recognizable names in the Liga Nacional were Daniel Parra, a great amateur lefty; Ramón (Colorao) Roger, also with a remarkable amateur and professional career; infielder Francisco (Sojito) Gallardo, who had played for Cienfuegos the previous year; and Orlando (Tango) Suárez.

The Liga Nacional scheduled its games so as not to compete head on with the Cuban League, banking on the demographic fact that Greater Havana, which included Marianao, Regla, and many other neighboring communities, now had a population of nearly 1.5 million. They had figured (*Carteles*, December 17, 1950) that at the Gran Stadium crowds of about 30,000 showed up only for Habana Almendares games, with the average attendance for other teams being 12,000. There had to be more fans willing to relive the days of old at La Tropical. Their (reasonable) contention was that maintaining an available talent pool of conditioned players in Havana would cut down the cost of replacements when players in the Cuban League were injured, or when Americans had to return home for whatever cause. It did not work. The Liga Nacional could not get around the Cuban League's commitment to player development with Organized Baseball. American players were paid by the Cuban League teams, but costs of replacing them (i.e., travel) were borne by their major-league clubs. The Liga Nacional did not succeed because no professional baseball could flourish (at least in Havana) outside the restrictions set up by the pact with Organized Baseball.

The Cuban League was thriving, however. The 1950–51, 1951–52, and 1952–53 seasons saw the reemergence of the Habana Lions and their leader, Miguel Angel González. The Reds won three years in a row with a core of Cuban and American players who gave the team stability, while the other three had problems of adjustment. Cienfuegos, for instance, fired Salvador Hernández as manager during the 1950–51 season and brought Billy Herman, the second American manager in the Cuban League (the first had been Vernon "Lefty" Gómez, also with Cienfuegos, in 1947–48). But the former star second baseman for the Cubs, and future Hall of Famer failed in Cuba, among other reasons because he spent a great deal of his time "under the influence." In that same season Marianao gave Cordeiro his release, and the veteran went back to Almendares as a coach. Meanwhile, the Tigers hired Luque away from his coaching job with Miguel Angel and made him manager. They eventually got Fermín Guerra from Almendares in 1952–53 when the Blues hired Bobby Bragan.

The Tigers got Miñoso back after the Indians had denied him permission to play in 1949–50, and he settled in at the core of the Marianao team, along with Lorenzo (Chiquitín) Cabrera and Claro Duany. Cienfuegos got a last burst of stardom from Silvio García, who not only batted at a .347 clip but also led in stolen bases despite his advanced age. Noble finally became a stable catcher, and his power hitting increased, while Crespo and Otero still had good years. At short Almendares broke in Willie Miranda, who took over from Avelino Cañizares. Héctor Rodríguez continued his brilliant play at third, but veterans such as Amaro and Mayor were virtually through, and Roberto Ortiz slumped badly in 1950–51. Guerra continued to manage courageously, but some of the imports did not come through or were not enough. Russ Derry hit a number of homers; Dick Williams had a good season in the outfield; and Tom Lasorda, traded from Marianao, became a steady performer for the Blues, returning virtually every winter to Havana. The Cuban League continued to bank on players from major-league organizations with ties to Cuba. These teams—principally the Cardinals, Dodgers, and Giants—had either trained in Havana earlier or were known for having Cuban players in the past. The International League Baltimore Orioles also sent several players because Almendares' Mario Mendoza had a connection with that team.

The Habana Reds of 1950–53 had remarkable stability for the era. Their prize rookie, Edmundo Amorós, turned out to be a star at bat and in the outfield, wearing out the league's pitching. Amorós had it all: speed, power, batting eye, and desire. He was also in the Brooklyn Dodger organization, which endeared him even more to the Cuban fans. Formental had strong years in the early fifties, even if his batting average dropped to the .250s: He hit eight to nine homers and drove in about forty runs a season. Chino Hidalgo's offensive production declined, probably because of fatigue, but he came back every year, even after losing his starting position at short to Lou Klein, the old Cardinal and Mexican Leaguer, who became a favorite for several seasons. Chino Valdivia stayed with the Reds, though from 1950 to 1953 Miguel Angel imported Del Wilber, Ray Katt, and Dick Rand, all promising Cardinal prospects, to add punch to the catching position. Gilberto Torres remained a Red, playing the infield and pitching once in a while, and Orlando Varona was a reserve infielder through these years. Veteran Crespo came to Habana from Cienfuegos and added power to the outfield. Among the native pitchers Miguel Angel had Moreno, Carlos (Patato) Pascual, and Adrián Zabala, obtained from Cienfuegos, along with Crespo, in exchange for promising Pablo García.[7] This was the core of Cubans playing for the Lions in their championship seasons.

But in addition, Miguel Angel managed to bring for at least two years in a row, and sometimes three, a number of Americans who had excellent performances. A slugger who came only once was Steve Bilko, a husky first baseman who early in 1950–51 had difficulties with Cuban League pitching, but recovered and wound up with thirty-nine runs batted in and six homers. I have already mentioned the hard-hitting infielder Lou Klein. Two favorites who became fixtures of the Reds were Bert Haas, who played first and third, and Johnny (Spider) Jorgensen, a wizard at second. A veteran who had played for the Dodgers in the later thirties and then bounced around the National League with the Reds, the Phillies, and the Giants, Haas was idolized by Habana fans. He was a hard-playing throwback to a rougher kind of baseball. He told me in Tampa that he liked to take a shot or two of whiskey *before* a game to get himself geared up for it. Lanky Bill Ayers, once a Giant, became a stalwart of the pitching staff during this period. Finally there was Hoyt Wilhelm, then a Giant rookie, who baffled everybody with his knuckleball and found in Chino Valdivia the best catcher he had ever had for the elusive pitch. Because *ayer* means "yesterday" in Spanish and *hoy* "today," their names were punsters' delights.

In 1950–51 Habana and Almendares actually tied for the championship with identical records, but Habana won the one game playoff and the right to go to the Caribbean Series for the first time. As would occasionally happen throughout the decade, an American player was not allowed to stay with the team for the Series; in this case it was hulking Steve Bilko, for whom the Cardinals had big plans (he flopped). So Habana took Chiquitín Cabrera in his place at first base. Cabrera had hit .342, losing the batting title to the rejuvenated Silvio García. With Amorós and Formental this gave Miguel Angel a powerful trio of lefties. The third Caribbean Series was held in Caracas, with Venezuela represented again by Magallanes, managed by Lázaro Salazar, Puerto Rico by Santurce's Cangrejeros, and Panama, champions of the second Caribbean Series, by Spur Cola. Puerto Rico had a super team that included Rodríguez Olmo, Bob Thurman, Willard Brown, Junior Gilliam, George Crowe, Pantalones Santiago, Rubén Gómez, and Roberto Vargas. They lost only one game, finishing 5 and 1 taking the Series, with Cuba close behind, at 4 and 2, and Venezuela and Panama bringing up the rear. Spur Cola only won once, though it had Scantlebury, Connie Johnson, and Jessup on their staff. Santurce had too much talent. Rodríguez Olmo was the leader in homers with three, and Santiago was the champion pitcher. Two Cubans led in offensive categories, except that one, René González, who drove in eleven runs for the crown, did it for Magallanes. Chiquitín Cabrera led in hitting with a record .619 average and in hits with thirteen. But to no avail. Cuba had not won since the first Series, in 1949.

Habana's loss provoked a good deal of grousing in Cuba. The teams from the other three countries were allowed to reinforce themselves for the Series with American players from the other clubs in their leagues, while Cuba was not. The reason for this was that Cuban League teams could field as many as nine Americans, while the number was lower elsewhere— as few as five.[8] Some called for a Series made up of all-stars from each Caribbean country, while others argued that the teams should carry only natives because Americans did not play with the same zest when their country's "flag" was not involved. There had already been some criticism of American players in the second Series, held in Puerto Rico. The conflict between nationalism and professionalism had no clear-cut solution, and there was nothing in these disputes that a Cuban victory could not cure. It finally came in 1952.

Miguel Angel's Lions arrived in Panama City for the fourth Caribbean Series after fending off Cienfuegos to win the Cuban League by a slim margin. The Reds were now being carried by Amorós, who had won the batting title with a .333 average, and Bert Haas, who hit .323 and drove in forty-four runs. Wilhelm was not allowed to go to the Series this year by his major-league club, so Miguel Angel chose Marianao's Tom Fine to take his place. He was a popular and successful pitcher in Cuba (earlier with Cienfuegos). This time, facing a Cervecería Caracas lineup that included Chico Carrasquel, Lorenzo (Piper) Davis, Camaleón García, Wilmer Fields, and Dalmiro Finol, the Texan pitched the first no-hit, no-run game in Caribbean Series history. Formental saved the day with a circus catch in center field. Amorós was the Series' batting champion at .450. He was about to move up to the Dodgers after eating up American Association pitching while playing for St. Paul (he hit .337). Inexplicably, the powerful Puerto Rican team lost every game, but for one it tied with Cuba, the only blemish on the Reds' record.

The fifth Caribbean Series, in 1953, marked the beginning of a second cycle and a return to Havana. Miguel Angel's Lions still had Amorós, Formental, Klein, Jorgensen, and Haas, but had added veteran Damon Phillips at short and Bob Usher in center. Formental was now in right with Amorós in left, while Klein moved to third and Dick Rand was the catcher. The greatest addition was Robert Alexander, a righty who never did well in the majors but who won 10 and lost 3 that winter. Amorós was batting champion at .373, and Formental led in doubles with 18 and in RBIs with 57. But this year's sensation was Klein, who broke Roberto Ortiz's home run season record by hitting 16, the equivalent of his entire major-league output. Klein was revered by the Habana fans, and it is fair to say that his performances with the Lions were the pinnacle of his career.

Playing at home, the Lions were favorites. Managed by "The Inmortal" Martín Dihigo, Venezuela's Cervecería Caracas had a combative team led by Carrasquel, Pompeyo Davalillo, Finol, and Piper Davis. No one seems to have asked why Dihigo was not managing in Cuba. Panama, represented by Chesterfield, had the weakest squad, though it still had Scantlebury and Cuban Roberto Fernández Tápanes at first. Puerto Rico, stung by the previous year's debacle, brought a terrific team. Santurce had Luis (Canena) Márquez in the outfield with Willard Brown and Bob Thurman. Víctor Pellot Power and Junior Gilliam were in the infield, and powerful José R. Montalvo and Valmy Thomas were behind the plate. The Cangrejeros did not lose a single game, led by Willard Brown, who had 4 homers, 13 RBIs, and 8 runs scored, to take the crown in all those categories. Known in Puerto Rico as "Ese Hombre" (That Man), where he was an idol, Brown was one of the many mature Negro Leaguers who suffered as a result of the quota system used by many big-league teams. He was forty at this time but was certainly much better than many white journeymen players in the American and National Leagues. This Caribbean Series in Havana must have been a vindication for him.

This was Miguel Angel's last hurrah in the dugout, though he would continue to own and manage Habana. Appropriately enough, the Cuban League honored him and Luque for their fifty years in baseball by placing a bronze plaque that is still in the Gran Stadium. The 1952–53 season was one of change. Almendares brought Bobby Bragan to manage, and he in turn imported, once the season started and Frank Kellert had failed to hit, Glenn (Rocky) Nelson, one of the most successful and popular American baseball players ever to perform in Cuba.

ROCKY NELSON: I went down there on December 18. I will never forget. I was out here working for the county engineers, and I tore my pants and came into the house. Before I went out she [his wife, Alberta] said, "Bob Bragan had called you from Cuba." "I don't know no Bob Bragan." At that time Bob and I had only spoken, I never saw him or knew him or anything. And they told me to call at six o'clock, and I call down at six o'clock and he says: "I got a job down here for you. Thirteen-fifty a month." I go down there and Monchy de Arcos meets me at the airport, and he says, "We'll go by the ballpark to put your stuff up." I go in there and I go out and we were playing. Almendares was playing. So I go out there, swung the bat a few times, and went back in the clubhouse. I got my glove and hung it up on the rack. I was sitting in the dugout and there were eight guys out on the field. The pitcher was on the mound and everything. I knew I wasn't playing. But Bragan comes over and says, "Would you like to participate?" And I said, "What are you talking about?" And he says, "We've got a spot out there for you." There was no first baseman. That's how he did things. So I go out and they had a guy Davis, he was with the Cubs, was pitching against us [this must be Jim Davis]. First inning, I'll never forget it, he hangs me a curveball, I loved to hit the curveball off of left-handers, and I hit a base hit to right field, and the right fielder lets the ball go through his legs and I end on third base. I called time and I said, "Bob, get somebody in there 'cause I've had it." He says, "What are you talking about? You've done great." And I says, "Man, I can't go any farther." Maestri was the umpire, so Bob gets into an argument with him so I could get my wind back.

Almendares was building up, adding Angel Scull, another Matanzas product, a fleet-footed, powerful black outfielder in the mold of Amorós, but right-handed. Yet another Matanzan was José Valdivielso, such a gifted shortstop that he would challenge Miranda for that spot. Veterans such as Agapito Mayor were being phased out. The 1953 season was his last on the active roster. Roberto Ortiz was traded to Marianao. Batista's *coup d'état* in March 1952 had quieted the political situation temporarily, although at a great cost. On July 26, 1953, Fidel Castro attacked the Moncada garrison in Santiago de Cuba, but at the other end of the island from Havana. The Cuban League was in a moment of true splendor, with the "eternal rivals" competing for championships and Marianao and Cienfuegos getting ready to take their place. The midfifties belonged to Almendares.

It seems clear that the Almendares leadership decided to put an end to Habana's hegemony by tightening the Blues' ties with Organized Baseball. They had hired Bragan to this end. He was a combative former third-string catcher with the Dodgers who had become a successful manager in the Texas League (and later in the Pacific Coast League and the majors).[9] Bragan did not best Miguel Angel in 1952–53, but he did during the middle years of the decade, winning the 1953–54 and 1954–55 seasons. What Bragan was unable to do was stop the string of Puerto Rican victories in the Caribbean Series. They won at home in 1954 and in Caracas in 1955 with teams of unmatched brilliance. Bragan brought an aggressive style of managing and made good on the plan to turn the Cuban League into a development circuit for the majors, either by preparing young players or by recycling old ones. He was quick to send home anyone who did not produce, and according to Rocky Nelson threatened his Almendares compatriots with backing up the truck and sending for a load of new ones. In 1953–54 he did just that, keeping a host of veterans, led by Nelson, that included Earl Rapp, Forrest Jacobs, Cliff Fannin, and Sam Chapman. He still had Héctor Rodríguez at third and Willie Miranda at short, while Scull started to come into his own. Nelson won the batting title with a gaudy .347; Rapp hit .345 and led in homers with 10; and Scull, Miranda, and Jacobs all hit over .300, with Chapman finishing at .295 and Héctor Rodríguez at .286. Fannin had a record of 13 wins and 4 loses with a 1.45 ERA. Veteran Dodger Joe Hatten also had a good season for the Blues. In addition, rookies such as Carlos Paula and José Valdivielso were waiting in the wings. Guerra and Ortiz were gone to Marianao and Mayor saw little action, though the latter told me that Bragan ripped his arm off by having him pitch batting practice constantly.

Miguel Angel González made the mistake of bringing back Dick Sisler, a legendary figure in Cuba because of his three home runs in a game at La Tropical in the 1946–47 season. Sisler told me that this was a gimmick to boost attendance because he had a badly injured throwing arm and was virtually useless on defense. He hit only .246. Haas was released, signed with Marianao, and had a terrible season at .204. Amorós "slumped" to .298, though Chiquitín Cabrera, now with the Lions, hit a very respectable .318. Two young players who would have significant careers in the Cuban League and the majors emerged this season: Marianao's first baseman (taking over from Cabrera) Julio Bécquer, and Cienfuegos shortstop Humberto (Chico) Fernández. They both hit in the .290s. Noble hit a solid .284 and tied Rapp for the lead in homers with 10, some of them of mammoth proportions.

Cienfuegos, on the other hand, hired Al Campanis as manager to strengthen its relationship with the Dodgers. The voluble "Greek" was popular in Havana but did not win. From then on, however, the Elephants fielded players such as Humberto Fernández, Don Hoak, and Don Zimmer, all Dodger infield prospects who played in the International League with the Montreal Royals. Charlie Kress, a Dodger reclamation project, failed with the Elephants. Among the pitchers, Bob Milliken, who had won eight games in Brooklyn in 1953, failed with Cienfuegos; Glen Mickens, who had lost one that summer for the Dodgers, did not improve in Havana with Cienfuegos. The Dodger connection continued, as it did with Almendares, so that games between the two teams must have seemed to the American players like intrasquad contests. Many of these Cienfuegos players, however, did not make the grade, were shipped back, and were replaced by other Americans or by Cubans. The Elephants would have their day, but not in 1953–54.

In 1954 the Caribbean Series returned to Sixto Escobar Stadium in San Juan, Puerto Rico where the local team would be Caguas' Criollos, managed by Mickey Owen. They had Canena Márquez, Víctor Pellot Power, Charlie Neal, Félix Mantilla, Tite Arroyo, Rubén Gómez, Jim Rivera, Carlos Bernier, and Brooks Lawrence. Venezuela's club this time was Pastora, managed by none other than Napoleón Reyes. To his dying day Reyes was proud of this team, which had future major-league stars Wally Moon, Johnny Temple, Ed Bailey, and Yankee veteran left-hander Tommy Byrne, who was winding down his career. Luis Aparicio, *fils*, made his Series debut, and Camaleón García continued his brilliant play at third. Almendares was weakened by the absence of Rocky Nelson, who had been traded from the Dodgers to the Indians. He was slated to be their starting first baseman, so they did not allow him to travel to San Juan. Bragan took instead Marianao's Bécquer, a left-handed hitter like Nelson. Cuba's highlight was venerable Conrado Marrero's shutout of Panama in the third game of the Series. But to no avail, Caguas gave Puerto Rico the title at home, to the delight of local fans. They did not sweep, however, but finished 4 and 2, against Cuba's and Panama's tough 3 and 3 and Venezuela's 2 and 4. The Venezuelan team was elated in having finally won a Series game against Cuba, having lost ten in a row until then.

In 1954–55 Almendares repeated as Cuban League champion. This time they were carried by Rocky Nelson, who led the league with 13 homers, in RBIs with 57, in runs scored with 60 and was walked 70 times. He finished with a batting average of .312. After being sold back to the Toronto Maple Leafs of the International League by the Indians, he had again tormented Triple-A pitching and frustrated major-league organizations who expected great things from him. Scull had blossomed to lead the league with an astronomical .370 average, with 5 homers, and promising young catcher Gus Triandos (a Yankee on his way to the Orioles) hit 7 out, with an average of .278. Román Mejías, a rookie outfielder who would go on to have a nine-year career in the majors, hit a solid .295, and strapping Carlos Paula, another rookie, hit .258 in a few games (he hit .299 with the Senators the summer of 1955, in 115 games). Bragan's pitching was led by veterans Joe Hatten (13 and 5) and George Munger (11 and 7) and got opportune performances from old Conrado Marrero, still baffling hitters with his curves and uncanny control.

Miguel Angel had tried to recover the crown by stepping down as manager and naming none other than Luque to take his place. Papá Montero had been fired by Marianao over a dispute about pitcher Red Barrett, considered by Luque to be a miscreant, and remained out of the Cuban League. It was a touching gesture by Miguel Angel, for Luque had not been very provident and probably needed a job.[10] Miguel Angel also brought the cream of the Cardinals' minor-league system to shore up his team. The Lions fielded the following St Louis prospects: Dick Rand as catcher, Ken Boyer at third, Dick Schofield as shortstop, Don Blasingame at second, and Bill Virdon in center field. Virdon hit .340 and dazzled fans with his defense, while Boyer averaged .303 with 6 homers. Blasingame finished at a respectable .284 and Rand at .248, but with 4 homers and 44 runs batted in. Amorós was back in form, hitting .307 with 5 homers, and Formental .292 with 7. Virdon's stellar performance in center led many to consider him as the best who had ever played that position in the Cuban League (Oms's arm was not as good, said Miguel Angel in an interview). This was a powerful team that led in most offensive categories, but it came in second because the pitching failed, with the exception of Dodger Ed Roebuck, a starter in Cuba (whereas he was a reliever in Brooklyn), who finished at 13 and 7. It could have been much worse. Habana was 12 games behind at the beginning of December, and it seemed as if Luque's comeback would turn into an embarrassment. Amorós had been injured, Schofield was having trouble, and no suitable first baseman could be found. But, as with other teams, Habana was saved by the emergence of several outstanding Cuban rookies. Oscar Sierra took over at first and hit sensational homers, Pedro Cardenal replaced Amorós in center, and Jackie Robinson Morales filled in at short. In addition, Vicente Amor, a right-handed pitcher, came into his own and turned into an overnight star.

The season's biggest gaffe was Marianao's Alfredo Pequeño, who traded to Cienfuegos a rookie pitcher who had finished with a record of 4 and 1: His name was Camilo Pascual. Pascual, who had a brilliant major-league career, went to the Elephants for a dozen bats (or so he told me in Miami recently), where he became the best pitcher in the league and one of the very top pitchers in all Cuban history, worthy of being mentioned with the likes of José de la Caridad Méndez, Martín Dihigo, Luque, and Ramón Bragaña. I remember watching from the first-base stands how right-handed batters flailed at Pascual's sharp, biting curve, which made his thumping fastball look that much faster. He told me that his older brother, the diminutive Carlos (Patato), actually threw harder, but had hurt his arm. Patato, who also pitched for the Senators, was with Habana in the Cuban League.

Two of the last standouts from the Negro Leagues to succeed in Cuba had an excellent season in 1954–55: Connie Johnson, who led the league in strikeouts with Marianao, and Bob Boyd, Cienfuegos first baseman, who led in hits with 88. They would both have good years with the Baltimore Orioles. It was a long time since 1906, when Rube Foster had starred in Cuba with a Fe team that was a winter version of the Philadelphia Giants. Johnson's domination of Almendares kept the championship from turning into a rout.

The 1954–55 season was a controversial one. Four Cuban major leaguers—Miñoso, Fornieles, Consuegra, and Camilo Pascual—were not allowed to play in Cuba by their American teams. This was the source of much bitterness, particularly because attendance was dropping noticeably at the Gran Stadium. Some clamored for a reduction in the number of American imports, claiming that many who failed had been replaced by more than capable Cuban rookies. Witremundo (Witty) Quintana and Asdrúbal Baró had become fixtures with Marianao when American players faltered. Lino Donoso, a lefty, won a few games for Almendares. The crop was impressive. Miguel Angel dissented, however, maintaining that Cubanization would drop the quality of the Cuban League, given that other Cubans had declined in their production. The controversy became acrimonious with the results of the Caribbean Series.

Venezuelan dictator Colonel Marcos Pérez Jiménez threw the ceremonial first pitch of the 1955 Caribbean Series, held again in Caracas, to Almendares catcher Gus Triandos. The new Stadium Universitario was full nearly every time, with crowds of well over thirty thousand. Magallanes was again managed by Lázaro Salazar, whose squad had Venezuelans dreaming of victory. Emilio Cueche and major-leaguer Ramón Monzant joined José (Carrao) Bracho on the mound, with Chico Carrasquel, Camaleón García, and Dalmiro Finol among the native players, joined by Bob Skinner, Bob Lennon, and George Wilson among the imports. Panamá's Carta Vieja brought budding pitching star Humberto Robinson, a skinny native who would make the Milwaukee Braves' staff and who pitched a brilliant game against Cuba in the Series. But the Santurce Cangrejeros brought from Puerto Rico one of the most formidable teams in the history of Caribbean baseball. Other than National League all-star squads, Santurce is the only club that can boast of having had Willie Mays and Roberto Clemente in the same outfield. With such a duo the Venus de Milo could have been the third outfielder, but they had glorious veteran Luis Rodríguez Olmo in addition to Bob Thurman and George Crowe. Hard-hitting, rifle-armed Don Zimmer, the Dodger prospect so well known in Cuba, was the shortstop. With Valmy Thomas behind the plate, the Crabbers had a staff that included Sam Jones, of Negro Leagues and major-league fame, Luis (Tite) Arroyo, and Rubén Gómez, the winner of 17 games the summer before, pitching for the New York Giants.

This was a bitterly fought Caribbean Series, which saw one of the wildest altercations in the history of the tournament. With Magallanes' Cueche pitching superbly against Almendares and Joe Hatten, Héctor Rodríguez made an errant throw to Rocky Nelson at first after a fabulous stop at third. Nelson had to leave the bag toward home, but put a swipe tag on the runner as he went by. The Venezuelan umpire Roberto Olivo called him out, whereupon Salazar began a dignified protest as debris began to rain from the stands. Olivo remained erect and unmoved, arms crossed and head held high in defiance, oblivious to the missiles landing near him. Meanwhile, the home-plate umpire, an American named Rice, called on Salazar to calm the crowd. A gesture of despair by the Príncipe de Belén provoked the throng even more, whereupon Rice ejected Salazar, making the situation worse. Enraged fans began to drop onto the field of play from the bleachers.

ROCKY NELSON: I go over and catch the ball, turn around, and hit the guy on the shoulder. You could see I'd hit him. The umpire is Venezuelan. He calls him out. The manager turns around and goes like this [raises his arms as in disgust] to the fans. They threw oranges, beer cans, and everything. So we all huddled on the mound. They were throwing things all over the place. So Bragan and I are chin to chin. The guy behind home plate was American and he threw the manager out of the game for inciting a riot. So then they called up to the colonel. He is the one that heads all the guards and the Secret Service men at the ballpark. They ask for police protection. He calls down and says, you put our manager back in the ball game and we'll give you police protection. I look over at Bob. As I said, we are all huddled on the mound, all the American ballplayers of Almendares, and they got these Secret Service men around us. I told Bob, I says, "Get him back in the game. It doesn't hurt us." We called the umpire over and told him, "You put him back in." And he said, "I can't do that." So Bob says, "You either do that or get us killed." So they put him back in. Anyway, we won the game.

In the midst of the melee, Olivo continued stiff as a statue courageously, while all the other umpires left the field to consult with the officers of the Confederación del Caribe, and even George Trautman, minor league commissioner. They reinstated Salazar. Cueche, meanwhile, cooled off during the forty-five-minute pause and lost a heartbreaker, 1–0, having given up only two hits. On the way out of the park, Nelson recounts, "They brickbatted in the windshield of our car in the back side. Carlos Paula was in the back and he had about six pieces of glass in his arm."

Venezuela fought hard, but lost a crucial sixth game when Mays hit a tremendous homer in the eleventh inning to give Puerto Rico the victory. Cuba finished third. Zimmer captured the home-run crown with three,

Nelson the batting championship at .471, Mays led in RBIs, and Clemente in runs scored. It was the last Caribbean Series won by Puerto Rico during the first period of these classics, which ended in 1961. But it was a magnificent one, won by a Santurce team that should forever be remembered. Cuba, on the other hand, protested to Trautman in Caracas the fact that Puerto Rico had been able to count on all its major-league players, as well as Americans of the caliber of Willie Mays, already a superstar with the Giants, while Cuba had been without the services of Miñoso, Pascual, Fornieles, and Consuegra. All of the critics who had denounced the pact with Organized Baseball reared up their heads again, claiming that Cuba had become the Cinderella of the Caribbean. The clear implication was that Trautman was partial to Puerto Rico because it was part of the United States. The situation was particularly galling because it was Cuba that had ushered the pact with organized baseball, which had led to similar pacts with Panama, Puerto Rico, and Venezuela, and in 1954 a league in Colombia (based in Cartagena, hence in the Caribbean), and the Liga de Veracruz in Mexico. Cuba would not lose another Caribbean Series.

The 1954–1955 season was critical because of this controversy, but also because the Class B Havana Cubans had become the Cuban Sugar Kings of the Triple-A International League the previous summer (more about this later). The bond with Organized Baseball was stronger than ever, while at the same time the Cuban League was suffering from the stranglehold. Branch Rickey, now running the Pittsburgh Pirates, who trained in Havana at the Gran Stadium in the spring of 1953, visited Cuba during the 1954–55 winter to scout talent for his hapless team. He liked what he saw in Mejías and Donoso, and both made the Pirates in 1955. Fresh Cuban talent was reaching the majors in record numbers now that both blacks and whites could play. Paula, Valdivielso, and Bécquer would make the Senators, as had Pascual and soon after, Pedro Ramos. But attendance had declined, and the Cuban magnates were worried. Baseball had to compete now against many other forms of entertainment, including television and many new movie houses, some of them lavish, showing not only American and European films but also very popular Mexican potboilers. Havana was a city with four home teams whose games were broadcast by radio and television, which must have hurt the gate. The Americanization of the Cuban League was a depressing factor, too, as was the decline of the Amateur League. Budding stars such as Amorós, Valdivielso, and Pascual were signed right out of the Juveniles, before they could acquire renown by playing for Fortuna or Hershey, as in the past. Moreover, after 1955 the only championship won by one of the "eternal rivals" was in 1958–59, when Almendares was crowned for the last time in its distinguished history. Cienfuegos and Marianao were ready to make their move as the Cuban League had hoped they would to expand the fan appeal. But, as in the past, if the Reds and Blues did not win, revenues diminished.

Habana and Almendares had won nine seasons in a row, but Cienfuegos had strengthened itself by the return of Pascual and the emergence of Ramos, also as a front-line pitcher. Consuegra, at the top of his form, was now with the Elephants, giving them three native major-league pitchers. Humberto Fernández had taken over short and had become a .300 hitter, and a rookie slugger, a natural, emerged from the provinces: Ultus Alvarez. He was a blond, blue-eyed country boy from the deepest woods in Pinar del Río, with shocking power at the plate, speed on the bases, and a strong arm. A right-handed hitter, Alvarez seemed destined for stardom, leading the league in homers with 10 in 1955–56. Two strong hitters joined him in the outfield. One was veteran Archie Wilson, who had played for Marianao earlier in the decade and was a favorite in Cuba; he hit 7 homers and finished with an average of .311. The other was Prentice Browne, a rugged left-hander who clouted 7 homers while hitting .248. Bob Boyd, who had failed with Habana earlier in the fifties, had become a fixture at first with the Elephants as a consistent .300 hitter and contributed five homers. Managed by Oscar (Barriguilla) Rodríguez, who had been very successful in that capacity for the Havana Cubans, Cienfuegos fielded one of the best teams in the history of the Cuban League.

The Elephants' pitching was the determining factor. Pascual finished with 12 victories and 5 defeats, while Ramos won 13 and lost 5 to finish first in winning percentage. Pascual was champion pitcher, with a fantastic 1.91 ERA. The right-hander was clearly among the top pitchers in all of baseball. Ramos, a taller man and also a righty, was a gifted athlete who was probably the fastest runner anywhere and a very good hitter. A blond, blue-eyed man with movie-star looks, the irrepressible Ramos was said to spend no small amount of time with his many female admirers. According to Fausto Miranda this curtailed what could have been an even greater career. Perhaps. But from the midfifties to the very end of the Cuban League, he excelled.

All of these Cienfuegos pitching accomplishments came in a season that was dominated by a Habana pitcher: Wilmer (Vinegar Bend) Mizell. Miguel Angel had imported him from the Cardinals, who wanted the big left-hander to get back into shape after two years in the army. He had also brought right-hander Gordon Jones for good measure. Mizell, who had a blazing fastball, became all the rage in Cuba. He set a strikeout record with 206 in 179 innings and led in complete games with 13. His duels with Pascual became as famous as those between Dihigo and Bragaña, Martin and Lanier, and Marrero and Patterson. Attendance once again rose at the Gran Stadium, and kids throughout the country, watching on television, imitated Mizell's high kick and elegant follow-through. I remember being at the stadium one night when Vinagre Mizell, as he was known in Cuba, struck out the side with the bases loaded against Almendares. I stood with the crowd for the last strikes as people around me began to throw hats and jackets in the air. Mizell was an idol to the legions of Habana fans, including Ernest Hemingway. Norberto Fuentes writes:

It was in these days, during his convalescence, that Hemingway enjoyed a rare indulgence. He would settle himself for hours in front of the TV set to watch the outcome of Cuba's championship baseball games. He was a fan of the "Havana" club, a professional team whose red uniforms bore the figure of a lion. His impassioned TV viewing and his heated arguments in defense of the "Havana" made [Dr.] Sotolongo at times fear for Ernest's health. There was a certain American pitcher, Wilmer Mizel [*sic*] (whom the Cubans called "Vinagre" Maicel [*sic*]) who was his special favorite and who broke a record that year, much to Hemingway's delight.[11]

I remember spotting the writer in Old Havana, surrounded by black American baseball players at a fruit-juice stand, surely not one of his habitual watering holes in the city.

Meanwhile, Almendares dropped precipitously that year under the direction of Marrero, who failed as a manager, and with a considerable plummet in production by Rocky Nelson. After the season the Guajiro de Laberinto returned to Sagua la Grande, as usual, came to one of our games—which we played at the local airstrip, where there had been a baseball field with a *glorieta* back in the twenties—and told us that the Blues had everything but a good manager. An unassuming, genuinely modest man, the premier seems to have always had a realistic perception of himself, which probably helped him on the mound. Marrero was not quite through as a player and had put himself in to pitch in a few well-chosen spots.

This championship saw the only interruption of a Cuban League game by the increasingly tense political situation that followed Bastista's controversial election to the presidency in 1954. The incident occurred during an afternoon doubleheader, on Sunday, December 4, with the "eternal rivals" facing each other in the second game and Mizell on the mound for the Reds. The time and the place had been carefully chosen, for a televised Habana-Almendares match on a Sunday would have the largest possible national audience. A group of university students jumped onto the field from the bleachers in right, at the point closest to center field. They appeared exactly where a billboard promoting Batista's candidacy had been prior to the elections, visible to the television camera behind the plate. The students were members of the Directorio Estudiantil Universitario, whose leader was José Antonio Echevarría (Fidel Castro's "26th of July Movement" was being organized in Mexico). The demonstrators were carrying a long banner, which they planned to unfurl as they marched toward the crowded grandstand. In their haste, the two students at the ends of the banner held it upside down as police dropped onto the field and began to clobber them mercilessly with their nightsticks. The students, unarmed, fled in various directions, with policemen in pursuit. Rocky Nelson told me that he saw from the Almendares dugout how one of them was surrounded near the shortstop position and brutally beaten. The group was finally rounded up and led out through the gate in left field through which the jeep that dragged the infield exited. The policemen still flailed at them as they were being herded out. The fans booed, but order was restored and no one else jumped onto the field.

I was watching on television from Sagua la Grande and saw the beginnings of the confrontation (one of the two channels broadcasting switched to the station's logo) as the inverted banner was opened and the police closed in. I was unable to read what the banner said, except for the word "Batista." My paternal grandparents and young uncle Eduardo were at the Gran Stadium, sitting along the first-base line, and witnessed the entire episode. Eduardo recalls how the crowd taunted the police for their cowardly abuse of force against unarmed protesters. Though the game resumed, my family left in disgust, and Eduardo remembers how, from the back of the stands, fans jeered at policemen down in the street, one of whom waved a submachine gun in their direction menacingly. Other policemen milled around flaunting their feared *vergajos,* an instrument described by the dictionary of the Spanish Royal Academy of the Language as "the bull's male organ, which once cut, dried, and twisted, is used as a whip." In Cuba it was generally feared that the police filled them with shot to inflict more damage.[12]

The Directorio Estudiantil Universitario's choice of the Gran Stadium as the site for its demonstration is evidence that the Cuban League games were the most universal spectacle in Cuba now that television was in full swing. The ritual confrontation of the "eternal rivals," which harked back to preindependence days, was now a truly national phenomenon. A Sunday Habana-Almendares match at the hallowed grounds of the Gran Stadium, site of the great 1947 deciding game, was charged with symbolic meaning. The fact that the students failed to incite the crowd at the stadium to riot, even though most people were appalled by the excessive force applied by the authorities, also shows that Havanans were both fearful of the police and not in a state of desperate opposition to the government. If baseball was the most public forum for nationalism, it was not quite ready to supply enough political energy to topple a regime. Games are, perhaps because of their ritualistic nature, agents of order, not of revolt. The game was played to conclusion. Still, the students' pummeling had shown the Batista police in the worst of lights to the entire country, and in this Echevarría and his followers scored a painfully earned victory.[13] Instead of the symbolic sports arena, the students took their action next to the real center of political power, the Presidential Palace, which they would attack unsuccessfully in March of 1957, with many, including Echevarría, losing their lives.

Cienfuegos went to the eighth Caribbean Series in 1956 as the favorite, and they did not disappoint, winning 5 and losing only 1 to take the flag. Pascual and Ramos won 2 each, and the Elephants enjoyed relief help from another newcomer, René (El Látigo) Gutiérrez, a lanky mulatto sidewinder known in the United States as René Valdés (he got into 5 games with the Dodgers in 1957). From a Cuban point of view the most interesting team, other than Cienfuegos, was Venezuela's Valencia Industriales, managed by Regino Otero, with Reinaldo Cordeiro as coach and two of Pelayo Chacón's sons in the outfield: Elio, who would reach the majors with the Reds and the Mets, and Pelayo *fils*. Otero, by the way, had barely defeated his brother-in-law Fermín Guerra, who managed the second-place team in the Venezuelan League. This was one of several Caribbean Series featuring two Cuban managers. Caguas, representing Puerto Rico, was not the powerhouse Santurce had been the year before and tied Panama for second, at 3 and 3. Still, this team had players of the caliber of Wes Covington, Félix Mantilla, and Victor Pellot Power. Mays, Clemente, and Olmo were gone. Panama played inspired ball before the home crowd, led by Héctor López, a rookie who would have a solid twelve-year career in the majors. Cienfuegos' Noble led in batting at .400, with Boyd leading in RBIs and Humberto Fernández in runs scored. In 9⅓ innings, Gutiérrez gave up no runs for the pitching title.

The 1956–57 season marked the start of a two-year Marianao reign under the leadership of Napoleón Reyes, and with the help of two superb American pitchers he scouted in the summer while he managed the Cuban Sugar Kings in the International League: Jim Bunning in 1957 and Bob Shaw in 1958. In addition to the peerless Bunning, the Tigers had in right-hander Miguel Fornieles an answer to Cienfuegos' Pascual. Fornieles was a full-fledged major-league pitcher about to reach his peak. Reyes also had Miñoso, the best Cuban in the majors then, at the top of his form. Marianao had Bécquer, fully developed at first, and Valdivielso, a major leaguer, at shortstop. Both were established with the Senators, who continued to sign Cuban players through Joe Cambria. When Fornieles was on the mound, the Tigers had four native major leaguers in the lineup. Asdrúbal Baró played right. He was a graceful fielder with speed on the bases and a consistent line-drive hitter. Baró, a soft-spoken, smart player, had tremendous seasons in the International League and elsewhere in the Dodger and Cardinal systems. He told me in Havana recently, without bitterness, that as a black he endured much discrimination in the American South. Had it not been for the quota system Baró would have made the majors.

Other than Bunning, who won 11 and lost 5 with a 2.10 ERA, Marianao's greatest import that year was Solly Drake, a marvelous center fielder who led the league in doubles, runs scored, and stolen bases. The Tigers had also developed Witty Quintana, one of the *gitanillos,* a defensive asset at third or second, and Rodolfo Arias, a left-hander who would pitch briefly for the White Sox and who had very good seasons with the Cuban Sugar Kings. They also counted on a youthful Andrés Ayón, a crafty, slight right-thander whose career continued in Mexico after the Revolution. Other

Cuban rookies of note with the Tigers during those years were outfielders Juan Delís and Orlando Leroux. The catcher in 1957 was Baltimore Oriole Hal (Harold Wayne) Smith.

Cienfuegos and Habana fought hard, with Pascual again running away with most pitching honors (he won 15 games), but to no avail. Habana, now managed by Gilberto Torres, as Luque's health declined, depended on Vicente Amor's and Billy Muffett's pitching, which was not enough, though the Cuban won 13. The "eternal rivals" had made a controversial trade, with Almendares sending Héctor Rodríguez, Román Mejías, Oscar Sardiñas, and Raúl Sánchez to Habana for Amorós. But the Blues dropped to the cellar, even though Bob Skinner, playing first instead of Nelson (who had not come that year), had a good season, as did left-handed veteran pitcher Joe Hatten, who finished with a 2.08 ERA. Napoleón Reyes took his Tigers to the Caribbean Series. It was not his debut, but his first time with a Cuban team.

The Series came to Havana for the third time. George Trautman, commissioner of the minors, threw out the ceremonial first ball, with Colonel Roberto Fernández Miranda, director of sports, and Dr. Arturo Bengochea, at the time president of the Cuban League, participating in the ceremony. Batista could not risk being booed by a baseball crowd, and he seemed to have lost interest in the game. Besides, Trautman's presence, along with that of other dignitaries from Organized Baseball, meant more to the Cuban baseball entrepreneurs, who had their sights on a major-league franchise.

Marianao lost only one, when Puerto Rico's Pantalones Santiago, with help from Humberto Martí, shut them out. But Puerto Rico's Mayagüez Indians won only one more game. Solly Drake was the star, leading in batting (.500), hits (11), runs scored (9), and stolen bases (4). He was one of several players whose performance in Cuba augured a great career in the majors that never materialized, whereas his teammate Bunning made the Hall of Fame. Veteran Puerto Rican Canena Márquez led the Series in homers with 2 and Miñoso and Smith in RBIs with 7 each. A highlight was again Marrero's pitching against Panama, in a game eventually won by Bunning, who had to rescue the premier in the fourth inning, when Panama scored its only run but was threatening to do more damage. Marrero was signed by the Tigers after he was dismissed as Almendares' manager, and this was to be his last hurrah as a player, showing once again that pitching was more brains than brawn. He was at this time forty-six years old and had not been very active in the past few years. In 1956–57 he had been in only 7 games without a record, but in his nearly 20 innings he had a 1.37 ERA. It was an emotional occasion for the fans who crowded the Gran Stadium. They surely preferred to cherish the memory of Marrero the pitcher than the memory of his debacle as manager of Almendares.

The Series awakened fan interest and was a social success for the visiting dignitaries and baseball celebrities. The Gran Stadium rocked again with great crowds in a nationalist frenzy. Meanwhile, as at the Congress of Vienna, the delegates danced. At Bengochea's country estate near Havana there was a lavish party. Pictures show Napoleón Reyes dancing to the newfangled rock and roll with his young wife, and Mrs. Trautman, with a worried look on her face, attempting a Caribbean rhythm with Angel Guillermo Grima, vice president of the Panamanian League. Scores of journalists, beauty queens from the participating countries, and government officials caroused in an atmosphere of prosperity and high expectations. The Series was a financial success, and the Cuban economy was peaking.

That summer, on July 3, 1957, a chapter, or rather a volume of Cuban baseball history was closed with the death of Adolfo Luque from a heart attack in his native Havana at age sixty-six. Papá Montero had been through it all, from army teams to the Vedado Tennis Club, to the Negro Leagues, the Long Branch Cubans, stardom in the Cuban League and the majors, to managing victories in Cuba and Mexico, and coaching with the New York Giants. The Pride of Havana had barnstormed through the United States and Cuba, been an arm for hire, even an entrepreneur. Luque managed all four major teams in the Cuban League, and led Almendares to victory on February 25, 1947, the most memorable confrontation between the "eternal rivals." His joining the "ineligibles" in 1947–48 at La Tropical in the rival Liga Nacional gained the admiration of the fans for his principles: According to the *Bohemia* feature on his death (July 14, 1957), this was one of his finest moments. Luque was a strong personality whom people never forgot, and he earned himself a memorable epithet embedded in the depths of Cuban culture: Papá Montero. He was brash, violent, vulgar, irascible, yet a great teacher and scout of talent. Sal Maglie learned from Luque how to "shave" batters by throwing at their heads, and Camilo Pascual how to break his knee-bending curve. He took a shot at one of his players for not giving his all. Always improvident, Luque died, if not in poverty, then at least far from the financial splendor his accomplishments deserved. He spent it all in this life. That is surely how he wanted it. Luque was lucky that he did not live to see the end of the Cuban League he had labored so much to advance. All Cuba wept for Papá Montero, that *canalla rumbero*. Baseball could never be the same without him.

Marianao repeated in 1957–58. It was a turbulent season in which the pact with Organized Baseball again became a bone of contention. By this time Havana was in a building fever, with new hotels and casinos going up stimulated by laws passed by the Batista regime to lure American tourists. The involvement of figures from American organized crime in Havana's gambling had increased, as well as that of prominent members of the administration. Baseball was not touched by any of this except tangentially. For example, on October 25, 1957, when gangster Albert Anastasia was gunned down in the barbershop of the Park Sheraton Hotel in New York, it came out that he had recently been in meetings "with a group of four

Cubans, headed by Roberto 'Chiri' Mendoza, a well-connected contractor who was building Havana's new Hilton Hotel, an edifice even larger than Meyer Lansky's Riviera, with 630 rooms to the Riviera's 440."[14] Mendoza, of the same family that had an interest in Almendares, had gone to New York to entice Joe DiMaggio to become a greeter at the new hotel-casino (the Yankee Clipper refused). Grumbling about the pact came when Bobby Bragan returned to manage the Blues, but, having been hired to lead the Cleveland Indians the next summer, he treated Almendares like a spring-training outfit. Four times he left the club in the (capable) hands of coach Sungo Carreras while he went to Cleveland to prepare for his assignment, and Mel Harder, the Indians' pitching coach, came to Havana to work with two Indians' prospects currently on the Almendares staff: Dick Brodowski and Jim (Mudcat) Grant. The press claimed that once Harder began to tinker with their deliveries, their performances, particularly Brodowski's, declined, as if they were more interested in preparing for the Indians than in winning for Almendares. In addition, Almendares had traded for Amorós, but in the process had given up favorites Héctor Rodríguez and Román Mejías to Habana. The Reds got a good season out of pitcher Billy Muffett, first baseman Norman Larker, and Mejías. Cienfuegos had to do without Pascual, again held back by the Senators, and Humberto Fernández, held back by the Phillies. Philadelphia had acquired the shortstop during the winter and forced him to quit playing for the Elephants in midseason, aggravating the complaints about how Cuban baseball was being treated by the Americans (there were insinuations that Fernández, and others before him, had been paid not to play in Cuba). Not even the splendid season that Oriole hopeful Brooks Robinson had played for the Elephants (9 homers) could help them. Oscar Rodríguez was fired amid protests by the fans, and Tony Castaño took over.

There also was turbulence on the field. Several fistfights erupted, one involving Miñoso, normally a restrained man, who scuffled with an umpire. In another game Raúl Sánchez left the mound and charged the plate (quite a reversal) to mix it up with Orlando Peña, his pitching opponent. And Almendares catcher Russ Nixon, after being violently bowled over by Delís and Valdivielso in succession, charged the slender Marianao shortstop as benches emptied, while Tiger third baseman Milton Smith climbed into the stands after a heckler. But the worst fracas involved Dodger left-handed pitching prospect Danny McDevitt, playing with Cienfuegos, who was bashed over the head with a mask by umpire Armando Rodríguez, suffering a broken skull. I was watching on television and saw a bleeding McDevitt being led off to the dressing room with a towel over his head. Several American ballplayers from both teams refused to take the field in protest, and it was a while before the game could be resumed.

Marianao brought back Drake and its stellar group of Cubans, to which it added fifteen-year major-league veteran catcher Clyde McCullough and rising pitching star Bob Shaw, who was, like Bunning the previous season, a Detroit Tiger prospect. Shaw won 14 games (as did Brodowski for Almendares), with a minuscule ERA of 1.48 to lead the League. Meanwhile, Milton Smith led in batting with .320, newcomer Casey Wise in doubles with 12, and Bécquer and Drake in stolen bases with 11. Even though Almendares and Habana put up a fight, and there were exciting duels between Shaw and Brodowski and between Almendares' Billy O'Dell and Habana's Billy Muffett, attendance declined alarmingly, as it had during the summer in International League games. Was it that Marianao just did not have enough appeal, no matter how good the team was?

The Tigers arrived in San Juan, Puerto Rico, for the tenth Caribbean Series as the absolute favorites. Regino Otero was back with his Valencia Industriales, winners of the Venezuelan League. He still had Chico Carrasquel, Elio Chacón, Carrao Bracho, Emilio Cueche, and major-league catching prospect Earl Battey. Veteran Athletics' receiver Wilmer Shantz (still active) managed Carta Vieja, again Panama's entry, with Héctor López and Humberto Robinson being the most prominent natives, and former Pirate Tony Bartirome at first. The home team, Caguas Criollos, was loaded, with Clemente, Pellot Power, Canena Márquez, Mike Goliat, Mantilla, Valmy Thomas, and a staff anchored by Pantalones Santiago and the sensational rookie Juan Pizarro. A lightning-fast left-hander, Pizarro was also a fearsome hitter and an excellent runner. He was a complete ballplayer.

Marianao won again, but in a tight Series that saw Puerto Rico and Panama tie for second with 3 and 3 records. There were two memorable games, one in which the twenty-year-old Pizarro, before a crowd of nearly fourteen thousand at Sixto Escobar Stadium that included Governor Luis Muñoz Marín, struck out seventeen Carta Vieja batters to set a record, allowing only two hits and no runs. Pizarro also went two for three at the plate, including a triple. The other game ended in a tumultuous altercation as violent as the Caracas one in 1955. Caguas and Marianao were playing their first game, with the Criollos beating the Tigers by two in the ninth inning late into the night. Cuba's Marianao, the home team for this particular game, tied it after a dramatic sequence of plays that culminated with Pizarro having to come in to relieve with the bases loaded. Orlando Leroux, batting for pitcher Pedro Ramos (a reinforcement with catcher Noble), slapped one to right that Allen caught as he slid and fell. The umpire ruled that he had trapped it and allowed the tying run to score from third and the bases to remain full with no outs. All hell broke loose as bottles and other missiles began to drop from the stands. Screaming Caguas players surrounded the umpire as fans began to run onto the field, with policemen in pursuit wielding nightsticks.

The chief umpire was Venezuelan Roberto Olivo, the same man who had faced a similar situation in Caracas. He went over to George Trautman, who had also been in the stands in Caracas, and who ruled that the game should be suspended and resumed the next day at the same point. Dr. Arturo Bengochea, president of the Cuban League, protested loudly that the game should be forfeited in favor of Marianao, and lunged toward Trautman, who squared off. Named after a Puerto Rican boxing champion, Sixto Escobar Stadium was about to become the arena for a Quixotic battle between two suited middle-aged men. The two dignitaries had to be pulled apart as Bengochea shouted that Trautman had no jurisdiction over the matter, which should be decided upon solely by Olivo, who had no business consulting anybody. The game was suspended—there were many arrests— and when it was picked up the next day, Marianao won. The decision went against Marion Fricano, who later pitched and lost the regular game against Panama to become the first and only pitcher in Caribbean Series history to drop two in one day. The near fight between Bengochea and Trautman was the culmination of all the controversies about the pact between organized baseball and Caribbean baseball.

The 1958–59 season of the Cuban League ran the risk of joining those in the early thirties that had succumbed to political turmoil. But the collapse of Batista's government on January 1 and the rise to power of Fidel Castro stopped competition for only a few games. Though the Battle of Santa Clara raged only two hundred miles away, Havana was mostly oblivious, with full nightclubs and casinos on New Year's Eve. At the Gran Stadium, however, fans were frisked as they entered because of the fear of bombs, quite a few of which had been exploding in Havana, and the number of policemen had increased. Rocky Nelson (back with Almendares) and his wife, Alberta, remember the roar of planes as they drove home westward to Marianao from a New Year's party in Havana. Since the Columbia military airfield from which Batista, his family, and his closest associates had taken off, was in that direction, it is quite likely that the noise the Nelsons heard was that of the engines carrying the former sergeant out of Cuba for good.

All of Cuba went berserk with happiness as the guerrillas moved toward Havana and the new government took power. Collective euphoria prevailed in a carnival atmosphere increased by the holiday. It seemed as if the New Year were going to really bring something new and beneficial to everyone. Crowds took to the streets in the capital and elsewhere. Very little damage was done by the mobs, however, except to the gambling casinos, the houses of prominent Batista men, and the parking meters, which were reputed to give a huge kickback to the First Family. But for a major metropolitan center suddenly left without a police force, calm was restored quickly in a joyous atmosphere of liberation. Ford Frick, commissioner of baseball, urged by Calvin Griffith, owner of the Senators, ordered the American players out of Cuba. Art Fowler, the Almendares pitcher, replied in the name of the players that they were staying, having been offered guarantees by the new regime. Only five days of games were lost, from the first to the fifth, on which date the Cuban League decided to resume the schedule the next day with a nighttime doubleheader beginning at 7:00 P.M., with Cienfuegos and Marianao in the first game and Habana and Almendares in the second. The *rebeldes,* now being called *barbudos,* because of their beards (the length of which indicated time of service in the hills), were invited to attend for free. This would be a *Día de Reyes*— an Epiphany—like no other. The crowd stood to sing the July 26 Movement's anthem and gave a long standing ovation to the soldiers, many of them white *guajiros* from the deepest backwoods who were in Havana for the first time. Players and soldiers fraternized. When Carlos Paula hit a homer a *barbudo* jumped onto the field and embraced him. Nelson and Tom Lasorda appeared in pictures published by *El País* on January 7 holding the rifles of smiling *barbudos.* It was a time of celebration at the Gran Stadium, as if all of Cuba (and quite a few Americans) had joined in a ritual of reconciliation on Epiphany Day, the Twelfth Night, at the anointed sports arena. Baseball was, again, the crucible of Cuba's nationalism, even though the new leader had yet to reach Havana. He was slowly approaching in a caravan from Oriente, a new magic king from the East.

Nelson was back with a restructured Almendares club that included pitchers Fowler and Lasorda, as well as new Cuban standouts Alejandro Peña and Miguel (Mike) Cuéllar, both on their way to the majors. The Blues had a formidable outfield made up of Paula, Amorós, and Scull, with slugger Bob Allison added for good measure. Tony Taylor was at second, Miranda at short, newcomer Jim Baxes at third, and Nelson at first. The catcher was Dick Brown, a good hitter from the Cleveland Indians. This Almendares club, managed by veteran Oscar Rodríguez, was again of major-league caliber.

Marianao brought back nearly the same team, with the addition of José Tartabull, a promising new outfielder who hit left, and massive catcher René Friol backing up import Charlie Lau, a left-handed hitter. But without a Bunning or a Shaw the Tigers were declawed, even with Miñoso, Delís, Baró, Bécquer, and Valdivielso. Al Cicotte threw 6 shutouts (and led with a 1.38 ERA), and Fornieles was all but unhittable. However, there was no front-line pitcher as in the past two seasons, and Solly Drake's production was not the same.[15] Cienfuegos had found in Leonardo (Chico) Cárdenas and Octavio (Cookie) Rojas a native double-play combination of the highest caliber, and in Rogelio (Borrego) Alvarez a Cuban slugger to play first base. The Elephants sent mammoth Panchón Herrera back to the Habana Reds. Another find was left-handed slugger and rifle-armed outfielder Antonio (El Haitiano—Tony) González, who was major-league-bound. Ramos lost 13 and Pascual was 9 and 9 (but with a 2.12 ERA). The Habana Reds finished last, with diminutive Albie Pearson in center and Buddy Peterson at short. But Miguel Angel's imported pitchers Chuck Churn and Charlie Rabe were bombed, and Vicente Amor pitched courageously but lost 13. John Buzhardt, brought in during the season, did pick up some of the slack. This was a season during which pitching prevailed, with a total of 44 shutouts. Miñoso could only hit .269, though he had finished at .302 with Cleveland that summer. The batting champion was Tony Taylor with a mere .303, and Jim Baxes led in homers with only 9.

As Pérez Jiménez had also been toppled in Venezuela, the ceremonial first ball of the eleventh Caribbean Series was thrown by Dr. Edgar Sanabria, president of the governing junta. Captain of the rebel army Felipe Guerra Matos, the new head of the Dirección General de Deportes, traveled to Caracas with the Cuban delegation to participate in the ceremonies. Almendares had added to its already loaded team Camilo Pascual, who made the difference. The Blues' manager, Oscar Rodríguez, took ill, so coach Sungo Carreras, a beloved figure in Cuba (and well known in Venezuela), took over the team. He was the first black manager Cuba had sent to the Series, but not the first black Cuban manager, as Dihigo and Salazar had managed Venezuela earlier.

Puerto Rico's Santurce looked like the team to beat, with Rubén Gómez, Tite Arroyo, and Pantalones Santiago among the pitchers, and strong-boy slugger Orlando (Peruchín) Cepeda and José Pagán, both San Francisco Giant rookies, added to veterans Victor Pellot Power, Saturnino Escalera, Antonio Alomar, and Felix Maldonado. Cocle, Panama's entry, was one of the weakest teams ever in Caribbean Series play. Its only real name player was Pumpsie Green, the fleet-footed infielder who was about to break the color barrier of the Boston Red Sox that summer. Cocle lost all six games. The home team this year would be Oriente, managed by Kerby Farrell, who had directed the Cleveland Indians in 1957. He had a strong squad, led by left-handed slugging first baseman Norm Cash, a White Sox rookie, and veteran Phillies pitcher Jim Owens. Farrell also had native star pitcher Ramón Monzant and Elio Chacón, a favorite in Havana with the Sugar Kings and about to embark on his brief major-league career. With Cuba and Venezuela just having toppled dictators, the countries were in a state of patriotic fervor. This was reflected in the Series, both in the fabulous gates and in the agitation of the fans, who were inflamed by the usual nationalistic pageants involving flags, marching honor guards, and a proliferation of salable iconographic trinkets.

Rubén Gómez beat Orlando Peña, 2–1, in a tight first game. Peña's superb performance was a harbinger of things to come. He, Fowler, and Pascual mowed down the opposition. Peña himself shut out Santurce in their next meeting, while Cuba crushed Venezuela behind Fowler. Pascual beat Panama, 4–1, and Venezuela, 8–2. Cash, Mora, and García were belting the ball for Oriente, and Birrer was pitching well. But Venezuela just could not defeat Almendares, who won with a record of 5 and 1, while the home team finished a close second, at 4 and 2. There was bitterness in Caracas because of the embarrassing record in their individual series against Cuba over the years (3 and 19), and mostly because Venezuela was the only country yet to win the Series, although it was the largest.

The frustration finally boiled over in the final game, as Cuba led Venezuela one more time and by a wide margin. Pascual was pitching and tired in the eighth, when he gave up two runs (to the seven Cuba already had). Carreras did not want to take any chances, so he had his young ace Cuéllar, a left-hander who was meant to neutralize Cash, warming up in the bullpen. Listening to the game in Havana, I heard with indignation that the Venezuelan fans were pelting Peña and catcher Enrique (Hank) Izquierdo in left field and that a major brouhaha was brewing. The situation worsened when the Almendares players began to return some of the missiles thrown at them. Rocky Nelson remembers:

I'm on first base and I'm looking down there and I see that somebody threw a bottle on the field, 'cause they were behind. You know, down South, anyplace from Cuba on down, when your team is behind you are mad, the people are. So they threw a bottle out there. Pascual was winding up to pitch and I'm behind him going to left field. I just happened to be looking at them. And just as I get over there I tackled Izquierdo, who had the bottle ready to throw it back up there. I grabbed his arm and wrestled him down, and here is the other one arguing, the pitcher. Just as luck would have it a couple of the other players came over and helped me and we got him out of there. Well, now it really started. When the game was over—we won the game, 8–2—we are going through the ramp to get in the clubhouse and there are guys hitting us with anything they got. We came out of the ballpark and they brickbatted everything in again. And I says, "I'll never go down there again. That's it." We were lucky to get out alive both times.

As in Havana during the student demonstration, the Caracas police brutally clubbed everyone around, including photographers and umpires Rubén Sánchez and the unlucky Roberto Olivo, in the fray one more time. Nelson added that they were hastily paid the winners' share—in cash—and hustled to the airport for the return flight to Havana. The Series had been a spectacular success in financial terms, with attendance records set even before the second round of games began.

    That spring, unexpectedly, Cubans heard on the radio that the Cincinnati Reds and the Los Angeles Dodgers were coming to Havana to play three exhibition games over the weekend because there was bad weather in Florida. I, along with thousands of others, headed for the Gran Stadium, where a miracle had happened: The Reds and the Dodgers were on the field, warming up for their first game. This was my first glimpse at major-league teams in the flesh, and I was elated. Somehow I managed to get a seat in a box just to the right of the screen and was able to fumble through conversations with the likes of Don Newcombe, Dutch Dotterer, and Vada Pinson. It was during this game that Dick Gray, a former Cienfuegos infielder who belonged to the Dodgers, hit the foul ball that bounced off the screen and I caught amid a crowd of *barbudos*. The next day a militiaman offered to take the ball around both dugouts to have it signed by the teams. I gave it to him reluctantly, but he came back a few minutes later with the ball signed by Duke Snider, Sandy Koufax, Don Drysdale, Pee Wee Reese, and many Cincinnati Reds. The series was splendid, and that year the Dodgers won the pennant and the World Series. American and Cuban baseball seemed to be a means of consecrating the coming of a new age.

The celebration on January 6, when the Cuban League resumed play under the revolutionary regime, and the triumph of Almendares in the Caribbean Series, were but heralds of what would be the apotheosis and finale of Cuban professional baseball: the victory of the Cuban Sugar Kings in the Little World Series in October 1959, days before the beginning of the opening of the Cuban League season. Caracas' Stadium Universitario, site of the Almendares victory in the Caribbean Series was not the Gran Stadium, and absent from it was the protagonist and master of ceremonies for an upcoming October triumph: Fidel Castro. Before chronicling the declining seasons of the Cuban League, I will now turn to the Cuban Sugar Kings, the most paradoxical and ironic venture that joined baseball, Cuban nationalism, and capitalism, and that gave off a final flash before extinguishing itself.

The strongest effort to link Cuban professional baseball to organized baseball was the creation of the Cuban Sugar Kings of the Triple-A International League by Bobby Maduro. The Havana Cubans had been popular, but they were in Class B. The International League, as Maduro and his associates saw it, was but a step from the majors, and indeed the new team's slogan was "One more step and we get there." In the parlance of Cuban politics the Cubans, as they were known on the island, were a kind of *anexionismo,* a joining of the Union, as it were, not being subservient or opposed to it. The new team was, perhaps unwittingly (hence more deeply so) steeped in tradition. By being called the Cubans, it reached back to the original Cuban Giants and the succession of teams with that name all the way up to the New York Cubans. It was hoped, of course, that the team would tap into nationalistic sentiment, and the Cuban teams that competed in the by now legendary Amateur World Series of the forties were invoked in press releases; in fact two of the stars in those teams, Jiquí Moreno and Conrado Marrero, played for the new club. By becoming a farm team of the Cincinnati Reds, the Sugar Kings joined the major-league organization in which the great Luque had enjoyed his best years and that had signed Rafael Almeida and Armando Marsans, the first Cuban major-leaguers of the century. Cincinnati was known in Cuba as *el querido Cinci* (beloved Cinci).

Although other reasons may have played a part, the fact that Maduro went with Cincinnati and not the Washington Senators, which had been the parent club of the Havana Cubans, shows that his goal was eventually to obtain a major-league franchise for Cuba. Cambria worked for Washington and was unlikely to be interested in creating a major-league team in Havana. Washington needed Havana as a farm, whereas Cincinnati, with no tradition of having a minor-league team in Cuba, might work as a stepping-stone. Furthermore, the inescapable fact was that the Senators were a weak team, one of the worst in the American League. Cambria represented an old tie with Organized Baseball, and a controversial one at that. Maduro represented a new front and a modern Havana ready to compete for a new team with Los Angeles and San Francisco, which were further away from other major-league cities, even if within the United States. The International League would eventually produce, in Montreal and Toronto, two clubs that became major-league franchises.

But the International League offered more. First, it was, indeed, international, with three Canadian teams: the Montreal Royals, the Toronto Maple Leafs, and the Ottawa Athletics. Second, with the exception of Richmond, all teams were located in the northern part of the United States. Buffalo, Rochester, and Syracuse were in upstate New York. This was important if the new team fielded, as it did, a large number of Cuban blacks. The Havana Cubans had been forced to play only whites because of the Jim Crow policies of most cities in the Florida International League. The race issue may also have played a role in Maduro's move away from the Washington Senators, who, by 1954, had yet to officially field a black player, in spite of their many white Cuban players in the past. In Canada and in the three upstate New York cities, blacks would be no problem.

In addition, many players in this circuit were familiar to Cuban fans. Two teams in the International League had working agreements with major-league clubs that had ties to Cuba: Montreal with the Dodgers and Rochester with the Cardinals. Toronto and Buffalo, which were independent, used many players from the now nearly defunct Negro Leagues who were well liked in Cuba. When the Montreal Royals came to Havana they brought Cubans such as Edmundo Amorós and Humberto Fernández on their roster, as well as Americans such as Tom Lasorda and Rocky Nelson, who performed regularly in the city during the winter with Almendares. Rochester brought players such as Bill Virdon and Dick Rand, Cardinal prospects who played for Miguel Angel González's Habana Reds. Toronto had Héctor Rodríguez for a good many years, and Buffalo Panchón Herrera. The Maple Leafs also had Jim Bunning and Bob Shaw, who starred for Marianao. Later in the decade, when Miami joined the league, the Marlins brought to Cuba none other than Satchel Paige, who became a tormentor of the Sugar Kings, and Cuban (and Habana Red) Panchón Herrera. I had the privilege of watching Paige baffle the Cubans several times, usually in the seven-inning first game of a Sunday doubleheader. In a sense, the International League could be like a summer version of the Cuban League, only that all the fans would root for one common team, with no abatement in passion or attendance, as when Cienfuegos played Marianao. With a team representing Cuba one short step from the majors and competing against Canadians and Americans, the Gran Stadium could become, like La Tropical in the early forties, another shrine to reenact the torrid nuptials of nation and sports.

Maduro wanted to tap not only the Cuban market but also make Havana the spearhead of a well-coordinated Latin invasion of organized baseball. The Sugar Kings would gather stars from Latin American countries, assuming the role Havana had played through the century as the capital of Latin American baseball and the center of dissemination and development of the sport in the entire Caribbean basin. Like the New York Cubans earlier, the Sugar Kings became a refuge for Latin American players from Puerto Rico, Venezuela, Mexico, and Panama, mostly blacks not in the majors because of the quota system. Maduro probably felt that he could corner a market that would produce instant results in the International League. He succeeded, with the team almost reaching the playoffs in their first season (1954) and actually making them in their second (1955). There was a decline until 1959, when the Cubans won the Little World Series. But on the whole the team was efficient in producing Latin players.

In fact, the Cuban Sugar Kings became a developer of Cuban stars, taking some of the initiative away from Cambria and the Senators. The Sugar Kings produced or polished Latin major leaguers of varying accomplishments, such as Octavio Rojas, Leonardo Cárdenas, Orlando Peña, Miguel Cuéllar, Raúl Sánchez, Vicente Amor, José J. (Joe) Azcúe, Saturnino Escalera, Pompeyo Davalillo, Elio Chacón, Daniel Morejón, Rogelio (Borrego) Alvarez, Rodolfo Arias, Tony (Haitiano) González, Julio Bécquer, and Luis Arroyo. Mature black Latin stars of no interest to the majors, again because of the quota system, played for the Cubans. Some, such as Asdrúbal Baró, a talented outfielder, and Amado Ibáñez, a slick infielder who had been a Newark Eagle, were still in their prime or about to reach it. Another was Angel Scull, who was rejected by the Senators because they were not quite ready to break the color line, and bought by the Cubans in 1954 for their first season.[16] In addition there were glorious natives such as Marrero, Guerra, Noble, Formental, Roberto Ortiz, Patato Pascual, and others. There were Venezuelans Emilio Cueche, Camaleón García, Julián Ladera, Pompeyo Davalillo, and Carrao Bracho, as well as Panamanian Pat Scantlebury. Davalillo and Cueche became team stalwarts. Cueche was a superb pitcher who could hit with authority and play the outfield if needed. Davalillo, a diminutive infielder, could play everywhere with skill and intensity.

Perhaps because of its ethnic identity, the Sugar Kings did not produce American players of note. Catcher Dutch Dotterer, who played for Cienfuegos in the winter, had a modest major-league career. Some of the Americans who came through were typical Triple-A players who shuttled back and forth to the majors, such as Ray Coleman, Clint (The Hondo Hurricane) Hartung, Johnny Lipon, Saul Rogovin, Jesse Gonder, Lou Skizas, Ted Wieand, Paul Smith, Ken Raffensberger, Ray Shearer, Jim Pendleton, Brooks Lawrence, Howie Nunn, Hal Bevan, and Zack Monroe. There were occasional reports in Havana that Cincinnati Red recruits were reluctant to report to the Cubans, fearful of what they would find outside the United States. It is not surprising that young Americans with little education and no worldliness would balk at having to spend the summer in a country whose language and culture were foreign to them. But the Latin American identity of the Sugar Kings was worth the cost of this inconvenience if it produced revenues and showed Organized Baseball that Havana was a worthy major-league site.

Sometimes the exotic side of that identity was exploited by other International League teams and by the Sugar Kings themselves. For instance, the *Montreal Star* of Tuesday, May 25, 1954, reports, after the first game the Cubans played in Canada: "The Sugar Kings started five Cuban Negroes. They are showy and flashy with more than a delicate shade of the 'showboat' which is rather refreshing." The paper refers to the Sugar Kings routinely as "Cuba." In that inaugural journey to Montreal the Cubans brought to Delormier Downs José Peláez's *charanga* (a small Afro-Cuban ensemble), which the *Montreal Star* delightfully called their "conga band," and described thus: "The Sugar Kings brought along 11 musicians (?) who serenaded their heroes with gourds, maracas, jungle trumpets, Cuban woodblocks and jungle drums. They offered the rhythmic beat of some weird jungle dance when the Kings were at bat" (May 1954, undated clipping). In 1958, when the Sugar Kings played in Toronto, the Maple Leafs offered free cha-cha-cha lessons.

But the Cubans did not draw well at home, except the first couple of years. In 1954 they almost made the playoffs, but finished fifth, and in 1955 they did make them, but lost to Columbus and did not make the Little World Series. It seemed as if support could not be sustained through so many months of summer, and for all its appeal the International League was not as strong as the Cuban League, where the best from the minors gathered along with not a few major-leaguers. In addition, because the Sugar Kings were a farm of the Cincinnati Reds, a player who was doing well could be suddenly summoned, regardless of standings in the International League. For the same reason, one who was not doing well could not just be sent home, as in the winter. The demanding Cuban fan did not suffer gladly mediocre minor-league players. The Havana Cubans had banked on the charisma of stars from the Amateur League, but by the fifties the most promising players were plucked from the Juveniles, which were teams without the appeal of clubs such as Fortuna or Hershey. Fading former amateur stars such as Moreno and Marrero did not last long with the Sugar Kings, and by the end of the decade none of the glorious veterans was with the club.

Maduro's plan was comprehensive, however, and its failure was due to many factors, including, of course, the worsening political situation. But he helped to create the Cubanitos (Little Cubans), a Little League–like organization that enjoyed some success. There had been youth baseball in Cuba before, though not much, and even a branch of the Little League in Havana sponsored by one of the social clubs, but nothing as widespread and well run as the Cubanitos, which made mandatory a report from the player's school guaranteeing that he was in good academic standing. Finals were played at the Gran Stadium, and some teams traveled to the United States for exhibition games against teams in the Little League.

Maduro's efforts did not make the Cubans as popular as Habana or Almendares, even though the Sugar Kings were managed by figures of the stature and drawing power of Regino Otero, Manager of the Year in 1954, Tony Pacheco, Napoleón Reyes, Preston Gómez, and Tony Castaño. Gómez, one of Cambria's boys from the forties, led the team to win the International League playoffs and the Little World Series in 1959. This was the culmination not only of the Sugar Kings but also of professional baseball in Cuba, ironically presided over by the man who would be instrumental in its demise: Fidel Castro. The Series provoked a paroxysm of nationalist sentiment like none other in Cuba since the Amateur World Series of the forties (presided over by the man Castro had toppled, Fulgencio Batista). Sports, militarism, and nationalism coalesced in a moment of political frenzy when Cubans thought that Utopia was at hand. The game played in Paradise would be baseball (*pace* Bart Giammatti). The fall of Batista's regime seemed to many, even to an old fox such as Cambria, a propitious development for professional baseball in Cuba. He wrote in the *Times of Havana* of February 9, 1959: "The potential of baseball talent in Cuba is tremendous, and now that the political situation is getting settled, the boys will be able to devote more time to the game."[17]

The Cubans finished the 1959 International League season in third place, aided by a brilliant infield combination that included Cárdenas, Chacón, Davalillo, and Rojas, the hitting of Daniel Morejón and Tony González, and a raw rookie with shocking power, Borrego Alvarez. Defensive specialist Izquierdo was behind the plate. The other catcher, Jesse Gonder, was a left-handed power hitter. The leading pitchers were Wieand, Cuéllar, and Sánchez, with Arroyo in relief. Larry Novaks and Roy Shearer also played in the outfield. When Izquierdo caught, Davalillo sat, and one of the Cubans pitched, this team fielded a nine that was 100 percent Cuban. But the American players were well liked and considered very much a part of the club.

Buffalo won the pennant and Columbus was second, with Richmond fourth. Buffalo had Panchón Herrera, who had a tremendous season, winning the Triple Crown and being named Most Valuable Player. The Cubans beat Columbus, sweeping them in four, and later Richmond, which had beaten Buffalo. The Cubans defeated Richmond in six games, the last of which was at the Gran Stadium. *Revolución* of September 23 printed photos of Fidel Castro in the Cubans' locker room with winning pitcher Raúl Sánchez and catcher Enrique Izquierdo. The Maximum Leader also posed with Arroyo, Cuéllar, and Tony González, and with the losing Richmond pitcher, Bill Short, and his manager, Steve Souchock. The team would now travel to Minneapolis to face the Millers, winners of the American Association playoffs, for the Governor's Cup, or Little World Series.

In Minneapolis, the Cubans won the first game. The Millers were managed by Gene Mauch and had catcher Eddie Sadowsky, veteran infielders Herb Plews and Johnny Goryl, and pitcher Tracy Stallard. They had promising infielder Carl Yastrzemski at second and powerful outfielders Chuck Tanner, Lu Clinton, and Tommy Umphlett. The front-line pitchers were Tom Borland and Billy Muffett. All these players belonged to the Red Sox, with whom the Millers had a working agreement. This was a solid Triple-A team made up of veterans and prospects about to reach the majors.

The third game in Minneapolis, after the Millers won the second, was called on account of cold. It was then decided to play all the remaining five games in Havana because more cold weather was predicted. A great reception was planned, and Fidel Castro announced that he would throw out the ceremonial first pitch. *Revolución* of September 30 said that during the season the Cubans had begun to win after Fidel threw out the ceremonial first pitch on Agrarian Reform Day. So the Commander's pitch would be a good omen. George Trautman, Ed Doherty, president of the American Association, and Frank Shaughnessy, president of the International League, would all be present. The ceremonies began when Fidel Castro made a grand entrance from center field, walking with two or three aides. The throng applauded, yelling *"¡Que hable!"* (Speech!). But when handed the microphone the Maximum Leader said he had come to watch the game like any other fan and would not deliver a speech, that as the revolution had won in Cuba he was sure the Cubans could win the Little World Series. Thirty thousand gave him a standing ovation when he threw out the ceremonial first ball. The Cubans won in ten. It was a game that Fausto Miranda called one of the most dramatic ever played in Cuba. He intoned in *Revolución* of October 2, 1959: "How different from the baseball with fans frisked at the gates, or the afternoon when the students were clubbed on this very field." Carl Yastrzemski hit a homer in this game. Cárdenas made a circus catch at short and fed Chacón for a spectacular double play. Morejón robbed Robbins of a home run with a fantastic leap in left. The popular radio announcer Cuco Conde was so excited that he screamed over the air *"¡Coño, la cogió!"* (Goddamn it, he caught it!) and got himself suspended. When Shearer got the winning hit to right, the fans carried him on their shoulders in triumph. Fidel Castro exited through the same gate in center on board the jeep used to bring in the pitchers from the bullpen. Another game was witnessed by Fidel Castro and Camilo Cienfuegos from the Cubans' dugout, and in yet another, President Osvaldo Dorticós and

Commander Che Guevara watched from a box behind home plate. The Cubans won that game in the eleventh, with Davalillo scoring the winning run. In the decisive contest, on October 6, Morejón got a hit that sent Raúl Sánchez diving home with the winning run. The fans jumped onto the field and carried the players on their shoulders toward Fidel Castro's box. *Revolución*'s huge headline the next day read: CUBA CAMPEÓN (CUBA CHAMPIONS).

The Cuban Sugar Kings had—it cannot be forgotten—American players. So the nationalism expressed at that point was not necessarily anti-United States. It was in line with the early aspirations of the revolutionary regime: to perfect a political system, not to destroy it, and to continue to profit from Cuba's relationship with the United States. In a few months this would change drastically.

The 1959–60 championship of the Cuban League began right after the Sugar Kings' victory in the 1959 Little World Series. A cracker factory, Galletería Unica, put out a guide to the new season that prominently featured a picture of Fidel Castro pitching, clad in the uniform of the Barbudos (Bearded Ones), the tongue-in-cheek baseball team organized that year with members of the rebel army (sports director Guerra Matos was the catcher). Beards gave this team (which looked like a Cuban House of David) a carnivalesque air because they had been out of fashion for such a long time. The *Guía del fanático: 1959–1960* has the following caption under the picture of the leader in midwindup: "FIDEL CASTRO RUZ: star pitcher of our glorious Cuba Libre Club." The mock-heroic tone is quite in line with the atmosphere of jubilation, of patriotic ecstasy and renewal that predominated in Cuba at the time, and yet symbolic of the profound, multifaceted niche baseball has in the nation's psyche. During this first year of revolutionary rule the game would undergo major transformations, sealing them with various rituals of collective bonding.

Fidel Castro threw out the ceremonial first ball of the 1959–60 campaign, which had the magnates hoping for a reawakening of fan interest that would be reflected in the attendance. At the start, with Habana jumping ahead in the first couple of weeks, that seemed to be the case indeed: a rekindled Habana-Almendares rivalry appeared possible. But the illusion did not last long. Cienfuegos had the best season since the Santa Clara Leopards of 1923, racing to the pennant with a record of 48 wins and 24 loses for a .667 average. Their closest pursuer, Marianao, finished 12 games out of first place. Meanwhile, Almendares, which finished last, had the worst year ever, with a record 47 loses, which, with their 25 wins, gave them an embarrassing .347 percentage.

Most of the season leaders were Cienfuegos' Cuban players. Tony González won the batting title with a .310 average and Román Mejías led in hits with 79, whereas Panchón Herrera, back with Habana, led with 15 homers and 50 RBIs. Camilo Pascual and Raúl Sánchez, both Elephants, were the leading pitchers, the first winning 15 and the second, 12. Pascual had 13 complete games and the most strikeouts, with 163. He was at his peak.

Cienfuegos, in fact, had a formidable team made up for the most part of natives. The most successful import was first baseman George Altman, an imposing left-handed slugger of heroic dimensions who blasted 14 homers. Don Eaddy, a third baseman, and like Altman a Cub prospect, hit .256 with 6 homers. The catcher, Cincinnati Red hopeful Dutch Dotterer, smashed 5 with a meager average of .212. But Cienfuegos had Rojas and Ossie Alvarez at second, with brilliant new shortstop Leonardo Cárdenas. He was a slender, wiry type who hit 11 homers, and like Rojas played for the Cuban Sugar Kings in the summer. Both were bound for the majors. Alvarez was also in the majors with the Senators and about to move to Detroit. The Elephants also had in the wings infielder Hiraldo Sablón, who would be known in the major leagues as Chico Ruiz. In the outfield they had a fantastic trio of natives: González, winner of the batting title who also hit 10 home runs; Mejías, who finished at .281 with 5; and the new strongboy, Rogelio (Borrego [The Ram]) Alvarez, also a first baseman and a Cuban Sugar King with astounding power from the right side, who blasted 12 homers and hit .248. They also had Ultus Alvarez, who did not have a good season. Behind the plate Cienfuegos still had Noble, at the end of his career, and up-and-coming Azcúe, another Cincinnati Red catching prospect, who would actually have a better major-league career than Dotterer. The pitching, with Pascual, Ramos, and Sánchez, was superb, with Cincinnati rookie Ted Wieand lending some support, along with Cuban Héctor Maestri, just coming into his own. Many of these players were or would be Cuban Sugar Kings, which showed the extent of the Cincinnati Reds' investment in Cuba. Rojas, Cárdenas, Sánchez, Borrego Alvarez, González, Dotterer, Wieand, and Azcúe all played for the Cubans.

Almendares had up-and-coming Daniel Morejón, Jim Baxes in the infield, and Gordon Coleman at first, trying to fill Rocky Nelson's shoes. He did not. Orlando Peña was the pitching ace, with Miguel Cuéllar, who had a poor season. Tony Taylor, already a regular with the Cubs, was at second, with Willie Miranda at short. The pitching was a fiasco. The Blues tried veteran Phillie infielder Granny Hamner as a pitcher, but he failed, and Lasorda had to be sent back home because of his ineffectiveness. Jim (Mudcat) Grant, a hard-throwing Indian prospect, was inconsistent.

Miguel Angel had entrusted Habana's helm to veteran Fermín Guerra. The Reds had a left-handed pitcher named Jim Archer, who hurled 5 shutouts, and who played for Kansas City in 1961–62. They also had Tom Cheney, then a Cardinal, who went on to have a modest eight-year career in the majors, and veteran Warren Hacker, a righty. Other pitchers were Cuban veterans Fernando (Trompoloco) Rodríguez and Látigo Gutiérrez. The Lions had Marv Breeding, an infielder who later played for the Orioles;

Dick Gray, who belonged to the Cardinals at the moment and had played for Cienfuegos earlier; and veteran catcher Ray Katt, who also belonged to St. Louis. A still spry Héctor Rodríguez was at third, with Humberto Fernández settled at short. Habana's tight infield and good pitching gave them the early lead, until Cienfuegos came roaring past everybody with their sluggers and pitchers. The 1959–60 season was one of the home run, and Cienfuegos was the main contributor. The league set a record of 209, with Cienfuegos reaching the individual team record of 72. Borrego Alvarez hit three in a game against Habana on December 17, and Cárdenas did the same against Marianao on December 29. The purists complained that the fences at the Gran Stadium had been moved in, which they had, but still the Elephants had quite an array of sluggers, with Altman, González, the two Alvarezes, and the surprising Cárdenas.

Marianao had reliever Manuel Montejo, a right-hander who got into 12 games with Detroit in 1961 but who was in 40 games with Marianao in 1959–60. They still had Fornieles, who threw 5 shutouts. Right-hander Bobby Locke did well, but left before the season was over. The rest of the team was a by now familiar group of Cubans: Bécquer, Valdivielso, Miñoso, and Delís. Quintana and Baró had been traded to Habana, where they languished as reserves. Import Steve Demeter, a Detroit Tiger hopeful, did well at third but did not last in the majors. Al Spangler, in center for Drake, also performed ably, and did play in the majors for thirteen years. He was a good defensive outfielder and left-handed hitter.

What would be the last Caribbean Series of the first era (the tournament was revived later, with Mexico and the Dominican Republic in place of Cuba and Panama) was played in Panama, where Cienfuegos swept with six victories and no defeats, with a surprising home team coming in second, Puerto Rico third and Venezuela last with only one victory.[18] Pascual's performance was decisive one more time: He won two games again, including a masterful one-hit shutout of Puerto Rico. His overall record from 1956 to 1960 was six wins without a defeat, to make him the most successful pitcher in Caribbean Series history. The Caguas team that Pascual blanked, managed by Victor Pellot Power, was outstanding, with native major leaguers such as Felix Mantilla, Orlando Cepeda, José Pagán, Félix Torres, and Juan Pizarro, and Americans Ray Ripplemeyer, Earl Wilson, and George Brunet. Panama's team (Marlboro, instead of Chesterfield—Panamanian teams represented either rum or tobacco companies) boasted native stars Humberto Robinson and Héctor López, plus promising rookie Ruthford (Chico) Salmón. Slugger Jim Gentile and slick Cardinal infielder Lee Tate were among the American reinforcements whom Wilmer Shantz, again the manager, counted on. Venezuela was represented by a team called Rapiños, instead of the Central League champions, because of a players' strike. This team still had Camaleón García, Luis Aparicio and Julián Ladera in the native contingent, and Willie Davis, Billy Muffett, and Ken Aspromonte among the Americans. Sánchez, Ramos, and Peña won, Borrego

Alvarez hit two homers, and Cuba, with its nearly all-native Cienfuegos, ran away with the title. It was the seventh time in twelve Caribbean Series that Cuba had won, and the fifth in a row—a fitting ending to the island's participation in a tournament whose conception was the direct result of the pact its professional league had signed with Organized Baseball. With the Cuban Sugar Kings' victory in the Little World Series in October 1959, the 1960 Caribbean Series was the grand finale of the Cuban professional game. But the Cuban League had one more season left and the Sugar Kings' history a dramatic conclusion.

By the summer of 1960 the character of the new Cuban regime was changing from a nationalist political movement to remove a corrupt, illegitimate government and reinstate the 1940 Constitution, to a radical revolution involving takeovers of industries and a shrill anti-American policy. I am not one who believes that communism was Fidel Castro's goal all along. In 1960–61 Cuba was still a capitalist country undergoing fundamental reforms within a liberal democratic framework; but pressed by internal forces defending their interests and by a U.S. reaction that was not unusual, it was pushed toward the Soviet camp. The memory of earlier American interventions radicalized those in power, who were determined not to allow the history of 1933 to repeat itself. The most telling blow was the reduction of the "sugar quota"—the sugar bought by the United States at fixed prices—in retaliation for the takeover of American companies. Deteriorating relations between Cuba and the United States were reflected immediately in the world of baseball, the passion these intimate foes shared.

At a meeting in Buffalo in January 1960, the International League ominously granted its president, Frank J. Shaughnessy, the power to move franchises and alter the schedule. Toronto and the Sugar Kings cast the dissenting votes. Throughout the spring there were rumors that the Cubans would be moved before the season began, and in March a scheduled series between the Baltimore Orioles and the Cincinnati Reds was canceled. (It was reported that Oriole players Gus Triandos and Willie Tasby were concerned about their safety in Havana, and *Revolución* countered that they were afraid to return because they had left unpaid bills and pending "women problems" in Cuba from when they played in the Cuban League.) The season opened against Rochester, with Fidel Castro (who else?) throwing out the ceremonial first ball. But in early July, while the Cubans were on the road, Shaughnessy decided to relocate them to Jersey City for the "protection of the players." The reaction in Cuba was sharp, and the team manager, Tony Castaño, resigned, along with his coach Reinaldo Cordeiro. Napoleón Reyes took over the team and was bitterly criticized in Cuba. Defections by Raúl Sánchez, Orlando Peña, and others did not materialize, because of their fear of being banned from Organized Baseball. Echoing a line of José Martí, Fausto Miranda wrote in *Revolución* on July 9 that Cuba was "without a franchise but without a master."

Because of these and other developments, it was clear in the spring of 1960 that the next season of the Cuban League was in peril. By May the league was aware that there would be no dollars to pay the American players. Appraised of this, Che Guevara, minister of finance, summoned league officials to tell them that the government would see to it that dollars became available for the Americans—to no avail, given that Organized Baseball was ready to pull the rug out from under the Cuban League. Before Commissioner Ford Frick could take action, the league announced that it would not import American players. The newspaper *Revolución* reported on September 1 that Frick had "recommended" to the owners of major-league clubs not to allow their players to compete in the winter leagues of Cuba and the Dominican Republic. The latter, of course, was not yet a member of the Confederación del Caribe, and hence not under the protectorate of Organized Baseball. Frick was rattling his saber to bring into line the Cuban and Dominican leagues, which were pulling away from the control of Organized Baseball. Rumor had it that Frick was contemplating banning all Latin American players, including the Cubans, from performing in Havana. The paper went on to say that at least ten American players had expressed their willingness to play in Cuba, and that the Cubans felt the same, even Orestes Miñoso, who was their leading star and president of the Association of Cuban Professional Baseball Players. The paper likened Frick's "aggression against" Cuban baseball to that of Shaughnessy's when he took the Cuban Sugar Kings out of Havana.

The lines were drawn. Fausto Miranda, writing for *Revolución* on September 9, 1960, declared that a championship with only Cuban players would be a great one because, in any event, not all the Americans who had come to Cuba were like "Max Lanier, Jim Bunning or Forrest Jacobs. . . . There was a large number of drunkards and malingerers who had to be sent back home in midseason." The all-Cuban season, of course, breached the pact in the sense that the Cuban League was not just allowed but also committed to use American players for development. The threat to Organized Baseball became even more imminent when plans were made to have Cuban League teams play in Venezuela. There was a meeting of the Confederación del Caribe every June in the country hosting the Caribbean Series the next year. In 1960 this meeting took place in Havana, and it was decided that the Cuban League teams would play games against teams in the Liga de Zulia (Maracaibo) and the Liga Central (Caracas). Each of the four Cuban clubs would play Thursday and Friday in one, and Saturday and Sunday in the other. Games and statistics would count in the Cuban League. The main reason for this was to allow the Cuban players to leave behind in Venezuela the money they earned there, which they could later draw from other countries, something they could not do any longer with what they earned in Havana. But this commingling of the Cuban League with the two Venezuelan Leagues was also a hint that an independent pan-Caribbean league could be established. The revolution could spread and the menace could become worse than the one that had been posed by the Mexican League, which led to the organization of the Confederación del Caribe and the signing of the pact. Frick stoked the fire by declaring that Puerto Rican players, who were, after all, American citizens, should not travel to Havana if the Caribbean Series were held there as scheduled. *Revolución* countered that, if asked, the Puerto Ricans would come because they surely felt more like Puerto Ricans than Americans.

But for all its defiance, the Cuban League faced serious difficulties. One was that CMQ, the leading television station, could not afford to put up the $240,000 for broadcasting rights that it had promised. A settlement altering the schedule of payments had to be reached just before the start of the season. This did not solve the problem because the government took over CMQ in October, and the new man in charge (an old Communist) was adamant about not paying anything to the Cuban League. But when the jovial director of sports, Captain Felipe Guerra Matos (a *barbudo*), intervened on orders from Fidel Castro, who wanted the season played as scheduled, the matter was solved at once. Another problem was that if only Cuban players were used, then the teams would have to be shuffled somewhat to attain parity and ensure reasonable competition. To make matters worse, the strongest teams were Marianao and Cienfuegos, which, in spite of recent successes, did not have the drawing power of Habana and Almendares. Cienfuegos had by far the best array of native players, with which it had won the previous year. Habana, probably because of Miguel Angel González's increased dependence on the Cardinals, seemed to be the weakest. Ticket prices were reduced to 60 cents for general admission, plus 5 cents for the Players' Association, with ladies paying 40 cents. As a result of all this, players' salaries had to be cut 25 percent. Equipment was another dilemma, now that it was not readily available from the United States. It was decreed that balls that went into the stands would have to be returned. The legendary ballboy Bicicleta would have a field day cajoling the fans into giving up their souvenirs. Narciso Camejo, the last president of the Cuban League, told me that this championship was played with the baseballs left over from the previous one.

The season proved that Cuba had more than enough native players to stock the four clubs and that the American imports were not really needed to keep up the quality of play. Indeed, the successful championship unmasked the greed behind the pact with Organized Baseball. It became clear that the pact benefited Organized Baseball and the owners of Cuban teams, who expected greater revenues with the performance of budding American stars. But it was certainly not beneficial for Cuban players. When squeezed by Organized Baseball, the Cuban League joined in the nationalist clamor that was sweeping the country and retaliated. It boasted before opening day that it had enough natives from the majors to offer a quality season. The players listed as major-leaguers by *Revolución* were: José Azcúe (Cincinnati), Orestes Miñoso (White Sox), Pedro Ramos (Senators), Miguel de la Hoz (Indians), Edmundo Amorós (Detroit), Humberto Fernández (Detroit), Miguel Fornieles (Boston), Camilo Pascual (Senators), Panchón Herrera (Phillies), Tony Taylor (Phillies), Leonardo Cárdenas (Cincinnati), Eduardo Bauta (Cardinals), Julio Bécquer (Senators), José Valdivielso (Senators), Tony González (Phillies), and Zoilo Versalles (Senators). But it was not just these major-leaguers who ensured the high caliber of play, but also the availability of many other players just about to reach the majors or who had been there in the recent past. Cuba was teeming with professional baseball players with various levels of accomplishment and experience, not to mention quite a few with marquee value, even if not in the majors. In fact, in the summer of 1959, Kansas City Athletics outfielder Whitey Herzog, playing against the Senators, hit into an all-Cuban triple play: He lined to Ramos on the mound, who fired to Bécquer at first, who nailed the man there and threw to Valdivielso at short, who tagged out the lead runner.[19]

One hundred professional Cubans from all ranks of Organized Baseball showed up at the Gran Stadium to try out for the four teams. It was the first time in years that they had a real chance of making one of them. There were many players from the highest minor-league classifications. For instance, there was Marianao catcher René Friol, a member of the Dodgers' organization, who was playing for St. Paul in the American Association. Lázaro Terry, a Habana infielder, was in the same league, with Indianapolis. Roberto (Musulungo) Gutiérrez, the Habana catcher, was with Columbus, in the International League. Many came from the Pacific Coast League, such as Héctor Rodríguez, and from Mexico, such as Carlos Paula, Jiquí Moreno, Asdrúbal Baró, and Juan Delís. Ultus Alvarez and Gonzalo Naranjo were with Nashville in the Southern Association, and so forth.

Given the opportunity, some players reached levels that propelled them to the majors or into regular positions there, such as Leonardo Cárdenas, who hit 8 homers and finished with a .302 average; Azcúe, who hit .290 with 6 homers; and Hiraldo Sablón, Cienfuegos' third-baseman who hit .274. José Tartabull became a Marianao regular and soon made the majors. Rookies who did very well included Luis Tiant, son of the great left-hander of yore, who had been playing in Mexico. Then a hard thrower, he won 12 that winter in Havana but led the Cuban League in walks with 90. Diego Seguí was another right-handed pitcher who came of age in the 1960–61 winter, as did outfielders Hilario (Sandy) Valdespino and Leopoldo (Leo) Posada. Miguel Angel had both men on his Habana club, having seen something in them (*Bohemia*, October 30, 1960). Musulungo Gutiérrez, his young catcher, also showed promise, though he did not reach the majors. Miguel Angel González talked enthusiastically about a Marianao rookie flamethrower called Roberto (Habichuela) Gómez. In that same interview he expressed the hope that the demanding Cuban fans not be too harsh on the rookies, a severe problem in the past.

Jiquí Moreno, the former amateur star hurler and former Senator, had a fantastic season with Habana. His superb performance also highlighted the fact that by importing Americans, Cuban veterans lost their right to wind down their careers in their own country. Many had been going to the Dominican Republic and Nicaragua, where new, less demanding winter leagues had been organized in the recent past. With all-Cuban teams Agapito Mayor, for instance, could have pitched longer, and Claro Duany and Chiquitín Cabrera could have played a few more years. Formental, too, had been forced to emigrate to Venezuela, where he hit .300, and later to the Dominican Republic. They had been replaced by Americans, many of whom were uncertain prospects, but investments for major-league organizations, while the Cuban players past their prime were not.

To shore up Habana, the Reds were given Daniel Morejón, Eduardo Bauta, and old Rafael Noble as reinforcements, and Rojas was sent to the Reds in exchange for two rookies. They still had Panchón Herrera, Héctor Rodríguez, and Humberto Fernández, with Valdespino and Oscar Sardiñas in the outfield, along with Morejón and center fielder Pedro Cardenal, a great leadoff hitter. Musulungo developed when Noble was injured, and manager Fermín Guerra came out of the blocks ahead of the pack with his Lions. This Red team battled until the end and finished only three games behind the winner. The sentimental favorite was Moreno, while Rojas became a star, compared with Almendares' Taylor as the best second basemen in Cuba, and the best in a long time, going all the way back to Bienvenido (Patajorobá) Jiménez and Euscbio (Papo) González. Both Rojas and Taylor excelled in the majors.

José María Fernández was finally named manager of Marianao, partly because of the resentment against Napoleón Reyes, who had agreed to manage the Cuban Sugar Kings when they went to Jersey City and thus went out of favor. Napoleón was also censured by the Cuban Players' Association. The Tigers finished last, but only four games out. Rookies Lorenzo Fernández and Zoilo Versalles made the team and got a chance to play when Valdivielso had to have an appendectomy. Bécquer had his best season in the Cuban League and Fornieles was masterful, with Montejo as an effective reliever backing him up.

Managed by Regino Otero, Almendares fought literally to the last game. Amorós had a great season at first base, his old position in the Juveniles. They had a strong staff led by Orlando Peña and Miguel Cuéllar, with Gonzalo Naranjo and Andrés Ayón. Miguel de la Hoz continued to show class, particularly on defense, Paula supplied the power, and Scull added hitting and defense in center. Taylor starred at second and Humberto Fernández at short. Enrique Izquierdo, one of the best defensive catchers Cuba ever produced, was behind the plate, backed up by brilliant newcomer Orlando McFarlane, who would reach the majors with the Pirates.

Cienfuegos, still managed by Tony Castaño, won again with virtually the same roster that had captured the championship and the Caribbean Series the season before. The batting champion was Habana's Octavio

Rojas, who finished at .322. The Elephants had been able to give him up because they had an embarrassment of riches in the infield with Ossie Alvarez, Hiraldo Sablón, and Leonardo Cárdenas. Pascual did not pitch much because of a sore arm. But Pedro Ramos was 16 and 7, with 17 complete games. The ERA champion was the surprising Moreno (Habana) at 2.03, though Ramos' was 2.04. Julio Bécquer led in homers with 15 and in RBIs with 50, while Rojas also led in hits, with 85. It was a hotly contested championship, with Cienfuegos prevailing over Almendares in the last game of the season, and of the Cuban League's history. Only four games separated the Elephants from the fourth-place Tigers.

In spite of the quality of play and the excitement of the race, attendance did not improve (René Molina, *Revolución*, December 14, 1960). As part of a campaign begun by the government to include the provinces in all aspects of Cuban life, but also as a result of the low revenues, games were played in cities other than Havana. Habana and Marianao, for example, inaugurated a stadium in Remedios, Las Villas Province, on Saturday, December 17. On January 7, Almendares and Cienfuegos played in Cienfuegos. Games were played at Matanzas' "historic" Palmar del Junco. Much enthusiasm was generated, but in view of what followed, it was futile. The country seemed too distracted by politics to pay much attention to baseball, and the exile of many of the people who used to attend the games in the capital did not help either. Narciso Camejo says that only twenty-nine people paid to see one game. He often had to send for schoolchildren, prison inmates, and senior citizens from old people's homes to fill some seats. There was also considerable government interference. Once a Sunday doubleheader, already in progress, was suspended by government decree because Che Guevara was about to speak on television. An announcement had to be read over the loudspeakers and the ongoing game stopped.

The championship was decided on February 8, the last day of the season, when Cienfuegos and Almendares played their regularly scheduled game, with the teams tied for first. Pedro Ramos defeated the Blues, 8–0, to complete a fantastic campaign. He also cracked a homer into the right-field stands, where future writer Jesús Díaz almost caught the ball (or so he told me). The Cuban League, nearly a hundred years old—redolent with a history of epic deeds that reached back to old Almendares Park—went with a whimper, not a bang, but endures in the minds of those who cherish it as part of their treasure of childhood memories. No ceremonies were held to mark its passing, and the veterans' games held for years in Miami and New Jersey to reenact its past glory cannot capture its flavor, so far from Cuba and so far removed in time.

The Caribbean Series, slated for February 10, was, of course, canceled, as the other countries were not quite ready to break with Organized Baseball. It was relatively easy not to play it because no country other than Cuba would be unduly affected. Had the Series been programmed for any of the other three countries it would have constituted a more serious loss in revenues and in investments made in preparations. A new era of the Caribbean Series would begin in 1970, but without Cuba it could not be the same, even though a strong Dominican Republic had replaced Panama and the Mexican Pacific Winter League was added, oblivious to geography. In March 1961, at the regularly scheduled meeting of the Cuban League— its last—Narciso Camejo was again elected president. He requested and was granted an indefinite leave and fled Cuba. Miguel Angel González was named provisional president. Presumably he held the office until his death, in Havana, on February 19, 1977.

For many players, the collapse of the Cuban League had tragic consequences. The diaspora began. Amorós, for instance, returned to Cuba broke, and could not leave for many years, during which he became an alcoholic and eventually a diabetic. When he did leave, the Dodgers put him on their roster for the few days he needed for his pension. He died in Miami after years of loneliness and neglect. The brilliant Habana center fielder Pedro Cardenal finished his career in Mexico, where he was killed in a crash. Many had to leave behind close relatives whom they would never see again, or only sporadically and after heroic measures. Others suffered great financial blows. Humberto Fernández, who had built an apartment house for his parents, lost it to urban reform laws. Many players, most from humble backgrounds and not a few colored, had to leave all their property behind to continue their careers in the United States and elsewhere. Borrego Alvarez hesitated too long about leaving, and he missed a chance to make it with the new Senators. Many saw with anguish the relentless clock of athletic vitality tick away their only source of income. Others, who did make it, such as Tony Oliva, did not look forward to the end of the major-league seasons because they had no home to return to. Adjusting to not having a country to return to was harsh on these men. It must have affected their performance on the field. A good number had the fortune of being able to play in Mexico, Venezuela, the Dominican Republic, Nicaragua, and Puerto Rico during the winter. But it was not the same, and it would never be again. The clock had struck the final hour.

As if to make its knell more lugubrious, definitive, and historic, Agustín (Tinti) Molina passed away in Havana on February 10, 1961, a mere two days after the last game of the Cuban League. Molina had begun playing in his native Key West when the War of Independence was being organized, and had been a key performer, manager, and entrepreneur, both in Cuba and in the United States, where he ran the Cuban Stars (West) in the fledgling Negro Leagues. It was as if the Cuban League was buried with him.

1 2 3 4 5 6 7 8 9 R H E

Baseball and Revolution

There has never been a case in which a head of state has been involved so prominently and for such a long period in a nation's favored sport as Fidel Castro has been with baseball in Cuba. So many controversies have surrounded the Cuban Revolution that few have taken notice or given serious thought to this phenomenon. To many, I suppose, it is a slightly humorous topic, frivolous by comparison to many painful ones concerning Cuba. To others, perhaps, it is evidence of the Maximum Leader's youthful, unaffected spirit. But because of the historical depth and relevance of baseball in Cuban culture and history, the commander in chief's relationship to the national sport is no trivial matter. Fidel Castro's role in the sport during the revolutionary period is necessarily an important subject. In a sense it defines baseball in Cuba from 1959 until today, a span as long as the era from the turn of the century to the Amateur World Series and the revival of the Cuban League in the early forties.

Given the inordinate length of Fidel Castro's tenure in power, it is impossible to find even a close second in this aspect of his performance, and only the most ludicrous hypothetical comparisons come to mind. It is, for instance, as if Franco had been deeply and visibly committed to the fate of bullfighting in Spain throughout his long rule and donned the *traje de luces* once in a while to try a few passes. I am not aware if Perón attended soccer matches in Argentina, or if Pérez Jiménez followed the fates of the Venezuelan Olympic teams. Somoza did take over the reigns of the Nicaraguan national team in an Amateur World Series being held in Managua, but the popularity of the sport in that country cannot compare to Cuba's, and Somoza was not in power as long as Fidel Castro. Moreover, neither soccer in Argentina, Olympic sports in Venezuela nor baseball in Nicaragua have developed in relation to a nearby political and cultural power such as the United States and an institution like Organized Baseball. The Maximum Leader's sports craze is itself a product of U.S. influence, unimaginable in less modern Latin American countries, tied to Spanish or European images of political deportment.

One thing appears to be clear: Cuban national, cultural, and political identities can only be carved out of their involvement with the United States. All the paeans to the Soviet Union in the recent past, to the sister countries of the Communist block, to the Third World, and to Latin America were largely propaganda. They never truly reflected the people's feelings. The focus of Cuba's attention is the mighty neighbor to the north, where one-tenth of its population has wound up in spite of punitive travel restrictions. The process through which national and political identity are defined on the island is a complex mixture of admiration for and rejection of the United States. Modern Cuba's identity was forged in the second half of the nineteenth century, just as baseball was being incorporated into the future country's culture. Baseball was present at the birth of the nation. A Cuba conceived during the sports-minded belle époque had to include play, physical prowess, and the arts as essential components of nationhood. It is for all these reasons that the commander in chief wears not only his olive green military hat but symbolically a baseball cap as well. He embodies the nation, and with it the martial yet ludic physical spirit of sport. The interlocking order of a game's rules projects a sense of stability as a method of shaping future events. A manager calling for a steal to stay out of a double play is like a general planning a battle. The implication of military leaders in sports earlier in Cuban history, from Machado to Batista, were only harbingers of what would come after 1959.

Fidel Castro's involvement in the last gasps of professional baseball were related earlier, as well as his performance with the Barbudos team in whose uniform he appeared in well-publicized pictures. But this was nothing compared to his participation in the game later. He has been invariably present to throw out the ceremonial first pitch in national competition and in international contests held in Cuba. But sometimes this was not enough. *Cuba Internacional* (March 1965) reported that the final game of the National Series drew 32,470 fans to the Stadium Latinoamericano—as the Gran Stadium was now called—and that the first pitch was thrown by Germán Lairet, representative in Cuba of the Venezuelan Liberation Forces (the regime was promoting revolution in the rest of Latin America then), whereupon Fidel Castro took the mound and pitched to the first batter of the game! It was not reported if the at-bat counted or if the Maximum Leader got into the books with his performance. Pedro Chávez, an early star of post-1959 baseball, reminisced in 1984 about how Fidel Castro would stay after games of the National Series to play a few innings with the guys, something they deeply appreciated (*Bohemia*, October 12). In August 1964 *Cuba Internacional* ran a graphic report on Fidel Castro's participation, as pitcher, in two games, one at Latinoamericano. In Camagüey he pitched for that province's team against Pinar del Río's, not allowing a hit for seven innings (were the hitters *really* trying?). After the game he sat on the grass with the players to lecture them on the regime's plans for sports. This paternalistic supervision and participation was also demonstrated by rewards from the *Comandante* after a great performance, or words of praise and encouragement as a team left for or returned from international play.

I find most Americans incredulous when I tell them that baseball is Cuba's *national* game. Those who know something about baseball are aware that the game is popular in Cuba, but the idea of holding in common the national game with a country with which the United States broke diplomatic relations years ago seems bizarre. It is like sharing intimate family habits and rituals with a stranger. How can two countries jointly hold something that is part of the unique essence of nationhood? Again, how can a game define a nation? How can the national game of the threatening imperial power also define the Cuban nation? This contradiction did not escape everyone in Cuba at the beginning of the revolution, and indeed some measures were taken to increase the country's commitment to soccer. But this did not succeed. Soccer had been rejected in the thirties in a fit of xenophobia against Spaniards, still viewed by Cubans as backward and out of step with the modern. Baseball was Cuban because it was modern and because it was shared with the Americans, not with the crass Spaniards.

To the revolutionaries the notion of beating the United States at its own game became a cherished dream, even if it meant perpetuating an undeniable American influence.[1] To common people the game was too deeply ingrained in everything a boy learned as soon as he was able to socialize and satisfy the need to play, to be easily abandoned. Memories of past games, even local or provincial, were too profound and could not be erased. So the decision had to be made very soon after 1959 to continue Cuba's commitment to baseball. It was in fact expanded to bring about something that many Cubans seemed to have wanted for a long time: a national championship that involved all regions of the island and that also broke down the racial apartheid of amateur baseball. To tie all this to the forging of a new sense of national identity, invested in the revolutionary government and its leaders, was a consciously followed plan that met with great success in many areas, but not without the same cost to human freedom and individual self-determination as in all other aspects of Cuban life.

To reshape baseball was a difficult task because the edifice of tradition had to be demolished and carefully rebuilt. In 1959, Cuban baseball memory reached back to the turn of the century and included mostly revered figures who had shined in the professional ranks, except for the few whites whose major exploits had come in the Amateur League. Méndez, Torriente, Dihigo, Salazar, Tiant, Luque, Miguel Angel González, Bragaña, Silvio García, Chacón, Mayor, and Miñoso were associated with Habana, Almendares, Cienfuegos, Marianao, Santa Clara, and Fe, all the great teams in the Cuban League. Older fans could still remember the Cuban Stars—both editions—and their legendary journeys through American independent baseball. Younger ones cherished Miñoso's triumphs with the Cleveland Indians and the Chicago White Sox, and all savored Amorós' decisive catch in the 1955 World Series, which brought victory to the beloved Brooklyn Dodgers, who had trained often in Cuba. It was easy to dismiss and deride the history of the Cuban Republic, but it was hard to erase these deep-seated memories, filled with pleasure, attached to longings for the innocence of childhood, and intertwined with one's link to family traditions. Many Cubans had in their heads a better idea of baseball's chronology than of Cuba's history.[2]

When Almendares and Cienfuegos played the final game of the 1960–61 season it was obvious to people running the Cuban League that there would not be a championship the next year. I do not think that anyone thought that professional baseball as it was known in Cuba was finished for good. As with everything else, changes appeared to be provisional, soon to be reversed when the new regime collapsed or was forced to correct its policies drastically. The revolutionaries were improvising under pressure. Most of those (of us) who left early believed that normalcy would return in the not too distant future, and with it Habana, Almendares, Cienfuegos, and Marianao. But the revolutionary leaders had other plans, and in February 1961 the INDER (Instituto Nacional de Deportes Educación Física y Recreación) was created. In March it decreed the abolition of professional baseball, and plans to hold a national amateur championship were laid out. By pure chance, an Amateur World Series was slated for Costa Rica in April 1961. This was to be number XV for this event, though none had taken place since 1953, and the tournament had long lost the prestige it had in the forties. The Cuban Olympic Committee, headed by Manuel González Guerra, hastily organized massive tryouts, out of which a powerful team emerged. It plowed through the competition in San José at the same time as the revolutionary forces were repulsing the Bay of Pigs invasion back home. The connections between the two victories were not lost, and the bond between baseball and the defense of the motherland was strengthened. The idea of rewriting Cuban baseball history by connecting the present to the glory years of the Amateur League and the World Series held at La Tropical began to take shape. But if professional baseball was finished in Cuba, certainly not professional baseball played by Cubans.

⊖

Paradoxically, even though after 1961 the legal flow of Cuban players to Organized Baseball was cut, there were more Cuban stars and greater achievements by Cubans in the majors after 1959 than ever before. In the sixties, Calvin Griffith's and Joe Cambria's dream of fielding a winning team stocked with Cuban players finally came to fruition. In 1965, at long last, the Senators won a pennant led by Cuban stars, only they did so as the Minnesota Twins, with Tony Oliva, Zoilo Versalles, Camilo Pascual, and Hilario (Sandy) Valdespino on their roster. Pascual had become one of the premier pitchers in the majors, and Versalles won the Most Valuable Player award that year. Pascual, Versalles, and Oliva were bona fide stars. Oliva won a Rookie of the Year award and three batting titles in his career. He was the first Cuban batting champion in the majors—indeed, the only one so far. Versalles, an aggressive, inspirational player, became one of the best shortstops in all of baseball; he was a good fielder who could hit with power.

The diaspora that began as the curtain came down on the Cuban League in February 1961 included many players on major-league rosters as well as others who were about to make them. Players who had begun their careers in the fifties enjoyed good seasons in the sixties and seventies. Tony (El Haitiano) González had a few good years with the Phillies and the Braves. Francisco (Panchón) Herrera did not quite live up to his promise with the Phillies, but had a few bright moments. Orlando Peña became a notable reliever for several teams, and Miguel (Mike) Cuéllar turned into one of the dominant lefties of the seventies and the cowinner of a Cy Young Award in 1969, the only one ever by a Cuban. An early defector from a Cuban national team, Dagoberto Campaneris (*né* Campanería), became one of the greatest base stealers in the majors while playing for the Oakland A's. He was one of the best shortstops in recent years, and performed memorably in the World Series. Marcelino López, a strapping black lefty who also left Cuba in the sixties, had some good seasons for the Phillies and other clubs. And Atanasio (Tony) Pérez, first baseman for the Cincinnati Big Red Machine of the seventies, made several all-star teams and is considered by many to have had a Hall of Fame career. Meanwhile, Luis Tiant, following in the footsteps of his famous father and going far beyond him, reached stardom with the Indians, Red Sox, and Yankees, and pitched some unforgettable World Series games.

There were quite a few other Cuban players with notable careers in the seventies, eighties, and nineties. Two, Hiraldo Sablón Ruiz (Chico Ruiz), a reserve infielder with Cincinnati and other clubs, and Minervino (Minnie) Rojas, a very good reliever with the Angels, were involved in terrible automobile accidents. Ruiz was killed and Rojas was paralyzed. Both had enjoyed good years, with Ruiz becoming one of the most effective pinch hitters in the business. José J. (Joe) Azcúe caught with distinction for the Cleveland Indians, as did Paulino (Paul) Casanova for the Pirates and the new Senators. A native of Banagüises, Casanova was another Matanzas-area product. Octavio (Cookie) Rojas had an outstanding career as an all-around player for the Phillies and other teams, and managed the Angels in 1988. He was the third Cuban to manage in the majors. Miguel Angel González had managed the Cardinals in 1938 and 1940, and Preston Gómez, one of Cambria's signees in the forties, managed the Padres, Astros, and the Cubs in the sixties, seventies, and early eighties. The fourth was Tony Pérez, who managed the Cincinnati Reds all too briefly in 1993.

Camilo Pascual was the last Cuban star to record great performances in both the majors and the Cuban League. He pitched last for the Indians in 1971, having completed a magnificent career that would have yielded even better statistics if he had not spent most of it with the lowly Washington Senators. He told me in Miami that his best season was 1959, when he won 17 for the Senators, not his 20-game seasons (1962 and 1963) with the Twins, which were a much better team. Winning for the Senators in the fifties was an achievement. Miñoso was really through by 1964; his plate appearances in 1976 and 1980 were gimmicks. The major-league stars of the post-1959 era were Oliva, Pérez, and Tiant. Only Tiant had a season in the Cuban League; the others never played in it. Yet these three, and younger stars of the eighties and nineties, José Canseco and Rafael Palmeiro, had better verifiable records than any Cuban player before, including the biggest names, such as Méndez, Torriente, Luque, Dihigo, and Miñoso.

Tony Oliva was one of Cambria's last finds. He was born Pedro Oliva, but only managed to get out of Cuba using a brother's passport, becoming forever Tony. A tall, lanky, left-handed hitter from Pinar del Río, in western Cuba, Oliva hit out of a crouch reminiscent of Stan Musial. Like him, Oliva was a deadly line-drive hitter who hit to all fields with power. He finished with 220 home runs, 34 more than Miñoso. After burning up minor-league pitching, Oliva joined the Twins in 1964 and led the American League in batting with a .323 average, hits (217), runs (109), and doubles (43). He also clouted 32 home runs and was named Rookie of the Year. He won the batting title again the next year, with a .321 average, and a third one in 1971, with a .337 mark. Were Torriente, Dihigo, or Silvio García as good batters? There is no reason to doubt that they could have been, but there are no records to prove it. Before his time, Oliva's only competition among the Cubans was Miñoso, and he bested him in every important category, including fielding (Oliva won a Gold Glove in 1966), except stolen bases and charisma. Oliva was not a flamboyant speedster like Miñoso and did not go for big cars. But his greatest lack was a country to revel in his glory and an adoring Cuban public to promote his virtues. One can only imagine what a prerevolutionary Cuba would have made of a three-time major-league batting champion. Though a respected and admired player in the United States, Oliva was not an American, and, given his quiet demeanor, did not fit or play up to any of the stereotypes of a Latin player, as others, such as Tiant, did.

Another demure star was Tony Pérez. Until Canseco, Pérez was the greatest Cuban home-run hitter in the history of the majors. He was the first Cuban to reach 40 homers in a season, and he finished with 379. Canseco has reached 40 three times, hit 46 in 1998, and has surpassed Pérez's total. But where Pérez is unreachable is in the RBI department, where his 1,652 is a Hall of Fame figure. Canseco has had several outstanding seasons in this category and could conceivably catch Pérez, but it is unlikely. Pérez was a steady, reliable performer, with a good glove at third and first, and a team player. Like Oliva, he was missing a country to celebrate him, though he did make a home in Puerto Rico, where he played ten seasons in winter competition. Was he better than the "Inmortal" Dihigo at the plate? Pérez finished with a lifetime average in the high .270s. Dihigo hit .311 in eleven seasons in the Mexican League, with 55 homers. Pérez hit far more homers, and all of them against major-league competition. But because he excelled before Cuban fans in Cuba, Dihigo will forever enjoy a higher place in Cuban baseball lore, and many if not most Cubans on the island have never heard of Pérez. It is also true that Dihigo was, in addition, an outstanding pitcher, perhaps his best position.

Luis Tiant managed to get in one season, the last, in the Cuban League, where he was outstanding. But he quickly left for Mexico, where he picked up where he had left off, married, and was probably going to settle there, as had so many black Cuban players in the past. But he was signed by the Cleveland Indians and went on to have a tremendous career in the majors. Older Cubans would always compare Tiant to his father, but they were completely different pitchers. The older Tiant was a slender left-hander with some speed and much guile and control, not to mention an uncannily deceptive pickoff move. It is not true that he had a bizarre pitching motion that his son may have copied or inherited. Young Tiant was born too late to see his father play. The younger Tiant was a stocky, fire-balling right-hander until he hurt his arm. He then became the sneaky, head-jerking, and twisting hurler notorious for his craftiness. Tiant had superb years as both kinds of pitcher, though he will always be remembered as the eccentric kind. He won twenty or more games four times, the only Cuban to do so, and he is the only Cuban pitcher to have won more than 200 games in the majors (229). He had memorable performances in the 1975 World Series pitching for the Red Sox. Was Tiant a better pitcher than his father, or better than Dihigo, Bragaña, or Marrero? Because of the anomalies, the comparison is not possible. Marrero did not reach the majors until he was in his forties, and old Tiant, Dihigo, and Bragaña starred in the Negro Leagues, Mexico, and Cuba. Tiant's real competition among contemporary Cubans is Pascual, who won fewer games (174), but pitched for lesser teams. Having seen them both perform and studied their records,

I believe that Pascual was the better of the two. Was Luque better? Probably. The Pride of Havana won 194 major-league games.

Of these postrevolutionary stars, Tiant was the one to acquire the most fame. Pascual and Oliva had very brief postseason exposure, compared to Pérez and Tiant. The two Twins played in a small market, away from media centers such as Boston and New York, where Tiant performed. But in addition, Tiant played up to some of the stereotypes of a Latin player and wound up with the ridiculous moniker of El Tiante in pig Spanish. He was often pictured smoking a postgame cigar, and much was made of his age, a common source of mirth in the media concerning Latin and black players, who often play longer because there are seldom jobs awaiting them in baseball or other fields. Oliva has had a long career managing in Mexico, and Tiant has recently been hired by the Dodgers as a roving pitching coach. Some Cuban players opened baseball academies in the Miami area.[3] Be that as it may, the figure of a very black Tiant sunk in a whirlpool of very white foam with a huge stogie sticking out of his smiling face became a cliché that carried into an inane biography of his published under the inevitable title *El Tiante*.

These players, who had every right to enter Cuban baseball lore, missed out. Few fans with living memories of the greats from yesteryear were able to see them in action to make comparisons and thereby to enshrine them in the constant debate that makes up baseball oral history. There was no Cuban baseball in the old sense to receive them. This is a great loss, not the greatest caused by exile and the diaspora, but a sensitive one nonetheless, as when a family loses all its picture albums in a fire. José Cardenal, who never did play at the Gran Stadium, once told me that he would have given anything to have had one at-bat in the Cuban League. His career in the majors was good, lengthy, and has now been extended as first-base coach of the Yankees. But because he remembered Cuban baseball, it is not enough.[4]

Those who came next had no memory of it, but the records of two of them compare very favorably with those of Cubans in the past. Canseco and Palmeiro were both born in Havana, but came to the United States as babies. They are Miami Cubans, or Cuban Americans, who developed as ballplayers in this country. The left-handed-hitting Palmeiro, a first baseman, hit .415 with 29 home runs and 94 RBIs at Mississippi State in 1984, the only Triple Crown winner in the Southeastern Conference. By 1986 he was with the Chicago Cubs, where he began a career of great brilliance that already includes well over 200 home runs, close to 1,000 RBIs, and a lifetime average of about .300. Palmeiro is challenging Pérez as the best Cuban-born first baseman ever and could catch up with him in many offensive categories. And then there is the irrepressible José Canseco, a strapping right-handed-hitting outfielder with astonishing power and explosive speed on the bases. Canseco's 1988 season has to be the best ever by a Cuban: He clouted 42 homers, hit for an average of .307, drove in 124 to lead the American League, and stole 40 bases, the only man in baseball history to have had more than 40 home runs and 40 stolen bases in one season. Some of the homers were of the tape-measure variety. Like Palmeiro, Canseco is also closing in on Tony Pérez's numbers. But Canseco's combination of power, average, and speed probably makes him the best Cuban baseball player ever—may I be forgiven by Dihigo, Torriente, Oms, and Pérez.

Because of his off-the-field antics, flamboyance, and immaturity, older Cubans have not always warmed up to Canseco, in spite of his epic exploits. In Cuba itself, broadcaster Eddy Martin told me, he is known as *el pesado* (the boor). When I asked Fausto Miranda, the dean of Cuban sportswriters, if he thought Canseco was the best Cuban ever, he twisted his face in a gesture of acute anguish and intoned: "Roberto, he has the body of a superman but the brain of a baby!" Still, the same could be said about Babe Ruth, and Torriente was a pitiful alcoholic. Camilo Pascual, who signed Canseco out of high school for the Oakland A's, told me that Tony Oliva, not Canseco, was the greatest Cuban hitter who ever lived. Who am I to argue with Pascual? But the numbers do not bear him out. While Canseco does not have Oliva's batting titles and has hit for an average at least thirty points below his left-handed compatriot, he has more homers and RBIs. One could say that a Canseco with Oliva's level head could have accomplished more, but as a physical specimen, the big baby has no peer. I think that older Cubans—including Miranda and Pascual—downgrade Canseco because, as a ballplayer, he is not really Cuban by development and has no memory of Cuban baseball lore. The same applies to Palmeiro, a typical American collegiate star who has excelled in the majors.

There are a few others, with lesser accomplishments, such as huge, switch-hitting first baseman Orestes Destrade, who spent several years in Japan. Except for a 20-homer season with the Marlins, he has struggled in the majors. He came from Cuba at age six and grew up in Miami. Left-handed relief specialist Tony Fossas is a Havana native who did not reach the majors until he was in his thirties. He has stuck in the majors because of his ability to dominate left-handed hitters in tough situations with guile and curves.

After these come the defectors and the American-born children of Cubans, among them those of Cuban ballplayers. I will deal with the former in a later section, and mention the latter briefly here to conclude this one.

There are some eye-catching names in the majors these days, particularly on the Phillies' roster. The most prominent is Danny Tartabull, the son of José. Danny is a slugger who has had excellent seasons with the White Sox, lesser ones with the Yankees, and who seems to be winding down his career. Another is Rubén Amaro, an outfielder who is the son of Rubén Amaro and therefore the grandson of Santos Amaro. The first Rubén was born in Mexico and the second in Philadelphia. Neither can compare with the old man, who was bigger, hit for average and power, and had a rifle arm. Yet another is catcher Bobby Estalella, the grandnephew of Roberto (El Tarzán) Estalella. Seattle has David Seguí, a first baseman who hits from both sides and is the son of pitcher Diego Seguí, who had a substantial career in the majors and played in the final season of the Cuban League. Tony Pérez's son Eduardo, a strapping right-handed hitter like his father, has been struggling in the majors. He was born in Cincinnati. The last father-son combination of native-born Cubans, as we saw, was completed when Aurelio Monteagudo made the Kansas City Athletics in 1963 (the pitcher put up modest numbers for seven years). He was the son of 1938 Senator recruit René Monteagudo. Both had identical 3 and 7 records in the majors.

Alex González, the current Toronto shortstop, is the son of Cuban parents, as is Fernando Viña, the Brewers' second baseman. Alex Fernández, an accomplished right-hander for the Florida Marlins, was born in Miami. So was Alex Ochoa, the powerful outfielder for the New York Mets. There are probably many others. With so many Spanish surnames in the majors today it is difficult to tell, and given the spread of the Cuban population, it has become even more so. Alex González was born in Miami, a good clue, but Viña was born in Sacramento, California. I thought, at first, that he was a Chicano. Given the length of our exile, there could be grandsons of Cubans in the majors. How far to count? The new Cubans on big-league teams today are the defectors, who bring with them a new Cuban baseball lore.[5]

Cuban government publications call baseball after 1959 "revolutionary baseball," to distinguish it from that of previous eras, but I will opt for "postrevolutionary baseball" so as not to imply that the game itself has been transformed in any significant way beyond its organization and role in society. But there is no denying that these changes in themselves have been revolutionary. The first was, of course, the abolition of the Cuban League, which together with severe travel restrictions, attempted to deny all Cubans the opportunity to play professional baseball. The glossy magazine *Cuba,* a clone of *Soviet Life,* published the following statement of the party line concerning the abolition of professional baseball whose directness and succinctness I cannot improve upon:

In 1961 Cuba eradicated the practice of professional baseball, considering it a form of the exploitation of man by man: Athletes were sold or traded like simple merchandise. Many critics were bold enough to predict the noisy collapse of baseball, thinking that once the material incentive was removed, enthusiasm and love for the game would disappear. It is evident that professionalism in sports is the product of a society in which young men without means and the chance to attain a certain cultural or technical level that would allow them to live normally, take recourse to their physical strength and ability in a given sport with the hope of excelling and thereby securing for a few years their subsistence [*Cuba*, December 1969, p. 17].

The issue of whether professional baseball was or is a form of exploitation of man by man, whereas the game now played under the system in Cuba is not, remains open for debate. But the radical change brought about in the game by the revolution and the relentless propaganda about its benefits in the Cuban press and other publications force me to draw a comparison.

There are several areas in which the advantages brought about by the revolution are undeniable. Perhaps the first has to do with the game itself. Baseball in Cuba is free from all the hoopla surrounding the actual contests in the majors and minors in the United States, where the game seems to be a pretext for a spectacle designed to entertain the fans and keep them consuming all the products sold at the stadiums. Discrimination in amateur baseball was abolished, though one might observe that until 1997 no black had ever been named manager of the Cuban national team, and that the sports bureaucracy in general gets whiter as one moves up the pyramid, as is the case with the regime itself. (Since 1997 the manager has been former second baseman Alfonso Urquiola, a mulatto) The game was effectively expanded to all areas of Cuba, including the Isle of Pines (now known as Isla de la Juventud), and stadiums were built to accommodate the new teams. A centralized, nationwide circuit, which includes minor leagues (or *ligas de desarrollo*), provides entertainment and participation everywhere. The production of baseball equipment in Cuba itself (Batos is the trademark) makes it more readily available because it is less costly than the imported kind.

The Cuban baseball calendar is quite crowded. The Serie Nacional plays from October to May, concomitantly with the *ligas de desarrollo,* in which each major team keeps a full roster of reserves who play a full schedule in uniforms that, but for a patch, are the same as those of the main club. The National Series consists of sixty-five games, whereas the Selective Series is forty-five. However, as the Selective Series is played, the circuits involving municipal teams start. Players not chosen for the Selective Series thus return home to begin again their quest to make their provincial team. Seasons overlap, and players perform the entire year whether they make the final four or not. Those who do, of course, receive the most attention and eventually compete for the Holy Grail of the Cuban national team and travel abroad.

The Gran Stadium was renamed Latinoamericano, and new, modern stands were built around the outfield in 1971 to increase its capacity to fifty-five thousand. Other parks built around the island, some with capacity for more than twenty thousand, are the following: Guillermón Moncada in Santiago de Cuba; Cándido González in Camagüey; Augusto César Sandino in Santa Clara; Victoria de Girón in Matanzas; Capitán San Luis in Pinar del Río, and Nguyen Van Troi in Guantánamo. Near Havana a new park was built in Bauta, another in Guanabacoa, and yet another at the Psychiatric Hospital in Mazorra (which used to field an amateur team called Los Dementes before 1959). There are others on Isla de la Juventud and in other localities. Except for a new park built in Morón, Camagüey Province, in the fifties, and another at the Ciudad Deportiva in Havana, Cuba did not have an array of baseball parks of this quality before the revolution. The benefits of other developments are more debatable.

The abolition of professionalism has prevented many Cuban young men from the anguish of years of toil in the American minor leagues, at meager pay, only to be frustrated in their aspirations to make a major-league team. This happens to many Dominicans and Puerto Ricans, as it did to many Cubans before 1959. At the same time, however, by abolishing the Cuban League and making it treasonous to leave the island to play elsewhere, many likely Cuban stars have been prevented from competing against the best in the world and realizing their earning potential. Without the Cuban League, fans have been denied the pleasure of seeing their best players compete against their budding American counterparts, thereby honing their talents further. For every defector there might be ten other players who have yearned to leave but have not done so because of the stigma attached to it, and because to do so would mean to abandon their country forever, not to mention their families, from whom they would be separated, probably for good. The very notion of "defection," which really implies "desertion," as from the military, to indicate an individual's choice of where to live and play, is abhorrent to me. This term expresses the totalitarian nature of the Cuban regime, which conceives of the nation as an army led by the Maximum Leader, to whom absolute fealty is due. The vigilance exercised over the players and the control of their lives turn participation in sports into a form of conscription. I continue to write "defector" for the sake of expediency, but the reader should be aware that I use the word without the implications of cowardice and treason given to it by the Cuban regime. On the contrary, in many cases the players who left their country did this at great peril and endured much anguish and suffering, as the recent flight of Orlando (El Duque) Hernández in a flimsy boat demonstrates.

The eradication of professionalism may have wiped out whatever corruption the system bred, be it in the form of illicit payments to players or, in the larger scheme of things, the Cuban game's subservience to Organized Baseball. But this benefit is mitigated if one considers that Cuba's sports authority is part of a self-perpetuating bureaucracy and has been in power for forty years without being held accountable by the people of Cuba, whom it often invokes as its beneficiary; hence it is a broader, more pervasive, and more insidious form of corruption. Given the control of the press, it is difficult to know what really goes on in Cuban baseball, although one hears and even reads of players who throw games for payoffs from gamblers, alcoholism among some players, and other common ills of organized sports everywhere. Gambling goes on openly and loudly at the Latinoamericano, as I witnessed on every one of the five or six games I attended between 1995 and 1996. I have been told that it is rampant all over the island.

Of course, the abolition of professionalism did not really take place, if one considers a professional someone who earns emoluments for what he does, and if the perfection of that activity or skill is the most important task in his daily life. Elite baseball players in Cuba—indeed, the better athletes in most sports—are subsidized. The system is corrupted by what is called *licencia deportiva* (sports leave), meaning that one is granted time off from work to practice a sport. But everyone knows that the better athletes do nothing else. The bad faith is patent and is akin to what prevails in American collegiate football. Top Cuban baseball players perform all year (some since they were children in sports academies), receive salaries for their work as well as many special rewards (such as traveling abroad), gain permission to bring goods into the country, are granted stays at expensive hotels along with their families, and are given automobiles. Great performances may be rewarded by "a car as Fidel Castro's gift." In recent times athletes, some of them baseball players, have been able to make substantial amounts of money abroad by playing professionally or by acting as instructors. I was told that retired slugger Agustín Marquetti had made $1,500 a month as an instructor in Japan, and that he, like others who played in that country's industrial leagues, was allowed to bring home all sorts of goods. In a Cuba beset by shortages, these athletes are an elite, sometimes so anointed by their "election" to the Asamblea del Poder Popular, that rubber-stamping body of chosen followers of the regime, a great many of whom hardly ever visit the regions they "represent."

The creation of sports academies gives a chance to a young boy to develop his talents very early by devoting a great deal of his life to the practice of baseball. But this turns the game into a profession at a tender age, does not necessarily ensure proficiency later, and excludes from competition boys who are not as talented. Late bloomers may be left out, as well as others who simply want to play the game, not strive to become a member of the Cuban national team. There are exceptions, to be sure. Osvaldo Fernández, currently with the San Francisco Giants, but a standout with the Cuban national team in the eighties and early nineties, told me recently that he learned the game on his own and made the municipal team and later the provincial team. He is, however, from a remote part of eastern Cuba. But the investment in sports academies belies the propaganda about mass participation and turns boys into professionals exploited more thoroughly than the teenagers signed by major-league teams and sent to baseball academies in the Dominican Republic (a shameful practice in its own right). In my travels to Cuba I have seen precious little baseball played by people of any age outside the pyramid of success described above.

The overarching organization of sports in postrevolutionary Cuba followed the pattern of twentieth-century totalitarian regimes. The model was naturally the Soviet one, but is parallel to what was developed in Nazi Germany and Fascist Italy during the thirties: the integration of medicine, physical education, and public health with the goal of creating citizens bodily and mentally prepared to defend the fatherland. Within that structure, the practice of sports in which international play could become an arena for ideological confrontation with capitalist powers was arranged as a funnel of achievement. Competition was designed to cull the best players to constitute the national team, an object of patriotic pride, political loyalty, and worldwide propaganda. All must be well in a society that can produce such splendid athletes. Tournaments and leagues became a series of ever-finer sieves through which the athletes were filtered until only the finest remained. The establishment of sports academies was the foundation of this system, which would identify talent as early as possible in order to cultivate it in the most efficient way, leading up to the national teams.

Children at the elementary-school level who show athletic talent are sent to these academies, whose purpose is to teach them a given sport in the most scientific way, developing their physiques to fit the game in question while also taking care of their education. When asked about this, Jorge Fuentes, manager of the Cuban national team, answered as follows: "In Cuba there are, in all provinces, two athletic institutions. One is introductory and is called Escuela de Iniciación Deportiva Escolar, or EIDE, which goes up to the tenth grade. From the tenth grade to high school [*preuniversitario*] there is the Escuela de Superación y Perfeccionamiento Atlético, ESPA." To Fuentes these academies were "pillars in the athletic development of Cuba." These academies have two sessions, one where the kids get the schooling proper to their grade, and another where they receive "theoretical" instruction in the sport of choice. This is followed by practices, including games against other academies. The process lasts the entire school year. Those who do well in EIDE are moved up to an ESPA, from which they can be integrated into their municipal teams, the National Series, the Selective Series, and so forth until the best group, normally enough for two squads, vies for the national team. They are sent to a sports complex called Cerro Pelado, where they are quarantined during the culmination of training for an international event. Given that there was no experience with baseball in the Soviet bloc, the system had to be adapted to fit the sport, and here the Cuban input, with not a small measure of American influence in training methods and techniques, played a vital role.

In the former Soviet bloc, particularly in East Germany, this system produced athletes who performed with robotlike efficiency: no flair, no creativity. In track and field and some team sports, the results were impressive. But baseball is a game in which athletic conditioning plays a lesser role than in most, and whose training and performance traditions are more artistic than scientific. The kind of lore passed on from one generation of Cuban players to the next about the practice of the sport and the way to be in shape for it differed from the grim, mechanical application of Soviet and East German axioms. Nevertheless, Cuban coaches and managers were given training of that sort, including, of course, sports medicine, physical education, and strategy. As the men with experience in professional baseball or the Amateur League grew old, the new mentors were trained in the Soviet system, with the unavoidable deviations. Fuentes told me that he had been coaching since age twenty-two, when he was selected along with others for formal instruction. He is an educated, soft-spoken man who ponders everything carefully and never shows emotion. He has been criticized and even lampooned for this. When I told Enrique Núñez Rodríguez, a journalist in his seventies known for his humor, that Fuentes had actually played little, he dismissed him as someone *de laboratorio,* meaning that he was manufactured in a lab. So there is an awareness among older Cubans of the difference in style of play, and many Cuban players continue to perform with a shrewdness that owes more to the lore of the game than to the manuals of the technicians.

The *Béisbol 1968: Guía Oficial,* a statistical summary of the eighth National Series, which was the first after a substantial expansion in the number of teams, states quite clearly what the INDER's goals were: "Our highest sports organization has never taken into account attendance or the parity of a tournament, because its greatest interest has always been the development of athletes, and there was no doubt that this expansion would work in favor of the more rapid development of players, as was the case." Though this artificial expansion did not kill interest in the game among the fans, others that followed, inspired by the same objectives, did diminish it. Teams with generic names designating their "selective" status could not possibly be of interest. The system did, however, continue to produce ballplayers, but at the expense of those who slid out of the pyramid of success and whose education was mostly in sports.

But the greatest failure of postrevolutionary baseball comes from what can only be termed an "epic deficiency." It is clear that sports in the modern world take the place of epic deeds, this being the reason why they can be assimilated by a regime or by a political movement in the process of founding a nation. But epic deeds need to be absolute in their greatness, unsurpassed in the strength, skill, and valor of the heroes who perform them. Needless to say, this is an assumed greatness that cannot be verified, as it can in the modern world. Achilles and Hector, Aeneas and Turnus were heroes of unsurpassed accomplishments anywhere in their known universe. No one was better. Together with this was fame. Heroes carried out their epic deeds, and these were sung by the poets, who spread their renown in such a way that they rivaled the gods. In our times, amateur sports rarely can aspire to these heights. There is always the feeling that no matter how great their feats, they cannot possibly compare with those of professionals.

This is particularly so in the case of baseball because of the existence of the major leagues. There have been countless amateurs of seemingly limitless potential who have failed in the majors, when faced with the best in the world on a daily basis. When it comes down to performance it does not matter if the individual is paid or not; all that is required is that he perform within the rules and limitations of the sport in question. There are some absolutes in the measure of human attainment, particularly in sports and the arts, that exist irrespective of circumstance. Outside of this all other considerations are moral, political, or both, as well as aberrant ones based on race. An athlete or an artist is either the best, among the best, or an "also-ran" soon to be forgotten. The achievements of Cuban baseball players after the revolution are tempered by this epic flaw. Sure, Omar Linares hit three home runs in one game during the 1996 Olympics, but against whom? José de la Caridad Méndez shut out the Cincinnati Reds, and Cristóbal Torriente wore out the best pitching in the American Negro Leagues. Miñoso hit .300 in the American League, and Camilo Pascual won 20 games. I believe that Linares would have shined in the majors, but we will never know if he would have turned out to be another of the countless "bonus babies" on whom fortunes were spent and they flopped. Clint (The Hondo Hurricane) Hartung was expected to be so great that he should have gone directly to the Hall of Fame. But he could not hit major-league pitching, and he also failed as a pitcher.

The question of fame is just as demanding and cruel. The fact is that, for all the importance Cuban authorities wish to attach to baseball amateur tournaments such as the World Cup, the Amateur World Series, the Pan American Games, and even the Olympics, very little attention is paid to them in the rest of the world. In the United States only a minority follows even collegiate baseball, and Team USA is followed by a tiny minority, even if more than fifty thousand showed up to watch Cuba beat them in the Atlanta Olympics. Everyone knows that the best young players are already in the professionals, and that an ordinary Class AA team could beat Team USA on any given day. Regardless of whether it is right or wrong, the fame of amateur baseball players, even the Cubans, is not that widespread. They have left no records against the highest competition. This is not the case in track and field, where the Olympics are the highest form of competition, and someone like Adalberto Juantorena is known to have defeated the best in the world and performed a deed fit for the ages. His accomplishments met the epic requirements.

Even in Cuba, although against the proclaimed collectivist spirit of the political system, local fame is bestowed on some of these athletes. Omar Linares enjoys star status in Cuba, as circumstances allow. But the renown of these luminaries is not as widespread as that of players before 1959. One of the reasons is the lack of press and media coverage. Cuba's press is tightly controlled by the government, which uses it as an instrument of propaganda. Sports are an important component of that propaganda, so it is unlikely that many pungent stories about athletes and games find their way into newspapers and magazines to enhance the aura of players. There is a dearth of publications about sports in comparison to what there was before. Coverage by radio and television is much more plentiful, but no record, or very little, is left. The lack of commercial advertisements cannot be offset by the political propaganda that uses the athletes but is out of focus except in ideology. The highest form of recognition for an athlete is to appear in the press or television with the Maximum Leader bestowing upon him or her the blessings of the fatherland, because, when all is said and done, in postrevolutionary Cuba there can only be one hero of epic proportions, and he is Fidel Castro. José de la Caridad Méndez, Martín Dihigo, and Roberto Ortiz were greater in the minds of fans than the politicians of their time. But no athlete can equal Fidel Castro, who is treated by his votaries as if he were the living embodiment of the Cuban nation.

Having said all this, it is undeniable that the reorganization of baseball after 1961, the creation of the National Series, and the durability and expansion of the entire structure through nearly forty years are quite significant accomplishments. Moreover, it would be symmetrically unjust in spirit to deny that the proliferation of teams, the construction of stadiums, the nurturing of rivalries, and the production of players have been sources of recreation and pride to many people in Cuba—if not the people, *el pueblo,* as the regime excessively proclaims. A game is a game, and when people watch, analyze, criticize, and praise the players in the here and now of a contest, very little time is left for sociopolitical reflections or the narcissistic contemplation of the greatness of the fatherland. People express regional loyalties, boast about their players and about how much baseball they know, and put up with the propaganda without really paying much attention to it. It is the same everywhere, as games, because of their mock martial spirit, are absorbed into nationalist propaganda, when they are really rooted in pleasure, and their link to war is a form of symbolic aggressiveness and even sadism, not the expression of the sublime spirit of sacrifice. As we have seen all along in this book, teams have been sponsored by beer manufacturers and tobacco companies, and in the United States, where the flag flutters at every center-field pole and "The Star-Spangled Banner" is sung before each game, a team is boldly called the Brewers. It would be naive to think that all the Cuban players believe revolutionary propaganda, or that they mean it when they claim that they would rather play for the Cuban people and Fidel Castro than for millions of dollars in the majors. All one has to do to be disabused of any such notion is to compare some of the statements made by players before and after they defected. The billboards with revolutionary slogans and the pageants before international competitions are probably as meaningful to most of the athletes as advertising in ballparks elsewhere. Players in Organized Baseball have been known to mouth pieties about sacrificing for the team and being proud of the city they represent. I suspect that the same rift exists in Cuba between patriotic propaganda and the realities of baseball.

In spite of the break with the past, postrevolutionary baseball prof-ited—as did boxing—from Cuba's living tradition—the veteran players who remained after the initial diaspora. Among those the most influential and prominent were Gilberto Torres, Pedro (Natilla) Jiménez, and Con-rado Marrero. Lesser figures, such as Asdrúbal Baró, Juan Vistuer, Juan Delís, Orlando Leroux, Andrés Ayón, Francisco Quicutis, and a few others also played important roles. Fermín Guerra was among the few top figures who remained, but after a brief stint as manager of Occidentales and later Industriales he fell into disfavor and (as he told me in Miami) was sent to Camagüey Province to pick potatoes. He eventually left. Miguel Angel González stayed in Havana, aloof and unmolested until his death in 1977. A curious form of continuity has been that of the ballboys at the Gran Stadium. After Faustino (Bicicleta) Zulueta retired, he was replaced by his nephew Teófilo Zulueta, who now sells peanuts at the park. He, in turn, was replaced by the current ballboy, Fernando Padrón. Like Zulueta, fans taunt Padrón, who takes it in stride and seems somewhat disoriented. All the ballboys have been colored, a retention that reaches back to the first Almendares Park.

Yet another link with the previous era is Eddy Martin, the most pop-ular broadcaster of the postrevolutionary period along with Bobby Sala-manca (their Americanized names could not be more telling). Martin (*né* Antonio Eduardo Martín Sánchez) worked as a commentator during the last decade of the Cuban League, both broadcasting and conducting inter-views with players before the game. He also did commercials for various products. Martin is a well-spoken man with a wealth of information about Cuban baseball. He is a keen analyst of the game and is well informed about major-league baseball. He is very much in the mold of Orlando Sán-chez Diago, Felo Ramírez, and Manolo de la Reguera, the principal baseball announcers of prerevolutionary Cuba, with whom he worked and learned. But the key figures in the transformation of Cuban baseball were the former players who remained on the island and managed or coached the new teams.

Gilberto Torres managed the early national team that played in the São Paulo Pan American Games and passed on his vast knowledge of the game to generations of players thereafter. Natilla Jiménez managed the Orientales for three years, did some coaching on the other end of the island, in Pinar del Río, and wound up in Santa Clara, where he managed for six years. He was the pitching coach of the national team in the Amateur World Series of 1969 (Dominican Republic), 1970 (Maracaibo), and 1971 (Cuba), as well as in the 1970 Central American Games in Panama, the 1971 Pan American Games in Cali, Colombia, and several other interna-tional competitions.

An October 5, 1984, article in *Bohemia* speaks of Juan Vistuer, a reserve outfielder with Almendares in the 1954 Caribbean Series, who eventually wore the uniform of all four teams in the Cuban League, mostly Marianao's. After the revolution he became an instructor, studied physical education in the USSR, and returned to Cuba to assist with the new baseball. In this interview he reminisces about Luque and Miguel Angel González with devotion. Asdrúbal Baró, a teammate of Vistuer's in the Cuban League, told me that he had coached in Pinar del Río and Las Villas in the early years of the revolution. Another transitional figure of importance was Pedro Chávez, manager of the Cuban national team in 1984. He played with the Círculo de Artesanos of the old Amateur League beginning in 1956 and was the Triple Crown winner in 1957. Chávez also played in the Liga de Pedro Betancourt before the revolution. In 1961 he was with the World Series champion Cuban national team in Costa Rica, and later won two batting championships in National Series.

Conrado Marrero remained in Cuba (though one of his sons was among the invaders at the Bay of Pigs) and has coached pitching for several teams, among them the Industriales, based in Havana. He has also been a roving instructor. The unflappable Premier has on occasion thrown out a ceremonial first pitch, but he makes no political pronouncements and travels often to Miami to visit his sons and grandchildren. The most active among the leading figures of the Great Amateur Era was Juan Ealo, who became a theoretician of the game and even published a manual on how to play it (see the bibliography). Ealo claims that the pitching in his time was better but that hitting is now superior. Espinacas, as he was known in the Amateur League, has been one of the mainstays of postrevolutionary baseball, and clearly among the most influential men in the transition to the game as it is played now in Cuba.

That transition took place at the national level with the organization of the first National Series, which included four teams: Occidentales, Orientales, Habana, and Azucareros. The four-team format was a clear echo of the Cuban League's. By 1962 the team number had increased to six, and a couple of years later to fourteen. Ealo sorts out this history in his book on baseball thus:

If we take the National and Classifying Series as the ultimate expression of the high quality of our baseball we can appreciate the development attained since the triumph of the revolution. Beginning with a first phase with four teams, the National Series were organized years later with six. Beginning with 1967 twelve teams were included, which represented the champions and an all-star from each of the then six provinces. In the 1974–75 and 1975–76 championships fourteen teams took part in the Classifying Series, which were finally split up into seven teams that participated in the Selective Series and Seven in a Special Series. Beginning with the 1977–78 championship eighteen teams played in the National Series, representing each of the provinces and the special municipality Isla de la Juventud, according to the new politico-administrative organization. Later six teams participated in the Selective Series, representing territories that traditionally belonged to the same province [p. 16].

One of the additional teams was the Industriales, so called because they came into existence at the time Che Guevara, minister of finance, had embarked on the harebrained plan of industrializing Cuba, one of the first economic catastrophes of the new regime. This Havana-based team caught on because, wearing blue, it inherited some of the Almendares fans, whereas the other early Havana team, called Metropolitanos, wore red, like the old Habana Lions. Industriales, whose name also rhymed with Almendares, is still in existence and is probably the team with the largest following in Cuba, while the Metropolitanos have apparently lost their link with the Lions. There is now a third Havana-based team, called Habana-Campo, which represents the rural area of the capital region.

The expansion and repeated reshuffling of teams was obviously intended to spread organized baseball throughout the island and to create regional loyalties. Obviously one of the problems at first was that a team such as Industriales, located in the area of highest population density, would dominate. And it did for the first four or five years. To avoid the concentration of talent in the capital facilities were built in the provinces and rules passed to prevent players from moving to the capital, and strengthen teams there. I was told that players have to play for the team in the area they are from, and that to change residency and play for another team a period of two years has to elapse and permission obtained from local and regional authorities. In this way it is ensured that players such as Víctor Mesa would remain with Las Villas and Omar Linares with Pinar del Río. The system is obviously also designed to sift out the better players to constitute the national team, but the return to a "selective series" involving former traditional regions (the old provinces) shows that, as I was told, fan following declined once Cuba, and baseball with it, abandoned its old division in six provinces to create more than twice that many smaller ones. This expansion, as in Organized Baseball, must also have diluted the quality of play at the National Series level. Another reason for the decline may have been the inanity of the teams' names, which, like "Industriales," tend to be based on a regional economic activity: Citricultores (Citric Producers), Salineros (Salt Producers), Cafetaleros (Coffee Growers), and so forth.[6]

Yet the fact is that, even in this period of decline and desperate economic need, baseball excites the fans as pennant races reach their climax, and players enjoy the thrill of competition and the elation and release provided by physical activity and collective bonding. Since a non-Cuban perspective is probably freshest and more valid, I record here the comments of Timothy Dwyer, of the *Philadelphia Inquirer*, who wrote a piece after a visit to Cuba to cover the finals of the National Series.[7] He reports on a night game between Industriales and Pinar del Río, the home team for this game:

By the time the national anthem is played, about 27,000 people have jammed into a park built to hold 22,000. Fans stand behind the outfield fence and inside the old scoreboard. They perch three stories high on the concrete light stanchions and they sit atop the billboard portrait of Captain San Luis (a local political martyr after whom the stadium was named). . . .

The most prominent sign at the park is a mural on the left-field wall depicting athletes in action, with this message: "And in addition to that, Soldiers of the Homeland," referring to the ballplayers. No one pays any attention to it:

The first pitch is a strike and sets the crowd off. One man has rigged a bicycle pump to a trombone and he pumps away, honking approval. . . . About 1,200 fans have made the trip from Havana. Now they are up, dancing, blowing whistles and ringing bells. . . . Usually there are only one or two police officers at the game. But earlier in the week, an umpire was attacked between games of a doubleheader between Havana and Matanzas in Matanzas, so more police officers attend this series as a precaution. . . .

The transition to postrevolutionary baseball was smoother than it may seem. First of all, INDER has to be seen as the heir of the DGD, which had been attempting to integrate amateur baseball since its creation in the thirties, by organizing the Juveniles and circuits such as the Liga de Pedro Betancourt and the Liga de Quivicán. In fact, if followed closely, the history of postrevolutionary baseball shows that the first championship held to break the hegemony of the Amateur League was organized by the DGD in 1960. The championship involved 240 teams and was truly national in scope. This "I Campeonato de Baseball Amateur de la DGD" (the only one) lasted seven months. Five thousand athletes took part (*Revolución*, December 2, 1960). The tournament was won by the Mulos de Nicaro, an integrated team from that town in Oriente, led by black slugger Daniel Thompson. They beat the Universidad de la Habana Caribs in the finals, which were played in Oriente Province. A subsequent game between the two teams was played at the new stadium in the Ciudad Deportiva on December 3.

Other than Pedro Chávez, the other key transitional figure in the evolution from the Amateur League to postrevolutionary baseball was Alfredo Street, a tall, right-handed pitcher from Boquerón, near Guantánamo, in Oriente Province. A black of Jamaican origin, he began playing in local tournaments near his hometown, where he became a pitcher at age fifteen. Street moved to Havana, where he was given a job at the telephone company as a guard so he could pitch for their team. He played for Teléfonos in the last three championships of the now integrated Amateur League (1959, 1960, and 1961). The telephone company was one of the first taken over by the revolutionary government, which explains the integration of its amateur team. Other blacks in Teléfonos at the time were Antonio (Kinko) Rodríguez and Rafael (Cachirulo) Díaz. Street was a member of the Cuban national team that did not fare well in the third Pan American Games, in Chicago in 1959. On July 15, 1961, he threw a no-hitter against San Francisco, pitching for Teléfonos at Stadium Latinoamericano. He was champion pitcher of the Amateur League in 1960. In 1961 he pitched for the victorious Cuban national team in the 1961 World Series in Costa Rica. He was twenty-four years old in 1960 and had rejected several offers to play professionally because he liked his job at the telephone company. As a result, he was able to join the new National Series organized by INDER, where he had an illustrious career and played on several national teams.

The early history of the National Series was dominated by the Industriales. After the Occidentales, managed by Fermín Guerra, won the first one, in 1962, Industriales won from 1963 to 1967, under Ramón Carneado. They were led by Urbano González, Pedro Chávez, Jorge Trigoura, and Antonio Jiménez, respectively. Their pitching was anchored by Street, Manuel Hurtado, Rolando Pastor, and Maximiliano Reyes. Their second baseman, Urbano González, won a batting championship in 1965 with a .359 average, led in hits three times in the sixties, and became one of the stars. He had a rival in Henequeneros' (Matanzas) second baseman Félix Isasi, a great hitter and base stealer. Other stars of the period were Miguel Cuevas, who played for Granjeros (Camagüey) and was one of the leading sluggers of the sixties. He also hit for average and had a record of 86 RBI's in 1968. Among the pitchers were Modesto Verdura (Azucareros), Rolando Pastor (Occidentales), Manuel Alarcón (Orientales), Aquino Abreu (Occidentales), and Gaspar Pérez (Occidentales). The premier defensive shortstop of the period was Rodolfo (Jabaíto) Puente. All of these men, with outfielder Fidel Linares, pitchers Lázaro Pérez, Rigoberto Betancourt, and Raúl (Guagüita) López, along with Felipe Sarduy, a slugger from Camagüey, shortstop Antonio (Tony) González, and a few others, are at the foundation of the lore of postrevolutionary baseball. They shined at the origin and in a period of ascendancy that included great victories in international competition. Interviewed for *Estrellas del béisbol,* they wax nostalgic about a period when there was "pride in the uniform," meaning team loyalty, and the game was played hard. They, too, suffer from the old-timers' perception of the present as a time of decline, marred by the players' selfishness. In their case, however, it may be based in fact, given that realignment broke up the traditional loyalty based on the old provinces.

These founders gave way in the seventies to what may have been a Golden Age of Cuban postrevolutionary baseball insofar as the production of stars. From the late sixties on, the game came to be dominated by a large black slugger, Agustín Marquetti, an outfielder and first baseman with enormous power. A left-handed hitter who played for Havana, Marquetti was rivaled by Antonio Muñoz, another left-handed slugger, known as "El Gigante del Escambray," and Armando Capiró, a right-handed basher who, like Marquetti, played for Havana, and hit a record 22 home runs in 1973. Another great hitter of the period was Elpidio Mancebo. The pitching was led by one of the brightest stars of postrevolutionary baseball: Braudilio Vinent (El Meteoro de La Maya—The Meteor from la Maya), a right-hander from Oriente Province. Between 1967 and 1983 he won 178 games. He performed brilliantly in international play, particularly against American teams, though he lost to them in the memorable debacle of 1981 in Edmonton, Canada. The other luminary, also a righty, was José A. Huelga, whose life was cut short by an automobile accident on July 4, 1974, at age twenty-six. By then he had accumulated 73 victories in Cuba, not to mention quite a few stellar performances in international play. Like Vinent, Huelga's feats were against teams from the United States. Close behind these two was lefty Santiago (Changa) Mederos, also an ace in international competition and a consistent winner in Cuba. The great catchers of the period were Lázaro Pérez and Ramón Hechevarría. Industriales' dominance had been broken in the late sixties and early seventies, though they won again in 1973, under Pedro Chávez. But the new powerhouse was Azucareros, which won in 1971 under young Servio T. Borges, who would go on to manage the Cuban national team.

The next superstar within the Cuban firmament of baseball was Víctor Mesa, a center fielder born in Sitiecito, district of Sagua la Grande in Las Villas Province. He played for Las Villas and for selections from the central region, and became a fixture on the Cuban national team. A right-hander, Mesa hit for average and power and was a flashy fielder with speed and a sense for the dramatic. But Mesa's signature was his reckless base-running, a real no-no throughout Cuban baseball history, which earned him the nickname "El Loco." Mesa, a handsome mulatto with a winning smile, was rambunctious, reacted to the fans' jeers and cheers, waved his arms in triumph, and became the quintessential *postalita*. But he produced, scorning the grim, mechanical maneuvers and training methods introduced by the Sovietization of the Cuban sports machinery. He was both admired and reviled, and because of his notoriety he was the most epic of baseball heroes in Cuba before the advent of Omar Linares. Mesa also gained notoriety for yet another eccentricity that linked him to the Cuban past: He is a fervent follower of Babalú Ayé (St. Lazarus) and makes a spectacular show of devotion during the yearly procession to the *orisha*'s shrine in El Rincón. During these pilgrimages many of the faithful fulfill promises to the saint by punishing themselves in various ways, such as making the long trek on their knees, or with stones attached to their feet. Though not exactly favored by the Communist regime, in recent years this parade of popular piety has been tolerated, and one of the most visible participants has been Mesa, whose political fealty, however, has never been questioned.

When, in 1984 (*Bohemia*, October 12), Pedro Chávez was asked to name an all-star team of postrevolutionary baseball, he chose the following men: "Ricardo Lazo, catcher, Antonio Muñoz at first, Alfonso Urquiola at second, Pedro José (Cheíto) Rodríguez at third, Rodolfo Puente at short, and Miguel Cuevas, Víctor Mesa, and Luis Giraldo Casanova in the outfield. The right-handed pitcher would be Manuel Alarcón and the left-handed one Santiago Mederos" (p. 47). As the eighties unfolded, some of these selections would be challenged, particularly at third, shortstop, and perhaps even first base and one of the outfield positions, not to mention the pitchers. Even without moving farther in time than 1984, one misses Marquetti, Capiró, and Vinent from this squad. In any case, there is little doubt that there were stars aplenty in this period, and that defections had not begun to thin out the ranks at the top.

Although expansion and the dilution of talent that began to take place in the eighties reduced fan interest, baseball development in areas other than the capital and the Matanzas region began to have an impact on National Series and Selective Series. Although the first to show this improvement was the central region, the most notable was Pinar del Río, which was considered the most backward area in the development of sports (although it had produced earlier professionals of the stature of Pedro Ramos, Ultus Alvarez, and Rogelio "Borrego" Alvarez). The Pinar del Río team and the selective Occidentales became a natural rival of the teams based around Havana, such as Industriales and Metropolitanos. But this was also due to the emergence of the most remarkable player in the history of postrevolutionary baseball: Omar Linares.

The emergence of Linares, which coincides with a period of both triumphs and defeats at the international level, as well as a dramatic rise in the number of "defections" to Organized Baseball, also saw a trend in Cuban baseball that reflected the major-league game: the "home-run mentality" and the decline of pitching, which could be connected. But Linares, all by himself, could make pitching decline. He is the son of Fidel Linares, who was an accomplished outfielder for Pinar del Río in the sixties and who had several notable performances in international play. Linares was born on October 23, 1967, in the town of San Juan y Martínez, in Pinar del Río. In Barquisimeto, Venezuela, at a Juveniles contest, Linares hit for an average of .307 at age fourteen. Two years later, at Kindersley, Canada, at another meet, he crushed 8 homers, 4 doubles, and 3 triples and finished with an average of .511. He was already on the Cuban national team that lost in Edmonton in 1985. He was chosen for the all-star team of the tournament after hitting .421. By then he was already known as "El Niño" (The Kid) and was dominating the National Series.

Linares filled out at a potent six feet and two hundred pounds but still was able to run the hundred meters in 10.6, a speed he uses to steal almost at will. He is a tremendously agile third baseman with a gun for a throwing arm: His pegs to first have been clocked at ninety miles an hour. His massive homers are legendary in Cuba and abroad. By 1995, with almost 5,000 times at bat, he had an average of .371 in Cuban National and Selective Series, including 333 homers. In international competition his batting average has fluctuated between the .400s and the .500s, with as many as 11 homers in one International Cup (1987). In the five or six games I have seen him play in Cuba he seemed to be so far above the average that he appeared bored. The last time I saw him in action at the Latinoamericano he was batting .521. Fuentes, his manager with both Pinar del Río and the national team, told me that Linares was running everything out and playing hard. Perhaps, but he looked to me as if he were still going through the motions unchallenged. My impression may be based on Linares' demure demeanor. He is spectacular, but unlike Víctor Mesa or José Canseco, he is not flashy. When I met Linares at the motel where Pinar del Río was staying for the series against Industriales in Havana, he looked more like a heavyweight boxer than a ballplayer. He is extremely gifted, and it is a shame that he has not played to his potential by competing against the best in the world. At thirty-two he is clearly beyond his peak, but it would still be interesting to see him face the likes of Roger Clemens, Randy Johnson, and David Cone on a regular basis. There is no reason to doubt that Linares would excel, but it would have to be proven on the field.

Playing alongside of Linares on the Cuban national team was shortstop Germán Mesa, a gifted fielder in the mold of Puente, his backup, Rey Ordóñez, and previous Cuban greats Willie Miranda and Avelino Cañizares. A smallish man—5 feet, 7 inches and 154 pounds—Mesa hit in the .280s for Industriales in the National and Selective Series. On the national team he paired with second baseman Juan Padilla and later Antonio Pacheco to form superb doubleplay combinations. Both Padilla and Pacheco are strong hitters for middle infielders. At first base the national team had Roberto Colina until he defected, while also using veteran Orestes Kindelán and newcomer (now also gone) Jorge Luis Toca. The leading pitchers of the eighties and nineties are now mostly in Organized Baseball: René Arocha, Osvaldo Fernández, Ariel Prieto, Euclides Rojas, Liván Hernández, Orlando (El Duque) Hernández, and Luis Rolando Arrojo. Omar Ajete, a hard-throwing left-hander for Occidentales and the national team, has had great success and recognition, as has lanky right-hander Pedro Luis Lazo. Francisco Santiesteban has been one of the leading catchers (he, too, recently defected). Rey Isaac, an outfielder from Santiago de Cuba, seems to be one of the budding stars, and Eduardo Paret, in the mold of Mesa but a better hitter, would have taken over as the leading shortstop, but he was recently suspended for attempting to defect. Osmani Santana, another promising young player, an outfielder, has just defected.

Penury during the "Special Period" (the era following the collapse of the Soviet Union), which has forced the reduction of the National Series schedule and the number of night games, together with the many defections, have diminished the quality of Cuban baseball and caused fan interest to decline. The memory of great international triumphs is now tempered by recent defeats, which probably makes less tolerable the squalor of the facilities made available to the players. Yet it is in the international arena that Cuban baseball must continue to prove itself, perhaps now more than ever, in spite of the presence of more agents ready to offer fabulous deals to its players.

⊝

Cuba's dominance of amateur baseball during the past three decades has been such that the most memorable games have been the ones its national team has either lost or come near to losing. Winning has become routine, and routs of their opponents common. Because of the natural political rivalry, the Cuban national team's contests against Team USA have usually been given top billing, and the two squads have been playing exhibition games regularly for the past ten years. But only in the past few have the contests been interesting, and then only because of the spate of defections from the Cuban team, and a gradual decline of the game on the island partly provoked by the crash of the economy after the demise of the Soviet bloc. For the most part, competition between the two countries has been— ironically—a contest of seasoned professionals (Cuba) and collegiate all-stars (USA). Except for the random and truly anomalous game, the Cuban national team's only competition has been against an occasional club from a professional league in Venezuela, Mexico, Japan, or Puerto Rico. Even then the Cubans have fared quite well. Until recently, the team's stiffest challenge, as in the past, has been at home, against other Cuban selections. I think it is safe to say that if Cuba had been allowed to field three squads in most international contests, they would have taken the top three positions in the standings.

Cuba's record in international competition has been more than adequately covered by the propagandistic *Viva y en juego* up to 1986, and virtually to the present by Peter C. Bjarkman's *Baseball with a Latin Beat* and other publications, so I will not cover it exhaustively here. It is made up of countless victories in a variety of fairly obscure tournaments, or in more visible arenas such as the past two Olympics, but always against competition far below the best in the world. I will concentrate on some of the high and low points, or on tournaments or games of special significance.

Cuba's first international triumph in international play was the already chronicled trouncing of the opposition in Costa Rica in April 1961. International pressure against the new regime led to the Colombian government's denial of visas to the Cuban team for the next World Series, following the old practice of "If you can't beat them, don't let them play." The Federación Internacional de Béisbol Aficionado (FIBA) wanted to prevent Cuba from competing, and therefore did not recognize the Juveniles world championship Cuba had just won over Canada in Havana. Trouble ensued at the tenth Central American and Caribbean Games, held in August 1966 in San Juan, Puerto Rico. There were delays in allowing the ship *Cerro Pelado*, carrying the Cuban delegation, to enter the port of San Juan. Once inside, only one-third of the Cuban athletes marched during the opening ceremonies because the rest had not yet disembarked. The team was cheered by some and booed by Cubans against the revolution, who also threw stones at them. Cuba won the first baseball game, 5–2, against Puerto Rico behind righty Aquino Abreu. Venezuela then beat Cuba, 1–0, behind Adán Morales. Cuba's Gaspar (Curro) Pérez pitched a great game but lost on errors, one his own. Pedro Chávez hit a long drive that was caught four hundred feet away in center by Alfredo Díaz. Cuba then bested the Dominican Republic, 1–0. Jesús Torriente gave up only three hits, and Miguel Cuevas got a double. Rigoberto Betancourt allowed Panama only one hit and Cuba scored seven runs as they bombed three pitchers. Cuba, Venezuela, Panama, and Puerto Rico tied for first place. Alfredo Street blanked Dutch Antilles, 6–0, striking out thirteen. Pedro Chávez hit a homer. Aquino Abreu blew up against Mexico, but a good relief effort by Raúl (Guagüita) López won the game, as Pedro Chávez hit a sacrifice fly in the ninth inning to drive in the winning run, scored by Antonio Jiménez. Cuba and Puerto Rico finished in a tie with 5 and 1 records, and Cuba won the playoff game. The following Cuban players made the games' all-star team: Ricardo Lazo, catcher; Urbano González, second base; Antonio (Tony) González, shortstop; Miguel Cuevas, left field; Felipe Sarduy, center field; Pedro Chávez, right field; and Rigoberto Betancourt, left-handed pitcher. The victory in Puerto Rico was a harbinger of things to come.

The sixteenth Amateur World Series, held in the Dominican Republic in 1969, was played under a great deal of political tension. This was perhaps a watershed tournament for Cuban postrevolutionary baseball. The United States fielded a team for the first time since the bogus 1942 squad that came to Havana and, like Cuba, won every game to reach the final confrontation for the title. In addition to Cuba and the United States there were teams from Venezuela, Panama, Puerto Rico, the Dominican Republic, Nicaragua, Mexico, the Dutch Antilles, Guatemala, and Colombia. The Dominican Republic finished third, with a 7 and 2 record. The team played its heart out before the home crowds. The Series was played with a lot of anti-American feeling because of the 1965 invasion of the Dominican Republic. Games were held in Santo Domingo, San Pedro de Macorís, and Santiago de los Caballeros. In the final, against the Americans, pitcher Gaspar (Curro) Pérez was brilliant in relief, drove in the tying run, and later scored the winning one for Cuba. Twenty thousand were at the closing game, along with seven thousand policemen! The team was managed by Servio Tulio Borges, with the technical assistance of Juan Ealo and Pedro (Natilla) Jiménez. Cubans again dominated the all-star team selected at the end of the tournament: Felipe Sarduy, first base; Felix Isasi, second base; Owen Blandino, third base; Agustín Marquetti, outfield; Fermín Laffita, outfield; and Gaspar Pérez, pitcher. The Cuban team also boasted stellar pitchers Santiago (Changa) Mederos, José A. Huelga, and Lázaro Santana, with Lázaro Pérez and Ramón Hechevarría as catchers.

Servio Tulio Borges, a very young manager and the first to emerge after the traditional figures had retired, led the Cuban national team to three pennants in Pan American Games and seven in Amateur World Series. In 1977 he managed the team in a series of nine games against professional Mexican and Venezuelan teams. Borges presided over the transition to the aluminum bat and the designated hitter. He was obviously also part of the move toward the Sovietization of sports.

The seventies are the high-water mark of Cuban postrevolutionary baseball. Cuba not only dominated but also often held the contests at home, showcasing its powerful national team and its new facilities. The team's superiority also demonstrated to the people the country's success in one area, in spite of the grave social, political, and economic problems. This was the same plan, but on a larger scale, that Batista had carried out with the famed Amateur World Series of the forties, and Machado with the 1930 Pan American Games.

In 1970 Cuba won the eighteenth Amateur World Series, held in Colombia, in spectacular fashion. This was, for a change, a fiercely contested tournament that saw the American and Cuban teams finish with identical 10 and 1 records. The American team was led by future major leaguer Burt Hooton, who baffled the Cubans with his knuckle-curve in their only defeat. But in the playoffs José A. Huelga bested Hooton in eleven innings, 3–1, in one of the classic games of international amateur competition. The second game was postponed several days, but when it was played, lefty Changa Mederos took the mound against Richard Troedson. Cuba prevailed in a tight game in which Manuel Alarcón and Huelga pitched masterfully in relief. Troedson won 8 and lost 10 over two years in the Majors. But Hooton went on to have quite a good career with the Dodgers, and the ill-fated Huelga became a hero back home. The twenty-first Campeonato Mundial de Baseball was played in Cuba. The games were staged all over the island, with Cuba emerging victorious, though the national team showed some weaknesses on offense (*Bohemia*, December 3, 1971). They won essentially because of their pitching, particularly that of Mederos, who was peaking. Capiró, however, did not hit as well as expected and neither did Isasi or Rosique. Elpidio Mancebo was the batting star.

The nineteenth Amateur World Series was also played in Cuba. This tournament was held during the propitious month of February, in 1972. There was an elaborate pageant during the inaugural ceremonies to celebrate Cuba's baseball traditions and the revolutionary regime. Cuba won, undefeated with a 9 and 0 record, followed by Colombia at 7 and 2. The United States did not send a team, owing to the increasing political tensions. Fifty-five thousand fans filled the Latinoamericano for the opener, but the tournament was again played in the new stadiums throughout Cuba. This has to be one of the high points of postrevolutionary baseball and a propaganda windfall both abroad and at home for the regime. After winning, Cuba played against an all-star team made up of the best players from the other countries and beat them, too. The article in *Cuba Internacional* (February 1972, p. 62) that I am following here crows about the triumphs up to 1972 of postrevolutionary baseball: "Besides winning the Amateur World Series in Costa Rica (1961), Dominican Republic (1969), Colombia (1970), and Cuba (1971), there were victories in the Pan American Games in São Paulo (1963) and Cali (1971), as well as in the Central American and Caribbean Games of San Juan, Puerto Rico (1966) and Panama City (1970)."

In February 1979 the fourth International Cup was played in Cuba. Cuba had not played in the previous three, which had taken place in Italy (1973), Canada (1975), and Nicaragua (1977). The United States sent a team to this competition. It was the first time an American amateur team had visited Cuba in thirty-seven years. The tournament was a great triumph for Pedro José (Cheíto) Rodríguez, a Cuban slugger who hit from the right side. He led in homers with 7, hits with 18, runs with 15, and RBIs with 18. He finished with batting average of .450 and a slugging percentage of 1.000 because he had more bases than turns at bat! Cheíto was then twenty-four years old and had the third-highest home-run frequency in history, behind Sendaharu Oh and Babe Ruth. Cheíto's was higher, according to a *Cuba Internacional* piece (February 1979) than Killebrew's, Williams's, Mantle's, and Aaron's. Cheíto was a stocky 5 feet, 7 inches and 195 pounds, and his fame reached the United States, where I heard rumors about scouts eager to sign him for the Yankees. In International competition he had, by then, an average of .360, with 55 homers in 444 times at bat, and an average of a homer per 8.1 times at bat. The cup was also a triumph for manager Servio Tulio Borges: "Ten years of uninterrupted victories . . . His debut as manager of the Cuban national team took place in 1969, when he was only twenty-two years old and won his first world championship in the Dominican Republic . . . six world titles, three Pan American, and three Central American and Caribbean, together with an International Cup. . . ." Fidel Castro was in attendance at some of the games and, of course, in the victory celebration.

In November 1980 the twenty-first Amateur World Series went to Japan. Cuba again won, undefeated (11 and 0) under Borges. Lourdes Gourriel got the decisive hit against the United States, but winning was a foregone conclusion. Cuba just rolled over everybody, mercy-ruling some of the teams. Gourriel was at this time one of the most popular players in Cuba. The Japanese setting gave the Amateur World Series a truly global quality, even if coverage in the United States and elsewhere was meager. It also served to underscore the differences between Asian and American (in the continental sense) baseball. The smaller, weaker Asians played an inside game, going for a single run even when far behind because they lacked the slugging power to go for a rally. They felt that their only hope was to inch back into contention. It was a very disciplined game, with pitchers seldom issuing walks and working tirelessly in games and in the bullpen. But they were no match for the Cuban bashers, who overwhelmed them on offense. The differences in style helped, even if only by contrast, hone the Cubans' play, which continued to be, although more conservative in general, a reflection of the Americans'.

In 1981 Cuba suffered a defeat that remains in postrevolutionary baseball lore as the archetypal warning against complacency. The fifth International Cup was played in Edmonton, Canada, after a Selective Series in Cuba that was considered among the best, and a leap forward in quality of play. Although the Cuban national team crushed the Americans in their first meeting, the Cubans lost consecutive games to Canada and the Dominican Republic. They made the playoff, however, aided by Vinent, who defeated the South Koreans in a crucial game. The Americans chose lefty Ed Vosberg for the deciding game, and Borges went with Rogelio García. The game went back and forth, with Vinent being brought in to relieve with only a day's rest. He was superb, and Pedro Medina hit a homer to tie the contest at five. But the Americans prevailed, 6–5, in ten innings (the team had future major leaguers Franklyn Stubbs, Oddibe McDowell, and Bruce Wolcott). In the purple prose of postrevolutionary reporting, this defeat "is a thorn stuck in the deepest feelings of Cuban baseball players, and especially in Braudilio Vinent's."[8]

In October 1984 the World Championship was played in Havana, and there was further evidence of the improvement of baseball in areas heretofore discounted on the map of international play. Fidel Castro attended the first game in the company of West Germany's Willy Brandt, who was visiting Cuba. There was, again, a lavish pageant, with a tribute to the nineteenth-century players who fought in the War of Independence. Baseball was being incorporated into the revolution's chiliastic version of Cuban history, which progressed in providential fashion from 1868, to 1895, to 1933, and finally to the "definitive liberation" in 1959. Conrado Marrero threw out the ceremonial first pitch to retired star Rodolfo (Jabaíto) Puente, probably because the Maximum Leader was too busy with the baseball-innocent Brandt. Fidel Castro must have had a scare, for these games provided a few surprising developments. In their first match, the Cuban national team reached the ninth inning trailing the Italian team! They were saved from utter embarrassment at the last moment by the hitting of Lourdes Gourriel and Alfonso Urquiola. Then they lost to Puerto Rico, 5–4. Manager Chávez came under attack for the way he used his pitchers. The batters were criticized for swinging at too many first pitches, and the whole club was accused of falling prey to the home-run mentality, a taboo in Cuban baseball strategy going back to Almendares Park and La Tropical. There was concern about the quality of the pitching. The Cubans finally won, with Antonio Muñoz hitting dramatic homers. The American team averaged nineteen years of age and had future major-league star Barry Bonds, described as a contact hitter who used the whole field. Panama's team, which did well, was managed by former Baltimore Oriole Ruthford (Chico) Salmón.

Played in venues throughout the country, the meet was a display of the density of Cuba's baseball history before and after the revolution. In addition to the opening pageant in Havana, there were similar ceremonies in other cities. In Santiago de Cuba, for instance, the luminaries in attendance were Manuel Alarcón, Elpidio Mancebo, and Andrés Telemaco, recent retirees, and old Aristónico Correoso, a Cuban League pitcher. The break between eras was being bridged with these ceremonies, in an effort to present postrevolutionary baseball as the culmination of Cuban baseball history. No mention was made, to be sure, of former Cuban stars in exile, or of current Cuban players excelling in the majors. A triumphant feeling was being promoted. Amateur baseball, the purest kind, was reaching a peak with this tournament, hosted by the country leading it, and with its Maximum Leader everywhere to celebrate.

In the late eighties the United States put together national teams that were worthy opponents of the Cubans. These Teams USA eventually lost the 1987 Pan American Games in Indianapolis and the 1987 and 1988 International Cup in Cuba and Italy, respectively, coming in second to the Cubans every time. But they acquitted themselves well and actually beat the Cuban team several times. The final confrontation, at the 1988 Olympics in South Korea, was aborted when Cuba boycotted the Games. (As in the 1984 Los Angeles games, when the Cubans also boycotted, baseball would be an exhibition sport, yet everyone concerned took the Seoul tournament quite seriously.) But there were memorable showdowns in a series played in Havana from July 16 to 21 as well as in the 1987 Pan American Games. In the summer of 1987, Team USA, coached by Ron Fraser (University of Miami), had players of the caliber of Frank Thomas, Ed Sprague, Scott Servais, Tino Martínez, Jim Poole, and Gregg Olson, all of whom would become major leaguers, with Thomas and Martínez becoming stars. But the hero of the team was Jim Abbott, who beat the Cubans at home in Havana in the mid-July tournament. Abbott, who went on to have an excellent major-league career in spite of having been born without a right hand, became a celebrity in Cuba. He was given standing ovations at Stadium Latinoamericano, the first when he deftly handled a chopper in front of the plate by the first hitter he faced. He mowed down the Cubans with his powerful fastball and control. The Maximum Leader greeted Abbott after one performance, hailing him as an example to all, of course. In Indianapolis, Cuba won the gold medal, but Team USA beat them once with a dramatic homer by Ty Griffin, and other games were close. In October the United States sent a different team (except for catcher Servais) to Cuba for the International Cup. This was a much tougher tournament because it included the Asian teams South Korea, Taiwan, and Japan. The Cubans won thirteen straight and finished undefeated, outscoring their opposition in the preliminary phase, 101–9, and 37–10 in the medal round. Only

Taiwan gave them trouble, in a ten-inning game in which the Cubans prevailed, 3–2. Omar Linares, then twenty years old, hit an incredible eleven homers, slugger Alejo O'Reilly blasted nine, and catcher Orestes Kindelán eight. The most impressive American player of this International Cup was Robin Ventura, who became a favorite with the Cubans.

In 1988, in preparation for the Olympics, the summer of 1987 Team USA was reconstituted and strengthened. It again competed strongly against the Cubans. Ventura was retained from the International Cup team and Abbott and Poole were back, but the staff was improved with the addition of Charles Nagy, Andy Benes, and Ben McDonald. It was already known that Cuba would not play in the Olympics, so all other tournaments acquired special interest. In Millington, Tennessee, during their traditional meet, Team USA won the first game but dropped the next four. Then came the World Amateur Championship in Italy. The twelve-team tournament was played in late August and early September. Cuba, which finished undefeated, beat the Americans twice by rallying in the ninth inning both times. In the championship game Abbott held the Cubans to three hits for eight innings and was winning, 3–1. But after a disputed tag play at first, Lourdes Gourriel hit a homer to tie the game. Another controversial tag play ensued, and Lázaro Vargas blooped one off Benes over a drawn-in infield for the Cuban victory. René Arocha had started for the Cubans and dueled Abbott, but the win went to reliever Euclides Rojas, who was involved in several heroic finishes during the tournament. But the star of the 1988 World Amateur Championship was Cuban second baseman Antonio Pacheco, who not only led in hitting but also was voted the top defensive player. Tino Martínez and Robin Ventura, along with Abbott, were the American stars. The Cuban Olympic boycott was disappointing not only to the Americans, who would not have another chance to beat Cuba, but particularly to the Cuban athletes, for whom international travel is one of the most coveted emoluments. There was trouble ahead.

The *New York Times* of August 1, 1991 (p. B12) reported that Lázaro Valle, the star pitcher of the Cuban national team, had a blood clot in his pitching arm and would miss the eleventh Pan American Games about to be held in Havana. "Edel Casas, a sportscaster for Radio Rebelde and the voice of Cuban baseball for the last thirty years, said the loss . . . could open the door for a United States victory." Worse still, René Arocha, another front-line pitcher, had just defected in a stopover at Miami on the way back from the yearly games against Team USA at Millington, Tennessee. The Cuban authorities insisted that he was only their third or fourth starter, but Arocha had a distinguished record in national and international competition. Omar Ajete, a powerful left-hander, became the number one starter, and Osvaldo Fernández moved up to number two. Cuba still swept in the Pan American Games, thrashing Puerto Rico, 18–3, in the last game; they had whipped them, 16–2, in the qualifying round. Ermidelio Urrutia went 6 for 6 in the last game, including 3 home runs. Linares connected twice, while Orestes Kindelán and Germán Mesa had one apiece. Cuba scored 136 runs in 10 games, and hit over .400 collectively. Jorge Luis Pérez, a lefty, won the final game to round out a team record of 33 and 1 in international play. Fidel Castro bestowed the medals and condescendingly told the American team to "keep on practicing because they have a good squad" (The *Miami Herald,* August 19, 1991).

In preparation for the 1992 Barcelona Olympics, the first in which baseball was an official competition sport, Team USA went to Cuba for a series of tune-up games. They were trounced in Holguín by the Cubans, who won all three games, two by scores of 16–1 and 17–6. Howard W. French, reporting the game for the *New York Times* (July 6, 1992), quoted a Cuban sportswriter who said about their national team: "It is almost unfair the burden they are carrying. They are the best in the world and are not expected to lose to anyone, but they know that a loss against the United States would be more than a sports defeat. It would be a national betrayal." The Cuban team, in fact, was peaking, and the new Team USA was no match for them. An excellent "Olympic Preview" by *Baseball America* (August 10–24, 1992) offered much significant information about recent competition between the Cubans and the Americans, as well as a forecast of the match in Barcelona. Interestingly, a chart of the games between the two teams between 1987 and 1992 shows that while Cuba was superior, the Americans had acquitted themselves honorably. Cuba was the winner in twenty-nine games, but Team USA had managed thirteen victories. But the disparity between the two teams as they approached the Olympics was stark. As Jim Callis, the author of the *Baseball America* article, put it: "The average age on Cuba's twenty-five-man pre-Olympic traveling roster was twenty-eight, and sixteen players had been with the national team for at least five years. Team USA's twenty players average a mere twenty years of age and include just seven veterans of the Pan American Games last summer. Each year, Team USA must start from scratch" (p. 4). The core of Cuba's team continued to be Gourriel, Víctor and Germán Mesa, Linares, Kindelán, Orlando (El Duque) Hernández, Pacheco, Osvaldo Fernández, Vargas, Rojas, Arrojo, and their manager Jorge Fuentes. They won, undefeated, in Barcelona, while Team USA did not even win a medal, finishing behind Japan and Chinese Taipei. In a game against the Americans, Cuba won, 9–6, after they were down, 5–0, in the first inning. Veteran American coach Ron Fraser declared: "The thing that hurts Cuba is the absence of competition. Most of the time they are kinda bored. If they played major-league clubs they could win" (the *Guardian,* July 31, 1992). In Madrid I watched on TV the semifinal game between Team USA and Cuba on August 4, 1992. Osvaldo Fernández won, 6–1, while Kindelán and Víctor Mesa hit homers and Linares went 3 for 3, with a walk. After the final out of the deciding game an ebullient Víctor Mesa wrapped himself in the Cuban flag and ran around the field, leading the team in a victory lap. Cracks were beginning to appear, however, particularly in the pitching. But the team was about to have a real test of its talent.

This was a most interesting game the Cuban national team played against the San Juan Senators, a well-known professional club from the Puerto Rican League. It so happened that the 1993 Central American and Caribbean Games were played that year in Puerto Rico at the end of November, during the winter season of professional baseball. The Cuban national team had won handily again, and a game against the Senators was arranged. According to a story in the *San Juan Star* of December 2, 1993 (p. 56), the contest was held the previous evening at Hiram Bithorn Stadium, in Hato Rey, Puerto Rico, with twenty-two thousand fans in the stands. Because of the presence in Puerto Rico of many Cubans opposed to the revolution, there was a great deal of tension. Scuffles erupted between Cuban exiles and members of the Cuban delegation sitting behind the Cuban dugout. The exiles also had a banner flown over the park with a phone number for potential defectors to call. There had been forty defections during the Central American and Caribbean Games, but none from the baseball team. The game itself proved to be a real contest.

The Senators had a typical winter-league squad made up of native major leaguers and American and Puerto Rican prospects of approximately Triple-A caliber, with a few journeymen filling out the roster. Their stars were Atlanta Braves catcher Javier López and Cleveland Indians second baseman Carlos Baerga, along with Toronto Blue Jays slugger Carlos Delgado. In the outfield they had Lee Tinsley, who had played for Seattle and Boston, and Ryan Thompson, who has had a modest career with the Mets. The pitchers were Carlos Reyes, who pitched for Oakland; Shawn Holman, who had a cup of coffee with the Detroit Tigers; lefthander Mike Hampton, who so far has had a modest career with Seattle and Houston; Mets right-hander Mel Telgheder, who has done little in the majors; and veteran Rafi (Rafael) Montalvo, who had a brief appearance with Houston in 1986. Led by Fuentes, the Cuban team did quite well, losing only in the ninth inning, when Javier López hit one out off Omar Ajete with a man on base and Cuba ahead, 3–2. Linares hit a homer, Pacheco and Gourriel went 2 for 4, and Lázaro Valle pitched a good game. This Cuban team was loaded with veterans. In addition to those mentioned, there were Víctor and Germán Mesa, Orestes Kindelán now at first, Ermidelio Urrutia in right, and Alberto Hernández as catcher. In the spring of 1995 Orioles star second baseman Roberto Alomar, a Puerto Rican who did not play for the Senators, told me in Fort Lauderdale somewhat defensively that the Cubans had the advantage of aluminum bats. But according to an article in the *San Juan Star*, "Eight of the nine Senators starters forsook their wooden bats for aluminum Wednesday night, negating Cuba's advantage," so the field of play was reasonably even. This was an impressive performance for the Cubans, suggesting that they, like the Senators, were of about Triple-A quality, except for a few players who were clearly major league—not only López and Baerga, but also probably Linares, Valle, and both Mesas. Although Fuentes claims that, overall, Cuba had a record of 16 and 2 against Mexican, Venezuelan, and Japanese professionals, this is the only recorded game against an opponent of near-major-league quality. But a debacle was around the corner.

In August 1995 the Cuban national team traveled to Millington, Tennessee, for what was already a traditional series of games against Team USA. This location was obviously chosen because of its distance from metropolitan centers where there could be trouble with Cuban exiles. The yearly games in Millington had become a showcase of talent that led to some defections (about which later). This time, Team USA, coached by Skip Bertman, had played about thirty practice games already and caught Cuba cold. They swept the four-game series with delirious fans waving brooms in the stands during the last contest. Troy Glaus singled to win the first game in dramatic fashion. Mark Kotsay had an extended hitting streak and finished above .300. Travis Lee went 2 and 5, chasing Lázaro Valle. Pitcher Ryan Drese struck out ten in one game. Other effective pitchers were Mark Roberts, Mark Johnson, and R. A. Dickey. All of them, according to Cuban broadcaster Eddy Martin, threw at more than ninety miles an hour. None of these players, however, has made an impact in the professionals yet. There were criticisms of manager Fuentes and concerns about the quality of baseball in Cuba. *Granma* of August 30, 1995, voiced some of these grumblings.

In spite of the Cuban triumph in the 1996 Atlanta Olympics, all was not well with Cuban baseball. For one, in spite of the batting heroics of Kindelán and Linares, who peppered the outfield stands of Atlanta Fulton County Stadium with their homers, the pitchers were hit freely. One of the factors had to be the defections, which had thinned out the staff. Another was the fear of defections, which led to a final roster made up of veterans, such as Kindelán, who would be in no danger of being lured by the scouts. Germán Mesa, who would eventually be suspended for dealing with agents interested in signing him, was not at his usual position at short. Eduardo Paret, presumably less desirable to the scouts, took his place—he was also suspended for the same reason two years later. All in all there was a sense of change and transition, and indeed some drastic measures were taken back in Cuba. Besides the suspension of Mesa and a few others, about sixty players were forced into retirement, reportedly to make room in the rosters of the National Series for younger, more deserving ones. But one wonders if, as in other areas of Cuban life, political fealty was not the strongest prerequisite. It was also a way of opening up roster spots for fresh talent at a time when the economy would not allow the creation of new teams. Be that as it may, the inescapable fact is that the performance of the Cuban national team not only declined, but also its very operation became troubled. Their traditional games against Team USA, which in 1997 would take them to the Northeast (including Yale Field, where I expected to see them in action), were canceled at the last moment for fear, according to the communiqué, of "the destabilization of our team." This was obviously a reference to the work of agents such as Joe Cubas, who were actively trying to sign the players to professional contracts. All of this led to their World Cup defeat in Barcelona (August 1997) to the Japanese, and another subpar performance later, in a tournament against Japanese semiprofessionals from industrial leagues. Defections have forced the Cuban national team to deal with the problem of turnover in the same way as amateur programs in other countries where the professionals periodically take the best players.

It is no accident that the spate of defections has taken place after the collapse of the Soviet Union, with catastrophic results in a Cuba subsidized by the Communist bloc. The system of rewards to players has necessarily shrunken and has made their future look bleaker than before. Those who travel abroad for international competition cannot fail to see how far their living conditions are even from those of minor leaguers, owing both to the crash of the economy and to the system of vigilance under which they play. The same article previously quoted by Timothy Dwyer, of the *Philadelphia Inquirer*, gives the following description of how the players live:

On the road, there are no luxury hotels. They live in the bowels of the stadiums. The living quarters smell like the pipes are perpetually backed up. The rooms, crammed with bunk beds, look more like prison cells than bedrooms. Water leaks steadily from the shower heads and most of the wooden commode doors are off the hinges or look as if they have been splintered by kicks and punches . . . They never leave the stadium. On a typical day, the players practice in the morning, eat lunch and then sleep in their tidy dungeons until it's time for batting practice. Those who don't sleep wander around the stadium in shorts and T-shirts.

When I visited Fuentes he was staying with his Pinar del Río team, which was playing against Industriales in Havana that night, in a motel for athletes at Mulgova, near the Havana airport far to the southwest of the city. It was like a cheap American motel in run-down conditions, far from the lures of the capital. The athletes who stay there are virtually quarantined. The team is bused back and forth to the Latinoamericano, which, given the near-absence of public transportation, is not reachable in any other way. I shook hands there and exchanged pleasantries with superstar Omar Linares, who could have easily commanded a suite at the best American hotel with a limousine and a driver waiting for him outside. No pink Cadillac for him, like Miñoso's, however. Tom Miller, who traveled with one of the current Cuban teams through the provinces, reported similar arrangements in his *Trading with the Enemy* (1992).

Before the spate of defections of the nineties, which continue to this date, quite a few Cuban players had managed to come to the United States and had tried to make it in Organized Baseball. Many came over in the 1980 Mariel boatlift. A story in the *New York Times* of May 18, 1980, reports of several who tried to get in shape while at a relocation camp in Florida and who were looked at by some scouts. The players, Julio Soto, a second baseman, Julio Rojo, a pitcher, Carlos Martínez Pérez, a catcher, and Román Duquesne and Eduardo Cajuso, whose positions are not given, appeared too old to have a chance. Rojo had set a record of 18 wins in the 1968 National Series. Soto was a .250 hitter in Cuba. Soto and Duquesne signed eventually with the Macon Peaches of the South Atlantic League, and Cajuso with the Detroit Tiger organization (*Miami Herald,* June 4, 1980). None seems to have made it very far.

The best of those who came in the Mariel boatlift was Bárbaro Garbey.[9] Born in Santiago de Cuba in 1956, a right-handed line-drive hitter 5 feet 7 inches tall and about 180 pounds, Garbey had enjoyed success in Cuba and made the national team. But he had faced disciplinary problems stemming from accusations about fixed games. In the United States he had excellent seasons in the Detroit Tigers minor-league system. He was brought up and hit .287 for the world champions, becoming the first postrevolutionary Cuban player to make the majors. Garbey did not get a hit in twelve at-bats in the World Series, hit .257 the next year, and was traded to Oakland, where he never played. He had been suspended twice while in the minors, once for threatening a heckler with his bat, and continued to have troubles in the majors. Garbey was also a poor fielder who could not find himself at first, third, or the outfield. From 1986 to 1994 he hit .335 in the Mexican League, playing third mostly for the Mexico City Tigers, with seasons of twenty-eight and twenty-nine homers. In 1988 he played in thirty games for the Texas Rangers but failed to hit.

René Arocha's defection in 1991 was the first from the Cuban national team and hence a watershed. His actions stimulated others to do the same, and he was himself involved in helping a few gain their freedom. As the national team made a stopover in Miami on their way home from their traditional games against Team USA in Tennessee, Arocha walked away and was picked up by family members. But when I spoke to Camilo Pascual in Miami shortly after Arocha's defection he told me that he and Orlando Peña had given him a tryout and had not been impressed. They felt that Arocha did not throw hard enough. But Arocha was signed by the Cardinals, had a good-enough minor-league stint with their Louisville Triple-A associate, and made the majors. His record there has not been stellar, however, and he has been injured for the past two years.

The *New York Times* of June 2, 1993, chronicles the defection of five Cuban players in the wake of Arocha's. They were being helped by a Los Angeles–based agent named Gus Domínguez: "The most likely candidate to succeed: Iván Alvarez, 22 years old, a 6-foot, 3-inch, 210-pound left-handed pitcher with a 90-mile-an-hour fastball. . . . The other four hopefuls are outfielder Alexis Cabreja, 24, 6-1, 205; shortstop Osmani Estrada, 24, 5-10, 175; first baseman Lázaro González, 24, 5-11, 200, and a distinct long shot, 32-year-old knuckleball pitcher Rafael Rodríguez, 5-11, 195." Alvarez, Cabreja, and Estrada defected during a tournament in Mérida, Mexico. The three were teammates for Industriales. Alvarez had been demoted from the national team, which he had made at age twenty. He claimed it was political. Cabreja "found all the outfield spots in the national team taken, despite his .336 batting average over seven seasons—the third highest career average in Cuba, according to Domínguez." Agent Domínguez explained, echoing his clients' complaints: "It's hard to break into the national team. . . . Usually the only guys who break in at an early age are pitchers or someone like Linares because he is such a super, super player. And once a Cuban player is established on the national team, no matter what he does during the season, they are going to keep him, because they have proven they can win with him." Rodríguez made it across the treacherous Straits of Florida on a raft in January. González hit .340 last year in a Canadian league after defecting. Cabreja, who had jumped from a Cuban Juveniles team, only hit .226 with Erie, in Class AA. He then went to Mexico, where he played for Puebla from 1994 to 1995, batting for an average of .325, but with little power. Cabreja played some exhibitions for the Yankees as a "replacement player" in 1995, the year of the strike. But none of the others has made it even that close to the major leagues.

In July 1993, during the University Games being played in Buffalo, two Cuban baseball players abandoned their team. One was Edilberto Oropesa, a twenty-three-year-old pitcher who jumped the chain-link fence at Sal Maglie Stadium in Niagara Falls, got into the waiting car of a relative, and drove to Miami. The other was today's brilliant Mets shortstop Rey Ordóñez, who left the next day. He was twenty-two then, and had left his wife and eighteen-month-old son back in Havana. Ordóñez, with a famous bullfighter's name, is such a flashy fielder that he made the Mets after hitting only in the middle .200s in AA and AAA. He did have one great winter season in Puerto Rico, in 1995–96, when he battled Roberto Alomar for the batting title until the end, coming in second but at a sparkling .351 average. Away from Caribbean weather and food Ordóñez has hit about .220 in the majors, but his fielding and quick mind in the field have made him a fixture with the Mets. He won a Gold Glove in 1997 and another in 1998. His play has awed everyone, placing him in the distinguished tradition that goes back through Willie Miranda to Silvio García, Pájaro Cabrera, and Anguila Bustamante among the all-time best Cuban shortstops.

After Arocha came Euclides Rojas, a right-handed reliever who depended on his breaking pitches. His is a moving story with touching elements of friendship and human solidarity. A *balsero* who played for the Cuban national team for several years, Rojas took to the sea in a makeshift raft in 1995. The rickety vessel was only fifteen feet long and carried fifteen people. While at sea, Rojas witnessed terrible scenes, as when a woman who began to hallucinate yelled, "I see lights, I am going to eat bread," jumped into the water, and drowned. I talked to Rojas in August 1995, when he was pitching for the Portland Seadogs of the Eastern League. He told me then that René Arocha, whom he has known since he was eleven and René twelve, flew to the Guantánamo Naval Base to get him out after he was picked up from the sea. Arocha talked to Rojas and his wife to reassure them and acted as their sponsor to enter the United States.

Rojas' career is a good illustration of how the sports system works in Cuba. He is a burly six-footer, with light eyes and chestnut hair. Born in Havana, he told me that he was recruited from school at age eleven and sent to a baseball academy, where he met Arocha. Rojas was recruited by a *comisionado*. There are provincial, regional, and municipal *comisionados* who act as scouts, he explained. He played for Industriales in the National Series and made the Selective Series teams and the national team. He played with them for three or four years, traveling to Spain, Holland, Italy, the United States, Mexico, and other countries. The broadcaster Eddy Martin told me in Havana that Rojas was known as "the hero of Italy" because of his brilliant relief performances in the World Amateur Championship played there by the Cuban national team in 1988. Rojas said that Cuban players are warned that Americans would treat them badly if they went to live in the United States, and were told about crime, drugs, and violence in the streets. I asked him how he thought the Cuban national team would fare in the Eastern League. He replied that they would win because they are very good, experienced ballplayers.

Most of the recent defections have been made possible by agent Joe Cubas, who has become the Joe Cambria of the nineties, except that he does not work for an individual team. He has obtained fabulous deals in the millions for most of the players, nearly all of whom happen to be pitchers. But the results on the field have been mixed.[10]

The next group of defectors was made up of three pitchers: Ariel Prieto, Osvaldo Fernández, and Liván Hernández. Prieto, like Arocha represented by Gus Domínguez, is a strapping right-hander who went almost directly to the majors with the Oakland A's after a brief stint with Palm Springs in the Western League. With Cuba he had won 76 games in international competition, averaging 9.3 strikeouts per 9 innings. He fanned 20 in one game against Nicaragua (*Baseball America*, June 26–July 9, 1995, p. 19). Fuentes told me that he thought Prieto had the best chance of all the defectors to make it in the majors. In his major-league debut he lost a heartbreaker to Cleveland and continued to do well, but later was injured. Prieto's main weapon, as opposed to Arocha's, Rojas' and Fernández's, is a blazing fastball, once clocked at 101 miles per hour. He returned to Oakland in 1977 after the injury, but he had a mediocre season with a bad team. He finished the 1997 season at 6 and 8 and did not play in 1998. Osvaldo Fernández, one of the top pitchers on the Cuban national team, who helped them win the 1992 Olympics, also made the majors. He has been a starter with the San Francisco Giants, but with modest success so far. He is now injured, and word is that it might be career-ending, though he recently told me at Shea Stadium in New York that he is on the mend. Liván Hernández, the most promising of the group because he is the youngest, did well initially in spring training with the Marlins but had to be sent down, where he was hit freely at the Triple-A level. He was then sent to the Portland Seadogs with Carlos Tosca, a Cuban American who speaks Spanish and managed to straighten him out. Liván, apparently, loved American food and gained too much weight. He got into shape, made the Marlins in 1997, and had a sensational season, winning 9 in a row at one point. Hernández struck out 15 Atlanta Braves in a National League championship game to help the Marlins win the pennant and then won 2 games and the Most Valuable Player Award in the 1997 World Series. His success upstaged, even in Cuba, Fidel Castro's high kitsch beatification of Che Guevara, a suggestive interference of baseball in Cuban politics and an indication of how the game and the Maximum Leader have parted ways in his dotage.

Liván's success probably stems from the fact that, being much younger than his compatriots, he has been trained better and has learned to adapt to Organized Baseball, and to the wooden bat (against aluminum, pitchers tend not to come inside enough and use more breaking stuff than against wood). Another case in which youth has been a determining factor in success in the majors is Ordóñez's.

Other recent defections have been those of Luis Rolando Arrojo, Vladimir Núñez, and Roberto Colina. Arrojo (who has dropped the Luis from his name), a right-hander, was probably the best pitcher in Cuba. Tall and slender, he has a ninety-plus fastball with movement. Because he signed with the expansion Tampa Bay Devil Rays he did not pitch in the majors right away. But he did well in the minors and had a great 1998 season with the Rays. Núñez, another right-handed pitcher, also signed with an expansion team, the Arizona Diamondbacks, and has seen little action in the majors, but has also been doing well in the minor leagues and is being touted as a sure shot. Colina, a slugging first baseman, is also in the minors. Even more recent defectors, such as catcher Francisco Santiesteban and outfielder Osmani Santana, have yet to sign professional contracts, but I expect that they will play winter ball, go to the minors, and be ready soon for the majors.

The official reaction to the defections in Cuba is in consonance with the totalitarian nature of the regime, and the patrimonial sense in which athletes, and sports in general, are regarded as soldiers of the motherland, owing allegiance to the commander in chief, who stands as the father figure. An article in the official newspaper *Granma*, of October 29, 1996, summarizes the regime's response to the defections, which took the form of criminal charges brought against Juan Ignacio Hernández Nodar, a Cuban American residing in Venezuela, and the suspension of several prominent players for entering into deals with him. The scouts are identified by

Granma as Mafia-linked elements of Cuban origin based abroad, mostly the United States, who "have dedicated themselves, in a vulgar, shameful, and unacceptable manner, to the task of approaching, harassing, pressuring, and making tempting offers to Cuban athletes, with the purpose of stimulating and provoking desertions of treason against the Motherland." Recent defectors, such as Arocha, Fernández, Hernández, Núñez, and Larry Rodríguez, all of whom "betrayed the Cuban people," are accused of remaining in touch with players in Cuba such as Orlando Hernández and Germán Mesa, inciting them to defect: "It is worth mentioning that these mafiosi also organized and carried out the clandestine departure from the country of the families of Osvaldo Fernández and Rolando Arrojo." Hernández Nodar was arrested in Sancti Spíritus, where he was attending the Juveniles World Championship, allegedly acting as agent for Joe Cubas. He is said to have violated Cuban laws controlling emigration and the organization of illegal departures from the country. *Granma* claims that ballplayers Germán Mesa and Orlando Hernández had close ties with Hernández Nodar and were making preparations to leave Cuba, hence their suspension. The article's conclusion is a paean to the system, whose central figure is the Maximum Leader, who embodies its purity of purpose: "Aside from these actions that injure the innocent feelings of the people, the overwhelming majority of our revolutionary athletes remain firm, faithful and unbowed; on the side of the Revolution, the Party and their Commander in Chief. They are the purest pride and joy of the entire Cuban people."

The recent suspension of Eduardo Paret and several others, including coaches, not to mention the defections of leading ballplayers, show that the repressive measures have not put an end to the problem. The schism between doctrine and practice is too severe. On the one hand, the government can (as in other realms) negotiate professional contracts for some athletes, including ballplayers in professional leagues outside Organized Baseball, but individuals are not allowed to strike their own deals. The issue, then, is not professionalism, but for whom one performs in exchange for money, and to whom the money is given. It seems to me, as it does to other observers, that baseball in Cuba is in the midst of a severe crisis from which it will not emerge unscathed. Further repressive measures will incite more defections; less supervision will have the same result.

Recent losses in Barcelona and Japan (against semiprofessional teams from industrial leagues) are clear indications that the sport is in disarray in Cuba. A colleague of mine at the University of Havana, Ana Cairo, writes to tell me that heads are rolling because of the defeats. As I feared, one was that of my friend Jorge Fuentes. Reynaldo González was removed as head of INDER and replaced by Humberto Rodríguez González, a member of the Communist Party's Central Committee. A recent report (October 1997) in the news says that INDER has been stripped of its convertible dollar budget as a result of allegations of corruption. It is difficult to foresee what will happen next, but it seems to me that postrevolutionary baseball as it has been known in Cuba for the past thirty-eight years is about to undergo radical changes.

The baseball season has also been revamped, scrapping the two parts—national and selective—in favor of a single, longer tournament beginning in mid-November and ending in April. Is this a reduction determined by economic need, or is it a way of keeping more ballplayers occupied through the year? Will this further dilute the quality of play? How can the regime keep the lid on players' defections after Liván Hernández's triumph in the World Series, followed by the $6 million contract for his half-brother Orlando (El Duque), and El Duque's brilliant performance with the world champion Yankees in 1998? El Duque's success and charisma are creating a momentum that will be difficult to contain. The hard-line, retrograde policies outlined at the Communist Party Congress in October 1997 seem like desperate measures by the aging ruling elite to hold on to power.

The harsh response to the spate of defections, however, may have been only the first reaction to the crisis, not the definitive one, or the one that became policy. On September 28, 1998, I met with Humberto Rodríguez González, the new INDER president in Havana, and discussed the situation with him. Rodríguez, a young man in his early forties dressed casually in blue jeans, made his mark as the mayor of Santa Clara, where his liberal policies included the securing of a space for the local transvestite community to gather freely. He admits that baseball in Cuba has experienced a decline in recent years, but says new measures are being taken to restore it to its former preeminence. When I ask him why bother to do so in the face of economic hardship, he answers that he considers baseball to be an integral part of Cuban culture. He underlines "culture," not politics, and says that his plan is to encourage massive participation at all levels. Among the new crop of bureaucrats in the regime, Rodríguez is, with Minister of Culture, Abel Prieto, among the most interested in culture. A classical music buff, he is proud that at the opening game of the next baseball season an orchestra will perform. Rodríguez, in fact, levels the same kinds of criticism of post-revolutionary baseball in Cuba that I have been putting forth in this book. He wants to move away from the pyramid system that encouraged the production of players for the national team to emphasize the participation of all—*participación masiva*. His aim is to have teams in all schools and municipalities (as in the old days, I tell myself). When I ask him about the ban on older players' participating in professional leagues in countries such as Japan, he replies that what he would like is that the top athletes, at their peak, compete with and against the best in the world, including professionals. Rodríguez cites the case of Cuban teams, such as a women's volleyball squad, that have played in professional circuits and brought back large sums of money to the country. He hopes the same can happen in baseball.

I cannot say that my solutions would be the same as those Rodríguez proposes, for they all assume a continuance of the current regime and political system in Cuba, and with Fidel Castro still the boss who knows how much can really change. But his critical view of the obsolescent sports establishment on the island and his fresh approach to renewing it are encouraging. Even granting his basic premises concerning the survival of the regime, one has to wonder if there are enough economic resources to bring about the change. I was told in Matanzas, six days after my interview with Rodríguez, that there were hardly any baseballs for the children in the baseball academy at the Palmar del Junco to practice with. And ordinary men in Havana expressed regret that they lacked the most basic equipment to play even softball after work. The best that one can hope for is that a significant transition can really take place and the fabulous wealth of Organized Baseball spreads to Cuba. Then, of course, the question would be at what cost.

What does the future hold? Could the collapse of the Cuban regime send an avalanche of players to Organized Baseball? I believe that any opening of relations between the United States and Cuba would bring about such an avalanche, probably preceded by a feeding frenzy of scouts trying to get first dibs on all the available talent, a huge pool in comparison to those of much smaller countries, such as the Dominican Republic and Puerto Rico. Would such an opening bring back professional baseball to Cuba? It is pleasant to imagine a resumption of the Cuban League history, with the "eternal rivals" resuscitated from their forty-year slumber, and new teams dotting the island. Perhaps these could be developed from those that now make up the National Series and a Miami team added to the Cuban League. But, like everything else in Cuba, it all depends on the will or the endurance of the Maximum Leader, and when he will make his last pitch.

The 1998 season in the major leagues was a memorable one for Cuban players, even though pitchers René Arocha, Osvaldo Fernández, and Ariel Prieto were all injured and unable to play. But established stars like Canseco, Palmeiro, and Ordóñez had excellent seasons. Canseco surprised everyone by clouting 46 homers, the highest single-year total of his career, driving in 107 runs, and stealing 29 bases. It is true that his average reached only .237, but his production, including 98 runs scored, was significant and almost helped Toronto reach the playoffs. Palmeiro had one of the best seasons ever by a Cuban player in the major leagues. The Oriole first-baseman finished with an average of .292 with 43 homers, his highest single-year total, and 121 RBIs. Like Canseco, he scored 98 runs, but unlike him he is also a fine fielder. Ordóñez, the Mets' flashy shortstop, won his second Gold Glove award in a row, and his .246 batting average was adequate for a defensive player with his outstanding skills. If to his 42 RBIs one could add all the runs that he kept from scoring with his acrobatic catches and improbable plays his contribution would look even better.

Meanwhile, last year's World Series hero, Liván Hernández, had a very good season, taking into account that the champion Marlins were dismantled by ownership and became a very weak team. He posted a 10–12 record with a 4.72 ERA, a more than respectable performance for a pitcher with so little support.

Two newcomers made their mark in 1998: right-handed pitchers Rolando Arrojo and Orlando (El Duque) Hernández. The rangy Arrojo had a great season pitching for the last place expansion team Tampa Bay Devil Rays. He had a record of 14–12 with an ERA of 3.56 and an impressive strikeout to bases on balls ratio (152–66). Arrojo had his best performance during the first half of the season and made the National League all-star team, a first for a Cuban defector. Had he not tired in the second half, he would have become a twenty-game winner.

But Arrojo's performance could not match that of Orlando Hernández, whose heroics eclipsed even those of his half-brother Liván the previous year. In Cuba, El Duque had been one of the best pitchers in the history of post-revolutionary Cuban baseball. In eleven years with the Havana-based Industriales he had amassed a 129–47 record. He had also enjoyed extraordinary performances in international competition and was considered, with Arrojo, among the top three or four pitchers on the island. El Duque was stellar in the 1992 Barcelona Olympics, and in the 1993–94 National Series finished with a 1.74 ERA. His successes, classy demeanor, and charisma had earned his moniker, something frowned upon by Cuban authorities, who claim to be against the idolization of individuals. His prominence, combined with the flurry of defections in recent years (particularly Liván's), made those authorities suspicious of him, and they suspended him from national and international competition in 1996. He was also a victim of the restructuring campaign to pare down the rosters of veterans, make room for younger players for whom teams could not be found or created, and reduce costs during the "special period." According to a Cuban baseball card issued in 1994, El Duque was born on October 11, 1965, so he was thirty-two years old in the summer of 1998. Cuban authorities perhaps figured that keeping him out of action so long past his prime would diminish interest in him by professional teams. Probably impelled by anxiety about his advanced sports age, not to mention the lack of freedom and bleak future in Cuba, El Duque reached the desperate decision to take to the sea in a small, rickety boat with seven others on December 26, 1997.

Their ordeal crossing the Florida Straits, the days of hunger endured when they did arrive in Anguilla Cay, in Bahamian waters, their rescue, and El Duque's subsequent signing with the Yankees are the stuff of movies. In fact, he received several offers from Hollywood by the time the season ended. As he had done with others, agent Joe Cubas had El Duque obtain a Costa Rican visa to avoid the draft and deal with professional teams as a free agent. In my mind El Duque's most remarkable feat was to gather himself together in Costa Rica, get into shape, and impress scouts enough to command a six-million-dollar offer from the Yankees, who beat out Seattle, Anaheim, and Cleveland in the bidding. He had not pitched in over a year and had just endured draining physical and emotional trials. As he was to prove later, El Duque is not only an exceptional athlete, but a man of character and steely will.

Doctors who gave El Duque a physical before the 1998 season spring training said that he was the best-conditioned athlete they had ever examined. He had kept himself in shape during his year of banishment from competition in Cuba. Ironically, El Duque's conditioning and the knowledge of physical education that allowed him to stay sharp are a tribute to the Soviet-style athletic program of Cuba's sports system. His selection as a physical specimen, his training, and his education on the physiology of sports he probably owes to this. His acrobatic pitching motion, which some have mistakenly compared to Luis Tiant's gyrations, suggests the balance and ballet-like motions of a Soviet-trained gymnast. Whereas Tiant's windup was part showmanship, El Duque's is a controlled flexion and balancing of weight and force to propel the ball in the most efficient way, while hiding the pitch from the batter. But El Duque's determination and courage he owes only to himself, and they were the main factors in his success.

Called up to New York in June, with the season already in progress, El Duque walked into a typically pressure-packed Yankee operation, made more so because the team had not repeated as champions the year before. Liván Hernández's success in 1997 was nothing to scoff at, but it is one thing to play for an expansion team like the Marlins, and another to play for the most famous sports franchise in the world in the media capital of the United States. El Duque was under intense scrutiny from the moment he arrived, and he conducted himself with courage and poise on and off the field. Liván arrived in the United States young and impressionable and eventually fit into the mold of current ballplayers: spoiled, frenzied consumers who cannot see beyond the benefits coming to them for playing a child's game in public. El Duque, charismatic but serious and aware of his responsibilities beyond baseball, including the political ones, showed maturity and wisdom. He became the darling of Cuban fans in the United States, and in my September 1998 trip to Cuba I discovered he had gained new respect and admiration among his fans on the island. Cubans realized that El Duque had proved himself on the most demanding of stages: with the champion New York Yankees in a World Series.

El Duque won 12 games during the season, but his greatest victories came in the crucible of the playoffs and World Series. With the Yankees down 2–1 to the Cleveland Indians in the American League Championship series, he won what his manager Joe Torre called the Yankees' most crucial game of the year. Had the Yankees lost that game and gone down 3–1, their chances of not reaching the World Series for the second year in a row would have dangerously increased. For a team that had established a record number of wins during the season, not reaching the World Series would have been particularly crushing. Pitching with confidence under trying circumstances—in cold weather and on the road—El Duque put away the Indians, as he would the San Diego Padres in the World Series. El Duque's style, relying on shrewdness, control, and deception, is like that of Cuban pitching greats of yore, such as Luque, Bragaña, and Dihigo, and more recent stars like Pascual and Cuéllar. It is the conservative style of Cuban baseball, so unlike the stereotypes of Latin flamboyance bandied about in the United States, which are unfortunately assimilated by some of the Latin players. It remains to be seen whether El Duque will continue to enjoy success in 1999, when he will be thirty-four years old. But whatever happens, his feats in 1998 are worthy of those by José de la Caridad Méndez and others before, and will remain forever enshrined in Cuban memory.

The present shatters into inchoate images, yet to be structured by the plot-making of memory.

I am sitting in a box in the Gran Stadium on December 5, 1995, watching a game between Pinar del Río and Havana's Industriales. This is the very same box where thirty-six years earlier I caught the foul ball hit by the Dodgers' Dick Gray in an exhibition game between Los Angeles and the Cincinnati Reds. A middle-aged fan in front of me seems to know a great deal about baseball. We strike up a conversation. He does know his baseball, including the current major-league season. The man is a serious-looking mulatto in his mid fifties. He furrows his brow and looks at me for a moment, pausing before making a solemn pronouncement: "You know, there are a lot of assholes in this country who think that you'd want to leave Cuba if you knew more about American baseball. Imagine, when I have endured thirty-six years of this shit." Having thus established his seriousness, he says that Havana's Germán Mesa, who is the starting shortstop for the Cuban national team, is very good, but not as good as Willie Miranda, the defensive wizard who played for the Yankees, Orioles, and Almendares in the fifties. "After all, Miranda was a major leaguer." He has not lost a sense of perspective. This is the kind of hard, critical stance I remember Cuban fans having.

I also strike up a conversation with three kids in the next box. They turn out to be part of Cuba's baseball team of nine- and ten-year-olds that is leaving for Barranquilla, Colombia, tomorrow, to play in an international tournament. Raimel Garteix Suárez is a second baseman, Naidel Ayala is a shortstop and pitcher, and Dusnel Morán is the left fielder. (Where do parents come up with these names nowadays?) The boys are all products of baseball academies. I have never met three more knowledgeable ten-year-old ballplayers in my life, and very few of any age with a better understanding of the game's nuances, not just who the stars are, or what so-

and-so's average was last year. These kids knew baseball strategy like seasoned professionals. A pitcher for Industriales threw what looked to me like a curve (one can tell by the change of speed) and I said something like, "Well, he threw him a curve in that spot," only to be corrected by Raimel, who tells me that it was too fast to be a curve, that it was a slider. I turn my head and give this little know-it-all a glance, but he is not cowed. He knows that he knows. When I asked him later why he was picked to be in a baseball academy, his answer came without hesitation: "Because I am good."

Could the best Little Leaguer in the United States know so much about baseball? I do not believe so, but the Little Leaguer would, I think, enjoy the game more. I am no advocate of the Little League, which I have always considered a form of entertainment for parents at the expense of their kids, but these Cuban ten-year-olds were hardened professionals. They have sold away their childhood much too early for the distant goal of making the national team. I am sure that their Cuban counterparts in Miami are under a great deal of pressure from foolish fathers who want them to be the next José Canseco. Nonetheless, the lives of these Cuban Americans are not completely taken up by the sport.

A measure of the deference shown to veterans of postrevolutionary baseball is that today's pitcher for Industriales is Agustín Marquetti's son. The middle-aged fan tells me that the only reason he is pitching is because of his father. The elder, retired Marquetti, a huge black with quite a few extra pounds around the middle, sits proudly nearby, surrounded by fawning fans and hangers-on. The young Marquetti is a tall, well-built right-hander who looks like a pitcher and has smooth motions, but is hit freely. Linares gets two singles off of him almost without trying. My learned friend turns around after the second one and mutters: *"No perdona."* (He shows no mercy.) The young Marquetti hung around until the seventh. The next day I heard on the radio about his "brilliant" performance. He has not graced the roster of any national team.

A few months later, on March 10, 1996, I am at Pro Player Stadium in Miami to watch Liván Hernández pitch for the Florida Marlins against the Toronto Blue Jays in a spring-training game. Liván is a tall, hefty black Cuban with a great deal of poise. He is only twenty-one years old; on this day, he is still a prospect, not yet a World Series M.V.P. I am behind home plate, surrounded by Hispanic spectators, mostly Cubans, but also a few Nicaraguans, like the man next to me, an extremely knowledgeable fan. He says, with impressive poetic flair, that John Olerud, then the first baseman for the Blue Jays, has such a sweet swing that he "caresses the ball when he hits it." The Cuban fans are yelling at Angel Hernández (no relation to Liván), the umpire behind the plate, who happens to be a Cuban, too, from "the Republic of Hialeah," says my Nicaraguan friend sardonically.

Liván is impressive and then some. He allows no hits in four innings, picked off first one of the two men who got on base on errors (Cuban-

American Alex González), and even hit a double. He throws hard, but more importantly, he has great control within the strike zone with all his pitches. He dominated Joe Carter on changes of pace inside both times he faced him. It was a masterful performance. Though a mere exhibition, the Marlins advertised the game as if it meant something. They are clearly trying to cash in on Liván's appeal in the Cuban community. His next performance, in Puerto Rico against the Cleveland Indians, was not as good, and Liván was sent to the minors right before the season began.

It is December 2, 1996, and I am at what used to be the ballpark of the Vedado Tennis Club. It is almost at the Malecón—in other words, very near Bayshore Boulevard, to the west of Havana proper. A practice game *(tope)* is taking place between two teams from a baseball academy and a few independent players. I sat behind the backstop, where a number of adults, among them the baseball instructors, addressed as *profesores,* are sitting on cement blocks or whatever else is available. There is the usual bunch of idlers also watching and making comments. One of the professors is umpiring balls and strikes from his position behind the screen and offering advice and instruction to the hitter and the catcher. The boys, of all colors, are about fourteen years old.

The equipment is old and scarce. The two catchers share the one set of equipment, and there is a total of three rather used-up baseballs. The gloves look fine, though not new, and the shoes are well worn but serviceable. The aluminum bats are excellent (Japanese). There is a very high technical level and a relentless critique of play. The catchers are constantly reminded of how to *mascotear* in the right way, how to move the mitt properly. It reminds me of Corcho and some of my own instructors as a child in the provinces. I ask questions about the academy in a casual way. One of the boys tells me that someone goes to the primary schools in a given district and holds tryouts. The most promising boys are chosen to attend the baseball academy. They are transferred to these, where they receive daily instruction on baseball and all other subjects. Baseball in the morning, other subjects in the afternoon, and later practice. Every day. These boys, like the ones I met last year at the Latinoamericano, know a great deal about baseball, and the game is played by the book.

Somebody spanks a hard liner to center for a single, and the next batter dutifully and skillfully bunts toward third base. But the pitcher pounces on the ball, turns, and makes a perfect throw to second to try to get the lead runner. Just like a professional. But the play is very close, and the runner is called safe. There is no criticism of the pitcher, who made the right decision. The next boy hits a vicious line drive over the center fielder's head. The setup for the relay throw from the outfield is perfect, but the batter makes it around the bases for a home run. The pitcher stands on the mound with his hands on his hips, yelling at his center fielder for playing too shallow. But the outfielder was in close, hoping to nail the runner at the plate on a single, not because he is stupid or does not know the game.

He gambled and lost, like the pitcher himself on the earlier play, and shouts back a few choice words himself.

One of the professors is Ihosvanny Gallego Montano, a former pitcher for Occidentales (in 1967 he had an ERA of 0.80 in 67 innings). He is a slender mulatto in a dust-covered baseball outfit made up of sundry pieces. A well-spoken, terribly didactic individual, Ihosvanny intervenes when a loud argument erupts on the field over an alleged "balk." With a runner on second the pitcher, a right-hander, pivoted to the right and threw to try to pick the runner off at second. It was an unconventional way of doing this, for the right-hander usually steps off the rubber and pivots around to his left. The opposition claimed that the pitcher had balked. Professor Gallego walks slowly to the mound and conducts a clinic on the balk rule. He declares that there had been no balk. His ruling is accepted without further argument. Gallego is an intelligent man who projects a benevolent air of authority.

Somebody brings up Ihosvanny's exploits in the National Series, but he pretends to brush these off by saying that these are in the past and would not buy him a thing at the store today. But when goaded a little more he launches into a long, detailed reminiscence of some of his records and most memorable games. He remembered clearly a shutout he pitched on a Día de Reyes, after a long rain delay, with Fidel Castro in attendance. The game had to be played to please the *Comandante* no matter what the conditions of the field.

Gallego also intervenes in an argument among the players and spectators about a new directive that was being considered for all contests among and within the academies: that all batters would have to alternate sides of the plate on each turn at bat through the game to make them all switch-hitters. The discussion is highly technical. Gallego is skeptical about the plan. Why not cultivate a batter's natural or strong side instead of wasting time with the other? Besides, he says, other than a couple of steps to first base, what real advantage does a left-hander have? I opine, just to keep the discussion going, that left-handed batters see fewer left-handed pitchers because there are fewer southpaws; hence it follows that they would fare better by hitting from the right side against those they did see. But he answers that the opposite is true of righties, who would wind up hitting more often from their unnatural side. His clincher is that Ted Williams could hit righties and lefties the same, and I counter that he was the exception. I am not defending the intended directive, but I can see the theory behind it. It sounds like the rational kind of approach to sports that a Soviet-trained coach would concoct. In fact, it would be abhorrent to have all these boys sacrifice their natural talent and their chance of having fun just to make them better-trained performers, but that is what the academies are all about anyway.

I spent three afternoons at the Latinoamericano watching a series between Havana's Metropolitanos and Cienfuegos in December 1996. The uniforms are chintzy, with adjustable caps, and the level of play seems to me to be below Double A in the United States. These are splendid afternoons, with the temperature in the high seventies, a mild breeze, and a few high clouds. I soon make several acquaintances. The first is Ernesto Morilla, a wiry old man who turns out to be a former professional who pitched briefly for the Habana Lions and the Cienfuegos Elephants of the Cuban League in the later forties and early fifties. He is obviously part of a group of mature fans and former ballplayers who spend their afternoons at the ballpark reminiscing and watching the game. I also meet one of my boyhood favorites, though he played little for Habana, Asdrúbal Baró. Baró was a remarkable outfielder for Almendares, but mostly for Marianao and in the end for Habana. He was fast, good defensively, and hit about .300 with some power.

Baró is a very intelligent, well-spoken man, with an air of worldliness about him. He says that the level of play of what we are seeing is about Class C. He means obviously the Class C he knew and experienced in the United States as a player in the forties and fifties, which was quite good. I would venture to say that it is equivalent to today's Class A. Attendance at the stadium is very sparse, and the most vocal group, high in the stands behind home plate, are the bettors. They wager not only on the outcome of games but also on the run spread. This explains to me why they get all excited at what seems to be odd moments of the game. The few fans at the park are critical as ever. One gets up and yells in a booming voice after the Metropolitanos blow a relay throw: *"¡Caballeros, qué malos son ustedes!"* (Man, you guys are lousy!) Baró observes the proceedings with an air of benevolent condescension, but after a bonehead play cannot resist shouting, *"¡Ay, qué bruto eres, muchacho!"* (Boy, are you a dummy!)

The other friend I make is Raúl Esteban Pérez, who is a professor of physical education at the University of Havana and a sort of stadium manager. Fernando Padrón, the ballboy, comes to ask him for new baseballs when the plate umpire complains that he is running short. Pérez is a thoughtful, well-spoken black man with graying hair. He is a true gentleman. His son is playing center field for the Metropolitanos. He, Baró, and Morilla are buddies who meet every afternoon here. They all know their baseball extremely well, but Pérez is a true scholar of the game and knows more than I do about current major-league play. I am stunned by his precise, detailed knowledge of Cuban ballplayers in the majors. On our second meeting he produces a huge sheet, with neatly drawn lines, where he has listed every Cuban who ever played in the major leagues, with statistics, years of service, and everything one would want to know. The whole thing, done by hand, looks like an old-fashioned ledger book from a store. How does he get the information? People bring him magazines, a friend gives him the tape from an old news-ticker machine whenever he sees something on baseball, and he watches some CNN and other programs with friends who have satellite dishes. The ones who have these charge to let people watch games, such as the World Series, of which Pérez saw a few games. He launches into a paean for Rafael Palmeiro and other current Cuban major leaguers, such as José Canseco. I tell him that Jorge Fuentes told me that the Cuban national team would give a good show against a major-league all-star team. He looks up and rolls his eyes until all I see are the whites and mutters: "The delusions that people suffer here are sometimes incredible."

The game in front of us is getting interesting, as the Metropolitanos threaten to even the score in the ninth—they are two behind. With runners on first and third they try a double steal, but the catcher throws to the pitcher, who throws back to him, and the runner at third is hung up in a rundown until he is tagged out. A journalist friend of my friends runs over, holding his head with both hands: "What a childish play; this is shameful." Another runner gets on, and Jorge Sanfrán, a large, right-handed batter, hits one late but deep to right. It lands in the stands, and the game is over. He is met at home by the entire team while Cienfuegos retreats to the dugout.

There are very few women and children at the stadium. It is true that the game is being played on a school day, in the early afternoon, but I have the feeling that baseball continues to be the adult male ritual that it has been in Cuba since the turn of the century. Once the game ceased to be a Sunday amusement for the well-to-do, it became a male contest involving a man's self-image, be it by his prowess as a player or by how much he knows about the game. Baseball became, since then, something like smoking cigars—slightly sinful, pleasurable, and male. Betting is another feature that removes it from the world of children and women. In this sense baseball is closer to cock-fighting and other male-dominated activities in which betting prevails.

Proofs of this are the notorious baseball *tertulias*—informal gatherings to talk about something that all present know passionately. There is one at Parque Central, in front of the famed Hotel Inglaterra, right under the statue of José Martí. The other is at a cafeteria called La Esquina Caliente (The Hot Corner), on 23 and 12 in Vedado. At the other end of the island, in Santiago, there is one at the Campo de Marte. Tertulias began in Spain in the eighteenth century and continue to the present in the Hispanic world. They are gatherings—cenacles—usually at cafés, where men for the most part discuss politics and literature, but in some only bullfighting. The baseball gathering at Parque Central takes place on the park's stone benches, but people mostly stand up. It is in continuous session every day from morning until late into the night. It is a large group of thirty people more or less, divided up into smaller discussion groups, but there always seems to be a main clique in which a big argument is taking place. Cubans do not say that they are going to *hablar de pelota* (talk about baseball), but to *discutir de pelota* (argue about baseball), so this institution is a natural outcome. To anyone not familiar with this custom, or with the volume and vehemence of a Cuban argument, the tertulia sounds like a fight is about to break out and that someone ought to call the police. Everyone is male, and while the color varies, I found in my visits that blacks and mulattoes predominate. In fact, I was warned by someone at the Writers' Union, a black himself, not to go there too late and alone for fear of the *negrada*—the bunch of blacks, an expression that goes back to the nineteenth century, when it referred to the group of slaves at a sugar-mill. The topics vary, but they center mostly on second-guessing managers or on who is or who has been the best at a given position, who should or should not have been included on an all-star or a national team, and so forth. The arguments on strategy are of a very sophisticated technical level. Only the ballplayers among the baseball commentators in the United States would stand a chance in this assembly of baseball scholars and theoreticians. Male pride is clearly involved in winning arguments and in simply *saber de pelota* (knowing about baseball). There were a few boys around when I visited the tertulia, but they would not dare to participate. They were learning by listening to their elders, waiting until they were older, when they would be able to jump into the fray.

Back at the stadium I ask Baró about his cane. He tells me that he had to have a hip-replacement operation and is convalescing. He walks slowly, leaning on the cane, but with great dignity. Aging is particularly painful in an athlete. It is not only that he loses his means of support, but also the ability that made him unique vanishes, leaving him an old man like any other. A frail Ted Williams, a tottering Joe DiMaggio, an emaciated Mantle are sad spectacles indeed. They are heroes who have suffered the worst of defeats, not at the hands of formidable enemies, but to the relentless, ordinary passage of time, like everybody else. Bodies that were once the wonder of multitudes turned into wrecks by age. I have seen my share of such spectacles in writing this book.

I will never forget peering through a window of Edmundo Amorós' apartment in Tampa, with Agapito Mayor, to see if the old hero of the 1955 World Series was awake. Every day, Mayor brought him a meal from a nearby restaurant with take-out service and cleaned up the apartment for him. I was deeply moved by Mayor's kindness, which he displayed without fuss, as if he were performing the most routine of chores. Once inside we find a withered figure, missing a leg from the knee down (diabetes), and with the ashen color of poor health. He speaks softly of leaving Cuba, of getting an offer to play in some independent league in Canada because they still remembered him there from his salad days with the Montreal Royals. But he knew that he was through, he says. His artificial leg is propped up against the wall. A small television set blares with some adventure movie. Mayor is puttering about, picking up things, tidying up. He has run Amorós to the hospital several times and is in touch with one of Amorós' daughters in Miami. In 1992 this forgotten boy of summer died.

Mayor, on the other hand, is still spry and vigorous, and when I first visited him, he had pitched batting practice to some youngsters. One can still see in his Popeye-like forearms the strength of a professional athlete. He became a house painter in Florida, worked a bit as a bird dog for the Twins, saw his daughter get married, and now lives modestly and without regret. Gloria, his wife of fifty years, still runs the house. Agapito, as white as can be, keeps his Afro-Cuban altar in the bedroom and pulls a red hand-kerchief from his pocket when I ask him what a *resguardo* (a protective talisman) is. Glad to reminisce about the past, he runs to the phone and calls Max Lanier in Dunellon. They gab about the past in grunts and scattered phrases. Mayor has not picked up much English.

I find the giant Claro Duany, who blasted tape-measure homers out of La Tropical, bent over and sick, also from diabetes. He has had one kidney removed. His neat little apartment in Evanston, Illinois, is very modest. The only other member of the family who comes out to meet us is a dog. Duany speaks softly, with the wisdom of age. A man who won the batting championship in the Mexican and Cuban Leagues in the same year, who had his share of glory with the New York Cubans, Duany is saddened by the way his business failed after baseball. He talks of a truck he had bought in Cuba and had to leave behind; then of the truck he crashed in the United States, which put him out of a job. A gentleman of flawless manners, he offers to call a taxi for me when the interview is over. He asks me to give warm regards to any friends of his I meet in my travels.

Rafael Noble is another diabetic. I catch the ceremonial first pitch he throws in a veterans' game at Roosevelt Stadium in New Jersey. He also seems to have shrunk, and one of his legs has been amputated, like Amo-rós's. That night, at the banquet, he tells me that he considered letting himself die rather than having his leg severed, but that he is glad he had changed his mind. Noble is well-spoken, serious, soberly dressed. Thousands of innings behind the plate in leagues from the sugarmills in Cuba to the National League, the Negro Leagues, the International and Pacific Coast Leagues, calling the pitches for the likes of Pedro Ramos and Camilo Pascual with Cienfuegos, have given him a wealth of experience and worldliness.

I visited the legendary Dick Sisler in a nursing home in Nashville, Tennessee. It was a plush affair, but a nursing home. I will never understand why Sisler, still tall and vigorous, was there. At the nursing home I spoke quietly with the slugger who had clouted three in a game against Maglie at La Tropical, and had propelled some balls to unimaginable distances in that vast yard. He told me how Pasquel had wanted to sign him for a fabulous sum, but that his "daddy" (none other than Hall of Fame member George Sisler, under whose shadow he played) advised him against it. He remembered taking a tour of Cuba by car, and how nice people had been to him. He seemed a bit confused about the years, but perked up at the mention of Agapito Mayor to recall the titanic homer he had hit off of him fifty years before.

Rodolfo Fernández is a proud gentleman, slowed down by age but quick and sharp of mind. He and his wife received me and mine in their modest Manhattan apartment. Rodolfo was not only a superb pitcher but also a smart coach and manager. In addition, he was a keen judge of talent, not easily impressed. I asked him if he had seen the Cuban national team on television and what he thought of them. He is skeptical, he said. Most of those players had already peaked, he thought, and would not make the majors. I saw him again at the veterans' game where I caught Noble's pitch. An old, paunchy Marcelino López was huffing and puffing on the mound. Rodolfo opined with his sharp wit: *"A Marcelino nada más le queda el casco y la mala idea."* (Marcelino only has left the shell and the shrewdness.) We correspond, and his letters are written not only in impeccable Spanish, but also in a beautiful script that he complains is not what it used to be because his hands now tremble.

Quilla Valdés is using a walker when I meet him, a gaunt old man in obvious poor health. Quilla is delighted to reminisce, and quite willing to explain the anomaly that a man of his talents and accomplishments never turned professional. He is happy to attend softball games of the Quilla Valdés League in Miami, but cannot go when the weather is cool, he says. He has hardly any memorabilia, having left most, if not all of it, in Cuba when he came into exile. Looking at current major-league baseball, he is sure he could have played at that level, and he decries the lack of effort by some of the better-paid players. Quilla reminded me of Don Quijote as he raised his skinny right arm to show me how he would finish each practice session by standing at home plate and hurling a ball over the left-field fence.

Perhaps the most bizarre post-baseball career was that of Pedro (Perico) Formental, my boyhood hero, whom I could never locate. I was told in Madrid by the distinguished Cuban poet Gastón Baquero, who was born and raised in the same region of Oriente Province as Formental and Batista, that Perico had wound up in Spain, where he lived for a while with Sungo Carreras, the former Almendares manager. They subsisted on public charity provided by other Cuban exiles and the Spanish government. One afternoon, when all they had left was a baseball glove they planned to pawn, they were sitting at an outdoor café, pondering what to do next. There they were spotted by movie producer Samuel Bronston, in Spain to make one of his epic films. He approached the two Cuban blacks and told them that he needed extras of their color for a project he was working on. He hired them on the spot, and both worked as voodoo priests in one film, and later as extras in battle scenes of *The Fall of the Roman Empire*. Once these jobs were over, Formental went to see Baquero, who suggested he go seek Batista's help in Estoril, Portugal, where the former sergeant had a home. The exiled general was, after all, their compatriot and both the poet and the player had been his followers. Formental showed up at Batista's complex, but the guards refused to let him in, whereupon he started to shout at the top of his lungs: "Batista, Perico Formental is here!" Eventually Batista emerged, let him in, and gave him money to buy passage to the United States. The last I heard was that the Habana center fielder was earning his living in Chicago as a *babalao,* an Afro-Cuban priest. Apparently, he has died.

Other than Amorós, who was in no condition to be interviewed formally, five other men I talked to died as I wrote this book, as far as I know: Fermín Guerra, Claro Duany, Quilla Valdés, Napoleón Reyes, and Dick Sisler. Guerra looked frail, and a stroke had affected his speech slightly. But he remembered everything and was still upbeat about his fistfight with the immensely bigger Don Newcombe: "I was tough," Guerra said. At the end of the interview a grandson chimed in to say that he was so proud that his grandfather had been able to accomplish so much being illiterate. I was startled. This man, who had managed successfully in Cuba and elsewhere, who was a leader in his time, could not read and write? His wife, the sister of Regino (Reggie) Otero, explained with some embarrassment that she had taught Fermín how to write his name to sign contracts and autographs, and then eventually how to read and write a little. Massive Napoleón Reyes was a shadow of his former self, limping and breathing with some difficulty. But his green eyes sparkled as he reminisced about his good times in Mexico, playing for Pasquel, and his exploits as an amateur playing for the University of Havana. He had finished a degree in chemical engineering. He told me with moist eyes the moving story reproduced in chapter 6 about his arrival in the United States.

It is uncanny to hear these men's words on tape, knowing that they are truly disembodied voices. They have become something that has only been possible in our century: oral relics. As I write these final words I marvel at how many games have been played in Cuba since Nemesio Guilló returned to the island with a ball and a bat in his student's trunk, and I wonder about the many days that have since then fallen forever into time.

Notes

Chapter One

1. *For Want of a Horse: Choice & Chance in History,* ed. by John M. Merriman (Lexington, Mass: The Stephen Greene Press, 1985), p. x.

2. It is unlikely that the game took place the day before because November 27 is a day of national mourning in Cuba, commemorating the death by firing squad of several medical students during the Spanish regime. Of course, given that Castro is such a common surname, the "F. Castro" in the box score could be someone else.

3. The final irony in all this is that even a reference work, the *Biographical Encyclopedia of the Negro Leagues,* has Clint Thomas hitting "a home run off a young pitching prospect named Fidel Castro, who would later lead a revolution and become president of Cuba" (p. 774). Since Thomas played in Cuba from 1923 to 1931 and Fidel Castro was born in 1926, that pitching prospect was really young when he gave up the homer. A book that advertises itself as "Baseball's Ultimate Biographical Reference," *The Ballplayers,* edited by Mike Shatzkin, devotes an entry to Fidel Castro (p. 169). Like malignant cells, misinformation is hard to kill.

4. Her name was Isora del Castillo, a Cuban third baseman for the Chicago Collens, of the Women's Baseball League in the forties. Born in Regla, near Havana, in 1932, she was the daughter of a great shortstop in the Amateur League, Argelio de Castillo. Known as "Chica" and "Pepper," she played in 1949 and 1950. A singer, she was often called upon to croon "Quiéreme mucho" before games. *The Pinch Scotch Whiskey Cuban Baseball Hall of Fame Gala,* June 28, 1997, a pamphlet with biographies of inductees and other interesting materials.

Chapter Two

1. Durocher had first come to Havana in the thirties as a member of the Gas House Gang (the St. Louis Cardinals), and later, in 1941, as manager of the Dodgers, when he staged a riotous protest in a spring-training game against a Cuban selection at La Tropical. He was tossed from the game by the legendary Cuban

umpire Amado Maestri, and came close to being subdued more forcefully by members of the Cuban Rural Police when he initially refused to leave. Batista, president at the time and in attendance, thought that Durocher's antics were part of a routine and asked if Leo could give a repeat performance the next day. Leo, as could be expected, had taken a liking to the Havana nightlife, and to the luxurious Hotel Nacional, where the team was staying. The casinos were of particular interest to him, and it is probably there that he came into contact with the unsavory characters whose presence at the Gran Stadium led to his suspension. There was, of course, no gambling at the hotel per se until the fifties, but Leo found where the action was in Havana.

2. Pasquel wanted respectability for his league but his own voluble character often got in the way. For instance, he jumped onto the field to meddle in a dispute involving Maestri, but the Cuban umpire, who had molded himself in the image of his admired Bill Klem, tossed Pasquel out and refused to let play resume until he left. He did, but Maestri quit the next day and flew back to Cuba after picking up his paycheck. Pasquel also made many players angry by moving them from one team to another.

3. The interview between Pasquel and Luis Orlando Rodríguez was included in a story by Ernesto Azúa in *El Mundo* (October 27, 1946, p. 30), titled "Pasquel continuará este invierno la guerra firmando jugadores de las Grandes Ligas."

4. Both Amaro and Orta had sons who made it to the majors.

5. A revolutionary from the thirties with ties to the notorious *bonche universitario,* a group of thugs who terrorized the university, Luis Orlando had once been shot six times and left for dead in a gutter. Somehow he survived, spent time in Florida as an exile (where he probably learned English), and lived to see some of his friends assume power once Grau rose to the presidency. Orlando carried some of the lead from the shooting in his body until the end of his life.

6. In an interview with Habana's second baseman, Heberto Blanco, September 29, 1998, in the squalid tenement house in which he lives in Havana, another version of the Lions' swoon was offered. After paying homage to Miguel Angel González, whom he says he revered as a teacher, Blanco hesitantly and carefully suggested that the Reds' manager had let the team slip by not pitching Martin at appropriate moments, in order to allow the race to become more interesting and profitable. A well-spoken, thoughtful man who invoked José Ortega y Gasset's dictum about man being a composite of "me and my circumstances" to excuse González, he also acknowledged that in the fateful play in rightfield on Fleitas' hit, his brother Carlos had simply misplayed the ball (*la toreó*).

Chapter Three

1. Black American players usually stayed at the same kind of hotel in Havana. During the previous season, an article in *Carteles* reported that many American blacks, Mexicans, and Spanish jai-alai players lodged at the Hotel San Luis, on Belascoaín Street in downtown Havana. Fausto Miranda told me that traditionally black players stayed at the very modest Hotel Boston, which is probably where Robinson and his black teammates stayed. White American players, even in the fifties, stayed in apartment complexes, or in houses near the exclusive social clubs and the beaches.

2. In its *Programa Oficial. Campeonato 1950–1951* (Havana: Official Baseball Records Advertising Comp., 1950).

3. Paige also feared a statutory-rape accusation against him in Cuba dating back to 1929, but he could have returned the money.

4. The Giants sold him to the Braves eventually, probably so as not to have two black outfielders—the other was Willie Mays.

5. De la Cruz returned to Cuba in shame and anger after being rebuked by those in Mexico who had joined the Asociación de Peloteros, played in the Liga Nacional, and not been paid their salaries. He had had a successful career in organized baseball, winning 9 games for the Cincinnati Reds in 1944 after a 21-win season for Syracuse (in the International League) the year before. He also had notable careers in Mexico and Cuba. In Mexico, de la Cruz, who had leadership qualities, good looks, and tremendous talent as a pitcher, worked as an announcer, and became a friend and confidant of Jorge Pasquel. De la Cruz's return to Cuba in the summer of 1948 was a precipitous fall from grace. But fate smiled on de la Cruz in a most unusual way. Back in Havana, his favorite lottery-ticket vendor (known as "Checo") practically forced him to buy a whole sheet of a given number, and the former Almendares star won first prize. $100,000.00! As if that were not enough, a few months later de la Cruz won the lottery again, this time about $25,000.00. With the money he bought an apartment building and a Cadillac convertible. He named the building Edificio Bárbara, in thankful homage to Santa Bárbara (Ochún, an Afro-Cuban *orisha*, or deity), to whom he attributed his unusual run of good luck. He also built an elaborate altar for her in his house. In 1950 de la Cruz was still considering a return to active duty in baseball (he was then only thirty-six), though he was now living comfortably off of the more than $1,000 a month in rent he was collecting, along with other earnings from a construction business. He was, by far, the most fortunate of the Cuban stars whose careers were on the wane in the late forties and early fifties. De la Cruz's luck ran short, however, when he died young in 1960.

6. "Malayo," or "Malaysian," is one of the many gradations of color among Cuban mulattoes, indicating bronze color but straight hair.

7. De Armas was a financial adviser to the league, Parga owned the sporting goods store Casa Tarín that had the concession for the (Wilson) baseballs used by the league, and Maduro was one of the owners of the Gran Stadium. With this clout Cienfuegos could counter that of the ten owners of Almendares, which, as we saw belonged to powerful Cuban families such as the Sanguilys, Mendozas, and Menocals, Marianao's newly acquired financial and political power, and Habana's financial stability under Miguel Angel.

8. I have a clipping from an unidentified newspaper of the time, given to me by Agapito Mayor, that is like an obituary note, with a cross and EPD (En Paz Descanse—Rest In Peace) embossed at the top. The "deceased" is given as Club Habana, which "Passed away of the Blue Disease, After Receiving Thick White Washes. The Burial is set for February 18. All Are Invited. Signed Mike González, Alberto Garrido ("Chicharito"), Chino Hidalgo, Sagüita Hernández, and Other Players. Grave-diggers: Morris Martin, Octavio Rubert, Fermín Guerra, Monte Irvin, Jethroe, Gionfriddo, Agapito Mayor, etc." The Almendares crowd was having its fun.

Chapter Four

1. As in the United States, baseball needs a pastoral cradle, even if the game had an urban birth. Perhaps the gardenlike lawns on which it is played (which reveal its English lineage) make the countryside a necessary setting.

2. Tinti Molina died on February 9, 1961, in Havana, at age eighty-seven. He was born in Key West on August 28, 1873. His father had emigrated there, persecuted by the Spanish authorities. In 1889 Tinti participated in a championship organized to raise funds for the independence movement, playing catcher for a team named Cuba. In 1895 he came to Cuba for the first time, carrying important documents of the conspiracy and, to avoid suspicion, played in the championship being held at Almendares Park, with the Matanzas B.B.C. He returned to Key West, then came back to Cuba with an expedition of revolutionaries. After independence he organized Team Cuba, and later played for San Francisco and Habana, the team with which he last played, in the 1908–9 season. He won the championship as manager of Fe in 1913 and in 1923 as manager of the famous Santa Clara Leopards. He was the Cuban League's *administrador* (manager) until the Gran Stadium was built in 1946. For twenty-five years he took the Cuban Stars to the United States. This information is drawn from obituary notes written by René Molina (no relation) and Fausto Miranda, in the February 11, 1961, issue of *Revolución*.

3. E. J. Salcines, "José Martí in Tampa: 20 Documented Visits (1891–1894)," *La Gaceta* (Tampa), June 27, 1997, p. 22.

4. Diego Vicente Tejera, "La indolencia cubana," printed in *Cuba Contemporánea* 28 (1922): 169–77. The lecture was delivered to the Sociedad de Trabajadores of Key West on December 12, 1897.

5. For instance: *El Sport. Semanario de Sport, Arte y Literatura. Organo Oficial de la Liga de Base Ball de la Isla de Cuba,* directed by Aurelio Granados and Ezequiel García, which is from the 1880s. *El Score. Semanario de Sports y Literatura,* also from the 1880s. It has many drawings of baseball players, and columns signed by "Truth" and "Dumb Bell"; the names are in English. The pictures of baseball players in uniform on the covers of this journal are superb and are the basis for my descriptions. *El Pitcher. Semanario de Sports y Literatura. Organo Oficial del Habana Base Ball Club,* edited by Luis Testar y Font, also from the 1880s. The Almendares authorities forbade the sale of this magazine at its park, which brought protests from its editors on March 15, 1891 (año 5, no. 11). The journal published excellent pictures of ballplayers, not exclusively from Habana. In that 1891 issue mentioned, Gálvez, who played for Almendares, is on the cover. *El Petit Almendares: Semanario de Sport y Literatura,* first published in April 1902, in answer to *El Petit Habana. Semanario de Sport y Literatura,* which Alberto Castillo had started publishing in 1900. This journal covers in some detail baseball activity in the provinces. *El Petit Almendares* boasts pictures of black ballplayers, who had just been allowed in the Cuban League in the 1900 season. At about this time there was also *Revista Deportiva: Semanario Ilustrado de Sport y Literatura,* which began publication on February 15, 1908. Also *La Cancha Habanera: Semanario de Literatura y Sport,* directed by Domingo Asensio, which began publication in 1902. It dealt mostly with jai-alai. Back in Havana, *Revista Deportiva: Semanario Ilustrado de Sport y Literatura,* directed by Víctor Muñoz, which began publication on February 15, 1908. *Hojas Cubanas,* whose first issue is of January 10, 1913, styles itself as a "Revista de actualidades, literatura, arte y sports." Although other Matanzas jour-

nals, such as *Artes y Letras,* which started in 1893, carried information on baseball, the principal publication in this respect was *El Album. Semanario Ilustrado,* edited by Nicolás Heredia, with graphic artist Ricardo de la Torriente, which was first out on July 12, 1887, carrying a detailed piece about a benefit for the Matanzas B.B.C. at the Palmar del Junco, where there was light theater and music. *El Album* chronicles the very active social side of games in both Matanzas and Havana. One issue contains a hilarious piece translating amorous courting with stages of a baseball game that attests to the erotic element of the sport. In Santiago de Cuba there was *Arte y Sport: Semanario Ilustrado de Sport y Literatura,* directed by Pedro Acosta, and which first came out on March 15, 1902. A search in Cuba's National Library did not turn up journals of this time in Santiago de Cuba. But this does not rule out their existence in the eastern regions of Cuba. In 1897 there was one called *El Sport* in Tampa.

There were other journals, lost in the mists of time, such as *El Sportsman Habanero, El Clipper Habanero, El Pelotero,* and *El Habanista.* Those that do exist are crumbling into dust at the National Library in Havana. They all deserve a much more detailed study than I can offer here.

After the *belle époque,* or in terms of the history of Latin American letters, after *modernismo,* baseball ceased to be associated intimately with literature. Baseball was no longer the sport of young, well-to-do men anymore, and as it was integrated into the myths of the nation it ceased being exotic, having lost its foreign appeal. But baseball, as part of Cuban reality, continued to appear sporadically in works of literature, such as Carlos Loveira's *Generales y doctores* and Alejo Carpentier's *¡Ecué-Yamba-O!* both quoted in this book. Since then, the most important manifestations of baseball in Cuban literature, as far as I know, are the following. In "Tú no sabe inglé," from *Motivos de son* (1930), the leading poet of the Afro-Cuban movement, Nicolás Guillén, chides a black for pretending to know English, but all he really knows are baseball words, which he mispronounces (contained in *Obra poética 1920–1958,* Havana, Instituto Cubano del Libro, 1972, I, 109–10). Guillén's most ambitious evocation of the sport, however, is his "Elegía por Martín Dihigo," a moving poem written on the occasion of the player's death (in *Obra poética 1958–1972,* Havana, Instituto Cubano del Libro, 1973, II, pp. 355–56). José Lezama Lima, the great poet and leader of the Orígenes Group (they published the important journal *Orígenes*), wrote an enigmatic text that appeared in *Diario de la Marina* on October 9, 1949, called "El juego de pelota o la historia como hipérbole" (The Game of Baseball or History as Hyperbole). It is known that the Orígenes Group used to attend games together at the Gran Stadium, but Lezama's text does not appear to be motivated by any specific contest. In it, Lezama speculates how the Mommsens of the twenty-fourth century would interpret the game of baseball, putting forth, obviously tongue-in-cheek, that they would see it as the synthesis of the Greek and Christian worlds, much like the art of Byzantium. He recalls the glass ball that Byzantine painters depicted in the hands of the Divine Child, and finds symbolic the persistence of the number 9 in the game. Lezama's text is most easily found today in José Lezama Lima, *La Habana* (Madrid: Verbum, 1991), pp. 55–56. In the sixties, Roberto Fernández Retamar wrote "Pío Tai," a poem in which he evokes the players he and others of his age admired in their youth, and whose colorful names now acquire a poetic aura ("Mosquito" Ordeñana, "El Guajiro" Marrero, and "El Inmortal Dihigo" are among those he remembers). "Pío Tai," "Pido *time,*" or "time out" among Cuban kids, is a meditation on time, memory, and the significance of popular culture. Fernández Retamar's poem ends by stating that the ballplayers recalled were as important to his education as Joyce, Stravinsky, Picasso, and Klee. "Pío Tai" can be found in Fernández Retamar's *A quien pueda interesar. (Poesía, 1958–1970)* (Mexico: Siglo XXI Editores, 1970), pp. 88–89. More recently, Eliseo Alberto devotes a few pages of his *Informe contra mí mismo* (Madrid: Alfaguara, 1996) to baseball expressions that are used in Cuba to describe situations in life.

6. The preface to Gálvez's book was written by Dr. Benjamín de Céspedes, who praises baseball for promoting health and vigor, including sexual, and criticizes old-fashioned (i.e., Spanish) mores for being too sedentary. De Céspedes was well-read, defiant, and irreligious. His view of sports reflects those prevalent in the industrial centers of the world, such as the United States.

7. There is a monument to Emilio Sabourín on H and 7, in El Vedado, at the place where the original Habana Glorieta stood. It reads: *"Emilio Sabourín y del Villar. Ilustre habanero, fervoroso patriota y revolucionario, pionero del base ball. Fundador del Club Habana, que en estos terrenos organizó el primer campeonato oficial de Cuba y laboró también por la independencia de la patria. Por acuerdo del ayuntamiento número 52, de 28 de agosto de 1952, se ha consagrado a su memoria este monumento en el centenario de su natalicio. 1853—2 de sept—1953."*

8. According to a historian I met at the National Library in Havana in December 1995, the Almendares River was named after Bishop Almendáriz. This august personage used to navigate down it to Havana from his country estate or the nearby sugarmills, when the river was called La Chorrera, to avoid the more treacherous route by horse-drawn carriage. The area, which became the fashionable Almendares neighborhood, took the name from the river. The Marquesado de Almendares was created by royal decree issued by Queen María Cristina de Borbón on May 12, 1838 (Royal Dispatch of December 14, 1842). The one upon whom it was first bestowed was Miguel Antonio de Herrera y O'Farril Pedroso for his services on the Board of Directors that brought about the construction of the railroad between San Julián de los Güines and Havana, the first in Cuba. Rafael Nieto y Cortadillas, *Dignidades nobiliarias en Cuba* (Madrid: Ediciones Cultura Hispánica, 1954), vol. I, p. 23.

9. Other retentions of bullfighting in Cuban baseball are calling a pitcher's work a *faena,* the word to refer to a matador's performance, and something about the color of infield dirt, reminiscent of the *albero,* the sand in a bullring.

10. A fragment of *Nicotina* was published in *Cuba Contemporánea* 5, no. 2 (1914): 474–87. A note about Gálvez says that he was at the time prosecuting attorney at Pinar del Río's court of appeals. The note goes on to say that he is one of Cuba's few comic authors, as he proved with the publication of his little book of epigrams titled *Cantáridas* (La Habana, 1912).

11. All of these inscriptions in the flags and on the medals were in English.

Chapter Five

1. The great Sam Lloyd was known in Cuba as "Bemba de Cuchara" or simply "Cuchara." *Bemba* means "nigger lips," and *cuchara* means "spoon." Lloyd's protruding lower lip led to this tasteless and racist name. Some say that he was also called Cuchara because he picked up a lot of dirt as he scooped up a

grounder, like a shovel. But there is no way of avoiding the racism involved in this as in other such nicknames.

2. As recently as 1995 Fausto Miranda, the dean of Cuban sportswriters, told me that Oscar Charleston, whom he saw play in a sugarmill team in the twenties, was the best baseball player he had ever seen, and he had seen Joe DiMaggio in action many times.

3. *Cuba: The Pursuit of Freedom* (New York: Harper & Row, 1971), p. 497.

4. An Asturian family, the Lópezes, came to Havana in the early part of the century and had several children but moved to Tampa, Florida, where their youngest, Alfonso, was born and eventually became a catcher and manager in the big leagues. But for a quirk of fate, Al López would have been a Cuban ballplayer (he was to help many later in his powerful positions with the Chicago White Sox and the Cleveland Indians).

5. San Francisco was a dock, as well as the neighborhood around it. It was a mostly black area of Havana, peopled by the dock workers, a highly organized group who often belonged to Afro-Cuban sects such as the *ahakuá*, much feared by the general populace.

6. In "El 'Cuba' y el 'Cubano,' " Solloso stated quite plainly: "Being opposed to the participation of blacks in what had been officially, up to then, a sport for whites, I never allowed team Cuba, nor its players, to cross their bats or ashs neither with "Franciscans" nor with "Alexandrians.". . . . When the new championship was convened, and even though Article 94 of the league's charter set forth clearly that the players had to be white and of Cuban nationality, the black club San Francisco had its secret defenders, some of them pure, others with profit in their minds." In *Official Spalding Base Ball Guide* (New York: American Sports Publishing Company, 1906), p. 67.

7. Kiko Magriñat spoke about Camps, saying: "Moisés [Pérez] used to remember that I had performed successfully as a base umpire in the United States, by order of Manuel Cans [*sic*], who was the owner of that era's *Cuban Stars*. . . ." Pedro Galiana, "Del diamante al cementerio," *Carteles*, 16 de enero de 1949, p. 64.

8. The evolution of Negro baseball in the United States was affected by Cuba. Foster moved to Chicago to found the Chicago American Giants, a powerhouse of a team that traveled by Pullman car and that was well organized and disciplined—and in black hands. The "American" in the name of this most significant team in the history of Negro baseball was an answer to the "Cuban" in Cuban Giants. It was also a defiant political statement about the nationality of its players. The Cuban Cristóbal Torriente would become one of Foster's stars on this team.

9. I have been able to locate four of these precious documents at the New York Public Library. The first is the already quoted *Official Spalding Base Ball Guide* (New York: American Sports Publishing Company, 1906). The title page within reads: *Guía oficial del Base Ball de Spalding*, redactor Henry Chadwick "El Padre del Base Ball." Nueva York: American Sports Publishing Company. The others are for 1908–9, 1910–11, and 1917. The title pages vary slightly and the contents substantially.

10. Albert G. Spalding, *America's National Game: Historic Facts Concerning the Beginning, Evolution, Development, and Popularity of Baseball, with Personal Reminiscences of Its Vicissitudes, Its Victories and Its Votaries*, cartoons by Homer C. Davenport (New York: American Sports Publishing Company, 1911), p. 378.

There is a 1992 facsimile edition by the University of Nebraska Press, with and introduction by Benjamin G. Rader.

11. Ira Thomas, "How They Play Our National Game in Cuba," *Baseball Magazine* 10, no. 5 (1913): 61–65.

12. Thomas, 62–63.

13. John B. Holway, "Cuba's Black Diamond," *Baseball Research Journal* 10 (1981): 142.

14. Fe began by representing Regla and as alternative to Habana and Almendares teams that not only hailed from the capital per se, but from two areas (Habana began in El Vedado) where upper-class families lived. Though the upper-class origin of these clubs is lost as baseball became professional, something of their original association remained. Fe, on the other hand, came from a modest town across the bay, hence was more open to blacks, and during its existence fielded many American players from the Negro Leagues.

15. In October 1915 there was even a Chinese season, with the visit of a team from China that played against teams called Havana Park and Almendares Park. They also played against two teams from the Amateur League, the Vedado Tennis Club, and Universidad. The Chinese finished with a record of 5 and 7. *Spalding Guide* (1917), op. cit., p. 109.

16. Peter C. Bjarkman, "First Hispanic Star? Dolf Luque, of Course," *Baseball Research Journal* 19, (1990): 28–32. In Cuban publications the Long Branch manager is sometimes called Enriquez, at other times Dr. Chas Henriquez.

17. See *Entertaining a Nation: The Career of Long Branch,* written and illustrated by the Writers' Project, Work Projects Administration, State of New Jersey (Long Branch, N.J.: sponsored by the city of Long Branch, 1940).

18. Helio Orovio writes, describing the development of rumba in the Matanzas region in this period: "The influence of rumba extended toward Sagua la Grande, where Pío Mobba, Cheché Mulú, Mulence, and, above all, the famous Papá Montero, stood out." "Unión de Reyes llora," *Revolución y Cultura* (Havana) 12 (December 1987): 40. In Alejo Carpentier's 1933 novel *¡Ecué-Yamba-O!* one reads: "¡Papá Montero . . . a pimp and great dancer! The marvelous tale was on everybody's lips. ¡Papá Montero, the son of Chévere y Goyito and María la O's lover! His shadow seemed to flutter among the still palm trees, moving to the sound of the music." (Madrid: Editorial España, 1933), p. 35.

19. Emilio Grenet, *Popular Cuban Music. 80 Revised and Corrected Compositions. Together with an Essay on the Evolution of Music in Cuba,* prologue by Dr. Eduardo Sánchez de Fuentes, tr. by Rachel Phillips (Havana: Ministerio de Educación, 1939), pp. 47–48.

20. Pi also reports in *El Fígaro* of November 9, 1913, that "During the fifteen games played by Birmingham at Almendares Park 42,003 fans have attended. The greatest number in attendance was during the November 5th game against Habana, which was 7,680. The least, also in a game against Habana on October 27th, was 564."

21. Charles Monfort Soberats, "La hazaña de Cristóbal Torriente: tres jonrones en un juego," *Carteles,* año 36, no. 46, November 13, 1955, pp. 78–79; John Holway, "The One-Man Team—Cristóbal Torriente," *Baseball Historical Review* (1981): 72–74; Jorge S. Figueredo, "November 4 [*sic*], 1920: The Day Torriente Outclassed Ruth," SABR, BRJ, 1982, pp. 130–31.

22. Leopoldo F. de Sola and José Sixto de Sola were athletes at Yale at the

beginning of the century, with Leopoldo being an accomplished and award-winning gymnast. Their father was among the founders of the Vedado Tennis Club. José Sixto was the author of an article of great importance to my topic in this chapter: "El deporte como factor patriótico y sociológico: las grandes figuras deportivas de Cuba," *Cuba Contemporánea,* Año 2, Tomo 5, no. 2 (Havana, June 1914), pp. 121–67. Sola's argument is that sports serve as a means to foster a nationalism in the population that transcends social, racial, and economic differences. He writes: "What Cuban, attending a game of baseball between Almendares and one of the great American teams who have visited us in recent years, has not felt himself bound to our players and the rest of the crowd by a powerful link?" (p. 128). Fervently opposed to American interference in Cuban affairs, Sola sees baseball, among other sports, as a way to demonstrate that Cubans need not feel inferior to anyone. He cites, with pride, the case of Méndez: "the modest black athlete, the best pitcher and athlete that Cuba has produced, who has astonished the great American critics with the incredible speed of his pitches, his intelligence, his fielding, and his hitting" (p. 168). Needless to say, Méndez would not have been able to gain admission to the Vedado Tennis Club. Sola's arguments, however, anticipate those of today's Cuban regime, and express clearly the ideology behind Cuban baseball in this century.

23. The *negrito* was a black who played opposite a Galician and who taunted each other. They were both poor and lived by their guile, which the *negrito* had in abundance, while the Gallego, a credulous simpleton did not. The *negrito,* a character that harkened back to nineteenth-century Cuban theater, was played by a white in blackface. These were the precursors of Chicharito and Sopeira, about whom we learned in a previous chapter.

24. Significantly, the best-known early set of Cuban baseball cards was issued also by a tobacco company, Cigarrillos Aguilitas Superfinos, which included only amateur players, in 1928. In that same year another tobacco company, La Gran Fábrica de Cigarros Vallaamil, Santalla y Co., put out a series of Cincinnati Reds players, including, of course, Adolfo Luque. Tobacco companies and Cuban printers had produced in the second half of the nineteenth century splendid series of vignettes to adorn their cigarette wrappers.

25. Roy Campanella, who saw Dihigo at his best both in the Negro Leagues and in Cuba, and who was later a major-league star, was among those who said it.

26. Championships around the town of Holguín, in eastern Cuba, were at this time as strong as or even stronger than those in Havana. Charles Monfort, who is from that region, tells me that duels between Dihigo, pitching, and a black right-hander called Conrado (General Sagua) Rodríguez, drew large crowds. Rodríguez played in the Cuban League from 1906 to 1912, but mostly preferred to remain in Holguín, where he had settled after leaving his native Sagua la Grande (hence his nickname). Another outstanding pitcher from the region was Armelio Acosta, known by his rising fastball. Many talented players from the provinces chose to stay home and play in championships, such as the one in Holguín, which were sponsored by the sugarmills (more about this in the next chapter).

27. I have been unable to ascertain when exactly Habana and Almendares adopted the lion and the scorpion, respectively, as their symbols. Habana's lion was probably chosen not only because of the ferociousness of the king of beasts but also because lions figure prominently in the Castilian coat of arms. The scorpion is the most dangerous insect in Cuba, an island where there are no lethal animals at all.

But there is also an Afro-Cuban dance to kill the scorpion that may also have intervened.

28. The guinea hen is, to Cubans, the fastest of animals, and has a reputation comparable to that of the road runner in the United States. Such is the guinea hen's penchant for running fast that it is reputed that at mating time the male takes a long lead and rushes the female at top speed for the quickest of quickies.

29. Other Monarch players came back to the United States with more conventional stereotypes, complaining about toothless women and a diet based on rice and plantains. American blacks were, well, American. See Janet Bruce, *The Kansas City Monarchs. Champions of Black Baseball* (Lawrence, Kan.: University Press of Kansas, 1985), p. 66.

30. Estalella was, according to Rodolfo Fernández, a *mulato capirro,* a light mulatto whose hair was somewhat kinky. He was signed to play in the majors ten years before Jackie Robinson because of the confusions about race and nationality concerning Cuba in the United States.

31. Elements in the continuity of the league were the presence of Kiko Magriñat as umpire, and eventually Raúl (Chino) Atán, as well as that of the Franquiz brothers as official scorers and statisticians.

32. Another linguistic factor was the creation of a peculiar slang in press accounts of games. We already saw what a *"laboratorio"* was. Second base was called *la adulterina,* probably because it was between first and third; third base was *la base de las angustias,* because players there were anxious to score. To score was *caer en los brazos de Margot* or *caer en la chocolatera.* A *peliculero* is someone who scores. Outfielders ran after balls *como vendedor de periódicos,* and a hot grounder was *un arranca margaritas.*

Chapter Six

1. Cubans of Chinese ancestry did play in the Amateur League, however, and the respected umpire Raúl (Chino) Atán often worked its games.

2. José Rodríguez Feo, *Mi correspondencia con José Lezama Lima* (Havana: UNEAC, 1989), p. 35.

3. The word, of Taíno origin, prophetically meant the square where the Indians played their own ball game, which, as we saw, was called *batos.*

4. The vocabulary of sugar had entered baseball: *pegarle dulce a la majagua* (to hit sweetly with the majagua bat), for instance. Majagua is a Cuban hardwood used in making bats.

5. *The Cuba Review* for August 1924 (vol. 22, no. 9), reports that "Baseball equipment in Cuba is purchased entirely from the United States. Uniforms, complete with shoes, are retailed at prices varying from $8 to $15, although those from $8 to $10 meet with the greatest demand" (p. 25). This situation would change. Quilla Valdés told me that the Central Hershey uniforms were made by El Lucky Seventh, a sporting goods store in Havana that became quite famous and that rivaled Casa Tarín and J. Vallés. Tarín, as we saw, distributed Wilson equipment, most notably baseballs, which came to be known as "la Wilson de Tarín." The Amateur League used Wilsons, as did the Cuban League. Luis Parga, owner of Casa Tarín—which fielded a semipro team—became a prominent figure and team owner in the Cuban League.

6. The Cuban Telephone Company, its name in English, was an American-owned company. Club Teléfonos was organized as a social club to comply with Amateur League rules. Sometimes, instead of script, the team's uniforms had a quaint old telephone on their front.

7. Other clubs were Víbora, Loma, Antiguos Alumnos, etc.

8. Given his last name, it is doubtful that this player was really of Chinese ancestry, though he could have had a Chinese mother. But in Cuba, as in much of Latin America, people of any race who happen to have slanted eyes are often nicknamed "Chino." The O'Farrills were a prominent Havana family.

9. Tomás Morales Fernández, *Los grandes juegos* (Mexico: S.C.L., La Prensa, 1970), p. 18.

10. Marrero's hesitations are due to the fact that, like many ballplayers of his time, he lied about his age. I have found several birth dates for him in various publications and baseball cards. I believe that at this stage of his life he would tell the truth, however, and that the one he gives here is the true one.

Chapter Seven

1. In 1942, clearly a reflection of the Cuban League's recovery, professional ballplayers built a fairly elaborate mausoleum at Havana's lavish Colón cemetery to bury their own. According to the inscription on the mausoleum, which still stands, it was built by the "Asociación Cristiana de Players, Umpires y Managers de Base-Ball Profesional." There is the statue of a ballplayer on top of the structure, and a small plaque with the name of Emilio Sabourín, and the years (1878–95) in which he played, but I do not know if he is actually buried there. Among the names of the players who were instrumental in building the shrine the best known are Miguel Angel González and José María Fernández. I have no reason to believe that either is buried there.

2. Another link between these two worlds was disease and vice. According to Emilio de Armas, many of the black ballplayers suffered from syphilis, and the use of drugs, particularly marijuana, was not uncommon. Fermín Guerra told me that Aristónico Correoso, for instance, liked to smoke cigarettes that were *un poco cargados* (a little loaded). Others referred to marijuana as *cigarrillos mexicanos* (Mexican cigarettes). Marijuana had a heavy stigma in Cuba and was thought to be used only by underworld figures.

3. "El Brujo Rosell: la dicha de recordar," in Cristina Pacheco, *Los dueños de la noche* (Mexico City: Editorial Planeta de México, 1990), p. 275.

4. In our interview, Al López told me that Latin American players tended to be ahead of Americans at the beginning of seasons because of winter play, so he waited longer to assess their talent and did not let himself be unduly impressed by early successes.

5. Soon to be followed by Angel—Jack—Aragón, who made the Giants in 1941 and whose father, Angel, had played thirty-three games for the Yankees between 1914 and 1917. Since then the only native-born Cuban father-son combo has been René and Aurelio Monteagudo. There have been three other sons of Cuban major leaguers in the majors, but the sons have been born in the United States: José and Danny Tartabull, Tony and Eduardo Pérez, and Diego and David Seguí.

6. Because it will come up again in reference to Raymond Brown, it may be

best to explain this term now. *Jabao* means a mottled rooster or hen—one with small black and white squares or dots—and is used to describe a light mulatto in Cuba. It appears to be a word of Taíno origin.

7. In 1944, in another *Carteles* article (February 27), Losada describes Cambria as: "Scout for the Washington Senators, co-owner of a Class D team in the minors, and outright owner of a laundry that washes dirty laundry, except Cambria's own."

8. Bob Considine, "Ivory from Cuba: Our Underprivileged Baseball Players," *Collier's,* August 3, 1940, pp. 19, 24.

9. In an interview with Pedro Galiana of which I only have the undated clipping, the eighty-two-year-old Pompez spoke Spanish somewhat haltingly, according to the reporter, but had a clear and proud memory of his New York Cubans, particularly the 1947 champions.

10. It was, in fact, a reorganization, for there had been a powerful and influential team named Azteca earlier.

11. Brinquitos Brown's career included many good seasons in Mexico. *The Biographical Encyclopedia of the Negro Baseball Leagues* reports that when he played for the Cuban Stars in the early thirties he was sometimes listed as "Brownez" in an apparent effort to add a little Spanish flavor to the lineup of the Cuban Stars (West).

12. De Armas brought the Folies Bergères to Havana in the 1950s and was involved in many other promotions, including a circus, throughout his long life.

13. Though race relations were—and are—much better in Mexico than in Cuba, black catcher Tommy Dukes was known as "La Changa" Dukes there. *Changa* means monkey in Mexico.

14. Fausto Miranda has written this story, as also told him by Monfort, in *El Miami Herald,* April 22, 1984 ("Lecturas de domingo: Josh Gibson, una leyenda"). I had heard it said that Gibson hit one at Sixto Escobar Park in Puerto Rico that reached the ocean. I visited that stadium to see if this was a figure of speech but it seems possible, though the shot had to have been cyclopean.

15. I am quoting from the Cuban League program for the 1942–43 season.

16 In the 1939–40 season a lanky, right-handed black pitcher, Isidoro (Cuchilla [Razor]) Thondike, threw a complete game for Almendares but lost. It was his only game in the Cuban League. Years later, in the fifties, I was to know him simply as Cuchilla, the shoeshine at the Liceo social club in my hometown of Sagua la Grande. Cuchilla had been a great pitcher in the region and was recruited by Luque. He always told the story that he lost the game because it was the end of the season and Luque played a bunch of rookies who made many errors. I was mesmerized by the tales told by this regal-looking man, proud still while performing his humble job.

17. "Honor y Gloria," now a videocassette, is an edifying melodrama about Ortiz's life, in which he is portrayed as the pure country bumpkin who is doggedly loyal to friends and family and is willing to make sacrifices to excel in baseball. Interlaced with the story of his life is that of a fictional Raúl Hernández, a first baseman who, in contrast to Ortiz, is a drinker who impregnates his girlfriend, and fails at baseball and life in general. Raúl's wife is a cabaret singer and dancer, which allows for the insertion of a couple of musical spots. But in spite of this kitschy plot, so stereotypical of the fifties, the film contains a number of valuable sequences at the Gran Stadium, as well as at Delta Stadium in Mexico City and the park where

the Venezuelan Liga de Zulia played. One can see in action, besides Ortiz, the likes of Agapito Mayor, Ramón Bragaña, Avelino Cañizares, Chino Valdivia, and Pedro Formental. The portion depicting Ortiz's early career with Hershey has several scenes at that sugarmill's stadium, and I believe that in one quick sequence the shortstop in action is the fabled Quilla Valdés. But besides Ortiz, the film is a homage to Havana's Gran Stadium, which we see both inside and outside, with clips about the fans and announcers, including Cuco Conde and Juan Ealo.

18. Miñoso's complicated names are the bane of English-language sportswriters and a bafflement to Americans in general. Saturnino Orestes Arrieta Miñoso Armas scans thus. Saturnino and Orestes are Miñoso's first and middle names. In Spanish his whole name should have normally been Saturnino Orestes Arrieta (his father's last name) Armas (his mother's maiden name). However, his mother was widowed and remarried, to a man named Miñoso, with whom she had four children who used that name. Miñoso came to be known, too, by that name, so he adopted it. Miñoso is clearly a Galician name that alludes to the Miño River, which runs through that northwestern part of Spain. Classical names such as Saturnino and Orestes are not uncommon in Spanish. Miñoso's teammate with Marianao was Asdrúbal Baró, who had a brother named Aníbal, following classical history to the letter. Then there are Alcibíades, Camilo, Aristónico, Heliodoro, etc.

19. In *Extra Innings* Miñoso tells an interesting story that allows me to mention the name of a great figure of Cuban baseball hardly ever remembered. When he went out to practice with Partagás for the first time, he noticed that the first baseman was a young woman. So when he took his first grounder at third, he lobbed the ball across the infield, which provoked the woman's ire, who yelled words questioning his arm (and perhaps his manhood). So Miñoso answered in kind by firing one over, which she fielded smoothly. It was then that he realized that his teammate was the great "Viyaya." Eulalia González, known as "Viyaya," which means someone who is full of energy and pep—a "live wire"—was a legendary baseball player who had defied all tradition by playing with boys and later men from the equivalent of Little League on up. In the forties and fifties she occasionally played exhibition games with teams in the Cuban League, and hired herself to play around the country. She was small and slender but could play a stylish first base, for which she claims to have been compared to Regino Otero. She complains that she was thrown at by men who were embarrassed when she got hits off their pitching and started a few brawls. She was signed by Racine, a team in the American women's league, but returned home before playing a game. She missed Cuba too much. In the interview from which I gather this information, laced with not a few *coños* (the word literally means "cunt," but Cubans use it merely as an expletive), one can see that Viyaya was feisty and fearless. See Roger Ricardo Luis, "Eulalia 'Viyaya' González: 'Yo jugué en los mejores terrenos de La Habana,' " *Cuba Internacional* 32, no. 293 (January, 1995): 60–62. In chapter 1 I already mentioned Isora del Castillo, another remarkable Cuban woman baseball player.

20. Pedroso could not be known by his nickname in New York, with so many Puerto Ricans. In this community *bicho* means male organ, while in Cuba it means bug, or more to the point, someone who is clever and resourceful, which the smallish and fast Pedroso obviously was.

Chapter Eight

1 Herrera's signing and early development were anomalous. He actually signed first with the Kansas City Monarchs, of the declining Negro Leagues, one of the last Cuban blacks to do so and one of the few rookies who went that route after Jackie Robinson. Herrera played for a rookie Monarch traveling club that barnstormed during the early fifties and "lived out of a bus," as he told me in Miami. That club included future Hall of Famer Ernie Banks.

2. The newspaper *Alerta* published a series of pictures of the Cuban League players as part of Antonio Alcalde's election bid. Some of these are superb black-and-white shots and still can be found for sale on the streets of Havana.

3. Valdivielso summed it up in what amounts to a "Yogi Berraism" when he told me that the Senators had very good teams, it was just that the others were so much better!

4. More than a thousand fans came all the way from Venezuela and hundreds from Panama and Cuba.

5. The Navegantes had been led by Cuban star player-manager Lázaro (El Príncipe de Belén) Salazar. But he had to dash back home to Mexico, where his wife had passed away. Salazar, himself, as recounted earlier, was not far from his own dramatic early death.

6. Rodolfo Fernández managed the Aguilas Cibaeñas in 1953–54, and the next season he went to the Estrellas Orientales, with Agapito Mayor taking over the Aguilas, Pollo Rodríguez Escogido, and Oscar Rodríguez Licey.

7. *Patato* means shorty—which Pascual was—but was misheard as "potato" by Americans, who called him that in the United States.

8. The reason Cuban teams could have more imports goes back to the origins of the pact with organized baseball. Because Cuba agreed to abide by the suspension of Cuban players who had performed in Mexico, the Cuban League teams was bereft of native talent, which, as seen before, went to La Tropical.

9. Bragan writes in a letter of February 18, 1992: "I was managing the Fort Worth, Texas team AA in the Texas League. Monchy de Arcos came to Vero Beach, Fla., Dodgertown, and would sit in the meetings of Mr. Branch Rickey with the managers and scouts each night during spring training. He was impressed with me, I suppose, at those meetings, and consequently asked me to manage his team."

10. Narciso Camejo, who was present at the meeting between the two patriarchs, says that Miguel Angel had left blank the space naming the salary in the contract, and when Luque asked, the old catcher said words to the effect that he could not dare put a price on the services of a figure such as Papá Montero, that the old pitcher should fill in what he though he was worth. Camejo disputes the popular belief that Miguel Angel was a tightwad, claiming that he kept many old ballplayers on the Habana payroll so they could make a living after their playing days were over.

11. *Hemingway in Cuba,* with an introduction by Gabriel García Márquez (Secacus, N.J.: Lyle Stuart, 1984), p. 66.

12. At the time of this incident Fidel Castro was in Mexico, plotting his landing in Cuba. It was perhaps knowledge of this event that led Don Hoak to later claim that he had batted against Fidel Castro when the leader had invaded the field of play during a game. The late Everardo J. Santamarina debunked the whole story in his "The Hoak Hoax," *The National Pastime. A Review of Baseball History* 14

(1994): 29–30. Hoak had played third for Cienfuegos in 1953–54, hitting .296. Fidel Castro was in jail for the 1953 Moncada attack and was not amnestied until May 1955, whereupon he went into exile.

13. The *Diario de la Marina* reported blandly on Tuesday, March 6 (no newspapers were published on Mondays), that the opposition had attempted to bring the issue of the students' beating before the Cuban Congress but that lack of a quorum had prevented it. They also ran, however, a caricature in which a fan is asking another who the two catchers are, pointing to a couple of ballplayers in full catcher's gear, and another replies: "They are not catchers but outfielders."

14. Robert Lacey, *Little Man: Meyer Lansky and the Gangster Life* (New York: Little, Brown, 1991), p. 301.

15. Cicotte had the misfortune that his name sounds exactly like the Spanish *sicote,* which in Cuba means toe jam.

16. Scull speaks bitterly of this in an interview in *Diario de la Marina* of April 17, 1954. In that same year the Senators would eventually bring up Carlos Paula, another Cuban black, who broke their color barrier.

17. In this column, called "Don't Die on Third," Cambria is arguing for the creation of a third major league, made up of Latin American cities and stocked with Latin players, that would play the winner of the World Series.

18. Felo Ramírez told me that a kind of Caribbean Series was organized in Nicaragua in 1964, including teams from Venezuela and Puerto Rico. The San Juan Senators, winners of the Puerto Rican League, took a team that many thought would win the tournament so easily that fan interest would lag. It included Roberto Clemente and Orlando Cepeda, among other luminaries. But Nicaragua won with a team made up of, for the most part, Cuban veterans such as Julio Moreno, then in his midforties, and others, such as the powerful Borrego Alvarez, who had been left out of Organized Baseball.

19. This incident was brought to my attention by my friend Tom Miller, who mentions it in his piece "Little Havana's Triple Play," *Hemisphere* (United Airlines magazine, April 1993), pp. 69–71.

Chapter Nine

1. I doubt very much that many Cubans thought of beating the Americans as an important goal. It is prudent, it seems to me, to distinguish between what the Cuban regime says the people feel, and what they may actually feel but have no free way of expressing.

2. The propagandistic *Viva y en juego,* a history of Cuban baseball produced by the regime, skims over professional baseball, which it dismisses with derisive terms such as *baseball rentado* (baseball for lease). But by exalting amateur baseball, which it attempts to connect with postrevolutionary baseball, it celebrates the Amateur League, which practiced apartheid. And by giving short shrift to the Cuban League, it condemns to oblivion all of the great black Cuban stars who were not allowed, and could not afford to be amateurs. The book, written by white Cubans, is the last gasp of the Amateur League and its racist policies. The same kind of omission is found in the Museo Nacional del Deporte, which stands at the Plaza de la Revolución. Except for Martín Dihigo's, the exploits of all the great black Cuban players who had to play as professionals or semi-professionals, are nowhere to be found.

There are, however, a few uniforms from the Amateur World Series of the early forties, sponsored by Batista and featuring Cuban teams that were virtually all white.

3. I have an August 1991 clipping from one of the many Cuban local papers from Miami, with an advertisement of an "Academia de Baseball" run by former Cuban big leaguers Orlando Peña and Miguel de la Hoz. Many retired Cuban players opened baseball academies in the Miami area. Some, such as former star Camilo Pascual, have been hired as scouts. Those with more education, such as José Valdivielso, have found positions in the Spanish-language media.

4. Rigoberto (Tito) Fuentes had good years for the Giants and Padres in the sixties and seventies, and because he was a show-off, or a "hot dog" in baseball parlance, received more attention than his performance deserved. Another Cuban infielder from the period was Jacinto (Jackie) Hernández, a good defensive player with modest offensive numbers, who played with the Angels, Pirates, Twins, and Royals. Right-handed pitcher Oscar Zamora played for the Cubs and Astros. Roberto (Bobby) Ramos, from Calabazar (Havana), was a second-string catcher with the Expos.

5. At a typical gathering of Cuban fans in Miami at Restaurante La Rosa, I was engaged in argument by my dear friend Manuel García (not Cocaína) about how many Cubans were on major-league rosters (July 1998). He produced a list that included not only the ones mentioned here, including those known to be born of Cuban parents, but also Jorge Posada and Tino Martínez of the Yankees. It seems that Posada, who was born and raised in Puerto Rico, is the son of Cuban parents and the nephew of Leopoldo Posada, the Cuban outfielder who played for the Kansas City Athletics. Martínez's ancestry had been discussed in the press, with his father explaining (a bit too vehemently for Cubans) that he was Spanish, not Cuban. It does seem, however, that Cardinal catcher Elieser Marrero is Cuban.

6. I am quoting from a crudely mimeographed copy of the schedule, rules, and rosters for the XXXVI Serie Nacional (1996–97) obtained at Stadium Latinoamericano from a friend.

7. "Baseball: Cuba's National Passion" (Sunday, May 20, 1990).

8. Fausto Triana, *Braudilio Vinent: la fama de la consistencia* (Havana: Editorial Científico-Técnica, 1985), p. 79.

9. Named after Santa Bárbara, one of the Afro-Cuban syncretic deities of the Afro-Cuban pantheon, known as Ochún. But Bárbara has no equivalent in the masculine, so to name a boy Bárbaro—which literally means "barbarian"—is a deliberate religious gesture, making him a son of Santa Bárbara.

10. Born in Miami of Cuban parents, Joe Cubas became an agent after following the Cuban national team for several years and determining that many of its players were of major-league caliber. He is actively opposed to Fidel Castro's regime, aiming to uncover the lies behind the propaganda involving sports. Cubas' activities have been denounced by the Maximum Leader himself. The agent apparently took considerable financial risks at first in signing Cuban ballplayers, but they have paid off with the fantastic contracts obtained for the likes of Osvaldo Fernández and Liván and Orlando (El Duque) Hernández. The name Cubas, by the way, is common in Spanish and means wine cask, having nothing to do with the country's name, which derives from a Taíno Indian word. The only printed information I have been able to find on Cubas has been Mark Winegardner's article "Patriot Games," *GQ* 68, no. 6 (June 1998): 150–58. I once called his office, but my call was not returned.

Bibliography

The statistical history of Cuban baseball lies buried in newspapers and magazines dating back to the 1860s. I have plumbed it as much as necessary and possible, but a good deal of it was beyond my reach and purposes. Much of that numerical record is crumbling into dust because of the inadequate current conditions that prevail in Cuba's National Library. A substantial part can be culled from collections in the United States and elsewhere, a task that would take a team of trained researchers several years of toil. Charles Monfort, an independent archivist and collector in Miami and a good friend, put at my disposal the fruits of his considerable efforts to cull and classify the material, which were invaluable in checking last-minute details.

Current books on Cuban baseball history are labors of love by amateurs in the original sense of the term. Being one myself and sharing similar motivations, I celebrate their existence. The *Anecdotario del baseball cubano* is particularly revealing about the lore as well as the shape of the game's history in the memory of Cubans. The same is true of Angel Torres' *La historia del béisbol cubano,* Jorge Figueredo's *Pelota cubana: momentos estelares,* and Gustavo Tápanes' two *Catálogo de postalitas de peloteros cubanos.* Torres' latest book, *La leyenda del béisbol cubano,* which is full of useful raw information, arrived late at my desk, but I was still able to profit from it. The biographies of Luis Tiant and Orestes Miñoso are, on the whole, quite poor, and those of Americans, such as Tom Lasorda, who played in Cuba, hardly worth consulting. Statistics on today's baseball in Cuba are copious and reliable, though the publications are sometimes difficult to obtain. Very little of any worth has been published in Cuba about prerevolutionary baseball. The most comprehensive effort is *Viva y en juego,* but it is marred and limited by political propaganda. *Estrellas del béisbol* is a much better book, in spite of the cant, because it affords rare glimpses into the lives of players in postrevolutionary Cuba. The recent biography of Martín Dihigo, *El Inmortal del Béisbol* (1998), contains much unprocessed but useful data and interesting accounts by people who knew him. It is, however, saturated with propaganda and written in a rhetoric to match, down to the point of lamenting that Dihigo, though presumably a leftist, did not master Marxist-Leninist doctrine well enough to probe deeply into Cuba's social and political ills. I hear of collectors and independent historians in Cuba who treasure valuable materials but are prevented by political and economic conditions from publishing them.

The old histories of Cuban baseball are indisputably significant, not only as sources but also as documents themselves. They are, however, unreliable and often confusing, with the exception of Wenceslao Gálvez's, a mine of information based on firsthand knowledge. I have used Raúl Díez Muro's extensively but have been often dismayed by his rounding up a roster with an "etc." The most authoritative and wide-ranging books on Cuban baseball are the *Guías* published by the Esso Oil Company in the forties. This is true particularly for amateur baseball. The four *Spalding Guides* that I found are also valuable. Beyond these, I have availed myself of programs, albums of stickers, baseball cards, yearbooks, and other publications I have been able to gather, some as gifts, others purchased on the streets of Havana and elsewhere. Among these, the most informative have been the season programs, of which I was able to collect a few, but not all. The 1948 *Quién es quién en el base ball en Cuba,* which I have sacked with caution, contains much unusual information, but sometimes a player's season record is given as "only a few games." But my chief sources, other than informants such as the old ballplayers, entrepreneurs, announcers, and newspapermen, have been *Carteles* and the newspapers listed below, particularly *Diario de la Marina,* available in microfilm at the New York Public Library. The recently published encyclopedia of Mexican baseball contains a wealth of information on Cuban players, but the biographical data about them are often in error.

Books on Latin American baseball in English are on the whole disappointing, but a higher level of accuracy and literacy was reached with the publication of Peter Bjarkman's *Baseball with a Latin Beat.* Scant knowledge of Latin American history and culture, and it seems that in most cases of Spanish itself, force these authors to see the game from a perspective based on popular American misconceptions of the region. Their books, predictably, tend to confirm those prejudices. A major fault is that they fail to take into account the significant differences between the cultures of specific areas of the Caribbean and Latin America. In spite of the obvious similarities, the singularity of Mexican, Venezuelan, Dominican, Puerto Rican, and Cuban histories and cultures makes generalizations about "Latin" baseball misleading. I have consulted these books as needed and used whatever could be sifted out that was of value, for which I am grateful.

The same can be said about the many books on the Negro Leagues that inevitably touch on Cuban baseball. The best of these is still the first, which founded the tradition: Robert Peterson's *Only the Ball Was White.* But two more recent books stand above the rest: John Holway's *Voices from the Great Black Baseball Leagues* and Mark Ribowsky's *A Complete History of the Negro Leagues.* James A. Riley's *The Biographical Encyclopedia of the Negro Baseball Leagues* I found very useful, but the information on Cuba was not always accurate. Still, it is a valuable tool, and I wish there were one as good on Cuban baseball. Biographies of Satchel Paige, Josh Gibson, and other black stars are long on lore and short on fact and reliability.

I have, needless to say, made constant use of the *Baseball Encyclopedia* in everything concerning Cuban players in the majors. James Charlton's *Baseball Chronology* has also been constantly at my side, as well as the superb *Baseball Uniforms of the 20th Century,* by Mark Okkonen, which was indispensable in dating photographs given me by some players.

I have limited the bibliography on Cuban culture and history to the most directly relevant items, given that specialists will know the rest, and others can consult very well-known sources. A good place to begin is the journal *Cuban Studies/Estudios cubanos,* but there are many other publications, including electronic ones, with abundant current and historical information.

Cuban Baseball

Album Caramelo Deportivo. Serie de Base Ball 1945–1946. Havana: Fabricado y Distribuido por Felices, 1946.

Alfonso, Gustavo. *Guía del fanático. Campeonato 1959–60.* Havana: Galletería Unica, 1959.

Anecdotario del baseball cubano. Miami: Federación de Peloteros Profesionales Cubanos., n.d.

Antero Núñez, José. *Series del Caribe.* Caracas: Impresos Urbina, 1987.

Arvelo, Alvaro, hijo. "Rodolfo Fernández: 'Trujillo no nos amenazó para que ganáramos el torneo de 1937'," *Ahora* (Sección Deportiva), no. 803, April 2, 1979, pp. 68–71.

Autógrafos Deportivos. Almendares B.B.C. Campeonato 1949–1950. Havana: Editorial La Milagrosa, 1949.

Azúa, Ernesto. "Pasquel continuará este invierno la guerra firmando jugadores de las Grandes Ligas," *El Mundo* (Havana), October 27, 1946, p. 30.

Béisbol 1968. Guía oficial. Campeonato nacional de aficionados. VIII Serie. Reglas y Estadísticas. Havana: Ediciones Deportivas Instituto del Libro, 1968.

Béisbol-73. Guía Oficial Cubana. Havana: Instituto Cubano del Libro, 1975.

Bisher, Furman. "Major-League Minnie," *Sports,* August 1954, pp. 44, 90–91.

Bjarkman, Peter C. *Baseball with a Latin Beat. A History of the Latin American Game.* Jefferson, N.C.: McFarland, 1994.

Campeonato de Baseball Profesional 1958–59. Schedule. Eight pages with cover, includes rosters of four teams. No publisher or date.

Cañizares, René. *Guía Esso de Baseball. Con las reglas oficiales y los récords de las Grandes Ligas y de las ligas Profesional y Amateur de Cuba.* Havana: Standard Oil Company of Cuba—Palacio y Cia., c. 1944.

———. *Guía Esso de Baseball. Con las reglas oficiales y los récords de las Grandes Ligas y de las ligas Profesional y Amateur de Cuba.* Havana: Standard Oil Company of Cuba—Palacio y Cia., c. 1945.

———. *Guía Esso de Baseball 1946. Con las reglas oficiales explicadas y los records de las Grandes Ligas, Profesional y Amateur de Cuba y México.* Havana: Standard Oil Company of Cuba—Compañía Litográfica de La Habana, 1946.

Casal, Julián del. "El base ball en Cuba," *Julián del Casal. Prosas,* Vol. II. Havana: Consejo Nacional de Cultura, 1963, pp. 11–12. Originally in *La Discusión* (Havana), November 28, 1889.

Casas, Edel, Jorge Alfonso, and Alberto Pestán. *Viva y en juego.* Havana: Editorial Científico-Técnica, 1986.

Club Teléfonos de Cuba. Memorias. Havana: Impresos Hermanos Núñez, 1962.

Considine, Bob. "Ivory from Cuba: Our Underprivileged Baseball Players," *Collier's,* August 3, 1940, pp. 19, 24.

Crespo, José R., and Alberto Aguila. *Así era José A. Huelga.* Sancti Spiritus, 1991. Appears to have been printed by Sectorial Provincial de Deportes.

Cuarta Serie Mundial de Base Ball Amateur. Habana. 1941. Havana: Radio Habana

Cuba-Cadena Azul, 1941. Pamphlet produced after the Series with a statistical summary of the games and previous series.

Cuétara Vila, José M., José Dávalos Rossié, and Felipe Coronado Prince. *Efemérides deportivas de la Provincia de Matanzas.* Matanzas: Equipo Provincial de Historia del Deporte, 1979.

Díez Muro, Raúl. *Historia del base ball profesional de Cuba. Libro oficial de la Liga de Base Ball Profesional Cubana.* Havana: no publisher indicated, 1949. Title page indicates third edition.

Ealo de la Herrán, Juan. *Béisbol.* La Habana: Editorial Pueblo y Educación, 1990.

Federación de Peloteros Profesionales Cubanos (en el exilio). Hall de la Fama. Miami, Trade Litho, 1986(?).

Figueredo, Jorge, ed. *Pelota cubana; momentos estelares.* Miami: Interal Trading Corp., 1981.

Fundamentos de béisbol. La Habana: INDER-Imprenta Nacional de Cuba, 1961.

Galiana, Pedro D., Antonio Conejo, and D. Crespo Varona, *Quién es quién en el Base Ball en Cuba,* primera edición. Havana: Ediciones Abela, 1948.

Gálvez y Delmonte, Wenceslao. *El base-ball en Cuba. Historia del base-ball en la Isla de Cuba, sin retratos de los principales jugadores y personas más caracterizadas en el juego citado, ni de ninguna otra.* Havana: Imprenta Mercantil, de los Herederos de Santiago S. Spencer, 1889.

Home Rum [sic]. *Periódico de Base Ball,* Año 1, no. 1, February 25, 1945. Contains records of the Amateur League for 1944.

Krich, John. *El Beisbol: Travels Through the Pan-American Pastime.* New York: Atlantic Monthly Review Press, 1989.

Libro Azul. Resumen general del campeonato de base-ball profesional 1946–47. Souvenir deportivo. Havana: Arrow Press, 1947.

Liga Social de Amateurs de Cuba y sus Federaciones Nacionales. Memoria. 1931–1943. Preparada por el actual Secretario General Honorario de la Liga, señor Gerardo Coyula Girart. Havana: Talleres Tipográficos de Bijol, 1943.

Luis, Roger Ricardo. "Eulalia 'Viyaya' González: 'Yo jugué en los mejores terrenos de La Habana,' " *Cuba Internacional* 32, no. 293 (January 1995): 60–62.

Martel, José, recopilador. *Los Segundos Juegos Deportivos Centro-Americanos.* Havana: Sindicato de Artes Gráficas de La Habana, S.A., l930.

Mendoza, Ramón S., José María Herrero, and Manuel F. Calcines. *El Base-Ball en Cuba y en América.* Havana: Imprenta Comas y López, 1908. Reviewed in *El Fígaro,* March 29, 1908, año 24, no. 13. "el libro de los tres simpáticos compañeros del *Diario de la Marina* . . ."

Miñoso, Orestes "Minnie," with Fernando Fernández and Robert Kleinfelder. *Extra Innings: My Life in Baseball.* Chicago: Regnery Gateway, 1983.

Miñoso, Orestes "Minnie," with Herb Fagen. *Just Call Me Minnie. My Six Decades in Baseball.* Champaign, Ill.: Sagamore Publishing, 1994.

Muñoz, Víctor. *Base Ball. Fundamentos. Técnica. Estrategia,* prólogo de Eladio Secades. La Habana: Editorial Martí, 1947.

Official Spalding Base Ball Guide (New York: American Sports Publishing Company, 1906). Title page within: *Guía oficial del Base Ball de Spalding,* redactor Henry Chadwick "El Padre del Base Ball." Nueva York: American Sports Publishing Co. I have seen three more editions, for the 1908–9, 1910–11, and 1917 seasons. The covers vary slightly, with some saying "Spanish American Edition," and the 1917 "Edición Hispano-Americana."

Oleksak, Michael, and Mary Adams Oleksak. *Béisbol: Latin Americans and the Grand Old Game*. Grand Rapids, Mich.: Masters Press, 1991.

Onigman, Marc. " 'Good Field, No Hit': The Image of Latin American Ball Players in the American Press, 1871–1946," *Revista/Review InterAmericana* 9 (Summer 1979): 199–208.

Padura, Leonardo, and Raúl Arce. *Estrellas del béisbol*. Havana: Editora Abril, 1989.

Pestana, Alberto, compilador. *Breve historial de las series mundiales de béisbol amateur*. Havana: Periódico Juventud Rebelde, n.d.

Pettavino, Paula J., and Geralyn Pye. *Sport in Cuba. The Diamond in the Rough*. Pittsburgh: University of Pittsburgh Press, 1994.

The Pinch Scotch Whiskey Cuban Baseball Hall of Fame Gala, June 28, 1997. Pamphlet printed in Miami with biographies of inductees and other interesting materials published to commemorate a gathering of the Cuban Baseball Hall of Fame in Exile.

Pozo, Miguel Angel (Chacho). *Historia del béisbol en Santiago de las Vegas: 1886–1970*. Boyeros, Cuba: Imprenta 19 de Abril, n.d.

Programa de la IV Serie Mundial de Béisbol Amateur, Habana, 1941, no covers.

Programa Oficial de la Comisión Nacional de Base-Ball Profesional. Campeonato 1942–43. Havana: Dirección General de Deportes, 1942.

Programa Oficial. Campeonato de 1950–51. Liga de Base-Ball Profesional de Cuba. Havana: Official Base-Ball Records Advertising Company, 1950.

Programa Oficial. Campeonato de 1951–52. Liga de Base-Ball Profesional de Cuba. Havana: Official Base-Ball Records Advertising Company, 1951.

Programa Oficial. Campeonato de 1952–53. Liga de Base-Ball Profesional de Cuba. Havana: Official Base Ball Records Advertising Company, 1952.

Ruiz, Yuyo. *Visita del Bambino a Cuba*. Appears to be privately published.

Santamarina, Everardo J. "The Hoak Hoax," *The National Pastime. A Review of Baseball History* 14 (1994): 29–30.

Santana Alonso, Alfredo. *El Inmortal del Béisbol: Martín Dihigo*. Havana: Editorial Científico-Técnica, 1998.

Smith, Marshall. "The Senators' Slow-Ball Señor" [About Conrado Marrero], *Life*, 11 June 1951, pp. 81–92.

Sola, José Sixto de. "El deporte como factor patriótico y sociológico: las grandes figuras deportivas de Cuba," *Cuba Contemporánea* 5, no. 2 (1914): 121–67.

Tápanes, Gustavo. *Folleto ilustrado de peloteros cubanos que jugaron en las Grandes Ligas 1871–1990*. Union City, N.J.: Leon Printing (Imprenta Cubana), 1990.

———. *Catálogo de postalitas de peloteros cubanos que jugaron en las Grandes Ligas, 1949–1989*. Union City, N.J.: Leon Printing (Imprenta Cubana), 1989.

Tejera, Diego Vicente. "La indolencia cubana" (conferencia pronunciada el 12 de diciembre de 1897, en la Sociedad de Trabajadores, Cayo Hueso), published in *Cuba Contemporánea,* 28 (1922), pp. 169–77 and in his *Textos escogidos*. Havana: Editorial de Ciencias Sociales, 1981, p. 171 (the quote).

Thomas, Ira. "How They Play Our National Game in Cuba," *Baseball Magazine* 10, no. 5 (1913): 59–65.

Tiant, Luis, and Joe Fitzgerald. *El Tiante: The Luis Tiant Story*. Garden City, N.Y.: Doubleday, 1976.

Torres, Angel. *La historia del béisbol cubano 1878–1976*. Los Angeles: Copyright Angel Torres, 1976.

———. *La leyenda del béisbol cubano*. Miami: Review Printers, 1996.

Triana, Fausto. *Braudilio Vinent. La fama de la consistencia.* Havana: Editorial
  Científico-Técnica, 1985.
Varona, Enrique José. "El base ball en La Habana," *Revista Cubana,* 4 (1887):
  84–88.
Vázquez, Humberto. *¿Conoce usted las reglas del béisbol? Sobre jugadas basadas en
  reglas oficiales.* Santiago de Cuba: Editorial Oriente, 1988.
Vistuer Valdés, Juan. *Béisbol: la acción de batear.* Havana: Editorial Científico-
  Técnica, 1994.
Washington Nationals 1953 Yearbook. Washington, D.C., 1953. Pictures and bi-
  ographies of several Cuban players.
*Washington Senators 1959 Yearbook. 100 Years of Baseball in the Nation's Capital
  1859–1959.* Washington, D.C., 1959. Contains "All-Time Senator Roster,"
  which includes many Cubans.
Winegardner, Mark. "Patriot Games," *GQ* 68, no. 6 (June 1998): 150–58.

Principal Articles from Carteles (in Chronological Order)

Jess Losada. "El Brooklyn en la Habana," March 22, 1931, p. 35.
———. "Nuestro deporte en ruinas," April 15, 1934, p. 38.
———. "Una semblanza de Mike González," November 18, 1934, pp. 38–39, 44.
———. "Resumen deportivo" (1934), January 6, 1935, p. 39.
Roig de Leuchsenring. "Las corridas de toros en La Habana," May 26, 1935, 38–
  39, p. 26.
Jess Losada, "30 años de deporte profesional," May 24, 1936, pp. 117, 129.
J. González Barros. "Valores de la Dirección General de Deportes: Dr. Arturo Ben-
  gochea, Asesor de Baseball," September 11, 1938, p. 54.
———. "Experiencias del campeonato de baseball," February 19, 1939.
Jess Losada. "Las grandes ligas de cerca," April 9, 1939.
Anonymous. "Primera serie mundial amateur en La Habana," June 11, 1939, p.
  56.
———. "La Serie Mundial Amateur," August 20, 1939, p. 52.
René Molina. "Los viejos del baseball," December 15, 1940, p. 56.
Jess Losada. "Los Dodgers de Flatbush en La Habana," March 2, 1941, pp. 53–
  55.
———. "Cómo ganó Venezuela el Campeonato Mundial de Baseball Amateur,"
  November 2, 1941, pp.12–13.
———. "Grandezas y miseria del amateurismo," November 9, 1941, pp. 8– 9.
J. González Barros. "Baseball vs. Balompié," November 9, 1941, p. 14.
Jess Losada. "Hace cuarenta años se jugaba baseball en Caracas," November 30,
  1941, pp. 8–9.
———. "La temporada de baseball amateur," March 29, 1942, pp. 56–57.
———. "Cómo vio la revista *Life* la visita de los Dodgers a la Habana," April 19,
  1942, pp. 39–40.
Gabino Delgado, Jr. "Cienfuegos, campeón de baseball amateur," May 17, 1942,
  p. 56.
———. "Los Yankees del amateurismo criollo," June 7, 1942, p. 54.
———. "Conrado Marrero," June 21, 1942, pp. 48–49.
———. "¡Fanático!" July 12, 1942, p. 47.

Jess Losada. "El base-ball organizado barre la línea de color," August 16, 1942, pp. 34–35.

———. "Baseball dominicano (una historia de valor y entusiasmo)," October 11, 1942, pp. 34–35.

Gabino Delgado. "Una breve historia de Coco del Monte," October 11, 1942, p. 46.

Jess Losada. "Puntos luminosos de la Serie Mundial de 1942," October 18, 1942, pp. 34–35.

Gabino Delgado. "Síntesis de la V Serie Mundial," October 18, 1942, pp. 47–49.

Jess Losada. "Venezuela en la Serie Mundial," October 25, 1942, pp. 34–35.

Gabino Delgado. "México en la Serie Mundial," October 25, 1942, p. 47.

Jess Losada. "Mucho Habana," November 15, 1942, p. 49.

Gabino Delgado. "Resumen deportivo," December 27, 1942, p. 55.

———. "Los cubanos en las mayores," January 17, 1943, p. 46.

Jess Losada. "La minerología al servicio del deporte," February 7, 1943, p. 49.

———. "Campeonato de baseball amateur," March 14, 1943, pp. 48–49.

———. "Temporada de 1943: Juventud racionada," April 18, 1943, pp. 34–35.

Gabino Delgado. "Moreno y su velocidad," April 25, 1943, p. 46.

———. "Los tres mosqueteros," May 2, 1943, p. 46.

Jess Losada. "Club Atlético Santiago de las Vegas," May 16, 1943, pp. 48–49.

Gabino Delgado. "Un equipo campeón para el V.T.C., aspiración de Reinaldo Cordero," July 4, 1943.

Jess Losada. "¡Serie Mundial de 1943! La selección cubana," September 5, 1943, pp. 32–33.

Gabino Delgado. "Natilla Jiménez, Veterano a los 25," September 19, 1943, p. 48.

———. "Resumen del Baseball Amateur," October 3, 1943, p. 36.

———. "Ganaremos esta vez—dice Burrolote," October 10, 1943, p. 46.

———. "Julio Moreno fue balompedista," October 17, 1943, p. 46.

Jess Losada. "Reinaldo Cordero, internacionalista del baseball," November 7, 1943, pp. 34–35.

Gabino Delgado. "Lanzadores, factor básico del Almendares," November 14, 1943, pp. 48–49.

———. "Cuando venga Estalella," November 21, 1943, p. 46.

———. "Amado Maestri las canta como son," December 12, 1943, p. 46.

———. "La Liga Nacional en acción," January 9, 1944, p. 47.

———. "Baseball cubano en la República Dominicana," January 23, 1944, p. 46.

———. "Un año habanista," January 30, 1944, pp. 46–47.

Jess Losada. "Ayer y hoy en la vida de Joseíto Rodríguez," January 30, 1944, pp. 48–49.

———. "Nuestro baseball de ayer . . . ," February 6, 1944, pp. 34–35.

———. "Un cubano en las Grandes Ligas (la historia beisbolera de Roberto Ortíz)," February 27, 1944, pp. 34–36.

Gabino Delgado. "Quilla Valdés, atleta y caballero," May 26, 1944, p. 48.

Jess Losada, "Julio Moreno es un Bob Feller tropical," April 2, 1944, pp. 34–37.

Gabino Delgado. "Latinos en el baseball norteamericano," April 2, 1944, p. 46.

Jess Losada. "Pedro Natilla Jiménez," April 9, 1944, pp. 34–37.

———. "Balance de una obra deportiva," April 23, 1944, pp. 34–36.

Gabino Delgado. "Moreno poncha sin querer," May 7, 1944, p. 49.

———. "La magia de Vitico Muñoz," May 28, 1944, pp. 46–47.

Jess Losada. "Y lo hice sin comer espinacas (apuntes de la vida deportiva de Juan Ealo)," July 16, 1944, pp. 34–37.

———. "Nació en Cidra, lo llaman Limonar y es el ídolo de Matanzas," September 10, 1944, pp. 34–36.

———. "Las siete vidas de la Serie Mundial de Baseball Amateur," September 17, 1944, pp. 34–37.

———. "Campeonato profesional," November 5, 1944, pp. 36–37.

———. "Del pasado deportivo," January 21, 1945, p. 47.

———. "Optimismo primaveral en las mayores," April 1, 1945, pp. 34–35.

———. "Joe Cambria contrata a un pelotero," April 15, 1945, pp. 34–36.

———. "La serie mundial amateur hace crisis," June 17, 1945, pp. 34–36.

———. "El campeonato de B.B. de las escuelas públicas," July 22 1945, pp. 34–35.

Gabino Delgado. "Una entrevista por Vía Aérea con Napoleón Reyes," August 19, 1945, pp. 46–47.

Jess Losada. "Los cubanos en México," September 9, 1945, pp. 34–36.

———. "Medio año deportivo," May 12, 1946, pp. 69–71.

———. "Las Grandes Ligas en plena zafra," May 26, 1946, pp. 46–49.

———. "Baseball nocturno en La Habana," June 2, 1946.

———. "Panorama mundial," June 16, 1946, pp. 46–48.

———. "La noche pasqueliana," July 14, 1946, pp. 46–47, 50.

———. "La noche pasqueliana," July 21, 1946, pp. 46–48.

———. "La noche pasqueliana," July 28, 1946, pp. 46–47.

———. "La Habana se convirtió en Plaza de Liga Grande," November 3, 1946, pp. 52–53.

———. "Figuras del torneo profesional," December 15, 1946, p.53.

Mario Vidal. "Furia de pelota," December 15, 1946, p. 57.

Jess Losada. "Televisión y deportes," December 29, 1946, pp. 48–49.

———. "Cocaína García," January 12, 1947, pp. 48–49.

———. "Vaticinios para 1947," January 26, 1947, pp. 48–49.

———. "Andrés Fleitas, el más útil," February 23, 1947, pp. 46–47.

Rai García. "Hotel San Luis. Cuartel General del Deporte," February 23, 1947, pp. 46–47.

Jess Losada. "El ensayo étnico de Jackie Robinson (no han desaparecido aún las barreras raciales)," March 16, 1947, pp. 46–47.

———. "Campo de entrenamiento en La Habana," March 23, 1947, pp. 46–47.

Gabino Delgado. "El poderío de los Havana Cubans," April 6, 1947, pp. 50–51.

Jess Losada. "Lo que hay detrás de la cesantía de Luis Orlando Rodríguez," April 13, 1947, pp. 48–49.

———. "Hay que ordenar nuestro baseball," April 20, 1947, pp. 48–49.

———. "Béisbol femenino: una nueva cantera deportiva," May 18, 1947, pp. 48–49.

———. "Brooklyn invita a un pelotero amateur cubano," June 1, 1947, pp. 48–49.

Gabino Delgado. "La reunión de Chicago," June 29, 1947, p. 46.

Jess Losada. "Justicia social por la vía deportiva," July 6, 1947, pp. 47–49.

Rai García. "Otros seguirán a Jackie Robinson," July 27, 1947, pp. 46–47.

Jess Losada. "Los Havana Cubans ganaron el campeonato bajo el látigo," September 21, 1947, pp. 52–53.

Rai García. "Play Ball," October 12, 1947, p. 50.

Jess Losada. "El fanático decide: problema beisbolero," November 23, 1947, pp. 52–53.

———. "El fanático decide: problema beisbolero," November 30, 1947, p. 51.

———. "Los deportes al día," February 22, 1948, pp. 52–53.

Rai García. "Miguel Angel González: 34 años dirigiendo el Club Habana," March 14, 1948, p. 50.

Jess Losada. "Iniciación de un rookie cubano. Moain García se viste de Big Leaguer," March 21, 1948, pp. 50–51.

Rai García. "La juventud en nuestro béisbol," March 21, 1948, p. 55.

Jess Losada. "Luis Rodríguez Olmo: ídolo beisbolero," April 11, 1948, p. 51.

Rai García. "Campeones y rompe-récords," September 12, 1948. pp. 50–51.

———. "De ripieras a millonarios," September 19, 1948, p. 51.

———. "Vuelve la pelota. ¡Play Ball!," October 10, 1948, pp. 50–51.

Gabino Delgado. "Figuras del campeonato," January 16, 1949, p. 59.

Pedro Galiana. "Del diamante al cementerio," January 16, 1949, pp. 64–65.

Gabino Delgado. "Tuve que jugar béisbol agresivo (impresiones del manager almendarista)," February 13, 1949, pp. 62–64.

Rai García. "300 marca difícil de lograr en Cuba," February 13, 1949, p. 65.

———. "La pequeña serie mundial del Caribe," February 20, 1949, p. 61.

Jess Losada. "Serie del Caribe," February 27, 1949, pp. 60–61.

Gabino Delgado. "¿Por qué perdió el Habana?: una entrevista con Miguel Angel González," February 27, 1949, pp. 62–63.

Jess Losada. "El deporte no reconoce los prejuicios étnicos," April 17, 1949, pp. 64–65.

Gabino Delgado. "Deporte contra radio y televisión," April 24, 1949, pp. 58–59.

Jess Losada. "Comienza la zafra beisbolera," October 9, 1949, pp. 68–69.

———. "Psiquis del home-run," October 30, 1949, pp. 54–56.

Rubén Rodríguez. "10 años de Base Ball Profesional," October 30, 1949, pp. 62–63.

———. "Dentro del palco de la prensa," November 6, 1949, pp. 64–65.

———. "Willy Miranda, átomo del diamante," November 20, 1949, pp. 62–63.

Jess Losada. "La pelota fuera del estadio," November 27, 1949, pp. 54–56.

———. "Miguel Angel no habla de ayer, de hoy y de mañana," December 11, 1949, pp. 58–59, 69–70.

———. "La vida de Roberto Ortiz es popular," January 1, 1950, pp. 58–59.

Gabino Delgado. "La vida pública de Napoleón Reyes," January 1, 1950, pp. 62–63.

Jess Losada. "El fanático de la sirena," January 29, 1950, pp. 58–61.

———. "Pedro Formental, legislador," February 5, 1950, pp. 58–61.

Gabino Delgado. "Su vida es la pelota y también su gran amor," February 5, 1950, pp. 62–63.

———. "Claro Duany, fuera del diamante," February 12, 1950, pp. 62–63.

Jess Losada. "La novela de Tomás de la Cruz," February 19, 1950, pp. 63–67.

———. "El coraje de Fermín Guerra," February 26, 1950, pp. 58–59.

Gabino Delgado. "Limonar Martínez protagonizó la más brillante hazaña," February 26, 1950, p. 69.

Jess Losada. "La serie del Caribe," March 12, 1950, p. 66.

Gabino Delgado. "Resurrección del béisbol amateur," June 4, 1950, p. 64.

Jess Losada. "La raza negra en el béisbol," June 18, 1950, pp. 60–62.

———. "La tierra de la caña," July 9, 1950, pp. 61–63.

———. "Baseball," October 15, 1950, pp. 94–95.

———. "Alejandro Crespo, su bate y su cráneo" November 5, 1950, pp. 58–60.

———. "Adolfo Luque," November 5, 1950, p. 95.

Ricardo Agacino. "Miñoso," November 12, 1950, pp. 64–65.

Gabino Delgado. "Steve Bilko," November 19, 1950, p. 92.

César Torres. "Jiquí Moreno: el pítcher que volvió," November 26, 1950, pp. 56–57.

———. "El Stadium también es mercado," December 3, 1950, pp. 58–59.

———. "Amorós, ¿el novato del año?," December 10, 1950, pp. 56–57.

Pedro Galiana. "Es beneficioso el pacto con el béisbol organizado," December 10, 1950, pp. 94–95.

———. "Archie Wilson, el outerfielder que todo el mundo olvida," December 17, 1950, pp. 62–63.

César Torres. "Los criollos de La Tropical," December 17, 1950, pp. 66–68.

Jess Losada. "Radiografía del Almendares," December 17, 1950, pp. 92–95.

———. "La feliciana historia de Happy Chandler," December 24, 1950, pp. 92–93.

On Cuban History and Culture

Aguilar, Luis E. *Cuba 1933: Prologue to Revolution.* Ithaca, N.Y.: Cornell University Press, 1972.

Arrom, José J. *Historia de la literatura dramática cubana.* New Haven, Conn.: Yale University Press, 1944.

Batista, Fulgencio. *Cuba Betrayed.* New York: Vantage Press, 1962.

Bergad, Laird W. *Cuban Rural Society in the Nineteenth Century. The Social and Economic History of Monoculture in Matanzas.* Princeton, N.J.: Princeton University Press, 1990.

Blanco Aguilar, Jesús. *Ochenta años del son y los soneros del Caribe: 1909–1989.* Caracas: Fondo Editorial Tropykos, 1992.

Carpentier, Alejo. *¡Ecué-Yamba-O! Novela Afro-Cubana.* Madrid: Editorial España, 1933.

———. *La música en Cuba.* Mexico: Fondo de Cultura Económica, 1972 [1946].

Diccionario de los sueños. Contiene la charada china o chiffá. Miami: n.d. or publisher.

Domínguez, Jorge I. *Cuba: Order and Revolution.* Cambridge, Mass.: Harvard University Press, 1978.

Franck, Harry A. *Roaming Through the West Indies.* New York: The Century Company, 1920.

Fuentes, Norberto, *Hemingway in Cuba,* with an introduction by Gabriel García Márquez (Secaucus, N.J.: Lyle Stuart, 1984).

———. "La Mafia en Cuba," *Cuba Internacional,* Año 10, no. 117 (August 1979) pp. 60–64.

Fuentes, W. de, and A. Valenzuela, eds. *Havana. Monumental City Plan and Gen-*

eral Guide, English edition. Havana: Imprenta y Papelería de Rambla, Bouza, y Ca., 1928.

Gálvez y Delmonte, Wenceslao. *Esto, lo otro y lo de más allá (mosaico literario),* 2nd. ed. con un prólogo del Dr. Rafael Fernández de Castro. Havana: Imp. de Alvarez y Cía., 1892.

———. *Nicotina. Costumbres cubanas. Novela.* Havana: Imprenta Molina y Cía., 1932. Printed in *Colección cubana* de libros inéditos o raros, dirigida por Fernando Ortiz, Vol. 10.

———. *Tampa. Impresiones de Emigrado.* Ybor City, Tampa, Fla.: Establecimiento Tipográfico "Cuba," 1897.

Grenet, Emilio. *Popular Cuban Music. 80 Revised Compositions Together with an Essay on the Evolution of Music in Cuba.* Havana: Carassa and Company, 1939.

Guerra Sánchez, Ramiro. *Azúcar y población en las Antillas.* 5th ed. Havana: Editorial Lex, 1961 [1927].

———. *Manual de historia de Cuba. Desde su nacimiento hasta 1868.* Havana: Editorial de Ciencias Sociales, 1971.

Havemann, Ernest, "Mobsters Move in on Troubled Havana," *Life,* March 10, 1958, pp. 32–36.

Healy, David F. *The United States and Cuba 1898–1902. Generals, Politicians, and the Search for Policy.* Madison: University of Wisconsin Press, 1963.

Hermer, Consuelo, and Marjorie May. *Havana Mañana: A Guide to Cuba and the Cubans.* New York: Random House, 1941.

Kutzinski, Vera M. *Sugar's Secrets: Race and the Erotics of Cuban Nationalism.* Charlottesville: University Press of Virginia, 1993.

Jenks, Leland Hamilton. *Our Cuban Colony. A Study in Sugar.* New York: Vanguard Press, 1928.

Le Febure, Roger. *The Blue Guide to Cuba,* 1948 edition. Havana: printing by Ramiro F. Moris, 1948.

Linares, María Teresa. *La música popular.* Havana: Instituto del Libro, 1970.

Moreno Fraginals, Manuel. *El ingenio. Complejo económico social cubano del azúcar.* Havana: Editorial Ciencias Sociales, 1978. Original edition 1964, 1 vol., trans. *The Sugarmill: The Socioeconomic Complex of Sugar in Cuba.* New York: Monthly Review Press, 1976.

Nelson, Lowry. *Rural Cuba.* Minneapolis: University of Minnesota Press, 1950.

Orovio, Helio. *Diccionario de la música cubana.* Havana: Editorial Letras Cubanas, 1981.

———. "Unión de Reyes llora," *Revolución y Cultura* (Havana) 12 (December 1987): 39–42.

Ortiz, Fernando. *Cuban Counterpoint: Tobacco and Sugar,* tr. Harriet de Onís, intr. Bronislaw Malinowski, pr. Herminio Portell Vilá. New York: Random House, 1970 [original ed., 1940].

———. *La africanía de la música folklórica de Cuba.* Havana: Ediciones Cárdenas y Cía., 1950.

———. *Los bailes y el teatro de los negros en el folklore de Cuba,* prólogo de Alfonso Reyes. Havana: Ediciones Cárdenas y Cía., 1951.

———. *Los factores humanos de la cubanidad.* Havana: Molina y Cía., 1940. Originally published in *Revista Bimestre Cubana* 55, no. 2 (1940).

———. *Los negros curros,* texto establecido con prólogo y notas aclaratorias de Diana Iznaga. Havana: Editorial de Ciencias Sociales, 1986.

Peraza y Sarauza, Fermín. *Personalidades cubanas.* Havana: Anuario Bibliográfico Cubano, 1958.

Pérez, Louis A. Jr., *Cuba Between Empires 1878–1902.* Pittsburgh: University of Pittsburgh Press, 1983.

———. *Cuba and the United States: Ties of Singular Intimacy.* Athens, Ga.: University of Georgia Press, 1990.

———. *Slaves, Sugar, & Colonial Society: Travel Accounts of Cuba, 1801–1899.* Wilmington, Del.: Scholarly Resources, 1992.

Pérez Firmat, Gustavo. *The Cuban Condition: Translation and Identity in Modern Cuban Literature.* Cambridge, Eng.: Cambridge University Press, 1989.

Phillips, Ruby Hart. *Cuba: Island of Paradox.* New York: Mc Dowell, Obolensky, 1960(?)

Pino-Santos, Oscar. *El asalto a Cuba por la oligarquía financiera yanqui.* Havana: Casa de las Américas, 1973.

Reynolds, Philip Keep. *The Story of Sugar.* Boston: United Fruit Company, 1924.

Robreño, Eduardo. *Cualquier tiempo pasado fue . . .* Havana: Editorial Letras Cubanas, 1979.

Rodríguez Feo, José. *Mi correspondencia con José Lezama Lima.* Havana: UNEAC, 1989.

Roig de Leuchsenring, Emilio. *La Habana: apuntes históricos.* Havana: Municipio de La Habana, 1939.

Rouse, Irving. *The Taínos: The Rise and Decline of the People Who Greeted Columbus.* New Haven, Conn.: Yale University Press, 1992.

Scott, Rebecca J. *Slave Emancipation in Cuba. The Transition to Free Labor, 1860–1899.* Princeton, N.J.: Princeton University Press, 1985.

Thomas, Hugh. *Cuba: The Pursuit of Freedom.* New York: Harper & Row, 1971.

Thompson, Robert Farris. *Flash of the Spirit: African and Afro-American Art and Philosophy.* New York: Random House, 1983.

Velie, Lester. "Suckers in Paradise: How Americans Lose Their Shirts in Caribbean Gambling Joints," *Saturday Evening Post,* March 28, 1953, pp. 32–33, 181, 183.

Venegas Fornias, Carlos. "La Habana Vieja: patrimonio de la humanidad," in *La Habana,* textos de Antonio Núñez Jiménez and Carlos Venegas Fornias, fotografías de Manuel Méndez Guerrero. Madrid: Ediciones Cultura Hispánica— Instituto de Cooperación Iberoamericana, 1986, pp. 31–49.

———. *La urbanización de las murallas. Dependencia y modernidad.* Havana: Editorial Letras Cubanas, 1990.

———. "El malecón habanero," *Revolución y Cultura* (Havana), Año 33, época 4, no. 4 (July–August 1994), pp. 46–50.

United States Army Dept. of Matanzas and Santa Clara. Annual Report of Brigadier General James H. Wilson, u.s.v., Commanding the Department of Matanzas and Santa Clara. To Which is Appended Special Report on the Industrial, Economic and Social Conditions Existing in the Department at the Date of the American Occupation, and at the Present Time. Matanzas, 1899.

Villoch, Federico. *Viejas postales descoloridas. La guerra de independencia.* Havana: Ministerio de Defensa Nacional, 1946.

Wilford's Seeing Havana Intelligently. Condensed History of Cuba and Complete Guide to the City of Havana and its Environs. Key to the Spanish Language with Comprehensive Index. Havana: R.Biosca Company, 1928.

Woon, Basil. *When It's Cocktail Time in Cuba.* New York: Horace Liveright, 1928.

On Latin American Baseball

Agundis, Teódulo Manuel. *El verdadero Jorge Pasquel: Ensayo biográfico sobre un carácter.* Mexico City: Asociación Mexicana de la Cruz Roja y Casa de Beneficiencia y Maternidad, 1956. Chapters on baseball by Alejandro Aguilar Reyes (Fray Nano) and Eladio Secades.

Album de toleteros. Colección de valiosos peloteros profesionales de Puerto Rico. Mayagüez: R. García y Co., 1949.

Alvarez, Ernesto. *Cantar del Jíbaro Olmo. Novela-Reportaje.* Arecibo, P.R.; Ediciones Boán, 1995.

Arbena, Joseph L., ed. *Sport and Society in Latin America.* Westport, Conn.: Greenwood Press, 1988.

Enciclopedia del Béisbol Mexicano, ed. Pedro Treto Cisneros. Mexico City: Revistas Deportivas, S.A., 1996.

Gillette. Series Mundiales. Libro de Datos, compilado por Hy Turkin, prólogo por Buck Canel. New York: A. S. Barnes, 1953 (contains glossary of Spanish terms in baseball and list of all Latin American players who appeared in the majors).

Jiménez O., Dr. José de Jesús. *Archivo de baseball.* Santiago de los Caballeros, Dominican Republic: Talleres Litográficos Amigos del Hogar, 1977(?).

Joseph, Gilbert M. "Documenting a Regional Pastime: Baseball in Yucatán," *Windows on Latin America: Understanding Society Through Photographs,* ed. Robert M. Levine. Miami: North South Center, 1987, pp. 76–89.

Klein, Alan M. *Sugarball: The American Game, the Dominican Dream.* New Haven, Conn.: Yale University Press, 1991.

Krich, John. *El béisbol. Travels Through the Pan-American Pastime.* New York: Atlantic Monthly Press, 1989.

Lara C., Joaquín. *Historia del béisbol en Yucatán (1890–1906).* Mérida: Editorial Zamná, 1953.

Mendoza Mancilla, Raúl. *28 Temporadas. Unión Laguna Algodoneros.* Mexico: Impresiones Gráficas México S.A., 1990.

"Mexican Baseball," *Life,* vol. 20, no. 25 (June 24, 1946), pp. 119–25.

Morales Fernández, Tomás. *Los grandes juegos.* Mexico City: Editora de Periódicos S.C.L, La Prensa, 1970.

Oleksak, Michael M., and Mary Adams Oleksak. *Béisbol. Latin Americans and the Grand Old Game.* Grand Rapids, Mich.: Masters Press, 1991.

Pieve, Carlos. *Los genios de la insuficiencia.* Santo Domingo: Editora Alfa y Omega, 1984.

Piña, Tony. *Guía del béisbol profesional dominicano (Dominican Baseball Guide) IV Edición 1985.* Santo Domingo: Edición Oficial de la Liga de Bésibol Profesional de República Dominicana, 1985.

Quién es quién en el béisbol Liga Mexicana 1996. Mexico City: Revistas Deportivas, S.A., 1996.

Regalado, Samuel O. *Viva Baseball! The Latin Major Leaguers and Their Special Hunger.* Urbana: University of Illinois Press, 1998.

Rodríguez Juliá, Edgardo. *Peloteros.* San Juan: Editorial de la Universidad de Puerto Rico, 1997.

Ruck, Rob. *The Tropic of Baseball: Baseball in the Dominican Republic.* Westport, Conn.: Meckler Corporation, 1991.

Salas, Alexis. *Momentos inolvidables del béisbol profesional venezolano 1946–1984.* Caracas: Miguel Angel García e Hijos, 1985.

Tijerino, Edgard. *Doble Play.* Managua: Editorial Vanguardia, 1989.

Van Hyning, Thomas E. *Puerto Rico's Winter League: A History of Major League Baseball's Launching Pad,* with a foreword by Eduardo Valero. Jefferson, N.C.: McFarland, 1995.

On the Negro Leagues and U.S. Black Culture

Brashler, William. *Josh Gibson: A Life in the Negro Leagues.* New York: Harper & Row, 1978.

Bruce, Janet. *The Kansas City Monarchs: Champions of Black Baseball.* Lawrence: University Press of Kansas, 1985.

Campanella, Roy. *It's Good to Be Alive.* New York: Little, Brown, 1959.

Chadwick, Bruce. *When the Game was Black and White: The Illustrated History of the Negro Leagues.* New York: Abbeville Press, 1992.

Cooper, Michael L. *Playing America's Game: The Story of Negro League Baseball.* New York: Lodestar Books, 1993.

Davis, Lenwood G., and Belinda Daniels, foreword by James E. Newton. *Black Athletes in the United States: A Bibliography of Books, Articles, Autobiographies, and Biographies on Black Professional Athletes in the United States, 1800–1981.* Westport, Conn.: Greenwood Press, 1981.

Flood, Curt. *The Way It Is,* with an introduction by Vida Blue. New York: Pocket Books, 1972.

For the Love of the Game. August 11–13, 1991. Reunion—Recognition—Celebration of the Negro League Players. Atlanta, Ga.: pamphlet published by Southern Bell Co. Copyright 1991.

Frommer, Harvey. *Rickey & Robinson: The Men Who Broke Baseball's Color Barrier.* New York: Macmillan, 1982.

Gibson, Bob, with Phil Pepe. *From Ghetto to Glory.* New York: Popular Library, 1968.

Hardwick, Leon Hubert. *Blacks in Baseball 1872–1980.* Los Angeles: Pilot Historical Association, 1980.

Holway, John B. *Blackball Stars: Negro League Pioneers.* Westport, Conn: Meckler Books, 1988.

———. *Voices from the Great Black Baseball Leagues.* New York: Dodd, Mead, 1975.

———. *Josh and Satch. The Life and Times of Josh Gibson and Satchel Paige.* New York: Carroll & Graf, 1991.

Manley, Effa, and Leon Herbert Hardwick. *Negro Baseball . . . Before Integration.* Chicago: Adams Press, 1976.

Paige, Leroy "Satchel," and David Lipman. *Maybe I'll Pitch Forever.* Garden City, N.Y.: Doubleday, 1962.

Peterson, Robert. *Only the Ball Was White.* Englewood Cliffs, N.J.: Prentice-Hall, 1970.

Ribowsky, Mark. *A Complete History of the Negro Leagues 1884–1955.* New York: Birch Lane Press, 1995.

Riley, James A. *Dandy, Day, and the Devil,* foreword by Monte Irvin. Cocoa, Fla.: TK Publishers, 1987.

Rogosin, Donn. *Invisible Men: Life in Baseball's Negro Leagues.* New York: Atheneum, 1983.

Rosengarten, Theodore. "Reading the Hops: Recollections of Lorenzo Piper Davis and the Negro Baseball League," *Southern Exposure* 5 (1977): 62–79.

Ruck, Rob. *Sandlot Seasons. Sport in Black Pittsburgh.* Urbana, Ill.: University of Illinois Press, 1987.

Rust, Art, Jr., *"Get That Nigger Off the Field": A Sparkling, Informal History of the Black Man in Baseball.* New York: Delacorte Press, 1976.

Rust, Edna, and Art, Jr. *Art Rust's Illustrated History of the Black Athlete.* Garden City, N.Y.: Doubleday, 1985.

Trouppe, Quincey. *Twenty Years Too Soon.* Los Angeles: S & S Enterprises, 1977.

Tygiel, Jules. *Baseball's Great Experiment: Jackie Robinson and His Legacy.* New York: Oxford University Press, 1983.

White, Sol. *Sol White's Official Baseball Guide. By Sol White, Captain Philadelphia Giants 1905–1906–1907,* ed. H. Walter Schlichter. Philadelphia, 1907.

Young, A. S. "Doc." *Great Negro Baseball Stars and How They Made the Major Leagues.* New York: A. S. Barnes, 1953.

Baseball in General

Alexander, Charles. *John McGraw.* New York: Viking, 1988.

———. *Our Game: An American Baseball History.* New York: Henry Holt, 1991.

Bealle, Morris A. *The Washington Senators: An 87-Year History of the World's Oldest Baseball Club and Most Incurable Fandom.* Washington, D.C.: Columbia Publishing Co., 1947.

Blake, Mike. *The Minor Leagues: A Celebration of the Little Show.* New York: Winwood Press, 1991.

Brown, Bill. "Waging Baseball, Playing War: Games of American Imperialism," *Cultural Critique* (Winter 1990–91), pp. 51–78.

Durocher, Leo, with Ed Linn. *Nice Guys Finish Last.* New York: Simon & Schuster, 1975 [using 1976 paperback ed.].

Gelber, Stephen. "Working at Playing: The Culture of the Workplace and the Rise of Baseball," *Journal of Social History* 16, no. 4 (1983): 3–22.

Giamatti, A. Bartlett. *Take Time for Paradise.* New York: Summit Books, 1989.

Gilbert, Bill. *They Also Served: Baseball and the Home Front, 1941–1945.* New York: Crown, 1992.

Goldstein, Richard. *Spartan Seasons: How Baseball Survived the Second World War.* New York: Macmillan, 1980.

Goldstein, Warren. *Playing for Keeps: A History of Early Baseball.* Ithaca, N.Y.: Cornell University Press, 1989.

Gregory, Robert. *Diz: The Story of Dizzy Dean and Baseball During the Great Depression.* New York: Viking, 1992.

Honig, Gerald. *Baseball Between the Lines: Baseball in the '40s and '50s.* New York: Coward, McCann, & Geoghegan, 1976.

Kahn, Roger. *The Boys of Summer.* New York: Harper & Row, 1971.

Lasorda, Tommy, and David Fisher. *The Artful Dodger.* New York: Arbor House, 1985.

Levine, Peter. *A. G. Spalding and the Rise of Baseball: The Promise of American Sport.* New York: Oxford University Press, 1985.

O'Neal, Bill. *The International League. A Baseball History, 1884–1991.* Austin, Tex.: Eakin Press, 1992.

Robinson, Brooks, as told to Jack Tobin. *Third Base Is My Home.* Waco, Tex.: Word, 1974.

Seymour, Harold. *Baseball: The Early Years.* New York: Oxford University Press, 1960.

———. *Baseball: The Golden Age.* New York: Oxford University Press, 1971.

———. *Baseball: The People's Game.* New York: Oxford University Press, 1990.

Spalding, Albert G. *America's National Game: Historic Facts Concerning the Beginning, Evolution, Development, and Popularity of Baseball, with Personal Reminiscences of Its Vicissitudes, Its Victories and Its Votaries,* cartoons by Homer C. Davenport. New York: American Sports Publishing Company, 1911. There is a facsimile edition by the University of Nebraska Press, 1992, with an introduction by Benjamin G. Rader.

Sullivan, Neil J. *The Minors: The Struggles and the Triumph of Baseball's Poor Relation from 1876 to the Present.* New York: St. Martin's Press, 1990.

Reference Works

The Baseball Encyclopedia. The Complete and Definitive Record of Major League Baseball, 10th ed. New York: Macmillan, 1996. This edition includes Negro Leagues records.

Charlton, James. *The Baseball Chronology. The Complete History of the Most Important Events in the Game of Baseball.* New York: Macmillan, 1991.

Johnson, Lloyd, and Miles Wolff, eds. *The Encyclopedia of Minor League Baseball,* 2nd ed. Durham, N.C.: Baseball America, 1997.

Neft, David S., and Richard M. Cohen. *The Sports Encyclopedia: Baseball,* 11th ed. New York: St. Martin's Press, 1991.

Okkonen, Mark. *Baseball Uniforms of the 20th Century. The Official Major League Baseball Guide.* New York: Sterling, 1991.

Riley, James A. *The Biographical Encyclopedia of the Negro Baseball Leagues,* foreword by Monte Irvin. New York: Carroll & Graf, 1994.

Shatzkin, Mike. *The Ballplayers: Baseball's Ultimate Biographical Reference.* New York: Arbor House, 1990.

Treto Cisneros, Pedro, ed. *Enciclopedia del béisbol mexicano.* Mexico: Revistas Deportivas, S.A., 1996.

Magazine and Newspaper Collections

Avance, Baseball America, Bohemia, Carteles, Casa de las Américas, Cuba Internacional, Cuban Studies, Diario de la Marina, El Fígaro, Nine: A Journal of

Baseball History and Social Policy Perspectives (Edmonton, Alberta), *Revolución, Revolución y cultura*

Interviews

Emilio de Armas, Miami, Fla., December 12, 1993.
Claro Duany, Evanston, Ill., December 28, 1990.
Rodolfo Fernández, New York, N.Y., January 26, 1991.
Andrés Fleitas, Miami, Fla., December 12, 1990.
Jorge Fuentes, Mulgova, Ciudad de La Habana, December 7, 1995.
Fermín Guerra, Miami, Fla., August 8, 1991.
Bert Haas, Tampa, Fla., December 7, 1990.
Francisco (Panchón) Herrera, Miami, Fla., August 12, 1991.
Max Lanier, Dunellon, Fla., December 9, 1990.
Al López, Tampa, Fla., December 8, 1990.
Conrado Marrero, Miami, Fla., December 10, 1993.
Eddy Martin, Havana, August 30, 1995.
Agapito Mayor, Tampa, Fla., September 8, 1990.
Fausto Miranda, Miami, Fla., December 11, 1990.
Charles Monfort, Miami, Fla., December 11, 1990.
Glenn (Rocky) Nelson, Portsmouth, Ohio, March 5, 1993.
Enrique Núñez Rodríguez, Havana, August 30, 1995.
Camilo Pascual, Fort Lauderdale, Fla., August 15, 1991.
Felo Ramírez, San Juan de Puerto Rico, April 30, 1991.
Napoleón Reyes, Miami, Fla., August 13, 1991.
Dick Sisler, Nashville, Tenn., April 6, 1991.
Quilla Valdés, Miami, Fla., December 12, 1993.
José Valdivielso, Mount Sinai, N.Y., January 12, 1991.

Other Documents

Fred Martin and Max Lanier, Plaintiffs-Appellants, against National League Baseball Club of Boston, Inc., et al., 1949.

Correspondence (in Chronological Order)

Gustavo Pérez Firmat, Miami, Fla., March 16, 1986.
Roberto Landazuri, San Francisco, Calif., April 4, 1990.
Rob Ruck, Pittsburgh, Penn., April 12, 1990.
Robert Heuer, Chicago, Ill., May 14, 1990.
Rob Ruck, Pittsburgh, Penn., May 29, 1990.
Rodolfo Fernández, New York, N.Y., December 30, 1990.
Adrián Zabala, Jacksonville, Fla., December 31, 1990.
Rafael Noble, Brooklyn, N.Y., January 1, 1991.
Rodolfo Fernández, New York, N.Y., March 29, 1991.
Rodolfo Fernández, New York, N.Y., August 27, 1991.

José Antonio Madrigal, Auburn, Ala., September 3, 1991.
Edmundo Mendieta G., Miami, Fla., September 4, 1991.
Jorge Pérez López, Falls Church, Va., September 14, 1991.
Bobby Bragan, Arlington, Tex., February 18, 1992.
Bobby Bragan, Arlington, Tex., April 1, 1992.
Frank Dellunde, San Francisco, Calif., April 7, 1992.
Carter Bancroft, Ph.D., Huntington, N.Y., April 8, 1992.
Jay S. Friedman, Decatur, Ga., April 9, 1992.
Tom Miller, Tucson, Ariz., April 4, 1992.
Mel R. Martínez, Orlando, Fla., July 1, 1992.
Rodolfo Fernández, New York, N.Y., July 7, 1992.
Isabel Alvarez Borland, Worcester, Mass., July 1, 1992.
Oscar N. González, Tampa, Fla., July 3, 1992.
Jorge Pérez López, Falls Church, Va., December 10, 1992.
Glenn "Rocky" Nelson, Portsmouth, Ohio, February 3, 1993.
Manuel "Cocaína" García, La Guaira, Venezuela, February 22, 1993.
Glenn "Rocky" and Alberta Nelson, Portsmouth, Ohio, March 8, 1993.
Everardo Santamarina, New York City, March 12, 1993. With manuscript of article
    "Don Hoak's Story."
Glenn "Rocky" and Alberta Nelson, Portsmouth, Ohio, April 15, 1993.
Roberto Ruiz, Attleboro, Mass., April 16, 1993.
Tom Miller, Tucson, Arizona, May 17, 1993.
Rodolfo Fernández, New York City, June 2, 1993.
Enrique V. Menocal, Philadelphia, June 11, 1993.
Narciso Camejo, San Juan de Puerto Rico, August 19, 1993.
José Cabranes, New Haven, Conn., July 18, 1995.
Ana Cairo, Havana, February 15, 1996.
Ana Cairo, Havana, October 6, 1997.
Rodolfo Fernández, New York City, March 29, 1998.

Index